Political change and the Labour party 1900–1918

Political change and the Labour party 1900–1918

Duncan Tanner

Lecturer in History, University of Wales, Bangor

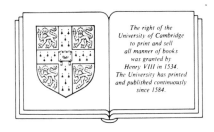

The right of the
University of Cambridge
to print and sell
all manner of books
was granted by
Henry VIII in 1534.
The University has printed
and published continuously
since 1584.

Cambridge University Press

Cambridge
New York   Port Chester
Melbourne   Sydney

Published by the Press Syndicate of the University of Cambridge
The Pitt Building, Trumpington Street, Cambridge CB2 1RP
40 West 20th Street, New York, NY 10011, USA
10 Stamford Road, Oakleigh, Melbourne 3166, Australia

First published 1990

Printed in Great Britain by The Bath Press, Avon

British Library cataloguing in publication data
Tanner, Duncan
Political change and the Labour party 1900–1918.
1. Great Britain. Political parties. Labour party
(Great Britain), 1900–1918.
I. Title
324.24107′ 09

Library of Congress cataloguing in publication data
Applied for

ISBN 0 521 32981 7

BS

To Christine

Contents

Tables

Preface

The political changes of 1900–18 have been analysed in a number of different ways. Some historians have emphasised events at the centre, some events in the constituencies. There are studies of national Liberal and of Labour organisation, leadership, policy, and ideology. Local studies of the position in municipal politics abound. Conflicting theories have developed because historians tend to stress the strengths of the party examined, and also because studies of different aspects of the question lead naturally to different conclusions. Moreover, major differences about the nature of politics and political change lurk beneath these discussions, disposing historians to look at questions in very different ways. There has been no single study which embraces all the layers of the debate. Research has progressed simultaneously on disparate lines, with conflicts over some points and interpretations serving only to cloud the real issues. The field is littered with books, articles, and theses, none of which provide a comprehensive explanation of the electoral and political changes.

This attempt to provide a more complete explanation of these changes is dominated by three considerations. First, the debate has taken place in a vacuum. Historians have not grounded their explanations in a full assessment of the electoral position of the respective parties in a sufficiently large number of areas and constituencies; instead they have extrapolated from limited information. Neither have they focused on the ideas and forces which created Labour's electoral strategy. In this area too there has been a good deal of speculation and only a modicum of detailed research. Secondly, by dealing only with fragments of the question, historians have glossed over the most fundamental issues: the nature and importance of the interaction between the centre and the constituencies, between municipal and parliamentary politics, between a party's strategic and ideological containment, and between social class and political behaviour. In all these areas assumptions have been more common than empirical validation. Thirdly, and building on this, empirical debate has masked significant differences over such questions as the role of cultural factors, economic needs, and political ideas in creating political change when these differences are central to the different arguments. Also historians have in the past assumed that the factors which governed a party's expansion have left an indelible mark on the nature of that party; this too is an important question which has become submerged by much narrower concerns. The concentration on just one aspect of the problem has resulted in unbalanced and partial accounts. As a result, the complex but fascinating dynamics of the political system as a whole are seldom appreciated, and the parties produced by change are only half understood. There is a need to add new information to the existing stock, to place that information in a new framework which ties all the ends together, and to reassert the importance of the fundamental issues and questions which have too often been passed over in recent years. Without such an approach the texture of contemporary politics will continue to seem one-dimensional, and a poor indication of the problems and obstacles – the context – of political development. Equally, there can be little development in our understanding of Labour's expansion, and of Labour and electoral politics in general, while the existing models and their themes dominate each new study which emerges.

The needs of the subject (and the indulgence of Richard Fisher at CUP) have made this a large book. I have tried to encompass all the elements in the existing debate, to produce material on these questions, to formulate an explanation of the political changes, to examine the nature of the Liberal and Labour parties in the period, and to suggest new ways of looking at Labour and at electoral politics. The book is the product of many years of my own thought and research and a crystallisation of information available in other works.

In writing this book I have incurred debts to scholarly works too numerous to mention individually; the footnotes and the introduction must tell this story. However, my debt to Peter Clarke's *Lancashire and the New Liberalism* and David Howell's *British workers and the Independent Labour Party 1888–1906* deserve specific notice. This is partially because they supply excellent information which I have used throughout the book, but even more for their inspiring treatment of Liberal and Labour politics after 1885. The authors of these books have also contributed generously with comments on the whole text; Dr Howell following a letter from a total stranger (which arrived eighteen months before the manuscript), Peter Clarke after years of taking his research supervisor's role well beyond the call of duty. I must also thank Martin Pugh and John Ramsden for reading the MS with great care, and Michael Hart for casting the diligent eye of an Oxford historian over the manuscript at a late stage in its evolution. Bill Purdue, Barry Supple, John Thompson, and Andrew

Thompson made comments on sections where their knowledge far exceeded mine. All have saved me from making errors of varying kinds. Those which remain are sadly mine.

My debt to the staff of record offices around the country is considerable, and I apologise for not having the space to mention all depositories individually. I am particularly grateful to the beleaguered staff at the National Newspaper Library, Colindale, and to Stephen Bird at the Labour party archives. I am also grateful to Microform Ltd of Wakefield (formerly E. P. Microform) for microfilming the records of many local Labour parties, and to the BLPES for buying them. I would also like to record a debt of thanks to those individuals, and the officials of local and national parties and trade unions, who responded to my letters of enquiry or allowed me to consult and cite information in their charge. I hope the owners of copyright material will similarly accept a blanket vote of thanks.

It has taken ten years to produce this book. It would not have been possible to undertake this project without the support of various educational bodies. The DES supplied funds for the initial three years. I am grateful to Michael Thompson and the Twenty Seven Foundation for a Scouloudi Research Fellowship, and to the British Academy for a 'Thank-offering to Britain' Research Fellowship. The Master and Fellows of St Catharine's College Cambridge elected me to a further Research Fellowship in 1985. My debt to their patience, and to the liberal attitudes which permitted the election of someone from outside Oxbridge, is considerable and sincere. I am also grateful to historians at Westfield College, London, and the University of Kent, where I held teaching appointments. Because of this support I have been able to conduct a lengthy research project at a time when the enforced contraction of academic employment has pushed many young scholars out of research, or towards 'manageable', narrower, topics. I have been comparatively fortunate, but I have no doubt that the recent climate has done nothing but harm to my own research and to the innovative historical research and teaching of many young and established scholars.

I owe more to my mother than one can write in the preface to a book. I hope what follows makes some of my parents' many sacrifices seem worthwhile. The selfless practical contributions of Cambridge friends kept our family functioning, and our spirits high, when problems seemed insurmountable. My copy editor, Anne Rix, eased the book through its final stages with admirable skill and patience. My wife Christine, and our children Eleanor and Megan have (gradually) come to accept my absences and late arrivals. I am grateful to Eleanor and Megan for keeping me sane (if tired). Christine has tolerated the financial and personal consequences which result from ten years of poorly paid and insecure employment, and made practical contributions over the years which are too numerous to acknowledge here. My debt to her is greater than even chocolate can repay.

Abbreviations

A.H.	Arthur Henderson
A.P.	Arthur Peters, Labour party national agent
A.R.	Arnold Rowntree (Lib. MP York)
AR	*Annual Report*(s)
AR &BS	*Annual Report and Balance Sheet*(s)
ASC&J	Amalgamated Society of Carpenters and Joiners
ASE	Amalgamated Society of Engineers
ASRS	Amalgamated Society of Railway Servants (becomes NUR)
BIHR	Bulletin of the Institute of Historical Research
BrSS	British Steel Smelters
BSP	British Socialist Party
BSSLH	*Bulletin of the Society for the Study of Labour History*
C.F.T.	*Cotton Factory Times*
C.P.S.	C. P. Scott, editor *Manchester Guardian*
C.P.T.	C. P. Trevelyan (Lib. MP Elland)
CR	*Conference Report*(s)
CRO	County Record Office
CVLL	Colne Valley Labour League
D.H.	*Daily Herald* (*Herald*, 1915–1918)
DMA	Durham Miners' Association
DWR	Dock, Wharf, Riverside and General Workers' Union
EC	Executive Committee
EHR	*English Historical Review*
F.J.	Francis Johnson, ILP Secretary
G.L.	George Lansbury
GUCJ	General Union of Carpenters and Joiners
H.G.	Herbert Gladstone, Liberal Chief Whip
HCLF	Home Counties Liberal Federation
H.H.A.	Herbert Henry Asquith
HJ	*Historical Journal*
ILP	Independent Labour Party

IRSH	*International Review of Social History*
J.B.G.	John Bruce Glasier
J.K.H.	James Keir Hardie
J.R.M.	James Ramsay MacDonald
J.S.M.	J. S. Middleton, Assistant Secretary of the Labour party
LA	Liberal Association
LCLF	Lancashire and Cheshire Liberal Federation (Lancashire, Cheshire and North-West Fed. from 1910)
L.D.P.	*Lancashire Daily Post*
L.G.	Lloyd George
Lib. Agent	*Liberal Agent*, journal of the Society of Certified Liberal Agents
L.L.	*Labour Leader*
LLRC	Liverpool Labour Representation Committee
LP	Labour party
LRC	Labour Representation Committee
M.B.	Minute Book(s)
MFGB	Miners' Federation of Great Britain
M.G.	*Manchester Guardian*
Mid. LF	Midland Liberal Federation
MLF	Manchester Liberal Federation
MR	*Monthly Report*(s)
MRC	Modern Records Centre, Warwick University
NAC	National Administrative Council of the ILP
NAFTO	National Association of Furnishing Trades Operatives
Natsopa	National Society of Operative Printers' Assistants
NAUL	National Amalgamated Union of Labour
N.D.T.	*Northern Daily Telegraph*
N.E.	*Northern Echo*
NEC	National Executive Committee of the Labour party
NLF	National Liberal Federation
NMA	Northumberland Miners' Association
NUBSO	National Union of Boot and Shoe Operatives
NUR	National Union of Railwaymen (formerly ASRS)
NWLH	*North-West Labour History Society*
PLP	Parliamentary Labour Party
PRO	Public Records Office
P.S.	Philip Snowden
R.R.	*Railway Review*, journal of the ASRS/NUR
SDF/SDP	Social Democratic Federation/Party
S.G.	*Sheffield Guardian*

S.H.	Sam Higenbottom, Labour party national organiser
SWMF	South Wales Miners' Federation
T.E.H.	T. E. Harvey (Lib. MP West Leeds), and Harvey Ms
TC/T&LC	Trades Council/Trades and Labour Council
TUC	Trades Union Congress
UTFWA	United Textile Factory Workers' Association
W.C.	Winston Churchill
W.C.A.	W. C. Anderson, Chairman, ILP
W.H.	William Holmes, Labour party national organiser
WLA	Women's Liberal Federation
WNC	War Emergency Workers' National Committee
W.R.	Walter Runciman
YMA	Yorkshire Miners' Association
Y.P.	*Yorkshire Post*

Introduction

I

The political changes of 1900–18 had three components. First, Labour changed its electoral strategy from a policy of limited parliamentary campaigns and alliance with the Liberals before 1914, to a policy of massive parliamentary campaigns and opposition to all parties beginning at the 1918 election. Secondly, Labour's electoral performance improved. It fared worse than the Liberal party before the war, but progressively outdistanced it thereafter. Thirdly, both parties appeared to change in the process. They developed features which would help determine their strengths, weaknesses and characteristics as parties of the centre-left.

These important changes have attracted a great deal of scholarly attention. Why, historians have asked, was the Liberal party replaced by Labour after the First World War, when before 1910 it was unquestionably the major working-class party? The conflicting answers revolved around the rise of class-based politics. In the 1950s and 1960s Marxist and Weberian sociologists and political scientists argued that class was the crucial determinant of electoral behaviour, all else being 'embellishment and detail'.[1] For Marx, changes in the nature of capitalism would inevitably throw up working-class organisations; Weber too had accepted the connection. The nature of the British political alignment, the fact of Labour's success and the Liberal party's failure, seemed to confirm Labour as *the* working-class party. As class replaced religion as the basis of political alignments, support

---

[1] P. G. J. Pulzer, *Political representation and elections in Britain* (1967), p. 98.

for Labour would (and did) increase, whilst for the Liberals it would (and did) decline.[2] Labour's rise was inexorable and inevitable.

Historians of the Liberal party and of Edwardian politics produced material which sustained a conflicting interpretation. Following Weber, Peter Clarke argued that a change from the 'status' politics of religion to class-based socio-economic politics did indeed take place. More contentiously, he argued that this was accompanied by a fundamental shift in the nature of Liberalism, in the Liberal party, and in the basis of its electoral support. The 'New Liberalism' supplied the ideological and political drive, and had the electoral purchase, to make the Liberal party a 'viable' medium for working-class interests. New, professional, politicians – particularly Asquith, Lloyd George and Winston Churchill – provided the institutional pressure. Their opinions were carried into the constituencies by the nationalisation of issues and the centralisation of political power. By 1910, the Liberal party had adapted to socio-economic change. It – not Labour – was rooted in the class sentiments which could give it permanence as a political force. The Liberal party did not decline in 1918 and after because of a change from 'religious' to 'class' politics; that change was already well under way. Clashes and divisions during the war split the party between Asquith and Lloyd George, and undermined its appeal.[3]

This thesis launched a debate which has raged ever since. The first major challenge was based on an excellent institutional history of the central Labour organisation during the period 1910–24, which also questioned the underlying assumptions, and the empirical basis, of Clarke's thesis. Ross McKibbin argued that the 'war' thesis had been stated, not established; Labour had also been split, but it had survived and grown more powerful. More positively, he suggested that post-war central organisational developments were well under way before 1914; so too was

---

[2] G. Dangerfield, *The strange death of Liberal England* (New York, 1935, Perigee edn., 1980), J. Glaser, 'English Nonconformity and the decline of Liberalism', *American Historical Review* (1958). This view is generally associated with Henry Pelling, in part because of comments in his own summary of a more complex argument (H. Pelling, 'Labour and the downfall of Liberalism', in his *Popular politics and society in late Victorian Britain* (2nd edn., 1979), pp. 119–20). In reality, Pelling paved the way for a less rigid view. See esp. his comments in F. Bealey and H. Pelling, *Labour and politics* (1958), pp. 284–5, 288 and his *Social geography of British elections* (1967).

[3] P. F. Clarke, *Lancashire and the New Liberalism* (Cambridge, 1971), esp. pp. 393–7. See also T. Wilson, *The downfall of the Liberal party* (1966), R. Douglas, *The history of the Liberal party 1895–1970* (1971), N. Blewett, *The peers, the parties and the people* (1972), esp. Chapter 12. Lloyd George or Asquith (whoever one blamed for the split) were thus the architects of Liberal decline in much of the literature on Liberal politics during the First World War. For a summary of this debate, T. Wilson, *The myriad faces of war* (Cambridge, 1986), pp. 408–23.

the party's organisational and electoral expansion in the constituencies. Liberal policies were irrelevant. *Labour* had become a 'class-based' party.

McKibbin pointed to three important developments which became apparent after 1910, as a result of increases in class consciousness. First, the changing attitude of trade unions to the Labour party supplied the party with money, workers and an established network for distributing information and propaganda. Secondly, Labour was gaining support in by-elections after 1910 and probably in municipal elections as well as a result of the trade union/Labour link. With improvements in constituency organisation, this gave the party a much broader and stronger platform. Thirdly, Labour's electoral strategy was changing to reflect the party's improved position. In 1914, Labour was about to terminate its unofficial electoral alliance with the Liberal party. It was no longer content to be the junior partner in a Progressive Alliance. Improvements in organisation and electoral circumstances were causing Labour to grow up as a political force. The strategy of electoral restraint and compromise was thus falling apart. Electoral results and organisational developments were not more substantial, because of structural constraints. The Osborne Judgement prevented trade unions contributing to local Labour organisation for a substantial portion of the period; a restricted electoral system excluded 'natural' Labour supporters and prevented electoral demonstrations of the party's full strength.[4]

A stream of complementary studies extended every aspect of this counter-thesis. McKibbin's brief, but favourable, tabulation of Labour's municipal performance was expanded and reinforced in national and local studies of the electoral trends. Local organisational improvements received similar attention.[5] Some historians drew comparisons with alleged Liberal organisational problems; a few actually produced some

---

[4] R. I. McKibbin, *The evolution of the Labour party 1910–1924* (Oxford, 1974).

[5] M. G. Sheppard and J. L. Halstead, 'Labour's municipal election performance in provincial England and Wales 1901–13', *BSSLH* (1979), pp.39–42. For local studies, e.g. K. Laybourn and J. Reynolds, *Liberalism and the rise of Labour* (1984) [Yorkshire], P. Thompson, *Socialists, Liberals and Labour* (1967) [London], A. Howkins, *Poor labouring men* (1985) [Norfolk], T. Moorhouse, 'The working class', in D. Fraser (ed.), *A history of modern Leeds* (Manchester, 1980), pp. 353–88, G. L. Bernstein, 'Liberalism and the Progressive Alliance in the constituencies, 1900–14: three case studies', *HJ* (1983), pp. 617–40, A. Fowler, 'Lancashire and the New Liberalism', *NWLH*, Bulletin no. 4 [Hyde], H. E. Mathers, 'Sheffield municipal politics 1893–1926: parties, personalities and the rise of Labour', Sheffield Ph.D. thesis 1980; J. White, 'A panegyric of Edwardian Progressivism', *Journal of British Studies* (1977), esp. pp. 146–8.

evidence.[6] By highlighting Labour's increased representation on municipal councils, or its victories or favourable performances in particular
three-cornered contests, labour historians could argue that beneath the
compliant, contained, Labour parliamentary campaigns in 1906 and 1910
lurked a municipal monster, whose tentacles reached out across the
country. Labour was gaining ground in a whole range of constituencies
(whether or not one accepted Clarke's account of what was happening
in Lancashire). By 1914 the Liberal party was being strangled and
devoured at the roots.

There was also considerable support for the notion that Labour was
about to break out of the Progressive Alliance in 1914. Some argued
that this reflected the expansion of Labour support in the constituencies.
For others, rank and file pressure, and municipal and parliamentary by-
election conflict, were also causing a breakdown in *local* willingness to
comply with the *national* strategy. If McKibbin and others argued that
pressure from below disrupted a carefully constructed national Labour
scheme of gradual expansion, Christopher Howard argued that by 1914
party leaders were willing participants in the expansion planned for the
election in 1914/15.[7]

With the assistance of two colleagues, McKibbin also extended his
observations on the structural constraints facing the Edwardian Labour
party. Matthew, McKibbin and Kay's seminal article attempted to show
that the pre-war parliamentary electoral system had placed an artificially
low ceiling on electoral manifestations of Labour's popular support, and
that it was the removal of this ceiling which allowed Labour to expand.
This important link in the chain has rightly received a great deal of attention. It was supported by other accounts, often with slightly different
intentions and emphases. It developed a municipal dimension which

[6] C. Cook, 'Labour and the downfall of the Liberal party', in A. Sked and C. Cook (eds.),
Crisis and controversy (1976), pp. 38–65. The better local studies include, K. O. Morgan,
Wales in modern British politics (Oxford, 1963), C. Parry, *The radical tradition in Welsh
politics* (Hull, 1970) [*Gwynedd*], R. Hills, 'The City Council and electoral politics, 1901–
71', in C. Feinstein (ed.), *York, 1831–1981* (York, 1981), p. 264, P. J. Waller, *Democracy
and Sectarianism* (Liverpool, 1981), pp. 265–7, G. N. Trodd, 'Political change and the
working class in Blackburn and Burnley, 1880–1914', Lancaster Ph.D. thesis 1978, R.
A. Wright, 'Liberal party organisation and politics in Birmingham, Coventry and Wolverhampton, 1886–1914', Birmingham Ph.D. thesis 1978, pp. 309–14.

[7] McKibbin, *Evolution*, p. 76, M. Petter, 'The Progressive Alliance', *History* (1973), pp. 57–
59, R. Gregory, *The miners in British politics, 1906–14* (Oxford, 1968), p. 191; C. Howard,
'MacDonald, Henderson and the outbreak of war, 1914', *HJ* (1977), pp. 871–2. For reflections of this, Bernstein, 'Liberalism and the Progressive Alliance', pp. 639–40, J. Hinton,
Labour and Socialism (Brighton, 1983), p. 95, K. Burgess, *The challenge of Labour* (1980),
p. 141.

argued that there were also structural impediments to Labour success in municipal politics.[8]

The counter-thesis became more elaborate as more elements of Liberal / Labour politics were scrutinised. Historians of Liberal social policies questioned the 'radicalism' of the Liberals' approach in some instances, and the extent to which New Liberal ideas influenced policy formation in others.[9] Some also suggested that Liberal reforms were unpopular with precisely the voters they were designed to attract.[10] More generally, political historians argued that in national and local politics, New Liberal ideas had not penetrated far beneath the surface. Old ideas and policies were still popular with those who held institutional power at Westminster and in the constituencies. Because of this influence, New Liberal currents were undermined from within by 1914.[11] To differing extents, the Liberals in Yorkshire, the North-East, Wales and even in some parts of Lancashire were more conservative than in those areas which Clarke examined in detail.[12] Liberal municipal politics in particular often proceeded in a different direction to the national approach. Building on this, others argued that the Liberals were thus not a radical, class-based party, but a conservative organisation, still dependent on status politics and Nonconformity (with a little genuine radicalism at the top).[13] Institutional obstacles, and the Liberals' position as a bourgeois party, blocked the spread of New Liberal ideas, and undermined the Liberals' prospects as a party of the left.

[8] H. C. G. Matthew, R. I. McKibbin, and J. A. Kay, 'The franchise factor in the rise of the Labour party', *EHR* (1976); C. Chamberlain, 'The growth in support for the Labour party in Britain', *British Journal of Sociology* (1973), esp. p. 481, H. F. Moorhouse, 'The political incorporation of the British working class: an interpretation', *Sociology* (1973); M. G. Sheppard, 'The effects of the franchise provisions on the social and sex composition of the municipal electorate 1882–1914', *BSSLH* (1982), and local studies by Mathers and others.

[9] J. R. Hay, *The origins of the Liberal welfare reforms, 1906–14* (1975), J. Harris, *Unemployment and politics, 1886–1914* (Oxford, 1972) [references to the pb. edn., 1984].

[10] P. Thane, 'The working class and state "Welfare" in Britain', *HJ* (1984), D. Powell, 'The New Liberalism and the rise of Labour, 1886–1906', *HJ* (1986).

[11] G. L. Bernstein, *Liberalism and Liberal politics in Edwardian England* (1986), R. E. Ellins, 'Aspects of the New Liberalism', Sheffield Ph.D. thesis 1980, and the elaboration of this in M. Bentley, *The climax of Liberal politics* (1987), G. Searle, 'The Edwardian Liberal party and business', *EHR* (1983), B. B. Gilbert, 'David Lloyd George: the reform of British landholding and the Budget of 1914', *HJ* (1978).

[12] K. O. Morgan, 'The New Liberalism and the challenge of Labour: the Welsh experience, 1885–1929', in K. D. Brown (ed.), *Essays in anti-labour history* (1974), Parry, *Gwynedd*, M. Pugh, 'Yorkshire and the New Liberalism?', *Journal of Modern History* (1978), Supplement, A. W. Purdue, 'The Liberal and Labour parties in North-East politics 1900–14: the struggle for supremacy', *IRSH* (1981), I. G. Hunter, 'Workers participation in local government on Tyneside to 1919', Newcastle M.Litt. thesis 1979. See also studies by Howkins, Laybourn and Reynolds, etc., above, fn.5.

[13] This was a widespread assumption. See e.g. Bernstein, *Liberal politics*, p. 200.

It took rather longer for labour and social historians to analyse the theoretical foundations of their belief in an inevitable, class-based, rise of Labour. In the earliest incarnations, Marxist labour historians argued that the Liberals were an employers' party, whereas Labour was linked to the workers' experience of conflict. Industrial unrest was regarded as the motor force of Labour expansion. The level of Labour support reflected the degree of class conflict: Liberal support amongst the working class before 1914 was the result of an incomplete, or scarcely formed, class consciousness; Labour's growth was the result of its intensification and growth in the First World War and the strife torn post-war period.[14] This was gradually modified by emphasising attacks on control of the workplace as the primary agent of class formation. The disintegration of skill and control of the workplace from the 1890s aroused the opposition of 'labour aristocrats' to the political system.[15] For some historians, the war accentuated these developments, radicalising the labour aristocracy and pushing it still closer to the unskilled.[16] Changes in the labour process were again seen by some as the catalysts of discontent and the agents of class formation. Class conflict was an important element in working-class life. A more Socialist party and stance had thus always been a possibility. Leadership passivity was the major obstacle.[17]

Those historians who emphasised the social and cultural reasons behind the emergence of the British working class developed a fuller explanation of political change. In these accounts, circumstances which had little to do with conflict at the workplace created a sense of working-class cultural unity, before the First World War, which was fundamentally inimicable to a Liberal political outlook. For some this was because there was 'some degree of turning back into the manual working class' by labour aristocrats as greater residential segregation, and declining social

[14] A. Howkins, 'Edwardian Liberalism and industrial unrest', *History Workshop* (1977), pp. 158–9, J. L. White, *The limits of trade union militancy* (1978), pp. 146–78, J. Hinton, review of Clarke, *Lancashire Liberalism, BSSLH* (1972), p. 63.

[15] G. Crossick, *An artisan elite in Victorian society* (1978), p. 250, R. Q. Gray, *The aristocracy of labour in nineteenth century Britain* (1981), p. 51, R. Price, *Masters, unions and men* (Cambridge, 1980), and the theoretical and historical elaborations of this in his 'The labour process and labour history', *Social History* (1983) and *Labour in British society* (1986).

[16] Comments by J. Winter and others on McKibbin's paper, 'Labour and politics in the Great War', *BSSLH* (1977), pp. 3–7; see also the elaboration of this in J. Winter, 'Trade Unions and the Labour party in Britain', in W. J. Mommsen and H.-G. Husung (eds.), *The development of trade unionism in Great Britain and Germany 1880–1914* (1985), pp. 364–9.

[17] Burgess, *Challenge of labour*, pp. 166–71, J. Hinton, *The first shop stewards movement* (1973), pp. 332–7, J. Schneer, 'The war, the state and the workplace: British dockers during 1914–1918', in J. E. Cronin and J. Schneer (eds.), *Social conflict and the political order in modern Britain* (1982), pp. 96–109, J. E. Cronin, *Labour and society in modern Britain 1918–1979* (1984).

mobility, helped to form a more homogeneous social stratum. For others, cultural habits and outlooks, the peculiar structure of British society and industry, created an insecure, conservative, but strong sense of class unity. McKibbin put these elements together, arguing that trade unionism could create *collectivist* views and still be compatible with socially conservative views.[18]

Political scientists and 'sociological' historians reinforced this thrust both indirectly, through their impact on the more well-known contributors, and directly in contributions to the historical debate. In their accounts, patterns of religious socialisation were undermined by a growing working-class cultural identity, based on shared experiences, living standards, and life styles, and reinforced by family and workplace socialisation, particularly through the trade unions.[19] For some, especially Arthur Marwick, working-class participation in the war effort, and the attendant revolution in attitudes, was a crucial accelerator to these changes. The political consequences became evident when the franchise was extended in 1918. Labour expanded.[20]

This body of literature highlighted various shortcomings in Clarke's evidence, and clarified and expanded an alternative thesis. The objections might be summarised as follows. First, Clarke *assumed* that the purchase of New Liberal ideas was sufficient to assure their adoption in Cabinet. Secondly, he did not establish that the nationalisation and centralisation of politics had influenced the majority of industrial areas in the same way as it had affected parliamentary politics in those parts of Lancashire which were the focus of his book. Moreover, he failed to establish that Labour was still contained after 1910, when industrial and political circumstances changed in its favour. Thirdly, he speculated on the explanation of the Liberals' downfall after 1918, making little attempt to examine the causes of the Liberal defeat, the origins of Labour support, or the precise explanation of why Liberal disunity should be more politically damaging than Labour's equally apparent division over the war.

These general points are in many respects valid criticisms of Clarke's

[18] P. Joyce, *Work, society and politics* (Brighton, 1980), pp. 332–4, Crossick, *An artisan elite,* p. 250, G. Stedman Jones, 'Working-class culture and working-class politics in London, 1870–1900: notes on the remaking of a working class', *Journal of Social History* (1974) (references to the reprint in *Languages of class* [Cambridge, 1983]); R. I. McKibbin, 'Why was there no Marxism in Britain', *EHR* (1984). McKibbin's work here resembles the classic article by D. Lockwood, 'Sources of variation in working-class images of society', *Sociological Review* (1966).

[19] Elaborated in D. Butler and D. Stokes, *Political change in Britain* (2nd edn., 1981), and K. D. Wald, *Crosses on the ballot* (New Jersey, 1983), pp. 227–37. For the use of these works, Matthew *et al.,* 'Franchise factor', pp. 733–5, Bernstein, *Liberal politics,* p.19.

[20] A. Marwick, *Britain in the century of total war* (1968, Pelican edn., 1970).

pioneering book. Some more specific points are also well established and argued. Yet this is not to say that social class 'explains' the rise of Labour, or that the Edwardian Liberal revival was inevitably temporary. Other historians have examined aspects of the debate and reached rather different conclusions. The *negative* emphasis on the deficiencies of Liberal politics at the centre has not been entirely accepted, although it has not exactly been debated. Although historians of Liberal ideas have in different ways accepted that there were general and specific weaknesses in Liberal ideology as a mobilising force during this period, they have at the same time reinforced the original emphasis on its potential ability to inform a popular and radical approach.[21] Liberal financial policy has also been defended as coherent and radical (even if it did not succeed).[22]

The position in constituency politics is also uncertain. Clarke attempted to fill some of the gaps in his previous work by arguing that the Liberal party fared perfectly adequately at the by-elections of 1910–14, when the politics of change were allegedly growing in strength. Increases in the Labour vote, he argued, resulted not from an absolute increase in 'secular' support, but from a predictable and temporary dissatisfaction with the Government. By-elections, then as now, were an opportunity to register a protest at Government inactivity: they did not signal any permanent change in the level of support. If municipal results were also a stick to beat the Government, then the whole empirical basis for the counter-hypothesis started by McKibbin may need investigation.[23] Regional studies by Davis, Hutchison and Howe point to the existence of powerfully radical tendencies in constituency Liberal politics before, and during, the Edwardian period.[24] Moreover, other local studies show that, despite limited local support for New Liberal policies, the Liberal

[21] P. F. Clarke, *Liberals and Social Democrats* (Cambridge, 1978), M. Freeden, *The New Liberalism* (Oxford, 1978). See also two limited but useful additional works: A. Vinson, 'The Edwardians and poverty: towards a minimum wage', in D. Read (ed.), *Edwardian England* (1982), A. Vincent and R. Plant, *Philosophy, politics and citizenship* (Oxford, 1984).

[22] A. Offer, *Property and politics, 1870–1914* (Cambridge, 1981), B. K. Murray, *The People's Budget 1909/10* (Oxford, 1980).

[23] P. F. Clarke, 'The electoral position of the Liberal and Labour parties, 1910–14', *EHR* (1975), pp. 832–36. See also, R. Douglas, 'Labour in decline', in Brown (ed.), *Essays in anti-labour history*, pp. 105–25, M. Pugh, *The making of modern British politics 1867–1939* (Oxford, 1982), pp. 147–8.

[24] J. Davis, 'Radical clubs and London politics, 1870-1900', in G. Stedman Jones and D. Feldman (eds.), *Metropolis. Histories and representations of London since 1800* (1988), I. G. C. Hutchison, *A political history of Scotland 1832–1924* (Edinburgh, 1986), Chapter 8, J. Howe, 'Liberals, Lib/Labs and Independent Labour in North Gloucestershire, 1890–1914', *Midland Hist.* (1986).

party remained the more important working-class organisation.[25] Recent
studies of political trends in neglected but significant southern towns
show that Labour had made little headway by 1914.[26] Analysis of Labour
politics in future Labour heartlands also shows that even here the party
was often distant from the needs of voters, and that it suffered electorally
as a result.[27] The interpretation and significance of these points is as
yet poorly integrated with the historical debate. However, it is increasingly uncertain that Labour was the inevitable beneficiary of social
change. Some political historians have also recently questioned whether
the electoral system was dramatically biased against potential Labour
voters before 1914, thus explaining poor pre-war performances, and the
subsequent electoral changes.[28] Moreover, some social and labour historians have argued that class fragmentation was *not* eradicated by the
First World War, and that those changes in industrial experience which
allegedly created a more homogeneous working class were not apparent
until *after* the political changes had taken place.[29] Furthermore, even
after 1918, and despite an allegedly 'fully formulated' class consciousness,
political change was slower, and more contingent on the parties' competing approaches, than historians have previously suggested.[30]

These counter-blasts are very convincing on their individual areas, and
several contain broader insights. Nonetheless, innumerable questions
remain unanswered, and innumerable areas of the debate remain unex-
plored. The various critical accounts noted above do not answer the
narrow question of why Labour replaced the Liberals, either by confirm-
ing Clarke's thesis or by supplying an elaborated alternative. They also
do not address the broader question of whether 'ideas' or 'culture' were

[25] e.g. those by Purdue, Hunter, and Pugh above, fn. 11.
[26] M. J. Daunton, *Coal metropolis: Cardiff 1870-1914* (Leicester, 1977), pp. 213–14, P.
      Wyncoll, *The Nottingham labour movement 1880–1939* (1985), R. C. Whiting, *The
      view from Cowley* (Oxford, 1983) and Howe, above, fn. 24.
[27] P. Stead, 'The Labour party in Wales', and W. Hamish Fraser, 'The Labour party
      in Scotland', in K. D. Brown (ed.), *The first Labour party 1906–14* (1985), J. Smith,
      'Labour tradition in Glasgow and Liverpool', *History Workshop* (1984), I. McLean,
      The legend of Red Clydeside (Edinburgh, 1983).
[28] D. M. Tanner, 'The parliamentary electoral system, the "Fourth" Reform Act and the
      rise of Labour in England and Wales', *BIHR* (1983), M. Hart, 'The Liberals, the war
      and the franchise', *EHR* (1982), p. 826.
[29] A. Reid, 'Dilution, trade unionism and the state in Britain during the First World War',
      in S. Tolliday and J. Zeitlin (eds.), *Shop floor bargaining and the state* (Cambridge,
      1983), J. Zeitlin, 'Craft control and the division of labour: engineers and compositors
      in Britain, 1890–1930', *Cambridge Journal of Economics* (1979), R. Penn, *Skilled workers
      in the class structure* (Cambridge, 1984).
[30] McLean, *Red Clydeside*, Chapters 13–14, Whiting, *Cowley*, Chapter 6, T. Adams, 'The
      formation of the Co-operative party re-considered', *IRSH* (1987), C. Howard, '"Expec-
      tations born to death": local Labour party expansion in the 1920s', in J. Winter (ed.),
      The working class in modern British history (Cambridge, 1983).

the basis of pre-war political success. While they contain ideas which may inform a new interpretation of why the Labour party grew in this period, they do not supply a coherent argument which can rival the older accounts. Moreover, questions relating to electoral and political change in general generally remain the preserve of political scientists or 'theoretical' historians writing in partial detachment from the historical material.

This book addresses two problems. The first is empirical. There is a shortage of information and there are technical doubts over how that information should be interpreted. However, the addition of new information is unlikely in itself to provide an adequate explanation of the electoral and political changes. As a few studies of Labour politics before and after this period are beginning to indicate, and as my own work suggests, the problem is more fundamental. New information has to be put in a new framework if it is to make sense of the complex pattern of change revealed in these and other studies. It is more instructive, I will argue, to treat the competing ideas of a class-based Liberal party, powered by New Liberal ideas on the one hand, and a class-based Labour party, powered by a limited, 'cultural', class consciousness on the other, as equally inappropriate guides to the political realignment of 1900–18. The question is essentially how to reconstruct and rephrase these debates in a manner which will explain the electoral changes, and the changes in the parties themselves. The older 'schools' do neither, while newer approaches have to be built into an overall view of the rise of Labour. This book attempts to supply a new bench mark and a way of going forward by developing new ideas and suggesting new approaches both to this narrow question, and to the related and implicit concern with electoral change in general.

II

Traditional means of examining political and electoral change are currently being reassessed, and recent work by political scientists, electoral geographers, sociologists and social historians has suggestive consequences for any analysis of the political map of Britain between 1900 and 1918. 'Class consciousness', some sociologists argue, may not inform political actions, even when it evidently 'exists'. Some social psychologists have argued that political actions are rational, individual, choices and are not based on group sentiment; political scientists have attacked the idea that simple shifts in the class structure can of themselves 'explain' realignment. They have developed hypotheses which stress the importance of factors other than social class in contemporary political behaviour. Voting, they argue, may be influenced by religion, housing tenure, occu-

pational interest and geographical region. While there is no consensus
on the weight to be attached to these (and other) factors, it is widely
accepted that intra-class differences may be more significant than notions
of a broader class unity in explaining electoral behaviour.[31] Those who
take this line are explicitly critical of older studies of voting behaviour,
and of the idea that 'class politics', the notion which implicitly and explicitly underpinned much of the earlier historical analysis of electoral
realignment, is a useful explanatory concept.[32]

New theories do not suggest that voting patterns are best explained
by a social determinism based on a larger number of variables. The logic
of much recent analysis is to recognise the difficulties of making connections between 'social' experience and 'political' responses. The state itself,
some argue, might take a hand in the process by 'contesting' the transformation of the working class into a single radical force.[33] Ideology, language, and policy – political factors – are ascribed a (differing) degree
of responsibility in determining the nature of political actions.[34] Voting
can best be explained by examining the interaction between social experiences and the political attempts to mobilise sentiments, interests, and
beliefs, not by assuming that either social conditions or ideas are paramount. However much they differ on the precise explanation of political
behaviour, most recent analysis agrees that the political map contains

[31] A. Giddens, *The constitution of society* (Cambridge, 1984). For electoral behaviour,
e.g. D. Robertson, *Class and the British electorate* (Oxford, 1984), A. Heath, R. Jowell,
and J. Curtice, *How Britain votes* (1985), P. Dunleavy, 'The urban basis of political
alignment', *British Journal of Political Science* (1979), R. Johnson, e.g. in *The geography
of British politics* (1985). For 'rational choice' and voting behaviour, H. T. Himmelweit,
P. Humphreys, M. Jaeger, and M. Katz, *How voters decide* (1981), esp. Chapter 5.
The older tradition is represented by M. Abrams and R. Rose, *Must Labour lose* (1960)
and M. Jacques and F. Mulhern (eds.), *The forward march of Labour halted* (1981)

[32] Political scientists have made some interesting observations on the historical uses, and
abuses, of psephological insights. See W. Miller, *Electoral dynamics* (1977), pp. 224–5
and Chapter 6, I. Crewe, 'Do Butler and Stokes really explain political change in Britain?'
European Journal of Political Research (1974). For a further critique of the *historical*
validity of the Butler/Stokes view, H. T. Himmelweit, M. J. Biberian, and J. Stockdale,
'Memory for past vote: implications of a study of bias in recall', *British Journal of
Political Science* (1978), R.J. Katz, R. G. Niemi, and D. Newman, 'Reconstructing
past partisanship in Britain', ibid. (1980).

[33] Stedman Jones, *Languages of class,* pp. 1–24, P. Joyce, 'Labour, capital and compromise:
a response to Richard Price', and his 'Languages of reciprocity and conflict: a further
response to Richard Price', *Social History* (1983 and 1984). See also for a summary
of the origins of the debate, G. Eley and K. Nield. 'Why does social history ignore
politics?', ibid. (1980).

[34] Historians wishing to unravel the *differences* between groups of modern political scientists may gain some guidance from the following: D. Kavanagh, 'How we vote now',
Electoral Studies (1984), J. R. Owens and L. L. Wade, 'Economic conditions and constituency voting in Great Britain', *Political Studies* (1988), M. Savage, 'Understanding
political alignments in contemporary Britain: do localities matter?', *Political Geography
Quarterly* (1987).

pronounced regional variations which cannot be explained by social class alone, and which have to be explained, in part at least, by examining the competing political approaches of the respective parties.

There is an additional question to be considered. The ideas of class-based voting behaviour, and class-based political action, are closely related. However, if electorates are not monoliths, neither are parties. They do not exist to serve a single body of ideas or a single interest. Ideas and interests vary; parties may represent several interests in differing ways and to differing extents. Party action, like electoral behaviour, may best be examined through studying the relationship between political factors (such as party ideology) and social factors (such as the economic/ social interests of the party's major electoral constituency). Yet there may be several ideological strands within a party, and several real, or potential, electoral bases. As participants in the debate already recognise, the nature of a party's electoral base, and the nature of its aims, are powerfully related. Reinterpretation of the pattern of electoral change, and reinterpretation of the *nature* of the parties, should logically go hand in hand.[35]

Yet policy is not just about the intellectuals' ideology and the voters' interests. Party actions are also influenced by the beliefs of those who control the political machine. The structure of the party, and the nature of institutional power at the centre and in the constituencies, may determine what issues are put forward, what issues are selected to dominate the party appeal, and what ideas are put forward as policy in office. Again, this is recognised implicitly in many historical accounts.[36] Institutional questions must be given due weight.

This book has its origins in three broad ideas: that the specific historical debate over the 'rise of Labour' needs greater investigation; that the ideas underpinning some accounts are questionable; that newer theoretical ideas and new historical evidence can be put together to their mutual benefit. The conceptual dissatisfaction, and the alternative put forward here, has four facets. First, political ideas are too frequently seen as part of intellectual history, while even those who stress the importance of a political context in the history of ideas have not always fully integrated the study of changing ideas with the study of political and electoral change. Secondly, national influences – be it ideology or class consciousness – are seen as the major, universalising, dynamic of political and electoral change. Yet the precise nature and meaning of ideologies or of class consciousness, and their political implications, are likely to differ

[35] See e.g. McKibbin, *Evolution,* p. 247, and Winter, 'Trade unions and the Labour party', in Mommsen and Husung (eds.), *The development of trade unionism,* pp. 364–9.
[36] See works cited in fns. 6, 9, 11.

from place to place. Most 'national' studies – and many theories of electoral behaviour – fail to identify the importance of a spatial or contextual perspective to electoral and political change, by passing over the role of a diverse social and economic structure, and an active local political elite, in determining political outcomes and images. Thirdly, and following from this, local social/economic conditions are often seen as determining forces, when they were only rendered politically operational by political factors. Popular perceptions of needs, I would argue, were influenced by political factors as well as 'objective' social realities. In sum, 'national' forces are worked out and made individually meaningful in electoral politics according to the balance of local economic interests, past political traditions, and current political approaches. 'Policy' and 'class' are not felt or expressed in the same way in all places.

The final point concerns the relationship between electoral politics and electoral change and shifts in the nature of the parties themselves. A contextual, disaggregated, and interactive view of electoral politics, requires a similar view of the parties as institutions. It is argued here that local political representations of particular economic or social perspectives can become distinct, if ill-formed, ideological strands. The advocates of these views within a national leadership (or party structure) may ensure that they become part of a composite national image. Changes in the institutional strength of ideological strands, or in the electoral purchase of their ideas, can thus alter the balance of the party as a whole. *Parties* are thus best understood not as representatives of a nationalising ideology or social force, but as unstable coalitions of ideological groups with different interests and aims.[37] *Policy* is best understood by examining the conflicting ideas of competing strands on several important considerations. These ideas became apparent in discussions concerning who the party's supporters were or who they should be; what this groups interests might be; how these interests might best be satisfied; and how satisfying these popular demands might be reconciled with the interests and views of the party activists themselves. Policy thus helps determine support (by contributing to the creation of a particular image); it also reflects the nature of the party's electoral base. In sum, electoral behaviour, and political parties, must be disaggregated and reassembled in a more helpful and constructive manner if we are to understand major electoral realignments and broad policy orientations. While this may require better theoretical models (of voting behaviour and class formation for example), these alone will not provide answers. Circumstances constantly change, presenting new opportunities and new challenges. The

[37] See the suggestive analysis by Stedman Jones, 'Why is the Labour party in a mess?' in his *Languages of Class*.

pattern of change will not be understood by constructing castles in the air; they need to be related to shapes on the ground.

Despite the use of insights common in modern political science, this book is a purposely historical study of the political changes which took place between 1900 and 1918. I have tried to place the analysis of change firmly in its contemporary context, to illuminate the forces which kept Labour confined within the Progressive Alliance before 1914, and allowed it to break out thereafter.[38] I have, it is true, attempted to establish the validity of contemporary perceptions, to substantiate some of them, and to explain the changes in a manner which is not subservient to contemporary language; to respect the past is important, but to become its slave and become buried in its views and vocabulary is a serious mistake.

This book draws on a variety of ideas and material. It addresses a historical debate which has been divided, for some years, into two, periodically warring, camps and several half-distinct approaches. Social historians, political historians, political scientists and others have all tackled the subject in partially different ways. Within its historiographical confines the book is fairly expansive, combining material and ideas from all these areas. It analyses why change took place and the effects which this had on British social democracy. It considers ideas, policy, *and* electoral and institutional change as it influenced *both* the Liberal *and* Labour parties. It deals with broad issues, which successive studies have increasingly shrouded in a mass of conflicting detail, but without neglecting to base these ideas on hard historical evidence. The argument of the book nonetheless rests mainly on its ability to make sense of the changes which actually took place, not on the 'validity' of its (eclectic) 'theoretical base' or the breadth of the research. I believe my conclusions are more consistent with the evidence, more thoroughly researched, and sustained by better empirical evidence than the alternatives, but I do not expect this to be the last word on the narrow question (the rise of Labour) or the broad question (ways of approaching Labour and electoral history).

Some parts of this book will no doubt by read by 'political' historians, some by 'social' historians, and some probably by neither. Political historians may think chapters dealing with social history are unnecessary and vice versa. Theoreticians and local historians in particular will also find many over-simplified summaries. I hope, however, that the book will be viewed as a whole, as a book which ties various strands together,

---

[38] One by-product of this concentration on the dynamics of the Progressive Alliance is the exclusion of Scotland from much of the early part of the book, as the Progressive Alliance did not operate there. A number of excellent recent texts on Scottish history nonetheless suggest that the pattern of political change in Scotland was not that different from England and Wales. For cross-references to Scottish politics, below pp. 200 fn. 3, 319 fn. 1, 336 fn. 38.

and builds these into a new account. A broad, all-embracing, historical account was necessary because theoretical accounts and case studies are too easily dismissed. It was possible only because so many historians, on both 'sides' of the debate, have produced material on aspects of the question which is serviceable and convincing. Since my argument stresses the *interactive* nature of politics, it will inevitably, and rightly, share some points with these accounts. I do not wish to claim that my approach is historically or conceptually without precedents or debts. However, I do not believe that a continuing emphasis on the extent to which research confirms or refutes either of the existing approaches is helpful. I have attempted to *build* on much of the existing research in this area, while adding new insights and information. The end product 'belongs' to neither side, and is not an attempt to mediate between them. The rejection of 'class politics' – created either by ideas or by other factors – as an explanatory concept is part of a broader trend which may provide a platform for the necessary reconstruction of the electoral and institutional history of the British working class since 1885.[39] The book should perhaps be seen as a very long essay dealing with a particular problem, which is itself part of a larger issue.

The book has a simple structure. Part I contains a discussion of debates over ideology and policy at the political centre. It also notes the policy consequences of these debates for the Liberal and Labour parties. It is concerned with the conflict within parties, and between them, as they acted in an uneasy, partial, alliance. It also examines the ways in which the resulting 'national' image could be transmitted to the constituency parties and to the electorate. Part II examines the way in which the party images were received locally, i.e. it involves recognising that constituency parties could emphasise particular aspects of the 'national' image. It also examines the way in which voters in vastly different areas, with different interests and political cultures, responded to the local/national image of the competing Progressive parties. In Part III, I put these elements together, and discuss the electoral position, strategic choices, and the nature of the Liberal and Labour parties on the eve of the First World War. Part IV shows how this position changed between 1914 and 1918. I look first at the extent to which structural conditions changed, creating the potential for a shift in political allegiances, and secondly at Labour's attempt to formulate new, popular, political, interpretations of that

[39] For works with related themes, D. Howell, *British workers and the Independent Labour Party 1888–1906* (Manchester, 1983), M. Savage, *The dynamics of working-class politics* (Cambridge, 1987), Adams, 'Co-operative party'. McLean, *Red Clydeside,* and J. P. D. Dunbabin, 'British elections in the nineteenth and twentieth centuries: a regional approach', *EHR* (1980) also identify new means of examining electoral change in this period.

experience at the 1918 election. The Conclusion briefly discusses the consequences which political realignment and political change had for the nature of British Liberal and Social Democratic politics in the years following Labour's emergence as a major electoral force.

Part I   Politics at the centre

Chapter 1

The origins and viability of
Progressive politics

The Liberals had become the principal working-class party in most parts of the country by the 1880s. Many trade unions sought political representation through Liberal channels. The formation of a Labour party in 1900 was thus a break with the past because it involved independent organisation and representation. Nonetheless, the Liberals did not abandon 'labour' or the working-class vote. On the contrary, they hoped that a tacit alliance with an independent Labour organisation would enable them to extend their appeal. Many Liberals believed that Labour might attract support from some Tory working-class voters. They also acknowledged that labour organisations were already a powerful force in some 'Liberal' areas. A Liberal/Labour pact thus had a dual justification. Labour parliamentary candidates – unopposed by the Liberals – might obtain support where the Liberals, unaided, would always fail; a pact which limited Labour intervention in 'Liberal' strongholds would also protect Liberal flanks. The Liberals would gain the support of a useful ally. Labour would secure the parliamentary foothold it had hitherto been unable to gain through direct competition with the older parties. An informal pact was drawn up in 1903, and this operated fairly successfully at the 1906 election (Section I).

In 1903, Labour was a junior partner with presumed, localised advantages over the Liberals. At the same time, the Liberals recognised that if Labour was to remain a supplementary ally, and not become a national rival, they would have to maintain and reinforce their credibility as a radical force. There were several competing strands in Liberal politics, and politicians representing these competing views hoped to supply the political means of maintaining the Liberal party as the primary anti-Tory organisation in British politics. They all, to differing extents, supported more interventionist, and more radical, social, and economic policies (Section II). Although the Progressive Alliance had some purely pragmatic supporters, who saw it as a tactical device, its formation also reflected the existence of considerable Liberal support for a vague, undefined, radical synthesis, which might bring policies supported by Labour to the foreground of Liberal politics. The Liberal party had began to change even before the formation of a Liberal Government in 1906.

Representatives from the various ideological strands in the Labour party also recognised the need for practical state intervention, although – as in the Liberal party – each strand had a partially different conception of what this should involve. However, if there was an area of shared Liberal/Labour political *interest*, certain 'Labour' and 'Liberal' ideological strands also shared a core of political *beliefs*. Nonetheless, there were 'Labour' aims which Liberals did not wish to accommodate, while even those Labour reformers who shared many radical Liberal views argued that a *composite* Liberal party would be unable to implement a radical programme because of the power of its conservative wing. On the Labour side, a coalition of disparate reformers thus hoped to co-operate with the Liberals over shared objectives, whilst working to replace them as the permanent party of the left (Section III). Even if a 'Progressive consensus' existed between key political leaders in both parties, these leaders wished to maximise their own party's political position. They wished to co-operate where necessary, not to merge.

The radical Liberals' primary weapon was the purchase of their ideas. If they could encapsulate most of the Labour party's needs and interests, then it would be difficult for it to escape from its position as a (useful) junior ally. However, the idea of a Progressive Alliance was not without its critics. Each party contained ideological/political forces which were dissatisfied with the national approach. This had important consequences. Policy formation and debate could result in the exposition, and adoption, of views which – if the ideas were powerful enough, or if their representatives were institutionally strong enough – could alter the composite image of the party in one of three ways. First, it might alter the balance of power between the two parties at the margins by making one slightly more attractive than was hitherto the case. Secondly, it might allow a more fundamental shift within the Progressive Alliance without dramatically undermining the broad ideological consensus. Thirdly, the secondary strands might more fundamentally shift the balance of internal power, either by a political/institutional coup, or by creating an ideological trajectory which made the Alliance strategy unnecessary. This might totally alter the nature of the electoral competition and shatter the Progressive consensus; it might also fundamentally alter the nature of the political parties. The Liberal and Labour parties were being drawn together, but the Progressive Alliance was under pressure from its inception.

I

The Gladstone–MacDonald pact of 1903 was formed against a background of Liberal and Socialist electoral failure. Despite the extension
of the franchise in 1884 to agricultural labourers and the large number
of industrial workers (particularly in coal and woollen textiles) who lived
in county divisions, the Liberals did not appear capable of even denting
the Tory ascendancy after 1885. Tory success did not stem just from
its sound organisation, from Liberal disunity, or from clever tactics.
Neither was its new support based solely on the impact of agricultural
depression and the growth of Villa Toryism. There was a third component. Liberal mishandling of the economy between 1892 and 1895, and
trade depression more generally, were significant factors in the continued
existence of working-class support for the Conservative party. The Tories
developed a variety of successful and material appeals to working-class
voters to reinforce their older approaches. A strong Empire, backed by
a strong navy, they argued, would create a secure market for British
goods. Fair Trade and Bimetallism were specific, locally popular, manifestations of this stance.[1] Some Tories also supported a degree of social
intervention. This included a municipal collectivism which embraced the
provision of certain services, the extension of municipal housing schemes,
and the relief of destitution. In some areas this reinforced an older popular
Toryism, based around a xenophobic Protestantism.[2] What worried
the Liberals, however, was not just that parts of working-class Lancashire,
the West Midlands, London, and some southern ports were becoming
Tory bastions; they were also now being threatened in 'Liberal' areas
such as Yorkshire and the North-East.[3]

The ILP was also under threat. Although able to mobilise an encouraging amount of support after its formation in 1893, it was declining by
1900. Nonetheless, two important features of ILP politics made it a potentially attractive partner for the Liberals. First, if working-class Tory col-

---

[1] This neglected question cannot be adequately dealt with in a book dealing largely with
the shift in Progressive politics, although it is touched on below where Tory politics
had a major impact on Labour. It is clear, however, that some of the problems, and
some of the debates, evident in Progressive circles were paralleled in Tory politics. [See
M. Pugh, *The Tories and the people 1880–1935* (Oxford, 1985), and E. H. H. Green,
The crisis of Conservatism (forthcoming, 1992).] See also Offer, *Property and politics,*
pp. 223–4.

[2] Pelling, *Social geography,* e.g. pp. 254, 259, Savage, *Preston,* pp. 137–45, Fowler, 'Hyde',
pp. 49–50, Waller, *Liverpool,* esp. Chapter 3, Hutchison, *Scotland,* Chapter 7 and esp.
pp. 205–6.

[3] See correspondence on the position in the North-East, H. Samuel and I. Mitchell to
J.R.M., 23 June 1903, LRC 9/369, 6 May 1903, LRC 8/174. See also correspondence
cited in Bernstein, *Liberal politics,* p. 71. For South Wales, L. Harcourt to H.G., 3
Oct. 1903, H.G. Add MS 45992 fos. 63–5.

lectivists would not support the Liberals, they might support Labour. Secondly, Socialists attracted support from dissident radical Liberals, particularly in areas, like Yorkshire, where their own party was extremely conservative. They also, in these areas, attracted Tory support.[4] An alliance with the new Labour party would remove the threat to Liberal success in its strongholds and establish a potentially more successful ally in areas of working-class Conservatism. By fielding only one candidate against the Tories, 'Progressives' (Liberal or Labour) would become a more powerful force. The Liberals could contribute a middle-class Nonconformist vote which Labour alone could not mobilise. Labour could contribute the support of ex-Tory working men who would not support a Liberal candidate. Both parties already appealed to Liberal radicals. The electoral logic was so compelling that, even before the national parties formed an arrangement, constituency organisations were conducting their own negotiations.[5]

The 'negotiations' involved in the 1903 pact have been ably discussed elsewhere.[6] MacDonald hoped for a free run in up to fifty-two seats. In return, he would encourage Labour constituency organisations elsewhere not to field candidates, but to vote for the party which had shown its 'good fellowship' by not opposing Labour candidates in other seats. It was an unofficial arrangement. Labour had to be independent from the Liberals if it was to attract Tory working-class support, and to appease its Socialist activists. Independence was also MacDonald's primary bargaining counter in negotiations with Liberal leaders. Herbert Gladstone, the Liberal Chief Whip, thought there would be no problem in obtaining free runs for Labour candidates in thirty-six of the fifty-two constituencies where Labour campaigns were likely. The bulk of these were working-class Tory seats and double member boroughs. The pact took shape so easily because Liberal party strategists were so pessimistic about their electoral prospects without such an alliance.

In 1906 the pact operated fairly successfully. Of the fifty-two Labour candidates who went to the polls, around two-thirds were in 'Tory'

---

[4] For the ILP's 'Tory' support even in 'Liberal' areas, see *Labour Chronicle* (Liverpool), Dec. 1898, referring to the East Bradford by-election, and Howell, *ILP*, p. 198. Dr Howell's book is an invaluable source and sure guide to the ILP in this period.

[5] The Lancashire examples are the most fully documented (Clarke, *Lancashire Liberalism*, pp. 162–4, Howell, *ILP*, pp. 221–4). For Yorkshire, e.g. Howell, *ILP*, p. 193 (Bradford), Leeds LF Cabinet Comm. Mins, 22 Aug. 1898, Halifax West Ward Lib. Comm. Mins, 2 Dec. 1901, noting opposition to 'the action taken in the last Municipal Elections, Liberal and Labour uniting together to forward the Progressive movement'.

[6] e.g. H. Pelling, *Origins of the Labour party 1880–1900* (Oxford, 2nd edn., 1965), and Bealey and Pelling, *Labour and politics*. The major correspondence is reproduced in F. Bealey, 'Negotiations between the Liberal party and the Labour Representation Committee before the General Election of 1906', *BIHR* (1956).

regions or double member boroughs. Almost all of these were elected. In 'Liberal' areas, there were a few 'concessions' in seats where Labour had a substantial base, and again Labour candidates were usually elected as a result. The pact also worked from the Liberal standpoint. There were only thirteen official three-cornered contests, leaving the Liberal flanks fairly free of disruptive attacks. The Liberals also benefited from Labour support in Tory areas. This was widely regarded as a major influence on the result.[7]

Nonetheless, the Progressive Alliance was a sickly child, the secret offspring of an illicit relationship. Although Liberal/Labour conflict in 1906 was not particularly widespread, there were many more constituency leaders who opposed the idea of a pact than the level of Liberal/Labour conflict in the constituencies would suggest. Indeed, there was no Liberal/Labour pact in Scotland, because Liberal anti-Progressives were so strong in the area.[8] In the North-East, nineteen of twenty-three Presidents of Liberal constituency organisations opposed the arrangement. Liberal opposition was rife in Yorkshire, where many ILP-dominated organisations also found it almost impossible to contemplate agreements with the conservative local Liberals. When the NEC refused to sanction Labour campaigns, dissident Labour activists often supported unofficial Labour or SDF candidates.[9] Neither was the opposition without some political rationale. In several Yorkshire seats (e.g. Bradford West, Leeds South, Huddersfield, and Wakefield) and a few mining seats in the North-East and South Wales, Labour polled so well that the Alliance appeared likely to restrict electoral expansion rather than help. If so, it would inevitably come under pressure. Once the threat to Free Trade either receded or assumed less significance, the Labour attack might grow and spread.

II

Liberal radicals were aware that Liberal conservatism was a major danger. They argued that it made the party liable to be outflanked. A continuing Liberal fascination with status issues and *laissez faire* economics would allow Labour to expand even in Liberal strongholds, simply by being a 'better' Progressive party. From the 1890s, the 'New Liberals' argued that the Liberal party must update its ideology and policies if (as J. A. Hobson wrote) it was 'to avoid the shipwreck which Continental Liber-

---

[7] Table of results, Bealey and Pelling, *Labour and politics*, pp. 290–2. 'Tory' and 'Liberal' regions are identified in Chapters 5–10.

[8] Bealey and Pelling, *Labour and politics*, Chapter 10 and Hutchison, *Scotland*, pp. 179–85.

[9] H. V. Emy, *Liberals, Radicals and social politics 1892–1914* (Cambridge, 1973), pp. 90–1; Laybourn and Reynolds, *Yorkshire*, Chapter 5. For SDF/ILP co-operation, see e.g. Howell, *ILP*, pp. 210–11 (Rochdale), and below, p. 264 (Bradford).

alism had suffered when it was driven on to the submerged reef of the economic problem'. The relative merits of 'Individualism' and 'Collectivism' became the focal point of Liberal ideological debate.[10]

By the 1890s the point of contention was not the need for *some* intervention, but the grounds, nature, and extent of collectivist action. It was increasingly recognised that liberty was a chimera without greater equality, and that a better, more 'moral' or civilised life was incompatible with current economic conditions. Historians have long recognised that these 'Individualists' split into two camps, the Liberal Imperialists and the Radicals. Although some of the Liberal Imperialists' leaders and MPs, like Haldane, Asquith, Crewe, Trevelyan, and Samuel, were Collectivists who happened to support the idea of Empire, many of the less well-known back benchers were arch-Individualists. At the constituency level, Liberal Imperialists were preponderantly Anglicans (or 'Protestant' Nonconformists). Their views were frequently closer to those of the average Tory than to the largely Nonconformist Radicals, whose enthusiasm for temperance, licensing reform, and Home Rule were dismissed as 'faddist' by some Liberal Imperialists.

The Radicals' *moral regenerationism,* as New Liberals and historians have noted, had an ideological core. Many emphasised the detrimental moral and economic impact of extensive state intervention. For T. H. Green, whose views inspired many Radicals, man's moral/ethical motivations were part of a General Will which corresponded with his 'higher' convictions, and with God's will on earth. There was no salvation in moral actions achieved through compulsion. Practical attempts to achieve individual improvement (through non-economic policies or through social work) were a duty and a Christian act. The religious were to create the conditions in which self-help could prosper. The Forward Movement in Methodism, Christian Socialism, and the Settlement House movement, reflected these intentions.

Radicals and Liberal Imperialists (with those – perhaps the majority – who stood somewhere between the two) could often agree over the need to limit state intervention in the 1880s. By the turn of the century at the latest, the climate was changing. Nonetheless, while men from both groups (like Morley and Rosebery) stuck to their guns, other Liberals – particularly leading Liberal Imperialists (like Haldane and Asquith) and leading Radical businessmen (like J. Brunner and W. H. Lever) –

[10] J. A. Hobson, *The Crisis of Liberalism* (1909), pp. xii-xiii. The following section draws heavily on the now enormous secondary literature on Liberal ideology, particularly S. Collini, *Liberalism and Sociology* (Cambridge, 1979), Clarke, *Liberals and Social Democrats,* Freeden, *New Liberalism.* Radicals (capital 'R') are those Liberals, the dominant element after 1885, who were interested in for example: temperance reform, education, Nonconformist issues, Irish Home Rule, etc.

increasingly saw state intervention as the proper means to provide the
conditions in which moral enlightenment (and private industry) could
prosper. Moreover, a different strand, which included religious radicals
like Rowntree and many of the London Liberals, who had followed their
religious beliefs and engaged in Christian mission to the poor, came to
think that environmental and economic conditions were blocking individual moral progress. 'Self-help' was only possible if the state intervened
to tackle the root causes of poverty which, they recognised, were social
and not personal. At the same time, a secular radical strand, identified
with the journalists and theorists L. T. Hobhouse and J. A. Hobson,
but also including a number of MPs, was also gaining in strength. Perhaps
paradoxically, given the New Liberals' distaste for religion, many of the
religious radicals became strong supporters of New Liberal policies, swelling the importance of this strand in Liberal politics.[11]

The emergence of 'new' men and new views created new ideological/
political groupings with broadly similar perspectives. The first new perspective, expressed in works by men such as F. W. Hirst and J. A. Simon,
and drawing support from sympathisers with the 'national efficiency'
movement, was not ideologically sophisticated. These men raised doubts
about the New Liberals' interest in Socialism and state intervention
because they began from a genuinely different premiss. Their views, as
the New Liberals knew, were shared by a substantial proportion of the
party, and thus had to be considered. The New Liberal 'advanced guard',
Hobson wrote, had to 'succeed in rallying round them the genuine support
of the Liberal "centre" in Parliament and in the nation'. This 'Centrist'
group, he continued, was 'alike in sympathy and in formal policy more
advanced than it has ever been before'. Their objection to 'the great
work of social reconstruction' rested 'not on points of practical detail
but on deep-seated notions respecting the ways and effects of social reconstruction'. They were particularly concerned that a socialistic Liberalism
would mean bureaucracy, higher taxation, 'encroachment upon private
profitable enterprise' and attacks on liberty and democracy. The party's
future existence depended on the conversion of this group to the New
Liberals' social programme.[12]

The key difference between the two groups was finance. Centrists were
concerned with the generation of wealth and opportunity, rather than
its redistribution. They were prepared to accept collectivist action where
it facilitated this, or where it did not prevent economic prosperity. The

[11] Vincent and Plant, *Philosophy, politics and citizenship,* esp. Chapters 3 and 6. For
examples of 'religious radicals', below, pp. 166–70, 272.
[12] Hobson, *Crisis of Liberalism,* pp. 133–8; Freeden, *New Liberalism,* pp. 62–4. For
Asquith's sympathy with these views, pp. 48–9, 65.

New Liberals, as 'moral reformers', shared many of the Centrists' basic Liberal beliefs, but augmented them with a belief in social justice, welfare and community. They wished to shift the balance of Liberal politics by addressing the issue of greater equality, although they were also concerned to show that greater state intervention was still compatible with individual liberty. Individuals could be convinced of the need for intervention; participatory democracy would continually reaffirm a voluntary consent. As the people

> could look upon the Government as their servant and the acts of the Government as their acts, it followed necessarily that the antagonism between democracy (or liberty) and governmental action fell flat.[13]

This was not a blueprint for sudden and wholesale state intervention. Change would be gradual. L. T. Hobhouse argued that psychologically all new ideas and experiences had to be reconciled with (more conservative) existing views; Hobson wrote of 'the futility of direct forcible assaults upon deep-rooted habits'. Nonetheless, there were no restrictions on how far change could proceed. If opinion demanded it, the state could extend its control indefinitely. As Russell Rea put it,

> there is no finality in (Liberal) Social Reform, given a universal, perpetual, never-satisfied desire for something better than anything that is ever realised.[14]

New Liberals argued that the national interest was paramount; they also recognised that certain groups needed particular attention – the 'greatest and most pressing need being the improvement of the condition of the working millions'. Society was not currently harmonious and class free because the balance of wealth and power weighted matters in capital's favour. On the economic front, the expansion of trade unionism would restore a balance; in the country as a whole, state intervention was necessary to underpin this position and to improve conditions for the unorganised. 'Competition and the forces of individual self-interest' had to be replaced 'by a deliberate and systematic arrangement of labour and commerce in the best interests of society as a whole'. The idea that society was an organic community, with each part dependent on the other, was used to support the emphasis on tackling working-class grievances. It was also used to justify the representation of organised labour in Parliament. Although the New Liberals were concerned that the 'sectional'

---

[13] Cited in P. F. Clarke, 'The Social Democratic theory of the class struggle', in Winter (ed.), *The working class*, p. 6. Freeden, *Liberalism divided*, p. 113 and Clarke, 'Social Democratic Theory', for the categorisation of social democratic and Liberal thought.

[14] R. Rea, *Social reform versus Socialism* (1912), p. 11. Hobhouse's views cited in J. T. Kloppenberg, *Uncertain victory: Social Democracy and Progressivism in European and American thought* (Oxford, 1986), p. 308, Hobson cited in Freeden, *New Liberalism*, pp. 256–7.

demands of organised labour groups would encourage them to act in their own self-interest, and that their concern to pass legislation in the working-class interest would reinforce this, they buried their concerns beneath a *moral populism* which saw 'goodness' and 'labour' as interchangeable terms.[15] Ideologically there was no reason for this. Since ethical conviction was seen to be the basis for individual action, and morality was not uniquely the preserve of the working class, *all* social groups might support social reforms. Many recognised this. The New Liberal theorists wished to preserve a role for the intellectual middle classes. Ideas – the New Liberals' currency – were the basis of political progress. Middle-class intellectuals were the life blood of the political system. New Liberals thus wanted to *convert* middle-class party members who were currently less convinced. They argued that their ideology was Liberal, that state intervention was Liberal, that Liberals of all social groups could support New Liberal aims, and that the necessary changes in Liberal politics would be gradual, rather than revolutionary. New Liberal philosophy was an ideological expression of the political need to change Liberal policy without destroying all the older Liberals' ideas, or antagonising the political constituency which they had established.

Ideological support for collectivism meant little if it was not reinforced by credible, materially relevant, policies. Many Liberal constituency parties shifted their position in the 1890s, accepting the need for a more material approach at the municipal level.[16] 'Municipal enterprise' was supported even by Radicals and Liberal Imperialists, who accepted public provision of utilities and services. Comparatively generous treatment of the poor, and provision for a more open educational system, became more evident in Liberal areas. The municipality also played an important role in Radical proposals for control of the drink trade; it was a means of making intervention and public control compatible. Although Radical/Centrist alliances would only go so far, where Progressives gained the upper hand, municipal policy became extremely radical. The London Progressives' administration of the LCC between 1895 and 1907, for example, was a model for Liberal organisations in other parts of the country, and for city authorities in other parts of the world. Change was under way.

[15] Quotations from Freeden, *New Liberalism,* p. 126 and Powell, 'The New Liberalism and Labour', p. 372. For the healing role of moral populism, Clarke, 'Social Democratic theory', p. 12.

[16] Much of the following is based on Offer, *Property and politics,* Chapters 15–16. For details of even conservative Liberal intervention, e.g. L. L. Jones, 'Public pursuit or private profit? Liberal businessmen and municipal politics in Birmingham, 1895–1900', *Business History* (1983), p. 255 and D. James, 'Paternalism in Keighley', in J. A. Jowitt (ed.), *Model industrial communities in Yorkshire* (Bradford, 1986).

The cost of these services pushed Centrists and New Liberals towards state intervention. Municipalities could not cope with the new demands without external financial assistance. One very popular solution was land reform. The Taxation of Land Values movement – which grew very substantially during the 1890s – was the lowest common denominator of contrasting schemes. Some prominent Liberal land reformers, like Lord Carrington, hoped to stem urban congestion and limit urban unemployment through a national policy of rural regeneration.[17] Other Centrist Liberals argued that the potential value of sites, rather than the current assessment, should be rated. This would shift the rateable burden to 'unproductive' landowners and speculators, not the 'productive' farmers and businessman who used the land to generate wealth. The balance of taxation would be altered, and the costs of increased local authority expenditure would be met by those who could afford to pay. More radical reformers also argued that land reform would bring land on to the market at lower rates (by making land hoarding unprofitable). It would thus facilitate cheaper and more numerous housing developments. Moreover, national taxes on land would give the Exchequer new funds. These could be used either for general social reforms or to nationalise expenditure on education and poor relief, enabling more generous, and more equal, provision across the nation irrespective of the local authorities' financial position.

A Centrist stance did not preclude an ideological or pragmatic interest in welfare reforms aimed at tackling poverty. Old Age Pensions might alleviate one cause of poverty; frictional and cyclical unemployment, and loss of income through temporary ill-health, should also be tackled. The problem of low wages was more difficult because legislation could influence industrial profits. However, amongst more radical Centrists, decasualisation and minimum wage rates in sweated trades were perfectly acceptable remedies, because this would drive the inefficient out of business and *reinforce* the work of the market.[18]

Nonetheless, Centrists did not see state intervention as the major cure for the economic problems which caused poverty. The market, and the production of wealth, were the basis of prosperity. However, many accepted intervention in industrial matters which would make prosperity easier to achieve. This might include support for conciliation and arbitration schemes, sliding scales, and technical education (an interest some Centrists shared with collectivist Liberal Imperialists like R. B. Haldane).

[17] The following discussion is based on Harris, *Unemployment and politics,* pp. 215–19, Powell, 'The New Liberalism and Labour', p. 384, Emy, *Liberals and social politics,* pp. 127–41.

[18] W. C. Churchill, *Liberalism and the social problem* (1909), p. 239. See also below, p. 181.

The more radical Centrists also supported trade unionism, for as Grey (later the Foreign Secretary) put it 'you can deal better with organised than unorganised Labour'. State intervention could also be justified if it increased productive capacity or efficiency. Thus Lord Carrington and Sir John Brunner supported Government control of railway freight charges or outright nationalisation, because it would lower costs to industry, and allow a more efficient development of the nation's economic potential. Mine owners similarly supported shifting the burden of taxation from those companies who produced coal to the 'unproductive' land owners who received revenue from their mineral rights. Co-operation and industrial harmony, backed by some welfare legislation, was as acceptable to Centrists as it had in the past been to many trade union leaders, who had found co-operation with employers (and with the Liberals) tolerably easy as a result. Many Centrists were proud of their party's Lib/Lab traditions. Politically, some at least still shied away from separate Labour representation, preferring to maintain the older tradition of co-operating with Lib/Lab elements within the Liberal machine.

New Liberals were willing to support Centrist economic measures, and to take them further.[19] They supported the nationalisation of any monopoly which the state might run to the benefit of the whole community (although they also recognised the need to improve conditions for state employees within these industries as a secondary aim). They wished to relieve unemployment by greater expenditure on public works, financed by Exchequer grants. However, as good classical economists (despite 'heretical' reputations), they also argued that the wage rates, and the tasks undertaken on relief work, should not compete with the private sector. The New Liberals' major contribution to policy discussion, however, was their emphasis on the redistribution (not creation) of wealth as a means of paying for reform. Since the community was an organic whole 'all sections may justly be called upon to share the costs of measures which in their direct and immediate application touch only the well-being of the poor'. Hobson's half-heretical notion that over-saving by the rich led to under-consumption by the poor, and hence to economic stagnation, reinforced the idea that the imbalance of wealth should be rectified by taxation.[20]

Even before 1906 there were changes in the ideological direction, and programmatic interests, of several Liberal ideological/political strands. They shared a core of general Liberal principles, and agreed on some policies. They disagreed over the applicability, and political repercus-

---

[19] For land reform and minimum wages, Collini, *Liberalism and Sociology*, pp. 106, 112–13. For Grey, Powell, 'New Liberalism and Labour', p. 384.
[20] Freeden, *New Liberalism,* pp. 126, 219, 221.

sions, of particular ideas and solutions, and over the extent to which these changes should be taken. Whilst New Liberals favoured alliance with Labour on ideological grounds, for some Centrists – and many other Liberals – it was largely a *strategic* decision. There could be more than one element in the Liberal elite's attempt to preserve the party's radical credentials.

III

British Socialist debate was equally concerned with the need for reforming politics and state intervention, although Socialists found their way to this position with difficulty. The founding fathers of international Socialism had left few detailed clues about how Socialism was to come about. Marx and Engels only tentatively discussed the allegedly inevitable transition from Capitalism to Socialism. They suggested that technological change would so sub-divide labour and remove its skill that work would lose 'all individual character and consequently all charm for the workman', who would become 'an appendage of the machine'. Dwindling profits, and the need for economies of scale, would *reduce* skill and income and *increase* the size and homogeneity of the proletariat. The clash of interests between labour and capital would intensify. Ultimately the downtrodden worker would revolt. Revolution would obliterate alienation and the consequent grasping materialism; it would change the system and its individual components. The working class, by the act of revolution, would 'succeed in ridding itself of all the muck of ages and become fitted to found society anew'.[21]

By the late 1880s and early 1890s it was clear that this economic analysis, and its political assumptions, were not an accurate description of European developments in two senses. First, they did not accurately describe changes in European society. Secondly, the general assumption that an impoverished working class could have the inclination and resources to make a revolution – and the capacity to operate an egalitarian post-capitalist system – seemed confounded by the evidence. In Britain in particular, 'factory' or 'craft' skill remained important to an economy still dominated by small work units and specialised production. Class fragmentation was as evident as class unity. Labour and capital were not homogeneous blocks; neither were they in constant opposition. Over the nineteenth century as a whole, income levels and profits had not

---

[21] Quotations from the *Communist Manifesto* and *German Ideology*. For Engels' later views (1895), see his Introduction to Marx's *Class struggle in France*, esp. fn. 1.

substantially diminished. The prospects of revolution seemed remote. Democratic politics (of varying kinds) were the norm.[22]

Socialists began to examine the relationship between participation in parliamentary politics and Marxist doctrine. In his influential text, *The class struggle,* Kautsky stuck puristically to the contemporary interpretation of Marx's text.[23] The expansion of the proletariat, he argued, would inevitably result in the success of working-class parties if these parties remained committed to proletarian organisation and aims. The experience of industrial and political struggle against capitalism would create the electoral support (and the human potential) from which Socialism would be forged. If in practice Kautsky was more pragmatic, and in later years more flexible, doctrinal purity was an essential ingredient of his written philosophy at this time.

Socialists in Europe and the USA reacted against this positivist stance. Bernstein's *Evolutionary Socialism* attracted the most attention and the most acrimony. He argued that Kautsky was fundamentally mistaken. Capitalism, he noted, had overcome many of its problems. Progress towards Socialism would consequently be much slower than Marx (and Kautsky) envisaged. Jaurès, the French Socialist, took a similar line, but he added – like Hobson and Hobhouse – that it was essential to build on what people understood. The language of change would inevitably be evolutionary. Belief and conviction – rational, ethical, choice – and its inspiration, radical ideas, should be placed alongside social and economic factors as determinants of change. These Revisionists emphasised the need to change human capabilities, as well as economic structures, if the revolution was to be more than the dictatorship of numbers. Kautsky, by contrast, argued that this 'ethical reformism' would just delay the inevitable downfall of capitalism. 'Bourgeois' reforms were capitalist sophistry; they were separated from the material super-structure and therefore an unsuitable vehicle for major transformations of social and economic relations.

There were comparatively few deterministic Marxists in Britain. Many of Marx's writings were unavailable in English, and few early Socialists appear to have read Marx in French or German. Most early British Socialists drew their inspiration from a moral, frequently religious, hostility to the effects of capitalism. Several mention their 'conversion' at the hands of Socialist/religious propagandists. The early Socialists set up Socialist

---

[22] R. Samuel, 'The workshop of the world'; C. More, *Skill and the English working class, 1870–1914* (1980); A. Reid, 'Politics and economics in the formation of the British working class: a reply to H. F. Moorhouse', *Social History* (1978).

[23] For this and the following sections, B. Hindess, *Parliamentary democracy and Socialist politics* (1983), pp. 17–24, Kloppenberg, *Uncertain victory,* Chapter 6.

Sunday Schools and Labour Churches, which taught such things as the Socialist Ten Commandments. Philip Snowden, one of the most popular Socialist propagandists, was a gospel preacher with a revivalist rhetoric. His classic lecture – *The Socialism of the Sermon on the Mount* – was extremely popular, especially in the North. In South Wales, the best-selling pamphlet was Keir Hardie's *Can a man be a Christian on a pound a week?*[24] For early Socialists, Socialism, as the title of one pamphlet put it, was *The politics of Jesus Christ*. 'We pioneers of the spirit', another early Socialist wrote, 'believed that we were preparing the way for Jesus the Socialist.'[25] Although many were dissatisfied with organised religion, they adhered to what they believed were Christian values. Others stayed in the church or sought spiritual consolation in fringe religious/mystical groups.[26]

These 'ethical socialists' saw themselves as crusaders for a better, more moral, world. Socialism was not solely about the common ownership of the means of production (although this, and other radical demands, were part of the ILP's immediate programme): 'if that were all Socialism meant it would die of dry rot'.[27] Socialism was about the abolition of immoralities (such as poverty) and inequities (such as opportunity based on, or denied, because of wealth, not individual worth). It aimed at the transformation of human attitudes. The origins of change were seen as individual, personal, and frequently emotional. Here was an ambiguity. Ethical socialists put great emphasis on education in their associational life. They were 'rational', often self-educated, men and women, who despised ignorance and wished to transform working-class life. Yet for some Socialism was 'more an affair of the heart than of the intellect'. It was the Socialists' job to stir hearts; the rest would follow.

Nonetheless, Marx *was* known in Britain. His work was studied in the ILP, and bowdlerised through the writings of William Morris and Robert Blatchford. However, some of those who studied Marx rejected his determinism as unsuitable to British conditions, while many who were influenced by Morris and Blatchford were nonetheless able to reconcile humanistic Marxism and ethical socialism. They did this by playing

---

[24] Howell, *ILP*, pp. 352–62 is a succinct and careful introduction. D. Clark, *Colne Valley* (1981) provides illustrative material. For the religious experience and Socialism in South Wales, W. J. Edwards, *From the valleys I came* (1958), p. 123, and J. Griffiths, *Pages from memory* (1969), pp. 14, 18.

[25] J. W. Kneeshaw, *The politics of Christ* (n.d.); T. Shaw Desmond, *Pilgrim to Paradise* (1951), p. 117. See also e.g. Rev. W. B. Graham, *Why Christians ought to be Socialists* (1909), R. Dixon Kingham, *Socialism: a religion* (n.d.), D. Hird, *Jesus the Socialist* (1898).

[26] See, for example, Clark, *Colne Valley*, p. 149.

[27] C. Ammon, *Christianity and Socialism* (1909), p. 11. For the following, Howell, *ILP*, p. 359.

down Morris' more revolutionary suggestions. To them, Morris was an emotional inspiration, not a practical prescription.[28]

British Socialist interventions in the European debate over the future of Socialism lacked theoretical rigour. Nonetheless, British debates addressed the same issues, and were part of the same historical/ideological process. Some British Socialists, following Theodore Rothstein, accepted Kautsky's views. This 'hard left' grouping of real determinists – always a minority – was essentially anti-capitalist. Although their support spread across the ILP/SDF 'divide', most sympathisers were found in the SDF. However, in keeping with the British Socialist tradition, others argued that of itself class struggle would lead only to 'individual animal consciousness'. Belfort Bax in particular recognised the strength of the past. Traditional, habitual, views, he argued, were so strong that it would be difficult to change values and beliefs and develop the 'social consciousness' which was necessary if economic conflict was to develop into the classless humanism of Socialism. He doubted the power of economic struggle to break the hold of the past, and to create the basis for a very different future. People had to change; they had to understand the need for a new form of social organisation. These *moral revolutionists* wished Socialist organisations to mobilise, and politically express, a distinct, latent, set of working-class values, which would become the basis for an entirely different form of social organisation. Class conflict, a purely proletarian struggle, could not be abandoned. However, it had to be actuated by a new 'ethic of Socialism', which would make public duty the central tenet of an individual's aspirations and help to arouse a latent working-class humanism. This would turn the 'negativities' of class conflict into a positive force. It would raise expectations, and encourage aspirations and dreams. These could only be satisfied by the left; they would lead (eventually) to revolution.[29]

Revisionists like Bernstein and MacDonald shared elements of this analysis. Like Bax, MacDonald argued that habit would make change difficult; he too doubted whether class struggle could generate a new Socialist consciousness. Yet MacDonald went further. He abandoned economic struggle as a mobilising agent, and substituted ethical choice. He believed that there were three problems with placing economic conflict

[28] For the rejection of Marx, W. Stephen Sanders, *Early Socialist days* (1927), pp. 28–31. For Morris' inspirational impact on reforming Socialists, L. Thompson, *The enthusiasts* (1971).
[29] S. Pierson, *British Socialists. The journey from fantasy to politics* (1979), pp. 82–4. See also Howell, *ILP*, p. 360.

at the centre of change.[30] First, the working class were both producers *and* consumers; they did not have a single economic interest. Skilled trade unionists might make gains through industrial conflict; the consequential price increases would only damage the unorganised majority of consumers. Secondly, MacDonald had less faith than the moral revolutionaries in the possibility of achieving broad working-class support for the construction of a new social order. The unskilled, whose whole experience was of exploitation, inequality and defeat, might sell their souls 'for a mess of pottage'. Thirdly, conflict, animosity, and class prejudice could not suddenly be transformed into the social spirit which was the true basis of Socialism. 'Any victory won as the result of siding with any one party in the struggle', MacDonald wrote, 'only perpetuates what it desires to eliminate.' MacDonald saw belief, rationality, and commitment as essential ingredients of electoral politics. He rejected class struggle.[31] MacDonald, like Bernstein, Hobson, Hobhouse, and many ethical socialists, was a moral reformer.

The political and strategic implications of this version of Socialism were significant. Because habit and capitalist concession were powerful disruptive forces, and because class struggle was no answer, Socialists would have to work at bringing about change. It was important to base political appeals on the past, on 'inherited habits, modes of thought, axioms of conduct, traditions both of thought and of activity'.[32] Change had to evolve from what existed already, not (and here MacDonald again broke from the moral revolutionaries) from the sublimated values implicit in working-class life. Moreover, because belief and commitment were not the exclusive preserve of the workers, it might be possible to persuade all members of the community to support socialistic changes. Change would come incrementally, through gradual progress.

In MacDonald's theoretical writing, the Marxist dialectic of progress by conflict was replaced by the organic evolution of rational men towards a distant, but inevitable, form of human perfection which the left called Socialism. The continuing emphasis on the inevitability of Socialism seems at variance with MacDonald's emphasis on the obstacles to its progress.

[30] There are many summaries of MacDonald's writing (see, for example D. Marquand, *Ramsay MacDonald* (1977), pp. 88–93). However these fail to recognise the extent to which his ideas paralleled those of European Socialists in some areas, and built on a traditional radical critique of the state in others. See D. M. Tanner, 'Liberalism, Labourism and Socialism – the ideological distinctiveness of the Edwardian Labour party', and P. Thane, 'Popular Radicalism and the rise of the Labour party, 1880s–1914' (Conference on Popular Radicalism and party politics in Britain, 1848–1914, Cambridge 1989).

[31] J.R.M., *The Socialist movement* (1911), p. 148. See also P.S., *Socialism and Syndicalism* (1913), p. 78.

[32] J.R.M., *Socialism: critical and constructive* (1921), p. 2.

But MacDonald the Revisionist was also MacDonald the party unifier and myth maker. He maintained his Socialist credibility by restating his belief in the transformation of society and the triumph of the left. He (safely) set the inevitable triumph in the (distant) future. MacDonald's 'organic' metaphor may have been the weak link in his political theory, but it was a vital part of his role as party theorist and unifier.[33]

Revisionists like MacDonald had ideological rivals. 'Fabianism' has become synonymous with the idea of state intervention and material improvement as ends in their own right. Yet many Fabians did not see state intervention and control as a panacea. Sydney Ball and William Clarke, for example, noted that collectivism 'may only be the substitution of corporate for private administration'. It was explicitly *not* an end in its own right:

it is merely ... a better way of doing business. It embraces the machinery of life, and so gives the higher self, the real individual, freedom for self-development and artistic expression which individualism can never furnish. It does this because it releases the mass of men from the pressing yoke of mere physical needs ... it furnishes in a right way, the physical basis on which the spiritual structure is reared.[34]

Many Fabians – and many of the trade unions who were most in favour of state regulation of their industry – saw that intervention as a means of securing greater prosperity or greater freedom. It was not collectivism for collectivism's own sake, and many were very suspicious of those who held such ideas. State intervention was not state control; it could serve the development of real freedom by controlling those aspects of economic life which took this away.

Even the 'bureaucratic' Fabians, Sydney and Beatrice Webb, had doubts about collectivism because of the ability of producers to engage in 'conspiracies against the public'. They thought that the *sectional* interests of producers had to be 'harmonized' into the interests of the community as a whole. They attempted to neutralise conflict through a corporate alliance of consumers and producers, with the ring held by an administrative elite. For moral reformers, an intellectual elite shaped action through the force of its ideas; for the Webbs, this was too elitist. Their corporate model was not anti-democratic, but it was less concerned with *individual* involvement, individual change, and with democratic control than the moral reformers or (particularly) the moral revolutionaries. Many Fabians – including to a lesser extent the Webbs – shared many of the

[33] R. Barker, 'Political myth: Ramsay MacDonald and the Labour party', *History* (1976), and his excellent essay, 'Socialism and Progressivism in the political thought of Ramsay MacDonald' in A. J. A. Morris (ed.), *Edwardian radicalism* (1974).

[34] Cited in Vincent and Plant, *Philosophy, politics and citizenship*, p. 65.

moral reformers' views, and cast doubts on the unions' abilities to act selflessly. Indeed, many unions themselves did not wish to become embroiled in the machinery of state regulation, even though the need to *regulate* Government intervention drew them in. There was a 'Statist' stand in Labour politics, but it was more ambiguous about 'collectivism' than is generally assumed.[35]

Even before the formation of the Labour party in 1900, there was an additional, if diffuse, ideological tendency in Labour/Socialist politics which distinguished it from the Liberal party. To some extent it is right to see 'Labourism' more as an outlook than a systematic theory. Indeed, many Labourists (like Herbert Smith, the Yorkshire miners' leader who joined the ILP in 1897) were contemptuous of 'theorising' and 'intellectuals'. 'Outsiders', the 'middle classes' – and Socialists very often – were disparaged for their assumption of a moral and social superiority. Many Labourist elements had plebeian views, a strongly conservative streak, and no faith in pronounced change as a practical (or desirable) proposition. This is often seen as the essence of British class consciousness, but this overstates its connections to class sentiment. Labourist horizons were often much narrower. To have called Herbert Smith 'miner-conscious', his biographer wrote, 'would have pleased him most. He would have understood that better: classes are abstract – and Herbert Smith had no time for abstractions'.[36] An awareness of class did not mean that class became a motivating feature of one's political life. However, Labourism (if we mean by this the views and outlooks of the trade union element within Labour politics) could be both more sophisticated and less defensive. Trade union attitudes varied according to a number of factors, including the degree of skill involved in an occupation, the security of particular groups, and the basis of their prosperity. To see 'Labourism' as a uniform, and strictly 'economistic' creed is to fit a complex situation into an ideological straitjacket.

In labour circles, as in the Liberal party, there was a widely perceived need for a change in policy. In the 1890s, radical and ethical socialists had adopted an emotive critique of capitalism and an 'educationalist' electoral strategy which gave the ILP an anti-Liberal image. Their imme-

---

[35] My definition of Statism differs from that of S. Yeo, 'Notes on three socialisms: collectivism, statism and associationism – mainly in late nineteenth and early twentieth century Britain', in C. Levy (ed.), *Socialism and the Intelligentsia 1880–1914* (1987), pp. 240–3. For reassessments of the Fabians, I. Brittain, *Fabianism and culture* (Oxford, 1980), esp. pp. 256–7, and L. Radice, *Beatrice and Sydney Webb* (1984). Although the New Liberals emphasised participatory democracy as a means of reconciling state intervention and industrial liberty, they did not generally discuss the more difficult question of how this should influence the details of party policies. It was thus easier for them than it was for the Fabians to appear as 'true democrats'.

[36] J. J. Lawson, *The man in the cap: the life of Herbert Smith* (1941), esp. p. 33.

diate programme included widespread nationalisation, pensions at fifty, and an eight hour working day. Some radical Socialists rejected parliamentary politics, and used this programme solely as propaganda. Ethical socialists tended to see parliamentary campaigns as a means to 'making socialists', rather than winning electoral victories. However, other ILP activists argued that semi-salvationist attempts at 'conversion' with utopian programmes were not enough. They did not have enough purchase with enough people, and had no impact on the social conditions which made Socialist ideas difficult to believe. As MacDonald wrote, 'Unless good emotion in society finds expression through a system of social relations (it) . . . will sink to mere sentimentality.' In moving from 'ethical socialism' to a 'Labour' moral reformism, members of the ILP who shared MacDonald's views recognised that poverty blunted perceptions of what was possible; it had to be tackled before many people could even contemplate Socialist ideals.[37] People had to be persuaded that by supporting Socialism they would improve their standard of living and their degree of security. Moral politics had to be supplemented with a hard, practical, materialistic thrust which would help create a 'practical' political image.

Labour policy was important because it was an indication of what the party stood for. Ethical socialists shared elements of a radical Liberal outlook; some also supported similar policies. Free Trade was sacrosanct; land reform was the 'economic bed rock' of all other progress. The redistribution of wealth, the attack on the 'unproductive' surplus, the doctrine of under-consumption, were all elements in the 'practical' Labour moral reformers' programme. At the municipal level, Labour proposals included housing reform, an extension of municipal trading and the provision of school meals. Yet these proposals were still frequently shrouded in a moral critique of capitalism. They drew strength from a 'common sense ideology' which saw 'middle class' ideas as a denial of the obvious, imperative, need to tackle iniquitous conditions. Despite MacDonald's accepted role as party theorist, many working-class and some middle-class moral reformers were not totally committed to his belief in rational conviction as a means of mobilising opinion. Some at least saw the working class as intuitively more 'moral' and 'decent' in their attitudes to people than the middle classes, whatever their 'rational' beliefs. Theirs was a part religious, part personal, belief in the irrational and inbred sides of human

[37] J.R.M., *Socialism after the war* (Manchester, 1917), p. 2. The widespread recognition of environmental considerations is discussed in L. Barrow, 'Determinism and environmentalism in Socialist thought', in R. Samuel and G. Stedman Jones (eds.), *Culture, ideology and politics* (1982). For the ILP programme, Howell, *ILP*, Chapter 15.

attitudes.[38] The 'Labour' moral reformist approach was a toughened up, but not transformed, version of ethical socialism. If (in MacDonald's hands) it was almost identical to the ideas of the New Liberals, not all broad sympathisers shared quite this perspective.

Labourist elements were primarily interested in practical politics and legislative change, and were evidently likely to support MacDonald's more reforming thrust, although they disagreed over the detail of some policy. Labourists who were members of trade unions for skilled workers might support craft representation as a means of securing action which was socially and politically in their interests. Several skilled unions only joined the LRC because Labour was perceived as a better, or in some cases the *only*, means to politically pressurise a Government incorporating some, but not all, of their views and aims.[39] Some Labourist and ethical socialist *leaders* also supported old Liberal political/religious issues such as Home Rule, and educational and licensing reform (although union *members* might be less convinced) again for good reason, and not through deference. In municipal politics, they might oppose high municipal expenditure on projects and policies which catered for the poor or the unemployed, or those who did not enjoy trade union benefits. Labourist leaders of skilled unions often supported the economic ideas of Liberal Centrists, believing in co-operation, conciliation, and progress.[40] However, expenditure on poor relief and public works to limit the impact of unemployment, the inclusion of fair wages clauses in Council contracts, and improvements in wages and conditions for Council employees could also be supported by non-Socialist reformers. In different economic circumstances, and particularly where employment was more casual, *unskilled* Labourist groups might support Labour representation from a conservative belief in Labour as a protective force, and a working-class hostility

[38] Tawney's attitude, cited in Winter, *Socialism and war,* pp. 72–4. The nature of working-class 'common-sense ideology', and the various strands within social democracy, need further investigation. For some preliminary observations on the former, Smith, 'Labour tradition in Glasgow and Liverpool', L. Barrow, *Independent spirits. Spiritualism and English plebeians, 1850–1910* (1986). For Labour leaders' views on land reform, C. Llewelyan Davis to L.G., 4 Aug. 1912, LG C/9/3/10. Cf. Land Union circular, reproduced in the *Locomotive Journal,* Aug. 1914: 'Our members should know by now that their whole economic existence is bound up in the land question, which is probably more important even than a wages movement.'

[39] See e.g. Boilermakers' *MR* Dec. 1901, for the 'pragmatic' support of a 'Liberal' union, and for unions with Tory and Liberal members supporting Labour as a neutral force, see the discussion of the textile workers' attitudes in Bealey and Pelling, *Labour and politics,* pp. 98–102.

[40] E. F. Biagini, 'British trade unions and popular political economy, 1860–1880', *HJ* (1987), esp. p. 837. See also A. Reid, 'Old Unionism reconsidered: the radicalism of Robert Knight, 1870–1900' (Conference on Popular Radicalism and party politics in Britain 1848–1914, Cambridge 1989), for the sophistication of one skilled unionist's moderate philosophy.

to 'moral' Liberal and Socialist doctrines. Leaders of unskilled unions also frequently had less faith in Liberal economics as a means of delivering material rewards for their members than those sympathetic to Centrist tenets.

Labour's support for collectivism could go further. In some areas it could hope to stand for, and express, the material interests of producer groups concerned with state intervention, and particularly the miners, railwaymen, and municipal employees. The Statist philosophy of the Webbs, which ascribed a greater role to the interests of 'producers' in public sector industries, thus had more purchase than a 'Labour' moral reformism.

Even before 1906, Labour politicians in the constituencies were beginning to try and merge these various practical stances into a more concrete programme. An alliance of Labour's moral reformers, Labourist elements of various kinds, and those with Statist interests was taking shape, despite the fact that these varying groups had very different views on aspects of policy and perhaps different end products in view. The municipal programmes developed by constituency groups with different orientations were remarkably similar, but differences in emphasis, and in voters' perceptions, meant that Labour had a spatially differentiated image.[41] Nonetheless, the broad commitment of all these groups was to concrete, legislative, change, swelling support for a reorientation of the party approach.

There was a final section of the Labour party which was also seeking the adoption of a practical programme. On the left some, like Lansbury, Fred Jowett, and even to an extent Keir Hardie, recognised, like the moral reformers, that Socialism had to come slowly: 'progress made in advance of the public opinion of the day rests on very unsafe foundations'. Originally they were moral revolutionaries, influenced by continental or British Marxists. However, they also saw the need for practical policies. Poverty prevented the liberation of the latent humanistic values which would make the working class the grave diggers of acquisitive, selfish, capitalism.[42] They attempted to attack poverty and insecurity through municipal intervention. In London, where poverty was rife and employment sporadic, they advocated generous poor relief and the employment of large numbers of unemployed workers on major housing developments. In addition to relieving poverty, they hoped this would undermine local

---

[41] Hunter (thesis), pp. 280–95 for the ILP's role in creating the Newcastle LRC programme (for which, see leaflet n.d. (c. 1907–8), LP GC 6/228). Other municipal programmes: Manchester and Salford T&LC AR 1902, Birmingham ILP Fed. Mins, 17 Sept. 1910, Huddersfield Labour and Socialist Election Comm. Mins, 17 Aug. 1909.

[42] F. W. Jowett, The Socialist and the city (1907), p. 3; F. Reid, Keir Hardie (1978), p. 148. See also Tanner, 'The Edwardian Labour party'.

labour markets by forcing up wage rates on private work (i.e., they accepted some orthodox economic ideas). In Bradford, where wages and conditions were poor, but less uniformly disastrous, this was not a viable strategy. Nonetheless, the provision of school meals was used to provide a more general (and 'moral') subsidy to local families. Moreover, this activity embraced a Labourist hostility to middle-class (state) interference, and the 'ethical socialist' belief that 'ordinary' working people (led by a labour aristocracy) could find their own salvation. These more Socialist moral reformers hoped to create a class conscious, self-confident, working class, which would have the self-reliance and the vision to support Socialist policies. The Socialists' role was to 'give expression to (sic) experience'.[43]

In both the Liberal *and* Labour parties, there was some overlap between the various ideological strands. The Liberal party's success in 1906 lay in its ability to mobilise support from a wide range of social groups and geographical areas. It was a coalition, which included Labour on the one hand and middle-class Nonconformist Radicals on the other. They all supported Free Trade, but this single issue alone was unlikely to be enough to maintain the coalition once the Tories had worked on an alternative. The crucial question for the Liberal party was what happened next. Even the radicals needed – and wished – to create a party which would retain as much electoral support, from as many social groups, and from as many sections of the party, as was possible. There were three aspects of Liberal politics which the party would have to consider in its attempt to fashion a popular electoral image. First, no individual strand of Liberal thought was likely to satisfy the interests and views of all Liberal activists or all those who voted Liberal in 1906. Even the adoption of New Liberal/Centrist ideas could create electoral weaknesses and alienate sections of the party. Nonetheless, these ideas would at least appeal to the working-class section of the party's electoral constituency. Secondly, the strength of conservative elements in the party would make it difficult to push such radical policies to the fore. It would also ensure that, once put forward, there would be serious, well-supported, attempts to modify them. Thirdly, unless there was an institutional coup by the reformers, a composite Liberal party would create a

[43] F. W. Jowett, *What made me a Socialist* (1925), p. 1. For local approaches, K. Laybourn, e.g., '"The defence of the bottom dog": the Independent Labour Party in local politics', in D. G. Wright and J. A. Jowitt (eds.), *Victorian Bradford* (Bradford, 1982). For London, N. H. Buck, 'The analysis of state intervention in nineteenth-century cities: the case of municipal labour policy in East London, 1886–1914', in M. Dear and A. J. Scott (eds.), *Urbanisation and urban planning in capitalist society* (1981), and the fuller account in J. W. Marriott, 'London over the border: a study of West Ham during rapid growth, 1840–1910', Cambridge Ph.D. thesis, 1984 Chapter 6.

fluctuating, inchoate, Liberal image. This might combine each ideological strand's electoral strengths; equally (and more probably) it might not. This was a dangerous game; if it worked the Liberals would maintain the support of the broad electoral coalition which enabled them to defeat the Tories in 1906. If the balance was slightly wrong, there might be small losses at the margins. If it was seriously awry, there might be a more dramatic polarisation of support which would strip away large parts of its electoral base. The coalition might disintegrate.

Labour also needed to construct a broad programme and strategy. 'Labour representation' and 'practical politics' were widely accepted as vital ingredients, but for very different reasons. MacDonald and Henderson, the principal party leaders, and the architects of the Liberal/Labour pact, unsurprisingly had the clearest vision of what should happen next. A pressure group which acted in alliance with the Liberals, MacDonald argued, could encourage the attack on poverty and insecurity which was necessary in order to release men's higher thoughts. Labour could prepare the ground for Socialism. Henderson had equally moral ideas, but more down to earth aims. Nonetheless, he and MacDonald both argued that Labour could use its differences from the *composite* Liberal party to gradually build an electoral base which would also reflect ideological/temperamental differences between Liberal and Labour voters. Labour would prepare the electoral, as well as the social, ground either for real social change, or simply to provide the means of achieving power and attacking poverty as an end in its own right. This preparatory work, they argued, had to be done in the constituencies. Propaganda work and municipal activity would maintain the party's idealism (its image of a better world) and build up its support. MacDonald wished to pursue legislative change in Parliament, and to change public opinion through work in the constituencies. Political action in Parliament and opinion formation were to be kept separate. If radical Liberals could dominate the Liberal party, and delivered legislative reforms, then Labour's independent electoral progress might be very gradual. If Labour's ability to exploit the Liberals' deficiencies was restricted to areas where the Liberals were weak (or where they could accept Labour expansion), its growth might *strengthen* the purchase of an alliance strategy; it would field fewer candidates than the Liberals and act as an ally. Its electoral campaign, and electoral base, would move in tandem. A Progressive Alliance was not MacDonald's long-term ambition, but its extended existence might be a consequence of Liberal ideological/political change.

The nature of Liberal ideology and policy, and the precise mix of its various standpoints, were important factors in determining the extent to which opportunities existed which Labour could exploit. The institutional balance of power in the Labour party would also help determine whether any opportunities were grasped. Labour had to present a credible, acceptable, alternative to the electorate. There was internal competition for the upper hand *within* the two parties, and an electoral/political competition *between* them for the position of senior anti-Tory party. The former helped to determine the latter.

The competition between competing internal ideological strands was more fundamentally significant. The pact, and the drift towards 'reforming' politics, were not universally popular. The reforming alliances in both parties were not rigid power blocs. Radicals and Liberal Imperialists (the Old Liberals) were the largest numerical group in the parliamentary party, and a powerful force in constituency Liberal executives. Many opposed Progressive politics and alliance with Labour. The Centrist Liberals' commitment to radical ideas, interventionist policies, and an alliance with Labour was also partial at best. They were quite capable of pulling the party in a different direction; but for this they needed ideas with purchase and representatives with institutional power. Neither was the Labour reforming alliance secure. The politics of the pact involved an emphasis on 'materialism' which ethical socialists abhorred; electoral restraint was a denial of the educationalist politics which were a part of the Socialists' 'operational ideology'.[44] In 1904 Keir Hardie – a party to the 1903 pact – argued that Labour's new moral reformism, and everything it stood for, was destroying the 'spirit' of the ILP, and its ability to 'make Socialists'. Bruce Glasier, a former ethical socialist and now a Labour moral reformer who was in broad agreement with Mac-Donald, 'heartily agreed, but pointed out that we must not fall away from reforming the State as well as ourselves'.[45] Nonetheless, many ethical socialists (and many ILP reformers with ethical socialist pasts) remained doubtful about the wisdom of party policy. Moreover, the 'hard left' hankered after 'pure' Socialism, while Socialist moral reformers, like Keir Hardie, were only vaguely committed to the Progressive Alliance. They had already developed a stance which was not unattractive to some unskilled Labourist groups. They too sought the institutional power, the ideas, and the policies, which were necessary to turn the party around.

One final point needs to be made. A 'reforming alliance' was attempting to dominate both parties. They had as yet neither *precise* policies nor articulated electoral strategies. Time and party actions would present new tests, and raise the opportunity for protest. Party leaders thought in terms of creating a composite party image, of taking with them as

[44] For the distinction between 'fundamental' and 'operational' ideology, M. Selinger, *The Marxist concept of ideology: a critical essay* (Cambridge, 1979), p. 4.
[45] J.B.G. Diary, 30 Sept. 1904.

many elements of the party as they could. The precise internal balance of power would help to determine the *nature* of the policies which were put forward. The electoral competition was not just about which party would triumph; it was also about what sort of party would dominate anti-Tory politics in Britain. The politics of the Progressive Alliance after 1906 had more than just a parochial significance.

Chapter 2

Ideas and politics, 1906–1914

Despite its victory at the 1906 election, the Liberal party still needed to reaffirm the validity of a 'Liberal' outlook. New circumstances presented new challenges. Initially, with a Cabinet reflecting the party's 'Old Liberal' roots, the party image was very conservative. The internal balance shifted with Asquith's elevation to the Premiership in 1908, and the increased institutional power of the party radicals. Nonetheless, the New Liberalism did not take over the party. Rival Liberal strands were still strongly represented. Their aims and objectives influenced aspects of national policy. They successfully modified the New Liberals' aims before 1910. They were also waiting for an opportunity to assume a more prominent role (Section I). However, so long as the New Liberals put forward ideas which had electoral purchase, they were unlikely to be displaced.

The Liberals' ideological success put MacDonald under serious pressure. His own attempt to forge an attractive, composite, party image was more severely affected by rival strands acting in a contradictory manner. Nonetheless, he retained the support and sympathy of a broad section of the party elite. MacDonald's ideological/strategic trajectory suited their aims and interests (Section II). The strength of Labour moderates, and the nature of Liberal policy, insured that the Progressive Alliance operated fairly smoothly at the 1910 election (Section III).

After 1910, as electoral problems intensified, tensions grew within the Liberal party. Despite a few Cabinet changes, policy formation was still heavily influenced by conservative Ministers. National radical leaders fought to ensure that the party image reflected their aims; rival elements grew more restless and sought alternatives. They did not succeed, but they moderated party policy and threatened to develop an alternative ideological/political/strategic approach (Section IV). Labour's moderate stance also came under threat. It had to change as new issues became more significant. Nonetheless, the authority of Labour's reforming alliance remained intact (Section V). Labour appeared a more 'practical' party; the Liberals' image appeared to be more conservative, and the

Liberal radicals a little less in control. There was, however, no sweeping change in the nature of Liberal/Labour politics.

I

The Liberal Cabinet assembled in 1906 reflected the whole spectrum of Liberal opinion. There were a smattering of peers, most significantly Earl Carrington. Fowler, Morley, Burns, Birrell, and Campbell-Bannerman, the Prime Minister, were old-fashioned Radicals. Nonetheless, there were signs of change. Herbert Gladstone, David Lloyd George, and Sydney Buxton (all with Radical pasts) had been advocates of action on unemployment before 1906, and now held Cabinet positions where they could – and to some extent did – initiate social/industrial reforms.[1] Of the Liberal Imperialists, McKenna, Carrington, Grey, Crewe, Asquith, and Haldane, only the last was a radical collectivist, and only Asquith and Carrington (as Chancellor of the Exchequer and President of the Board of Agriculture respectively) had major domestic portfolios. However, even Grey and Crewe were pragmatic or ideological Centrists. They were neither totally preoccupied with foreign affairs, nor financially reactionary.[2]

Genuine New Liberals, Centrist reformers, and Fabian collectivists held important junior offices. The Liberal party was being 'radicalised from below'. Emy estimates that a tenth of the parliamentary party were 'advanced' radicals and that at least a fifth were strongly committed to interventionist action. This may understate the true balance of opinion. The MPs who voted against the Government on a series of 'radical' measures (Emy's means of determining collectivist commitment) were the assertive tip of a less abrasive (or more career-minded) iceberg. A much larger group were pledged to broadly similar policies at the 1906 election. The Land Values Group, for example, which was committed to land reform of some kind, claimed 280 members, most of them Liberals. Change was already under way.[3]

---

[1] Gladstone was Home Secretary, Lloyd George President of the Board of Trade.

[2] For Carrington's reforming tendencies, A. Adonis, 'Aristocracy, agriculture and Liberalism: the politics, finances and estates of the third Lord Carrington', *HJ* (1988). McKenna's unorthodoxies became most apparent in the 1920s. See P. F. Clarke, *The Keynesian revolution in the making* (Oxford, 1988), pp. 14–15, 39–40, 100, 120–4.

[3] Emy, *Liberals and social politics*, pp. 184–7; Offer, *Property and politics*, pp. 317–19, A. K. Russell, *Liberal landslide* (Newton Abbot, 1973), p. 65. New Liberal junior ministers included H. Samuel (Under Sec., Home Office), J. M. Robertson (Under Sec., Board of Trade), R. D. Denman (Under Sec., Post Office), F. D. Acland (Under Sec., War Office). More moderate, Centrist, reformers included W. S. Churchill (Under Sec., Colonies), Walter Runciman (Parl. Sec., Education), and A. Ure (Solicitor-General, Scotland).

Nonetheless, Free Trade and other old Liberal issues appeared to have won the election. The numerical and institutional preponderance of Old Liberals was thus reinforced by the apparent purchase of their ideas. Prominent conservative Liberals wished to capitalise on their position and resist the collectivist drift. The Master of Elibank, Chief Whip after 1908, and a Scottish Whip before this, was their principal mouthpiece. Campbell-Bannerman was half-sympathetic. The 'two sops to Labour' which his Government introduced between 1906 and 1908 were balanced by traditional Liberal legislation. Government policy was uninspiring, and often unpopular. As a result, the Liberals suffered a series of municipal and by-election defeats in 1907–8.

Liberal radicals attempted to continue the collectivist momentum generated before 1906. L. C. Money carried the attack into the press: 'The Master of Elibank has told us that the Liberal party must crusade against collectivism. He might as well advise the Liberal party to rebuke the ocean.'[4] Liberal radicals, including Money, Masterman, Aneurin Williams and C. P. Trevelyan, argued that only collectivism could preserve the Liberal party. The *Speaker*, the *Nation*, and other radical papers argued the case: radical back-benchers put pressure on the Government; there were a series of revolts, particularly over the Government's inaction on unemployment. Winston Churchill and others welcomed Socialist by-election successes in Colne Valley and Jarrow as a spur to their hesitant party leaders.[5]

A major change took place in 1908. When Campbell-Bannerman died Asquith assumed the party leadership. This is often seen as a turning-point, and to some extent it was. Yet Asquith himself, despite having initiated some financial reforms as Chancellor of the Exchequer, was in practice less of a New Liberal on policy (especially on social/labour questions) than is sometimes assumed. In fact, he listened carefully to non-Progressive voices in Cabinet, and sometimes supported their case. There was no radical coup. Lloyd George replaced Asquith at the Exchequer; Churchill replaced Lloyd George; Runciman was promoted to head Education. Those spurned by Campbell-Bannerman, including C. F. G. Masterman and C. P. Trevelyan, took junior positions. Nonetheless, there was still a powerful conservative element at the top. Asquith's Cabi-

---

[4] Ellins (thesis), pp. 130–1. See also A. C. Murray, *Master and Brother* (1945), p. 48.

[5] G. Hosking and A. King, 'Radicals and Whigs in the British Liberal party 1906–14', in W. O. Aydelotte (ed.), *The History of Parliamentary Behaviour* (Princeton, 1977), pp. 141–2, Emy, *Liberals and social politics*, p. 146, Churchill to J. A. Spender, 12 Dec. 1907, Spender Add MS 46388 fos. 220–1, A. D. White, 'Radical Liberals and Liberal politics 1906–c 1924', Kent Ph.D. thesis 1980, p. 43.

net represented a broad spectrum of Liberal opinion, and whether by inclination or to preserve balance, the PM took notice of their views.[6]

The question of how to proceed, of which traditions to tap, had still to be faced. Although some historians have portrayed the party's sub-sequent radical thrust as 'New Liberal' in tone, and the party's major reformers as exploiters of this intellectual current, the position was more complex. The problems of translating theory into practice, the attitude of Civil Servants to policy proposals, and the core of similarity between the hitherto ignored Centrist strand and the ideas of New Liberals, ensured that the policies adopted did not obviously reflect one political stance. The principal reformers, Churchill and Lloyd George, shared a desire to attack poverty and insecurity through the reconstruction of chaotic labour markets and the creation of a national minimum. The social investigations of Masterman, Rowntree, and the Webbs, and their proposed solutions, were familiar to both men. Nonetheless, within months of the Cabinet changes, Churchill and Lloyd George were setting out not a New Liberal agenda but half-competing 'Centrist' and 'New Liberal' schemes.[7]

In December 1908, Churchill formally proposed attacking unemploy-ment. In Cabinet he deployed the Centrist arguments which he had advanced publicly in the preceding months. His solutions revolved around the need for Labour Exchanges, unemployment and health insurance, public works, technical education, and railway amalgamation. He was always more concerned with economics, with the limits of Socialism, and with the generation of wealth than most New Liberals.[8] Lloyd George, by contrast, chose to emphasise land reform as the major plank in his proposals. In the New Liberal mould, his reform proposals were to be financed not by insurance, but by the taxation of the rich: 'My mind has been working on a Land Tax ... I feel that if there is to be an extension of the pensions system on contributory lines, the property which is improved by the labour of the community should contribute its share ...'[9]

Lloyd George, like the New Liberal theorists, supported insurance as an important *adjunct* in the fight against poverty. Many New Liberals

[6] For Trevelyan's initial rejection and later promotion, H.H.A. to C.P.T., C.P.T. to G.O. Trevelyan, 13 Apr. and n.d. Apr. 1908, CPT 21, P. Jalland, *Women, marriage and politics* (Oxford, 1986), pp. 244–5. For Asquith, fns. 14 and 18 below.
[7] For their familiarity with these ideas, E. P. Hennock, *British social reform and German precedents* (1987), pp. 160–4, and W.C. to J. A. Spender, 22 Dec. 1909, Spender Add MS 45388 fos. 20–1. For L.G., A. Briggs, *Social thought and social action* (1961), pp. 63–4.
[8] See W.C., *The people's rights* (1910) and his *Liberalism and the social problem*.
[9] Cited in Offer, *Property and politics*, p. 323, and ibid., pp. 176–8 for Churchill.

had initially opposed the measure. As Hobhouse complained, contributory national insurance was not a tax on the 'surplus' of industry to which all (as members of the community) were entitled. This was a regressive, partial, scheme. Only the skilled and those in a few other occupations 'earned' the right to benefits through payments to the fund. New Liberals, by contrast, had advocated subsidised wages, minimum wages, and the nationalisation of poor relief payments as a means of raising living standards. Churchill's proposals – part of a respectable, improving, Centrist, Liberalism – were accepted, but not with enthusiasm.[10]

The Liberal reformers – Centrists or New Liberals – had a more serious problem. Many Liberal Cabinet ministers belonged to an older, more conservative, Liberal tradition. They were concerned that traditional Liberals were deserting the party. They wished to adopt a more conservative approach. Morley opposed even Old Age Pensions, arguing that it was 'injurious to us with the lower middle class, who after all are no inconsiderable contingent of our party strength'. He discerned 'the long arm of Social Revolution' in the Trade Boards Act of 1909. Runciman and others opposed the Miners Eight Hours Act and Workmen's Compensation. Bryce, W. S. Robson, Loreburn, and Burns opposed the feeding of school children, insurance, and land reform. Asquith himself was doubtful about several aspects of Centrist and especially New Liberal proposals.[11]

The problem came to a head in 1909. Lloyd George attempted to push land reform, the creation of a Development Commission to finance counter-cyclical 'national development' schemes, and the redistribution of wealth to the forefront of Liberal policy. Burns, as President of the Local Government Board, had responsibility for reforms in this area, but he refused to contemplate intervention. He was by-passed. Unemployment legislation was first delegated to a Cabinet Committee designed to submerge him and subsequently transferred (when this only half-worked) to the Board of Trade. Masterman, Burns' reluctant assistant, was used to tap the Local Government Board's expertise. Lloyd George made similar attempts to by-pass the Treasury in collecting data to support his case on land reform. He went directly to sympathisers at the Inland Revenue to counter reluctant Cabinet members (and officials).[12]

<hr>

[10] Collini, *Liberalism and sociology*, pp. 110–11, Clarke, *Liberals and Social Democrats*, pp. 122–4. For Churchill's policy, and its failure to utilise New Liberal ideas, Harris, *Unemployment and politics*, pp. 22–3 and Chapter 6; E. David, 'The New Liberalism of C. F. G. Masterman', in Brown (ed.), *Anti-labour history*, p. 22.

[11] Quotations cited in Ellins (thesis), pp. 352, 395–6. See also R. S. Churchill, *Winston S. Churchill* (1967), ii, p. 308, Offer, *Property and politics*, p. 323.

[12] David, 'C. F. G. Masterman', p. 26, Harris, *Unemployment and politics*, pp. 275–6, Emy, *Liberals and social politics*, p. 176.

Lloyd George merged these measures in a single Finance Bill, calling this his 'Budget'. It was a superb tactical device. The Lords – and conservative Liberals – risked popular displeasure if they rejected such a measure. At the same time, however, the threatened wealth taxes aroused the opposition even of Liberal Centrists. There were protests from provincial leaders, like Charles Furness and Sir Walter Runciman. Around thirty Liberal MPs declined to stand for a party which could contemplate such excesses. The policies – and the populistic means of presenting them to the electorate – were too radical.[13] In Cabinet, Charles Hobhouse, Financial Secretary to the Treasury, Wolverhampton, Loreburn, and Fitzmaurice provided support for the calculated financial objections of Harcourt, Runciman, and McKenna. They thought – rightly – that Lloyd George had underestimated tax yields to make a better case for increased taxation. 'We have no justification', Runciman argued, 'for taking from the taxpayer more than is really necessary.' Asquith was thought 'squashable' on an issue so determinedly argued by the centre/right. The fight was on.[14]

Lloyd George's actions in 1909–10 were limited by the constitutional constraints imposed by the need to cram measures into a Budget, and by Asquith's pledges. A number of drafting manoeuvres had to be introduced to make the proposals hang together. These muddied the waters of the proposals. Moreover, in order to minimise opposition within the Cabinet, the responsibility for implementing the various schemes was spread over several Ministerial Departments.[15] However, and at the same time, public opinion outside the House, whipped up by party radicals, was forcing the Cabinet's hand, making it impossible to water the proposals down to any considerable extent. The more moderate Cabinet repackaged some of the proposals, ensuring that lower middle-class Liberal voters were not adversely affected. They had hoped to go further, to avoid more taxation, and to prevent Lloyd George concentrating on capturing working-class votes through attacks on the rich. However, the nature of the campaign was now out of their hands, as politics moved towards a populistic over-simplification of what the Budget was really about. 'At the Cabinet (today)', Runciman wrote:

we have re-arranged the Budget figures – a process which was necessary but (which) has been performed after a manner which has rather disgusted me. I

[13] Emy, *Liberals and social politics*, pp. 211–16, Sir W. Runciman, *Before the Mast – and after* (1924), p. 281, Harcourt to Crewe, 7 Apr. 1909, Crew MS C1/17. For resignations, Blewett, *Peers*, pp. 71–2, 215.
[14] Harris, *Unemployment and politics*, pp. 341–4. Runciman cited in Offer, *Property and politics*, pp. 325–7. For Asquith, Lady O. Morrell, *Ottoline at Garsington – Memoirs of Lady Ottoline Morrell* (1974), p. 175.
[15] Murray, *People's Budget*, Chapter 6.

have never been on the Board of a bogus company, but I can imagine now how they touch up their balance sheets.[16]

Runciman and his allies did not get all they wanted, but they did not totally fail. The Budget did not attack the lower middle-class. In fact they benefited. Moreover, in party terms, the amended Budget was *more* successful as a means of securing support because of their intervention. Old Liberal resignations and contemporary comment apart, the Budget, when merged with an assault on the Lords, could be seen as an attack on the unearned increment, and unearned influence, traditionally awarded to land and the landed elite. This, pragmatism, and the attraction of other Liberal policies were important factors in retaining the support of some conservative Liberal MPs and some very moderate Liberal voters. Crucially, as far as the Liberal party was concerned, the nature of the 1909/10 approach meant that the parameters of Radical and even Centrist belief had been stretched, but for some at least they had not been broken.

Some Old Liberals and Centrists also doubted the advisability of an alliance with Labour. Ideologically *and* strategically, they argued, too much had been conceded to the Socialists. The Centrists' co-operation with labour on the industrial front had been, and continued to be, compatible with Lib/Lab political sympathies. Provincial leaders like Furness, Clegg, and Israel Hart, who opposed the alliance in 1906, continued to do so in 1910. The NLF hinted at sympathy with them. Liberal/Labour municipal and by-election conflict fuelled discontent.[17] Runciman, McKenna, Hobhouse, Harcourt, and Bryce in the Cabinet, and Elibank and Pease at the Whips' Office, lent a sympathetic ear. Harcourt, Runciman, Pease, Carrington, and Robson (the Attorney-General) argued that the Osborne Judgement could revive Lib/Lab politics and end the need for an independent Labour party. Asquith listened attentively and opposed the 'thoughtless pledges with regard to the Osborne Judgement', made by 'weak-kneed' Liberals. The plan was rejected because Labour support in Parliament and in the country was useful. Moreover, despite the anti-Progressives' claims, alliance with *Labour* was keeping *Socialism* in check.[18] The Progressives rested their case.

[16] W.R. to H. Runciman, 21 Oct. 1909, WR 303. For the manipulated pressure of public opinion, Crewe to H.H.A., and reply, 19 July 1909, Crewe MS C1/40.
[17] M. E. Petter, 'Liberals and the Labour party 1906–14', Oxford D.Phil. thesis 1974, pp. 123–4, 138, 223.
[18] C. Wrigley, 'Labour and the trade unions', in Brown (ed.), *First Labour party*, pp. 142–5; HHA to WR, 25 Sept. 1910, WR 302.

II

There were comparable differences in the Labour party over ideology, policy, and strategy. MacDonald's idea that Labour should proceed through gradual reform, legislative achievement, and incremental expansion through, and within, a Progressive Alliance – his Revisionism or Labourist 'moral reformism' – was at the root of the problem. The ideological nature of the opposition was made explicit in the widely debated pamphlet, *Let us reform the Labour party*, published in 1910.[19] The authors, regionally elected NAC members, wrote of the 'two schools of thought within our movement' – 'revisionism and revolutionism'. They were 'revolutionists', who would fight MacDonald's views until party members 'got the notion that Revisionism was one of the seven deadly sins'. Their strategy paralleled Kautsky's now revised views on the future of Socialism in Britain. Like other European Socialists, J. M. McLachlan, principal author of the document, felt that the working class naturally possessed superior values and feelings. Unlike MacDonald (and Bernstein) he did not believe that 'reason' should be central to the conversion to Socialism:

Students of human nature ... scarcely need to be reminded that men are stirred to action by their emotions, not by cognition or reason. Cognition of itself can never produce action. It is only emotion which can stir men to action – with or without cognition.[20]

The left dissidents wished to mobilise the innately cohesive and co-operative sentiments which were characteristic of working-class life. However, like previous humanistic Marxists, they argued that this repressed tendency had to be pointed in a new direction, and had to find expression in total social reconstruction.

The 'Green Manifesto' drew support from some deterministic Socialists who supported an old ILP Socialist rallying cry, the unity of the Socialist left, as an alternative to a restricting alliance with moderate trade unions. However, its authors initially looked more to those ethical socialists who were dissatisfied at MacDonald's lack of respect for ILP principles. They harked back to a (perhaps mythical) Golden Age of the ILP. As C. P. Douthwaite argued in 1910, 'the revisionist policy that MacDonald stands for was not the policy represented by the ILP in the past'. The dissidents emphasised an affinity with the ILP's operational ideology. Whether or

---

[19] Written by L. Hall, J. M. McLachlan, C. T. Douthwaite, and J. M. Belcher, and popularly termed the 'Green Manifesto'. All quotations concerning this from D. Morris, 'Labour or Socialism? Opposition and dissent within the ILP, with special reference to Lancashire', Manchester Ph.D. thesis 1982, Chapter 8.

[20] *L.L.*, 29 May 1908.

not this was based on their declining power and status in the ILP need not concern us here. They gave form to escalating, more broadly based, discontent and to a vague sense of dissatisfaction with the direction (and 'failure') of the party.

The dissidents had developed a four point critique of MacDonald's policy between 1906 and 1910. They aired these views in the Socialist press and at party conferences. The first point concerned PLP passivity in Parliament. Labour MPs, they argued, should dramatically demonstrate their opposition to Liberal inactivity by verbal aggression and the obstruction of legislation. Contributing to an extensive debate in the *Labour Leader*, H. Russell Smart, one of the ILP's founding fathers, wrote that the PLP should make opinion, not follow it. 'It is not Statesmen we want in Parliament at present, but agitators, who will use Parliament as a platform.' There was considerable rank and file support for this view.[21]

The second point concerned the leadership's attitude to fighting by-elections. MacDonald argued for a cautious policy, although he was willing to fight if a good result might inspire the party or if victory seemed possible. A series of by-election defeats, he argued, would reinforce the Liberals' claim that a Labour vote was a wasted vote. By contrast, a series of successful contests would create a bandwagon effect which would enhance the party's prospects. The left by contrast wished to see constant Liberal/Labour by-election conflict. Russell Smart went further, calling on the party to field 200 Labour candidates at the next election. A bold lead would elicit a bold response. An increase in Labour representation would inevitably follow. The electorate would demand more than the Liberals could offer; Socialists would step in. In the election after next, in seven to eight years, a radical Labour party could achieve a parliamentary majority.

Smart went on to attack party policy. Anti-Liberal, propagandist 'activism' in Parliament and in the constituencies should be mobilised behind a single 'talismanic point' – the need to tackle poverty.[22] Victor Grayson's Independent Socialist campaign and victory in the Colne Valley by-election (1907) was the spark which ignited this discontent. Many Graysonites put forward few concrete proposals – indeed, they disparaged them. However, Grayson's victory also inspired Labour's Socialist moral reformers, Lansbury, Jowett, and O'Grady, to attack on similar lines. They argued that Centrist Liberal solutions to the problem of poverty – particularly national insurance – were inappropriate to the unskilled and insufficient

[21] *L.L.*, 17 May 1907. For support, ILP *CR* 1908, pp. 34–7, 1909, pp. 35–6. These and the following points are amplified in the *L.L.*, 3 Jan. 1908.
[22] *L.L.*, 22 May 1908, *Clarion*, 4 Dec. 1908.

to tackle the problem. They targeted the need for material improvements in wages and conditions (as opposed to 'welfare') and coupled this with support for working-class self-activism and class confidence. Labour support for Centrist Liberal policy, and its pro-Liberal stance on 'radical' issues such as women's suffrage, were also seen as a betrayal of the dispossessed.[23]

Nonetheless, this approach was over-shadowed. Grayson's action in Parliament excited more support. He inspired nationwide 'Right to Work' campaigns, which focused attention on unemployment particularly at the 1908 municipal elections. Support for 'Graysonite' political action grew. The Lancashire/Yorkshire dissident leaders McLachlan, Hall, Douthwaite, Joseph Burgess, and Russell Smart joined ranks with leading SDF figures such as E. G. Hartley and Dan Irving. The national Socialist newspapers, *Justice* and *Clarion*, and regional papers like the *Huddersfield Worker*, spread the gospel of revolt. To an extent (and particularly in Irving's case) this reflected a long-standing, if minority, SDF desire to work within the Labour party. Right to Work campaigns were conducted by the merged forces of the ILP, SDF and sometimes the trade unions. As John Paton, the Glasgow Socialist, noted there was widespread hostility to the Labour leadership: 'a persistent minority emerged in every branch asking always, was it for this that the party had struggled and fought'. Grayson's 'plain action' was 'joyfully received'. He demonstrated that the 'self-sacrifice and the spirit' of the ILP had not disappeared.[24]

However, Grayson and many of his 'hard left' allies were increasingly divorced from ethical socialists and Labour's Socialist moral reformers by personality and ideological purity. For them, moral reformers such as Hardie were insufficiently Socialist, too concerned with 'middle-class' concerns such as women's suffrage, too willing to accept the crumbs from the rich man's table. Most 'hard left' elements came to favour the creation of a new, and purely Socialist, party. For many Socialist reformers, torn between a recognition of past radical Socialist failures to achieve political support or alter current conditions, and the rhetorical attraction of Graysonite Socialism, this was a difficult decision to make.[25]

The final dissident proposal was support for greater internal party

---

[23] Thane, 'Working class and welfare', pp. 896–9. For Russell Smart's economic analysis, which attacked the idea of under-consumption, see his *Revolution and reform* (1917). Joseph Burgess was involved in similar assaults on Hobson and L. C. Money. See his autobiography, J. Burgess, *A potential poet* (Ilford, 1927), pp. 201, 205.

[24] J. Paton, *Proletarian pilgrimage* (1935), p. 208; S. Desmond, *Pilgrim to Paradise*, p. 112. See also below, p. 264.

[25] Morris (thesis), pp. 175, 217, 228 for the impact of Grayson on prominent left leaders 1907–8. For a contemporary charting of Grayson's declining standing, esp. following personal attacks on Hardie, J.S.M. to his parents, 17, 28 Nov. 1908, MID 8/15 & 16, and J.S.M. to his parents, 1 Mar. 1909, MID 8/18.

democracy. If the *electoral* problem was the absence of radical leadership, the *political* solution was to change it. Russell Smart and Leonard Hall proposed changes in the ILP's constitution. They had three major sugges- tions: a three year maximum period of office for elected representatives; the exclusion of MPs and paid officials from the NAC; and committee control of the *Labour Leader* and the National Conference agenda. The oligarchical control of MacDonaldite moral reformers could thus be chal- lenged and (given the rank and file support which they took for granted) removed. The *organisational* issue – aired more fully by European Social- ists like Michels – was closely related to the question of ideological control and ideological direction.[26]

Statist elements and 'Labour' moral reformers did not accept this analy- sis. Although MacDonald accepted the left's aims ('to make Socialists is the one vital thing') and attacked party lassitude in Parliament,[27] he opposed the dissidents' philosophy, politics, and strategy. 'Parliament', he wrote, opposing Graysonite tactics at Westminster, 'is a place for applying Socialism – not for holding Hyde park demonstrations ... Our work inside Parliament should consist mainly in making those socialistic changes in social organisation which are ripe; our work outside should consist in ripening others.' Barnes, the PLP Chairman in 1910, and many other influential MPs agreed. Grayson's tactics, Bruce Glasier wrote, were 'the footlight heroics of a blatant wind-bag'.[28] Like the Webbs, Mac- Donald hoped to improve the performance of Labour MPs, but as practi- cal critics, not parliamentary demonstrators.

The strategy of extensive by-election conflict was also rejected. As the Boot and Shoe union told its members, by-elections: 'should not be fought for propaganda purposes ... Local elections should be the propaganda contests until the constituency has ... shown by the support of our local candidates that they are favourably inclined to our principles'.[29] The strategy of conflict was defeated.

It might appear that the left's attack on policy was successful, because Labour introduced several Right to Work Bills in the House of Commons. However, the translation of Right to Work proposals into parliamentary language removed much of the propagandist criticism of capitalism to

---

[26] For Michels' views on oligarchy as a force in Socialist politics, see his *Political parties* (1st edn., 1911). Many historians, following Michels, have seen organisational control, rather than ideological factors, as the key to explaining the nature of Labour politics. For Smart's proposals, *L.L.*, 15 May 1908.

[27] J.R.M. to J.B.G, n.d. 1907, JBG 07/89. For MacDonald's attack on the parliamentary ineffectiveness of Labour MPs, JRM Diary, 26 Oct. 1910, JRM circular to the PLP, 7 Feb. 1911, LP/MAC/09/1.

[28] *L.L.*, 10 May 1907, J.B.G. to E. Bruce Glasier, 30 Oct. 1908, JBG 08/12.

[29] Boot and Shoe operatives' *MR*, Apr. 1909.

leave a more practical, but less distinctive, product. These Bills could, and did, receive support from Labour *and* Liberal MPs (although some radical Liberals thought they were mere sentimentality). Moreover, Liberal action (through the Development Bill) blurred many of the remaining distinctions between Labour policy and the Government's stance.

The very real underlying differences between the Labour left and Labour moral reformers on welfare policy became more evident as the Liberals' full programme became clear.[30] Labour's reforming alliance lent considerable if qualified support. Skilled unions in particular had no objection to Centrist insurance schemes provided control of the schemes was kept in the unions' hands; land reform and shifts in the distribution of taxation were even more palatable. Pensions, Workmen's Compensation, unemployment measures and minimum wages all attracted some Labour support.[31] Education policies and the Liberals' attitude to the House of Lords attracted many practical Labour moral reformers, ethical socialists and some Labourist and Statist elements. As A. E. Fletcher, writing in the *ASE Journal*, put it, 'All other considerations are now over-shadowed by the question of whether the people or the peers are to control the people's destiny.' A hostility to domination by an unproductive class of aristocrats was a feature of popular radical politics earlier in the century. It was still strongly represented in Labour politics in the Edwardian period.[32] Moreover the Liberal Budget – to which the Lords issue was attached – was seen as a sign of the Liberals' real commitment to sweeping change.[33] The Liberals' policies would provide some material benefits to the working class. They were allied to a crusade against the rich and their control of authority. It was a politically attractive package. The left could not rival this appeal as far as most voters were concerned, or show how municipal interventionism – the Socialist moral reformers' favourite scheme – could become part of a *national* alternative.[34] They

---

[30] For Labour and Labour policy, Harris, *Unemployment and politics*, pp. 254 fn. 6, 264–72, Thane, 'The Labour party and state "Welfare"', in Brown (ed.), *First Labour party*, pp. 196–202.

[31] See the ASE's comments that policy on Workmen's Compensation was 'a great step forward' and Old Age Pensions 'a big instalment of social justice' (ASE *MR* June 1906, Oct. 1909). See also Thane, 'Labour and State Welfare', p. 201. For differing Labour views on minimum wages, Tanner, 'The Edwardian Labour party'.

[32] ASE *MR* Dec. 1909. For the importance of democratic control of the Lords to MacDonald, and the position of these views in the history of Labour and radical politics, P. Thane, 'Popular Radicalism and the rise of the Labour party 1880s–1914', Conference on Popular Radicalism and party politics, Cambridge 1989. For Labour, educational reform, and equality of opportunity, R. Barker, *Education and politics* (Oxford, 1972), pp. 24–5.

[33] ASE *MR*, Oct. 1909, J.B.G. to J.K.H., 25 Feb. 1909, JBG 09/65A.

[34] Their only 'national' programme involved 'Liberal' solutions such as land reform or heavier taxation of the rich: *L.L.*, 11 Nov. 1910 (Jowett).

could not create a 'class-based' appeal which was generally applicable. They were not ideologically or politically convincing enough to undermine moderate policies, or their strategic consequence, the Progressive Alliance.

The leftward movement of the Liberals in 1910, and the Labour left's inability to create a popular alternative, ensured the ascendancy of MacDonald's ideological/political/strategic trajectory within the party. The hard left alternative of ignoring the 'irrelevant' Budget in 1909–10, and the Socialist moral reformers' uninspiring strategy of ascribing it only secondary importance, were rejected. As MacDonald warned, the adoption of the left dissidents' views could only alienate moderate support and bring about the emergence of a moderate Socialist/Liberal alliance of the kind which existed in France. The unions, and the moderate moral reformers in the ILP, declined to sacrifice important material gains for ideological purity and the (uncertain) prospect of greater gains in the (distant) future.[35]

III

MacDonald's ideology, policy, and strategy received considerable institutional support before 1910. Bruce Glasier, Arthur Peters, the majority of other party organisers and MPs, and all the resources of the centre were thrown into the task of limiting Liberal/Labour electoral conflict. Between 1906 and 1910 there were just ten three-cornered Liberal/Labour by-election conflicts in nearly 100 by-elections. Most of these contests were approved by MacDonald, although some, like the 'fiasco' at Croydon in 1909, went through because left-wing elements were able to manipulate the party machinery, while local parties in Montrose, Dundee, Newcastle, and Pudsey rebelled against central decisions not to field candidates and supported Independent Labour or Socialist campaigns.[36] In the main, however, there was enough institutional support in the unions, on the NAC, and even in the constituencies to ensure that candidates were not asked to stand, or were dissuaded from standing even after their names had gone forward. Conflict was contained.

When a General Election was called in January 1910, the position was no different. Labour's performance in by-elections had not been encouraging, and its municipal progress was slow. The creative diversity of Labour organisations, and their attempts to exploit local deficiencies in the Liberal

---

[35] Blewett, Peers, p. 236; LP AR 1910, p. 46, UTFWA CR 1910.
[36] For Croydon, J.R.M. to J.B.G., 30 Mar. 1909, JBG 09/98, accusing Hardie of forcing through the candidature of his friend Frank Smith.

image, had only been successful in a few areas. The number of proposed parliamentary candidatures was pruned from around 130 to just 78.[37]

In order to limit the party's electoral campaign, the central party leadership had to control the dissident left in the ILP and in the unions. The opinion of union executives – who financed most party candidatures – was thus vital to the strategy of electoral concentration. MacDonald found most unions amenable. The miners and the textile workers were the largest of the politically active unions. The YMA and SWMF had proposed fielding five and three extra candidates respectively, all of them in Liberal-held seats. The YMA withdrew four of these new candidates; the SWMF withdrew them all. Warnings that intervention would damage the Progressive cause were heeded. Poor prospects of success in three-cornered contests also caused the UTFWA to withdraw their interest in contesting additional seats (Oldham and Stalybridge). They too fell in line with national policy.[38]

The ASE, the next largest union, was equally compliant. It declined to take on new responsibilities (such as contests in Liberal-held Cardiff and Rochdale), preferring to concentrate its energy on five winnable seats, 'rather than diffusing energies (over several seats) . . . with less likelihood of success'. The Socialist attack on the Liberals in 1909–10, was 'painful to perceive':

> During the coming battle let organised Labour in the first place make sure that no ground is lost . . . that every opportunity of adding to the present number of Labour members be taken (sic) and then in constituencies where Labour is not contesting let all votes be cast for the candidates whose word and honour is pledged to safeguard the rights of the people's House of Commons and its authority over finance and taxation.[39]

The ASE had asked the NEC to recommend 'acceptable' seats. The NEC declined; it was unconstitutional. Nonetheless, all the constituencies which the ASE contested had NEC approval at the time of sanction. A 'dissident' ASE candidate, F. H. Rose, refused to withdraw and received official backing from the national union. Nonetheless, the union members in Crewe were unenthusiastic. Like the ASE national leadership, they recognised the benefits of Liberal policy, and the advantages of MacDonald's approach.[40]

---

[37] NEC Mins, 1909–10 passim. Blewett's figure of 110 includes only sanctioned candidates, and not those seeking or presuming sanction.

[38] For the politics of coal and cotton, Gregory, *Miners*, pp. 128–30, 112; Oldham LRC Mins, 1 Dec. 1908, NEC Mins, 2 Dec. 1909, UTFWA *AR* 1910.

[39] ASE *MR* Feb. 1908, Dec. 1909; NEC Mins, 2 and 17 Dec. 1909.

[40] G. N. Barnes to J.R.M., 3 Jan. 1908, JRM PRO 30/69/1152. Rose was a 'political adventurer' who had made a spurious 'conversion' to Labour politics (J.B.G. Diary, 15 Mar. 1910).

The miners, textile workers and the ASE together sponsored around thirty candidates in January 1910, nearly half the trade union contribution. However, Labour's strategy of limited campaigning reflected the broader union support for Centrist and New Liberal reforms which existed amongst skilled and white-collar unions (many of whom were not even affiliated to the Labour party). The Boilermakers' union executive noted that its members supported 'a closing up of the Progressive ranks'. The union had attempted to place its candidates in 'acceptable' Progressive seats (i.e. those where there would probably not be a three-cornered conflict), failed, and therefore refused to let any candidate stand in 1910.[41] The Shipwrights supported Liberal legislative achievements *and* the Progressive strategy. The carpenters' unions turned down at least three constituencies which neither met with NEC approval, nor offered 'a reasonable hope of success'. ASLEF, the Stonemasons, and the Bleachers and Dyers withdrew support from candidates in seats where they would have divided the Progressive vote. Even unions, like the Typographical Association and the ASRS, who were far from happy with Liberal policy with regard to their own industries, nonetheless did not increase their parliamentary aspirations.[42] Moreover, many *unskilled* unions found New Liberal support for minimum wages more attractive than the idea of supporting Labour when it appeared to be the party of the skilled working man. This applied particularly to unions in sweated trades, but even large unskilled workers' unions, like the NAUL and the Workers' Union, did not finance Labour candidates in 1910. Resilient Lib/Lab sentiment, a preoccupation with benefits, and limited faith in the state as a means of influencing living standards were the major reasons.[43]

'Socialist' unions were often too divided to support a more aggressive strategy. When they financed candidatures, their Socialist candidates proved as pragmatic as Labour moderates. Ben Tillett, for example, declined to fight Liberal-held Eccles because there was no prospect of success. The NUBSO, the Gasworkers, and the Steel Smelters also declined to finance anti-Liberal campaigns, in part because they feared retaliation against other union candidates dependent on Liberal support. The BrSS withdrew from Swansea despite having appointed an agent. The *political*

---

[41] Boilermakers' *MR* Dec. 1909; J. Hill to J.S.M., 11 Oct. 1909, LP/CAN/06/1/14, and above, p. 55.

[42] F. Chandler, D. Richards, W. Matkin, A. Heaton to J.R.M., LP/CAN/06/1/68, 108–9, 33; ASC&J *Monthly Journal* Mar. 1911; NEC Mins, 15 Dec. 1908, 7 July 1909.

[43] R. Spencer to J.R.M., 1 Mar. 1906, LP/CAN/06/1/227; NAUL Mins, esp. 10 Oct. 1909; *Workers' Union Record*, Nov. 1913.

difficulty of opposing the Liberal party was such that they had to stand down.[44]

Socialist organisations also nominated parliamentary candidates (20 per cent of those standing in January 1910 were financed by the ILP or the Fabians). It might be assumed that they would support an anti-Liberal assault. The moderate 'Big Four' (MacDonald, Snowden, Hardie, and Bruce Glasier) had resigned from the NAC in 1909, at the same time that the ILP dissidents Smart, McLachlan, and Hall were elected as regional members. However, J. R. Clynes and W. C. Anderson (elected as replacements for the older leaders) combined with others, like T. D. Benson, the ILP Treasurer, to support MacDonald's broad ideological/political/strategic approach. The NAC reduced its list of sanctioned candidates in 1910 from sixteen to twelve. The Fabians (who sponsored three candidates) *opposed* campaigns which were unlikely to succeed.[45] With Socialist/trade union support, MacDonald was able to limit the number of candidatures and preserve the Progressive Alliance.

MacDonald's strategy was made more convincing because it appeared to succeed. There was some expansion of the campaign and of Labour's parliamentary representation in 1910. The most important contributive factor was the MFGB's affiliation to the Labour party, since the MFGB had a large number of MPs and candidates. However, in Attercliffe, Whitehaven, and Wigan, where Labour had demonstrated its strength in varying ways between 1906 and 1910, there was no Liberal opposition by December 1910. There were also seats which Labour happily fought against Liberal candidates or MPs. The Progressive Alliance strategy kept Labour/Liberal conflict to just nineteen seats, and some of these were 'justified' (in MacDonald's terms) by the close local position. Labour's electoral campaign only just exceeded the level of its popular support. As MacDonald had anticipated and hoped, his ideological/political aims, the party's electoral/organisational strength, and its electoral strategy were closely linked. The party had reaped a substantial legislative crop; it had secured increases in craft representation; in a few additional seats, there had been some electoral progress. This was better than nothing. It was not enough to worry the Liberals, but it did suggest that in a

---

[44] DWR *AR* 1910, *Dockers' Record*, 1 Feb. 1909; BrSS EC Mins, 11–13 Nov. 1909, in *MR* Nov. 1909, and NEC Mins, 2 Dec. 1909 (NEC advice to withdraw) and 17 Dec. 1909 (compliance).

[45] Pierson, *British Socialists*, pp. 164–5, Blewett, *Peers*, p. 238. The Fabians financed two three-cornered contests. In Portsmouth, a double member borough, it had been assumed that there would only be one Liberal candidate. In Huddersfield, it was realistically believed that Labour had every chance of success. For Benson and Anderson's views, e.g. T. D. Benson to Ensor, 15 Jan. 1909, Ensor MS, W.C.A. to J.R.M., 24 Sept. 1908, JRM PRO 30/69/1152.

climate of Tory revival, there was every reason for Liberals to try and maintain Labour's support.

IV

The Liberals' plans for the 1911–15 session were a balance between the 'Old' and 'New' Liberalisms. Ireland, the Constitution, Welsh Disestablishment, education and licensing reform were all mentioned in their sixteen point programme, along with National Insurance, the Poor Law, housing reform and land/rating reform. Liberal radicals were nonetheless worried that the party would drift. Some were concerned that it would concentrate on regaining its agricultural and middle-class vote. The loss of this support, they argued, was a blessing faintly disguised.[46] Yet few members of Asquith's reconstructed Cabinet agreed. It still contained a majority of Radicals and Centrists. In the Cabinet reconstruction of 1910–11, the allocation of posts and promotions depended on service and ministerial needs as much as on political/ideological questions. To the disappointment of the radicals, the conservatives Jack Pease (formerly Chief Whip) and Charles Hobhouse (the Gladstonian junior Minister at the Treasury) became respectively President of the Board of Education and Chancellor of the Duchy of Lancaster.[47] Haldane and Churchill were happily moved to the War Office and the Admiralty (the latter after a brief spell at the Home Office) to tackle problems evident before 1910, and to embark on a programme of military reconstruction.[48] John Simon and McKinnon Wood gained positions as Solicitor-General and Secretary of State for Scotland on their intellectual merit. Nonetheless, there were signs of change. McKinnon Wood had sound Progressive credentials; Simon was a Centrist and a career politician. Other promotions pushed the party still further to the left. Runciman moved from the political graveyard of Education to Agriculture, where action was being planned; McKenna was moved to the Home Office.[49] Although Haldane and Churchill did not have reforming departments, and Runciman was

---

[46] R. L. Outhwaite to C.P.T., C.P.T. to Grey, 1 Feb., 18 Mar. 1910, CPT 27. Contrast H. Samuel to H.G., 22 Jan. 1910, HG Add MS 45992 fos. 235-6: 'It is the abiding problem of Liberal statesmanship to raise the enthusiasm of the working class without frightening the middle classes. It can be done, but it has not been done this time.'

[47] H.H.A. to Crewe, 7 Oct. 1911, Crewe MS C1/40; A. H. D. Acland to Haldane, 21 Oct. 1912, Haldane MS 5909 fo. 270; C.P.T. to W.R., 18 Oct. 1911, WR 44.

[48] Haldane to his Mother and to E. Haldane, 24 Oct. 1911, 5 Feb. 1908, Haldane MS 5986 fo. 167, MS 6011 fo. 270; W.R. to H. Runciman, 15 Feb. 1910, WR 303. For the mixed motives behind these moves H.H.A. to W.R., 14 Oct. 1911, WR 302.

[49] W.R. to H.H.A., 24 July 1909 and W.R. to H.H.A., 18 Oct. 1911, Asquith MS 13 fos. 52-3. For some of the continuing difficulties with education and the general lack of interest in educational reform, J. Clifford to W.R., 27 Oct. 1911, WR 144, Pease Diary, 19 Nov. 1913, Gainford MS 39 fo. 80, Bernstein, *Liberal politics*, p. 142.

'doubtful as to the [desirability of a] minimum wage' for agriculture, the changes had been made with action in mind, and action was expected. Moreover, Haldane, Lloyd George, Grey, Churchill and Asquith became the core of an inner Cabinet, which met regularly and dealt with a range of business which crossed departmental lines. The political climate favoured further reform.[50]

Movements at the junior level were even more encouraging. Masterman, Addison, and T. E. Harvey, the Quaker radical, were to work on Insurance, which Haldane was to handle in the Lords. In 1914, Masterman was brought into the Cabinet, and a new, and potentially powerful, position of national party organiser was being seriously discussed. Wedgwood Benn was the favourite for the job (although Illingworth opposed him) but the other candidates were radicals with strong Progressive leanings. Addison, L. C. Money, J. A. Baker, R. D. Denman, Charles Roberts, and Trevelyan sat on committees of enquiry into 'radical' issues and featured as junior appointments in contemplated and actual reshuffles between 1910 and 1914. The party at the centre was changing.[51]

Despite this radical tide, the parliamentary party became involved largely with Ireland, Women's Suffrage, Education, naval expenditure, and Welsh Disestablishment after 1910. The Cabinet Radicals did not regret this. As the left had anticipated, they wished to win back the party's lower middle-class and agricultural vote. These old Liberal measures, allied to support for retrenchment (an issue which gained them Centrist allies), were believed to be popular with the party's 'lost' electoral base and with a portion of its new constituency.[52]

Elements of this argument were patently absurd. Educational reform was impossibly difficult and a vote-loser in areas like Lancashire. Ireland and Welsh Disestablishment were widely thought to be of only local importance. '(Opposition to) Home Rule is of little use as an electioneering asset', Steel-Maitland noted in 1914, and Liberal intelligence confirmed that their supporters found support for Home Rule equally uninterest-

---

[50] H. W. Massingham to W.R., 8 Oct. 1912, WR 68; W.R. to H.H.A., 18 Oct. 1911, as above fn. 43 for Runciman's commitment to reform and for the Government's plans. For the informal Cabinets, Haldane to his Mother, e.g. 5 Aug. 1911, 23 Jan. 1912, Haldane MS 5986, 5987 fos. 116, 25.

[51] L.G. to H.H.A., 5 June 1914, LG C/6/11/15; H.H.A. to Crewe, 13 Feb. 1914, 14 Sept. 1910, Crewe MS C1/40; K. O. and J. Morgan, *Portrait of a Progressive* (Oxford, 1980), pp. 13–26. Reforming views were not, of course, the only criteria for posts in the party organisation. See C. Hazlehurst; *Politicians at war* (1971), pp. 129–34.

[52] Comments on Morley, Harcourt, Burns, McKenna, and Loreburn, M. Asquith to Elibank, 14 Jan. 1912, Elibank MS 8803 fo. 6; memo dated 29 June 1914, by J. Simon, Beauchamp, McKenna, Hobhouse, Runciman, MacKinnon Wood, Asquith MS 25 fos. 170–2; C. Hobhouse to Harcourt, 15 Jan. 1914, Harcourt MS 444 fo. 4.

ing.[53] Home Rule was important because the Liberal party needed to maintain Nationalist support in the House of Commons, and because the Liberal rank and file needed to be satisfied that the Government was both truly Liberal and evidently resolute. Women's suffrage divided the party and could have a deadening impact on the organisationally important Women's Liberal organisations.[54] Nonetheless, if the Liberal appeal to the working class was failing, then the ability to attract a lower middle-class and rural vote would be a powerful force in determining party policy and in determining the internal balance of Liberal politics. There was pressure from within to move to the right.

There was also pressure from without. The electorate was restless. The economic position (for some workers) was worsening. Management/ union relations deteriorated as the workforce struggled to keep incomes in line with inflation. Union recognition became a serious issue. Industrial unrest, and demands for state intervention, increased. The Liberals could have reacted by seizing the initiative, but even radical Liberals were unsure of their attitude to these problems. They were particularly ambiguous about their relationship with the trade unions. They supported involving them in the administration of national insurance, for example, and showed a willingness to discuss and amend this legislation in the light of union experience. Yet they were wary of embracing the unions, and their demands, too closely.[55]

They were equally unhappy about industrial action. Discussions on the Trade Union Act of 1913 revealed considerable hostility to trade union demands.[56] The Liberal Cabinet, including 'radicals' like Haldane and Churchill, reacted almost hysterically to the industrial unrest, and particularly to the 1911 transport strikes. Troops with fixed bayonets were sent to quell 'riots'. Thirty thousand troops stood ready to prevent the 'storming' of London. Signalling posts were established at strategic vantage

[53] Hazlehurst, *Politicians at war*, pp. 26, 29, *Liberal Magazine*, May 1912, and below, p. 306.

[54] R. Adkins *et al.* to Harcourt, 5 Aug. 1914, Harcourt MS 444 fos. 124–5; C.P.T. to W.R., 25 July 1914, WR 135. For the impact on Liberal women's organisations, S. S. Holton, *Feminism and democracy* (Cambridge, 1986), esp. Chapter 6.

[55] H. A. Clegg, *A history of British trade unions since 1889, vol. ii 1911–1933* (Oxford, 1985), pp. 24–6, R. Davidson, 'The Board of Trade and industrial relations, 1896–1914', *HJ* (1978), and below, p. 65. For the unions and national insurance, *Hansard*, 5 Mar. 1914, c.s 737–8, 747–8, speeches by Clynes and Macnamara. For nationalised industries, e.g. R. D. Denman to the editor of the *Cumberland News*, 8 Dec. 1912, Denman to J. A. Spender and S. W. Belderson, 11 Oct. 1911, Denman MS 1A fos. 2–3. Denman argued that, while he would like Government servants to renounce the right to strike: 'The facts of Government service make the contingency sufficiently remote without special legislation.'

[56] Wrigley, 'Labour and the unions', pp. 144–5, J.S.M. to his parents, 3 Jan. 1913, MID 11/3.

points (including the top of St Paul's Cathedral). 'It is like a state of
siege', Haldane wrote from London, 'troops marched past all night.'[57]
The prosecution of strike leaders, such as Tom Mann and James Larkin,
following public statements calling on the police not to intervene in trade
disputes, revealed the political and ideological tensions in the party. As
C. P. Trevelyan warned, this action was contrary to individual liberty;
it was contrary to the 'very widely' held working-class view 'that soldiers
ought not to shoot in strikes', and was taking a hammer to crack a nut.
Moreover, in laughing at the 'treason' uttered by Carson and the Ulster-
men, and taking the 'follies' of Syndicalism seriously, 'in the eyes of the
working class you are ... making a differentiation between the indiscretion of the poor man and the indiscretion of the rich man'.[58] Yet
for many Liberals, it was a public order question and no more. The
Liberals' reaction to manifestations of popular economic aspirations was
a contributory factor to their unpopularity, since it seemed to reflect
their only partial commitment to working-class living standards.

Liberal Progressives, led by Lloyd George and Buxton, were sympathetic to the demands made in many of the strikes.[59] They attempted to
keep control of industrial relations in their own hands and to make concessions. There were difficulties. The workers' demands in the transport,
mining, and municipal workers' disputes could only be met through state
regulation of wages and hours, enforced union recognition, nationalisation, or forced decasualisation. Fabian Liberals like R. D. Denman were
quite happy to embrace a corporate understanding with the unions. They
wanted industrial problems to be settled by political campaigning, discussion, and limited state control. Yet if some New Liberals, like Hobhouse,
also supported nationalisation, they did not do so with great force. Other
Liberals were even more hesitant. As C. P. Scott privately commented,
while nationalisation of the British railway system would come in time,
it was impolitic to suggest such a radical change at that moment. J.
A. Spender, editor of the Centrist *Westminster Gazette*, was even more
cautious. These journalists had assessed the party position accurately
enough. Liberal leaders emphasised the need for better conciliation procedures, rather than state control, and permitted employers to increase

[57] Daily correspondence between Haldane and his mother, Aug. 1911, esp. 18 Aug. 1911,
   Haldane MS 5986 fo. 126. For a general discussion of the strikes and the Liberals'
   reaction, J. Morgan, *Conflict and order. The police and labour disputes in England
   and Wales 1900–39* (Oxford, 1987), Chapter 3.
[58] C.P.T. memo, 25 Mar. 1912, CPT 30. See also C.P.T. to Bishop Gore, 2 Apr. 1912,
   CPT 29, G. O. Trevelyan to W.R., n.d. 1912, WR 68; *Yorkshire Herald*, 12 Nov.
   1913.
[59] L.G.'s comments in Cabinet, Pease Diary, 11 Nov. 1913, Gainford MS 39 fo. 79.

prices in order to cover the wage increases which ended the transport strike.[60]

The Liberals' problems in dealing with industrial demands became more evident during the 1912 miners' strike. Lloyd George supported the strikers' calls for a national minimum wage publicly and in Cabinet. Using New Liberal language, he argued that if the mineowners were unwilling to concede a national minimum, 'he would justify the state stepping in and acquiring the mines and working them'. Morley objected, finding no 'Liberal' basis for intervention: 'To fix fair wages by law was alone justified on grounds of expedience.' The Cabinet pragmatists, led by Grey and Pease, decided that a major miners' strike, widespread violence, and the potential collapse of the economy, justified pragmatism. Nonetheless, they moderated Lloyd George's proposal. They argued for a *regional* minimum wage, to be set by negotiation and in accordance with local conditions. Centrists could quite happily accept this; it recognised the primacy of profits, and of the market, in determining wage rates. The reforming alliance was maintained, but Lloyd George's 'New Liberal' policy had been watered down.[61]

The Liberals also had to face the dissatisfaction of workers in unskilled occupations. For these workers the problem was low wages and sporadic employment. Centrist remedies were inappropriate. Lloyd George tried to make the best of things by presenting national insurance as a confiscation of employers' profit, which was designed to meet the problems of unemployment, and some Progressives anticipated electoral rewards 'when the benefits begin to be paid'.[62] However, even when the unskilled were covered by the legislation, its short-term effect was to take money from their pockets. As a regressive form of taxation, it was poor value for money. Neither did it solve the problem of low pay. The Tories were not slow to point this out. Again, the Liberal working-class vote was being squeezed.

State-regulated wages, the New Liberal solution, was one possible response. The Liberals had made a start with the Trade Boards Act in 1909, but very few trades were covered by this legislation, and the Government was slow to extend the experiment. It encouraged the adoption of Fair Wages contracts by local authorities, but it made no attempt to encourage the adoption of minimum wage rates for poorly paid munici-

[60] C.P.S. to Denman, J. A. Spender to Denman, 1 Oct. and 30 Sept. 1911, Denman MS 3; Hobhouse article, *M.G.*, 19 Aug. 1911. Several Progressives voted against the Government over its handling of the strike. See e.g. A.R. to M. K. Rowntree, 23 Oct. 1911, AR MS, J. Henry to H.G., 26 Aug. 1911, HG Add MS 46038 fo. 52 (T. E. Harvey).

[61] Pease Diary, 16 Mar. 1912, Gainford MS 39 fo. 36.

[62] H. Samuel to his Mother, 10 Mar. 1912, 19 Jan. 1913, Samuel MS A/156 fos. 401, 426. For the Tories, e.g. below, p. 171.

pal workers. The Departmental power of Liberal conservatives like Charles Hobhouse ensured that requests for minimum wages in some 'public sector' industries (like the Post Office) were rejected. Unions in other low paid industries, including the Bakers, Shop Assistants, and Tailors, sought to secure minimum wage rates, but found national Liberal leaders slow to react.[63]

Lloyd George and other radicals recognised that the party had a problem. In February 1912, twenty-five radical Liberal MPs supported a Labour motion demanding a national minimum wage. This was the start of an attempt to make the proposal party policy. In March, the *Nation* group – which included theorists like Hobson and Hobhouse, and MPs like Alden and Rowntree – supported the introduction of a minimum wage in a Cabinet memorandum. The 'time has come', they argued, 'to have in mind as the distinct objective of Liberal policy, the general principle of a living wage for every worker'. They formulated a programme. In May 1912, the Liberal press floated the idea that the Government might nationalise land, railways, and mines, with minimum wages *initially* in all three.[64]

Pressure began to mount. At the Cabinet meeting on 11 June, Lloyd George, supported by Buxton, Haldane and partially by Runciman, introduced a proposal to enforce a 'scale of wages on employers in the trade within a given area, if associations of masters and men had agreed to the scale, and no matter how many masters or men stood outside the agreeing associations'. The decision was 'postponed' after opposition from several leading figures (including Asquith). A few days later, Lloyd George warned the *Nation* group that he was 'doubtful whether anything could be done until after another General Election'.[65] The New Liberals suffered another setback.

The Liberal party nonetheless needed a policy. Runciman as Minister of Agriculture was already considering land reform. Some hoped that this would restore the party's lost rural support, and tilt it back towards the politics of the 1890s. However, for others, land reform was a means to tax the rich and end the maldistribution of wealth.[66] For the *Nation*

[63] For fair wages and minimum wages on Admiralty work, and in the Post Office, F. D. Acland to Haldane, 29 Oct. 1911, Haldane MS 5909 fo. 167, *Hansard*, 15–21 Mar. 1914. See also A. Clinton, *Post Office workers* (1984), pp. 174–90, reporting the unfavourable verdict of the Hobhouse Commission and the Government's attested concessions. Below, pp. 324–5 for minimum wage pressure in other industries.

[64] Memo cited in White (thesis), pp. 32–3. Discussions noted in A.R. to M. K. Rowntree, 16, 18 Apr. 1912, AR MS.

[65] Hobhouse Diary, 12 June 1912, in E. David (ed.), *Inside Asquith's Cabinet* (1977), p. 115. L.G.'s views noted in A.R. to M. K. Rowntree, 18 June 1912, AR MS.

[66] H.H.A. to W.R., 14 Oct. 1911, WR 302; Samuel to H.G., 22 Jan. 1910, HG Add MS 45992 fos. 235–6; Samuel to H.H.A., 12 Oct. 1911, Samuel MS A/63 fos. 79–80.

group, land reform was part of its package of proposed changes. By relieving local rates it might enable greater local expenditure on poor relief; it would free money (and land) for housing development. State control of land would lead naturally to state control of other monopolies. This in turn would lead to control of wage rates, and to a better planned economic system. Having failed with a frontal assault, Lloyd George recognised that he would have to appropriate elements of the moderate 'official' party programme of reforms and popularise the 'radical' version of these proposals. He set about the task with typical guile and gusto.

Lloyd George was involved in the Liberal land campaign, which was run and partly financed by the Rowntrees, from its inception. He hoped that public support for the radical aspects of land reform would force the party to make this its policy. He encouraged sympathetic Liberal editors like C. P. Scott and J. A. Spender to publicise the aims and findings of the land enquiry. Donald of the *Daily Chronicle*, with one eye on his circulation figures, joined in.[67] Most dramatically, in the summer of 1912, Lloyd George privately encouraged the Single Tax land reformers to engage in a series of by-election campaigns designed to demonstrate the electoral popularity of the 'radical' version of land reform. As Lloyd George had told MacDonald, he was 'anxious to run a vigorous land agitation to recover for the Liberals the ground lost by the Insurance Bill and that the only men he can rely on are the Single-Taxers'. It was the Single Taxers, led by Wedgwood, who forced a three-cornered by-election at Hanley in 1912, despite the opposition of many Progressives and the Chief Whip. Hanley was a Lib/Lab stronghold at the local level, and had been represented by a former Lib/Lab miner at the parliamentary level since 1906. On his death, the land taxers decided to win the seat back for the Liberals, and demonstrate the electoral utility of their scheme. They received support from Lloyd George. Following their success, the campaign gained momentum throughout the Summer of 1912. Its popularity was not unnoticed.[68]

The Hanley campaign did not mean that Lloyd George had decided to abandon the Progressive Alliance. He recognised that the Liberals needed to stay ahead of the field, to keep Labour in a cleft stick which made deviation from the ground occupied by the Liberals politically impossible. He also needed to convince his more conservative colleagues – and the electorate – of the need for a radical Liberal land policy. Hanley was a public message. This approach was a common feature of Progressive

[67] Briggs, *Social thought and social action*, Chapter 3; Koss, *Political Press*, ii, p. 204. For Scott's views, C.P.S. to L.G., 7 June 1913, CPS 333/20. See also below, pp. 308–9.
[68] L.G. cited in J.B.G. Diary, 5 July 1912. See also *D.H.*, 14 Aug. 1912, for the land campaign at subsequent by-elections, and above, pp. 311–12 for Hanley.

politics. The electoral side of the Progressive Alliance worked through informal displays of strength, rather than discussion and agreement between party leaders. As the Liberal Chief Whip put it, 'we never negotiate. Things simply "happen".'[69] That the Alliance worked this way was a *strategic* problem; that the Liberal party had to be prodded into adopting radical policies was more *politically* serious.

The Liberal radicals attempted to tackle the strategic problem on several occasions. Towards the end of 1912, at the end of the Single Tax land campaigns, and after several further clashes with the Labour party, the Master of Elibank, a known anti-Socialist, bizarrely transformed himself into a Progressive. He publicly stated that Labour should be allowed to field the only Progressive candidate in Midlothian (a solidly Liberal mining seat, where Elibank was the retiring MP) at the 1912 by-election. This was Lloyd George's visiting card. He followed it up immediately. Through his (and Elibank's) close friends, Isaacs and Mond, he offered Labour closer co-operation and a free run in eighty seats at the next election. MacDonald and W. C. Anderson floated the idea in the press. The reaction was such that the idea of a *formal* agreement had to be shelved. Nonetheless, both parties continued to work together, when drawn together, but sought what party advantage they could the remainder of the time.[70] The old, *informal*, Progressive Alliance was still intact.

The intention of using land reform to keep ahead of Labour, and to maintain the Progressive Alliance, became even more central to Lloyd George's plans after the Hanley victory. In February 1913 he obtained Asquith's approval to launch an official land campaign. By June he had accepted the Single Taxers' demand that the reform of local rating – the means to free land and money for municipal expenditure – would be a central part of the programme. Almost simultaneously, Wedgwood offered Labour a new pact, knowing, he told MacDonald, that 'you will be forced to attack the vested interests I hate in order to cover the union'. His offer was rejected. It was repeated in March 1914, when the army appeared to be ready to sabotage Government policy towards Ulster; this offer too was turned down.[71] Nonetheless, Lloyd George did not give up. MacDonald had told him, and others publicly hinted, that radical Liberal policies were likely to create 'tacit' Progressive co-operation of the kind apparent in 1909/10. Lloyd George still needed to push on.

[69] P. Illingworth to A. G. Gardiner, 8 Aug. 1913, Gardiner MS 1/8. For the general position, R. H. Davies to C.P.S., 4 May 1912, C.P.S. to Elibank, 5 Dec. 1911, CPS 332/107 and 55.

[70] See the lengthy discussion of this in G.L. to M. Coates-Hanson, 31 Oct. 1912, Lansbury MS LL 6 fos. 77–9.

[71] J. Wedgwood to J.R.M., 12 June 1913, JRM PRO 30/69/1157. For 1914, below, pp. 76, 344.

He allowed the land campaign to build momentum, and expectations, before bringing specific land reform proposals before the Cabinet at the end of 1913. It was then too late for Cabinet conservatives to resist the radical interpretation which Lloyd George's allies were publicly reading into the proposals. His subterfuge continued. As in 1909, he planned to combine his reforms in a radical Budget, using outside advisers to by-pass (hostile) Cabinet and Treasury influences. A supporting campaign was launched in the country (with allies like Addison in useful co-ordinating positions). The stage was set for a repeat of the 1910 election.[72]

The 1914 Budget had enormous radical potential. Yet it failed to become law. In under-estimating the technical problems, Lloyd George was forced to link his plans for current expenditure to revenue which would not be available for several years. As in 1909, he had not done his homework, and the Cabinet had not been given time to fudge the figures. He was found out. The Budget was labelled unconstitutional. Fifty Liberal MPs rebelled in the lobbies, and it was consequently withdrawn. Revenue plans were temporarily shelved. Instead, income tax (which did not affect the working class) was cut, despite radical hopes for a reduction in sugar duties as a more attractive campaigning issue with working-class voters. Land reform – as an immediate legislative proposal – was suspended.[73]

This gave the opponents of radical change an opportunity to reenter the race. A Centrist/Radical alliance had already been taking shape around opposition to armaments expenditure. They had now succeeded in reducing taxation on (middle-class) incomes. They could point to the likely electoral impact of the (reportedly popular) *rural* land campaign.[74] They certainly argued that a moderate approach could be electorally profitable. Lloyd George's Budget failure was not the only favourable circumstance for their counter-attack. The Progressive/Centrist alliance in Cabinet was crumbling. Churchill's fascination with Dreadnoughts had severed his competitive alliance with Lloyd George; Samuel had cast covetous eyes on the Local Government Board and land reform, which made him suspect in Lloyd George's eyes. Masterman – promoted to the Cabinet – had been defeated at two successive by-elections. Runciman gloated at their disarray.[75]

---

[72] Murray, *People's Budget*, pp. 303–10, K. O. and J. Morgan, *Portrait of a Progressive*, p. 28; Samuel to his Mother, 11 Jan. 1914, Samuel MS A/156 fo. 452. See also below, pp. 151, 271, 308–9.

[73] Gilbert, 'The Budget of 1914', pp. 117–41, A.R. to M. K. Rowntree, 13 Mar. 1914, AR MS.

[74] L.G. to W.R., 12 June 1914, W.R. to R. Chambers, 24 June 1914, WR 116.

[75] For Grey/Buxton, Grey to W.R., 18 Mar. 1912, WR 300; W.R. to Chalmers, above fn. 68. See also W.R. to C.P.T., 4 Jan 1914, CPT 33, Samuel to his Mother, 11 Jan. 1914, Samuel MS A/156 fo. 452.

The radicals were down but not out. A New Liberal/Centrist Cabinet alliance might be rebuilt by appropriating elements of their opponents' strategy and attaching it, once again, to radical policies. The first half of the equation was easily accomplished. Lloyd George and many Progressives had always opposed armaments expenditure; Lloyd George discussed sacrificing Churchill by engineering his resignation. The radical reinterpretation of the Irish crisis in 1914 (as an assault on democracy by the army, several Tory Lords, and by implication the whole class they represented) displayed Lloyd George's talent for building on older radical traditions in a populist manner; his involvement in the negotiations over Home Rule increased his popularity with the Radicals.[76] Neither was the Centrist/Radical alliance secure. The 'Cave' against the 1914 Budget had contained many, like A. G. C. Harvey and Percy Molteno, who were keen land reformers. They opposed the *form* of the Budget, not its content. Moreover, a Tory electoral revival, and the possibility of Labour opposition, had to be countered if the Liberals were to stay in office. The best that the Old Liberal/Centrist alliance could offer was a return to the position in the 1880s and 1890s, when the Liberal party was in almost permanent opposition.[77] This was not an attractive proposal for a party which was now used to power.

By August 1914, the Progressives were beginning to regroup and hit back. The land campaign in the country had carried on despite the problems in Cabinet, and Progressives at the centre refused to back down. 'Going forward', Haldane noted, 'is the only thing to do.' The full *Nation* programme had included an urban minimum wage and limited nationalisation as vital parts of the land reform programme. Land campaign intelligence saw this as the only way to win the towns. Lloyd George acknowledged that 'something has to be done to educate the urban population'. There were rumours of a forthcoming commitment to women's suffrage, and hints that Lloyd George would adopt the much-needed, broader, more materialistic, New Liberal programme at the next election. This programme had the potential to create a broad alliance in the country and in the party. It linked old and new issues; it advocated general reforms at the expense of the rich, and could justify catering for sectional interests if these were in the interests of the community. Whether this would satisfy a majority of the working-class electorate, or a large enough section of it to maintain the party's position as a broad reforming alliance with Labour support, remained to be seen. The Progressives at the centre had at least a viable package which might keep the Liberals' reforming alliance, and the Progressive Alliance, together. Their success or failure

[76] L.G. memo, n.d., Asquith MS 25 fo. 148.
[77] See below, p. 152.

would depend in part on the Labour party's ability either to chip off large sections of the Liberals' electoral base with a more attractive reforming package, or the Labour left's ability to create an attractive, class-based, alternative which would sweep the Liberal party into oblivion.[78]

V

The reason for Labour's electoral failure in 1910 was perfectly clear and frequently identified. The Liberals' electoral programme combined a sense of moral injustice with a new socio-economic radicalism. 'Collectivism' was gaining ground in both municipal and parliamentary politics: 'The general movement of thought and tendencies towards Socialism is most encouraging', Snowden wrote. The Liberals, he continued, were becoming the expression of that movement. Labour was divided and bitter.[79] Labour's moral reformism, and the composite Liberal package offered in 1909/10, were not sufficiently different to create a new political climate.

The left argued that Labour's current approach could bring neither real benefits nor electoral gains. The debate developed against the background of the 1912 Liberal land campaign. Fred Henderson, a long-standing ILP activist and journalist, put the left's view:

A Labour party which is preaching the virtues of the minimum wage ... or any social reform within the existing order instead of Socialism and the expropriation of the master class, cannot fight the New Liberals ... because to do so would be to include its own clap-trap in a common condemnation with Liberalism.

The Liberals' paternalistic collectivism, Henderson wrote, would only create what Hilaire Belloc and G. K. Chesterton had popularly labelled the 'Servile State'.[80]

The left maintained their belief in an 'educationalist' Socialism. 'There is no success', Fred Henderson wrote, 'that will stand the wear and tear of life, other than the success of converting public opinion to Socialism.' Unless *people* were changed, Keir Hardie similarly argued, the Servile State would stifle true Socialism in a 'Fabian' spider's webb of compromise and adjustment.[81]

The left had recently received a boost. The discovery of Kropotkin, Sorel, and Nietzsche, with their emphasis on irrationalism and emotion,

---

[78] Haldane to his Mother, 15 July 1914, Haldane MS 5991 fo. 253; L.G. to W.R., 12 May and 12 June 1914, WR 112; Holton, *Feminism and democracy*, p. 125. L.G.'s speech at Criccieth was reported in all the major Liberal papers and journals. See also below, pp. 412–16.

[79] P.S. to S.H., 18 Apr. 1911, SH MS. See also *L.L.*, 30 Oct. 1913.

[80] *Clarion*, 19 July 1912 and debate between Henderson and Chesterton, *Clarion*, 14 Mar. 1913 and *D.H.*, 22 Mar. 1913.

[81] *Clarion*, 12 July 1912; *Scotsman*, 5 Jan. 1914.

had reconvinced some activists that working-class sentiment could be the basis for change.[82] Industrial and social unrest after 1910 appeared to confirm the fact of working-class alienation, and demonstrate that the electorate possessed the oppositional consciousness from which Socialism could be forged. It demonstrated 'a new spirit actuating the working class ... a degree of solidarity and class consciousness which would have been considered impossible a dozen years ago'.[83]

George Lansbury and the *Herald* 'rebels' embodied this new confidence. They aimed to create a permanent 'spirit of rebellion'. 'The main thing to do', Lansbury wrote, echoing William Morris, 'is to make the workers want & want badly better conditions.'[84] The *Herald*'s faith in industrial unrest as a means of creating a class base often merged into Syndicalism; its support for the 'spiritually' related women's suffrage movement led it to contemplate an extra-parliamentary alliance of the alienated. Practical suggestions were limited.[85] Like Fred Henderson and McLachlan before them, the *Herald* argued that, if the PLP gave a lead, 'there will be such an uprising as will astonish the country'. Lansbury and Hardie obliged with some aggressive assaults on the Liberal front benches. They also urged the PLP to vote against all Government measures until the Liberals changed their policy on (successively) women's suffrage, national insurance, Ireland and naval expenditure.[86]

From around 1909, Fred Jowett began to construct a more sophisticated critique. He argued that 'State Collectivism' was unlikely to create 'real' change unless the role of the bureaucracy and 'officialdom' was checked and controlled. Parliament should therefore be reconstructed in such a way that committees would control the Executive (as they did in local government). MPs would vote on the merits of the case, to obviate the power of the political machine. By voting as its principles dictated, Labour would advertise the distinction between Socialist and semi-Socialist ideas and policies. This would increase Socialist credibility as an honest, consistent force; it would improve its *moral* purchase. Yet the left also needed to demonstrate that supporting Labour was *materially* meaningful. Recognition of the state as a non-benevolent force was accompanied by

[82] Paton, *Proletarian pilgrimage*, p. 212, R. M. Fox, *Smokey crusade* (1937), p. 54. See also Sanders, *Early Socialist days*, p. 14, and for a fuller discussion Tanner, 'The Edwardian Labour party'. Contrast Bruce Glasier's statement that Nietzsche's views were 'the philosophy of the Baboon'.

[83] *D.H.*, 15 Apr. 1912.

[84] G.L. to B. Webb, 28 Oct. 1913, Webb MS 11 4f fo. 166.

[85] C. Pankhurst to H. D. Harben, 7 Aug. 1913, A. Kenney to Mrs Harben, 4 Aug. 1913, Harben Add MS 58226. Cf. S. G. Hobson, *Pilgrimage to the left* (1938), p. 99, *Justice*, 1 Mar. 1913. See also below, pp. 178–9.

[86] *D.H.*, 3 July 1912; J.B.G. Diary, 11 Oct. 1911; K. O. Morgan, *Keir Hardie. Radical and Socialist* (1975), pp. 248–50; J.K.H. to J.B.G., 8 Feb. 1911, JBG 1911/31.

an attack on state reforms as inadequate and confiscatory. Jowett supplied an ideological justification for attacks on contributory national insurance and the Poor Law. Rejection of these legislative attempts to 'control' the people was accompanied by the rejection of ('middle-class') state 'preaching' on thrift and sobriety, and allegations of a reluctance to tackle real economic deprivation. Moderates like Thorne, F. W. Goldstone, and even Snowden and the Webbs were drawn into the campaign. Yet these Socialist moral reformers still did not know how to make the transition from concrete, locally relevant, issues to a 'national' means of mobilising opinion.[87]

This approach had strategic implications which were incompatible with MacDonald's electoral strategy. If the PLP was using Parliament to advertise the differences between Socialism and Liberalism, then party leaders would logically have to continue with the publicity at election time. Inevitably, Liberal/Labour electoral conflict would escalate. In the short-term, the *Herald* and others conceded, this might mean a temporary reduction in parliamentary representation; but (they added) Labour would immediately bounce back. Privately, leading left wing figures argued that no Labour representation was better than Labour representation on the existing lines.[88] Support for this approach grew in the constituencies. Its adherents became institutionally stronger at the centre. Although Grayson, Douthwaite, and other hard left elements departed and formed the British Socialist Party in 1911, McLachlan, and G. H. Stuart decided to fight from within and were soon elected to the NAC. Jowett and Lansbury topped the national ILP ballot, and gained positions on key committees as a result. From 1910–12 the political balance on the NAC was fairly even; on at least one occasion, Lansbury's efforts to change policy failed by just one vote.[89] However, to the annoyance of those who were working to change Labour from within, Lansbury's patience snapped. In 1912 he resigned his seat to fight a by-election in protest at Labour policy on women's suffrage (in particular) and its support of Liberal legislation in general.[90] Hardie's resignation from the NEC in support of Lansbury further weakened the left's position. Both men were isolated by 1914.[91]

[87] F. W. Jowett, *What is the use of Parliament?* (1909); Morris (thesis), pp. 308–16, Thane, 'Labour and welfare', pp. 204–9. Snowden's involvement was widely seen as an attempt to become MacDonald's successor.
[88] *D.H.*, 27 Nov. 1912; Harben to B. Webb, 8 Dec. 1913, Webb MS 11 4f fos. 168–9; T. Mann and B. Tillett to G.L., 27 Nov. 1912, Lansbury MS 28 fos. 87 and 89.
[89] J.B.G. Diary, 6 Oct. 1911.
[90] See e.g. J.S.M. to his parents, 2 Feb. 1913, MID 11/32: 'Lansbury's close association with the Pankhursts and the WSPU has not only cost him his seat at Bow but has also gone far to lose the sympathy of many of his admirers in the movement.'
[91] For Lansbury's isolation, A. Salter to G.L., 27 Sept. 1914, Lansbury MS 7 fo. 172; B. Webb Diary, 2 Apr. 1914; J.B.G. Diary, 6 Jan. 1912.

Nonetheless, the vote-on-principle policy was passed at the ILP annual conference in 1914.

Despite this apparent 'victory', the left had made little real headway. The leadership was unconvinced. MacDonald's union allies shunned the idea that conflict and irrationality could be the basis for successful action; strikes were divisive, they argued, because they imposed the greatest hardship on the workers themselves.[92] G. J. Wardle, for example, opposed the ILP left's calls for parliamentary demonstrations, noting their 'arrogant assumption of superiority', and the 'disloyalty' of their call for autonomy of action within the PLP. Many unions agreed: 'Labour . . . (should) conserve its strength and not waste it on vain heroisms . . . The "irreconcilable" game has been played in the House of Commons itself and has shown itself to be not worth playing.'[93]

Many moderate Labour reformers shared the Labour left's hostility to MacDonald's close contacts with the Liberal Whips. They complained when he traded Labour parliamentary support for the Liberals' National Insurance legislation in return for legislation which gave MPs a salary. Some thought he was 'leading the party into Liberalism'. Bruce Glasier and other long-standing ILP activists were uneasy at the lack of 'idealism' in Labour policy. Fabians were disgruntled by Labour's inability to act as efficient critics of the Liberals' half-radical measures. However, Lansbury's Graysonesque outbursts in Parliament – his denunciation of Asquith as a 'murderer', for example, because of his policy on the forced feeding of suffragettes – did not attract support. 'I hope I am not ungenerous', Bruce Glasier noted, with typical ungenerosity, 'in regarding this as a mere outbreak of self-consciousness and see-what-a-good-boy-am-I-ism.'[94] It was one thing to attract sympathy, another to create a broad and credible internal opposition to the party hierarchy.

The left's case for fighting by-elections gained more support. However, party strategy appeared to be changing. Organisational reform was being encouraged. Grants were given towards the cost of employing constituency agents; trade unions were encouraged to spend time and money on candidates and organisation. Party leaders were less stringent in their attitude to fighting by-elections. The NAC endorsed a candidate at Kilmarnock Boroughs in 1911: 'We have done this with some misgiving, because although we feel that a fight is necessary and that a good result

[92] e.g. W.C.A. in *D.H.*, 10 June 1913, P.S., *Socialism and Syndicalism*, p. 78, J.B.G. Diary, 6 Sept. 1911, and *Socialist Review*, Apr. 1912.

[93] *R.R.*, 31 Mar. 1911. See also ASE *MR* July 1913, *Typographical Circular*, Feb. 1914, BrSS *MR* Feb. 1914.

[94] J.K.H. to J.R.M., 4 Mar. 1914, FJ 1914/77; B. Webb Diary, 1 Dec. 1912; J.B.G. Diary, 6 and 7 Jan., 26 June 1912.

would lift up the whole movement, we are not convinced that the Kilmarnock Boroughs are the best fighting ground.'[95]

MacDonald opposed this and several other campaigns; the refusal to fight at Leicester in 1913 caused a major crisis. There were bitter reactions in the press, which culminated in debates at the ILP and Labour Conferences in 1914. Nonetheless, MacDonald carried the party with him on Leicester and on the party's election strategy in general. In part this was because he was willing to fight by-elections where the prospects were good, or where a fight might secure a seat. He, and the leadership generally, warmly approved of the decision to fight the Oldham by-election in 1911 for example (albeit as a tool to engineer a Liberal withdrawal before the next election). He reacted strongly to the Liberals' attempt to capture Hanley, and encouraged a second contest in nearby Crewe in retaliation. The mining constituencies, which frequently contained no Labour organisation, were earmarked as areas of potential expansion. The miners' unions were encouraged to pay them considerable attention. MacDonald made anti-Liberal speeches at several by-elections in mining seats in 1913–14.[96] Yet the speeches were meant as threatening gestures, which would encourage the Liberals to make further concessions. MacDonald wished to expand *within* the Progressive Alliance. Important members of the party were increasingly converted to this extension of the stance adopted before 1910, and the ideological/political aims behind it.[97]

Jowett's 'vote-on-principle' policy did not convince most trade union or soft-left MPs. As Joseph Pointer, the Sheffield MP argued, it would involve throwing over a Liberal Government because it proposed a single 'bad' measure. Given the current parliamentary arithmetic, Labour might remove the Liberals from office over an issue which had no electoral appeal. It would leave the working class to face Tory policies without good cause. 'In that case', he wrote, 'we shall be like Ephraim following the east wind – we shall not get very far.'[98]

'Radical' elements, including powerful provincial Socialist newspapers, like the *Huddersfield Worker* and the *Forward*, argued that ideological purity was better than immoral compromise: to sit voting for reactionary

---

[95] NAC report by W.C.A., 7 Sept. 1911, ILP H.O. Circ./6.

[96] J.R.M. to F. Hall, 30 Apr. 1914, LP/PA/14/1/58, and, more generally, McKibbin, *Evolution*, pp. 54–62. For Oldham, J.R.M. Diary, 18 June 1911, JRM PRO 30/69/1753, J.S.M. to his parents, 28 Oct., 11 Nov. 1911, MID 10/34 & 37.

[97] Morris (thesis), pp. 317–21 for Leicester, and for the 'MacDonaldite' soft left in Lancashire. See also M. Phillips to J.R.M., 10 Mar. 1909, LP/CAN/06/2/241, W.C.A. to J.R.M, 24 Sept. 1908, B. Riley to J.R.M., 25 Jan. 1909, JRM PRO 30/69/1152 and 1153. For the opposition of even men like Hardie to fighting some by-elections, e.g. J.B.G. Diary, 3 Feb. 1911 (N.E. Lanark).

[98] J. Pointer, S.G., 17 Jan. 1913.

Liberal measures was to 'commit suicide in a more . . . fundamental way'.[99]
Once again, however, MacDonaldites came back to an old argument:
Liberal reforms were neither unpopular nor reactionary. The parliamentary position, the danger of causing the return of a Tory government,
was a cloak to justify compromise between groups with a core of similar
ideological aims. W. C. Anderson, the ILP Chairman and a moderate
moral reformer, demonstrated the emotional and electoral weakness of
the left's case. Given the left's reasoning, he argued,

When workmen ask for an eight hours day it should solemnly be said to them,
'Social reform which still leaves the master class in possession of the sources
of wealth is futile.' When hungry children ask for bread, or old people for a
pension, or injured workmen for compensation, the Labour party should impress
them with the grave and high-sounding fact that 'nothing really matters so long
as private ownership remains'.[100]

Many of the trade unions who financed Labour politics were sympathetic to this criticism of the left. Liberal policy was not accepted without
question, but it was not unpopular. The details of the Insurance Act-
were often attacked, but the principle was widely applauded by the skilled
unions once the Government agreed to place its administration in the
unions' hands. 'The Insurance Act is the largest measure of social reform
which has ever been adopted', one ASLEF journalist noted; many union
members would 'have reason to thank God for it'. The Boilermakers
thought it 'a very distinct advance along the path of progress' and 'certainly
the greatest measure of social reform ever placed on the Statute Book'.
Other unions concurred. Insurance, as Beatrice Webb noted, was 'an
obsession of the public mind'.[101]

New Liberal policy was even more attractive. The Boilermakers saw
the miners' minimum wage legislation as the first step to the nationalisation of mining and railways. It 'must lead in the near future to the establishment of a national minimum in all trades, below which no private
employer shall be permitted to exploit our labour'.[102] State intervention
was not seen as a panacea, but as a means of controlling monopolies
and reinforcing labour's independence. The land/minimum wage/nation-
alisation programme was recognised as a powerful and attractive combination even by anti-Liberal Socialists. As G. H. Stuart put it, the adoption
of these proposals would complete the Liberals' transformation into a
radical party:

[99] Forward, 14 Jan. 1911. See also Huddersfield Worker, 4 Feb. 1911.
[100] Manchester Weekly Citizen, 23 Aug. 1912.
[101] B. Webb Diary, 6 Mar. 1911; Locomotive Journal, Jan. 1912; Boilermakers' AR 1910,
1911. See also BrSS MR Aug. 1911, Shipwrights' AR 1911.
[102] Boilermakers' AR 1911.

Of course, the mere Nationalisation of Railways, or even the establishment of a Minimum Wage, does not constitute Socialism, but when you add to this a vast scheme (sic) dealing with the land you get so near Socialism that the difference is not perceptible by ordinary people.

The ASE, ASLEF, and others were all enthusiastic.[103] Many union leaders also supported Liberal policy on issues like Irish Home Rule. When the army attempted to dictate policy to an elected Government, J. H. Thomas noted, 'all other questions become of minor importance'. This was not an unusual view; neither was it without presumed electoral relevance. Labour representatives argued that the Irish vote was the difference between success and failure in a large number of seats.[104] There was a good deal of principled and pragmatic acceptance of Liberal policy. As Barnes noted of the Liberals:

with all their faults ... they have done much wise things in the direction of the betterment of the conditions of the people. We are convinced that Mr Lloyd George's sympathies are with the workers and the poor, and that he would go much further than he has gone and promises to go if he were sure of carrying his Bills.[105]

Nonetheless, Labour moderates were able to make some headway against the composite Liberal image. Labour's response to the industrial unrest was particularly significant in this respect. It supported the unions' industrial campaigns, moving resolutions and amendments which criticised Government policy. In the autumn of 1911, W. C. Anderson abandoned the ILP's prospective land campaign to concentrate on advocating the nationalisation of the railways. This, he told the branches, 'would allow us to drive home many lessons of the recent strike'. The NEC also proposed a 'new departure' in the party's propagandist style, 'the idea being not so much to present for the approval of the public a series of disconnected measures, each one good in itself, but a conception of general reform which would arouse the imagination and enthusiasm of our supporters'. The Committee recognised that Labour calls for mini-

[103] *Postman's Gazette*, 1 Nov. 1913; ASE *Monthly Journal*, Feb. 1913, *Locomotive Journal*, Mar. 1913. Bruce Glasier argued that there was no Socialist alternative, and even those dissatisfied with the leadership recognised that his views had some force (*Huddersfield Worker*, 22 Apr., 22 May, 30 Sept. 1911).

[104] *R.R.*, 3 Apr. 1914. See similarly *Typographical Circular*, Mar. 1914, ASC&J, *Monthly Journal*, Aug. 1914. For MacDonald's view, below, p. 344. For the Labour view on Irish votes, *S.G.*, 11 July 1913, *Worker*, 2 Dec. 1911, *L.L.*, 5 Mar. 1914 (Leith), *Sheffield T&LC AR* 1914/15 (N–W Durham).

[105] ASE *Monthly Journal*, Feb. 1914. Cf. J.S.M.'s comments, expressed on the occasions of the Trade Union Bill, the national insurance discussions and finally Ireland: 'it's a choice of two evils, & the government have never done the wrong thing from our point of view without the Tories having urged them to be a jolly sight worse' (J.S.M. to his parents, 26 Apr. 1914, MID 12/22 and also MID 11/31, 35).

mum wages would be met with the claim that these would only damage the consumer. Labour's answer was to be nationalisation and taxation of wealth. The former was to focus on land, railways, and mines. It was to be 'a propaganda of ideas and principles, setting the whole idea in a conception of social necessity and human justice'. For skilled and organised labour, hours of work and the nature of housing provision were the issues; this was 'not so much a programme as the interpretation of a human claim to leisure, fair dealing, and social opportunities in terms of certain definite proposals'.[106] For organisations with 'Statist' interests, particularly the miners and the railwaymen, Labour was showing tangibly that it was on their side, that it would fight for them in Parliament. It was beginning to argue that it had proposals (particularly nationalisation) which would aid their cause. For the remaining skilled workers, it was showing that it cared about social security and moral justice. For the unskilled, it had little to offer.

Labour's attitude did not guarantee that it would assume a primary political role. Much of this duplicated what the Liberals offered, although Labour was more solidly committed to nationalisation of mines and railways. Labour politicians did not feature prominently in the settlement of industrial disputes; they were not the automatic political reflex of industrial aims. Industrial action and direct negotiation with Government were the norm. There was little space for Labour to exploit. On the one hand, Guild Socialism and Syndicalism – doctrines of industrial action – challenged the right of capital to make profit a prerequisite for wage settlements. On the other hand, the Liberals' willingness to force industry to make substantial concessions suggested that spending funds on Labour representation was unnecessary. Moreover, Labour was seen as largely a skilled workers' party; MacDonald even *opposed* minimum wage legislation (as the skilled unions did), arguing that it would not solve their problems. This may have been correct, but it was not good propaganda. The leaders of unskilled unions were reluctantly (and very partially) 'converted' to the idea of Labour representation as a means of influencing the Liberals.[107] State control was in fact increasingly congenial. By 1914 they found National Insurance legislation and decasualisation acceptable, largely as a means of regularising the work and wages of a (growing) unionised elite.[108] Miners were also only partially converted to Labour by their industrial needs. Support for a national minimum wage through

[106] W.C.A. H.O. report, 25 May 1911, ILP MS, H.O. Circ./3; NEC Mins, 8 Dec. 1911.
[107] *Baker's Magazine*, Sept. 1913, Sept. 1914; *Blind Advocate*, Sept. 1912; UK Society of Coachmakers' *Quarterly Report*, Oct. 1914, *Government Workers' Advocate*, Dec. 1914. For MacDonald and others on minimum wages, Tanner, 'The Edwardian Labour party'.
[108] Watermen and Lightermen *AR* 1913; National Union of Dock Labourers, *General Secretary's report 1912*.

nationalisation was officially MFGB policy, but in reality only the SWMF executive regarded it favourably.[109] Neither the unions, nor Labour, were fully confident that state control was the right way forward. Labour had come some way, but it did not have a national, 'class', solution to the Liberals' popularity which would mobilise support in all conditions, and amongst all groups.

As far as the Labourist, Statist, and 'moderate' moral reforming strands of the Labour leadership were concerned, a substantial proportion of Liberal policy was attractive. Nonetheless, there were weaknesses in the Liberals' position, and aspects of policy which some Labour elements found objectionable. Liberal radicalism had also lost some momentum by 1914, even if the radical leaders were attempting to make up lost ground in 1914. It looked as if the *balance* of the Liberal/Labour electoral competition may have shifted a little in Labour's favour. Within the Labour party, the 'reforming alliance' which hoped to exploit any Liberal failures of this kind had half-beaten off the left's challenge by 1914. It had developed a more relevant, sympathetic approach particularly to the interests of Statist groups. National politics would suggest that the party competition was a little closer in 1914 than in 1910. The Labour leadership had emphasised that it had something positive to say in areas where Liberal policy was only half-convincing and only partially attractive.

Politics at the centre was one thing; politics in the constituencies was another. Westminster politics, and central strategic planning, meant nothing if these ideological/political/strategic approaches did not leave their mark in the constituencies. Whatever the national balance, the local perception of that balance was of vital importance in determining political behaviour. Local economic circumstances and political actions were an important aspect of this, and they will be dealt with at length below. However, the centre's ability to influence the party image in the constituencies was also important in determining the nature of the political map. It is that question which must be addressed first.

---

[109] See below, pp. 209–11, 372, and report of nationalisation debates, R. Page Arnot, *The Miners* (1953), p. 123.

Chapter 3

The centre and the constituencies

New ideological stances, and new, more materially relevant, policies, were an important part of Progressive politics. So too was a 'national' willingness to overcome institutional obstacles to Progressive co-operation. However, the nature of politics and of institutional power in the constituencies was equally significant because local parties could undermine the 'national' image and strategy. 'Westminster' debates were repeated in 'constituency' politics. The local balance might be an improvement on the national position, since the local party might be better adapted to meeting local needs and views. It could also, however, cling to views which were no longer popular except with party activists. It could undermine the basis of the Progressive Alliance and make the prospect of permanent improvements over the position in the 1890s more suspect.

The 'national' ability to redefine the local party image in the constituencies was strongest where Progressive parties were weak, and had little to lose through change. Political desperation and financial problems ensured that local party members accepted central party dictates. It was easiest to operate the Progressive Alliance in 'Tory' working-class areas – principally parts of the North-West, the West Midlands, London and the south coast ports. Although the 'centre' exercised some influence in 'Liberal' areas, its influence was much weaker. The often informal links between the centre and the constituencies left scope for local organisations to determine the full extent of the local party image. The existence of powerful and electorally popular local groups also meant that a national strategy was not easily imposed on the party in the country.

Gradual Labour expansion in the Tory areas was not a danger to the Progressive Alliance. Liberal Progressives in fact regarded it as a means to achieve 'Progressive' victories in areas where their party had hitherto usually been unsuccessful. However, Labour expansion had to be confined to these areas. If Labour began to threaten Liberal strongholds – as it had to in order to become the principal party of the left – the

Progressive Alliance, and the Liberals' ability to hold office, would disintegrate.

There were already marked geographical variations in the level of party support before 1906. The Liberals did not satisfy working-class political needs in whole areas of the country. Local Liberal and Labour/Socialist organisations were not necessarily perceived in the same way in 'Liberal' areas as they were in 'Tory' areas. There were certainly forces operating which encouraged the 'nationalisation' of politics, but, despite these forces, voters in varying areas still had very different interests, expectations, and attitudes. Indeed, given these differences, it was not necessarily wise to emphasise the same aspects of a 'national' party image in quite different parts of the country. What was appropriate in Yorkshire, for instance, was not necessarily appropriate in the West Midlands. There would continue to be spatial variations in support and spatially distinct political approaches (Section I).

It was nonetheless evident by 1906 that *all* local variations of a 'national' image had to change a little, because they were not successful enough to give the parties the political results which they wanted. It was this which encouraged Liberals to 'radicalise' their national image, and this which encouraged MacDonald to shift 'Socialism' closer to 'practical' concerns.

A localised Liberal version of a composite national image had nonetheless been the basis of party success in whole areas of the country, and could not readily be abandoned. In 'Liberal' areas, 'national' politics had only to modify a local Liberal image; in Tory areas, 'national' politics had to transform the local party image, because the existing approach was a hopeless failure. The continuing power of constituency parties to influence how the party was perceived could have an adverse impact on the Liberals' electoral prospects. The adverse image created by constituency autonomy could allow Labour to capture all the Tory areas, by not putting up a serious resistance. It could allow Labour to expand more than it might have done in Liberal areas by ensuring that the local party did not seem sufficiently concerned with economic problems and social reform. The constituencies' contribution could preserve the 'old' politics where a measure of the 'politics of change' was necessary to produce better results. At the same time, local *Labour* resistance to reformist politics could itself prevent Labour grasping what opportunities existed as a result of local Liberal deficiencies.

National influences on local politics were evident and growing in Liberal *and* Labour politics after 1906. The party leaders had the ability and the will to influence politics in the constituencies, but their effect could be minimised (Section II). It was therefore necessary that 'radicalisation from above' (through national policy and propaganda) should be accompanied by a 'radicalisation from below' which would ensure the effective implementation of national views (Section III). If the national strategy of a Progressive Alliance was to be effective, local parties had to comply with central dictates.

Local politics had a second, less commonly identified, significance (Section IV). The creative diversity of local organisations could provide a basis for alternative approaches to the composite policy currently dominant at Westminster. The success or failure of the ideological approaches adopted by constituency parties would determine whether the advocates of that particular ideological approach at the centre had *electoral,* as well as *institutional,* purchase. If Radicalism and Liberal Imperialism continued to attract electoral support, then Radicals and Liberal Imperialists would not easily be removed from the party leadership. If a Socialist moral reformism, or if 'Labourism', had electoral purchase, then these strands in Labour politics would continue to exercise influence at the centre. The nature of the ideas and policies which attracted votes would inevitably influence the policy orientation of the party. The party at the centre could not afford to ignore the ideas which attracted its electoral support. The constituency parties would help determine whether ideological strands at the centre had the capacity, not just to undermine elements of the national approach, or to influence the parties' composite image, but to sustain a viable alternative. They could totally change the balance of the party's aims and image. This chapter examines the relationship between the centre and the constituencies; subsequent chapters show how politics in the constituencies were a mixture of 'national' and 'local' strategies and images, and discuss the consequences for the parties' aims and level of support.

I

The electoral map of Edwardian Britain was determined by a complex range of religious, material, and ideological factors. Non-economic factors were an important influence on voting behaviour. The spatial distribution of Nonconformist and Anglican religious attendance continued to be closely correlated with the distribution of (respectively) Liberal and Tory support. Middle-class Nonconformists and working-class Anglican attenders seem to have been more likely to deny their 'class' position and vote for the party associated with their religious preference. Some 'religious' issues – particularly the question of sectarian education – could have a considerable electoral impact in parts of the country. The 'politics of the past' still contained, for some, an over-riding importance.[1]

The 'politics of change' were also significant. This is not to suggest that 'religious' voting was being replaced by 'class' allegiances, and that the criteria for Liberal success was the extent to which a national party image penetrated the constituencies and formed a uniform 'class' allegiance. Political behaviour was more complex than this. The first, and most important, influence on an individual's political behaviour was the extent to which a party's broad image suggested that it would improve that voter's standard of living. However, 'interests' were not uniform. 'Liberal' Free Trade, for example, might mean economic prosperity to workers in export related industries, but it meant economic death to those suffering from international competition. Interests were occupationally and spatially different. Neither were they always rationally or objectively determined. Economic dependency on a particular industry or firm might encourage voters to pay close attention to the expressed interests of their local employers. The voters' perceptions of their interests and of desirable policies were more significant than any other criteria. Here the past had a further hold, and played an important role in creating regionally distinct outlooks. Nonconformist areas, for example, continued to be strongly Liberal (and subsequently Labour) long after formal religious attendance had declined. The values and attitudes associated with Nonconformity, and inculcated through family socialisation, and through political localism (or 'regionalism') did not disappear overnight. New experiences were viewed in the light of older views. Conceptions of what was desirable policy would be influenced by religion in a 'formal' sense (i.e. on the grounds of whether the party supported the aims of a particular religious group) and in a 'social' sense (i.e. whether it expressed historically respected values). The latter was evidently more common by 1910 (although the former did not cease to exist).

This is not to suggest that attitudes were based purely on 'religious' factors. The political parties had evolved alongside these religious forces, and had helped mould religious values into patterns of political opinion. They had forged genuinely *political* cultures. Subjective conceptions of history and politics were the basis of political knowledge and expectations, and one of the standards by which new policies were judged. As collections of potentially conflicting ideas and symbolic reference

[1] Miller, *Electoral dynamics,* Chapter 6 is the best source for religious affiliations after 1918, although the material and conclusions are not uniformly accepted. For the persistence of 'old' ideas, and their importance in 'new' contexts, F. M. L. Thompson, 'Social control in Victorian Britain', *Economic History Review* (1981), pp. 192–6, B. Harrison, 'Traditions of respectability in British labour history', in his *Peaceable Kingdom* (Oxford, 1982), pp. 157–8.

points – economic and social – a voter's outlook contained the potential for supporting a variety of political postures; but the nature of ingrained views is such that the political consequences were less fluid than this would suggest.[2] In the areas where the Liberals were historically very strong, for example, a Liberal/Nonconformist political culture ensured that the Liberals' political base was not simply dependent on instrumental allegiances, but on perpetually reinforced conceptions of what was right and attainable. This ensured that politics would not change overnight; that 'class' allegiances would not easily overcome older patterns of political allegiances. It also ensured, as MacDonald and the New Liberals argued, that if the presentation of politics in the present did not reflect in some respects the politics of the past, those new policies would probably not prove acceptable.

The complex means by which parties maintained support need not concern us here.[3] This analysis is based on the evident fact that parties clearly *did* establish themselves in particular regions; that they were not easily displaced in areas where they had always been strong, and that they were buttressed by their use of older, accepted, ideas and views about what was acceptable policy. Family socialisation, regionalism, and political habit, helped determine whether particular issues were regarded as salient to particular individuals or groups.

At the same time, these processes were not uniformly significant. Allegiances were not fossilised. In strongly Tory areas in particular, Liberal allegiances were less firmly rooted. They rested on weaker economic and social foundations, and perhaps more on a hostility to Toryism ('negative partisanship') than on a positive commitment to Liberal policies.[4] The existence of weak links in the Liberal armour gave Labour an evident opportunity to expand in these Tory areas, provided it could create an acceptable local image. Its presumed ability to gain support by virtue of its links to local working-class social views and occupational interests explains why even some Liberals who were not known for their radicalism supported an electoral compact in 1903. At the same time, however, Labour's progress in traditionally Liberal areas would be slower and more difficult. It might also require a different political approach. Even Liberal parties with little sympathy for social reform were deeply rooted in important, and 'valid', socio-economic circumstances, and in political habit. Labour could try and build on a radical tradition whose

[2] A. Brown and J. Gray, *Political culture and political change in Communist States* (2nd edn., 1979), pp. 1, 257, D. Kavanagh, *Political culture* (1972), esp. pp. 28, 60, 67.

[3] For general observations and specific suggestions on the importance of style and symbol, M. Billig, *Ideology and social psychology* (Oxford, 1982), pp. 217–22, H. M. Drucker, *The political uses of ideology* (1974), esp. pp. 47, 57.

[4] Crewe, 'Political change', p. 73 for negative partisanship.

longevity was reinforced by a radical Nonconformity and an economic analysis which did not see current conditions as unalterable. However popular radical ideas were not so self contained – so detached from aspects of a Liberal, or Tory analysis – that Labour could establish a secure constituency.[5]

The nature of local political cultures was thus an important feature of the electoral process, and past political tradition was of paramount importance in determining the nature and extent of political and electoral change in the Edwardian period. As the following chapters indicate, parties which worked against the grain of established local maxims of belief did not necessarily fail; new 'class' ideologies *could* break the hold of the past, particularly if they were functional to material interests. There was a geographical pattern to political support, based on a variety of factors, but there was also an economic or functional dimension which could counter these influences.[6] However, if 'rooted' parties themselves presented materially relevant policies, which *also* built on an existing outlook or language, they were not easily replaced. Where appeals were reinforced by economic prosperity, or an ability to determine what was seen to be possible, then their support was doubly secure. In attempting to influence voters the Liberals had a distinct advantage over Labour (in Liberal areas), but were more vulnerable where the Tories were historically the stronger party, or where Labour had links with the occupational interests of a particularly numerous local group.

II

The Liberal party at the centre possessed several important means of influencing the party in the constituencies. Foremost amongst these was the national Liberal press. 'Heavy' Liberal dailies, particularly the *Westminster Gazette,* addressed the Liberal elite in a loyal, moderate, and 'rational' language. As Spender, the editor, put it, the Liberals needed 'the demonic energy and vehement eloquence of its advanced friends . . . but we in our paper are appealing to an audience which wants every step proved to its reason'. Papers like the *Gazette* were unlikely to undermine the essence of party policy; they were equally unlikely to force the pace of change. Nonetheless, the radicals were not badly served. The intellectual journals, particularly the *Nation,* contained innumerable discussions of 'theoretical' and 'practical' New Liberal views. Even con-

[5] See in particular Reid, 'Old Unionism reconsidered', and Tanner, 'The Edwardian Labour party'.
[6] Analysis by geographical and functional units is now common practice. (See e.g. discussion in R. J. Johnston, C. J. Pattie, and J. G. Allsopp, *A Nation dividing* (1988), esp. pp. 2–9).

servative Liberals came into contact with radical Liberal writing. Members of the Cabinet were more aware of this than is sometimes recognised.[7] Moreover, provincial radical newspapers took the message to the local political elite. The Progressive *Manchester Guardian* and *Northern Daily Telegraph* covered much of Lancashire. Their influence is well-documented. The *Bradford Observer, Sheffield Daily Independent, Northern Echo, South Wales Daily Post,* and other papers filled a similar (if less well-documented) role elsewhere. Even Labour and trade union newspapers discussed radical Liberal ideas and policies.

The 'popular' national Liberal newspapers – the *Daily News* and *Daily Chronicle* – reached a wider audience. They were enthusiastically Progressive. They sensationally exposed poverty, making 'political' comparisons between (for example) the 'immoral' and 'extreme' wealth of (Tory) plutocrats and landlords on the one hand, and the acute and total distress of the (Liberal) poor on the other.[8] Yet between them they had less than three-quarters of a million readers in 1910 (less than the Tory *Daily Mail* alone).[9] Their editors enjoyed close contacts with Liberal leaders, but they did not dictate policy. If they were to change the party's stance it would have to be by encouraging popular pressure for a more radical approach. Their limited circulation was thus a serious handicap.

Labour's national stance was less easily disseminated. MacDonald set up the *Socialist Review* to be a Revisionist organ. Like the ILP paper, the *Labour Leader,* and the 'popular' *Daily Citizen* (set up in 1912) it was dominated by MacDonaldites. They wrote leaders, dictated editorial policy, and could stifle criticism. Labour MPs, the majority of whom were moderate trade unionists, also generally wrote loyal columns for local newspapers and trade union journals. Philip Snowden's columns spread through journals as diverse as the *Staffordshire Sentinel, Christian Commonwealth* and the *Blind Advocate.* Some local Labour/Socialist newspapers, such as the *Manchester Weekly Citizen,* the *Leeds Weekly Citizen* and the *Sheffield Guardian* reflected national policy (and took a great deal of their material from the national Labour news service). However, the 'national' moderate stance *was* challenged. The dissident national 'intellectual' journals, particularly *Justice* and the *Clarion,* were widely read by ILP and Labour activists. Many local and national party

---

[7] Spender speech notes, 31 Jan. 1914, Spender Add MS 46392 fo. 123. The footnotes to Dr Freeden's exhaustive study of the Edwardian intellectual press demonstrates the widespread dissemination of these discussions. For Old Liberal familiarity with them, Burns Diary, 2 Apr. 1909, cited in Harris, *Unemployment and politics,* p. 367, and comments of T. P. Whittaker, the Gladstonian back-bencher, below, p. 258. For Lloyd George and Churchill, above, p. 47.

[8] Above, p. 66 and below, p. 169.

[9] Blewett, *Peers,* p. 301.

journals carried 'dissident' articles; some local papers, particularly the *Huddersfield Worker,* were openly hostile to party policy. Moreover, by 1913 the *Daily Herald,* despite its precarious financial position, was rivalling the *Citizen* as the best-selling labour newspaper. It provided a platform for dissident opinion of all kinds. In terms of popular impact, however, both papers were minnows compared with the Liberals. The combined popular labour newspapers only reached 180–250,000 households.[10] Most towns and cities did not have a local Labour/Socialist newspaper; many that did had one only for a short while.

Both parties relied on the distribution of party literature to reach a wider audience. The Liberal Publication Department, the various 'fringe' Liberal organisations, and the various Labour/Socialist groups and publishing companies produced a vast array of leaflets, posters, pamphlets, and press information. In the Liberal party, this was well-organised, particularly at election times. In 1910 the LPD issued over 41 million separate items, whilst even the Labour party managed nearly 6 million posters, leaflets, and copies of the (very brief) party manifesto. Groups such as the Budget League and the Free Trade Union lent the Liberals valuable support. In 1909, Henry Norman, the Budget League's Secretary, organised conferences with more than twenty Liberal newspaper editors to co-ordinate policy. His Literature Sub-Committee, chaired by Masterman, produced pamphlets, leaflets, and cartoons, which were disseminated to Liberal news-agencies. The League's 'Weekly Column' was taken by over 140 local weekly newspapers, while Spender's 'Budget Points' were equally popular with the daily Liberal press.[11]

In the Liberal party, the party leaders' speeches were keenly reported by the local press, often at great length. By 1913–14, MacDonald was also attempting to direct his MPs' speaking tours towards the seats which the party hoped to contest at the next election, and towards issues which he wished to emphasise. Both Progressive parties regularly launched campaigns on set themes, using the combined resources of the local and national machine and 'fringe' organisations. In this respect the Liberal party, as the party of Government, was often on the defensive. Campaigns generally had to reflect current parliamentary concerns. After 1910 politics became bogged down in Old Liberal issues. The result was unedifying to radical eyes. 'It's really too awful', Masterman wrote in 1913, 'to think

---

[10] R. J. Holton, 'Daily Herald v Daily Citizen, 1912–15', *IRSH* (1974), esp. p. 374, J.B.G. Diary, 19 Dec. 1911, 10 Sept. 1912. The *Citizen,* like most provincial Labour papers, ran at a loss and constantly verged on collapse. See e.g. J.S.M. to his parents, 26 Apr. 1914, G. H. B. Ward to J.S.M., 22 Dec. 1914, MID 12/22 and 50. For branch reading material, e.g. Keighley ILP Mins, 3 May 1909.

[11] Blewett, *Peers,* p. 312; Murray, *People's Budget,* pp. 189–90, 203–4. See also J. Paul to C.P.T., 7 Dec. 1909, CPT 23.

of an "Autumn Campaign" of thousands of speeches by Liberal MPs
and candidates on the blessing of Free Trade, Home Rule and Welsh
Disestablishment'.[12]

Party officials shared Masterman's view. They were keen to move away
from these issues. Handbooks and pamphlets produced by the national
leaders of Scottish and English organisations for women and the young
(always an elastic term in Liberal circles) show a deliberate attempt to
address Progressive themes. The major national propaganda innovation
in this respect was the *Liberal Monthly*. After 1912, constituency organisations were encouraged to engage in regular deliveries of this (free), populistic, cartoon and slogan dominated publication. However, as
constituency parties were encouraged to append localised supplements,
it was hardly a totally 'nationalising' force.[13]

The power of the party at the centre might have also influenced the
action and comments of parliamentary candidates, who frequently played
a major part in constituency campaigning. The ambitious professional
politicians who were increasingly moving into Liberal politics recognised
that support for 'Old Liberal' ideas was not going to make them popular
with the party at the centre.[14] This was important. The Whips very
often 'recommended' candidates to constituency organisations, and could
therefore help to determine who got safe seats. This power enabled them
to encourage the selection of radicals in working-class areas, particularly
where the weakness of local Liberal associations made them dependent
on the advice (and funds) of the Whips.[15] In weak areas, the regional
federations were not a means of challenging the centre; they were its
local voice.[16]

---

[12] Cited in David, 'C. F. G. Masterman', p. 31. A Labour propaganda committee, which
      aimed at central co-ordination of campaigns, was set up in 1913. (J.S.M. to M. Phillips,
      10 Apr. 1913, LP/PRO/13/15 [and this file generally] and NEC Mins, 11 Dec. 1913.)
[13] Hutchison, *Scotland,* pp. 235–7 and J. Aubrey Rees, *Our aims and objectives* (LYL
      pamphlet, No. 1).
[14] See attitudes of e.g. Crawshay-Williams and Hamar Greenwood, below, pp. 293, 254.
[15] For the Whips' role in finding candidates in areas of Liberal weakness, e.g. C. C. Bigham,
      A picture of life 1872–1940 (1941), p. 232, T. Barclay, *Thirty years* (1914), p. 318,
      E. Crawshay-Williams, *Simple story* (1941), p. 73. Mid.LF and LCLF minutes show
      the depths of Liberal financial problems in the Tory part of the country. See also,
      HCLF *AR* 1910, and for the same area, L. Harcourt to W. Crook, 12 Dec. 1911, Crook
      MS Eng. Hist. d. 389 fo. 94. See also the Whips' reported preference for suffragist
      candidates, Holton, *Feminism and democracy,* p. 120.
[16] For close co-operation, e.g. W. Finnemore (Mid.LF) to Elibank, 13 Aug. 1912, Elibank
      MS 8803 fos. 107–8. Liberal Federations were officially the first point of contact in
      the search for a candidate. The Whips had a representative on each Federation board,
      and received quarterly reports of local activity from the Federations' election agent/
      organiser.

At the same time, the centre did not always dominate the constituencies. The Whips were aware of local conditions and circumstances. It was in the party's interest to consider local interests and views, and to choose a candidate who, at least in part, reflected them.[17] Moreover, local associations had the constitutional right to choose their own candidate, and (particularly in areas where the party was strong) they frequently exercised it. They referred to the Whips only when their own attempts to find candidates were unsuccessful. In these circumstances, belief or pragmatism ensured that candidates followed the *local* party's line.[18] In Cornwall, constituency associations dominated by Liberal Imperialists selected Liberal Imperialists; in Wiltshire, opponents of land taxes secured similar successors; in Liverpool, and other parts of Lancashire, candidates were frequently local men or imported carpet baggers chosen by members of the constituency elite. In other conservative Liberal areas (e.g. northern Yorkshire and the North-East) politics operated in a similar manner. Moreover, even when the party at the centre attempted to intervene, local Liberal associations might resist this interference, or reluctantly accept it with poor results for party morale.[19]

Yet wealthy Liberals were not always conservatives. Millionaire Progressives from the Brunner, Cadbury, and Rowntree families, for example, financed Progressive newspapers, Progressive political campaigns, and made large contributions to national party funds. They also backed Progressive candidates financially and through their position as local Liberal leaders. There was a rival radical 'network'. Local Progressive notables, especially MPs, formed bridges between radicals in the constituencies and the party at the centre. Some, like C. P. Trevelyan, regularly attempted to procure radical candidates; others, like H. J. Wilson, the Rowntrees and Wedgwood, made sporadic interventions within their own

[17] For central party knowledge of constituency affairs, J. Herbert to Elibank, 9 Nov. 1910, Elibank MS 8802 fo. 129. For the period before 1908, Clarke, *Lancashire Liberalism*, Chapter 8.

[18] Crawshay-Williams, *Simple story,* pp. 83, 87, A.R. to M. K. Rowntree, 3 Mar. 1910, AR MS. For this selection process in Leeds, e.g. W. Harvey to T. E. H., 22 Oct. 1903, TEH MS, J. Henry to H.G., 30 Oct. 1909, HG Add MS 46037 fos. 157–8.

[19] Blewett, *Peers,* pp. 217–18; Clarke, *Lancashire Liberalism,* Chapter 9. Politics of the Liberal Imperialists from H. C. G. Matthew, *The Liberal Imperialists* (Oxford, 1973). See also the imposition of 'national' figures at by-elections, and the resentment of this in Ipswich and Bethnal Green, H.H.A. to Elibank, 18 Sept. 1910, Elibank MS 8803 fo. 107, J. Herbert to W.R., 4 Oct. 1911, WR 44, P. Harris, *Forty years in and out of Parliament* (1949), pp. 47–8 and *Lib. Agent,* Apr. 1914.

geographical areas.[20] This was necessary because local radicals were not always in a position to secure the kind of candidates who they wanted, and because, even when they were, they could not always find one. The official Liberal machine, whether for institutional reasons or because of the Whips' deficiencies, did not run smoothly; it creaked. 'Grubby little complications', one organiser noted, 'cumulatively clog up the wheels.'[21] There was no guarantee that the right candidate would land in the right seat.

In the Labour party, by contrast, potential candidates were nominated by affiliated organisations (sometimes after a ballot of members) and placed on a national list. The trade unions directly financed three-quarters of Labour candidates. The NEC and NAC, and the local parties, had little control over the views of the party candidates, or over the image they presented to the electorate. Constituency parties *could* select their own nominee, and then seek endorsement and finance from his union. If this took place before the union had established a list of candidates, the applicant *might* become an official union candidate. However, the union's candidates had frequently already been chosen when applications were made. The available resources might already have been allocated.[22] The local parties could choose whichever candidate they pleased, provided he had financial backing from an affiliated organisation, but the strength of particular local groups, and the limited number of candidates available, meant that their hands were tied.

The power of the centre to determine politics in the constituencies hit several additional obstacles. National newspapers not only had a limited circulation; the regional concentration of their readership meant that, in huge areas of the country, 'national' views were not disseminated through this medium. Although 'democratic' voters in London may have read nothing but the radical *Daily News* and *Morning Leader,* the radical Liberal press did badly in other Tory areas like Lancashire and the West Midlands. Many Tory rural areas received no national, or even local,

---

[20] See pp. 233, 271, 302. For Trevelyan's broader role, see e.g. reports of discussions between Illingworth, Lloyd George, and E. D. Morel, with Trevelyan as the link, Morel to C.P.T., 28 June, 30 Oct. 1912, Illingworth to C.P.T., C.P.T. to Morel, 19 Aug., 4 Nov. 1912, CPT 29, M. Levy to C.P.T., 15 Jan. 1909, CPT 23. In order to ensure that E. D. Morel could pursue a political career, Cadbury paid him a salary, promised a pension, and agreed to pay most of his election expenses. He also contributed to some Labour campaigns (like other Progressives) and contributed to the costs of Labour newspapers (see e.g. below, pp. 184, 404).

[21] C. Beck to Masterman, 20 May 1914, LG C/5/15/5, also reporting problems with the 'independent' Grimsby LA. For the growing intervention e.g. W.R. to Elibank, 9 Apr. 1912, Elibank to 'P' [Illingworth?], 15 June 1915, Elibank MS 8803 fos. 43–4, 170, H.G. memo, 8 Dec. 1922, WR 192. The Whips' expenditure increased from £16,000 (1899–1906) to £100,000 p.a. after 1908.

[22] See below, p. 328.

Liberal daily. The Labour press was even more confined.[23] Moreover, many voters did not read national newspapers. A very large percentage, however, read the local evening or weekly papers. The *Bolton Evening News,* for example, reached 90 per cent of homes in its area of circulation. The image of parties put forward by the local press could have a more significant impact than national publications. The constituency leaders, who in many areas (including Bolton) were also newspaper proprietors, had a powerful means of excluding the aims of the 'national' party if they so wished.

The local autonomy of constituency politicians was particularly pronounced between parliamentary elections. Local organisations were thrown back on their own resources. The views of local party leaders, Liberal editors, and parliamentary candidates assumed far more significance. This is significant because 'national' Liberal and Labour politics would inevitably be judged in the light of the general local experience of what these parties stood for. It is in part for this reason that municipal politics assume such significance, for municipal political campaigning was the means of presenting a party image to electors in the constituencies. Moreover, municipal policy was very significant because social policy was still considerably influenced by the political nature of the local Council. Their actions influenced the type of services which were available, and their cost to the local community. They influenced the nature of local educational provision, the level of poor relief, and the availability of municipal housing. Voters took municipal politics seriously. As Jowett rightly noted in 1907: 'It is by no means uncommon in the North of England towns where the Labour movement is strong, for seventy-five to eighty-five per cent of the number of persons entitled to vote, to exercise their right at a municipal election.'[24]

All parties recognised the importance of municipal policy. The LCC Progressives' radical municipal programme was studied by other Liberal local authorities, and adopted in Manchester. The national party encouraged certain forms of local intervention in national statements and guidelines (for example, on the need for fair wages contracts).[25] The developing Liberal programme for land and housing reform linked radical policies for national *and* municipal problems, and in part aimed at increasing the capacity for local intervention. However, resistance to expenditure

---

[23] R. Donald to Elibank, 12 Mar. 1912, Elibank MS 8803 fos. 25–7; J.S.M. to his parents, 9 Nov. 1912, MID 10/20. For the following, G. Jones, 'National and local issues in politics: a study of East Sussex and the Lancashire spinning towns, 1906–1910', Sussex D.Phil. thesis 1964–5, p. 163.

[24] Jowett, *The Socialist and the city,* p. 10.

[25] e.g. TUC *AR* 1912, p. 143 noting Liberal attitudes to Fair Wages clauses; Clarke, *Lancashire Liberalism,* p. 162 for Manchester/London policy.

was as common as support for reform in local Liberal politics, and 'national' Liberal politicians were powerless to alter this emphasis.

Local Labour municipal policy was also beyond national control. Given the long history of Socialist activity in municipal politics, Labour had to face the fact that local parties had established municipal policies before the national LRC had even considered the question. MacDonald recognised this, as he recognised the need for municipal policies which were tailored to local conditions. He published a national guideline policy, but not the specific literature to back it up. In this sense, he too left the local parties to find their own solutions. MacDonald's critics were not reluctant to step into the breach. Local organisations, anxious to find concrete proposals and arguments, made full use of their literature.[26]

It is not possible to ascertain the precise importance of 'local' and 'national' contributions to the party image. It will become clear, however, that support built up in municipal elections, or evident at by-elections, often dissipated as a parliamentary contest polarised support.[27] National issues had assumed primary importance by 1910, and local election results were often a comment on a party's national standing. However, support built up in local contests did not necessarily return to its exact previous level after general elections. Although support then frequently polarised, where local parties had established a credible image, national factors and traditional allegiances could be undermined. Local political stances were not insignificant.

The central organisations' ability to impose a strategic alliance is also important. In the Liberal party, local associations alone decided whether or not they should find a candidate. For Labour, the process was more complex. The constituency party had to convene conferences of affiliated Socialist groups and all local trade unions (affiliated or not). These conferences discussed whether a candidate should be sought. Candidates were then sought, and the nominees' names sent to the NEC. The national party had to be informed of the initial conference and represented subsequently at the selection meetings. This representative would assess the situation or give the NEC's view on whether a candidature should proceed. National opinion was related to the conference, the candidates, and sometimes to the candidates' union, by a growing organisational bureaucracy of party agents and election advisers, including Arthur Peters

---

[26] e.g. ILP/Fabian pamphlets and conferences, Joint ILP/Fabian Comm. Mins, 12 Dec. 1912, 14 Apr. 1913, ILP MS. For the municipal circumstances in 1906, J.S.M. to NEC, 13, 20 Oct. 1906, J.S.M. to J. E. Smith, 10 July 1906, LP GC 8/304-6, 6/153. For Fair Wages and Labour, LP/PA/07/1/68-87.

[27] Clarke, 'Liberals, Labour and the by-elections', and e.g. pp. 149, 301-2. For the general relationship in modern politics, e.g. R. Waller, 'The 1979 local and general elections in England and Wales: is there a local/national differential?', *Political Studies* (1980).

(the national agent), and the English and Scottish organisers appointed in 1913.[28] ILP organisers, ILP MPs, and other figures – like Bruce Glasier – also put the 'national' view at meetings with local organisations anxious to fight Liberal seats.[29]

The national advice settled into a pattern. MacDonald's wish to proceed cautiously has already been noted. In concrete terms, this meant that he would continue to discourage three-cornered contests unless Labour looked capable of defeating the Liberals.[30] At the same time, he did not simply refuse all such requests. Intervention was perfectly acceptable if a good result was likely to lead to Liberal withdrawal at the following election; by-election campaigns might be considered in seats which the party would not fight at the general election. He was no Liberal stooge. He opposed the idea that Labour organisations should endorse Liberal candidates – 'if the local organisation supports the (Liberal) candidate, it is simply absurd for it to try to bring a candidate out against him at a subsequent election'.[31] He disparaged the Liberal tendency to 'offer' Labour hopeless seats; he refused to consider 'arbitration' or to consult the Liberal Whips over individual constituencies.[32] MacDonald argued that it was the constituency organisations' job to develop a political base, to be so evidently popular that the Liberals would decline to risk splitting the Progressive vote and strategically withdraw.[33]

This policy developed a municipal adjunct. Municipal campaigns were to be concentrated, in the early stages of activity, on (at most) a few wards. Political work was to be constant, practical, organisational. Ideally, it would involve saturation canvassing and leafleting and the emulation of the SPD's system of sub-divided organisation (the Berlin block system). 'Better only cover a part of the area and (have) something to show from it', Catlin, the ILP's Midlands organiser noted, 'than a hurried fight over a large district and no result.'[34]

By 1909, the NAC and NEC had linked the sanction of a parliamentary campaign to the constituency's ability to pass a 'test of fitness' which covered the local electoral, organisational, and financial position.[35] They

---

[28] The national organisers were Sam Higenbottom, William Holmes, and Ben Shaw.
[29] See below, e.g. p. 262.
[30] J.R.M. to W. Pimblott, 9 May 1905, LRC 23/196; J.R.M. to C. Horne, 8 Dec. 1902, LRC LB 1/146–7.
[31] J.R.M. to G. Wyver, 25 July 1905, LRC 24/485.
[32] J.R.M. to W. A. Appleton, 5 Jan. 1903, LRC LB 1/163–4; J.R.M. to R. C. Hall, 29 Mar. 1905, LRC 21/109; J.R.M. to W. Wainwright, 30 Mar. 1905, LRC 21/265.
[33] J.R.M. to W. Wainwright, 29 Aug. 1905, LRC 25/356.
[34] 'Suggestions to the Midlands Council and branches', n.d., H.O. Circ./3 and S.H., 'How to organise', S.G., 16 May 1913.
[35] See NAC circulars, 9 Sept. 1909, 6 Apr. 1910, ILP MS H.O. Circ./6. It was also debated at the Labour conference in 1909.

aimed to create a controlled expansion of the parliamentary campaign which matched the party's ability to defeat the Liberals.

The central Labour party, and its agents, could not constitutionally refuse endorsement to properly selected and sanctioned candidates. However, they could refuse to send constituency organisations lists of candidates, they could delay the adoption of chosen representatives, dissuade sponsoring bodies from proceeding, and deny sanction to last minute candidates. They could try to persuade local parties that electoral campaigns in seats where the Liberals were very strong were undesirable, but organisational, electoral, and financial criteria alone could be utilised in rejecting applications. This suited the leaders' aims. They too wished to expand if the conditions were favourable. They too hoped that the electoral and organisational criteria would justify campaigns on a broad front. The only problem with this 'informal' control was that, sometimes, electorally 'justifiable' campaigns did not always seem to be in the party's short-term strategic interests. In these circumstances, the party leaders did not always get their way.

The powers which the central party possessed were more likely to carry weight with weaker local organisations. As in the Liberal party, it was Labour organisations in parts of the North-West, the West Midlands, London, and the south coast ports who were the most likely to be influenced by national dictates. Organisations with a stronger base, or more money, would be less easily controlled. In 'Liberal' areas constituency organisations, on both sides, were stronger and less easily controlled in 1906. They were also less resolutely committed to the reforming consensus which was growing up between the parties.[36] Liberal allegiances were stronger and more easily reinforced. Labour could expect to make headway against the Liberals in Tory areas, where Progressive co-operation would also be more likely, but it was the historically *Liberal* areas which would be the real strategic/electoral test.

III

For the Progressive Alliance to really work smoothly, 'change from above' had to be accompanied by 'change from below'. It was necessary to ensure local compliance with national strategic dictates. It was necessary to ensure that 'old' ideas and strategies were 'modernised'. Failure to effect local compliance would ensure either that the mechanics of the Alliance would fail, or that one side would gain a partial advantage by being more (or less) radical than opinion dictated.

Local political attitudes and structures *were* changing. In 1885, the

---

[36] See Chapters 5–10 below.

Liberals had to reconstruct their organisations to cope with new boundaries and a new electorate. Some constituency radicals also argued that
it was time to revitalise constituency Liberal associations, to make them
more democratic and less dominated by small oligarchical groups. The
decline of elite participation in local politics generally, and Liberal politics
in particular, may also have opened up opportunities for less affluent
men to assume positions of importance. The unanswered question is
how far, and with what results, had this taken place by 1914.

MacDonald also recognised the need for constituency allies. He encouraged the formation of local organisations which replicated the national
model and involved the local unions. He was concerned to develop
'responsible' constituency leadership. He hoped local parties would move
away from their dependence on the ILP for everyday political activity
and for strategic guidance, as at the national level he hoped to make
the Socialists' views subservient to policy decisions by the PLP and the
full *Labour* conference.[37] The degree of sympathy for radical aims in
constituency Labour politics was as important for Labour as the degree
of constituency conservatism in the Liberal party.

Elements in both parties encouraged the development of a reforming
consensus at the centre and in the constituencies. Their success or failure
would help to determine how far the Liberal domination, and the Progressive Alliance, remained intact.

IV

The degree of local compliance with the ideas of the Progressive consensus
could materially influence levels of local support. However 'moral
reformers' did not have a monopoly on popularity. A local emphasis
on particular aspects of a national party image could also be very significant. The occupational structures, interests, and traditions of areas and
constituencies varied considerably. There was ample scope for parties
to vary their approach in a manner which would be more suited to these
particular circumstances. Local Old Liberal/Centrist alliances might still
successfully cater for local interests and ideas. In the Labour party,
'Labourist' or Statist elements might develop a substantial local electoral
base. The existence of varying interests, and the use of local politics
as a means of catering for or 'making' local opinion, was the basis of
Labour's strategy. It was a strategy which was not without foundation.

[37] McKibbin, *Evolution,* Chapter 2. For MacDonald's views on 'responsibility' and party
structure, see the minutes of his talk to the hostile South London Divisional Council,
30 Jan. 1909, Ensor MS, and J.R.M. to E. Whitely, 8 July 1907, LP/PA/07/1/92.
MacDonald resigned from the NAC, and gave Divisional Councils more power, as
part of an educative process. Anderson, Snowden, and others shared his views.

'Britain' was not a single entity. There were sharp occupational differences within the working class, and sharply differing political habits. Moreover, the geography of British politics ensured that there would not be a uniform response to political approaches and electoral campaigns even if 'national' views were uniformly disseminated. The question – from Labour's standpoint – was whether it could build these spatially distinct interests into a platform from which to attack the Liberal party.

The nature and success of these competing local strategies had a second significance. If the continuing local and national institutional power of these elements was combined with evidence of continuing electoral purchase, the Progressive Alliance was doubly insecure. 'Dissidents' at the centre would have their arguments reinforced by evidence of electoral credibility. They would have the capacity not just to undermine the Progressive Alliance in a few seats, or to modify Progressive policies; they might be able to create a credible case for a rival ideological/strategic trajectory for their respective parties. Ideological/political strands at the centre had ideological/political allies in the constituencies. If they represented a body of party activists and Liberal voters, they would become more than just a potential irritant to the onward march of progress. It was the capacity to win support which gave each group its real institutional permanence and power. If the dissidents retained this capacity, they would ensure that neither party was easily moulded into a completely acceptable 'social reforming' organisation. They would influence what issues the party would campaign on, and what kind of legislation that party would implement if elected. It is therefore necessary to determine the extent to which those elements who were not part of a moral reforming consensus represented a body of electoral opinion.

In order to survive as the major radical party, to stave off a reversion to the electoral problems of the 1890s, the Liberals had to maintain the Progressive Alliance intact, and keep Labour as its junior component. This was the key to its success in 'Tory' working-class areas. At the same time, they had to remain popular, and keep ahead of Labour in the working-class areas which were its electoral heartland. They hoped to combine this with the continuing support of the party's more conservative wing. Even New Liberals did not wish to create a party based on class conflict. They wished to see ethical progress, intellectual strength, and organic reform as the dominant elements in Liberal politics.

This challenge had been faced at the political centre. The national party could hope to influence supporters in the constituencies; it had some general powers, which were particularly important in the 'Tory' areas, and was developing sympathetic allies in the constituencies. These local/national alliances were becoming more significant, and more institutionally powerful. Yet 'change from below' and 'change from above' had to meet up if the 'politics of change' were to dominate the party. Labour, which was conducting a similar process of change, faced similar problems. Both parties competed to develop the strongest and most complete stance, to maximise their ability to exploit the strengths and weaknesses displayed at the national level.

Local parties might depart from the 'national' aims and emphasise particular components of the national image. While this could undermine the attraction of Progressive policies, and create electoral spaces which the Progressive rival might exploit, 'local' rival approaches could also prove popular. This might improve the overall electoral performance of the party, but it might also become the basis for a rival view of how the party should proceed. The nature – and success – of local approaches would determine the rate of electoral progress and influence the nature of the parties themselves. No party could ignore the views of its most successful elements without risking substantial internal opposition and electoral failure. Politics at the centre and politics in the constituencies merged to create competing local/national, ideological/political blocs. Constituency politics could be part of a political and ideological challenge to the ideas of the Progressive reformers. Constituency party leaders could undermine some of the national leaders' aims, or they could reinforce and replicate the central thrust; they could provide support for party dissidents, and even the basis for a political coup. 'Low politics', were as important, and as complicated, and as varied, as politics at the centre. The constituency conflict took place in a variety of settings; the balance of electoral support, and of successful strategies, would determine the strength and nature of the Progressive Alliance. This could influence the nature of British radical politics. Moreover, as the position in the early 1920s indicates, it could also seriously influence the electoral future of the Tory party. The dynamics of Progressive politics had considerable electoral and political significance.

Part II Politics in the constituencies

Chapter 4

The electoral framework of
Edwardian politics

The electorate is the politician's judge and jury. Perceptions of its nature
and composition helped to determine when late Victorian and Edwardian
elections were fought, and how the issues were portrayed. Its *real* nature
and composition could influence the outcome of the electoral competition.
If the (restricted) franchise affected one party more than another, if the
jury was packed, then some verdicts would be more likely than others.
For many historians, the system was seriously biased against the working
class, and consequently against the Labour party. Nonetheless, the precise
structure of the electoral system has not been thoroughly investigated.
The national legal and administrative framework (Section I) was complex,
but much less complex than the local application of these vague principles.
The system broadly favoured older men, particularly in provincial towns
(Section II), but also, to a lesser extent, in the cities (Section III). Younger
men suffered more than anyone else (Section IV). There was a secondary
bias against working-class men, especially those living in fluidly populated
metropolitan areas, but this bias was not dramatic; nor did it prevent
any party mobilising a substantial amount of support. There was a small,
general, anti-working-class bias, and isolated instances where it became
much more substantial. Plural voting was the major cause of inequality
(Section V). The nature of the parliamentary boundaries had a more
pronounced effect. There were a substantial number of seats whose social
construction suggested that they could become political 'ghettos' (Section
VI). The municipal electoral system was subject to similar laws and constraints; the net results were broadly similar (Section VII). The overall
impact was such that Labour *and* the Tories had the potential to develop
a political base from which to attack the Liberals' position. On the other
hand, 'ideal' seats were not so numerous that these parties could become
a Government without broader electoral support.

I

The electoral laws, as one franchise expert put it, were 'an almost hopeless mass of complications and anachronisms'.[1] The Reform Acts of 1832 to 1884 had been designed to incorporate, rather than repeal, former franchises. The parliamentary draughtsmen thus ensured that few people were disfranchised; they also ensured 'that each new babe ... (would) inherit its share of original sin'. The result was an accumulation of different parliamentary franchises, put at between eleven and seventeen by two Liberal authorities.[2] Nonetheless, with a little over-simplification, it is possible to identify seven major categories (Table 4.1). There was also a registration requirement, the details of which varied between franchises. For householders, this was twelve months continuous residence. Women, felons, certified lunatics, peers, and aliens were automatically excluded. If the rates on a potential voter's accommodation were unpaid, even by the landlord, or if a voter accepted parochial (i.e. non-medical) relief, then he would also be ineligible for the franchise.[3]

Most of those registered under the university, freemen's, and property franchises, and a substantial portion of occupiers, had more than one vote. There were roughly 450,000–475,000 plural voters in England and Wales. Most of these were small property owners, with two homes or a home and a business. Conservative Central Office estimates put the number of men with four or more votes at around 2,000.[4]

The electoral register was compiled by the Poor Law Overseers in the provinces and the Borough Clerks, after 1900, in London. The Overseers' work was frequently supplemented by the political parties. The law actively encouraged this by excluding even evidently qualified lodger and ownership voters from automatic inclusion in the lists.[5] The Liberal and Tory national organisations encouraged constituency associations to begin their annual registration work in June, concurrently with the Overseers. This the Walsall Liberal agent noted 'was the only method

[1] G. P. W. Terry, *The Representation of the People Acts, 1918–28* (1928), p. xvi. In unravelling the myriad complexities of the electoral system I have found the following invaluable: *Rogers on Elections* (18th edn., 1909), J. R. Seager, *The Franchise Act 1884* (1885) and his *Notes on Registration* (1903), and for reference, *Saint's Registration Cases* (1903). Some of the material has appeared in Tanner, 'The parliamentary electoral system'.

[2] J. H. Linforth, *Leaves from an agent's diary* (Leeds, 1911), p. 42; N. Blewett, 'The parliamentary franchise in the U.K., 1885–1918', *Past and Present* (1965), p. 31.

[3] F. Rowley Parker, *The powers, duties and liabilities of an election agent* (2nd edn., 1891), p. 67.

[4] J. R. Seager to Pease, 24 Apr. 1912, Gainford MS 64; Conservative Central Office memo by W. A. Gales, n.d. Oct. 1916, A. Steel-Maitland MS G.D. 193/202 fo. 6.

[5] For the administrative complexities of the registration process, which ensured that some householders would always be excluded, *Municipal Journal*, 24 Aug. 1906 and registration diary, PRO HO 45/10075/B7422.

Table 4.1 *Voters registered under parliamentary franchises, England and Wales, 1915*

Franchise	Qualifications	No. of votes	% of electorate
Property[a]	40 shillings freeholders, other freeholders, copyholders, and leaseholders	569,914	8.42
Freemen	Freemen by birth or apprenticeship in boroughs where such a qualification existed pre-1832[b]	20,610	0.31
University	(a) Oxford and Cambridge: graduates provided they hold an MA and pay annual charge of £20 (b) Other universities: all graduates and teaching staff	21,323	0.31
Occupation	Occupiers as owner or tenant of any land or tenement to the yearly value of £10		
Household	Inhabitant occupiers either as owners or tenants of any dwelling house or portion of a dwelling house defined as a separate dwelling	5,665,330[c]	83.67
Service[d]	Inhabitant occupiers of separate dwellings, not as owner or as tenant, but by virtue of office, service, or employment	146,477	2.16
Lodger	Occupiers of lodgings separately occupied and valued at £10 p.a. unfurnished	347,610	5.13
	Total	6,771,264	100.00

Notes:

[a] Exclusively a county franchise with the exception of 1,588 freeholders in four towns which were counties in their own right.

[b] In the City of London it was also necessary to be a liveryman, but the right to be a freeman could be purchased.

[c] These were not registered separately in the electoral registers.

[d] The service franchise was a sub-division of the household franchise, but service voters were registered separately under Division 2 of the register.

Source: Based on Blewett, 'Franchise in the UK', p. 32 with minor alterations. Figures are from *P.P.* 1914–16 (Cd 120), Lii, 583–604, as are all 1915 electoral statistics in the book.

by which it was possible to secure complete and satisfactory revision'. Party claims which were ready by August could be merged with the Overseers' list. Bearing the stamp of officialdom, they would be more difficult to oppose in the registration court held to consider disputed and late claims in September and October of each year. Adjacent local associations also co-operated to ensure efficient registration of supporters who moved across constituency boundaries, and city federations allocated duplicate registrations to chosen seats.[6]

Householders excluded from the Overseers' lists, and all new lodger and ownership voters, had to be prepared to prove their claims in the registration courts. Claims were generally made by a party agent and might be opposed by his political rival. Those agents who completed their registration work by the August were free to investigate claims and accumulate evidence to support objections. A revising barrister, selected from the local circuit, was appointed to adjudicate. If the Appeal Court dismissed any subsequent appeal, the original barrister's decision officially and instantly became Common Law.

In 1915 there were around 10,250,000 adult males in England and Wales. Allowing for a plural vote of 450,000, there were only 6,250,000 individuals on the parliamentary register. Some 4 million men were excluded. By digging beneath the surface of the Edwardian electoral system, it is possible to construct a picture of the electorate which shows that age and housing patterns (not class) were the primary factors in determining enfranchisement. Class was only a secondary influence.[7]

II

Householders received favourable treatment at each point in the electoral process. Initially there were some problems differentiating lodgers from householders. By the 1890s the law had been clarified. Occupants of divided buildings in which the landlord was resident were lodgers; those who occupied a section of a house in which the landlord did not reside were householders. The so-called 'latch-key cases', which went through the legal process on four occasions between 1906 and 1911, disrupted this simple definition but contemporaries estimated that only 130,000

[6] Liberal circular from Tom Ellis, Chief Whip, Stockport LA Mins, 4 May 1896; Walsall LA Mins, 10 Nov. 1908. For instances of co-operation, Coventry LA Mins, 13 Sept. 1897, *Birmingham Gazette,* 10 Sept. 1912; Halifax West Ward LA Mins, 4 June 1907. See also below, p. 123.

[7] 1915 population figures throughout the chapter are from the *Registrar General's Deccenial Supplement* (1933), pt. iii, p. 8. Figures for the electorate are from *P.P.* 1914–16, Cd 120, Lii, 585. All calculations based on 98 per cent of the adult male population, the maximum level of enfranchisement even by 1931.

Table 4.2 *Householders qualified through successive occupation, 1915*

		Successive occupiers	
Constituency	Householders on register		% of household elect.
Undivided provincial constituencies			
Gateshead	19,675	3,111	15.81
Worcester	8,076	989	12.25
Walsall	15,319	1,827	11.93
Wednesbury	13,148	1,276	9.70
Brighton	20,271	1,644	8.11
Glam., Gower	15,470	868	5.61
Divided parliamentary boroughs (1911 and 1915)			
Leeds, W. (1911)	18,733	4,280	22.85
Liverpool, Scotland (1911)	4,985	960	19.26
Bradford, E.	17,917	2,069	11.55
Islington, S. (1911)	6,370	709	11.13
St Pancras, E.	6,097	618	10.14
Bradford, W.	16,217	1,514	9.34

Source: Calculated from individual entries in electoral registers.

men were affected, most of them in London, and after 1911 the older interpretation was reestablished.[8]

The twelve month residence requirement was a more serious problem. Urban historians have shown that in the 1850s and 1860s residential mobility was so pronounced that few householders remained in the same home over a ten year period. In the Edwardian period it was estimated that in the counties about 5 per cent of the population moved each year, in the boroughs 20 to 30 per cent, in London frequently more. However, at mid-century 25 to 60 per cent of residents moved within the same area, usually venturing no more than a mile from their first identified residence.

[8] *Lib. Agent,* Oct. 1906, for the estimate that only 10–20,000 'latch-key' voters would be found in the provinces. There were four latch-key cases (*Kent v Fittal,* 1–4) because each case dealt with a different aspect of electoral law. After the first case, men could qualify as householders if their landlord lived on the premises, provided they could prove 'control' over their rooms. Chaos ensued. F. D. Acland noted that one latch-key voter had lost his vote 'simply because he had a parrot, for his landlord had inspected the bird when it shrieked, and this established his right of entry' (F. D. Acland, *Adult Suffrage* (1910), p. 13). Full details of the latch-key cases are given in *The Times,* 8 Sept. 1911.

This pattern of mobility had important, often over-looked, effects on the potential for working-class enfranchisement. Continuity of occupation was maintained in law if householders moved within the constituency or from one division of a Parliamentary Borough to another. 'Local' moves might not end the entitlement to vote. As Table 4.2 shows, this 'successive occupation' clause ensured that perhaps a quarter of the household electorate in fluidly populated constituencies was not disfranchised.[9]

Successive occupation mitigated the effects of the residence requirement, but three groups were still adversely affected. First, all men who claimed under a new franchise, or moved to a distant constituency (perhaps a suburb) in search of a better lifestyle, would lose their vote. The average re-qualification period was two years, the maximum 2.5 years. This *occasional* disfranchisement must have affected the middle classes. Younger middle-class householders, who were particularly inclined to move to suburbs, may have been *more* affected than the working classes, judging by the extent of middle-class suburban expansion. The upwardly mobile moved at least as frequently as the very poor, changing houses to match their growing financial security.[10]

Secondly, some householders suffered *periodic* disfranchisement because the nature of their employment meant sporadic moves over substantial distances. Engineers, masons, carpenters, and other mobile artisans, especially in the building trade, were affected. So too were some middle-class professionals. Studies of residential mobility in Liverpool show that 70 per cent of *all* residents, but 80 per cent of *working-class* residents, clung to the area they knew best.[11] A. L. Lowell notes the case of the forty year old, prosperous, married teacher, who complained that frequent promotions and subsequent moves had always prevented his enfranchisement. Aspiring bank managers, successful clerks, those in government employment, commercial travellers, and Wesleyan Ministers (the Edwardian Liberals' favourite example) were periodically disfranchised by the residence requirement. Finally a third group – mainly casual workers who moved very frequently – would suffer *frequent* disfranchise-

---

[9] Blewett, 'Franchise in the U.K.', p. 36. Urban material summarised in R. Dennis, 'Stability and change in urban communities: a geographical perspective', in J. H. Johnson and C. G. Pooley (eds.), *The structure of nineteenth century cities* (1982), pp. 270–3 and C. G. Pooley, 'Residential mobility in the Victorian city', *Transactions of the Institute of British Geographers* (1979), esp. p. 260.

[10] In Battersea's Shaftesbury estate, more clerks than artisans were moving out to the suburbs (J. McCalman, 'Respectability and working-class politics in late-Victorian London', *Historical Studies* (Australia) (1980), pp. 111–12). The scale of suburban development is ably demonstrated in F. M. L. Thompson (ed.), *The rise of suburbia* (Leicester, 1982) and A. Simpson and T. H. Lloyd (eds.), *Middle-class housing in Britain* (1977).

[11] Dennis, 'Urban communities', p. 272, Pooley, 'Residential mobility', pp. 270–1.

ment. Nonetheless, 'successive occupation' ensured that, in law, these 'flitters' only lost the vote if they 'flitted' too far.[12]

It was also comparatively easy for householders to get on to the electoral roll. Unlike lodger and ownership voters, they were placed on the register by the Overseers irrespective of their interest in politics or the quality of their accommodation. Where there were many claims to be examined in a short period of time, good information on residential mobility was hard to come by. As a result many may have qualified despite not satisfying the residence requirement. Moreover, in the 1880s and 1890s many qualified householders were omitted by inefficient Overseers, or those who did not feel compelled to trace successive occupiers. By 1914 they were more efficient, and legally obliged to trace as many voters as they could. The once common complaints about the Overseers' work became less frequent.[13] In Worcester, for instance, registration work had 'almost (reached) a state of perfection'.[14] Overseers were becoming more familiar with the routine, and professional registration officials were appointed. The Local Government Act of 1900 transferred the registration process in London to the Borough Clerks' department. The appointment of a Registration Officer at Ipswich in 1912 improved registration to such an extent that the number of Liberal claims and objections fell from 104 and 106 in 1912 to 14 and 25 in 1913. A further factor was the simplicity of the household franchise once the 'latch-key' problem was settled: there was no longer such scope for objections.[15] Finally, co-operation between Overseers and political parties, which resulted in Overseers including 'political' householders' claims with their own lists prior to their publication, became more pronounced. The genuinely qualified were now identified and registered. The dubiously qualified were less likely to be investigated. As Table 4.3 shows, in provincial towns very few householders found it necessary to appear in the revision courts. In the cities,

[12] A. L. Lowell, *The Government of England*, i (1908), p. 213; C. Dilke, *Electoral Reform* (1909), p. 11, *Southport Guardian*, 24 Sept. 1911, *Lib. Agent*, Oct. 1903 and 1904, *Hansard*, 8 July 1912, c. 1675.
[13] Compare MLF Mins, 31 Aug. 1911 with Manchester Central Registration Committee Mins, 3 June 1890. For other favourable comparisons, e.g. *Bristol Times*, 20 Sept. 1912, *East Anglian Daily Times*, 10 Sept. 1912 (Colchester). For a fuller discussion of householders evading the residence requirement, J. Davis and D. M. Tanner, 'The electorate and the cities, 1867–1890', unpublished paper. I am grateful to Dr Davis for bringing this point to my attention.
[14] *Birmingham Daily Post*, 11 Sept. 1912. Cf. similar comments, *Shields Daily Gazette*, 9 Sept. 1913, *Cheshire Daily Echo*, 12 Sept. 1913. Legal changes in the 1890s appeared to make it necessary for Overseers to make more strenuous efforts to trace voters (J. Davis, 'Slums and the vote', *Historical Research*, forthcoming).
[15] *East Anglian D.T.*, 19 Sept. 1912. Some London Borough Councils were taking steps to improve their registration techniques before the changes in 1900 (Davis and Tanner, 'The electorate and the cities').

Table 4.3 *Party claims in provincial cities and towns, 1913*
Divided boroughs

Area	Party	Div. 1	New lodger
Manchester	L	2,405	419
	C. & Lab.	1,700	628
Leeds (1912)	L	692	75
	C. & Lab.	894	260
Hull	All	1,901	680[a]
Nottingham	All	2,172	369

Note: [a] Inflated by unusual local conditions.

Single boroughs

Area	Party	Div. 1[a]	New lodger
Derby	L. & Lab.	46	72
	C.	26	189
Tynemouth	L. & Lab.	17	49
	C.	23	117
Halifax[b]	L. & Lab.	37	4
	C.	49	54
Dudley	All	56	163

Notes:
[a] Occupiers' claims in these constituencies represent less than 1 per cent of the household electors.
[b] Sustained claims only.

Source: Local press and party minutes.

however, the scale of successive occupation and other problems, made the position rather different (a point dealt with in Section III below).[16]

Enfranchisement became relatively easy for householders in provincial towns and rural areas. After some investigation, Conservative experts suggested that voteless householders made up only a small percentage of the unenfranchised; the majority of those excluded were young, unmarried, men. Other contemporary estimates suggest that perhaps 750,000 householders were excluded compared to the 5 million who had the vote. Almost 90 per cent of householders were enfranchised, and voteless

[16] For Manchester, Clarke, *Lancashire Liberalism,* p. 107, and for London, Thompson, *London,* p. 71, report by J. R. Seager on London registration, 21 Oct. 1901, HG Add MS 46023 fos. 231–3. See H. J. Hanham, *Elections and party management* (1959), Chapter 11 for the earlier period.

householders made up just one fifth of those who were still excluded. Householders, of all social classes, generally qualified with ease.[17]

Contemporary estimates could be misleading or simply wrong. To establish their accuracy, one would need to compare (unavailable) *Census* data on age, housing tenure, and occupation, with the electoral lists. However, comparisons can be made for earlier periods. Joyce's examination of the occupational and electoral structure of Blackburn in 1871 identified little anti-working-class bias in the electorate. Moreover, the household franchise at this time was *more* restrictive than in Edwardian times because of the less generous registration procedures. A recent study of electoral politics in East Anglia during the 1880s and 1890s ingeniously used extrapolations from 1881 *Census* data to reach similar conclusions.[18] The best information, however, is for Edwardian Scotland. Scottish electoral registers contain information on a voter's occupation, whilst published Scottish *Census* data is occasionally detailed enough to permit comparison between the occupational structures of the adult male population and the electorate.

The mixed constituency of Haddingtonshire is a reasonable surrogate for wider analysis because its social structure broadly reflects that of the British population. The data (Table 4.4) suggests that whereas the working class made up a little more than 77 per cent of the constituency's adult male population (almost exactly that of the British population as a whole) they made up 76 per cent of the household electorate. Skilled working-class householders were a little more likely to be enfranchised than either the unskilled or the semi-skilled, but the differences were not substantial. There is no reason to believe that because this data relates to a Scottish constituency it is untypical of the position in provincial England and Wales.[19]

This picture is also confirmed in Table 4.5. Comparisons between levels of constituency enfranchisement and the number of inhabited households (derived from the Census) is consistent with the view that only around a quarter of the voteless were householders (Column 5 of Table 4.5). In the provinces, the level of householder disfranchisement was remarkably even between constituencies of a radically different social complexion. Thus the difference between householder disfranchisement in middle-class York and working-class South Shields or Warrington was

---

[17] *Hansard*, 8 July 1912, c. 1713, memo by W. A. Gales, 3 Feb. 1917, Steel-Maitland MS G.D. 193/202 fo. 33, *Conservative Agents' Journal*, Apr. 1912.

[18] Joyce, *Work, society and politics*, pp. 106, 202; K. Langford, 'Success, failure and division – the Liberal electoral performance in East Anglia (with special reference to the Suffolk County division)', Cambridge BA dissertation 1985, pp. 6–7, 83. Ninety per cent of labourers were enfranchised.

[19] See Appendix 1.

Table 4.4 *Occupational structure of population and household electorate, Haddingtonshire, 1911*

Social category[a]	Male population 20 + (%)[b]		Household electorate[c] (%)	
Class I[d] ⎫ Class II ⎭	18.18		21.71	
Class III	15.28 ⎫		15.94 ⎫	
Class IV ⎫ Class V ⎭	43.37 ⎬ 77.21		44.88 ⎬ 76.39	
Miners[e]	18.56 ⎭		15.57 ⎭	
Retired/OAP	3.48		0.58	
Others[f]	1.13		1.32	

Notes:

[a] Based on the 1951 *Census* categorisation, using the techniques and information in R. Lawton (ed.), *The Census and social structure* (1978), pp. 179–223.

[b] Refers to the administrative county of Haddingtonshire, which made up 99 per cent of the parliamentary constituency.

[c] Excludes those whose normal residence according to the *Electoral Register*, 1911–12 was outside the constituency boundaries. These were mainly property-owning plural voters. The household electorate in this case includes service voters, who in Scotland were not registered separately.

[d] Differs from the classification in Lawton, *The Census*, by including students and those with private means. Household voters with no stated occupation in the electoral roll, but who are identified as owners/proprietors of houses/other property are also included.

[e] Includes other mine workers, some of whom may also appear in Cat. III or IV above.

[f] Includes voters of unstated/no occupation who were not property owners.

Source: *Census*, 1911 and *Electoral Register*, 1911–12.

apparent but not pronounced. Table 4.5 also shows that constituencies in the larger cities (like Woolwich in London) were not typical of the rest of the country. Clearly they require separate attention.

III

The situation in the cities was different. Mobility was more pronounced and, although large numbers of successive occupiers qualified, the Overseers could not cope with the scale of the problem. The political parties supplemented their work with more impact than in provincial towns. Nonetheless, at least half the unenfranchised in Woolwich were

Table 4.5 Non-separate households and the voteless population, 1911

Constituency	Adult male pop.[a]	Residential electorate[b]	Voteless men	Separate male households[c]		Non-separate male households	
				(approx.)	% voteless	(approx.)	% voteless
Shrewsbury	8,064	5,081	2,943	5,394	10.64	2,630	89.36
York	21,850	13,087	8,763	14,937	21.11	6,913	78.89
South Shields	26,065	18,709	7,356	20,484	24.13	5,581	75.87
Warrington	19,570	11,077	8,493	13,333	26.56	6,237	73.44
Hull (3)	74,889	46,658	28,231	56,362	34.37	18,527	65.63
Woolwich	34,462	16,888	17,579	24,798	45.00	9,669	55.00

Notes:

[a] Estimated by taking the percentage of men aged over 21 in the borough, for which full figures are available, and applying this figure to the male population of the constituency. Since the boundaries in each case are substantially comparable, errors will be small.

[b] Excludes only freemen. Figures which excluded all plural voters, and not simply the easily identifiable freemen, would produce more accurate results, but these are not available.

[c] Figures for separate households in the 1911 Census include women. A figure for men only has been calculated by subtracting from this the number of female householders who qualified for the municipal vote. However, the best available figures are for 1904, so the result is approximate on a number of accounts. For women voters, see ILP Census material.

householders (Table 4.5) compared to no more than a quarter elsewhere. This had a marked impact on the level of enfranchisement; in working-class constituencies in the larger cities just 48 per cent of the adult male population had the vote. The figure for provincial working-class seats was nearer 62 per cent. Only part of this can be explained by the large numbers of ineligible aliens in some city constituencies (such as Whitechapel in London).[20] In general, it reflected the broader problem of inner-city mobility – even some middle-class constituencies in the city centres had levels of enfranchisement below those for provincial working-class divisions.

Nonetheless, the inner-city electorate did not consist of a social elite. Lowell tellingly argued that slums (and hence slum-dwellers and slum voters) were always there; Burns that the characteristic of the 'street-corner men' was that they congregated always at the same, local, street-corner, hardly indicating geographical mobility. Dilke and others argued that in the East End of London a 'hovel franchise' already existed by 1910: 'We have already enfranchised the poorest of the population', Charles Roberts declared, 'We have enfranchised those who live in the slums'.[21]

This much is evident from the electoral registers. There were substantial numbers of voters in parts of London where the only resident middle-class elements were likely to be clergymen or Settlement house workers. Despite the late Victorian religious enthusiasm for the London poor, the electorate in these areas must have come overwhelmingly from the slums. Comparison of Booth's social survey data with electoral registers suggests that, even in the 1890s, there were numerous enfranchised householders in some of London's least salubrious streets.[22] Once legal decisions enforced the registration of householders in multi-occupied tenancies, even the very poorest of resident 'householders' could obtain the vote. Close comparison between *Census* data and electoral registers shows this clearly. By 1883, around 90 per cent of the identifiable voters in the Nicholl,

---

[20] Calculations based on 1911 *Census* population figures and the 1911 electoral register (P.P. 1911 (Cd 4975) Lxii, 679). Constituency classification from Blewett, *Peers,* pp. 489–94 and Pelling, *Social geography.* Full details in D. M. Tanner, 'Political realignment in England and Wales, 1906–1922', London Ph.D. thesis 1985, p. 52 fn. 53. For the impact of alien immigration on East London electoral registers, G. Alderman, 'The political impact of Zionism in the East End of London before 1940', *London Journal* (1983), pp. 35–8.

[21] Lowell, *Government of England,* i, p. 213; C. Dilke, *Woman Suffrage and Electoral Reform* (1910), pp. 13–14. For Burns and Roberts' views, *Hansard,* esp. debate of 8 July 1912, and 12 July 1912, c. 2120.

[22] e.g. the Long Lane/New Kent Road area of Bermondsey, 'one of the poorest spots in London' (C. Booth, *Life and labour of the people in London* (1902), ii, App. 2, p. 35).

one of East London's most poverty-ridden areas, were working-class. A third of the electorate were street traders and labourers, and around 50 per cent were artisans. Examination of Booth's unpublished survey case books suggests that these 'artisans' were invariably low-paid furniture and clothing workers. There was probably a bias towards the more geographically immobile elements in the London electorate, and against the tenants of sub-divided buildings (who were presumably more mobile, and more difficult to trace). At the same time, *all* social groups in London moved more frequently than equivalent social groups in the provinces, so the effects were not uniquely felt by one section of the working class. There were numerous very poor voters on the register in the 1880s, and it seems likely that by 1914 registration improvements would have made lower working-class enfranchisement even more complete.[23] Although greater mobility contributed to lower working-class disfranchisement, it was not pronounced enough to massively alter the composition of the electorate. Moreover, although there was a substantial 'seepage' of householders through the registration net *in the cities,* this was not typical of the country as a whole. [24]

IV

Most older, non-single, men obtained the vote fairly easily because of their position as householders. The contrast with younger and single men is dramatic. As Table 4.5 shows, men who were not 'separate occupiers' constituted around half the voteless in the cities (where mobility disfranchised even many householders) and usually three-quarters of the voteless in provincial boroughs. Most of the unenfranchised were single men. Although some older single men might have been householders, for most single men the lodger or service franchises were the only possible sources of votes.[25] In 1915 there were roughly three million single men, but only half a million service and lodger voters. Somewhere in the region of 2.5 million single men from all social groups were excluded.

The service and lodger franchises were as complicated as the household franchise was simple. The service franchise, a division of the household franchise, was included in the 1884 Act to enfranchise certain Scottish hinds and shepherds. It applied to men who occupied rooms free by virtue of their office, service, or employment. Subsequent legal decisions

[23] Quantitative data is from Davis and Tanner, 'The electorate and the cities'.
[24] See also below, pp. 388–91.
[25] Many widowers almost certainly lived in lodgings, and like younger single men would have problems qualifying under any other franchise. See also below, p. 120.

widened the Act's scope. In *Stribling v Halse* it was ruled that a man qualified as a service voter even if his landlord controlled parts of his accommodation, provided he 'separately occupied' a bedroom. This was qualified by *Skinn v Phillips, Barnett v Hicks,* and *Ladd v O'Toole,* which restricted the wider application of *Stribling v Halse,* but without returning to the *status quo ante.* As the *Liberal Agent* put it, the service franchise was 'a glorious specimen of judge made law'.[26] By 1910, it was generally assumed that four stipulations had to be satisfied – that the employer lived off the premises, that the nature of the employment made it impossible to live elsewhere, that the landlord was not the claimant's father, and that no rent was paid.

There were fewer than 150,000 service voters by 1914. A concentration of service voters in the mews and malls of West London, and in the financial centres, and shopping areas, indicates that domestic servants, caretakers, and shop assistants made up the bulk of the service electorate. C. T. Ritchie, who managed to obtain a service vote for No. 11 Downing Street, was an exception. Few middle-class men could hope to qualify as service voters.[27]

The lodger franchise was the most complex and anomalous franchise of them all. The residence qualification, which caused some problems to householders, applied to lodgers in an even tougher form. The successive occupation clause, which enabled so many householders to qualify, was largely inoperative. A lodger was allowed to change his rooms only within the same house without it interrupting the residence period. Even this token concession was withheld in some areas.[28]

Franchise stipulations were also stringent. All lodgers who separately occupied rooms to the value of £10 per annum unfurnished were theoretically eligible, but this simple definition masked a host of difficulties, obstacles, and problems. To prove 'separate occupation' the lodger had to establish he had complete control over his bedroom; the franchise was designed for men who, despite being technically lodgers, lived as independently as householders. 'Separate occupation' was also taken to mean 'sole and exclusive use'; a lodger who shared rooms would therefore usually be excluded. Men who permitted sharing, retaining control and their position as 'independent tenants', could in theory get the vote. Married lodgers sharing rooms with their wife and children were thus technically eligible, following *Searle v Staffs County Council,* but newspaper

[26] *Lib. Agent,* July 1897; *The Times,* 12 Sept. 1907, for its application.
[27] Dilke, *Electoral reform,* p. 13. *Stribling v Halse* was widely known as the 'shop assistant's case', after the group which benefited most from the ruling.
[28] It was not allowed in Cheshire, allowed in Croydon, and each case was decided on its merits in Islington (*Worcester Daily Times,* 12 Sept. 1912, *Croydon Express,* 23 Sept. 1911, *Islington Daily Gazette,* 16 Sept. 1913).

accounts and informed opinion suggest that most lodgers were single men.[29] The cumulative effect of these rulings was to exclude around 180,000 indoor servants, 75,000 soldiers and all policemen resident in barracks. However, the most important effect was on men living with their parents.[30] They were not *automatically* debarred from the franchise; however, revising barristers found it difficult to accept them as truly independent tenants; distinguishing sons who were 'tenants at will' from the genuinely independent proved to be one of the barristers' most persistent problems.[31]

Financial obstacles also helped limit the level of lodger enfranchisement. A lodger's rooms had to be valued at more than £10 per year (usually stated as a weekly amount of between 4s 0d and 4s 6d for an unfurnished room, 4s 6d to 6s 0d for a furnished room, 14s 0d to 15s 0d if food and services were provided, as they usually were).[32] It is difficult to ascertain how important this was. Most contemporary housing surveys do not detail the cost of rented lodgings. Scattered evidence (and common sense) suggests a distinction between London (and a few other areas with a similar housing structure) and the provinces. Even in the 1880s and 1890s, one room tenements in London were seldom rented at less than 4s 0d per week unfurnished. However, 80 per cent of rented lodgings in Cardiff and Bradford, for example, were let at less than 4s 8d per week even in the Edwardian period. As house rents in Wales and northern counties were only 65 per cent of the average London figures for comparable properties, it would seem that the distinction between London and

[29] For separate occupation, *Nottingham Guardian*, 16 Sept. 1912. See also *Lib. Agent*, Apr. 1911, *L.D.P.*, 10 Sept. 1910. For lodgers as single men, e.g. letter from S.H., *L.L.*, 18 June 1914. In Exeter, 15 per cent of all lodgers, and 24 per cent of all male lodgers were married men, and 70 per cent of all male lodgers were under forty [J. Emerson, 'The lodging market in a Victorian city: Exeter', *Southern History* (1987), pp. 107–9].

[30] Russell, *Liberal Landslide*, p. 5; S. Rosenbaum, 'The general election of January 1910 and the bearing of the results upon some problems of representation', *Journal of the Royal Statistical Society* (1910), esp. p. 476; W.C. memo, 7 Jan. 1911, PRO CAB 37/114; *Croydon Guardian*, 9 Sept. 1911.

[31] As vigorously affirmed by the revising barrister for South Shields, *Northern Mail*, 18 Sept. 1911.

[32] The value of rooms held in common with the landlord was not taken into consideration, but the value of rooms shared with another lodger often was. William Wedgwood Benn thought that 'Most furnished lodgers ... pay for Board and Lodgings inclusive': 'Scheme of constituency organisation for the London Liberal Federation', n.d. 1914, Stansgate MS ST/21 fo. 145. Figures for Colchester suggest that nearly 72 per cent of lodgers in 1915 paid for board and lodgings. This calculation is based on the unusually full figures contained in the *Electoral register* 1915. Similar, sporadic, references in other electoral registers and in the press suggest that this was not unusual.

the provinces applied to all kinds of property, and that in provincial seats many lodgers would pay less than the amount necessary to qualify.[33]

Lodgers also had to prove that the lodgings were of 'sufficient value', i.e. that they were actually *worth* £10 per annum unfurnished. Some barristers divided the rateable value of a house by the number of rooms in order to ascertain the value of each one. However, according to *McRea v Buchanen*, a room was worth £10 or more if it commanded that market value. Some barristers preferred this ruling. Others adopted a slight variation, taking local market conditions into account in order to determine whether the lodging was 'worth' the amount paid. A further group treated each case on its individual merits.[34] For a larger number this was too time consuming. They declared that no lodging would be deemed of sufficient value unless the rateable value exceeded a certain predetermined amount. Often this was £8, because market conditions might cause a lodger to pay a little more than the lodging was in fact worth.[35] In other constituencies the stated figure was £10. These were the most common figures, but some barristers put the limit lower, some higher, and some at different levels for town and country.[36] The permutations were almost endless. As one franchise expert wrote, 'no clause of any Representation Act has been interpreted in so many ways'.[37]

In most provincial seats in order to qualify the potential lodger voter had to pay an above average rent, for a house with an above average value. Although this militated against the working class, others were affected. The £10 limit, one MP stated, was 'felt keenly by the "intellectual middle classes"'. Dilke claimed that in many rural areas lodgers of a 'superior class' were excluded because of low local rents.[38] Farmers' sons

[33] R. Williams, *London rookeries and colliers' slums* (1893), p. 21, M. Pember Reeves, *Round about a pound a week* (Virago edn., 1979), p. 22, *Eastern Argus,* 14 Aug. 1880 (all London); Daunton, *Cardiff,* p. 100, and the *Worker,* 11 Nov. 1913. For house rents, *Year Book of Social Progress* (1913–14), p. 374, referring to the extensive, but flawed, Board of Trade survey.

[34] As in Halifax and Leeds (*Y.P.,* 13 Sept. 1910). For the previous practice, see e.g. *Sheffield Daily Telegraph,* 10 Sept. 1910.

[35] *Birmingham Daily Post,* 11 Sept. 1913, for the situation in Dudley. For Lincoln, *Yorks. Herald,* 16 Sept. 1911.

[36] *Devon and Exeter Gazette,* 12 Sept. 1911, *West Bromwich Free Press,* 15 Sept. 1911, *Sheffield Independent,* 13 Sept. 1911. For lower figures in Sunderland (£6.10s 1895, £7.10s 1912), *Lib. Agent,* Dec. 1895, *Yorks. Herald,* 11 Sept. 1912. For higher figures, *Exeter Gazette,* 12 Sept. 1912.

[37] J. King, *Electoral reform* (1908), p. 39. See also M. Ostrogorski, *Democracy and the organisation of political parties* (1902), i p. 374.

[38] *Hansard,* 8 July 1912, c. 1714; Dilke in discussion of Rosenbaum, p. 521.

often provided services in lieu of rent, but not all barristers would accept this as a valid substitute for actual cash payments.[39] Poorly paid members of the lower middle-class would also be affected even in many urban areas. The average skilled working-class wage, and the salary of the average clerk were almost identical; many younger clerks were paid less than the average rate.[40]

Barristers had considerable powers of discretion. Each barrister controlled an average of five constituencies. Linforth notes how in one seat a change of revising barrister led to 500 lodger voters being removed from the register; similar illustrations abound. His conclusion – 'our present law affecting lodgers makes the franchise entirely dependent upon the personality of the revising barrister' – is too extreme, for it implies that barristers could, and did, ignore laws and concrete realities when (usually) they did not. Nonetheless, the views of individual revising barristers could considerably influence the level of enfranchisement.[41]

Other extraneous factors also influenced whether an individual lodger obtained the vote. Where one party was entrenched, registration was often left entirely to the Overseers. Because the Overseers were not empowered to put lodgers on the register, lodgers who were supporters of the weaker organisation would be handicapped. Although the Liberal Whips made registration grants to organisations in these circumstances, this did not solve the problem.[42] At the same time, in safe seats, such as North-West Durham, neither party tackled registration work, 'one because they are always sure of a thumping majority & the other because it was always so helpless. There are plenty of lodger & occupation claims to be fought.'[43] If the stronger party carried out registration work with little opposition, it could pack the register. If a third party intervened and reintroduced an element of competition, all parties might fight for

[39] It was allowed in Hackney, Wandsworth, and Sheffield, but rejected in Middlesbrough (*Lib. Agent,* Oct. 1909, *Yorks. Herald,* 11 Sept. 1912). Material included in the electoral register for the Buckinghamshire division of Aylesbury suggests that nearly half of the lodger vote in this fairly rural constituency qualified through service; in Colchester the figure was only 5 per cent.

[40] For details of lower middle-class income, F. D. Klingender, *The condition of clerical labour in Britain* (1935), G. Crossick (ed.), *The lower middle class in Britain, 1870–1914* (1977).

[41] Linforth, *Agent's diary,* p. 36. See similar comments in, *Lib. Agent,* Dec. 1895, National Society of Conservative Agents Mins, 23 Mar. 1899, 1 Oct. 1903. Details of the numbers of revising barristers and the costs of the system are given in PRO HO 45/10075/B7422.

[42] List of registration grants for London in 1901, HG Add MS 46105 fo. 179, LCLF Mins, 12 Nov. 1912, YLF Mins, 4 June 1903, Mid.LF Mins, 13 July 1909.

[43] W.H. to J.S.M., 8 May 1914, LP/ORG/14/2/15. See also the table in J. Ramsden, *The age of Balfour and Baldwin 1902–1940* (1978), p. 53, for indications that this could still affect political prospects in these circumstances. It should be noted, however, that local officials' claims of registration gains were not always accepted by the other side.

an advantage by scouring the constituency for potential lodger voters.[44] However, because there were so few potential lodger voters, the political rewards from expensive attempts to track them down did not always repay the very substantial costs. If both parties engaged in similar activity, the net political gains might be negligible, the net financial cost quite dramatic.

The adversarial approach to compiling the electoral register also threatened to cripple the whole registration process. In law the lodger's claim was *prima facie* proof of his entitlement to the vote. This encouraged a competitive dishonesty which threatened to submerge the court beneath an avalanche of bogus claims.[45] Barristers therefore invariably called for further proof of the claim if an objection was made. They could, and did, 'receive and entertain as evidence against a lodger claimant any gossip, story or hearsay put forward ... the onus of correcting and disproving this lies upon the claimant'.[46] Lodgers were often asked to support their claim in court. This could act as a deterrent. Going to court could mean losing a day's pay.[47] Contested claims could lead to embarrassing discussions of the lodger's domestic circumstances. Many 'better class men' (in addition to many members of the working class) objected to this. However, if the claim was not personally supported, it was often automatically rejected.[48]

This policy was part of an informal alliance between legal officials and political agents designed to make the whole process manageable. It was often taken still further. At Swansea in 1911, 2,500 lodger claims were settled by agreement before the court came into session. Agreements between the parties in Bristol ensured that not a single contentious point was raised in the actual court hearings.[49] All sides recognised that without

---

[44] In Manchester, the dramatic increase in the number of lodger claims between 1896 and 1904 could possibly have been the result of Labour's intervention (Manchester and Salford LRC, *First Annual Report 1904*).

[45] For the very frequent complaints concerning fraudulent claims, e.g. *The Times*, 14 Sept. 1907, *Nottingham Guardian*, 12 Sept. 1913.

[46] *Conservative Agents' Journal*, Oct. 1910.

[47] In some areas evening sittings were held, and in others compensation – usually a fixed amount – was paid if the objection was fatuous.

[48] Excellent examples of this inquisitorial cross-examination may be found in the *Croydon Expr.*, 30 Sept. 1911 and *Midland Daily Telegraph*, 18 Sept. 1903. See also the article 'Modesty at a discount', *Lib. Agent*, Apr. 1905, and comments of a similar kind, *Primrose League Gazette*, 2 Dec. 1895. (I owe this reference to Dr Martin Pugh.) For rejections for non-attendance, *Birm. Daily Post*, 12 Sept. 1913, *Croydon Expr.*, 23 Sept. 1911, *Bristol Times*, 25 Sept. 1913.

[49] *Cambria Daily Leader*, 14 Sept. 1911; *Bath Observer*, 23 Sept. 1911; *Bury Times*, 23 Sept. 1911; *Chesh. Daily Echo*, 11 Sept. 1913. Cf. *Cambridge Chronicle*, 6 Oct. 1913: 'amicable arrangements between the party agents have caused the removal of much which in previous years has resulted in a great deal of friction'.

flexibility, tact, judgement, discretion, and compromise the registration process would 'extend into many months'.[50]

Many of the lodger franchise's numerous pitfalls applied with greatest severity to sons, of all social classes, who lived with their fathers.[51] The (normally sceptical) revising barristers received claims from these men with great suspicion.[52] Before 1907, the revising barrister in Blackburn, for example, rejected all such claims. In Bristol, Reading, and Cambridge, they had to be supported by written contracts between father and son.[53] The formal and informal rules of the registration process ensured that this particular group was particularly disadvantaged.

In the country as a whole there were only 350,000 lodger voters by 1915: 100,000 were in London; a further 100,000 were spread over the provincial boroughs; and the remaining 150,000 were in the 'counties'. While the low level of lodger enfranchisement reflects the bias against young men in general, this does not account for particular local variations. However, the broad pattern of enfranchisement is simply explained. There were usually more lodger voters where housing conditions created more lodgers, and even older, married, men were forced to live in rooms (as in London). There were generally fewer lodger voters where younger men lived with their parents, and there were fewer 'commercial' lodgings. Concentrations of 'genuine' lodgers caused by a shortage of housing affected market conditions by increasing both prices and a property's rateable value.[54] Although this meant more lodger voters, it did not necessarily mean higher overall levels of constituency enfranchisement, for it was still more difficult to qualify as a lodger than it was to qualify as a

---

[50] *Local Government Chronicle*, 29 June 1912. See also e.g. comments of one western circuit barrister, A. Mortimer, to the Under-Secretary of State at the Home Office, 23 May 1901, PRO HO 45/10075/B7422.

[51] A point made by some Tories: 'there are many of these sons, well-conducted men, and men of mature age, well-qualified to have a vote, who cannot get it'. In public Liberals argued that votes for middle-class men could be fabricated by their fathers, a point which they conceded in private was not always the case (*Hansard*, 17 June 1912, c. 1426; Pease to Elibank, 17 Aug. 1911, Gainford MS 64). Historians have accepted the *public* propaganda, rather than the measured *private* analysis.

[52] See comments by the revising barristers for Kingston-upon-Thames and Morley, *The Times*, 30 Sept. 1913, *Morley Obs.*, 12 Sept. 1913. This is not to suggest that these men could not obtain the vote. Analysis of electoral registers suggests that in provincial England and Wales frequently between fifty and seventy-five per cent of enfranchised lodgers had the same name as the landlord/lady. However, around half of these had landladies of the same name – perhaps a widowed mother or elder sister – and men in these circumstances were less usually regarded as 'dependent' tenants at will. In London, only fifteen to thirty-five per cent of lodgers had the same name as their landlord/lady, a reflection of the different social and housing conditions.

[53] *M.G.*, 12 Sept. 1907; *Reading Standard*, 14 Sept. 1912; *Cambridge Daily News*, 19 Sept. 1911.

[54] Tanner, 'Parliamentary electoral system', p. 211, gives examples of middle-class and rural seats with fewer lodger voters than working-class constituencies.

Table 4.6 *Occupational structure of population and lodger electorate, Haddingtonshire, 1911*

Social category	Male population 20 + (%)[a]		Lodger electorate (%)	
Class I } Class II }	18.18		37.58	
Class III	15.28		20.27	
Class IV } Class V }	43.37	77.21	16.32	58.54
Miners	18.56		21.95	
Retired/OAP	3.48		0.78	
Others	1.13		3.10	

Note:

[a] Figures are for the occupational structure of the entire male population over twenty. Figures for the occupational structure of lodgers alone are not available.

householder. It could in fact work the other way around. Where there were major concentrations of lodgers, because older men were not house-holders, a larger percentage of the adult male population faced a complex and anomalous system which made enfranchisement very difficult.

This is not to argue that social class had no impact on lodger enfran-chisement. Within an area, richer lodgers *were* more likely to qualify than poorer lodgers. However, circumstances varied so much between areas that affluent lodgers in one area might fare no better than poorer lodgers in a different part of the country. The system discriminated first against all lodgers; it discriminated second against sons living with their parents; only finally did it discriminate against the working class. Indeed, even if only lodgers in largely working-class and mining seats were from the poorer social groups, then 100,000 enfranchised lodger voters, around one third of the total, were working class.[55]

More concrete evidence (from contemporary reports, Scottish electoral registers, and detailed analysis of the position in Bethnal Green) confirms that many lodgers, even in socially mixed seats, were working class. Analysis of Haddington's lodger electorate (Table 4.6) shows that 60 per cent of registered lodgers were working class in a constituency where approaching 80 per cent of the local male population belonged to that social group. If this was reflected across England and Wales, then 175–200,000 lodgers (one half to two-thirds of the total) were working class.[56]

[55] Ibid., p. 213 fn. 52.
[56] This figure allows for there being lodgers in socially mixed and middle-class seats. It is a more realistic basis for the calculations.

V

Analysis of the electoral system thus suggests that age and housing tenure were the most significant determinants of enfranchisement, with class a secondary factor even on the lodger franchise. It is possible to use the information assembled above to estimate the size of the residual class bias. In 1915 there were 500,000 lodger and service voters. Almost all service voters (150,000) and around 200,000 of the enfranchised lodgers were working class. There were around 150,000 middle-class lodger voters, but 600,000 single middle-class men in the population as a whole. Around 450,000 single middle-class men were thus unable to qualify for the lodger vote. Some richer or older single middle-class men owned or rented houses or flats, and qualified as householders, but there is no indication that this was common. On the contrary, Dr Emerson's work on Exeter suggests that lodgings were a perfectly respectable, and common, type of accommodation even amongst moderately affluent single men (and women). Moreover, many newly married, older and widowed middle-class men were probably excluded from the electorate, perhaps temporarily, by the householder's residence requirement. The estimate of 450,000 disfranchised middle-class men is similar to the estimate made by Conservative Central Office in 1916. The fact that so many middle-class single men were disfranchised would also help explain why single men of *all* classes were unable to obtain the municipal vote after the First World War (there was considerable continuity between the pre-war parliamentary franchise and post-war municipal franchise).[57]

These figures may be used to estimate the class composition of the electorate as a whole. In 1915, there were roughly 2.1 million middle-class men in England and Wales. If the plural vote is added to this (+ 470,000), and the number of excluded middle-class men is subtracted (− 450,000), then the propertied vote stands at around 2.1 million, or a little over 30 per cent of the electorate. It follows that the working class comprised nearly 70 per cent of the total. If plural voters are excluded from the calculations, then the working class comprised 76 per cent of the electorate. This is still less than its share of the population as a whole (80 per cent), but it is hardly a dramatic bias. Moreover, the geographical distribution of the plural vote was uneven. It was spread thinly across the country, with a sizeable proportion of the total concentrated in commercial centres, university seats, and those county divisions which either bordered on urban centres, or contained several smaller, affluent,

[57] M. Pugh, *Electoral reform in war and peace* (1978), p. 92. For the post-war franchise, below, p. 389, and for the means of calculating the number of single men, based on the *Census* and the Registrar-General's population figures, Tanner, 'Parliamentary electoral system', pp. 212–13. See also Emerson, 'Lodgings in Exeter', p. 107.

boroughs, and therefore contained their freehold votes.[58] The class bias in these constituencies would be very high, but the class bias in the remaining constituencies would accordingly be reduced. Probably typically, in the Haddington constituency, taking all franchises together, the working class was only under-represented by 3 per cent. Despite the bias in the lodger electorate, the household franchise was broadly class representative, and there were few plural voters (Table 4.7). If nationally the working class was a larger element in the electorate than most historians have presumed, in the 'average' constituency the bias against it would be further reduced because plural voters were comparatively scarce.

Many Edwardians knew, as Lowell put it, that 'no considerable class in the community was aggrieved'; an extension of the franchise would give the vote to the 'unenfranchised members of enfranchised classes'. They recognised that married men, as householders, were favourably treated: 'the vote in this country has been a married man's vote (because) "married man" and "householder" are as a rule synonymous terms'. It was almost axiomatic that single men were excluded: 'he was unmarried', one contemporary biographer of a future Labour minister wrote, 'and therefore in those days had no vote'.[59] Keir Hardie regarded the failure to introduce a full Reform Bill before 1914 not as an attempt to restrict Labour's support, but as a plan 'to keep youth off the register'. Those who got the vote in 1918 were 'chiefly at the younger end of the scale'. Labour in fact did not anticipate major electoral benefits from an extension of the franchise. As Clynes wrote, 'It may be that a mere addition to the number of voters, however welcome and proper this would be, would not give any advantage to the Labour party.'[60] This distinction between older enfranchised householders and younger unenfranchised lodgers should not be surprising. The average age of marriage for men was thirty. Urban historians and urban geographers suggest that in this period few young men formed households before they were married, and being a householder was the easiest pathway to enfranchisement.[61]

---

[58] Blewett, 'Franchise in the U.K.', p. 46.
[59] Lowell, *Government of England*, i, p. 274; *Spectator,* 3 Feb. 1917; F. Blackbourn, *George Tomlinson* (1936), p. 36. See also London Labour Council for Adult Suffrage, *Adult suffrage* (1917), p. 1, J. J. Lawson, *A man's life* (1932), p. 175.
[60] *L.L.,* 10 Apr. 1913; *The Times,* 23 Sept. 1918. Cf. *Liverpool Post and Mercury,* 25 Oct. 1924, and E. G. Pretyman, *Hansard,* 8 July 1912, c. 1656: 'the bulk of new voters (would be) just over twenty-one years of age'. Clynes' comments from the *Manchester Weekly Citizen,* 10 Feb. 1912.
[61] *73rd Annual Report of the Registrar-General, 1910* (1911), p. xviii. For this situation in Liverpool and Glasgow, Pooley, 'Residential mobility', e.g. pp. 274–5, J. Butt, 'Working-class housing in the Scottish cities, 1900–50', in G. Gordon and B. Dicks (eds.), *Scottish urban history* (1983), p. 241.

Table 4.7 *Occupational structure of population and electorate, Haddingtonshire, 1911: compilation and summary*

Social cat.	Householders	Lodger elect. (%)	Residential elect.[a] (%)	Full elect.[b] (%)	Male pop. (%)
Class I \} Class II	21.71	37.58	22.59	22.94	18.18
Class III \} Class IV	15.94 \} 76.39	20.27 \} 58.54	16.06 \} 75.15	16.20 \} 74.7	15.28 \} 77.21
Class V	44.88	16.32	43.09	42.66	43.37
Miners	15.57	21.95	16.00	15.84	18.56
Retired	0.58	0.78	0.60	0.65	3.48
Others	1.32	3.10	1.67	1.72	1.13

Notes:
[a] Household and lodger electorate taken together.
[b] Residential electorate plus plural voters.

Nonetheless, some contemporaries argued that there *was* a class bias. They were generally franchise reformers attempting to get the system abolished, or opponents of change who argued that civilisation would disintegrate if an unenfranchised 'new proletariat' were given the vote. The former never quantified the degree of bias; the latter's claims were rhetoric founded on ignorance. If the voteless men had been very different from the existing electorate, as the anti-suffragists (and some subsequent historians) claimed, they might indeed have voted *en masse* for a particular party. However, they were not a 'new proletariat' infused with values which the older parties could not accommodate. On the contrary, perhaps three-quarters of them were the sons of existing voters. We do not know precisely how the generational transmission of political partisanship operated, and particularly how many families had established political traditions, but it seems likely that, under normal conditions, most of these young men would reflect family views, and vote either Liberal or Tory.[62] In a seat like Haddington, which did not have a great many plural voters, extending the franchise would barely have increased the working-class share of the electorate (from 74 to 77 per cent at best).[63] Parties based on working-class support might have benefited a little from an extension of the franchise, but, because the voteless were not a single social/political bloc, the increase was unlikely to have been considerable.

Labour did suffer from several minor electoral obstacles which limited its support at the margins, and had a more pronounced effect in a few particular seats. First, the exclusion of younger men. Even in the altered post-war conditions inter-generational voting patterns were remarkably stable, but Labour would no doubt have found it easier before 1914 to convert younger voters, who had only partially fixed views, than those with established voting patterns. Secondly, Labour suffered a little from the method by which the electoral register was compiled. Labour supporters benefited from the Overseers' efforts, and from Liberal activity, as Liberals generally looked at Labour supporters as potential allies.[64]

---

[62] I refer here to Butler and Stokes, *Political change in Britain*. Although I have questioned *applications* of this thesis to events in the past, and would accept some of the revisions suggested by political scientists such as Heath, Jowell, and Curtice, the importance of the generational transmission of ideas cannot be over-emphasised. For an example of the contemporary comment on the franchise which misdirected earlier historians, L. C. Money, *Things that matter* (1912), pp. 189–94.

[63] In most constituencies the margin of Labour's defeats before 1910 was too substantial for this to be significant. In fact, the actual working-class share of the electorate even in 1918 would have been less than its share of the population as a whole, because plural voting was not abolished. For this, below, pp. 387–8.

[64] F. Plant to J.R.M., 9 July 1904, LRC 16/384, W. Marshall to J.R.M., 20 May 1903, LRC 9/331; Leeds LF EC Mins, 15 Oct. 1912, Finance Comm. Mins, 5 Nov. 1914, showing results of claims in Labour-held Leeds East.

However, in seats where there was some prospect of a three-cornered contest, Labour lodgers were unlikely to benefit from Liberal support. Despite some progress by 1914, Labour organisations were ill-equipped to fill the gap. At Sheffield in 1908, for example, twenty Labour lodger claims were rejected because penury prevented a Labour agent's appearance.[65] Finally, a number of working-class constituencies, like Pudsey in Yorkshire, were swamped by plural voters. In the inner-cities, Liberals and Conservatives might also direct the duplicate votes of their propertied supporters to vulnerable working-class areas.[66] However, the Liberals also suffered from the nature of the electoral system. In part this was because they, like Labour, were a less affluent party than the Tories, and had a more working-class electoral base. In December 1910, the plural vote allowed the Tories to retain around thirty seats which they would otherwise have lost (Appendix 2). The plural vote did most to create a 'class' bias in the electoral system; it also gave the Tories an enormous political advantage over the Liberal party.

VI

The nature of constituency boundaries was a more important factor in the electoral competition. The basic details of the electoral map are well-known.[67] Ireland was considerably over-represented; expanding suburbs were considerably under-represented. However, the Liberal advantage from 'inflated' Irish support was partially countered by an over-weighting of small boroughs and the generous treatment of rural areas, both of which favoured the Tories. There was no shortage of predominantly working-class seats which Labour might hope to capture. Blewett identified more than 110 in England alone, and there were many more in Scotland and Wales. Moreover, although many mining seats, particularly in South Wales, were extremely large, there were still at least thirty-six

---

[65] Sheffield T&LC Mins, 13 Oct. 1908. For similar problems, Huddersfield Labour and Socialist Election Comm. Mins, 14 June 1910, Oldham LRC Mins, 3 July 1913 and below, pp. 244, 246.

[66] *Lib. Agent,* Oct. 1906, correspondence between J. Walker of the local ILP and F.J., FJ 1908/156, 160, 202, 208, 212 and B. Riley to F.J., FJ 1908/238. For inner-city Leeds, Leeds LF Finance Comm. Mins, 10 Sept. 1912. See also *Hull Daily News,* 13 Sept. 1912; MLF Mins, 20 Jan. 1910. Other constituencies in this group would include Finsbury Holborn, Sheffield Central, and Liverpool Exchange, although the allocation of duplicates could influence Labour's performance at municipal elections in any town with a central shopping area (e.g. Keighley LA Mins, 23 Sept. 1904, and *South Wales Argus,* 2 Nov. 1907). For the half a dozen seats where young men were reputedly disproportionally Labour, memo by J.R. Seager, 16 Nov. 1911, PRO CAB 37/108/148, but see below, pp. 410–11, for the extent of this after 1918.

[67] For the following, Blewett, *Peers,* pp. 364–8, 488–94, Gregory, *Miners,* Appendix B. See also below, p. 392.

in which this occupational group (generally more Labour-inclined than most) was a preponderant element.

Three other features of the constituency map deserve comment. There were twenty-two grouped boroughs. This meant that in Wales, for example, the industrial ports, Newport and Cardiff, were attached to small agricultural market towns. This watered down the radicalism of the industrial areas, and at the same time created a solidly agricultural constituency; both factors generally helped the Tories, and damaged the Progressive parties.[68] On the other hand, the Progressives benefited from the fact that there were twenty-three double member boroughs. This eased the often difficult problem of which Progressive party was to contest a seat. There were also thirty Parliamentary Boroughs, divided into 111 constituencies, many of which were dominated by a single social class. This favoured parties with a homogeneous social base, but there were other repercussions. As in the double member boroughs, negotiations between Liberal and Labour parties could be easier, since the *quid pro quo* of a free run in one division of a Parliamentary Borough would inevitably be the absence of opposition in another. There was no gerrymandered limit to the size of the Labour party; the nature of the parliamentary boundaries *favoured* its attempt to become established as a political force.[69]

VII

It is unnecessary to analyse the municipal franchise in depth because in most respects it was plagued by the same laws, and the same problems, as the parliamentary franchise. The relationship between the parliamentary and local franchise became fairly straightforward following the Municipal Corporations Act of 1882 and the Local Government Act of 1888. The local franchise differed by excluding freemen, lodger, and service voters. It included occupiers whose property was valued at less than £10 and unmarried female householders.[70] Subsequent Acts created a wider franchise for all local elections in Scotland, Ireland, and London, and for Parish, Rural District, Urban District, and Guardians' elections in provincial England and Wales, by adding all parliamentary voters, including non-resident property owners, to the register. The more 'signifi-

---

[68] Pelling, *Social geography,* pp. 352–4, and also pp. 403–5 for the similar position in Scotland.
[69] See below, e.g. pp. 145–6, 260.
[70] Established by *Drax v Ffooks* (1896), i, 238. This was intriguingly ignored by the revising barrister in Birmingham, who enfranchised a married woman (*Lib. Agent,* Oct. 1912, *Local Govt. Chron.,* 13 Sept. 1913).

cant' County and Municipal Borough contests, outside London, were still held on the narrower franchise.

The bulk of the municipal electorate in the provinces thus consisted of the 5.5 million male householders (who also had the parliamentary vote). To this should be added 900,000-1,000,000 unmarried female burgesses, and an unknown, but no doubt numerically less significant, group of property owners with low-value properties.[71] The political effects of the difference between the municipal and parliamentary franchises were probably not substantial. The exclusion of service and lodger voters from the municipal roll may have been to the Progressives' advantage. Service voters were often working class, but grooms, caretakers, chauffeurs, and shop assistants were not known for their Progressive views. The service franchise, one Liberal commented, could be abolished 'without (it) costing the Liberal agent a day of regret'.[72] The lodger vote was also not overwhelmingly Liberal. In Edinburgh and Glasgow, the Liberals claimed the support of 45 and 28 per cent of the lodger vote respectively. Figures for lodger claims in the revision courts cited earlier suggest a general Conservative advantage on the lodger franchise.[73] Conservative election agents favoured lodger and service voters being granted the municipal vote, a further indication of their political views. Nevertheless, in most constituencies lodger and service voters were a small part of the electorate, and their exclusion was therefore of no great advantage to the Progressive parties.[74] The inclusion of small property owners (around 2 per cent of the municipal electorate in Colchester, for example) could hardly have had a broad impact. However, the people enfranchised by this provision were mainly small shopkeepers, and in the wards which contained the town's main shopping area, they could be a considerable municipal force.[75]

The major difference, and the crucial question, is the political attitude of the female householders who made up perhaps 16 per cent of the municipal electorate. Urban geographers analysing the 1881 Census have

---

[71] J. Burns memo, n.d. Feb. 1912, LG MS C/17/3/7. The more usual estimate was 1 million (Pugh, *Electoral reform,* p. 35). In Colchester 82 per cent of municipal voters were householders, 16 per cent women, 2 per cent property owners (*Electoral Register,* 1915).

[72] *Lib. Agent,* July 1897.

[73] Blewett, *Peers,* p. 362, and above, p. 106. See also *Lib. Agent,* Oct. 1897. For Labour lodgers in e.g. Chester-le-Street and Woolwich, G. Jacques to J.R.M., 16 Apr. 1906, LP GC 3/140, W. Barefoot to J.R.M., 18 May 1906, LP GC 4/450. The position may have been rather different in London.

[74] Nat. Soc. of Cons. Agents Mins, 26 Feb. 1897.

[75] In the Bolton Exchange ward, for example, half the electorate qualified by virtue of their ownership of shops, warehouses or offices (*Bolton Burgesses' Roll, 1911*). Peers also had the municipal vote.

shown that there were numerous working-class women who were heads of households, at least where employment prospects were reasonably good. However, there has been no systematic attempt by political historians to determine whether these women were part of the municipal electorate. Fortunately, contemporaries were very concerned with this issue, because at one time it appeared that female municipal voters might also obtain the parliamentary vote. The results of Edwardian enquiries varied. A WLF survey concluded that 65 per cent of women municipal voters were working class; an ILP survey put the figure at 82 per cent; a limited survey of some northern towns put the figure slightly higher. Investigations held for the Liberal Cabinet showed that the women's franchise reflected the social composition of the constituency. The ILP survey was the broadest, but the results were strongly attacked. Much of the criticism of the survey methods was justified.[76] The ILP defined 'wage-earners' as 'working class', in order to make the task of gathering data more manageable. The branches which gathered the information cut even more corners. The Hull and Glasgow branches, for example, presumed that all enfranchised residents of working-class areas were working class, and conversely that all residents of middle-class areas came from this social group. Usually, however, the work was done by constituency canvass. Forty ILP branches canvassed nearly 60,000 women. There were returns from Norwich, Shrewsbury, and York, as well as from more industrial areas, although the sample was not weighted. Given this, and the definition employed, the figure of 82 per cent probably overstates the working-class proportion of the women's municipal electorate. Contemporary investigations, and the 1881 Census returns, show that in working-class districts many older, single, working-class women and widows were lodgers. Some widows in particular would have received poor relief. In either event they were ineligible.[77]

Nonetheless, and as contemporaries recognised, class composition was only an indication of the problem which really concerned them: the women's likely voting preferences. Many Liberal Federations argued from experience that women municipal voters were overwhelmingly Conservative. Some Labour candidates also blamed the 'women's vote' for their defeat in municipal elections, although at the same time others claimed

[76] People's Suffrage Federation, *Facts about franchise: working women and the limited suffrage bill* (1910); S. Rowbotham, *Hidden from history* (2nd edn., 1974), p. 83. For the 1881 Census information, Savage, *Preston*, pp. 72–3, Emerson, 'Lodgings market in Exeter', pp. 105–8. See also Pugh, *Electoral reform*, p. 34.

[77] ILP Census records, ILP MS; J. King and F. W. Rafferty, *Our electoral system: the demand for reform* (1912), p. 28; deputation of women's suffrage societies to Sir George Cave, 14 Nov. 1917, PRO HO 45/10842/337622; Savage, *Preston*, p. 73, Emerson, 'Lodgings market in Exeter', pp. 107–9.

it as the explanation of their victory.[78] The Secretary of the East of Scotland Liberal Federation argued that in working-class areas women were as Liberal as the men. This is close to being a sociologically defensible statement, although, because the enfranchised women were mainly elderly widows and unmarried women, we might expect them to be marginally more Conservative.[79] The exclusion of the more Tory lodger and service voters may have balanced any political bias in the women's electorate. The political balance of the women's vote might have influenced delicately balanced contests – if the women voted – but it did not introduce a major class or political bias into the municipal electorate.

The electoral significance of the difference between the municipal and parliamentary franchises could be tested by examining party votes in comparable parliamentary and municipal contests (provided voters in municipal elections did not switch their allegiance). If the municipal franchise was prejudiced against one particular party, then its municipal performance would suffer *vis-à-vis* its parliamentary showing. Unfortunately, mismatch between boundaries, and differences in the candidature patterns of local and parliamentary contests, makes extensive comparison for elections in this period very difficult.[80] However, the West Ham example (Table 4.8) suggests that disparities between a party's performance in local and parliamentary elections were small and easily explained by factors such as differential turnout. The inclusion of women voters, in West Ham at least, did not create a distinctly more Conservative electorate.

The second aspect of the electoral framework – the nature of the boundaries – was again a more influential factor in determining electoral outcomes. The existence of solidly working-class wards in most areas made it possible for parties dependent on this group to build an electoral base in a number of constituencies. As ward electorates were often small, concentrated occupational or religious groups could be very electorally powerful: 'Catholic', 'Dockers', or 'Railwaymen's' wards *were* differentiated, but candidates respected and supported by these groups had a

---

[78] For Labour comments, *East Anglian D.T.,* 3 Nov. 1913, *Wakefield Express,* 8 Nov. 1913, *Accrington Division Gazette,* 8 Nov. 1913.

[79] Women's voting behaviour in the inter-war years has been examined in several recent and little known studies, albeit with scant attention to the real nature of the post-war franchise (J. G. Francis and G. Peel, 'Reflections on generational analysis: is there a shared political perspective between men and women?', *Political Studies* (1978), J. Rasmussen, 'Women in Labour: the flapper vote and party system transformation in Britain', *Electoral Studies* (1984), Savage, *Preston,* pp. 172–3).

[80] See also below, pp. 149, 459–61.

Table 4.8 *Municipal and parliamentary polls compared, West Ham South parliamentary constituency and wards of West Ham CB, 1910*

	Municipal election, November 1910		Parl. election, December 1910	
	MA[a]	Lab.	C.	Lab.
West Ham	1,402	1,118	4,820	9,508
Tidal Basin	329	1,161		
Plaistow	1,119	1,378		
Hudson's	951	1,314		
Custom House	566	1,390		
Canning Town	293	965		
Total votes	3,660	7,326	4,820	9,508
	33.31%	66.69%	33.60%	66.40%

Notes:

[a] Municipal Alliance. The Municipal Alliance was a Tory-backed group.

Source: Stratford Express and F. W. S. Craig, *British Parliamentary Election Results, 1885–1918* (1974).

clear advantage.[81] There was every opportunity to embark on political campaigns which would be both cheap and effective. The nature of ward boundaries was ideal for a developing party with a socially or occupationally 'homogeneous' electoral constituency.[82]

The electoral framework in which Edwardian political parties operated was not overwhelmingly biased against the working class, or against parties which were based more heavily on this social group. It gave the Tories, as the party of property, a small general advantage, and an important cushion of support in areas where the plural vote was concentrated. The major bias was against women and younger men. All women were excluded from the parliamentary franchise by law, and married women were also excluded from the municipal electorate. The restricted municipal franchise consisted largely of widows and elderly spinsters. The only means by which single men could qualify for the parliamentary vote were the complex and anomalous lodger and service franchises (they were still excluded in provincial England and Wales from most municipal con-

---

[81] The Labour party suffered a number of electoral setbacks in 1908 because of its views on Catholic education. This was 'particularly common' in Lancashire (A.P. to F. Hargreaves, 11 Nov. 1908, LP/EL/08/1/61).

[82] Some boroughs (e.g. Bolton, Bootle, Dudley, Mansfield, and York) contained double member wards. As with double member boroughs, these could be used to facilitate inter-party co-operation.

tests). Age and housing tenure were the best guides to enfranchisement in the provinces. If the causes of disfranchisement in the larger cities were a little different, the electorate was still not substantially prejudiced against any one particular party. The nature of ward and parliamentary boundaries allowed parties with a spatially or occupationally concentrated base to build a core of support. Labour *and* the Tories might expect to benefit from this. However, the fact that these occupationally dominated wards seldom dominated parliamentary seats, except in mining areas, also made it essential for a successful party to have a broader appeal if it was to become a major force. If Labour was to turn a platform into a stage, it needed to convince a range of people that it had the policies, and the commitment, to represent their interests.

Chapter 5

The North-West

The North-West had a pivotal role in the two-party politics of the 1890s. The vast majority of the area's innumerable working-class seats returned Conservatives. This made a very substantial difference to a party whose principal support came from the middle class and farmers. The Liberal party's reversal of this position in 1906, and its ability to hold much of the captured terrain in 1910, ensured that the national electoral balance tilted sharply in its favour. The Progressive Alliance had been formed in part to facilitate this change. The North-West was the foundation-stone of the Liberals' new ideological/strategic stance, and the platform for its success. Alliance with Labour was meant – by the Liberals – to reinforce their position. However, if Labour expanded beyond the position of a useful ally, and the agreement broke down, it could return the Liberal party to its late Victorian depression.

In discussing the impact and significance of the electoral changes in this area, it is important to note that the North-West was not a single geographical and political unit, but a series of partially over-lapping sub-regions with quite distinct political traditions and economic structures.[1] Liverpool had its economic and political hinterland extending northwards to the Ribble (West Lancashire) as did Manchester (the textile belt). In the northern part of the region, Cumbria was as much a part of Scotland as it was of Lancashire, while the weaving towns around Accrington and Burnley had more in common with the adjacent towns in Yorkshire than with seats in South or West Lancashire. Where the economic/political spheres met (roughly along a line through Blackburn, Leigh, and Warrington) there was a confused mix of political and social forces.

West Lancashire was unshakeably Tory. The combination of casual, unskilled, and dangerous employment, and squalid social conditions, helped create a conservative and pessimistic culture, based on short-term interest, drinking, gambling, violence, fatalism, the pawnbroker, and

[1] This distinction forms the central theme of J. K. Walton's, *Lancashire: A social history* (Manchester, 1987). See also Pelling, *Social geography,* esp. pp. 258–9, 264–5, 331.

an acerbic hedonism. Irregular earnings and probable injury made 'Liberal' support for forward planning, education, and self-help seem an irrelevance. A xenophobic Protestant Conservatism had powerful roots in a religious/ethnic/economic hostility to the Catholic Irish. Political Conservatism also stressed an affinity with male working-class social interests, particularly the right to pleasure. The Tories were also frequently collectivists. They used municipal intervention to support and maintain a troubled local economy, and began to advocate similar remedies at the national level. Municipal collectivism, hostility to alien immigration, and support for tariff reform, were all portrayed as pathways to economic security.[2]

In most textile towns economic and social conditions were much better. A tradition of economic progress via co-operation with Liberal employers, and a Liberal sympathy for labour's interests and religion (Nonconformity) was welded into a Liberal political culture. However, this political culture was never totally dominant in the cotton spinning belt or in the Cumbrian industrial towns. The workforce in these areas was occupationally and religiously fragmented. The spinner's status as a labour aristocrat was very brittle; the workforce in shipbuilding towns like Barrow was dependent on the prosperity of single (Tory) employers, and on military orders.[3] Economic conditions encouraged a social conservatism which was reinforced by the Anglican-dominated educational system. Many cotton towns had a sufficiently weak local economy, a large enough Catholic element, and a strong enough tradition of working-class Conservatism, to embrace a close copy of Liverpool's abrasive Tory collectivism. There were some areas in and around Manchester where the economic/political pattern was even closer to the Liverpool model. It was only in the more economically and religiously homogeneous weaving towns in north Lancashire that a Liberal political culture was almost unchallenged. Here Free Trade and industrial co-operation seemed vital to prosperity. Liberal employers pragmatically accepted union demands on specific issues. Nonconformity reigned supreme. A Radical/Centrist alliance created a relevant, and usually electorally acceptable, political image.

---

[2] Savage, *Preston*, pp. 137–45, Fowler, 'Hyde', pp. 49–50, Clarke, *Lancashire Liberalism*, Chapter 3; J. R. Harris and T. C. Barker, *A Merseyside town in the Industrial Revolution. St Helens, 1750–1900* (Liverpool, 1954), p. 476, Waller, *Liverpool*, passim, Howell, *ILP*, pp. 204–9. For Tory municipal collectivism in 'Liberal' areas, e.g. *Burnley Express*, 3 Nov. 1909, 2 Nov. 1910.
[3] For this and much of the following, White, *Trade union militancy*, Chapter 3 and H. A. Turner, *Trade union growth, structure and policy* (1962), pp. 108–14.

The Liberals nonetheless had to challenge the Tories' hold over at least a portion of the working-class vote in the North-West if they were to solve the problem of the 1890s and become the party of government. The New Liberalism took root in Manchester and gradually spread into the surrounding area. However, before 1910 in particular the New Liberal message was mediated, and at times diluted, by the balance of institutional power within constituency Liberal parties. This was not necessarily disastrous. The degree of New Liberal penetration of constituency Liberal politics was not the touchstone of political viability; other Liberalisms retained some purchase especially in the textile belt either because they appeared to deliver economic prosperity, or because they incorporated prejudices which were more popular than the New Liberals' ideas. To differing extents, even these Liberal parties supported Centrist policies which aimed at making economic prosperity more secure. A leaven of New Liberal populistic hostility to the rich and support for the redistribution of wealth could help to reinforce local Liberal allegiances. Parties which rejected this injection of new ideas (perhaps because of institutional conservatism) might be weakened, but, if older ideas still retained their purchase, then the absence of a New Liberal input would have little effect.

Because a Nonconformist Radicalism had little purchase in West Lancashire, and in some parts of Manchester, Liberal Imperialists frequently dominated Liberal constituency politics. Nonetheless, by 1906, New Liberal ideas (as opposed to Radical/Centrist policies) were being adopted in seats in and around Manchester and in parts of West Lancashire in part because change was essential if the Tories were ever to be defeated. However, some weak organisations were in the pockets of a powerful conservative Liberal elite, and this institutional power kept new ideas in check even when they were more likely to be successful than old practices (Section I).

Labour similarly had to cope with its (Socialist) past. If it was to alter its electoral position, it had to abandon its disdain for humdrum aspects of working-class life. It had to support policies which people struggling to stay one step ahead of poverty could regard as sufficiently tangible. Where Socialist politics persisted after 1906, Labour's attempts to be seen as a realistic party of reform were undermined. However, there was growing party support for an accommodation with local material and social interests. In West Lancashire, where the ILP had put down few roots, the process was comparatively easy once some momentum was generated. The process was much slower in the textile belt, since Socialist activity had a long history and deep roots. There were bitter internal power struggles, and few electoral successes (Section II).

After 1910 the Liberals tightened the screw. Although New Liberal policies were not perfectly adapted to the economic problems faced by workers in West Lancashire, who needed higher, more regular, wages, not state welfare, the New Liberalism at least offered some action and a more assertively pro working-class rhetoric. It became a significant element in Liberal politics. In the textile belt, New Liberal candidates and ideas added a leaven of economic and social radicalism to the party image. The emergence of new industrial problems was a challenge which local Liberals did not ignore, nor one which necessarily undermined their position on a broad front (Section III).

Labour also continued its process of adapting and growing in accordance with local structures and needs. In West Lancashire, and in the similar, formerly Tory, parts of Manchester, Labour aligned itself with defensive working-class needs, and adopted a political language which at times differed dramatically from the Liberals'. However, the factors which told against the Liberals were only partially countered by Labour. A revitalised Conservative party remained in control in West Lancashire at least (although a Progressive pact was more successful in Manchester). Moreover, when the Liberals in West Lancashire adopted a radical approach, Labour's advance was partially retarded.

In the rest of Lancashire, Labour's gradual accommodation to local interests, and to a political culture which was already represented by an evolving Liberal party, meant little progress. Change was contested and restricted. The expansion of trade unionism and industrial unrest after 1910, and an imbalance in Liberal politics which gave old Liberal issues an unpopular prominence, together created some opportunities, particularly in northern Lancashire. Labour could occasionally construct an alternative by exploiting particular configurations of circumstances. It could also capitalise on the disaffection of Statist groups whose interests were currently under-represented. In the main, however, the weaving *and* spinning seats in the textile belt remained Liberal; Labour echoed the Liberals or floundered in disarray (Section IV). The geographical distribution of Liberal–Labour electoral support thus made the Progressive Alliance pragmatically sensible. Co-operation might win seats in West Lancashire; conflict meant certain Progressive defeats. Elsewhere, Labour was too weak, and the Liberals too popular, to justify conflict. Moreover, the balance of power in Liberal and Labour institutional politics made Progressive accommodation a more feasible option than ever before. The Progressive Alliance survived (Section V).

I

Nonconformist businessmen and the classic old Liberal issues of Free Trade, education, and temperance reform dominated Liberal politics in 1906. Old Liberal magnates governed Liberal politics in most of West Lancashire and in many textile towns. The ultra-traditional *Liverpool Daily Post* and *Lancashire Daily Post* (based at Preston) were the major Liberal means of communication in West Lancashire. They sympathised with the Liberal Imperialists; and, like most Liberal Imperialists in the constituencies, they showed little interest in 'national efficiency', domestic reform, or collectivist programmes.

Nonetheless change was under way. In the 1890s Manchester radicals effected a coup. They drew support from Arthur Haworth and George Agnew, members of prominent local Liberal families, and from politicians active in working-class areas. With the Whips' support, financial and executive power was concentrated in the hands of the newly formed Manchester Liberal Federation. The radicals used this to give the interests of working-class areas a primacy in policy making which they would not otherwise have enjoyed. Municipal candidates were selected with 'advice' from the MLF, and with the assistance of William Royle, the Progressive organiser and wirepuller. They were increasingly drawn from the party's radical wing. The MLF municipal programme (based on that of the LCC Progressives) encompassed many Labour demands. Labour municipal candidates were given free runs in some areas as part of a Progressive electoral strategy.[4] Parliamentary candidates, like Haworth and Schwann in Manchester, Agnew and Byles in Salford, took the radical message into their parliamentary campaigns.[5] The *Manchester Guardian*, staffed by Hobson, Hobhouse, C. P. Scott and his allies, became the mouthpiece and the medium for Manchester's New Liberal radicalism. It was the largest, most prestigious, Liberal newspaper in the area. It helped make Manchester the political, as well as the economic, fulcrum of the textile belt.

Manchester Liberalism was easily reconstructed. There were few prominent and powerful conservative Liberals to resist change, and most of the wealthy local Liberal families were willing to embrace New Liberal ideas. Their financial support, and the centralisation of power in the MLF, made it easier to seize the reins of power. Moreover, Conservatism

[4] Manch. Liberal Union Mins, esp. 2 Mar. 1894; D. K. Royle, *William Royle of Rusholme* (Manchester, 1924), esp. pp. 26–32; E. D. Record to H. J. Wilson, 28, 31 Aug. 1909, Wilson MS 5919, J. Hill, 'Manchester and Salford politics and the development of the Independent Labour Party', *IRSH* (1981), pp. 190–2.

[5] Byles, formerly editor of the Progressive *Bradford Observer,* had been a *Labour* candidate in 1900.

was so strong in parts of the city that the Progressive strategy had considerable purchase. The institutional position in West Lancashire was less favourable to change. The existing leadership was unlikely to lead a radical reconstruction of Liberal politics, and in some areas it was too powerful to be displaced. In the textile belt, Liberal millowners played a significant role in local life, and also frequently owned, or dominated, local newspapers which reflected their views. New Liberal views penetrated these areas (especially through the *M.G.*), and they were well-received by the Liberal rank and file. However, an Old Liberal/Centrist alliance would not easily step aside.

Nonetheless, the basic structure of Liberal politics was changing. The radicals were gaining influence. The extension of the franchise in 1884–5 meant that many 'county' seats were swamped by working-class textile workers and miners. The ILP's emergence further intensified the competition for working-class votes. The pace of political activity was stepped up. Municipal elections were hotly contested.[6] Most parties had professional agents by 1910, but the volunteer was the backbone of party organisation. Registration work, public meetings, and literature distribution were deemed essential. During parliamentary elections, activists were called on to distribute thousands of leaflets and hold several meetings each evening. This was only possible if parties had a large and involved membership. Formerly 'exclusive' Liberal organisations and Clubs had to lower their sights in order to attract new members; central Liberal Clubs declined as neighbourhood Liberal Clubs grew. In Bolton, Chorley, Leigh, Preston, and Rochdale, for example, the minimum subscription rate for Liberal membership was lowered to just one shilling by 1906. There was also a growing number of organisations for women and the young. In Preston, Rochdale, Middleton, and probably other seats, the newly 'popular' Reform Clubs, and other groups, were integrated into the Liberal machine. Many of these groups urged political changes on constituency leaders. New 'ginger groups' such as the New Century Society in Liverpool, the Progressive League in Preston and Warrington, the Forward Movement and 95 Club in Rochdale, and Gladstone League in Burnley, aided in many instances by the Young Liberals, were actively pressurising party leaders to adopt new policies.[7]

More political work put a strain on constituency finances. This could lead to the continued influence of a conservative elite. In Manchester

---

[6] Towns such as Ashton, Bury, Hyde, and Stalybridge contained few wards, and all of these would be contested. In larger towns (or those with more, and smaller, wards) it was more common to find solidly Tory enclaves which might go uncontested.

[7] G. Jones (thesis), pp. 205, 213–15, 229–36; Trodd (thesis), p. 362; *Widnes Examiner*, 14 Mar. 1914. For Rochdale, F. W. Hirst, *Alexander Gordon Cummins Harvey* (1926), pp. 33, 40, 61; *Rochdale Observer*, 9 Jan., 6 Mar., 16 June, 10 July, 6 Oct. 1909.

the problem was in part circumvented by the centralisation of power in the MLF. In the cotton spinning district a more numerous, more stable, and more involved, membership, and an elaborate system of Liberal Clubs, played a larger part in the financial solvency of constituency parties. Small, regular, bazaars, organised by party activists, helped to pay a major proportion of constituency running costs. Larger bazaars, held perhaps once every ten years, usually raised at least £1,000. Given occasional contributions from wealthy Progressive sympathisers, a contribution of perhaps £50 per year from a radical MP., and election expenses from the Whips' Office, many Liberal associations could escape a financial dependence on 'Old Liberal' manufacturing interests. However, if Old Liberal money played a progressively less significant part in local politics in some parts of the textile belt, in West Lancashire, and in some parts of northern Lancashire in particular, a few individuals still frequently continued to exercise financial and political control.[8]

As the rank and file members' prestige and role increased, so the party machinery had to change. Ward committees and other groups were more frequently guaranteed representation on the Divisional executive. Moreover, as some millowners abandoned their central role in Liberal politics, they were replaced by men who were more amenable to New Liberal policies. The radical parson, newspaper editor, or journalist entered the political leadership. Blackburn had the Rev. Fred Hibbert and T. P. Ritzema, editor of the Progressive *Northern Daily Telegraph*; Rochdale had the Rev. T. P. Spedding and W. W. Hadley, editor of the Progressive *Rochdale Observer;* F. L. Tillotson, owner of a Lancashire newspaper empire, and at least some of his staff were prominent in Bolton. In Oldham, the local Liberal newspaper supplied Councillors Rennie and Hurst. Many Oldham Councillors and municipal candidates, local Labour officials also reported, were former working-men or still practising artisans.[9] As more Councillors and candidates were drawn from these social

---

[8] *Todmorden Advertiser,* 24 June 1913 (noting an income from 'levies' of £36 from just two Liberal Clubs); *Rochdale Obs.,* 13, 27 Feb. 1909, 12 Feb. 1914; G. Jones (thesis), pp. 219, 234–6; *Rossendale Free Press,* 3 Jan. 1914; Clarke, *Lancashire Liberalism,* Chapter 8, ? to R. D. Denman, n.d. Aug. 1909, Denman MS 3; *Eccles and Patricroft Journal,* 15 May 1914, noting a bazaar which raised £1,600; Waller, *Liverpool,* pp. 224–5.

[9] G. Jones (thesis), esp. p. 187; Hirst, *A.G.C. Harvey,* pp. 32, 39–40. For Oldham, ? to A. P., 16 Nov. 1908, LP/EL/08/1/128. For problems finding men of substance to stand for Liberal positions or as Councillors, Stockport LA mins, 1908–9 passim. The local press was so important that the Liberal Chief Whip secretly bailed out the Liberal *Carlisle Journal,* which was on the verge of collapse (J. Herbert to H. K. Campbell, 8 Feb. 1912, R. D. Denman to H. K. Campbell, 23 Feb. 1912, Denman MS 4/1).

and political groups, municipal politics changed. The provision of municipal services became more widespread. Liberal Councils moved to the
centre-left.[10]

Nonetheless, Liberal politics in the cotton-spinning towns were not
simply dominated by New Liberal social reformers. Centrist Liberals
shared local trade union leaders' concerns with industrial prosperity (the
latter because it determined their members' financial security). In addition
to the Liberals' contacts with local voters through the Liberal Clubs,
in seats like Rochdale the major textile union leaders were also important
figures in local Liberal politics, and (as in Oldham and Bolton) the Liberals
and the 'Labour' Trade Council were on good terms. Economic issues
of particular interest to the union (such as fair wage contracts on council
work) were readily supported. Industrialists like George Harwood (MP
for Bolton) supported 'Labour' policy on unemployment. Trades Councils, and rank and file union activists, found that a Liberal party which
combined support for some New Liberal principles with Centrist attempts
to protect their economic prosperity catered for many of their interests
and needs. State-promoted social reforms – the provision of a social and
economic safety net as a means to individual improvement – did not sap
industrial success or replace it.[11] They were a bonus and a supplement.

In the 1890s, Liberals in the northern weaving towns had rigidly adhered
to a tough-minded, localist, Liberal conservatism to such an extent that
the Liberals' image was not even reinforced by the 'labourist' politics
of the Liberal Centrists. Self-help, temperance, and Nonconformist status
issues reigned supreme. Even after 1906, municipal politics were comparatively untouched by new policies or new patterns of thought.[12]

In West Lancashire too local Liberalism was unmoved by the forces
of change. Party membership was low; organised radical pressure groups
were defeated.[13] However, radical Centrists and New Liberals were
stronger on the outer fringes of the Liverpool hinterland, where other
traditions and economic structures were stronger. There were at least

[10] For the Liberals' views, *Oldham Chronicle* leader, 6 Apr. 1914, J. Hill, 'Working-class
      politics in Lancashire 1885–1906: a regional study in the origins of the Labour party',
      Keele Ph.D. thesis 1969, pp. 360–1 (Bolton), T. P. Ritzema to P. Illingworth, 10 July
      1913, LG C/5/4/2 (Blackburn). See also views of Liberal Housing Reform Association
      Councillor, and candidates from working-class wards in Rochdale, *Rochdale Obs.*,
      3 July 1909, 2 Nov. 1910, 2 Nov. 1911.
[11] W. Ratcliffe to A.P., 11 Nov. 1908, LP/EL/08/1/22, J.S.M. to his parents, 5 June
      1908, MID 8/13 [Bolton]; J Firth to J.R.M., 28 Dec. 1902, LRC 5/149, *Rochdale Obs.*,
      2 Nov. 1910, 3 Nov. 1913 (Rochdale). See also below, pp. 151–3.
[12] Trodd (thesis), esp. pp. 355–7 for an excellent analysis of Burnley politics.
[13] For the defeated Liberal radicals in Preston and Liverpool, *L.D.P.*, 23 Mar. 1910 and
      Liverpool Courier, 2 Nov. 1907.

two Trades Council members on the twelve man Liberal executive in Blackburn and the Liberals in Widnes, Warrington, and Birkenhead enjoyed good relations with local trade union leaders. Some Liberals began to support more municipal intervention. Moreover, Liberals throughout West Lancashire already recognised Labour's right to independent representation in municipal and parliamentary politics. Although the more conservative were unwilling to become members of a *Progressive* Alliance, they would accept strategic concessions for pragmatic reasons.

The chosen parliamentary candidates tended to reflect the locally dominant views. In Manchester and the surrounding areas, radical candidates became more common. In 1906, A. H. Scott, a provision merchant and former Secretary of the Bolton Shop Assistants' union, became the MP for Ashton-under-Lyne. Scott's views on unemployment and nationalisation placed him clearly on the Liberal left. He went on to vote with Labour, and against the Government, on several issues, and was generally seen by Labour MPs as a friend of the cause. In 1908, Churchill became a Manchester MP. At the same time, the younger sons of Old Liberal businessmen, as much professional politicians as anything else, became Liberal candidates in Leigh, Warrington, Radcliffe, and Bolton. Reinforced by Winston Churchill's deliberate and considerable focus on questions of trade and the production of wealth in his Lancashire speaking tour, they brought Centrist issues to the fore. In 1910, the New Liberal side of the reforming axis was strengthened by further changes in the Manchester area. C. T. Needham, a Manchester Progressive, was elected in South-West Manchester. Two London Progressives, Charles Russell and Spencer Leigh Hughes, replaced more conservative Liberal MPs in Salford South and Stockport. Francis Neilson, the land reformer, became MP for Hyde.[14] The radical Liberal message found sympathetic and enthusiastic expression. Nonetheless, the Centrists' weakness on some aspects of the radical Liberal programme, and the conservatism displayed by Liberals at the municipal level (for example in Stockport and Ashton), could modify or nullify attempts to create a new image. The Liberal image was not defined solely by Progressives or even by Centrists. Local perceptions of the party's image, and the rhetoric of that party's opponents, were bound to have an effect.[15]

In 1910, Liberal leaders in West Lancashire and the northern textile

[14] See Scott's own analysis of his politics, *West Ham Express,* 5 Nov. 1919. For Spencer Leigh Hughes' views, and those of Stockport Liberals, Stockport LA mins, 6 Dec. 1909, 6 Sept. 1910, and his autobiography, *Press, platform and parliament* (1918). For Needham, A.R. to M. K. Rowntree, 4 May 1911, AR MS. For Churchill, see introduction to his 1910 speeches, *The people's rights,* pp. 6–7.

[15] *Ashton under-Lyne Reporter,* 4 Nov. 1911, *Manchester Courier,* 2 Nov. 1909, both noting Liberal/Tory pacts.

towns ensured that the parliamentary election was fought on Free Trade and other old Liberal issues. The candidates in West Lancashire were Liverpool merchants and Welsh barristers, supplied by the Liverpool Liberal elite. Local politicians sought candidates who could reflect elements of a Tory political culture. The former Liberal Unionist, Thomas Barclay, was steamrollered into Blackburn; the former Tory Democrat, John Gorst, fought Preston.[16] However, this did not involve rejecting reform. Crawshay-Williams (Chorley, 1906) and Gorst (Preston, 1910) were keen collectivists. Moreover, by December 1910 Blackburn radicals were able to engineer the adoption of Henry Norman, formerly of the *Daily Chronicle* and now Secretary of the Budget League.[17] In the northern part of the region, two hitherto conservative Liberal associations (Burnley and Carlisle) adopted Philip Morrell and R. D. Denman as their candidates (apparently at the instigation of the Whips). Morrell was a New Liberal. Denman was a Fabian centralist. Both supported New Liberal proposals, although Denman also paid particular attention to the Statist interests of the numerous local railwaymen. Despite being opposed by Socialists, they praised local *Labour* organisations; Denman declared he would not have stood if Labour had fielded a candidate.[18]

The complexities of Lancashire Liberalism could not be ironed out by the *Manchester Guardian*. Neither could a radical candidate simply and easily counteract a contradictory local Liberal image. However, the Liberal party was not *necessarily* weaker because the New Liberalism did not assume a total primacy. Local roots in an accepted language and culture were extremely important for all parties. In the textile areas, a secular, middle-class, New Liberalism was less rooted than a Centrist Liberalism, which appeared to be the ideology of economic success. However, where these roots were maintained by grafting New Liberal support for social justice and security on to an economically successful Centrist Liberalism, the Liberal party became a more powerful force. The Liberals' optimum approach was to amalgamate old and new in a manner which created a positive party image. Labour's minimum task was to expose the weaknesses, fractures and inconsistencies in this Liberal image. It might also hope to provide a new approach which would sweep the Liberal party away.

[16] Bigham, *A picture of life,* pp. 229–32; Barclay, *Thirty Years,* pp. 319–20; Clarke, *Lancashire Liberalism,* pp. 235–6.

[17] Crawshay-Williams, *Simple story,* esp. pp. 50–2, 83–7. (C-W was Lloyd George's PPS, and had a similar temperament (see below, p. 293).) For Gorst, speech in Clarke, *Lancashire Liberalism,* p. 304 and for Norman, Murray, *People's Budget,* pp. 182, 189–90, 202–3.

[18] Trodd (thesis), cited above, fn. 12 and Carlisle LP AR 1907; Morrell, *Memoirs,* pp. 121, 125; *Carlisle Journal,* 7 Dec. 1909; *Carlisle Evening Journal,* 4 Nov. 1910.

II

Labour advocates of a more reforming political orientation had to overcome a powerful, institutionalised resistance to their ideas. SDF/ILP cooperation had been common in many parts of Lancashire before 1906, and it remained an institutionally popular option. Moreover, the Socialists' advocacy of ethical change, combined with a powerful condemnation of the immoral consequences of capitalism, had brought a degree of success in the more Nonconformist parts of the textile belt.[19] It grew from within a radical Liberal political culture. Socialists were a powerful force particularly in Blackburn, Burnley, and Manchester.[20] Nonetheless, their position was still weak. Ethical socialism was strong on hope, short on the means to convince the electorate that major economic change was possible. Socialism suffered from its rivals attempts to emphasise Socialist 'excesses'. Even by 1906, most trade unions in the cotton spinning belt were reluctant to throw their weight behind a Labour party associated with these groups. A Centrist Liberalism and Collectivist Conservatism represented powerful, and attractive, combinations of religious and economic appeals.

Labour had to prove its worth in a competitive environment. However, devising an alternative was no simple matter. There was no anti-Tory vacuum to fill; there were few workers whose economic and social position was not catered for by existing approaches. Although Liberals might co-operate with Labour in the double member boroughs, in seats like Accrington and Burnley strong, conservative, Liberal organisations had no desire to come to an arrangement. Moreover, Socialist organisations were themselves loath to sacrifice their independence or their radicalism and accept 'reforming' policies and electoral co-operation. Although Labour elements thought that moderation and co-operation were essential, this idea was fiercely resisted within the ILP.

The attempt to adopt a more moderate approach was most successful in West Lancashire. Here ethical socialism had proved as unpalatable as a 'moral' Liberalism (except in Preston, where, partially as a result of trade union involvement, the ILP had taken a more practical stance even before 1906). Socialist organisations were consequently pitifully weak. The Widnes ILP, for example, consisted of a dozen stalwarts, who met in a room over Boots the Chemists. In 1909, Labour officials found 'no evidence of any live fighting force' in the constituency which

---

[19] Howell, *ILP,* pp. 61–7 and Chapter 9. Lancashire *Socialist* leaders were often small businessmen and retailers, unlike *Labour* leaders, who were frequently union officials. See, e.g., *Rochdale Obs.,* 25 Oct. 1910, municipal candidates' nominations.

[20] For Manchester ILP politics, Hill, 'Manchester and Salford politics', N. Reid, 'Manchester and Salford ILP: a more controversial aspect of the pre-1914 era', *NWLH* (no number or date).

they might dignify by calling an 'organisation'. In Liverpool, the ILP was little more than 'an amateur dramatic society'.[21] It had been stronger in Blackburn, and to an extent in Preston and Barrow during the 1890s, but only in Blackburn was it still a powerful force by 1906.

In fact, Blackburn had one of the largest ILP branches in the country. A complex neighbourhood based political network was ably mobilised by Sam Higenbottom, the ILP's very competent agent. Local groups campaigned actively, drawing support from the party newspaper and from the inspirational rhetoric of Philip Snowden, the Labour MP. However, Blackburn was fairly close to the Pennines; it was more strongly Nonconformist, and less predominantly 'Irish', than any other major centre in the area.[22] The structural position was more favourable.

The *positive* attractions of Labour's stance in West Lancashire nonetheless need to be stressed. Perhaps 40 per cent of ILP activists in Blackburn, for example, were formerly Tories. Like Labour organisations in Preston, Barrow, and Liverpool, where many activists were also often former Tories, the Blackburn ILP survived by building on elements of a Tory political culture. It abandoned much of its ethical socialist ideological baggage. The new style Labour organisations advocated working-class municipal representation to ensure that their increasingly materialistic municipal policies on wages and hours were implemented. In 1905–6, James Sexton, the leader of the Liverpool dockers, and a powerful force in local Labour politics, demonstrated this attachment to 'Tory' political traditions even more fully. He focused attention on the threat to housing and jobs presented by the employment of Chinese and Jewish workers. This version of a traditionally 'Tory' economic/ethnic chauvinism was a potential means of overcoming the sectarian fragmentation which made Progressive victories so difficult. Equally, in Barrow, which was dominated by the Vickers shipyard and by the engineering union, Labour's success stemmed from ASE interest in craft representation, and from the party's support for specific union/industrial interests, rather than any affinity with Liberalism.[23]

Ethnic/religious issues still mattered. Indeed, they were so important that Labour's parlous unity, and its attempts to create an electoral base larger than the old Liberal vote, was soon endangered. In 1907–8 a

---

[21] J.S.M. to J. Hill, 22 Dec. 1909, LP/CAN/06/1/22, referring to Widnes, and G. E. Diggle, *A history of Widnes* (Widnes, 1961), pp. 119–20, 124, 126–7; Waller, *Liverpool,* pp. 159, 199. In Birkenhead, Labour was more moderate (Birkenhead T&LC *AR* 1908).

[22] *Workers' Tribune,* Aug. 1909; P.S. to I. Wainwright, 8 Jan. 1908, SH MS.

[23] Trodd (thesis), esp. p. 334 and election details, *Blackburn Labour Journal,* Oct. 1906; Waller, *Liverpool,* pp. 216–17 and Smith, 'Glasgow and Liverpool', esp. p.40. For Liberal recognition of the cultural/economic deficiencies of its policies in Liverpool, C.P.S. to Elibank, 5 Dec. 1911, CPS 332/55.

Liberal/Labour alliance at Westminster supported legislation to repeal the 1902 Education Act and introduce nonsectarian education. Many local Labour parties supported this traditional Liberal/Nonconformist policy. The 'Tory' working class, encouraged by the populistic campaigns generally associated with the Anti-Socialist Union, made its hostility clear. In Liverpool, the ASC&J withdrew from the LRC because it was 'propagating Secularism'. In Preston, the textile-dominated Trades Council and the ILP both disaffiliated from the LRC, the former because LRC policy was too 'Liberal' (i.e. it opposed separate religious education in the schools), the latter because it was not 'Liberal' (i.e. nonsectarian) enough. The Preston Tories, reinforced by new, popular, Catholic organisations, kept religious conflict to the fore. Labour's approach was seriously threatened by its continued links with the Liberal party and 'Liberal' views.[24]

Labour came through its trial in Blackburn and Barrow with greater ease. It had fewer Catholics to contend with. Moreover, in Blackburn the Trades Council demonstrated the party's roots in popular 'Tory' ideas by forcing the LRC to drop its commitment to nonsectarian education.[25] In both Blackburn and Barrow, Labour began to build on its success. The Barrow LRC, propped up by ASE money, and skilfully organised by Arthur Peters and later E. P. Wake, became a 'model' party. The close integration of the ILP and trade unions in Blackburn resulted in a 'practically perfect' organisation by 1908. Nonetheless, the revival of 'educationalist' and anti-capitalist tendencies (through the inspiration of Grayson's Right to Work campaigns), following in the wake of the education controversy, effectively decimated most weaker Labour organisations, and dented Labour's progress even in Barrow and Blackburn.[26] In Liverpool the organisation was already 'absolutely rotten' in 1907.[27] By 1908 there was 'no organisation worthy of the name'.[28] The Osborne Judgement 'became an excuse for those unions who, through indifference or hostility, preferred to save their coppers'. The party became financially dependent on a few middle-class activists.[29] In Preston, Labour was

---

[24] Waller, *Liverpool,* p. 235; Savage, *Preston,* pp. 157–60 and Morris (thesis), p. 52.

[25] Morris (thesis), p. 53. For the education issue generally, A. Thompson, 'The Liberal party and English Nonconformity *c* 1895–1914, with particular reference to education and licensing reform', Cambridge Ph.D. thesis in progress.

[26] Barrow LRC *AR* 1905–6, H. Hoyland to J.R.M., 27 Aug. 1903, LRC 10/3 and *Barrow News,* 21 Sept. 1907, 19 Sept. 1908 for labour's forces in Burnley, J. Frankland to A.P. 10 Nov. 1908, LP/EL/08/1/18, and Trodd (thesis), p. 345 for municipal campaigns extending into three-quarters of the constituency. For the Liberals' continued importance, below, p. 156.

[27] Mary Middleton to Mrs Middleton (J.S.M.'s mother), 11 Oct. 1907, MID 8/6. See also Boilermakers' *MR* Oct. 1907.

[28] J. Edwards to A.P., 8 Nov. 1908, LP/EL/08/1/103.

[29] LLRC *AR* 1910 and 1911. See similarly C. Anders to J.S.M., 2 Nov. 1910, LP/AFF 5/125.

'routed' in 1907, fielded no municipal candidates in 1908, and was in no position to fight the parliamentary election in 1910.[30] Elsewhere, attempts to form local organisations were immediately crushed.

These problems only compounded existing failures and deficiencies. In Blackburn, Labour was worried about its electoral prospects. The 1906 victory in Preston (a double member borough where Labour had considerable help from the Liberals) seemed even more fragile, while parliamentary campaigns in the Liverpool seats of Kirkdale and West Toxteth were outright failures. Municipal success was unusual. In Liverpool, Sexton captured the St Anne's ward (1905) and held it unopposed in 1908. Popular individuals won in Kensington (1905) and Edge Hill (1910), but only because the Tories were split. Nonetheless, and despite its problems, Labour was still a more viable political force than the Liberals. It was the only regular opposition to the Tories in six to seven wards. Similarly, by 1910 municipal Liberalism had almost disappeared in Barrow and had seriously declined in Blackburn. Both seats were Labour marginals in 1910, with success or failure being dependent on Liberal support.[31] Labour had established itself as an effective anti-Tory force in Blackburn and Barrow, and as a weak, but still potentially 'viable', anti-Tory party in Preston and Liverpool. It scarcely existed in some of the Tory seats which had a smaller working-class electorate. It was slowly and partially replacing the Liberals; it was not ready to challenge the Tories.

The Tories were able to practise 'Liverpudlian' politics in some parts of the textile belt, with a degree of success. However, only sections of a few seats in the Manchester/Salford area were Liberal deserts in 1906.[32] In the rest of the textile belt, Labour had to compete with a stronger, more rooted, Liberal opponent, in addition to a powerful Conservative party. Nonetheless, Labour performed very well in the Clitheroe constituency and in Manchester. The common feature was Labour's ability to adapt to specific local circumstances, to exploit local electoral spaces, and to offer a 'practical' alternative to the existing parties. The importance of early Socialist activity in the Clitheroe division is well-attested, but it is possible to overstate the extent to which Socialism influenced Labour politics and the party's subsequent electoral expansion. The seat was overwhelmingly Liberal until 1902, when the textile unions' interest in craft representation prompted the Liberals to concede the parliamentary seat to Labour. The most substantial political progress thus came *after* the

---

[30] *L.D.P.*, 2 Nov. 1907 and Savage, *Preston*, pp. 160–1.
[31] Waller, *Liverpool*, pp. 214–18, 247; *Barrow Herald*, 22 Jan. 1910.
[32] Hill (thesis), pp. 264–6, 506 fn. 103. For details of the East Manchester and West Salford constituencies, which contained some very poor areas, Hill (thesis), p. 18.

weavers', union became involved, and Labour became the political expression of the union membership's broad interests and outlooks. Each town in this weaving-dominated constituency had its own, closely knit, local weaving union.[33] The local Labour parties which the unions almost immediately set up were based on the unions' extensive network of local committees and collecting agents. Union funds, and an excellent union agent, turned this into an organisation which performed its formal functions with remarkable efficiency by 1906, and which remained in close contact with the electorate.[34] These popular links also ensured that there was nothing radical about official party policy. Shackleton, the MP, and the Labour Councillors who controlled Nelson's municipal politics from 1905-7, were Methodist temperance reformers and textile men. They opposed municipal 'extravagance' (cutting the rates in 1905), blamed unemployment on intemperance, and created a dour, protective, conservative image for the party. Reflecting local opinion, and contrary to the dictates of ILP policy, Shackleton supported the continued employment of 'half-timers', the teenagers who supplemented family income by spending half their time working in the mills and half their time at school. Some Labour policies were compatible with the views of local ILP activists, but others evidently were not. The Labour Councillors' conservatism and their reluctance to consider the views of party activists led to considerable internal opposition. The Nelson SDF was expelled from the LRC for its pains. Labour's roots in the community – and its base in 'loyalty' to a highly integrated union – combined to create a powerful, monolithic, centre-right Labour dynasty, similar to that established in mining areas after 1918. The new Labour party was playing to a wider audience than in the days when the ILP dominated labour politics, and it was succeeding. By 1907, it was reported that 'to all appearances the Liberal party in the Division has ceased to have an official organisation'. Labour had absorbed the Liberals' support by building a similar, but more socially rooted, appeal. In the 1910 parliamentary elections, it polled around 70 per cent of the vote.[35]

A similar process was taking place in the hitherto more Tory parts of Manchester, although a more diverse economic and social structure, and the absence of such a singly dominant trade union, ensured that the centre-right grouping was less institutionally powerful and less electorally successful. By 1906, MacDonaldite Labour moral reformers such as

---

[33] Howell, *ILP*, pp. 62–6 for the background material.

[34] Morris (thesis), pp. 29, 40; *Clitheroe Advertiser*, 3 Dec. 1909, *Colne and Nelson Times*, 28 Jan. 1910. There was a Nelson LRC News (and a Nelson Socialist Journal). See also Clitheroe Div. LP, *Agent's annual report* 1915.

[35] Hill (thesis), pp. 338–9, Morris (thesis), pp. 29, 55–6, 58, 67; *Colne Times*, 4 Oct. 1907. For the education question, Barker, *Education and politics*, p. 23.

T. D. Benson and J. R. Clynes, and powerful Lib/Lab elements, led
by George Kelly, had combined to moderate the ILP municipal programme. Moderate trade union activists became municipal candidates,
and (subsequently) moderate Labour Councillors. Some also became MPs
(Hodge in Gorton, Clynes in North-East Manchester, Kelly in South-West
Manchester). ILP branches and other ward organisations enjoyed some
autonomy, but not real power. Control over the city election agent, and
over the selection of municipal candidates, lay with the increasingly union-
dominated Manchester and Salford LRC.[36] There were no divisional
parties and therefore no constituency executives to rival the city Labour
elite. Even more than in Clitheroe, it was Labourist ideas, rather than
more radical ILP policies, which came to the fore, and which created
a positive image. Nonetheless, the tone of politics was different. 'Godless'
Manchester (unlike the Nonconformist Clitheroe division) was not the
place to put forward 'Liberal' policies such as temperance reform. The
greater significance of the Manchester Corporation as an employer, and
as a provider of economic benefits, encouraged a concern with municipal
wage rates and other, similar, questions. Labour tapped a 'Tory' collectivist tradition in appealing to the poorer, traditionally Tory, voters in
some parts of the city. Its electoral support in Manchester was noticeably
stronger in traditionally Tory areas. The Liberal party had collapsed
in the East Manchester and Gorton constituencies during the 1890s, and
Labour gradually came to dominate at least half of the municipal wards
in these seats (Bradford and Ardwick in East Manchester, Gorton and
Openshaw in the Gorton constituency). Labour or Socialist candidates
were also often successful in the poorest wards in Salford, although electoral defeats at the time of the education controversy reflected Labour's
ambivalent position with Salford's working-class Catholics (a function
of the ethical socialist tradition). The Liberals dominated the more
affluent, the more socially mixed, and the suburban wards, including
some which were in the Gorton and East Manchester seats: in these
wards, Labour usually came third.

Manchester's parliamentary politics generally reflected this position.
Gorton was captured by labour in 1906 and narrowly held in 1910.
Although the hitherto Tory constituency of East Manchester was captured
by a 'labour-minded' Liberal in 1906, Labour was the main Progressive
party in local elections. In 1910 the Liberals withdrew their parliamentary
candidate (despite some dissent) in recognition of this fact. Local organisational problems prevented a Labour contest in the docks-dominated West

---

[36] Hill, 'Manchester and Salford politics', pp. 198–9; Morris (thesis), pp. 72–3; Manch.
and Salford LRC AR, esp. 1905, 1906, 1909.

Salford seat.[37] There were no signs of a broader Labour 'breakthrough'. Liberal and Labour support was spatially distinct. Moreover, Labour's parliamentary representation was only secure if the Liberals did not split the 'Progressive' vote. The Progressive Alliance made sense here.

There was another side to Manchester politics. The ILP remained a powerful force. The Manchester Central branch, for example, continued to demand action on women's suffrage and opposition to the Liberal party with equal energy; other groups augmented and expanded the critique. In 1910 the Progressive Alliance, the symbol of Labour's more moderate approach, was disrupted by Socialist campaigns in South-West Manchester (McLachlan) and West Salford (A. A. Purcell). McLachlan was an official Labour candidate, despite his contacts with Socialists (like Purcell) who were outside the Labour party. However, both men fought without the support of local Labour MPs and against the wishes of many Labour officials.[38] McLachlan and Purcell had in fact already combined with local ILP leaders like Leonard Hall and others to develop a full critique of MacDonaldite Revisionism.[39] They had supported the 'Right to Work' candidates who conducted ill-prepared propagandist candidatures at the 1908 municipal elections. They had co-operated with the SDF during Dan Irving's parliamentary by-election campaign in North Manchester (also in 1908). McLachlan and Irving wished to fight for Socialist policies *within* the Labour party. Others disagreed, and formed the Manchester and Salford Socialist Representation Committee in 1909. McLachlan, Irving, Purcell, and the Right to Work candidates were convincingly defeated. In December 1910, South-West Manchester and West Salford were left to the Liberals. It appeared to contemporaries that the left's strategy, and its ideas, had taken a beating.[40]

Although Conservatism was an important force in the southern spinning belt (and an under-estimated force in some northern weaving towns), in the textile belt as a whole the Liberals were stronger than in Manchester. In the southern part of the textile belt, Labour faced more hostile con-

[37] J. Nuttall to A.P., 5 Nov. 1908, LP/EL/08/1/113 and report on West Salford by Peters, n.d. 1909, NEC Mins, n.d. 1909 (BLPES Coll. fo. 135). For the offer of the South Salford seat before 1906, Bealey and Pelling, *Labour and politics,* pp. 245–6.

[38] There was widespread support for concentration and the Progressive Alliance but not for subservience to the Liberals (J. Harker to J.R.M., 9 and 24 Oct. 1903, LRC 11/296 and 7, C. A. Bamford to J.R.M., 14 Mar. 1904, LRC 13/184/1, F.J. to J. E. Sutton, 13 Dec. 1909, F.J. 09/582, and J.S.M. to J.R.M., 28 Nov. 1910 and reply, 29 Nov. 1910, LP/MAC/09/1/13 and 14; Nuttall to A.P., above, fn. 37).

[39] See above, pp. 51–6. For local effects, N. Reid, 'Manchester and Salford ILP', Nuttall to A.P., above, fn. 37.

[40] Morris (thesis), pp. 239–43, N. Reid, 'Manchester and Salford ILP', p. 29, *ETU Journal,* Aug. 1909.

ditions than in Manchester or Clitheroe. A Centrist Liberalism was often
reinforced by some New Liberal influences and policies. Unlike Labour
organisations in Clitheroe and Manchester, Labour did not have the trade
unions full, moderating, support in most textile belt constituencies. The
moderates were institutionally weaker. This was particularly important
in the northern textile seats because here the weakness of Liberal organisations on economic and social reform (and their connections with local
employers) had created an electoral opening long before 'Labour' existed.
Some (large) SDF, supported by (small) ILP, branches and artisan activists
from the craft unions did quite well. In the 1906 elections, there were
several SDF/ILP candidates (in Burnley, Rochdale, Accrington) who
polled respectably despite Liberal opposition. If Socialists were unsuccessful, they were nonetheless a powerful and threatening force. With some
changes to accommodate more moderate voters, they could even become
a serious danger to the Liberals' ascendancy.

It could of course be argued that the Socialists did not need to moderate
their appeal, since they had already showed that voters could support
the radical left. Hyndman (the Burnley SDF parliamentary candidate in
1906) had argued in the election 'that it was absolutely necessary under
present conditions that one should go to the polls pledged to revolutionary
socialism and to nothing else'. However, Dan Irving (the local leader)
and the local party had consistently demanded action on unemployment,
housing, the scale of outdoor relief, and the provision of free school
meals. They aimed at establishing a link between Socialism and the desire
for a secure lifestyle, and had opposed the national SDF decision to work
outside the Labour party. They were successful because they had cornered
Labour's market as the 'practical' organisation. Nonetheless, they encouraged a degree of class confidence and conflict, were at least temperamentally different from many moderate Labour Socialists, and were fiercely
anti-Liberal.[41] It would not be easy to build such a base into a platform
for absorbing Liberal voters.

Attempts to expand the appeal of the more Socialist moral reformers
in Burnley came to grief. The Burnley LRC, formed in 1905, fell apart
in 1908 because of the SDF's insistent support for nonsectarian education.
Similarly, in Carlisle, Labour organisation collapsed when the SDF
insisted that municipal candidates should carry the 'Labour and Socialist'
label. As in Rochdale, further action on Labour lines seemed imposs-

---

[41] Hyndman cited in Clarke, *Lancashire Liberalism*, p. 300. Burnley Socialists showed
more distaste for formal organisational work (L. Rippon to A.P., 28 Nov. 1908, LP/EL/
08/1/46). The results of Liberal/Labour (and Socialist) clashes in parliamentary elections
are given in Appendix 3, pp. 452–3. For the major municipal results, pp. 459–61.

ible.[42] Moreover, in some southern cotton spinning seats where an ILP/SDF alliance was also strong (notably Ashton and Stalybridge), the Liberals and Tories had taken the opportunity and absorbed so much moderate union support that the position became fossilised. The only remaining electoral space was on the far left. Labour scarcely existed: the Socialists were unpopular and weak.

At the other extreme, by 1906 the double member boroughs of Bolton and Stockport had Labour MPs, and moderate organisations. This reflected the institutional power of the moderate spinning unions (Bolton) and the railwaymen (Stockport). The Bolton Trades Council acted in close alliance with the Liberal party and supported its policies. The Stockport LRC, which was more concerned with the railwaymen's particular grievances, campaigned aggressively in municipal politics but largely in those wards inhabited by railwaymen. The ILP in both seats was receptive to calls for Socialist unity. In Stockport it proposed adopting a second parliamentary candidate, and establishing a broader municipal campaign. Its advice was disregarded. The Bolton ILP wished to maintain its independence from the Trades Council; the Trades Council and the trade unions were happy to keep things that way. Hyde was the only seat in the southern cotton spinning area where a largely Socialist organisation was a powerful force. This well-led and well-organised party concentrated on welfare issues, in a similar manner to Irving in Burnley, and (aided by local economic problems) with a similar degree of success.[43]

Most parties in the textile belt stood someway between these two extremes. Weak Labour organisations were the norm. In Oldham and Eccles, Labour attempted to seize the initiative from radical ILP branches, but without the concerted aid of the textile unions it faced an uphill battle. In Oldham, there was an annual debate over which ideological/ strategic stance the party should take at the municipal elections. Moderation and concentration generally won, but larger campaigns and Liberal–Labour conflict had a good deal of support.[44] The ILP was strong and bitter enough to destroy the prospects of the joint Liberal/Labour parliamentary campaign which was being actively considered in 1908–10.

[42] Morris (thesis), p. 62; J. Hope to A.P., 12 Nov. 1908, LP/EL/08/1/52 and Carlisle T&LC AR 1909, 1910; J. Barnes to J.R.M., 3 Jan. 1908, JRM PRO/30/69/1152. There were only isolated Socialist campaigns in Rossendale (J. Bateman to A.P., 17 Nov. 1908, LP/EL/08/1/4).

[43] ILP HO Report, 20–1 May 1909, ILP HO Circ./6 (Hyde), ? to A.P., 16 Nov. 1908, LP/EL/08/1/128, Morris (thesis), pp. 34–5, noting limited initial support from textile unions even in Hyde; H. Earnshaw, J. Shaw to J.R.M., 16 Sept., 8 Nov. 1908, JRM PRO/30/69/1152 (Bolton). See also below, p. 157, for Oldham textile workers.

[44] H. Chadderton to J.R.M., 6 Feb. 1908, JRM PRO 30/69/1152, Oldham LRC Mins, e.g. 28 Jan. 1908, 3 Aug., 21 Nov. 1909.

Moderates replied by undermining the ILP's attempt to field a radical candidate (first Russell Smart and then James Whitehead) in the January 1910 election in Oldham. In Eccles the ILP was more institutionally successful. Although it failed to retain Ben Tillett as candidate (he regarded the prospects of victory unfavourably), it finally secured the adoption of the anti-Liberal Socialist, G. H. Stuart, late in 1909.[45]

The Labour/Socialist groups in Burnley and Hyde had created an electorally viable approach. They drew level with the Liberals at the 1909 municipal elections despite the earlier problems over education. Elsewhere, more radical Liberals, or less dynamic and convincing Labour organisations, contributed to Labour's stagnation. Three-cornered municipal contests in Oldham, Accrington, Bury, Rochdale, and Carlisle resulted in Labour/Socialist candidates coming third. Municipal polls of more than 20 per cent of the vote were unusual. In 1910, politics polarised even in Burnley and Hyde. Despite the 1909 results, the local Labour/Socialist groups had not forged a more attractive image. Labour support plummeted. The Labour/Socialist poll in the Eccles, Rochdale, and Burnley parliamentary contests was *lower* than in 1906. In Carlisle and Ashton, Socialist candidates scarcely managed 10 per cent of the vote. Even when Labour had a clear, successful, municipal stance, the Liberals' national standing and policy marked it as the party best fitted to fight the working-man's corner. Burnley and Hyde were still Labour's flagships, but it was in Bolton and Stockport that there were MPs. Liberal policies and the strategy of Progressive Alliance produced the results[46] (Appendix 4, pp. 459–61, for municipal results).

III

Institutionalised Liberal conservatism did not disappear after 1910, although the defection of so many conservative Liberal employers and businessmen as a result of the Budget weakened its hold. At the same time, however, industrial conflict and attendant 'sectional' interests provided a new challenge to the party radicals.

Manchester still set the pace. The newly formed Municipal Progressive Association pushed municipal policy further to the left. It advocated more municipal intervention and an expansion of opportunities, particularly

---

[45] BrSS EC Mins, 12–14 Aug. 1909, *MR* Aug. 1909, *Oldham Daily Standard,* 4 Nov. 1909, 24 Oct. 1910. For Eccles, *Dockers' Record,* Feb. 1909.

[46] See e.g. contrasting reports on 'Labour' and 'Socialist' strategy and performance in e.g. Carlisle T&LC *AR* 1908 and J. Hope to A.P., 12 Nov. 1908, LP/EL/08/1/52. In Bolton, Labour was successful in some Tory wards. In Stockport, they polled well only in the railwaymen's ward of Shaw Heath. Socialists intervened elsewhere but were easily defeated.

in education. Liberal Councillors in Warrington urged the adoption of a minimum wage rate for council employees. The Liberal Council in Eccles proposed spending nearly £100,000 on housing.[47] Land reform was one means of raising the money. By 1913, Liberal parties in Warrington and Eccles at least were supplementing the national land and housing campaigns with well-attended meetings of their own. The Middleton Liberals circulated every house in the constituency with copies of the populistic *Liberal Monthly* (which was increasingly given over to land reform).[48] Liberal radicals stepped up the pace.

Industrial relations are often seen as something of a problem for the Liberals, and to an extent this is correct. Even New Liberals were ambiguous over the demands for a closed shop which lay behind the weaving strikes of 1911–12. Those workers who turned to the state for legislative help with their industrial aims did not *necessarily* find the Liberals unsympathetic. Liberals continued to support fair wages contracts, minimum wage legislation, and other changes which were of material interest to those in low paid private and public sector industries. Liberal radicals regarded strikers in these industries at least as justified campaigners against obscene conditions. In Widnes, for example, J. T. Martindale, the radical Young Liberal, and parliamentary candidate, carefully cultivated Trades Council sympathy by supporting its industrial aims (Widnes was notorious for its low pay and sordid conditions). Neither were interventionist arguments confined to low paid industries. R. D. Denman in Carlisle argued (privately) that national industries (like the Post Office) or public services (like the railways) should be run through corporate understandings with the unions. Public sector industrial problems could thus be settled by pursuing parliamentary legislation, not by striking. It was politically difficult to say this in public (since it smacked of compulsory arbitration). Denman's public statements were therefore confined to the observation that the 1913 Trade Union Act had been insufficiently receptive to Labour demands. Political action by the trade unions was to be *encouraged* because it would ensure that politicians paid legislative attention to the unions' grievances (and that harmful strikes were therefore avoided).[49]

---

[47] *Widnes Exam.*, 14 Mar. 1914; *Eccles Journal*, 22 May 1914, reporting on the 'crowded' summer programme of meetings. For municipal policy, *Oldham Chron.*, 12 Apr. 1913, Manch. Municipal Progressive Ass. Mins, esp. 4 Oct. 1912–12 Mar. 1913, M. Stocks, *Ernest Simon of Manchester* (Manchester, 1963), Chapters 4–5.

[48] *Eccles Journal*, 31 Sept. 1914; *Widnes Exam.*, 4 Nov. 1911; *Todmorden Adv.*, 23 May 1913.

[49] *Crewe Guardian*, 1, 19 May 1914; Denman to J. A. Spender, 29 Sept., 11 Oct. 1911, Denman MS 3, Denman to S. W. Belderson, 11 Oct. 1911, Denman MS 2, *Carlisle Evening Jour.*, 4 Nov. 1910.

The New Liberal solution to industrial problems was state intervention
to remove the economic and social discrimination which caused unrest.
Local New Liberals advocated this with enthusiasm. Hobson, Hobhouse,
C. P. Scott and the *Manchester Guardian* became even more closely
involved with the formation and dissemination of Liberal policy. Rural
land reform and minimum wage rates in agriculture, they argued, would
soon be followed by an urban minimum. The ownership of one common
monopoly asset (the land) might be followed by others. Land reform
opened the way to both municipalisation and nationalisation of key services or assets such as gas, water, tramways at the local level, land,
mines, and railways through national control. E. D. Morel (Birkenhead's
candidate from 1912), Martindale, Morrell, and others took this up. The
Liberal party had been snowed under by Old Liberal policies. Much
of the textile belt, and the fringes of West Lancashire, were thawing.
The 'left-Liberal' momentum grew, even when faced with difficult problems.[50]

Opposition was not extinguished, particularly where industrial matters
were concerned. Liverpool, and at least some of the surrounding seats,
remained conservative bastions. Men like R. D. Holt were still in charge,
despite the (articulated) strains on their loyalty which resulted from
national Liberal policy on wealth and taxation. Holt's response to the
1911 transport strike reveals the depth of the problem. The Liverpool
Liberal party supported the Conservatives, and formed an electoral pact
to avoid 'politicising' the industrial conflict. Holt's answer to the problems
which lay behind the strike was the revival of (Liberal) good sense and
reason. The direct and indirect importance of conservative Liberal opinion
was such that Denman was advised (by fellow radicals) not to *publicly*
advocate nationalisation of the railways. He could argue that the reduction of railwaymen's hours of employment, for instance, was compatible
with Liberal politics, and ultimately inevitable; but he could not place
important trade union interests at the top of his political agenda. Liberal
conservatism worked in diverse ways to weaken the party's attempt to
meet the problems which led to industrial unrest.[51]

The Centrist Liberals often shared the Old Liberals' opposition to
nationalisation, and some were increasingly unsympathetic to the drift
of Liberal policy. Moreover, they remained institutionally stronger than
the New Liberals in a great many seats. The pressure exerted by the

[50] Clarke, *Liberals and Social Democrats*, pp. 144–5; C. A. Cline, *E. D. Morel* (Belfast,
      1980), p. 96.
[51] Waller, *Liverpool*, pp. 251–60. *Preston Herald*, 20 June 1914, reporting the Liberals'
      selection of a conservative candidate. For Holt's opposition to Liberal radicalism, Mur-
      ray, *People's Budget*, pp. 305–8. See also C.P.S. to Denman, 30 Sept., 1 Oct. 1911,
      Denman MS 3, on the need to placate moderate Liberals on industrial matters.

Gladstone League and the Young Liberals in Burnley, for instance, did not radicalise municipal policy. The Stockport Liberals clung to a municipal pact with the Tories; new parliamentary candidates, like Taylor in Bolton or Stanley in Oldham, were hardly radicals, but Taylor was respected locally. In the textile belt a hostility to nationalisation did not matter. Nationalisation was irrelevant. A Centrist approach retained its political credibility. It was also beginning to influence even some resolutely conservative parties in northern textile seats like Rossendale, an overwhelmingly Nonconformist seat where Radicalism was still immensely popular. Neither were Centrists forming centre-right alliances with Radicals or Liberal Imperialists. Although A. G. C. Harvey, the Rochdale MP, *opposed* the 1914 Budget, and the idea that the state should impose minimum wage rates even in 'monopoly' industries, he *favoured* the nationalisation of land, with all its radical implications. For Centrists like Harvey, land reform was a means to shift the burden of taxation to 'unproductive' wealth, and lower industry's costs. There was still considerable scope for a centre-left alliance with the New Liberals.[52]

The apparent validity of Centrist economics was reinforced by the economic boom in the textile belt after 1910. The Centrist response to industrial unrest in the cotton industry was also pragmatic and successful. Centrists, like many union leaders, identified a connection between industrial success and higher wages. Neither group believed that Statist Labour policies were the answer to their industrial needs. On the contrary, the unions were able to obtain closed shop agreements, for example, *without* state intervention but through negotiation with pragmatic employers. Unions occasionally flexed their muscles; employers responded. Neither side wished to fundamentally alter the rules while they were doing fairly well, and while negotiation and compromise were able to secure some benefits. The 'Liberal' system of industrial relations worked.

The Centrists and New Liberals were potentially rivals on both policy *and* strategy. Anti-Socialist Radicals in Labour areas (particularly Clitheroe and Manchester) wished to fight Labour with a distinct policy, and some Centrists with Lib/Lab tendencies were sympathetic.[53] The Centrist Oldham Liberals, for example, objected to running a joint campaign with W. C. Robinson, the ILP textile worker, and Labour's chosen representative for the 1914–15 election in this double member borough. Nonetheless, there is little indication that Lancashire Centrists wished to

[52] Hirst, *A.G.C. Harvey*, pp. 76–7, 95–8, *Rochdale Obs.*, 30 Aug., 27 Nov. 1913 (Rochdale), Trodd (thesis), pp. 364–8 (Burnley), Clarke, *Lancashire Liberalism*, p. 227 for Taylor, and *The Times*, 15 Nov. 1911 for the Whips' frustrated desire to select the Progressive land reformer E. Hemmerde in Oldham.

[53] *Colne Times*, 25 Nov. 1910, 1 Dec. 1911, 31 Oct. 1913, 13 Feb., 6 Mar. 1914, Clarke, *Lancashire Liberalism*, pp. 328–9.

abandon the New Liberals, embrace the party's more conservative wing, and court electoral defeat by opposing Labour candidates. Centrist politics and policies were making a generally positive contribution to a composite Liberal image.[54] It was even possible for Radicals, Centrists, and New Liberals to reach broad agreement on defence, education, temperance, and Free Trade. The Liberal party was a coalition, and a successful coalition. A Radical/Centrist alliance was unnecessary and politically divisive.

Liberalism in the North-West, even in 1914, had many faces. The policies advanced by Lloyd George and his allies were gaining support. Their dissemination spread laterally from Manchester and Blackburn. However, a Centrist Liberalism with its emphasis on the production of wealth, as opposed to its distribution, was dominant in the textile belt. This reflected its salience to the local population. However, each strand within the party needed the others. Where these strands were successfully merged together, the Liberals' strength rested on several strong props. Where Radical/Centrist alliances were established, the party did not always seem sufficiently committed to social reform, and to a crusading support for the poor in their attempt to obtain justice from the rich. There were other localised weaknesses. The Liberal party had few roots in West Lancashire. Even the New Liberals were ideologically ambivalent on the Statist interests of some trade unions. This did not nullify the New Liberals' faith in progress, in the redistribution of wealth, and in state intervention as a means of bringing about a more moral and equitable social order. However, these cumulative 'failings' meant that there were electoral spaces, of varying sizes, for Labour to exploit. Despite this, in 1914 it appeared that only a powerful rival could open up these potential fissures in the Liberal coalition. A portion of the Liberals' base could be undermined if Labour could exploit localised deficiencies and become a more credible and effective reforming alternative. However, it would need changed circumstances, or a new Socialist stance, if Labour was to expand beyond these confines, and replace the Liberal party in the North-West as a whole.

IV

By 1911 it seemed that Labour might exploit the partial weaknesses in the Liberals' position in West Lancashire and create a major electoral realignment. During the 1911 transport workers' strike, the LLRC fielded twice as many municipal candidates as was usual. The unions involved

[54] *Oldham Stand.,* 16 June 1914; *Daily Cit.,* 3, 20 Feb 1914 and *Colne Times,* 17 Oct. 1913, 6 Mar. 1914, reporting LCLF, MLF, and Whips' opposition.

added a further five. There were seven victories (including one in the docks-dominated Garston ward, which was in Widnes for parliamentary contests) and more widespread increases in Labour's popular vote. Simultaneously, a series of labourers' strikes in Widnes itself were accompanied by a campaign of unionisation, and by the revitalisation of Labour politics.[55] Strikes increased the size of the unionised workforce, the number of unions affiliated to local Labour parties, and the general level of commitment to Labour politics.

Nonetheless, Labour needed to be seen as the *political* expression of attempts to obtain a higher standard of living. After the strikes, with the Tories' arguments for municipal collectivism and Protestant chauvinism still popular, Labour was left arguing that its expansion was essential in order to prevent the economic abuse of the working class. This was insufficiently positive. Support slipped away. There was a marked contraction of effort. Nonetheless, there were some permanent changes. The scattered Liverpool Labour forces were moulded 'into one sound striking unit'. The ILP imported a successful organiser, Sam Higenbottom, who formed a party newspaper, the *Liverpool Forward*, encouraged ward organisation and concentrated activity. The West Derby constituency, already more 'Labour' than Liberal, received the most attention. All three wards returned Labour Councillors in 1911; despite the general decline of municipal activity in Liverpool as a whole, all the wards continued to be fought between 1911 and 1913.[56] There were similar changes elsewhere. The fusion of the ILP and Trades Council in Blackburn (1913), and the growing power of an ASE-dominated central party in Barrow, was accompanied by an expanding individual membership and an even more vigorous prosecution of formal organisational work.

There were also some changes in policy. Housing became the primary issue in Barrow, and an important issue elsewhere. Municipal housing provision was not necessarily controversial or uniquely 'Labour'. It did not shift Labour parties to the left. On the contrary, an emphasis on housing reform was often accompanied by the spread of a 'bureaucratic' organisation, and by the concentration of power in a conservative trade union elite. It was also associated with increasingly tense relations with the Socialists, who resented the movement away from an 'educationalist' strategy and more inspiring slogans. Moreover, active involvement with material issues increased the purchase of the centre-right. Politicisation of working-class grievances demonstrated that 'craft' or 'working-class'

---

[55] For the strikes and their aftermath, Smith, 'Glasgow and Liverpool', p. 41, Waller, *Liverpool*, pp. 251–64; *Liverpool Forward*, 25 Apr., 9 May 1913 (Widnes).

[56] *Liverpool Forward*, esp. 4 May 1912. See also 9 Aug., 15 Nov. 1912, 24 Jan. 1913, 6 Feb., 6 Mar., 17 Apr., 5 June 1914.

representation really mattered.[57] Labour became more firmly established in its strongholds. More frequent campaigns in wards deserted by the Liberals established a broader base. By 1913 constituency-wide municipal polls suggested that Labour was marginally ahead of the Tories in Barrow. In West Derby, it was still perhaps 10 per cent adrift; nonetheless, it was more clearly the principal opposition party.

Despite this localised success, 'class' appeals had not obliterated 'religious' voting. Two of the three wards in the Liverpool Kirkdale constituency , fought five times by Labour at the parliamentary level between 1906 and December 1910, were 'Protestant' (Tory) and 'Irish' (Liberal/ Nationalist) in municipal politics. The potential Labour vote was squeezed by rival 'religious' interpretations of local experience. There was a number of working-class seats in West Lancashire where Labour had still to become established as the major anti-Tory organisation. Moreover, the Liberals continued to be the major anti-Tory force in socially mixed areas. Religious fragmentation and a substantial middle-class electorate made it difficult for Labour to replace the Liberals in Bootle, Preston, and some Liverpool seats. In Widnes and Birkenhead, a radical Liberalism added an extra obstacle. This made little difference at the municipal level. Conflict was often avoided either by local alliance (as in Birkenhead) or by Progressive campaigning in separate 'spheres of influence'. These factors made further independent parliamentary expansion difficult in West Lancashire (although not impossible). More seriously, it ensured that in Barrow, and to an even greater extent in Blackburn, the Liberals were consequently strong enough to deny Labour a parliamentary victory if they chose to oppose its candidates.[58] Progressives needed to pool their support if they were to rival the Tories.

In the textile belt, Manchester and Clitheroe continued to be Labour's most productive areas. They also continued to be dominated by a conservative centre-right approach. However, after 1910 there was more of a struggle to maintain the course which moderate leaders had previously

[57] *Barrow Guardian*, 24 Jan. 1914 (LP ann. meeting) and J.S.M. to S.H., 28 May 1914, LP/ORG/14/1/37. For this in Blackburn, Trodd (thesis), pp. 376–7.

[58] *Barrow Guard.*, election reports, 5 Nov. 1912, 8 Nov. 1913; *N.D.T.*, 3 Nov. 1913, and Tanner (thesis), pp. 163–4, 168–9 for more detailed analysis. There had been little successful LRC activity in Preston since 1909. However, by 1914 the ILP had reaffiliated and, there were signs of some union support for the LRC *(Preston Herald,* 9 May 1914, Savage, *Preston,* p. 161). For Liberal attitudes, see e.g. comments by Blackburn's Liberal leader, following Liberal withdrawal and Labour victory in the St Matthew's ward: 'it did not matter . . . whether seats were won by Liberal, Labour or Independent' *(N.D.T., 2 Nov. 1912)*.

charted. Labour continued to pile up support in parts of East Manchester, Gorton and Nelson and Colne. However, Socialist opposition or defection temporarily and seriously reduced the party's organisational superiority, particularly in North-East Manchester. In Salford, Labour's potential, which had been evident in the 1911 municipal elections, was subsequently unrealised. As the Manchester LRC rightly argued, Labour's failure to field candidates was 'not to be explained by lack of Labour support in the electorate, but (by) weakness in organisation'. The formation of a Salford Divisional LRC, a commitment to tackle registration work and field five municipal candidates (financed by Manchester LRC funds) was evident by 1914.[59] Labour's position here was set to improve. Labour's organisation and its political image had changed in an area where an electoral space already existed.

Labour's growing emphasis on the provision of municipal housing in these areas was unlikely to diminish the party's appeal. On the contrary, it may have helped it begin to make some municipal progress in towns like Denton (part of the East Manchester constituency), which had previously been a weak point. However, in Denton (and Salford) economic factors were also important in creating a climate of dissatisfaction with the Liberal party.[60] The decline of the hatting industry, and of Salford docks, suggested that traditional economic philosophies were failing to deliver the material goods. Labour at least offered to fight for the unemployed, and to try and prevent an economic decline which market economics suggested would be permanent. Its standing improved.[61]

Nonetheless, Labour's support in Manchester was still largely confined to areas where the Liberals were historically weak. There was little broadening of the base. Labour's strong stance on unemployment may have helped it gain some ground in the poor, inner-city, Harpurhey ward (part of the Liberal-held Manchester North seat), but this was no basis for parliamentary expansion. Once plural voters were taken into consideration, Labour's greater support in the seat was swamped by Liberals and Tories. In 'Labour' North-East Manchester, and the remaining Manchester seats, the Liberals successfully resisted Labour's attempt to expand. Labour's limited success in its strongholds, and the portents of change in Salford, demonstrated that Labour was performing its pre-1910 role more efficiently. Liberal and Labour success continued to be

[59] Manch. and Salford LRC *AR* 1912, 1914; *Daily Dispatch,* 29 May 1914. Labour won the Seedley ward in Salford in 1911, despite Liberal opposition, and performed well elsewhere. For internal division, often augmented by differences over women's suffrage or internal democracy, Manch. Central ILP Mins, 12 Dec. 1911, 7 Jan. 1913, Morris (thesis), pp. 255–64, 265–6.

[60] For Salford and Denton, *Ashton Reporter,* 11 Apr. 1914, *Daily Dispatch,* 29 May 1914.

[61] See below, pp. 394, 413.

complementary. Moreover, Labour could neither expand in Salford, nor hold its existing seats in Manchester, if the Progressive Alliance disintegrated. The logic of co-operation remained.

The problem in most other textile belt seats was more acute. Labour organisation after 1910 was frequently devastated by the Socialists' fratricidal assaults on party moderates. There was a series of Labour/Socialist municipal conflicts (Bury 1913, Burnley 1911, Eccles 1913, Hyde 1913). The number of contested wards fell almost uniformly. Many unions remained uninterested in Labour politics. Most textile union branches in the Oldham constituency, for example, and those in Stockport, Stalybridge, and Leigh, voted against forming a political fund in the 1913 trade union ballot on Labour representation. [62]

Nonetheless, there were some signs in northern textile towns that Labour was rebuilding, reshaping, and redefining its image and its approach. Industrial unrest (and dissatisfaction with the Liberal response to 'sectional' grievances) had caused some textile union branches to alter their attitudes to the Labour party (although their members were still unwilling to support Labour candidates when opposed by Liberals). Before the industrial unrest, the railwaymen's wards in Carlisle, the mining areas of Burnley, and Accrington, and some 'weaving' areas of Accrington and Bury, had been fought by 'union' or 'Trades Council' candidates. There was now more formal co-operation between the unions and the LRC. Labour 'politicised' their grievances. [63] The party concentrated its activity on wards dominated by the members of unions sympathetic to the Labour party. This produced some positive, if localised, improvements but it was more difficult for Labour to substantially broaden this approach, and expand its electoral base. The Liberals had developed a political language which was not easily broached. In more isolated, more Nonconformist, areas, the position was even worse. Labour had to reflect the shape of its local surroundings. In devoutly Liberal and Nonconformist Rossendale, for example, the ILP was dominated not by attacks on Liberal economic conservatism, but by the ethical/moral observations of the Reverends Turner and Shield. [64] Liberal adaptation to 'new' issues seemed to match the pace of local opinion. 'Old' politics, modernised to varying degrees, still seemed relevant.

Labour lacked the same opportunities in the southern textile seats. There was not a single economic or religious experience to build on.

---

[62] White, *Trade union militancy*, pp. 153–5; S. Carter, 'The ILP in Ashton-under-Lyne, 1893–1900', *NWLH*, No. 4, p. 84; *M.G.*, 2 Nov. 1913.

[63] For divisions in Accrington, *Burnley Expr.*, 2 Nov. 1908, and partial resolution of differences, *Daily Cit.*, 5, 10 Jan., 19, 20 Feb. 1914. See also *Bury Times*, 4 Nov. 1911 for a concentration on minimum wages and unemployment.

[64] *Rossendale F.P.*, 14 Mar., 30 May 1914.

Fragmentation was more pronounced. The dominant cotton spinning industry was booming. The dissatisfaction associated with hard, poorly paid, manual work was less in evidence. There were fewer voters whose recent experience might lead them to question their existing political views. The Statist side of Labour's image was unattractive (except in Stockport) because of the occupational structure of the population. At the same time, the Liberals and Tories continued to maintain and update their credentials as representatives of local working-class interests and views. Labour made little electoral headway. In Hyde and Oldham, it fought different wards each year, but never once defeated the Liberals, who in Oldham at least won all six three-cornered contests.[65] Labour's 25 per cent poll at the 1911 Oldham parliamentary by-election (a poll inflated by Liberal unpopularity over national insurance) was the height of its success. In seats like Stalybridge and Ashton, Labour fared even worse. In Bolton, Stockport, and Middleton, Labour 'gains' at the municipal level were made with active or tacit Liberal support (see Appendix 4, pp. 459–60 for municipal results in Oldham). Liberalism was hardly being undermined at the roots.

V

Before 1910, Liberal and Labour organisations were generally successful in spatially segregated areas. This had not markedly altered by 1914. Labour's enhanced appeal to certain specific occupational groups augmented its base in some seats, but not sufficiently to form a viable alternative to the Liberal party. The purchase of Liberalism, and the decline of 'educationalist' Socialism, ensured that there was both the electoral justification for co-operation and the political ability to implement a Progressive strategy. There is every indication that policy and strategy at a 1914–15 election would have reflected this general accord.

Progressive agreement was easiest in West Lancashire: it was the only way to defeat the Tories. In 1906 Labour had fought parliamentary campaigns in Liverpool (Kirkdale and West Toxteth) and in Barrow, Blackburn, and Preston without Liberal opposition. In 1914 the Liberals tacitly offered Labour the Liverpool seat of West Derby by not adopting a candidate. Significantly, West Derby was the seat which Labour hoped to fight, on the grounds that it was organisationally and electorally its best

[65] By margins of 25, 20, 17, and 13 per cent (twice). See also reports of comparatively good Liberal performances in the outlying areas, *Oldham Chron.,* 12 Apr. 1913, 11 Apr. 1914, Oldham LRC Mins, 15 July 1914. For comments on Labour's performance in the general area, *C.F.T.*, 14 Nov. 1913, noting that industrial unrest here had little impact (cf. G. Pilling to A.P., 24 Nov. 1908, LP/EL/08/1/48, for similar circumstances in Bury).

prospect. It was also to fight Barrow, Blackburn, Preston, and probably Liverpool Kirkdale, all without Liberal opposition. Nonetheless, Labour was not yet the senior partner in the Progressive Alliance even in West Lancashire. Its base was too narrow. Attempts to expand beyond these confines failed. In Widnes, for example, the Carpenters and Joiners argued that Labour's position was 'not good enough for them to run a candidate'. There is no evidence that other seats received a more favourable response. The Liberals in Warrington, Birkenhead, and in Widnes itself seemed stronger than ever.[66] Labour had shown that it had the capacity to expand, not that this expansion was imminent.

In the rest of Lancashire, the Progressive strategy was less easily implemented. The Progressive organisations had more distinct images and aims. The Liberals had less need to co-operate, and Labour was more assertively anti-Liberal. To some extent, and especially in Manchester, the expansion of Labour's parliamentary campaign could be accepted by Liberals once Labour had demonstrated the electoral purchase of its ideas or the benefits of concession. There were plans to accept its potential strength in Salford by conceding the West Salford seat when Agnew retired in 1914–15. Moreover, Labour's demonstration of strength in the 1911 Oldham by-election was rewarded, as MacDonald had always hoped, by the Liberals' decision not to field a second candidate. The opposition of some Oldham Liberals to Labour's candidate – an ILP activist as well as a textile union official – soon evaporated.[67] Manchester East and North-East, Gorton, Clitheroe, and Stockport and Bolton (both double member boroughs) were to be fought without Liberal opposition.

There was inevitably some friction. Despite the shift towards moderation, the ILP was still a powerful force. The branch in Liberal-held Eccles managed to obtain NAC sanction for a parliamentary campaign. No other seat in the cotton spinning area could justify a campaign. Hyde, fought in 1910, was dropped. In the northern textile seats, the level of prospective Liberal/Labour conflict in 1914–15 reflected the closer electoral position and the ideological gap between the local Liberal and Labour parties. Accrington had a selected and sanctioned textile union candidate. Burnley would also probably have been contested, despite the financial problems of the BSP. Labour organisations in seats like Rossendale – where the NUWSS wished to finance a Labour candidate because the sitting Liberal was an anti-suffragist – were given short shrift

[66] LLRC Mins, 26 Sept. 1913. See also *Daily Dispatch*, 25 June 1914. For the failure to find alternatives in Widnes, and attempts to find a candidate for Kirkdale and West Derby, LLRC Mins, 27 Mar., 16 Apr., 1 May 1914.

[67] *Daily Cit.*, 10, 12, 19, Feb. 1914; J.R.M. Diary, 18 Nov. 1911, JRM PRO 30/69/1753, *Leicester Pioneer*, 23 Nov. 1911.

by the NEC. Accrington had not been contested in 1910; Rochdale (with its now declining Socialist party) had. The overall position, in terms of the degree of Liberal/Labour conflict, would remain the same.[68] The North-West, cockpit of Edwardian elections and home of the Progressive Alliance, was unlikely to witness an expansion of Liberal–Labour conflict. Labour was strategically trapped by the logic of its local position.

Liberal/Labour politics in the North-West did not follow a simple pattern. The Liberals had a strong political base in the textile belt. A Nonconformist-inspired sympathy for religious, political, and individual liberty, and for self-development, was reinforced by a perception of economic progress through Free Trade, co-operation between labour and capital, and 'sane' reform. The continuing salience of this Liberal political outlook after 1906 was reinforced by support for New Liberal and Centrist social reforms, particularly where the institutional barriers to the adoption of new ideas were falling. Yet Liberal strength was also based on the fact that it was seen as the party whose ideas and administration delivered economic prosperity. In West Lancashire, a more casual, unskilled, economy, more threatened by economic decline, had always proved less sympathetic to the Liberals approach. Although (where institutional factors allowed it) the Liberals' could adopt radical policies, the salience of a Tory political culture, based on Protestant politics, and a national/municipal collectivism which promised to protect employment, remained unchallenged. The Liberals made little headway. Labour, by contrast, could put down roots more readily in these circumstances, once it abandoned its Socialist past, by adopting a political style, and interventionist policies, which seemed more in accordance with local conditions. The Liberals could hold up Labour's advance, but in the working-class parts of West Lancashire, the writing was increasingly on the wall. In the textile belt, by contrast, craft representation, a respect for existing political cultures, and solidly practical proposals allowed Labour to establish itself as a distinct force in Clitheroe and Manchester. However, substantial lateral expansion into the more numerous, and, to the Liberals, more electorally significant, textile belt was blocked by the Liberals' ideologically and politically dynamic approach and the scarcity of disaffected occupational groups who might respond to aspects of Labour's appeal. Labour exploited the Liberals' over-conservative leanings, particularly in northern textile seats. Its image as a moderate moral reformist or a Socialist moral reformist party, with a particular interest in state intervention and municipal welfare, was attractive enough to create some

[68] *Daily Dispatch,* 30 May, 10 June 1914.

electoral support, but not usually enough to substantially erode the Liberals' lead. There was no indication that Labour's position was dramatically improving, even after it lost the support of those left-wing elements whose presence in Labour politics had prevented the party realising what potential existed. On the whole, Liberal/Labour strengths were complementary. In 1914, the Progressive Alliance was still in place because it still made electoral and (to a lesser extent) ideological sense.

Chapter 6

The Tory regions

The Tory areas outside the North-West were numerically and strategically very significant. The traditionally Tory areas of London and its hinterland, the West Midlands, and the South coast ports, collectively contained *more* working-class seats than the North-West and were as important to the Liberal victory in 1906. New Liberal policies and a Progressive Alliance were as much a part of Liberal politics in these areas as they were in the North-West.[1] As in the North-West, however, Liberalism's historic weakness in some parts of these areas suggested that there was an electoral space which Labour might exploit. The economic realities of many Tory working-class areas were very different from those areas where the Liberals were generally successful. 'Liberal' conceptions of what was possible and desirable were less of an obstacle to the creation of a 'Labour' political allegiance. Labour historians have thus tended to argue that the Liberal revival was temporary because it was lacking in cultural foundations.[2] Nonetheless, the conditions were not obviously favourable to Labour. Nonconformity and trade unionism were weak in most of the areas discussed in this chapter. Moreover, Liberal policy – which was not ideally suited to the conditions of people in parts of these areas – was not without its economic attractions, while Labour had yet to construct a viable alternative. Social forces did not point in a single direction; economic factors did not necessarily help Labour to appear a more credible force. There were both opportunities and constraints. The precise outcome of the competition could influence the Progressive Alliance in several respects. Partial Labour advance (i.e. on a small scale and within the Progressive Alliance) might *augment* the Liber-

---

[1] Blewett, *Peers,* p. 197. The results of Liberal/Labour (and Socialist) clashes in parliamentary elections are given in Appendix 3, pp. 452–3. For the major municipal results, Appendix 4, p. 461. While most ports elsewhere had Tory enclaves, few of these constituencies were dominated by the docks and consistently returned Tory MPs.

[2] Thompson, *London* passim; Stedman Jones, 'Working-class culture and working-class politics in London', in his book, *Languages of class.* See also G. Jones, *Borough politics: a study of the Wolverhampton Town Council, 1888–1964* (1969).

als' position and strengths. However, if Labour expanded on a broader front, if it became a serious rival in this key section of the electoral map, then the Liberals' ability to rival the Tories would be seriously threatened. These areas were vital to Labour's future. They were also vital to the Liberals' ability to sustain the Progressive Alliance, and hence to its future as a party of government. This complex position cannot be fully covered here, not least because historians have scarcely begun to investigate or appreciate the nature of London Liberalism. What follows is the skeleton of an argument.

In London, one very important obstacle to Labour success after 1906 was the attitude of its political competitors. The Liberals (and Tories) both put up strong resistance (Section I) by pursuing radical policies even more enthusiastically than Liberals in the North-West. Their Liberalism also developed in line with specific local conditions. The moral reformism of many Liberal radicals was only half appropriate in the East End of London. Local Liberals responded with a reforming moral populism, augmented by a 'Statist' support for legislative regulation of wages and hours in sweated East End trades. A New Liberalism more akin to national policy was evident in the stably populated, and more affluent, North and South-West London constituencies, with their skilled and lower middle-class electorates. London radical politics did not depend on a secular New Liberalism imposed from above. It predated the primacy of radical Liberalism on the national stage, and drew on a local religious and secular radical tradition. In some parts of London, radical Liberalism had a broad institutional base; in others it depended on the active involvement of a small professional elite.

Labour found it very difficult to escape the hold of Socialist policies which had flourished in the past, and to offer a 'reformist' alternative. This was partially because of the Socialists' institutional power, but also because the Liberals occupied so much of Labour's 'natural' ground that moderate Labour politics had little electoral purchase. When Labour did manage to change, it could not easily avoid supporting Liberal policies. Many of its supporters shared the Liberal radicals' reforming views, and were inspired by the same religious impulses. Often party leaders came from similar social backgrounds (Section II). In some circumstances, however, the party embraced a Labourist moderation which brought a degree of localised success. However, the conditions which sustained this success were seldom duplicated. Labour's only other successes were in a handful of poverty-ridden seats, where energetic campaigns by parties advocating extensive municipal intervention, a Socialist moral reformism, challenged the economic assumptions of both Liberals and Tories in a manner which the local Socialists made credible and acceptable to the electorate.

The political climate in much of the West Midlands was less favourable for all non-Tory parties. No Progressive party made much headway before 1910 (Section III). Most local Liberal organisations responded to their electoral problems by accepting radical policies. Nonetheless, a developing 'Labourism' began to undermine the Liberal party's position and slowly came to challenge the Tories. However, Labour did not seem capable (even in 1914) of defeating its rivals and increasing its parliamentary representation if it stood as an independent force. Moreover, outside Birmingham and its hinterland, a stronger Liberal tradition was reinforced by a more favourable economic climate, and more relevant Liberal policies. This generally prevented Labour from establishing more than a localised alternative positive appeal as an anti-Tory force.

On the south coast (Section V) a traditional Liberal/Socialist hostility to naval expenditure hampered both Progressive parties in many (but not all) of the dock/military dominated working-class constituencies. However, in some instances local Liberal organisations could be a serious political force. Policies which were economically relevant to the Liberals' 'old' electoral base (which was reasonably substantial in ports dependent on Free Trade), were augmented by newer radical initiatives, and a concern for the specific needs of dockyard workers. In these circumstances, Labour found it impossible to break through. It was only where the Liberals lapsed that it had an opportunity to expand.

As a result of this complex interaction of competing forces, Labour's substantial growth was generally confined to a few seats where the Liberals had been least successful. It was threatening to become a more serious rival in rather more former Tory seats in 1914 than in 1906. It looked capable of still further expansion in the future. The Liberals were happy to accept the logical result of Labour's electoral position, i.e. a slight expansion of Labour's parliamentary campaign. They were also happy to make concessions in double member boroughs. Labour's reciprocal support in marginal seats where Liberals were fighting Tories, it was still assumed, might be sufficient to ensure Liberal victories. The pattern of Liberal/Labour politics was entirely compatible with a general Liberal ascendancy, and with the continuation of the Progressive Alliance. As an election approached in 1914, the Progressive parties moved closer together.

I

There were two Londons. The political/electoral problems which the Liberal party faced were most acute in the East End seats, and to a lesser extent in the sink holes of poverty which littered West London.

Voters worked in an enormous variety of ill-paid, casual, or sporadic occupations. Tory success was built, as in Lancashire, on cultural affinities with working-class social activities, on attendance to ethnic tensions, and, allied to this, on support for the protection of British values, British jobs and British international prestige. The attraction of this appeal was far less apparent in the socially mixed and more affluent artisan and lower middle-class settlements in North and South-West London. This division forms the essential backdrop for the following discussion of Liberal and Labour politics in London.

In London, as in Lancashire, there were institutional obstacles to the spread of radical Liberal ideas. Some prominent Liberals, like J. Scott Lidgett in Bermondsey, were economically conservative and socially 'municipal puritans' (i.e. they opposed such things as liquor licences for music halls, and Sunday street trading). They were not typical. As in other areas which did not have a powerful and conservative Liberal manufacturing elite, Liberal radicals were a major force in local Liberal politics. After the 1884–5 redistribution of seats, Liberal organisation in London was totally reconstructed. By the late 1880s, 'London Radicalism had emerged as the most "advanced" section of British Liberalism, led by spontaneous and frequently working-class organisation in the (Liberal) clubs'. The decline of this Liberal artisan base led to organisational and financial problems in some parts of the East End.[3] Many constituencies suffered from a shortage of supporters and funds by the later 1890s. Wealthy conservative Liberal elements *could* have become more important as a result. There is little evidence that they did. Wealthy contributors to party funds (e.g. Evan Spicer [Norwood], H. C. Lea [St Pancras], or William Pearce [Limehouse]) were unusual; none of these can be described as conservatives, or as unchallengeable forces in their constituencies. When Lea *did* oppose radical ideas in 1909–10, he was deselected by his Liberal association as a result. It was more usual for Liberal associations to get by without the assistance of wealthy patrons. The largest annual subscriptions in Hackney were from £5 to £10.[4] This was hardly enough to 'buy' institutional power. Most Liberal leaders were not chosen for their financial power. Pickersgill, Bethnal Green's MP, was 'as poor

---

[3] Davis, 'London politics', esp. pp. 115–18 supplies excellent information. For localised Liberal problems, Strand LA AR 1888–90, Holborn Lib. and Rad. Ass. AR 1887–91, memo by J. R. Seager, 21 Aug. 1901, HG Add MS 46033 fos. 231–2. For similar problems in the West End, HCLF AR 1903. For Scott Lidgett, W. F. Lofthouse in R. E. Davies (ed.), *John Scott Lidgett* (1957), pp. 44–5, 69. In the 1920s, Labour policy was often compared with that of the LCC (H. Gosling, *Up and down stream* (1927), p. 84, *Nation*, 14 Oct. 1922).

[4] J. Cox, *The English churches in a secular society. Lambeth 1870–1930* (Oxford, 1982), pp. 116–17; *Hackney Gazette*, 9 Nov. 1893; Blewett, *Peers*, p. 216.

as a church mouse'. In St George's, the MP, John Benn, supplied his own election agent (his son), donated £25 per year to the Liberal association, and gave up a room in his house as his contribution to constituency expenses. Dr Cooper, the Bermondsey MP, 'practically directed all local activity', including registration work, until his death in 1909. He had to cope with the fact that there were few Liberal activists in the constituency, and little spare money for organisational work, but he did not 'buy' his primacy in local Liberal politics. He owed his position to hard work and commitment.[5]

In many working-class constituencies in East London, institutional power lay in the hands of religiously inspired social or Settlement House workers. The East London constituency of St George's relied heavily on members of the Benn family; Bermondsey relied on H. J. Glanville and Dr G. J. Cooper. In Finsbury, J. A. Baker and T. E. Harvey, Quaker Settlement House workers, shared the burden of municipal work with other middle-class social workers. Most of these Liberal leaders were popular because of their considerable commitment to local social improvement. They had good records as community workers. William Wedgwood Benn, for instance, was the third generation of his family to become active in remedying the myriad social evils of St George's. His grandfather (an approved school teacher and subsequently shopkeeper, social worker, and preacher) and his father, John Benn, were well-known and popular campaigners for improvements in public health and housing. Cooper, the Bermondsey MP, was a 'poor man's doctor' who, it was noted, had frequently declined the (lucrative) offer to move 'over the Bridge' to Harley Street. Addison – another doctor and the MP for Hoxton – was respected for his vigorous support of LCC reforms and for the economic interests of hard-pressed local traders. Liberal activity in Lambeth was heavily dependent on Frank Briant, founder of the local Philanthropic Institute, and his colleague F. H. Stead.[6]

Little is known about Liberal activity in the London suburbs, although there is some evidence that radical middle-class professionals were assuming dominant positions in Liberal politics. There was also a much larger Liberal membership in the suburban seats than in the inner-city constituencies. In Ilford, and in the more socially mixed seat of North Islington, the Liberals boasted a paying membership of over 500. Party members

---

[5] Harris, *Forty years*, p. 47; A. G. Gardiner, *John Benn and the Progressive movement* (1925), p. 195; *Southwark Recorder*, 15 Oct. 1909.
[6] F. W. Soutter, *Fights for freedom* (1925), esp. pp. 121–2; T.E.H. to A. M. Harvey, 23 Jan. 1904, 24 Apr. 1904, TEH MS; Gardiner, *John Benn*, esp. p. 131; K. O. and J. Morgan, *Portrait of a Progressive*, pp. 8, 10.

were not all professionals and tradesmen. Trades Councils in working-class suburbs such as Tottenham, Walthamstow, Hackney, and (after some problems) in Battersea worked closely with the Liberals.[7] The radical Liberal artisans who formed the basis of Liberal organisation in the 1880s and early 1890s did not disappear. Liberal associations in St Pancras, and to a lesser extent in Islington, had taken up the 'democratic' mantle of the Liberal Clubs. They formed radical Liberal associations, with elaborate networks of local committees, and proudly proclaimed the fact that rank and file Liberal activists controlled the constituency machine. The Young Liberals also played an important part in constituency activity, and in attempts to push radical policies and candidates to the fore.[8]

Liberal organisations could even flourish in the East End and its adjacent areas. After Cooper's death, for example, largely working-class ward committees were formed in Bermondsey to help the party fight the 1910 election. By 1914 they were campaigning as energetically as Labour's celebrated local organisation.[9] In Bethnal Green, where there was no lack of voluntary workers at the 1914 by-election, the Liberal executive contained a chimney sweep, wheelwright, billposter, and a prominent local trade union official.[10] Jewish leaders and Irish organisations also lent support to the Liberal machine. To an extent this made the Liberals vulnerable; some of this support was based on Liberal commitment to specific ethnic issues. However, a few immigrants were becoming active members of the Liberal party, and (whether at their instigation or not)

---

[7] *Islington News,* 2 Jan. 1914, *East London Advertiser,* 18 Apr. 1914. For suburban leadership and politics, discussion of James Chuter Ede's early career in Epsom, K. Jefferys (ed.), *Labour and the wartime coalition* (1987), p. 3. For Battersea, C. Wrigley, 'Liberals and the desire for working-class representatives in Battersea, 1886–1922' in Brown (ed.), *Anti-labour history,* pp. 141–50. The Liberal/Labour alliance in Battersea collapsed in 1909, but was reformed by 1912. For close, willing, Progressive agreements in working-class suburbs before 1907, correspondence in LRC 9/429, 11/334, LPGC 9/159, and for similar circumstances in South and North London, e.g. correspondence and papers in LP GC 3/146, 4/108, 331–2, 390, LP/ISL/08/1.

[8] *St Pancras Chronicle,* general Liberal advertisements, Feb. 1913 and for union involvement, e.g. 15, 22 Jan., 23 July, 26 Nov. 1909; *Morning Leader,* 30 Dec. 1909, 7 Jan. 1910, and Thompson, *London,* p. 268.

[9] *Southwark Recorder,* 10 Dec. 1909, 27 Feb. 1914, F. Brockway, *Bermondsey story* (1949), pp. 30–2. For the position before 1909, Soutter, *Fights for freedom,* p. 189, A. Salter to C. Hesse, 10 Dec. 1906, Hesse MS 1980/54/5/2 and Salter to J.K.H., 1 Nov. 1909, FJ 1909/480. There were still problems in some seats, such as Shoreditch, where the artisan population *had* disappeared.

[10] Harris, *Forty years,* p. 36.

Liberal leaders were attempting to merge the 'economic' concerns of immigrant workers with their ethnic or 'cultural' attitudes and interests.[11] The moral motivation of many Liberal leaders did not lead to an obviously unpopular and patronising political stance. Nonconformists like F. H. Stead had no interest in issues such as Welsh Disestablishment. The Quaker, T. E. Harvey, was concerned with the 'Nonconformist' issue of education, but as a means to working-class improvement and as an element of his service to the poor. The Mansion House settlement in West Ham, Toynbee Hall, and other, similar, institutions, produced a crop of radical Liberal activists. George Gillet's Peel Institute was, according to one (unsympathetic) commentator, 'a hothouse of *Daily News* style Liberalism'. Briant and Stead built a political base in Lambeth around their advocacy of better social and housing provision, not around their religious work. 'No man', one Liberal claimed, 'had done more to humanise the poor law' than Briant. Stead, warden of Briant's Settlement, and men like Caleb Hutchinson, a prominent Liberal leader in the area, followed his lead.[12]

Neither were Liberal politics necessarily 'dry' and 'intellectual'. Many Liberal leaders were committed to a more popular form of politics. John Benn, a former stage entertainer, 'had a great sense of the dramatic' and believed that 'an ounce of practical illustration and description created more impression than a pound of argument'. Moral reform became 'moral populism' with consummate ease. The poor were eulogised. Benn, for example, declared his aspiration to 'the honour of being the member for the backstreets'.[13] In this respect, Liberal radicals drew important support from the press. The *Daily Chronicle* and the *Daily News,* and London's dailies, the *Star* and *Morning Leader,* were very widely read, and populistic, purveyors of a moralistic collectivism. They pointed to the dire poverty which existed alongside extravagant wealth, and publicised the radical Liberal remedies of minimum wages and land reform. They kept the Liberal party on its toes, and gave its radicals ample and excellent publicity. A dry morality did not sell newspapers; 'morality'

[11] G. Alderman, *The Jewish community in British politics* (Oxford, 1983), pp. 42–85; D. M. Feldman, 'Immigrants and workers, Englishmen and Jews: Jewish immigration to the East End of London 1880–1906', Cambridge Ph.D. thesis 1986, pp. 213–16, 310–12; A. O'Day, 'Irish influence on parliamentary elections in London', in R. Swift and S. Gilley (eds.), *The Irish in the Victorian City* (1985), pp. 98–101. See also below, p. 171.

[12] For Briant and Harvey, Cox, *Lambeth,* pp. 160, 173, T.E.H. to A. M. Harvey, 6 Dec. 1908, T.E.H. MS. On the Peel Institute see G. A. Aldred, *No traitor's gait* (1955), p. 77. The reorientation of Liberal social workers' attitudes towards the causes and political consequences of poverty are discussed in S. Meacham, *Toynbee Hall and social reform 1880–1914* (New Haven, 1987), Chapter 5.

[13] Harris, *Forty years,* p. 42; Gardiner, *John Benn,* pp. 114, 128–32, 189–90.

tied to an attack on the rich was different. Moreover, the Liberal press had considerable public influence. As Alfred Salter, contesting Bermondsey for Labour in 1909 noted, the '"advanced democratic" elector scarcely reads anything in our part of the world but the "Morning Leader" and the "Star"'. 'Moral' radicalism became part of populistic crusades. This is evident, for example, in Wedgwood Benn's campaigns against brothel owners (exploiters of the poor) and even, by 1914, in ordinary Parish magazines: 'The Progressives draw support from all followers of Jesus Christ – the Moderates (Tories) from company promoters, slum landlords, drinksellers, bookmakers and brothelkeepers.'[14]

Liberal policy was not conservative. The Progressive LCC administration between 1889 and 1907 introduced fair wages contracts, minimum wage rates, housing programmes, and health and educational proposals which were supported by Labour representatives (who were generally elected on a Liberal slate). Municipal Liberals subsequently argued that poor law reform and welfare provision should be financed by taxing site values, a reform which, they claimed, meant taking money from 'idle' rich landowners and giving it to the poor.[15]

Local opposition to radical policies was frequently inhibited or crushed. In South London, Briant and Stead helped radical allies and protégés into positions of influence in local Liberal politics. The radicalisation of Liberal politics squeezed out many of the remaining Liberal conservatives. If, in Battersea at least, they fought back, this does not appear to have been the norm. Liberal politics were moving rapidly to the left as a result of local, as much as national, factors.[16]

The radicalism of the LCC Progressives and the borough parties was reflected in the adoption of innumerable 'advanced' Liberal parliamentary candidates. Sydney Buxton, the Poplar MP and senior radical, was 'a real social reformer', who demonstrated his reforming credentials at the Board of Trade and in Cabinet. Other East End MPs, including Wedgwood Benn, Masterman, Percy Alden, and J. A. Baker, were nationally known and respected radicals (who were also being tipped for future office). Cooper, the Bermondsey MP, frequently supported radical, Irish, and Labour amendments aimed at prompting reforms (as did his

[14] Cited in Cox, *Lambeth*, p. 173. See also A. Salter to J.K.H., 1 Nov. 1909, FJ 1909/480. There were comparatively few Liberal weeklies. For the role of the Liberal press, Koss, *Political Press,* ii, pp. 64–75, 204.
[15] The complexities of Liberal policy, and its political implications, are admirably dealt with in J. Davis, *Reforming London* (Oxford, 1988).
[16] *Brixton Free Press,* 10 July 1914; Wrigley, 'Battersea', pp. 147–9.

replacement, H. J. Glanville).[17] Addison and Chancellor (Shoreditch), who were added to the radical ranks in 1910, were later to join the Labour party.

This radicalism extended beyond the East End. All four St Pancras constituencies had radical candidates by 1910. In St Pancras East, H. C. Lea was replaced by Joseph Martin, a land reformer and barrister (who later joined Labour). Like P. W. Wilson, the Settlement worker, he supported the full radical programme. 'What was wrong with England', Wilson declared in Hobsonian terms 'was not the lack of money. There was quite enough money in this country, but it was unequally distributed.' In Lambeth and Camberwell, Macnamara (prominent in the NUT) and Collins were long-standing and respected radicals. Gosling (Lambeth North) was Secretary of the Lightermen's union. Cotton and Spicer, Dulwich's candidates in January and December 1910, had pronounced Labour sympathies. After his defeat, Cotton considered joining the ILP.[18]

After 1910, even more Liberal radicals were selected as parliamentary candidates. C. R. Buxton, author of the 1912 Land Report, and another religious radical, was selected in Central Hackney. L. W. J. Costello, an advanced radical with similar religious beliefs, was selected in North Islington after Young Liberal pressure. He was still not radical enough for many local activists. This, as one local newspaper commented, 'furnishes a striking commentary on the breakneck speed at which Radicalism is moving towards the arms of Socialism'. Frank Briant, Cooke-Taylor, and J. D. Gilbert (N. Lambeth, Dulwich, and Newington) joined Macnamara to create a phalanx of South London radical parliamentary candidates for the prospective 1914/15 election.[19]

Liberal parliamentary campaigns after 1910 were seldom fought purely on old Liberal issues. In the East End, Wedgwood Benn considered ethnic issues, but refused to let them dominate 'economic' considerations. In Stepney, despite its large Irish population, Liberal and Tory candidates

[17] This was true of many London Liberals, including W. H. Dickinson, H. C. Lea, J. Martin (St Pancras); J. A. Baker (Finsbury); T. J. Macnamara (Camberwell), and H. G. Chancellor and Dr C. Addison (Shoreditch). For Buxton and Cooper, C.P.T to W.R., 6 Oct. 1911, WR 44, Davidson, 'Board of Trade', pp. 580–1; Soutter, *Fights for freedom*, p. 168.

[18] *St Pancras Chron.*, 29 Jan. 1909; *Islington News*, 2 Jan. 1914, and above fn. 6; H.E.A. Cotton to J.R.M., 23 Mar. 1910, JRM PRO 30/69/1154.

[19] V. de Bunsen, *C. R. Buxton* (1948), pp. 51, 91; *Brixton F.P.*, 20 Feb. 1914, describing Costello as 'a disciple of what he calls Christian politics'. For Costello's selection in Lambeth, *Young Liberal*, May 1914 and K. Lindermann to C.P.T., 20 July 1912, CPT 28, *Islington News*, esp. letters, 2–16 Jan. 1914. For Cooke-Taylor and Gilbert's views, *S. London Press*, 29 May, 3 July 1914.

argued that incomes and employment, not Ireland, were the major issues.
As Preston, the Tory, put it:

> At the coming general election they would hear a tremendous lot about Home
> Rule, Welsh Disestablishment and taxation of land. All these were very important
> things, but they did not vitally affect them. The Insurance Act affected everyone
> … and he wanted them at the election that was coming to be selfish for once
> and say 'I am going to vote for the thing that affects me'.[20]

In the East End, most Liberals backed practical proposals, such as the
extension of minimum wage legislation (which many local trade unions
supported with enthusiasm).[21] The land campaigns of 1912–14 complemented the longstanding LCC proposals for the taxation of land values,
and were pushed hard by parliamentary candidates and constituency associations. In the East End, land reform was portrayed as part of an assault
on West End landowners (and West End jews) in favour of the poor
(of all races) in the East End constituencies. In North and South London,
land and rating reform had three selling points. It was a means of relieving
the burden of taxation, which fell disproportionately on lower middle-class
households; it was a means of enabling the extension of municipal housing
provision; and it would be a means of clearing the way to better opportunities and living standards.[22] When this was added to the long-standing
importance of Free Trade to dock-related employment, Liberalism must
have appeared as the 'natural' choice for many working-class voters.

Despite the growth of radical politics in London, and its success even
in 1910, the Liberal party was not totally secure. In most parts of the
East End, and perhaps also in the poorest areas of West London, it
was a fragile coalition. Ethnic fragmentation and competing economic
interests were not easily countered. Success was dependent upon the
ceaseless activity of small organisations, and on reform proposals (such
as minimum wages) which were a little too vague, and perhaps a little
too conservative, to be an entirely satisfactory means of countering the
divisive impact of the local social and economic structure. The Liberals'
radicalism was also perhaps at times a shade *too* moral. However (and
contrary to the views of many labour historians) on the fringes of the
East End, where the economic situation and the political traditions were
a little more conducive to Liberal success, and in the more socially mixed

---

[20] *East London Adv.,* 28 Mar., 30 May 1914. For Wedgwood Benn, Alderman, *Jewish
community,* pp. 74–5. Wedgwood Benn's papers contain numerous ephemeral pieces
which display his close attention to populist issues.

[21] For the unions' interest, *Journeyman Bakers' Magazine,* June, Aug. 1913, UK Society
of Coachmakers, *Quarterly Report,* Oct. 1914, *Government Workers' Advocate,* Nov.
1913, M. Stewart and L. Hunter, *The needle is threaded* (1964), pp. 135, 141–2.

[22] For land and housing, *South London Press,* 29 May, 12 June 1914. For sweating, *East
London Observer,* 13 Dec. 1913, *East London Adv.,* 1 Feb. 1913.

suburbs of North and South London, the Liberal party looked extremely healthy in 1914.[23]

II

The institutional structure of 'Labour' politics did not make it easy to construct a moderate Labour alternative to the Liberal party. Trade unionists were less numerous than in other areas because of the nature of the London labour market. The SDF had strong roots which were not easily dislodged. In most London seats, whether in the East End or in the suburbs, the SDF (and/or the ILP) were sympathetic to 'Socialist' policies and strategies, and often to calls for Socialist unity. Labour organisations frequently did not exist. Anti-Liberal sentiments, and anti-capitalist rhetoric, were the norm.

The SDF's views were reinforced by elements in the ILP, which is hardly surprising given their historically close contacts. Like the Liberals, the ILP tended to rely, particularly in the poorer areas, on middle-class leaders for organisational drive and financial support. These leaders were frequently either ethical socialists or more radical proponents of 'old' Socialist tactics. Clement Attlee of Haileybury and Oxford, a voluntary social worker of independent means, became Secretary of the Stepney ILP within weeks of joining. He was unpaid organiser, soap-box orator, and local candidate. When the ILP set up its local headquarters (above a funeral parlour) Attlee provided the furniture and part of the rent. In Bermondsey, Dr Alfred Salter, a prominent local doctor, founded the local ILP and LRC, was a candidate for the Borough Council, the Board of Guardians and the LCC, and was also the party's driving force and chief organiser. Three of Salter's four partners in the Bermondsey medical practice were ILP members; Mrs Evelyn Lowe, a partner's wife, was Secretary of the election fighting fund in 1914. Salter's second in command, the postal clerk Charles Ammon, was a Methodist lay preacher; the branch contained at least three other ministers, and displayed a 'chapel feeling'.[24] In Poplar (where most religious ministers were also Socialists by 1910) George Lansbury, an ardent Anglican and a local employer, and R. C. K. Ensor (the journalist and Oxford historian) made major contributions. ILP

[23] Reports of constituency Liberal associations, *Islington News*, 13 Feb., 20 Mar., 24 Apr. 1914 (S. Harringay, N. and W. Islington); *S. London Press*, 1 and 29 May 1914 (N. Lambeth and Kennington); *East London Adv.*, 18 Apr. 1914 (Romford).

[24] K. Harris, *Attlee* (1982), pp. 28–32. For Bermondsey, Brockway, *Bermondsey story*, Chapter 4, *Monthly Messenger*, Dec. 1913, Mar. 1914. Salter and Ensor's important role is evident from the constituency correspondence in the Ensor and Hesse MSS. For direct acknowledgement of Salter's role in Bermondsey, A. Salter to Hesse, 10 June 1919, Hesse MS 1980/54/5/2.

branches in West London were the children of the affluent middle-class radicals Frank Smith and Dr Davidson; the Bethnal Green party was kept alive by C. M. Lloyd of Toynbee Hall.[25] Ensor knew of:

no branch which would not welcome a middle class candidate for membership; the danger usually is that the less educated members will defer to him far more than he is worth ... Few branches do not contain some, many contain many, and some contain a majority.[26]

This had a serious political impact. Some middle-class ILP leaders, like Frank Smith, were moral revolutionaries and Graysonites. Neither Smith, nor ethical socialists like Dr Salter, allowed their views to be submerged by the need to construct a more reforming alternative to the Liberal party. In his 1909 parliamentary election address, Salter, formerly Treasurer of the Bermondsey Liberal party, described Socialism as 'the practical application of the message of Jesus Christ'. His support for temperance reform was honestly displayed. The branch aimed its propaganda at the respectable and the 'thinking population of Bermondsey'.[27] Salter's Socialism, like the views of many Liberal radicals, was perhaps too moral, and too elitist, to appeal to a majority of the electorate. Obviously, the local Labour party did not replicate every aspect of Liberal policy, or allow the views of radical or ethical socialist leaders to become the sole criteria for what action it should take. Labour contained fewer economically conservative, culturally aloof, moral regenerationists than the Liberal party. Labour's middle-class Socialists (like Tawney) may have been more likely to respect the 'good sense' and 'morality' of the working-class than some Liberal reformers. Nonetheless, the nature of the party leaders' views, and the fact that Socialism required a revolution in human attitudes and behaviour if it was to work, made it easy for the ILP to appear as patronising, impossible, and impotent.

The radical and ethical socialists often enjoyed an unchallenged institutional primacy. Not only were unions weaker; with the exception of some branches of the Gasworkers, Typographical Association, Municipal Employees, NUR, and the ASE, they were not usually sympathetic to

---

[25] Thompson, *London*, p. 232; E. I. Champness, *Frank Smith M.P. Pioneer and modern mystic* (1943), esp. pp. 25, 30, 33–4.

[26] Brockway, *Bermondsey story*, p. 33.

[27] *Monthly Messenger*, Mar. 1914 and addresses and cuttings, Hesse MS. Frank Smith, a close friend of Keir Hardie, was Secretary of the Graysonite Right to Work Council in 1908 and a propagandist candidate in several parliamentary contests. He also, with Hardie's help, unsuccessfully attempted to stampede a reluctant Lambeth LRC into contesting the Lambeth seat in Dec. 1910 (Champness, *Frank Smith*, pp. 32, 35, NAC deputation report, 29 Apr. 1910, ILP MS). Hardie had manipulated NAC sanction for Smith's candidature at Croydon in 1909 (J.R.M. to J.B.G., 30 Mar. 1909, JBG 09/98).

the Labour party. The Government Workers' Federation, the tram workers, bakers, cloth cutters, and tailors – all interested in minimum wages – gave little support to local Labour parties before the First World War. Those skilled trade unions who had members active in Labour politics did not share the interests even of the unskilled members of their own trade. Their political involvement, like that of trade unions such as the municipal employees and gasworkers, was not necessarily going to produce policies, and a party image, which unskilled or 'Tory' workers would find attractive.[28]

Moderate labour elements frequently acted in alliance with the Liberals in Borough and LCC elections. They had places on the Progressive slate. In Liberal working-class suburbs, such as Islington and St Pancras, in south London radical strongholds, and some seats in and near the East End, Liberalism satisfied many potential Labour voters. Nonetheless, this approach was increasingly questioned after 1910. Local Labour organisations were formed even in the radical Liberal strongholds. Moderate Labour supporters began to insist that Labour organisations should adopt 'reforming' policies. There was a partial, shaky, compromise between some moderates and members of the old 'radical' left.

Labour politics in Bermondsey, where the ILP was the bastion of 'Labour' activity before 1910, exemplify the partial nature, limited success, and the fragility of this change. By October 1909, the Bermondsey ILP had 150 members, a paid organiser, and a reasonably efficient organisation. In the 1909 parliamentary by-election, however, Salter obtained just 16 per cent of the vote, and came some 20 per cent behind Spencer Hughes, the second-placed Liberal candidate (and a *Daily News* journalist). The result was thought to be 'dismal'; the results in the November municipal elections confirmed that progress was 'disappointingly slow'.[29] Salter agreed to 'settle down to steady spade work for several years and then try again'.[30] A Labour party was formed in 1910; the ILP formed ward committees, extended propaganda campaigns, acquired new premises, and founded a newsletter, the *Monthly Messenger*. It became involved in local strikes, assisted with relief work, and helped materially by drafting resolutions and letters. Salter, despite his objections to industrial action, was heavily involved. In 1913 the NAC expressed its 'great satisfaction with the reports that were submitted concerning your methods

28 Thompson, *London,* Chapter 12; C. Hill to J.R.M., 29 Oct. 1910 LP/ISL/08/1/11; A. Brine to A.H., 10 Jan. 1914, LP AFF 8/47; J. A. Gillespie, 'Economic and political change in the East End of London during the 1920s', Cambridge Ph.D. thesis 1984, esp. pp. 362, 416–17. See also below, p. 176.
29 ILP report, 8 Oct. 1909, ILP H.O. Circ./6; Blewett, *Peers,* p. 35.
30 A. Salter to Ensor, 10 Dec. 1909, Ensor MS. For the following see also F.J. to P. Scott, 16 Nov. 1913, Bryan MS IVB fo. 13, Brockway, *Bermondsey story,* pp. 40–5.

of organisation and the amount of propaganda work that was being conducted'. Yet electorally the party was still stagnant. In the 1912 and 1913 local elections, Labour polled around 22 per cent of the vote in its strongest wards, at a time when the Liberals nationally were extremely unpopular. The attempt to construct a slightly more practical image was forgotten. Salter blamed Labour's moderate national strategy for the local party's difficulties:

All work in our branch has come to a complete standstill the members refusing to touch anything. We are paralysed for the time being and it will take up to 12 months to get over the blow dealt us by the NAC. We shall lose 50 per cent of our membership at least ...[31]

This reflected a wider hostility to Labour's new approach even amongst those committed to a degree of change. More radical Socialists also dug in their heels and attempted to halt the slide towards moderation. ILP branches in Islington, St Pancras, Fulham, Marylebone, and Erith (amongst others) had supported Victor Grayson in 1908. Grayson's approach was viewed sympathetically even by the more 'moderate' Bermondsey party. As Salter's observations suggest, this unrest did not disappear after 1910. The Islington ILP, for example, supported the BSP's plans to adopt a radical Socialist parliamentary candidate in 1913–14. While some parties genuinely did settle down to steady spade work, and made a little headway, Labour was frequently squeezed between a radical Liberalism (which had trade union support) and the left's impatient, often destructive, Socialist wing. An electorally floundering party could easily turn to the left.[32]

Radical socialist/ethical socialist alliances without some 'practical' element failed completely. The Limehouse ILP 'succeeded' in increasing its membership from sixteen in 1908 to a little over seventy in 1911, but as its most famous member records, it 'met weekly in a small dingy church hall', ran a newspaper (for three weeks) and an ambitious club (which swiftly failed). Local trade unions (in so far as they existed) could not be persuaded to form a Labour party or even a Trades Council. In the 1909 municipal elections, Attlee polled just sixty-seven votes. Labour's municipal activity was not taken seriously. Candidatures were 'propaganda contests ... to get a hundred votes was a moral victory'. The

[31] Salter to S. London Fed. Sec., 28 June 1913, Bryan MS IVB fo. 27; Tanner (thesis), p. 150. See also GGL, *Biennial Congress Report 1912*, reported lack of LRC funds in Bermondsey.

[32] See esp. *Islington Daily Gazette* and *Balham News,* 4 Nov. 1912. For additional information, ILP South London Fed. Mins, 1 Jan. 1914, *Islington News,* 16 Jan. 1914. Long-standing political divisions were made worse by personal conflicts (G. Wyver to J.R.M., 24 July 1905, LRC 24/484, correspondence in LP/ISL/08/1).

radical ILP branches in East Ham and Shoreditch also got into considerable difficulty after 1910. By 1914 the Bethnal Green LRC had 'practically ceased to exist'; the formation of the BSP meant that its small band of workers was so seriously depleted that it could not carry on.[33]

There were isolated cases of Labour making progress on moderate lines, most obviously in Deptford and Woolwich in South-East London. Both seats had been strongly Tory. By the 1890s, Woolwich Liberalism had disappeared, and Deptford's Liberal organisation according to Benn was 'very deficient'.[34] Labour was able to exploit the Liberals' weakness. The ASE, which dominated Woolwich, and was also a powerful force in Deptford, took over Labour politics and dictated a moderate approach. This allowed Labour to absorb 'Liberal' support, and to expand the Liberal base by converting hitherto unpoliticised or Tory voters. In 1903 the moderate former Liberal, Will Crooks, was returned without Liberal opposition in Woolwich. He was elected again in 1906 with 56 per cent of the vote. In Deptford, a divided Liberal association fielded a last-minute candidate against the very moderate Labour representative in 1906, without Liberal Head Office approval. Labour won, but not convincingly. The third-placed Liberal managed just 6 per cent of the vote, although municipal election results suggest a stronger Liberal position.

After 1906, Labour established a powerful organisation in Woolwich. There were large ward committees, 3,000 individual members, an agent, a weekly journal, the *Woolwich Pioneer,* and an active municipal campaign in the whole borough. An elaborate social, organisational, and propaganda structure kept activists involved and in touch with both the electorate and the party officials. In Deptford, by contrast, Liberal/ Labour co-operation continued. It was not until 1914 that the LRC finally and reluctantly disaffiliated the Liberal Clubs and appointed a Labour registration agent.

Labour's municipal policy consisted of support for craft representation, and for the Statist interests of some local groups. The party only gradually adopted a concrete and positive programme. It did little to attract the large unskilled and middle-class elements in the local electorate. Its housing policy, for example, reflected the interests of skilled workers (some of whom owned their own homes) rather than the interests of the dockland slum-dwellers. Minimum wage legislation was seen as either unnecessary or as a potential threat to existing wage differentials. In Woolwich,

[33] Harris, *Attlee,* p. 30, C. R. Attlee, *As it happened* (1954), pp. 35–7, J. Mylles to Ensor, 12 Oct. 1911, Ensor MS; ILP South London Fed. Mins, 1 Jan. 1914; C. M. Lloyd to A.H., 10 Jan. 1914, LP AFF 8/18. Labour's *potential* in these areas was half-demonstrated by the SDF's creditable performance at the 1908 Shoreditch by-election.

[34] Thompson, *London,* p. 252; Gardiner, *John Benn,* p. 289. For the following, see Thompson's account, esp. pp. 228, 240–1, 243–7, 256.

Labour was consequently much weaker in the wards where the unskilled (and the middle classes) were numerous. In Deptford, the middle-class wards were left to Liberal Progressives. Both Woolwich and Deptford were Labour marginals by 1910, and there was no subsequent improvement. Liberal intervention – leading to a damaging split in the Progressive vote – had to be avoided at all costs.[35]

Socialists wanted both electoral success *and* a policy which was more radical than that offered by the Woolwich/Deptford parties. They needed something which was practical, but which had the ability to attract *all* working-class voters. Organisations in West Ham and Poplar, both extremely poor areas, whose electorate consisted mainly of unskilled workers, made a bold, innovative, attempt to create a broad class base. In West Ham, the ramshackle Liberal coalition had fallen apart in the 1890s. Keir Hardie was elected as an Independent Labour MP in 1892, and there was a 'labour' majority on the council for a brief period in 1898–9. This labour/Socialist group attempted to reconstruct the local economy. The Council employed people to undertake socially useful tasks (particularly to build houses). The direct labour approach would ensure adequate remuneration, and maximise the employment effects. The adoption of (generous) fair wages clauses on Council work might also encourage local employers to increase private sector wages in order to compete. Labour members of the Board of Guardians used Poor Relief payments to cushion the impact of poverty. They saw their action as a struggle for justice and human decency, conducted *by* local working-class people, *for* local working-class people. They wanted the working class to stand up for itself, to become a socially independent group. They also wished to show that Socialism was part of their kind of lifestyle, experiences, and interests. They wished to demonstrate that Socialists attached real importance to the concerns of ordinary people.[36] They were seizing the initiative by creating a Socialist party with 'material' policies.

They achieved good results. The ILP/SDF alliances were backed by the Trades Council and by the Gasworkers' union (whose members formed a substantial proportion of the electorate). In Poplar, there were over 1,500 local activists. Although the 'educationalist' tradition was such that formal organisation, especially in West Ham, was weak until after

---

[35] For organisational problems in Woolwich, especially in the central wards, and for the left's disruptive impact, *Pioneer and Labour Journal,* Jan. 1914, ILP No. 6 Div. Mins, 7 Dec. 1911–17 Mar. 1912, 4 Dec. 1913. Contrast Crossick, *An artisan elite,* p. 247, for presumed working-class 'unity' as an explanation of Labour's electoral expansion. The membership figures here are lower than those given by Thompson, the same source notes that LRC membership was less than 200 before 1908 (J.B.G. Diary, 5 Sept. 1909).

[36] For this period, Marriott (thesis), Chapter 6, and Buck, 'Municipal labour policy in East London'.

1910, municipal campaigning was carried out systematically across the constituencies. This is hardly surprising given Labour's insistence on the economic importance of municipal intervention. In West Ham, electoral support came from both the gasworkers (the local labour aristocrats) and from the casual labourers and dockers. 'Labour' often polled over 70 per cent of the vote in Council elections. Will Thorne, General Secretary of the Gasworkers' union, captured the West Ham parliamentary seat in 1906 with over 67 per cent of the vote, and held it in 1910. In Bow and Bromley, Lansbury was opposed by a Liberal candidate at the January 1910 parliamentary election, against the wishes of many local Liberal radicals and the Whips. He polled a third of the vote, 9 per cent more than the Liberal, although not enough to win (there was no Liberal opposition in December 1910 and Lansbury was returned).[37]

The position in Bow and Bromley illustrates one aspect of the problem which Labour faced in making this approach work. The Liberals here (and in other poor working-class areas) had a radical and popular image. Many supported elements of Lansbury's programme, particularly his desire to humanise the poor law and improve housing conditions. On the Board of Guardians, it was Liberal votes which ensured that 'Labour' ideas on poor relief were implemented. Direct labour schemes in West Ham (and on the LCC) had been initiated by the Liberals. It was not easy for Labour to establish a separate identity. Only the *extent* of Labour's commitment to intervention (their willingness to go beyond what was economically possible), and its support for *class* independence, made it different from radical Liberalism. Although this was enough to persuade some local Liberals to abandon their municipal alliance with Labour at the 1912 Borough Council elections, others remained committed to radical Liberal ideas as the only means of tackling the problems. Moreover, as the position in West Ham demonstrated, the Labour/Socialist strategy could only be taken so far. Ultimately the threat of bankruptcy or of ratepayer rebellion loomed too large. In order to avoid defeat, the Labour Council in West Ham supported only those schemes which it could afford to finance.

In West Ham, the moderation of policy, and of rhetoric, but the retention of a 'working-class' ethos helped create a more Labourist party image. This shift was not necessarily unpopular, but it could cause internal party problems if the Socialist wing attempted to block change. The Socialist

---

[37] Thompson, *London,* pp. 240–1, Marriott (thesis), Chapter 6 and Conclusion, p. xxv. For pre-war 'Poplarism', P. A. Ryan, 'Poplarism, 1894–1930', in P. Thane (ed.), *The origins of British social policy* (1978), pp. 56–83. The Bradford ILP adopted a similar strategy and watched the Poplar position carefully. See (Bradford) *Forward,* 9 Dec. 1905, 17 Nov. 1906, and below, pp. 258–60, 273–4.

resurgence of 1911–14 encouraged the reconsideration of a 'pure' Socialist strategy. It had some impact in West Ham, but the most evident impact was in Poplar. Lansbury's characteristically principled resignation from Parliament in 1912 was made in protest at ILP subservience to Liberal policy, with particular reference to women's suffrage. Neither the particular nor the general issue were the basis of Labour's local success. The party's municipal popularity half countered Lansbury's unpopular stance at the ensuing parliamentary by-election, but it was not enough to ensure victory.[38] The party had apparently abandoned the tangible, 'working-class', radicalism which it had previously represented. Lansbury's forces split. The largest section followed Lansbury and disaffiliated from the Labour party. However, many sympathisers in the constituency, and throughout the country, thought the issue and the tactic to be inappropriate. Politics in Poplar had been polarising in Labour's favour, but the reversion to radical socialism brought this process to a halt.[39]

The Poplar party's materially minded Socialist reformism had worked in Lansbury's poverty-ridden Bow and Bromley constituency, because municipal interventionism was materially relevant to many local people, and because Lansbury displayed real political skill. In different conditions, this approach was less relevant and less popular. Even in the adjacent, but slightly more affluent, seat of South Poplar, the Liberals easily defeated a local Socialist candidate at the 1914 by-election. The scale of the Socialist defeat might be explained by the disfranchisement of several hundred 'paupers' and the lack of NEC support. Municipal results certainly suggest a slightly stronger local position. Nonetheless, the result also reflects the difficulty of creating support where conditions were less than ideal. Lansbury's stance was hardly a 'model' strategy for the Labour party in London as a whole.[40]

There were no easy solutions to Labour's problems. The hard left Socialists condemned capitalism, emphasised alienation, revealed a distaste for the realities of working-class life and aspirations, and did little to promote individual material self-improvement or security. By contrast, the partial 'material' solutions offered by radical Liberals (minimum wages, insurance, attendance to specific economic grievances, and poor

[38] G. Sanders Jacob to G. L., 27 Nov. 1912, Lansbury MS 6 fos. 24–5. National developments are dealt with below, pp. 337–47. For a fuller account of the MacDonald/Lansbury ideological positions, above, pp. 71–6.

[39] For divisions, Ensor to G.L., 4 Feb. 1910, Lansbury MS 28 fos. 59–6, and Thompson, *London,* p. 230. At the LCC elections in 1913, the Liberals took second place, but were only narrowly ahead of the Socialists *(East London Adv., 3 Mar. 1913).*

[40] J. Jones, *My lively life* (1928), pp. 25–6, by-election coverage, *The Times,* 16–18 Feb. 1914. For organisational problems, e.g. J. Mylles to Ensor, 12 Oct. 1911, Ensor MS.

relief financed by the rich) created a fairly positive and attractive image. If the left's more Socialist moral reformism was a potentially useful weapon, it was not easy to maintain its primacy or purchase. Moreover, in areas where 'affluence' encouraged ideas of improvement, or where a different labour market structure made living standards less dependent on municipal intervention, the 'municipal' approach seemed irrelevant. In North and South London, Labour was checked by a radical, responsive, and fairly open Liberal party, whose approach suited local conditions. Some seats stood between these two extremes. On the fringes of the East End, in Bermondsey and Bethnal Green, Labour's image was formed from an amalgam of competing ideological/political strands. It faced a tough and radical Liberalism. It secured a core of support, but this was insufficient to threaten the Liberal ascendancy. The position was not encouraging.

Nonetheless, Labour did have strongholds. Labour parties in Woolwich and Deptford had exploited the weakness of local Liberalism, and had become the major Progressive force. The West Ham party had been more radical, and continued to represent a more municipally interventionist approach. However, like the Woolwich/Deptford parties, it was increasingly moving towards MacDonald's agreed municipal strategy and policies. By 1914 these groups represented different kinds of Labourism. Like the Poplar party, West Ham's Labour sympathisers were socially and culturally rooted in the poorer areas in a way that the Woolwich party in particular was not, but it had abandoned attack in favour of protecting its constituents. These successes represented exceptional, half-conflicting, responses to difficult conditions. The approaches were not easily transposed to other seats. It was not easy to raise the necessary hope, interest, or unity in socially and ethnically fragmented seats like Whitechapel and Limehouse, where there was as much poverty as there was in Bow and Bromley. Woolwich, Deptford, Poplar, and West Ham were not the first stage of a more general, and inevitable, Labour advance within London. The pre-war ideological tensions, and political problems, were to continue even in the 1920s.[41] Labour had made localised breakthroughs. It had not found a simple and generalisable solution to its electoral and political problems.

III

Conservative strength in the West Midlands stretched beyond Birmingham to include Black Country seats such as Wednesbury and Handsworth, whose electorates were largely employed in metals and

[41] See Gillespie (thesis), Chapter 8 and below, p. 438.

manufacturing, the more mixed industrial seats of West Bromwich and
West Wolverhampton, and even coalfield seats such as Nuneaton and
Tamworth. Employment was spread over a range of industries; social
conditions varied. If Birmingham was fairly affluent, the Black Country
was generally depressed and squalid. One broadly common factor was
the nature of 'Tory' politics. Even in the Black Country many enlightened
employers shared the ideas and practices of the Birmingham paternalists.
The Liberal Unionists who dominated local politics embraced support
for a degree of municipal (and later national) collectivism. This could
be used to protect living standards (where conditions were poor) or to
offer opportunities for educational and social improvement (where the
population was more affluent).[42] Liberal Unionist organisation was elaborate and accessible. There was little space for *any* anti-Tory force in
Birmingham or its immediate hinterland before 1906, although as in the
North-West – and in London – the Liberals could achieve some success
further from the epicentre of radical Tory politics.

In the 1890s, flimsy Liberal associations were organised and (poorly)
financed by tradesmen and professionals in both 'Tory' and 'Liberal' areas.
They adopted radical policies (by the standards of their times) and forged
close contacts with the (few) trade union leaders who were politically
sympathetic. There was a number of Lib/Lab municipal and parliamentary candidates in Birmingham, while Liberal/trade union relations were
even closer in Wolverhampton, Walsall, and Coventry.[43]

In 1906, the Liberals won seats, such as Wednesbury and West Bromwich, for the first time since before 1885. Free Trade so clearly affected
people's pockets that only Birmingham remained overwhelmingly Tory.
However, the Liberal revival seemed secure only where victory was reinforced by a long-standing Liberal political culture. These areas – with
their booming local economies – were unlikely to benefit from the Tory
policy of introducing tariffs. Liberal success in affluent Nonconformist
centres such as East Wolverhampton, Walsall, and Coventry seemed
solidly based. Elsewhere it still seemed precarious.

The 1906 victory did not transform Liberal politics. The regional
Liberal federation, together with small local groups of party activists,
struggled to keep organisations going in former Tory strongholds like

[42] For this and the following, D. Smith, *Conflict and Compromise* (1982), pp. 233–47.
For pro-Tory Catholic voters, J.B.G. Diary, 14 Jan. 1906, J. Simpson to J.K.H., 8
May 1909, FJ 09/158. For employers in the Black Country, S. Blackburn, 'Employers
and social policy: the Black Country chainmakers, the minimum wage campaign, and
the Cradley Heath strike of 1910', *Midland Hist.* (1987).
[43] J. Corbett, *The Birmingham Trades Council, 1866–1966* (1966), pp. 67–71, Jones,
'Municipal enterprise', pp. 240–5; G. Jones, *Borough politics*, p. 37. See also below,
pp. 184, 399.

Handsworth and Wednesbury, despite the fact that they now had Liberal MPs. Birmingham Liberalism barely existed. Only the West Bromwich party developed a convincing radical profile. 'Your right position', one local Socialist said of Dr Hazel, the local Liberal leader and MP, 'appears to be in the ranks of the socialist and Labour party.'[44]

Hazel had been able to transform Liberal policy in West Bromwich so rapidly because there was no entrenched, institutionalised, conservative elite. The process of moving Liberal politics towards practical social reforming policies could not, and did not, take place so rapidly where there was a stronger Liberal tradition, and party leaders were more attached to old Liberal rallying cries. Nonetheless, a local radicalisation *was* taking place and it was accompanied by, and associated with, the creation of a more efficient and democratic party machine. The reconstruction of the Walsall Liberal association in 1909–10 finally persuaded the conservative Liberal Imperialists to leave. Their ideas, and now their institutional power, were being undermined. In Walsall (and Coventry) strong, radical, ward committees became stronger. Branches of the Young Liberals and the WLA were rapidly expanding. In Walsall in particular, Liberal working men's clubs played a major role in party activity. Because there were so few wealthy Liberals, subscriptions, bazaars, and socials were the major means of financing local political activity. Larger contributions from the Whips financed parliamentary elections, and occasionally supported registration work.[45] Already moderately radical Liberal associations became even more open to pressure from below and from the centre.

In municipal politics, many Liberal organisations operated a policy of divide and rule, of minor 'Progressive' concessions to moderate Labour candidates, accompanied by support for realistic reform. In Coventry and Walsall, Liberal ward committees in Labour strongholds intensified support for 'sane' Labour candidates, although formal pacts were rejected. If some traditional and Centrist Liberals wished to avoid increasing the rates, political expediency persuaded them to accept fair wages contracts, municipal minimum wages, and housing reform. In Coventry, for example, the Liberal party suggested building up to 600 municipal houses

[44] *The Free Press*, 6 Mar. 1914; Mid. LF Mins, 28 Oct. 1913 (Wednesbury), 13 July 1909 and (e.g.) 28 Oct. 1913, 29 Jan. 1914. For Liberal unpopularity in 1914, *Midland Advertiser*, 25 July 1914. Hazel was also a Liberal Imperialist and this may have helped him project a political image which was more acceptable to local Tory voters.
[45] Cov. LA Mins, 5 Oct. 1910; Walsall LA Mins, 25 Feb., 11 June 1913. For bazaars in Walsall (£1,700) and Wolverhampton South (£600), *Wolverhampton Chronicle*, 22 Oct. 1913 and *Midland Counties Express*, 9 Nov. 1912. The Walsall Liberal Imperialists set up a branch of the Liberal League (Walsall Lib. League Mins, 5 Mar. 1910). For Liberal clubs in West Bromwich, *Free Press*, 16 Jan. 1914.

by 1914.[46] The Liberal party advocated other policies which Labour in principle supported. It also retained sections of an older electoral estate. This gave it added strength in the immediate electoral competition.

Parliamentary candidates were also increasingly drawn from the Liberal left. They campaigned for an extension of national insurance, land reform, and increased taxation of the rich in the interests of the poor. They emphasised what land reform meant to urban areas: less competition for employment from displaced rural labourers, more land on the outskirts of cities for municipal housing development, and lower rates through land reform. Some also argued that the logical extension of rural minimum wages was an urban minimum and state control of key monopolies. William Brown, an Eighty Club Liberal and the Walsall candidate, thus rightly declared that, on the main issues of the day, he and the Labour members 'were not divided by a hair's breadth'. He was even willing to defend the trade unions' sectional interests. If the Tories won the next election, he warned, 'every privilege which trade unionists held dear would be in danger the next day. Even in opposition they threatened things which were bad; what they would do with power in their hands he dreaded to think ...'.[47] This approach was reinforced and spread by Progressive papers such as the *Birmingham Gazette*.

Liberal Centrists like G. R. Thorne and D. M. Mason (East Wolverhampton and Coventry) were more typical of the candidates consciously adopted by Liberal associations which were hoping to attract working-class votes, whilst maintaining traditional Liberal support.[48] They merged 'old' and 'new'. Mason's hostility to rearmament, although unpopular with his constituency executive, forged a useful link with the Radicals' hostility to an active foreign policy and to 'unnecessary' public expenditure. It was also a useful counter-weight to the ILP's similar stance. The Liberal party was not without internal tensions, but an evolving strategy eased the problems.[49]

Labour was presented with an opportunity to expand in Birmingham and the surrounding area. Further afield, the position was less favourable. In 1906, however, it was in no position to do anything. The Tories had an entrenched hold; the Liberals had their Lib/Lab contacts. This, and the fact that Socialist organisations had little interest in compromise,

[46] *Coventry Standard*, 4, 5 Nov. 1910, Cov. LA Mins, 14 Mar. 1912, *Walsall Observer*, 25 Apr. 1914. For support of Labour moderates only, *Cov. Standard*, 4, 5 Nov. 1910, Wolv. T&LC Mins, 24 Oct. 1907, 8 May 1908, 2 Nov. 1911.
[47] *Walsall Obs.*, esp. 17 Jan. 1914, but also 24, 31 Jan., 21 Feb., 23 May, 5 July 1914.
[48] Cov. LA Mins, 31 Mar. 1911; Jones, *Borough politics*, p. 37.
[49] For Mason's problems with the Coventry Liberals, Cov. LA Mins, 22 Jan., 1 Oct. 1914 and for Wallhead, the ILP's prospective parliamentary candidate, *Cov. Standard*, 29 and 30 May 1914. William Brown shared these views (*Walsall Obs.*, 17 Jan. 1914).

meant that in most seats 'Labour' barely existed. Even in Coventry, one of the few seats with a Labour organisation, only a few of the skilled unions lent support, and middle-class Socialists led the party. When Labour fielded parliamentary candidates in Birmingham Bordesley and West Wolverhampton in 1906 (with Liberal support), the party's independent position was so weak that Liberal views dominated consideration of policy (while Liberal money paid for one of the campaigns). Richards in Wolverhampton unconstitutionally courted Liberal support in order to stand any chance of election. The Liberals presumed that Labour had considerable potential. However, there was little evidence of its intrinsic strength in 1906, except in East Birmingham, where a concentration of railway workers (in particular) meant that the Labour candidate (a railwayman) did much better.[50]

When Labour organisations did exist, they were hampered by sharp divisions between Socialists and trade unionists. The respective merits of a propagandist, 'educationalist', Socialism (and numerous assaults on the Liberal party) or organised, concentrated campaigning with 'practical' policies was a constant source of conflict. In Wolverhampton, the annual debate on this issue was embittered by the trade unionists' continued support for Lib/Lab and radical Liberal candidates. In 1908, inspired by Grayson and the Right to Work campaign, the ILP proposed fielding ten municipal candidates. The Trades Council said no. It prevented changes in the party constitution which would make the sanction of candidates suggested by affiliated organisations effectively automatic. Disputes of this ideological/strategic kind also disrupted Coventry's union/Socialist relations, and caused similar problems (albeit rather later) in Birmingham.[51]

Few Socialist campaigns were successful. Occasional Liberal/Socialist conflicts resulted in Socialist humiliation, except in a few party strongholds. In 'Liberal' Coventry, the seat with the most active Labour party, Labour did well in only three of the eleven wards. In other (working-class) wards poor performances became poorer as the onset of an election polarised support (Appendix 4, p. 461). Unless the Liberals were willing to step down (and despite Labour's hopes, they were not) Labour had

---

[50] H. Wilson to J.R.M., 25 Nov. 1905 and reply, 27 Nov. 1905, LRC 28/180 and 181; LRC 28/28–33, esp. J.R.M. to T. Richards, 19 Dec. 1905, LRC 28/31. Bruce Glasier was the Bordesley candidate. For the local position, S. D. Shallard to J.B.G., 4 Dec. 1905, JBG 05/37 and J.B.G. Diary, 1 Jan., 6 Feb. 1906. For Coventry, Whiting, *Cowley*, pp. 26–7, and for East Birmingham, below, pp. 187–8.

[51] J. Whittaker to A.P., 6 Nov. 1908, LP/EL/08/1/322, Wolv. T&LC Mins, 8 Nov. 1908, 1 Oct. 1908, 27 June, 18 Aug. 1909; *Mid. Daily Tel.*, 2 Nov. 1907; Birm. LRC Mins, 14 Nov. 1912 and Birm. ILP Fed. Mins, 7 Feb. 1913. In Wolverhampton, the parliamentary campaigns were discussed with the Liberals (Wolv. T&LC Mins, 29 Mar., 28 Nov. 1910).

little chance of becoming the major anti-Tory force in parliamentary politics.[52] Elsewhere, even in 'Tory' seats, the position was worse. Birmingham Bordesley, fought in 1906, had a moribund LRC by 1910. In the parliamentary election, Labour fought 'Tory' East Birmingham and West Wolverhampton, without Liberal opposition, but semi-Liberal campaigns, conducted with Liberal support, mobilised a Liberal vote, and led to a crushing defeat.[53] Both seats went uncontested in December 1910, as the ASE in Birmingham, and the Boot and Shoe workers and Postmen in West Wolverhampton, declined to waste money on such improbable seats.[54] Labour was not a threat; it was not even a useful ally.

IV

There was some change after 1910. This change is best examined by concentrating on the impact of two events: the rent strikes of 1912–14, and the Birmingham and Black Country municipal workers' strikes of 1913. The local left's desired ideological/strategic conception of how the party should proceed (a Socialist reformist/ethical socialist mixture, occasionally shrouded in a more aggressively anti-capitalist language) depended upon graphic experience of conflict and alienation to arouse class hopes and expectations. Struggles over housing and minimum wages were thus good in their own right, but the left also tried to make them the occasion for converting the Labour party and the electorate to Socialism.

At the same time, 'Labour' also sought to represent these experiences, and to use them to create political 'lessons'. Poor housing and poor pay for municipal workmen were 'moral' questions, given appalling housing conditions, and the profits made in municipal service industries. Labour added a materially relevant solution to its moral assault. This was a powerful combination. Labour's attacks on the problems had considerable credibility. James Whittaker and the Revd J. A. Shaw, prominent

---

[52] The local Labour party was first allowed, and then refused, permission to adopt a parliamentary candidate because there were unfulfilled hints of a pact (S. G. Poole to J.K.H., 7 Aug. 1909, FJ 1909/285, NEC Mins, 2 Dec. 1909, *Mid. Daily Tel.,* 6 Dec. 1909).

[53] Birm. ILP Fed. Mins, 11 Dec. 1909, F. Spires to F.J., 7 May 1909, FJ 09/157, NAC Mins, 26 Nov. 1909, NEC Mins, 2 Dec. 1909. Labour's vote in East Birmingham fell to 32 per cent. In Wolverhampton it fell only slightly to 47 per cent, but this was no higher than the Liberal poll in the 1890s.

[54] Richards, candidate in 1910, was directed to Northampton, where the prospects seemed better. Stuart accepted and withdrew on the same day after Liberals advised him against the campaign (NEC Mins, 24 Feb. 1910, Wolv. T&LC Mins, 22 Nov. 1910).

Labour activists, had also been visible leaders of the Tenants Defence League in Wolverhampton. The Workers' Union organiser, who represented the municipal workers' industrial demands, combined his strike and union work with the formation of ILP branches.[55] Birmingham Labour Councillors argued the case in the Council chamber. Labour stood for the strikers' interests; it was 'their' party.

The varying reactions to the strike illustrate how Labour groups tried to form a new political culture, and break the hold of the past. For the left, the 'radicalising' experience of 'conflict' had to be kept to the fore. There was consequently a revival of support for 'educationalist' propaganda campaigns. In Birmingham James Kneeshaw, the West Birmingham parliamentary candidate, rejected the 'Labour' strategy of concentration, moderation, and formal organisational work. ILP activists in Wolverhampton and Smethwick were evidently also dissatisfied with a 'moderate' approach to the strikes. In Coventry R. C. Wallhead, the prospective Labour parliamentary candidate, had sympathised with the left over its opposition to national insurance, and to the tenor of party policy. His views were not far removed from Lansbury's or Jowett's.[56] For Labour moderates, however, the lessons of the strike were more mundane. If Labour had held office, then the workers' attempts to achieve a better standard of living would have been more sympathetically considered. They were interested in the immediate cause of discontent, not on attacking the underlying causes, as the left viewed them. The Labour newspaper, the *Wolverhampton Worker,* immediately argued that the Council should attack the housing problem by building 250 homes. Labour was supporting morally defensible needs with practical proposals. It was the party to ensure that what was 'right' actually happened; 'practical' policies came to the fore.[57]

This moderate approach was the culmination of changes which were evident even in 1910. The development of a 'soft left' and the 'conversion' of the unions to Labour politics predated the strikes. Birmingham's unions – particularly the municipal workers and the railwaymen – became involved initially through the Trades Council. Unions and Socialists came together to form Labour organisations in Smethwick (1909) and in West

---

[55] *Wolverhampton Worker,* esp. June/July 1914; Jones, *Borough politics,* p. 49; *Midland Adv.,* 31 Jan. 1914.
[56] See p. 189 below.
[57] It also praised 'practical' reformist measures implemented by other parties *(Wolv. Worker,* Sept. 1913, June–Aug. 1914).

Bromwich and Walsall (1912); only the formation of the Wednesbury LRC can be traced to the strikes.[58]

Many Labour organisations had also abandoned 'educationalism' in favour of electoral organisation and moderation before the industrial unrest. The Birmingham LRC concentrated its forces and attempted to fund a full-time organiser. East Birmingham, with its electorate of municipal workers and railwaymen, received the most attention. The West Wolverhampton Trades Council selected a new, moderate, parliamentary candidate, A. G. Walkden of the Railway Clerks. Walkden, and his union, insisted on the formation of a 'model' party, on more organised campaigning, and improvements in the formal machinery. Local committees were to be set up. They were to meet regularly and undertake a greater proportion of the municipal work. Street captains were to organise literature distribution, particularly of the union-financed free newspaper, the *Wolverhampton Worker*. Local supporters were to begin canvassing and registration work, aided by a full-time agent and paid secretarial assistance.[59] The union – which dominated the constituency executive – agreed to pay 90 per cent of constituency expenses.

Labour organisations focused on material grievances in municipal politics. Cheap public housing and transport, the improvement of services, and municipal trading for service – not profit and rate reduction – were at the centre of its programme. Municipal election campaigns, a vital element in the dissemination of propaganda, increased in size and scope. The only limitations were money and the need to placate residual Liberal support by leaving middle-class wards uncontested.[60] By 1913, for example, every ward in East Birmingham and Smethwick, the largest element in the Handsworth constituency, had Labour candidates.

The results were encouraging. In Smethwick, Birmingham, and Wolverhampton West, the major breakthroughs came in 1910–11. In the 1911 Birmingham municipal 'General Election' (occasioned by boundary changes), at least one Labour candidate was returned in all three major East Birmingham wards. The strikes simply reinforced changes which were already under way. In 1913 Labour obtained more than 60 per cent of the vote in the East Birmingham wards captured in 1911. Labour also took seats in Rotton Park, part of which was in the West Birmingham

---

[58] Corbett, *Birmingham Trades Council*, p. 92 and TC Mins, esp. 14 Feb. 1912, 11 Mar. 1914; K. Richardson, *Twentieth century Coventry* (1972), pp. 190–1 and T&LC *AR* 1913; *Midland Chronicle*, 1 Nov. 1912; K. J. Dean, *Town and Westminster: a political history of Walsall* (Walsall, 1972), p. 21; *Smethwick Telephone*, 9 Oct. 1909.

[59] Wolv. T&LC Mins, esp. 29 Feb., 5 Mar. 1912, 4 July 1912, 21 Jan. 1913.

[60] There was some tension in West Wolverhampton, over Labour's expansion into 'Liberal' wards (*Wolv. Worker*, Dec. 1913).

constituency.[61] First contests in Wednesbury and West Bromwich resulted in strong (if unsuccessful) polls, while in Smethwick, where all the wards were contested, Labour candidates gained 44 per cent of the vote. Labour's potential as an anti-Tory force was slowly being realised. It was forming a new political culture, and developing a positive electoral appeal. It was a practical party, with a practical general programme, and a willingness to support the Statist interests of particular occupational groups. It was not yet the *automatic* choice for anti-Tory voters. Its organisational and political progress was limited. The left did not always give the new policies and approach an easy passage. The Liberals sometimes put up a fight; the Tories were far from defeated. Nonetheless, the pattern of change was established.

Labour also shifted its approach in the more Liberal areas. Despite Wallhead's support for the left, the Coventry labour movement was not dominated by Socialist ideas. Wallhead's stance *may* have been attractive to the growing numbers of unskilled workers, but the LRC's municipal moral reformism largely reflected the interests of the skilled engineers who were the major element in the party. Housing, cheaper tramways, and the provision of more free places in grammar schools were the major planks in its local political platform. The Trades Council's support for rent strikers' *demands* was not carried over into support for their *tactics*.[62] A strategy of concentration replaced the strategy of widespread and dispersed campaigning. With occasional lapses, Labour fought the same three wards in municipal and Guardians' contests from 1910 onwards. There was some organisational and electoral expansion, but it was confined to these party strongholds. The immature Walsall organisation, although weaker than the Coventry LRC, was moving in the same direction.[63]

Even by 1914, Labour had not swept all opposition aside. In some strongly Tory seats its organisational and electoral position was better than in 1906, and better than the Liberals', but it was still weak. In West Wolverhampton and East Birmingham it became the major anti-Tory organisation by being a 'reforming' party with a strong material attraction to

---

- [61] Nonetheless, the All Saints ward, which covered half the West Birmingham seat, was uncontested by Labour throughout this period, although there were plans to attempt a campaign in Nov. 1914 (Birm. LRC Mins, 9 Apr., 14 May 1914).
- [62] *Coventry Herald*, 23, 24 Jan. 1914; Richardson, *Coventry*, pp. 190–1 and *Cov. Herald*, 9, 10 Jan. 1914, Whiting, *Cowley*, p. 26. Contrast D Englander, *Landlord and tenant in urban Britain 1838–1918* (Oxford, 1983), pp. 143–52.
- [63] *Walsall Obs.*, esp. 23 May 1914. The strength of both organisations can be exaggerated. See anti-Labour attitude of Trades Council delegates, Walsall TC Mins, 20 Mar. 1918. Four trade union branches disaffiliated from the Coventry TC in 1909 because of its involvement in Labour politics. See also below, p. 396.

certain Statist occupational groups (especially the railwaymen). However, the middle-class wards (between a quarter and a third of these
constituencies) were still Liberal, while Labour's support in the working-
class wards was not so pronounced that it could win these parliamentary
seats without Liberal backing.[64] In a range of Tory seats, including
West Birmingham, Wednesbury, Handsworth, and West Bromwich,
Labour/Socialist groups were gradually becoming the major anti-Tory
force. They had not completed the political transition made by the East
Birmingham and West Wolverhampton parties. In West Birmingham,
Wednesbury, and West Bromwich, ILP municipal campaigns in 1913 did
not signal a commitment to more systematic political activity and 'practical' campaigning.[65] Strong Socialist elements resisted this approach. Some
sympathised with Jowett and Lansbury's dissident stance, and argued
for a return to unspecified, but radical, policies and an 'educationalist'
strategy. Others were emotionally, or ideologically, opposed to anything
short of Socialism. Institutional change was necessary before Labour
could make more of its potential.[66]

In constituencies with a more Liberal tradition, the radicalisation of
Liberal politics reinforced an existing Liberal political culture. Free Trade
and the market brought prosperity. The local economy was booming.
Liberal welfare politics catered for the insecurity felt even by skilled
workers. Labour's moderate moral reformism was thus too close to the
Liberals' own policies for it to be a politically successful stance. Labour
had a toe-hold in small sections of several 'Liberal' constituencies. This
was enough to encourage the moderates, but not to quell support for
a more radical approach. Problems persisted, as Labour made only slight
progress.

The Progressive Alliance in the West Midlands still had a *raison d'être*
in 1914. Labour's 'success' was confined to Tory seats. It appeared that
more of these seats might fall into its hands in the future. However,
its success was not so pronounced that the party could win even Tory
seats if faced with Liberal opposition. In Liberal seats it had not come
near finding an ideological solution to its electoral impasse. Progressive
co-operation was mutually beneficial.

---

[64] Birm. LRC Mins, 7 Feb. 1914; Wolv T&LC Mins, esp. 5 May, 2 July 1914. Wolverhampton West was not a working-class seat. The Liberals retained a middle-class vote and
some working-class Nonconformist support.
[65] Birm. LRC Mins, 14 Nov. 1912; *Midland Adv.*, 6 June 1914; *Midland Chron.*, 1 Nov.
1912.
[66] For the ILP opposition, e.g. J. D. Davis to J.R.M., 2 Apr. 1910, JRM PRO 30/69/1154
(co-operation with the Liberals); Birm. ILP Fed. Mins, 5 July 1912 (women's suffrage);
Birm. ILP Finance Comm. Mins, 26 May 1913, 29 May 1914 (suggested disaffiliation).

V

Few South Coast ports elected Progressives even in 1906. Several contributory factors can be identified. The occupational fragmentation of shipbuilding and dockyard work hardly encouraged notions of class
solidarity. Local conditions and practices did not encourage the idea that
political reforms could create greater prosperity or security. The labour-
force in the Admiralty dockyards (Chatham, Portsmouth, and Devonport)
was ununionised, but workers nonetheless enjoyed stable and continuous
employment. They could often secure employment for members of their
families. They became individually and economically committed to their
industry, and to existing employment methods and structures. Moreover,
when problems did arise, informal political pressure enabled them to
settle their grievances without industrial or openly political action. They
had little active tradition of hostility to authority. Moreover, Conservative
support for British naval strength was not only economically in their
interest (since their employment was wholly dependent on the level of
naval expenditure); it also had personal resonance. In addition to current
and former naval personnel, the electorate contained many dockyard
workers who had friends or family in the navy or merchant marine.
The Tories were the 'natural' party of the southern ports.[67] There seemed
little reason to support Progressive parties, with their commitment to
state intervention, and traditional hostility to the military and military
expenditure.

The Conservatives' clever propaganda reinforced their position during
the naval race/invasion scares of 1906–14. No Progressive response
seemed as politically dynamic. Nonetheless, the parallel, and even more
virulent, developments within German Conservatism had evoked a successful reply from the German SDP, which was based on patriotism and
reform, but not on militarism. Although many contemporaries observed
that radical Liberalism bore a strong resemblance to German Social
Democracy, there were few signs that the Liberals were embracing this
particular aspect of SPD philosophy.[68] Frequently, they relied on Free
Trade. Its continued material relevance to 'commercial' ports may explain
the Liberal success in 'Tory' Southampton, for example, at the 1906
election; its comparative unimportance in military towns may explain

[67] J. M. Haas, 'Trouble at the workplace: industrial relations in the Royal Dockyards,
1889–1914', *BIHR*, (1985), M. Waters, 'Dockyard and Parliament: a study of unskilled
workers in Chatham yard 1860–1900', *Southern History* (1984).
[68] The various naval/anti-German scares are dealt with in A. J. A. Morris, *Scaremongers*
(1984), Chapter 14. For the SDP, R. Fletcher, *Revisionism and Empire* (1984), pp. 73–7
and C. E. Schorske, *German Social Democracy 1901–17* (New York, 1972). For the
comparison, W. John to J.R.M., 29 Jan. 1913, JRM PRO 30/69/1157.

the Liberals' sweeping defeats in Chatham and Gravesend. In Devonport and Portsmouth, by contrast, the Liberals had a history of at least occasional success. In these Nonconformist towns, Liberal MPs managed to simultaneously satisfy the Radicals, while also adopting the kind of Imperialist line on defence which Radicals generally found uncongenial. H. E. Kearley, the Devonport MP, also had a good record of obtaining naval contracts and of dealing with dock-related employment problems. After 1904, Kearley's Liberal Imperialism (and the similar views of Bramsdon and Mallet in Portsmouth and Plymouth) was supplemented by the reforming politics of Sir John Benn (Devonport, 1904), Aneurin Williams (Plymouth), and R. C. Lambert (Portsmouth). When Bramsdon and Lambert stood down after their defeat in January 1910, they were replaced by the land reformer E. G. Hemmerde and the Fabian collectivist and Imperialist H. D. Harben. Local radical elements, backed for a while by a very radical Liberal daily newspaper, encouraged a more dynamic approach. The Liberals merged a popular old Liberalism with new 'working-class' policies; they remained attractive to some Nonconformist elements in this fiercely Nonconformist area. Significantly, after 1910, F. D. Acland, a Devon MP and a New Liberal sympathiser, began to suggest that the Government adopt model employment conditions in Admiralty dockyards. Liberalism was a broad, and not unattractive, coalition.[69]

Labour, like the Liberals, was generally handicapped by its history of opposition to naval expansion and expenditure. In Southampton, however, it faced neither a Progressive Liberalism nor an electorate which was so completely concerned with the services. The SDF-dominated Trades Council was attentive to industrial questions, pushed social reforms and dockyard conditions to the fore, and took a strongly Imperialist, 'Blatchfordite', line on defence. Only its Socialist rhetoric prevented more complete comparison with Labour's approach in other dockland towns (such as Liverpool).

Initially the SDF vote was 'strongly Tory', but after 1910 the SDF also expanded at the Liberals' expense. A 'tacit understanding' between the Progressive organisations in this double member borough was increasingly attractive, for, although the Liberals were being pushed into third place in the three largest, working-class wards, they were still strong in several mixed/middle-class Nonconformist wards. It would also appear that a Liberal revival was under way by 1914. The Liberal associa-

[69] F. D. Acland to Haldane, 29 Oct. 1911, Haldane MS 5909 fo. 167. Harben was proprietor of the Labour *Daily Herald.* For his observation that Liberal policy 'does not go nearly far enough', H. D. Harben to E. Pease, 7 Dec. 1911, Fabian MS A7/2 fo. 62. See also above, p. 65.

tion was being reformed, ward groups were urging the adoption of a more radical municipal policy (particularly with regard to unemployment), and the executive was declaring its support for Lloyd George's programme.[70] Neither the Liberal party nor the BSP could hope to win the seat on their own; both had substantial electoral bases which, if pooled, would be more threatening.

It was more difficult for Labour to succeed where the Liberals put up a stronger fight, or where militarism was a more potent force. The trade unions in the 'services' constituencies worked hard at attacking long-standing material grievances after 1905. Labour also generally selected parliamentary candidates from unions, like the Shipwrights, who could claim expert knowledge of local problems, and who could utilise the (limited) support for craft representation evident amongst local shipyard workers. They were conspicuously unsuccessful in parliamentary elections, seldom achieving even a fifth of the vote when confronted with both Tory and Liberal opposition. The politicisation of trade grievances did not appear to be popular, as many had always anticipated. Sexton of the Dockers had seen 'little hope of (such dockyard) constituencies'. Bruce Glasier had argued that 'There are far more important places to be considered.'[71] They were proved correct. In 1912 Peters reported that the position in Plymouth and Devonport was such that 'neither their strength nor their finance at present justifies a serious move'.[72] As the Secretary of the Devonport LRC noted, there were scarcely 2,000 Labour voters in the seat (electorate 12,125 in 1910), which was 'largely swayed by "Big Navyism"'. He added, 'the future bristles with difficulties for us locally and I feel utterly incapable of diagnosing the complaint or of finding a remedy for "Yardies Fever"'. Middleton could only tell him to 'keep pegging away'.[73]

This uninspiring advice made sense. Devonport, Portsmouth, and Southampton were double member boroughs. The Liberals might accept a joint campaign if Labour produced evidence of its ability to attract some support. In 1910, the defeated Labour candidate at Portsmouth had reported, with some Liberal encouragement, that 'the way is now clear for one Labour and one Liberal candidate at the next election'.

---

[70] J. H. Weber to J.R.M., 3 Mar. 1903, LRC 21/273, J. Laing to J.R.M., esp. 20 May 1903, LRC 9/395; *Southern Daily Echo*, 3 Nov. 1913; Guardians' results and reports of ward and divisional Liberal groups, *Southampton Times*, 11 Apr. and 21, 28 Feb., 4 Apr., 11, 18 July 1914.

[71] J. Sexton to J.R.M., 7 Oct. 1902, LRC 5/359; J.B.G. to J.K.H., 10 Oct. 1902, JBG 1902/47. For the unions, Haas, 'Royal Dockyards', pp. 220–4.

[72] NEC Mins, 11 June 1912, and similar reports on the withdrawn candidature in Plymouth, T. D. Benson to Ensor, 26 July, 30 July, 2 Oct. 1909, Ensor MS.

[73] W. H. Weston to J.S.M., 29 Feb. 1912, and reply, 1 Mar. 1912, LP/AFF 7/151–2.

Outside Southampton, where Labour was able to expand on its merit, a Progressive pact, with Labour as a very junior partner, was the party's only hope.[74]

VI

In London, the West Midlands, and the southern ports, as in the North-West, Labour was not in a position to launch a substantial anti-Liberal campaign. In the more 'Liberal' fringes to these 'Tory regions', it had made little headway. Only Coventry, Bermondsey, and Portsmouth had sanctioned candidates in 1914. In Coventry and Bermondsey, Labour's dedicated and half-successful parties made the most of local Liberal deficiencies on matters of social reform. They were amongst the most practical, and the most active parties; they showed some sympathy for the Socialist moral reformism espoused by Lansbury and Fred Jowett. However, both Coventry and Bermondsey had prospective Labour parliamentary candidates in 1909–10, and both had been denied sanction at the last moment by the NAC. They had made only limited progress since that time.[75] In Portsmouth, Labour was organisationally and financially even weaker, and had failed dismally in 1910. The Liberals, by contrast, seemed stronger than ever. However, this was a double member borough, and Labour may have held the balance of power. The Liberal Whips also wished to improve the 'national' party's pro-Labour credentials. This ensured the concession of the seat. As in 1910, other threatened campaigns either had their origins in the unthinking enthusiasm of local party members, or were unlikely to materialise.[76]

The socio-economic and political conditions in London's Liberal constituencies were not evidently more favourable to the Labour party, and only in West Ham and Bow and Bromley (both to be fought in 1914/15) was Labour the more successful anti-Tory party. However, Labour *was* developing a broader base, largely through the Socialist moral reformist approach successfully pioneered in West Ham and Poplar.[77] Here, and in parts of West London, Labour's organisational position and electoral performance improved, while the Liberal party was gradually

---

[74] *Fabian News*, Jan. 1910. Labour had expected a compact before the election (Fabian Soc. AR 1910).

[75] NEC Mins, 7 Oct., 2 Dec. 1909, NAC Mins, 26 Nov. 1909, vote of 7–6 against fighting in Bermondsey.

[76] J. MacTavish (candidate) to J.R.M., 15 July 1914, JRM PRO 30/69/1158, *Daily Citizen,* 10 Feb. 1914 and for the Liberal revival, *Southern Daily Post,* 22 Jan. 1912. For London 'campaigns', e.g. cutting in LP/ISL/08/1/25, referring to Central Finsbury, and J. W. Spear to J.R.M., 21 Apr. 1914, LP/PA/14/1/39.

[77] For Lansbury's selection and campaign, *East London Obs.,* 4 Apr., 2, 9 May 1914.

collapsing.[78] Nonetheless, Labour was not yet in a position to replace them. If the Labour party in Poplar was on the verge of adopting Gosling, the former Lib/Lab Secretary of the Watermen's Union, as its prospective candidate in 1914, Labour had not created comparable openings in seats like Bethnal Green. No other 'Liberal' constituency in London was likely to be fought.

Nonetheless, there were 'Tory' areas where Labour had made more progress in replacing the Liberals. Woolwich, Deptford, West Wolverhampton, and East and West Birmingham would all certainly have been contested, without Liberal opposition. West Wolverhampton and West Birmingham had not been fought by Labour in December 1910.[79] The Liberals in Southampton offered Labour a free run (as they had done in the past). However, the institutional power of the Socialists ensured that, as in 1903–6, 1909–10, and 1912, these 'negotiations' failed. The SDF-dominated Trades Council adopted a constitutionally 'irregular' (i.e. BSP) candidate whom the NEC refused to sanction. Nonetheless, 'Progressive' sentiment, always there, was now growing in strength. Local Liberal groups urged municipal co-operation, and a section of the local labour movement, including the ILP, was disassociating itself from the BSP.[80]

These few exceptions were the advance guard of a potentially larger electoral base. The Liberals were willing to accept further Labour expansion, provided Labour demonstrated its strength. In Tory naval boroughs like Chatham or Gravesend, and in seats in the Birmingham hinterland, Labour was not yet mature enough to force Liberal concessions in 1914.[81] In seats like West Bromwich, where the Liberals were very radical, the party met a further, serious, obstacle. Yet changes *were* taking place. In Wednesbury, Labour's prospective candidate was received with greater enthusiasm than the Liberals'. There was little Liberal municipal activity or organisation in West Bromwich, and none at all in Wednesbury and Handsworth. Nonetheless, in both Wednesbury and West Bromwich, the Liberals had candidates in the field and possession was nine-tenths

---

[78] Labour was particularly active and successful in Hammersmith, and to a lesser extent in Lambeth.

[79] Railway Clerks' *AR* 1916, p. 29; *Wolv. Worker,* 11 Nov., 4 Dec. 1913, 2 July 1914. Shann, the Labour candidate for East Birmingham, had to agree to find the bulk of the prospective election expenses (Birm. LRC Mins, 7 Feb. 1914).

[80] LRC 9/395–7, LRC 21/273; NEC Mins, 31 Aug., 7 Oct. 1909. See also NEC Mins, 29 June 1914, ILP Southern Div. Mins, 7 May 1914, H. Dubery to H. Bryan, 7 May 1914, Bryan MS IVB/3 fo. 15. The ILP and eight trade union branches refused to attend a selection conference in 1914 *(Southampton Times,* 23 May 1914, and for Liberal/Labour municipal agreement, 14 Mar. 1914).

[81] For the position in Gravesend, E. P. Wake to Ensor, 28 Sept. 1909, Ensor MS, H. Bryan to F.J., 12 June 1913, Bryan MS IVB/3 fo. 131. For NEC support for Liberal/Labour campaigns in Devonport, NEC Mins, 24 Feb. 1910.

of the debate. The Wednesbury LRC backed down from its commitment
to fight the seat; the West Bromwich Labour 'campaign' – which only
existed on paper – was financially and politically impossible. Even if
the NEC did not actively discourage the idea of a campaign, it was unlikely
to sanction a contest. Only Handsworth, where steps were being taken
to find a candidate in 1914, was a realistic *immediate* possibility.[82] If
Labour wished to expand its campaign, *and* its parliamentary representation, it could do so by co-operating with the Liberals and acting within
the Progressive Alliance.

The Tory regions were the new battlegrounds. If the Progressives could
not hold their own, and were forced back on Liberal strongholds as
a result of an imminent Labour assault on their position in the Tory
regions, they would lose their electoral primacy. However, there was
little indication that Labour was breaking out of the Progressive Alliance
in 1914 and hence undermining the Liberals' ability to compete. With
everything to win, nothing to lose, and few institutional obstacles to
the adoption of Progressive views, Liberal organisations had often moved
to the left in an attempt to turn defeat into victory. Despite this, the
Liberal party was *most* electorally successful where Centrist/New Liberal
parties built on the interests, and the existing perceptions, of local electorates. 'Radicalisation from below', as well as from above, was successfully
helping the Liberals to hold Labour in check, particularly where conditions were suitable (as in North and South London, in parts of the
Black Country, and in a few south coast seats, such as Devonport and
Portsmouth). Often the Liberals had captured so much of the reforming
ground that the Socialist case for a more radical approach, strong in
the period before 1910, was still seriously considered in 1914. However,
there was also growing support for a moderate alternative. This enabled
Labour to chip away at the Liberal lead on a very limited front. It was
a long-term programme.

The position was electorally a little better in some poverty-stricken,
often 'Liberal', parts of London. The Socialist moral reformism adopted
with some success in West Ham and Bow and Bromley involved extensive
municipal intervention. It was intended to restruct the local labour market. Improved conditions and higher expectations would develop work-

---

[82] Mid.LF Mins, esp. 29 Jan., 8 Oct. 1914, Birm. LRC Mins, 9 Apr. 1914 (Handsworth).
    For West Bromwich, NEC Mins, 9 July 1914, NAC Mins, 29 Aug. 1914. For Wednesbury,
    Midland Adv., 14 Feb., 4, 25 Apr., 25 July 1914. Wednesbury had been considered
    by Gladstone as a possible Labour seat in 1903. Other possibilities included Dudley,
    Burton, Kingswinford, or Aston Manor. See e.g. rumours of a campaign in Dudley,
    discussion of a campaign in Burton. *D.H.,* 29 Apr. 1912, *Burton Evening Gazette,*
    20 Oct. 1909.

ing-class self-confidence in themselves and their confidence in Socialism. The 'radicalism' of this stance was not easily maintained. Labour could slip to the right, and go for the attainable. It could become *more* radical, and adopt less material policies, or those more associated with the operational or fundamental ideology of the left (as Lansbury did over women's suffrage). The approach was also not easily transferred to other, even poverty-ridden, areas, particularly where ethnic conflict could be used to prevent a 'class' unity. Moreover, Liberals also attacked poverty, and developed a popular and dynamic image. Their moral populism was augmented by an economically relevant support for minimum wages and other state reforms. It was mobilised by locally important, and popular, individuals and ideas. Liberalism could prove a difficult obstacle. Moreover, the Tory strategy of Tariff reform and immigration control created an equally dynamic and popular image. There was no obvious electoral space for Labour to exploit.

By contrast, in the 'Tory' areas Labour moved much closer to becoming the major radical party. In Birmingham and its hinterland, and in some parts of London (particularly Woolwich and Deptford) union-dominated Labour organisations directed the party away from a sterile 'Socialism' and towards an economically more relevant approach. Although Labour was beginning to develop a 'political' stance, and to merge policies with an attachment to a Tory political culture, with practical reforms in Woolwich and Deptford, it was often dominated by craft unions and craft interests. In Birmingham and its hinterland, however (and even in West Wolverhampton), Labour built up its image as a reforming party more completely. It worked for real improvements in living standards; it paid particular attention to the interests of locally numerous Statist groups, such as the railwaymen and municipal workers. However, if Labour seemed to be the party of the future, it had not yet made its position secure. Consolidation would come before expansion could even be contemplated.

Labour had not broken through on a broad front by 1914. It needed the Progressive Alliance to help it gain and hold Tory seats. It needed to make these seats secure, to expand its appeal in Tory areas, and develop a new means of undermining the Liberals before it could become a serious rival to the Liberal party. Meantime, Labour could benefit by co-operation, and only lose by attacking such an attractive force as the Liberal party. The Liberals also needed Labour as an ally to help them secure the formerly Tory seats which were an important part of their electoral coalition in 1910. In 1914, it appeared that Liberal/Labour aims might still be compatible.

Chapter 7

The coalfields

In 1911 there were a million miners in England and Wales, spread over seven major coalfields. They constituted at least 30 per cent of the electorate in thirty-six constituencies, more than 10 per cent in another thirty-eight.[1] Before 1906, most of these seats were consistently Liberal. Labour's challenge in these areas could thus be of major significance. However, despite Labour's post-war success in mining areas, there was no sign of a simple and inevitable transfer of support from the Liberals to Labour even by 1914. Liberal strength was based on more than a (waning) Nonconformity and trade union support which was passing to Labour. Regions had differing economic interests, and their miners different practices and traditions. How parties acted politically and represented or interpreted these facts was of considerable importance. Popular political attitudes did not automatically change once the MFGB affiliated to the Labour party in 1909. It was one thing to convince the leading figures in the MFGB and its constituent elements, another to convince local members to become active in Labour organisations or to vote for Labour candidates. They needed convincing, and 'union politics' were not on their own a sufficiently powerful argument. To imply an inexorable march of Labour overstates the power of the pre-war Labour dynamic, and fails to put sufficient stress on the varying elements behind a regionalised, and partial, pre-war Labour advance in the mining areas.[2]

Initially, Labour made most headway in the North-West (Section I). Here, and unusually, miners divided between the Liberals and the Tories. It was thus difficult for the LCMF to engage in political activity. It sup-

[1] Figures from Gregory, *Miners*, Appendix B. This chapter deals mainly with mining-dominated constituencies, although reference is made to the semi-mining seats. A few constituencies which were *politically* dominated by miners are also included. The results of Liberal/Labour (and Socialist) clashes in parliamentary elections are given in Appendix 3, pp. 453–4.
[2] I am aware that there were differences within regions (as I point out in several instances below). Nonetheless, the regional approach offers a valid, and manageable, means of analysing the overall pattern of political support.

ported the Labour party, even before 1906, because this 'independent' approach to political campaigning was the only means by which it could secure craft representation. The Liberals were too weak to resist LCMF attempts to elect Labour candidates. However, Liberal associations often did not *wish* to oppose Labour candidates, most of whom were earnest ex-Liberals, especially as they were intending to stand in seats where Liberal associations were half-derelict. Nonetheless, Labour's combination of craft representation and Liberal policies was not a strong platform, given the existence of an attractive rival in Tory collectivism. Socialism was no alternative. In the few seats where Socialist organisations existed, a weak 'Labour' position was further undermined, particularly where the Liberals were enthusiastic reformers and could assume some of the moderate Labour ground. By 1914, however, there were signs of a compromise between Socialist supporters of a more active and independent stance, and moderate supporters of reforming policies. This was based on support for local municipal reform, along the lines laid down in the national municipal programme, and further state intervention in the coal industry. Deterministic Socialism, ethical socialism, and a belief in craft representation as an end in its own right were being left behind.

In the North-East, South Wales, and Yorkshire coalfields, the Liberals were historically much stronger (Section II). Liberal allegiances had been in part based on a common cultural bond between Liberal leaders and the generally Nonconformist miners. In the North-East and South Wales, these bonds were reinforced by a belief in Free Trade, stemming from the importance of coal exports to local prosperity. Although in Yorkshire miners were already showing their support for a more industrially militant approach (supporting eight hours legislation and the formation of a national union in the 1890s), Liberal economic assumptions (including the idea that wages should fluctuate according to prices) were widely accepted. In Yorkshire and the North-East, mining-influenced Liberal associations buttressed an economically attractive Liberalism with support for municipal reforms, labour representation (under Liberal auspices), and the preservation of local mining interests. By 1910, New Liberal influences were also beginning to augment the local Centrists' support for social reform. The oligarchical strength of implacably conservative, usually Radical, elements – who dominated Liberal politics in South Wales – was much less evident in the 'Liberal' Yorkshire and North-East coalfields, even if Radicals were still significant.

In the Midlands, Centrist economic conceptions were reinforced by high wages, company paternalism, a record of joint 'progress' by negotiation, and strong links between the miners' unions and local Liberal parties (Section III). This Liberal political culture was not remotely threatened

in the East Midlands before 1914. Economic prosperity appeared to reinforce its validity. Union leaders in South Wales were, however, beginning
to question Liberal economic views. In Yorkshire and the North-East
attitudes stood somewhere between the two extremes. Nonetheless, rank
and file members were less convinced than party leaders in Yorkshire
and the North-East, and not convinced at all in the Midlands. A Liberal
political culture had strong foundations and substantial support.

   Labour's political intervention in Yorkshire, South Wales and the
North-East was initially conditioned by ILP ethical socialists. They had
some success in South Wales. A local belief in the ideals of communal
social provision, reinforced by a radical Nonconformity, were not easily
accommodated by conservative local Liberal parties (Section IV). Labour
successfully demonstrated that it could provide an attractive alternative
to the Liberal party, but only in a few instances. It abandoned ethical
socialism, built on a Lib/Lab tradition, and expanded its support (Section
V). Even when ethical socialists were institutionally important, however,
Labour was beginning to try and broaden its social base by including
support for more material, less esoteric, policies in its political rhetoric.
However, it was not until the 1912 miners' strike that the importance
of political power to the economic position of miners was properly demonstrated. The strike, and the nature of the Liberals' response to it, helped
undermine the Liberals' claim to be 'the miners' party'. Experience and
politics then merged. Labour made only limited headway in the coalfields
as a whole until the political lessons of the strike (the limited attractions
of the Liberal party) and a more 'practical' political approach from Labour
came together. By 1914, it had reached parity with the Liberals in most
mining areas in South Wales, and in some parts of Durham. In these
coalfields at least, the 'new' approach was beginning to resemble the
appeal of those few candidates who had previously succeeded in displacing
the Liberals. Nonetheless, the Liberals put up a fight by adopting new
ideas and updating old allegiances. In most parts of the Yorkshire and
many parts of the North-Eastern coalfield, Labour had not undermined
the economic arguments, or the social appeal, of a popular, modernised,
Liberalism (Section V). In the Midlands (Section VI) Labour had not
even dented the Liberals' lead.

   Before 1914 Labour did not appear to be a credible party with the
ability to deliver real changes in miners' living standards. Although
nationalisation had appeared as an issue, and could be seen as a means
of protecting coalminers (particularly those in less profitable areas) from
the ravages of the market, considerable state control did not appear to
be economically sustainable before the war. Labour could obtain some
mileage from this issue, and from other aspects of its positive appeal

to miners. However, even in the 'militant' South Wales coalfield, Labour was not evidently the only party which a miner could contemplate supporting. As a result, Labour was in no position to attack the Liberals in 1914–15, and was not about to do so (Section VII). It was developing its strength generally and establishing a hold in South Wales and some parts of Durham. In the longer term this might have endangered the Liberals' position. In most regions, however, and especially in the Midlands, there were few signs of its total post-war ascendancy in 1914.

I

Most of the North-West coalfield seats returned Tory MPs in the 1880s and 1890s. In mining seats, as in other North-West constituencies, ethnic divisions, religious traditions, and local economic circumstances supplied the conditions in which a populist Protestant Conservatism could thrive. Moreover, a precarious prosperity could appear to be dependent on the decisions of Tory coalowners and the exclusion of immigrant Irish labour. There were few religious, economic, or cultural affinities with the Liberal party. The miners – who lived in towns, rather than in classic 'mining communities' – were not readily 'unified'. Union leaders, themselves politically divided, did not try and persuade their members to support the Liberals. Although Eccles and Leigh fell under Manchester's radical spell, in mining or semi-mining seats like East Manchester, Ince, St Helens, Wigan, and Westhoughton, the Liberals barely existed in the 1890s, and made little subsequent recovery.[3] Liberals hoped that a Labour party with LCMF support would be electorally more successful because it was the expression of *all* miners' industrial and material interests. It could thus succeed where the Liberals' only prospect was defeat. The Liberals *encouraged* Labour expansion.[4]

By 1906 there were Labour candidates in Ince, St Helens, Newton, and Westhoughton. Wigan, also dominated by miners, was fought by a Labour-backed Independent Suffragist. Local Liberals generally cooperated. In Newton they offered to raise funds for the Labour candidate. Labour had to refuse, but unofficial relations were cordial, and tacit assistance very much in evidence.[5] The results were encouraging. All

[3] For social matters, R. Challinor, *The Lancashire and Cheshire miners* (Newcastle, 1972), Chapter 15, Walton, *Lancashire*, pp. 319–20. Political background from Hill (thesis), pp. 264–6, 362–9, Clarke, *Lancashire Liberalism*, pp. 321–3. Religious conflicts and the ILP's inappropriately moralising Socialist response to working-class life also helped limit Labour's expansion in the Scottish coalfield, although here the Liberals were more successful. See e.g. Hamish Fraser, 'Labour in Scotland'.
[4] See above, pp. 145–6, 148, 158–60.
[5] J. Herbert to J.R.M., 15 and 17 May 1905, JRM PRO 30/69/1149, LP Circular, n.d. 1905, LRC 4/10/5, Clarke, *Lancashire Liberalism*, Chapter 12.

the official Labour candidates were elected. Although the Tories won Wigan, the Independent Labour candidate pushed a semi-official Liberal into third place.

The Progressive strategy was comparatively unhindered by Socialist counter-proposals or objections. Only St Helens had an ILP branch. With the exception of Wigan (where the railwaymen were active) the LCMF *was* the Labour party. It appointed agents and formed divisional Labour organisations, in an attempt to create better machinery; it made no attempt to 'make' opinion, or persuade other unions to participate in Labour politics.[6] In St Helens, local Labour/ILP activists complained in 1908 that 'at the time of municipal elections they got no help' from the miners' agent. Propaganda work was almost unknown; organisation – outside Ince – was admitted to be poor, since the miners' political agents were often unsuited to their task.[7]

Labour did not really have a distinctive policy. The Wigan LRC, for example, adopted Liberal policies (like the Nelson textile workers) on education, and opposed high rates and 'maladministration'.[8] Its parliamentary candidate in 1910, Harry Twist, was an earnest ex-Liberal who stressed his faith 'in the social side of Christ's gospel'. T. Glover in St Helens was only a little more radical; W. T. Wilson and J. A. Seddon were too conservative for most radical Liberals. All four Labour MPs stressed conventional Liberal issues in 1910. Glover even praised the Liberals' eight hour day legislation, despite its local unpopularity.[9] Labour politics – as an independent entity – consisted of the mining unions' desire to get their parliamentary candidates elected. This did not substantially increase the old Liberal vote. Labour scraped in at the January 1910 election, but following the December campaign only Ince and Westhoughton still had Labour MPs. As in other Lancashire seats, Labour's vote rose and fell with that of the Liberal party.

This approach reflected one strand of opinion within the LCMF's politically active membership. Almost all Labour Councillors and activists in Leigh, for example, were ex-Liberals. They had joined Labour because

---

[6] Hill (thesis), pp. 326–8, Morris (thesis), Chapter 2, I. Scott 'The Lancashire and Cheshire Miners' Federation 1900–14', York Ph.D. thesis 1977, pp. 126–38. The LCMF also paid considerable attention to East Manchester, which was already dominated by the Labour party at the municipal level in 1906. A Labour contest in 1910 was accepted by the local Liberals as a natural reflection of the electoral position (see above, p. 148).

[7] ? to A.P., 15 Nov. 1908, LP/EL/08/1/319, Scott (thesis), pp. 237–8, 361, Leigh LP *AR* 1915. Several agents were dismissed during this period.

[8] Ibid., LP/EL/08/1/319, W. Farshaw to A.P., 5 Nov. 1908, LP/EL/08/1/144, *Liv. Post*, 2 Nov. 1907. See also above, p. 144.

[9] Scott (thesis), pp. 232–3; J. Wedgwood to E.P., 30 June 1908, Fabian MS A9/2 fos. 86–7; *Worker*, 23 Sept. 1911.

they 'did not think that the (Liberal) party was going fast enough'.[10] However, union politics were changing. The LCMF Executive was captured by the ILP in 1908, and Socialists grew in strength on the Cumberland miners' executive. Socialist union leaders tried to adopt a more anti-Liberal approach. The regional organisers, Greenall, Sparling, and McGurk, encouraged the dissemination of Socialist views. Three Socialist candidates were selected to fight Liberal-held seats (Cockermouth [1906], Whitehaven and Leigh [1910]). Nonetheless, this produced parallel political tendencies; it did not transform union opinion. In Leigh, the LRC's leader, the Rev W. J. Bull, opposed the LCMFs decision to field a Labour candidate and divide the Progressive vote. At least one Leigh miners' lodge asked the Liberals to oppose Greenall, Labour's candidate in 1910, and many Labour activists worked for the Liberals when he withdrew for the December election. A poll of Labour activists almost succeeded in replacing Greenall, whom they regarded as too extreme, with a moderate Progressive.[11] Miners in Whitehaven, Cockermouth, and Eccles would have little to do with the local ILP-dominated, and only nominally 'Labour', organisation. In Cockermouth, Smillie had to 'build from the very bottom' in 1906 and the position had not improved by 1910.[12] The election results confirm that whilst a miner, irrespective of his policies, attracted some mining votes, the radical, anti-Liberal, approach failed where the Liberals had a strong past reputation and a radical present. In Cockermouth, Leigh, and Eccles, Labour trailed its Liberal opponents by around 15 per cent of the vote. However, in Whitehaven (with a stronger Tory tradition) it ran the Liberals very close, and, as in Cockermouth, the Tories were consequently successful. To the annoyance of ILP radicals and some Tory miners, and the satisfaction of moderates, the Progressive parties in Cumberland struck a bargain. Labour got a free run at Whitehaven in December 1910, and the Liberals a free run in Cockermouth. There were consequently two Progressive victories, instead of two possible defeats.

At the LCMF Conference in 1910, the three LCMF MPs defended their refusal to speak for the union's Socialist candidate at Leigh in January 1910. Delegates were only just dissuaded from passing a vote of no confidence. This was only partially a victory for the left. Socialist delegates were supported by many Tory miners. They had supported LCMF affiliation to the Labour party because (this was before the 1906 election pact)

---

[10] *Leigh Journal*, 6 Nov. 1908. See also, for the party's campaign, *Leigh Chronicle*, 21 Jan. 1910.

[11] Scott (thesis), pp. 231, 359, 421; G. Jones (thesis), p. 49; Morris (thesis), p. 23. However, see the conflicting impression, LP *AR* 1910, pp. 62–3.

[12] *Whitehaven F.P.*, 9 May 1914, LP *AR* 1911, p. 127, *West Cumberland Times*, 8 Aug. 1906, 22 Jan. 1910.

it seemed to be independent. However, by 1910, Labour's close association with the Liberals ensured that, for example, it supported Liberal policy of legislative restrictions on the number of hours which miners could work. The threatened loss of earnings for miners working long hours on piece rates did not create a favourable view of 'Labour' policy. Although the Liberals' minimum wage legislation was fairly well received in Lancashire, where wages were low, many miners thought the minimum was *too* low to be useful. They wanted Labour to amend the Liberals' decision. Craft representation should not be Liberalism by the back door.[13]

The response to this was a less passive attitude to the Liberals, not the adoption of Socialism. At the local level, Labour began to create and adopt its own views. In constituencies such as Leigh, Labour developed policies on housing – of particular importance locally – which were more radical than those of a (municipally) conservative Liberal association. Some mining lodges began urging the regional unions' annual conferences to consider funding municipal activity. Labour politics were beginning to be more than just craft representation plus Liberal policies.[14]

This change was accompanied by minor organisational and electoral improvements in Labour's local position. Ward committees were spreading. An ILP branch was formed in Wigan, and a Labour/ILP alliance was coming together in Whitehaven. Registration work was being tackled with greater enthusiasm.[15] In Leigh, a new and more efficient agent opened three Labour clubs, appointed ward secretaries, and encouraged the formation of ward committees which included trade union leaders from non-mining organisations. Labour's municipal activity picked up and gained support. The four mining-dominated Pemberton wards (in Wigan for municipal purposes, but a major part of the Ince constituency) were contested regularly after 1910. By 1913 all four were returning Labour candidates with substantial majorities. In Wigan, the Progressive vote at the 1913 municipal elections topped 55 per cent. National party organisers thought that, at the next parliamentary election, Labour might hold Ince and regain St Helens, Wigan, and Newton. Labour-held Westhoughton, with fewer miners, and a larger Liberal municipal vote, was still doubtful.[16] In the Leigh constituency, despite its Liberal past, Labour

---

[13] R. Church, *The history of the British Coal Industry*, 3 (Oxford, 1986), p. 745.
[14] Scott (thesis), p. 243, Morris (thesis), pp. 22–3, 59, *West Cumb. Times*, 28 Jan., 25 Mar. 1914.
[15] Morris (thesis), pp. 59, 297, Leigh LP *AR* 1915, *Wigan Obs.*, 31 Mar. 1914. See also National Union of Dock Labourers', *AR* 1914, reporting registration expenses of £176 in St Helens; *Whitehaven F.P.*, 14 Mar. 1914.
[16] *Wigan Obs.*, 11 June 1914, S.H. to J.S.M., 13 June 1914, LP/ORG/14/1/51; *Horwich Chronicle*, 11 Apr. 1914, S.H. to J.S.M., 16 Feb. 1915, LP/ORG/14/1/110. For a similar change in Eccles, above, p. 159.

had nearly as many Councillors in Leigh itself as the Liberals and Tories (Leigh supplied around half the constituency electorate). There was also some improvement in Tyldesley, a mining-dominated area and a weak spot in the Leigh constituency at the January 1910 parliamentary election.[17] Higenbottom argued that there was 'no enthusiasm' for the Liberals in the division by 1914. He regarded the seat as winnable. Nonetheless, despite all the efforts, and the localised progress, informed opinion and municipal election results both suggest that the Liberals were still ahead of Labour.[18] Much of Leigh and Atherton, many of the textile workers, and a good proportion of the miners were still Liberal. Labour did not appear to be a sufficiently distinct and attractive rival. It did not have the means to counter the radical image constructed by Raffan, the Leigh Liberal candidate (who was prepared to support a full New Liberal programme, including nationalisation) and by his allies.[19] Labour still had an uphill struggle in 'Liberal' mining seats if its Progressive partner put up a fight.

The Liberal *and* Labour parties needed the Progressive Alliance. Although as Labour put down roots, and expanded its appeal, it became more popular, it was not in a position of authority and control. It (like the mining unions who supported it) could only lose if the Progressive Alliance disintegrated. By contrast, if the Alliance continued, Labour might hold Ince, Westhoughton, and Whitehaven, and regain Wigan, Newton, and St Helens. If the arrangement of 1910 prevailed, the Cumbrian mining seats would again probably return Progressives, and the Cumbrian miners would have an 'agent' in Parliament. The Liberals recognised Labour could not succeed without their support. They let it be known that they could, if necessary, undermine Labour's prospects of success in a number of seats. This was a shot across the bows, not a declaration of war. If conflict, on a limited front, was not impossible, Labour was unlikely to be responsible for a major change of strategy. When it had tried to expand at Cockermouth (1906 and 1910), and at Eccles and Leigh (January 1910), it had failed. It had only slightly eroded the Liberals' lead in these seats by 1914. The Liberals still had the ability to undermine Labour's prospects in 'Tory' mining seats. The Alliance made sense.[20]

[17] Scott (thesis), pp. 359–61, Leigh LP *AR* 1915. Reports of meetings and UDC results, *Leigh Chron.*, 22 May 1914, *Leigh Journ.*, 7 May 1913.
[18] S.H. to J.S.M., 13 June 1914, LP/ORG/14/1/52.
[19] *Leigh Chron.*, 15 Jan. 1914, *Leigh Journ.*, 1 May 1914. For textile workers' hostility to Labour representation in ballots under the Trade Union Act of 1913, White, *Trade union militancy*, p. 154. For Raffan and his support, *Leigh Chron.*, 14–28 Jan. 1910, *Leigh Journ.*, 3 Dec. 1909.
[20] For continuing Liberal strength, *Wigan Obs.*, 31 Jan., 4 June 1914. It was likely that in 1914 Labour would fight Whitehaven, the Liberals Cockermouth (*Whitehaven Free Press*, 7 Mar. 1914, *West Cumberland Times*, 25 Mar. 1914).

II

The leadership *and* rank and file members of the Yorkshire, South Wales, and North-East miners' unions were overwhelmingly Liberal before 1906. The unions' politics were an important aspect of the Liberals' success, particularly in those constituencies where a union member was the Liberal candidate. This was most common in the Midlands, although there were Lib/Lab candidates in most coalfields. The miners' Liberal allegiances, however, were the result of a deeper commitment to Liberalism. Indeed, the miners' Liberalism was so intense, their loyalty so pronounced, that some Lib/Lab MPs continued taking the Liberal whip, even after the MFGB affiliated to the Labour party in 1909. Their mining constituents did not insist that they change their party label. The continuing existence of a Lib/Lab strand was most prevalent in the Midlands coalfields, but Thomas Burt (Morpeth), J. Wilson (Mid-Durham), and Charles Fenwick (Wansbeck) in the North-East, and (after a while) J. Wadsworth (Yorkshire, Hallamshire) also took the Liberal Whip. In the North-East, it was unlikely, as one ILP organiser claimed, that 'with Burt and Fenwick out of the way the miners would be practically solid for Labour'; that did not happen in Burt's seat (Morpeth) even in 1918.[21] Morpeth (like Hallamshire and possibly other Lib/Lab seats) was not a Lib/Lab seat out of personal loyalty. The Liberal association had dominated the electoral campaigns, and had created the party image. Miners joined Liberal associations; the Liberal party had not become subsumed by the union. In January 1910, some of the most 'earnest and enthusiastic' Liberal workers in the Durham mining seat of Bishop Auckland were miners, despite the fact that Labour's parliamentary candidate was William House, a local man and Chairman of the DMA.[22] The nearby Houghton-le-Spring Liberal association, like those in Morpeth and Hallamshire, reportedly consisted very largely of miners. When House stood against a Liberal at Houghton-le-Spring in 1913, local lodges were split by the conflict. Every lodge in the constituency was represented at the Liberal candidate's selection conference, and many lodge officials spoke for him during the election. In North-West Durham, a large number of mining lodges declined to attend the Socialist Labour candidate's selection conference in 1913. Again, leading local miners spoke for the Liberals at the

---

[21] M. Simm to F.J., 24 Nov. 1909, FJ 09/536. Union politics had *officially* changed (W. Straker to J. Corrie, 13 July 1909, NMA Letter Book, fo. 650, noting Straker's resignation from the Northern Liberal Federation). However, for the real position in the North-East, N.E., 2 Feb., 2 Mar., 6 May 1914, Gregory, *Miners*, pp. 79, 112, NMA EC Mins, 9 Feb., 17 Mar., 13 May 1914.
[22] *Lib. Agent*, Apr. 1910.

ensuing by-election. Mining lodges in Jarrow, Gateshead, South Shields, and in the Yorkshire seats of Rotherham, Barnsley, and Osgoldcross, refused to join their local LRCs.[23]

The active involvement of individual miners, and sometimes of lodge-based Liberal associations in Liberal politics, reflected the fact that local Liberals were not unresponsive to material questions. In many parts of the Yorkshire and North-East coalfields, Liberalism was not a dry, conservative, creed; even many Old Liberals supported municipal intervention and reform. The Barnsley Liberals supported such 'radical' policies as fair wages clauses. The Bentley UDC near Doncaster built fifty houses under the Town Planning Act in 1913, 'and this', the local newspaper reported, 'in a Council which is not by any means dominated by Labour influences'. Liberal Boards of Guardians attempted to humanise conditions in workhouses, and to keep people out of them whenever possible. Barnsley's Liberal Guardians adopted illegally high scales for outdoor relief. Poor Law authorities in the North-East were tough but not ungenerous; municipalities were far from backward.[24]

This is not an apologia for Old Liberalism. Some of these policies were not incompatible with a desire to keep down the rates. Municipal enterprise could be used to finance social expenditure without major rate increases; it was a sound business proposition. There were weaknesses. Some Radicals made it abundantly clear to local voters that they disapproved of such working-class interests as drinking and Sunday entertainment. However, they were not all municipal puritans, and those that were were not always entirely unpopular even with some members of the working class. By linking *excessive* alcoholic consumption with immorality and social irresponsibility, the Liberal stance was not unattractive to tough-minded, respectable, working-class individualists.[25]

Old Liberalism had a second weakness. Its adherents did not always attempt to involve miners in local politics. In Doncaster, for example, there was no political organisation except for a few ward committees in 1914; miners' support was taken for granted. Before 1910, Liberal activity in Bishop Auckland and Houghton-le-Spring consisted of registration work and occasional meetings of known supporters. Neither were miners necessarily allowed to influence Liberal executives. In Bishop

[23] Gregory, *Miners*, p. 80, N.E., 6 Jan. 1914; NMA Special Comm. Mins, 26 Aug. 1912; Marsden Lodge Mins, e.g. 12 June 1910, 10 Dec. 1911, 23 Nov. 1913, referring to Durham, Jarrow, South Shields LRCs. See also South Shields LP Mins, 14 Jan. 1915 for the attitude of St Hilda's lodge.

[24] *Barnsley Chronicle*, 15 Nov. 1913, 24 Jan., 14 Mar. 1914; *Doncaster Gazette*, 13 Feb. 1914; *Sheffied Ind.*, 2 Apr. 1913; Hunter (thesis), pp. 167–8.

[25] *Barnsley Chron.*, 1, 8, 15 Nov. 1913. For the opposition of the Pontypridd TC to Sunday entertainment on Council property, Pontypridd TC Mins, 5 July 1911.

Auckland, for example, there were complaints of oligarchical control
by a conservative elite. The accusation was no doubt justified. Richer
men were a powerful force in North-East Liberal politics.[26]

The problem for the Liberals was much worse in South Wales. Even
when the mineowners were often Tories, and the Liberals could not therefore be dismissed by association as a 'bosses party', control of Liberal
politics was still in the hands of a conservative, non-industrial, elite of
Welsh-speaking, small businessmen, lawyers, doctors, auctioneers, and
Nonconformist ministers. 'In a political sense', one party worker noted,
'everything was taken for granted. As the election approached some
professional man or other, with an eye to business, would call together
haphazardly, a number of people from different districts and thus some
sort of preparation was made for the election.'[27] In Mid and East
Glamorgan, the 'Labour and Liberal Association' met once a year;
'organisation' was the preserve of the registration agent. In Merthyr the
'organisation' from 1888 to 1909 consisted of two Liberal Clubs, a local
Liberal association, which covered just a portion of the constituency,
and the personal supporters of the MP, D. A. Thomas.[28]

Few Liberal leaders in South Wales were as advanced as Liberals in
other coalfields (let alone other industrial areas). The majority, one
Liberal agent reported, 'care not a toss for many of the proposals of
the present Government'.[29] The basis of Liberal propaganda was a distinctly Welsh cultural and nationalistic Liberalism, albeit one which
stopped short of support for Welsh Home Rule. After 1910 Liberals began
a populistic, aggressive, anti-Socialist, campaign. The leaders, Clem
Edwards and W. F. Phillips, were former Labour sympathisers; Phillips
had been a member of Newport ILP. The campaign was conducted
through their journal, Y Gwerinwr: Monthly Democrat, through the
Young Liberals, and through pulpit propaganda.[30] This Nonconformist/
Liberal revivalism had nothing to do with social reform. As one Liberal,
the Rev J. Morgan Jones, wrote, Jesus Christ's

attitude towards the social problem was essentially and exclusively religious.
His message to the poor and oppressed of his time was to reveal to them a

---

[26] Doncaster Gaz., 15 May 1914; Auckland Chronicle, 13 Nov. 1913.

[27] Comments of the Merthyr Liberal agent, M.D., Sept. 1912. See also Llais Llafur, 6
June 1914.

[28] Cf. comments in the Merthyr Express, 23 Oct. 1909, and K. O. Morgan, 'The Merthyr
of Keir Hardie', in G. Williams (ed.), Merthyr Politics (Cardiff, 1966), pp. 62–4. More
generally, see Morgan's Wales in British Politics, pp. 243–4.

[29] M.D., Sept. 1912.

[30] For these views, C. Howard, 'Reactionary Radicalism: the Mid-Glamorgan by-election,
Mar. 1910', Glamorgan Historian, 9 (1973), pp. 29–42, Cambria Daily Leader, 19 Dec.
1910, Rhondda Socialist, 11 Apr. 1912. Merthyr's Liberal candidate in 1910 and
T. A. Jones, who was adopted as a second candidate in 1911, were both Young Liberals.

Father in Heaven, and to lift them out of their apathy and despair into the blessedness of Faith in that Heavenly Father and the love that springs from that Faith.

Religion might act 'to quicken in men's mind the sense of personal responsibility', but no more.[31]

In South Wales only a few activists and radical theologians argued for a more responsive approach to industrial questions. Only occasionally could a radical, such as D. A. Thomas, become a Liberal parliamentary candidate in the coalfield (and Thomas was an odd 'radical' at that). On the fringes of the coalfield, in semi-mining seats like North Monmouth and East Carmarthenshire, radical elements, aided by radical newspapers, made some impact, but (as Thomas found out) the coalfield itself was a conservative Liberal stronghold.[32]

Change was more apparent, however, in the Yorkshire and North-East coalfields. Some Old Liberal MPs became emphatic Centrists or pragmatic reformers. In 1914, the Barnsley Trades Council admitted that its collectivist MP, the former Liberal Imperialist Sir Joseph Walton, was 'not a bad representative'; Atherley-Jones (North-West Durham), despite his hesitancy over trade union immunities, was respected for his commitment to radical policies. J. M. Robertson (Tyneside) was an advanced radical and a keen Progressive. Even Pease in Rotherham, and other Liberal conservatives, were pragmatic or ambitious enough to allow supporters to promote New Liberal land campaigns.[33]

The threat of Labour intervention also increased Liberal activity, and escalated the pace of change. The Liberal MP for Bishop Auckland decided not to stand again in 1913 because of the new demands being made upon his time.[34] His replacement, D. V. Rutherford, was more active and more radical. This was not unusual. Many of the new candidates adopted after 1910 – including Aneurin Williams (North-West Durham) and Tom Wing (Houghton-le-Spring) – were active left of centre radicals. Even when MPs themselves were unconvinced, New Liberal policies were filtering through as politics became 'nationalised', or as Liberal associations were being pushed forward by their more radical members.[35] The national press circulated more efficiently in the North-East and Yorkshire coalfields than in the geographically (and in some parts still culturally) isolated Welsh coalfield seats. More significantly,

---

[31] *M.D.*, Feb., May 1912.

[32] Morgan, 'New Liberalism in Wales', pp. 166–7; *Free Press of Monmouthshire*, 23 Jan., 6 Mar., 17 Apr. 1914, and below, pp. 232–3.

[33] For the widespread land and housing campaign, e.g. *Rotherham Advertiser*, 25 Oct. 1913, 31 Jan. 1914.

[34] Contrast reports in *Auckland Chron.*, 20 May 1909, with LA annual reports, 6 Apr. 1911, 30 Oct. 1913, 14 May 1914.

[35] Purdue, 'North-East politics', p. 11.

the Rowntree-owned *Northern Echo*, the North-East's largest Liberal newspaper, was consistently Progressive. It was supported by a stable of much-read weeklies, in particular its subsidiaries, the *Auckland Chronicle* and *Yorkshire Herald*. The Progressive owners of these papers supported radical proposals for an urban minimum wage and an extension of state insurance and housing provision.[36]

New Liberal influences should not be over-emphasised; Centrist elements continued to dominate. They played a vital role in merging Old and New Liberal proposals in a manner which maximised support. Their attitude to mining legislation is the best illustration of this. Liberal Centrists defended what they portrayed as the interests of *local* mining organisations. Even more than in Lancashire, rank and file miners in the North-East opposed their Government's (and the MFGB's) call for an eight hour working day. In Durham, the Eden Lodge argued for a coalfield ballot on the issue. The Dean and Chapter Lodge called for the resignation of all DMA officials and Labour MPs because of their support for the legislation. In Gateshead and Bishop Auckland, Labour reportedly did badly at the 1910 election because of its support for the legislation.[37] Local *Liberals*, by contrast, realised that miners thought this particular Government measure would hit their pockets or affect their family life (by forcing changes in shift patterns). They argued against the legislation, or called for its amendment. They protected their reputation as 'the miners' party' by being more materially responsive than Labour parties which were tied to national (MFGB) policy.

The nature of the Liberals' minimum wage legislation also demonstrates the ability of Liberal Centrists to combine the interests of local miners with ideologically 'acceptable' forms of state intervention. North-East Liberals – particularly Grey and Pease – played an important part in ensuring that a regional, as opposed to national, minimum wage became Government policy following the 1912 miners' strike. The Act guaranteed a minimum degree of financial security, and created a safety net against bad times or temporarily adverse conditions and circumstances. It supplemented endeavour, and protected the prosperous from the sudden decline in income which was common in the export-oriented North-East coalfield. It was of more direct and general value to miners in poorer pits and to surface workers. There was nothing here that proud, self-sufficient,

[36] See pp. 66, 232.
[37] *Auckland Chron.*, 27 Jan. 1910. In Gateshead, where Labour was badly beaten, the miners felt strongly enough to march into the town on election day carrying banners proclaiming their hostility to the Act (*Lib. Agent*, Apr. 1910, Blewett, *Peers*, p. 254). For lodge hostility, Eden Lodge Mins, 23 Nov. 1909, DMA Mins, 22 Jan. 1910. Middleton thought that the eight hours legislation was still a factor in Labour's unpopularity when House stood again in 1913 (J.S.M. to his parents, 21 Mar. 1913, MID 11/43).

miners, with a mixed collectivist/individualist tradition, would find unattractive. Indeed, many regional mining federations, including the DMA and NMA, got the legislation they wanted. The DMA had argued that each district should have the power 'to secure a minimum wage in keeping with its circumstances'.[38] They already had some protection against the low wages which could result from poor conditions (the cause of the 1912 dispute), and they were keen to build on this arrangement without destroying the perceived economic foundations of their prosperity. Profits meant prosperity. 'Wages follow prices', the Socialist Jack Lawson ruefully noted, 'that is Durham philosophy'.[39]

The DMA and NMA supported the (largely) South Wales inspired strike for a national minimum, but without enthusiasm. In the generally prosperous South Yorkshire coalfield, the strike had also initially been unpopular. A sense of occupational solidarity and long-term common interest vied with more particularist views. Even more than in the North-East, high wages supplemented and reinforced a 'Liberal' economic and social outlook. A *national* minimum wage was an economic impediment, if set too high, or an irrelevance if set too low. Most areas thus supported a measure which was not perceived to be in their interests. This was not a good basis for industrial action, and support soon began to slip away in some areas. The political consequences were not entirely in Labour's favour. Liberal attempts to cajole reluctant employers to grant a regional minimum wage were contrasted with Labour's failure to exact any toll from the Government or the employers, and with the confusion and chaos which resulted as the strike ended.[40] The Liberals' policy and action had not been perfect; Labour could not as yet take full advantage. The political consequences were not obviously in Labour's favour.

Only the SWMF continued to support a national minimum wage after the strike ended. As Asquith commented to a delegation of miners arguing for the amendment of the Act in 1914: 'It was satisfactory that after nearly two years full experience of its working, the points which the Federation had raised were not points which went to the principle of the Act, or indicated that it was founded on a false basis'.[41] This was

[38] DMA EC Mins, 23 Sept. 1911. Cf. NMA Mins, Ann. Council Meeting, May 1912. For the individualist/collectivist tradition, R. Moore, *Pit-men, preachers and politics* (Cambridge, 1974), esp. Chapters 6–7 and B. Williamson, *Class, culture and community* (1982), esp. Chapter 4.

[39] J. J. Lawson, *A minimum wage for miners* (1911) p. 6. For the importance of cavilling and the county averages policy in allaying 'abnormal places' grievances, Church, *Coal Industry*, 3, p. 745.

[40] For Yorkshire politics, R. J. Neville, 'The Yorkshire miners 1881 to 1926: a study in labour and social history', Leeds Ph.D. thesis 1974, Chapter 7 and YMA Conference report, *Barnsley Chron.*, 18 Oct. 1913, 7 Feb. 1914.

[41] Asquith's observations, DMA *Monthly Circular*, Mar. 1914.

putting it too highly. Regional unions did not think that the legislation, or its administration, was flawless, and generally they would have preferred a higher minimum. However, the Labour/South Wales proposal of a national, state imposed, minimum – irrespective of local conditions – was not compatible with continued private ownership; nationalisation, although formal MFGB policy, was not really taken seriously outside South Wales. Even there state intervention was not always portrayed as a means to preserve the livelihood and jobs of miners and their communities. It was as much an expression of the Syndicalists' belief in total change as it was an 'economic' policy which would rival a 'Liberal' outlook. The Liberals' lead had slipped, but 'nationalisation' was not so obviously the answer to Labour's problems that miners took to it and the Labour party as the obvious way forward.[42]

III

The strength of Lib/Lab feeling in the Derby, Leicestershire, Nottinghamshire, Staffordshire, Warwickshire, and Somerset coalfields before the war is well-documented. In 1906, all the Midlands/southern English coalfields (except the tiny Bristol district) voted against affiliation to the Labour party. By 1908, despite a heavy propaganda campaign and the official alliance between Liberals and Labour, only the Somerset coalfield changed its decision. Some political historians tend to regard the demise of Liberal support as imminent and inevitable. There is little evidence with which to sustain such a conclusion. In Nottinghamshire, even Labour lodge officials were reluctant to collect the political levy in 1914, fearing that it would disrupt the union's imperilled unity. Despite the decisions of regional executives, local miners wished to remain Liberal.[43] Many miners were actively involved in Liberal politics. Between half and two-thirds of active Liberal workers in North-East Derbyshire, for example, were miners or members of some other trade union.[44] In Chesterfield, Barnett Kenyon, the Lib/Lab MP, spoke of an active Liberal association, 'to which we have always been in some way allied, and very largely from a membership point of view'. Even in seats like Mansfield or Rushcliffe, which did not have miners as MPs, there was little hostility to the Liberals. In the less affluent Staffordshire/Warwickshire coalfield

[42] M. W. Kirby, *The British coalmining industry, 1870–1946* (1977), p. 32, and discussion of MFGB Conference debates, Page Arnot, *The miners*, p. 123.

[43] A. R. Griffin, *Mining in the East Midlands, 1550–1947* (1971), pp. 200–1. The votes in 1906 and 1910 are recorded in Howell, *ILP*, p. 51.

[44] Gregory, *Miners*, p. 166 has 150/200 members of the Liberal association as miners. A by-election report by the Liberal agent states that half the people attending the Liberals' selection conference were miners or other trade unionists (*Lib. Agent*, July 1914).

there was a pronounced 'attitude of intimacy' between the Liberals and the unions' members.[45]

As in Yorkshire and the North-East, Liberalism was not an unpopular or reactionary creed. National legislative reductions in hours, for example, did not apply to the Midlands coalfields, because the mineowners had already, voluntarily, made the reduction. Mineowners provided a range of social facilities. Liberalism also drew strength from a history of mutually profitable co-operation in the industrial sphere. In Derbyshire in particular, a shared belief in progress through enterprise was also important. J. P. Houfton, the son of a miner, who became a mineowner and Liberal candidate, represented what local people regarded as the results of hard work and personal initiative. The Notts/Derby system of sub-contracted work, like the Somerset system of 'free-miners' running their own small pits, helped institutionalise this belief.[46] The radical policies adopted by the Liberal Government were often enthusiastically supported by local Liberal newspapers and MPs. In the Somerset/Gloucestershire coalfield, Charles Dilke, the veteran radical, was the MP for the Forest of Dean until 1911. Most other local candidates were advanced radicals. A. B. Markham (Mansfield) and J. E. B. Seely (Ilkeston) were strong supporters of the Budget in 1910 for pragmatic or ideological reasons of the kind adopted by many Centrists. Mineowners like Markham benefited from the taxation of mining royalties in the 1909 Budget, at the expense of the landowners who had leased them the mining rights; they could claim that the Budget was likely to create work; they could argue that it would create the funds for social reforms; they could portray it as a fight against the Radicals' old enemy.[47]

The Liberals were in a strong position. Continued affluence, and Liberal support for social reforms, ensured that, even in 1914, their political culture was not faced with a serious economic/political challenge. 'Affluence' itself does not explain the Liberal popularity. The Somerset and Staffordshire miners were generally Liberal despite their low wages. Economic perceptions were vital. The Somerset pits were uncompetitive. Pits would close, miners argued, if militant action pushed wages too high. Their union *opposed* even the idea of a regional minimum wage, arguing that it would price them out of work. Once the legislation was passed, the regional minimum set by the local arbitrator was higher than

---

[45] B. Kenyon to A.H., 7 July 1913, LP/JSM/DM/1; T. J. Harris to J.R.M., 7 July 1910, LP/MF/11/23. See also for Mansfield, J.R.M. to S.H., 10 Feb. 1911, SH MS and more generally, Gregory, *Miners*, pp. 170–1.

[46] C. Griffin, 'Conciliation in the coal-mining industry before 1914. The experience of the Leicestershire coalfield', *Mid. Hist.* (1987), esp. p. 79, for the economic benefits of co-operation. Church, *Coal Industry*, 3, p. 353 for hours of employment.

[47] Howe, 'North Gloucestershire', pp. 117–37.

the miners themselves proposed.[48] Liberalism seemed to provide a popular interpretation of the miners' experiences and beliefs.

IV

Despite the entrenched nature of the Liberal party, there were political, social, and economic traditions and circumstances which Labour could use to sustain a rival party to the Liberals. The nature of underground work, its isolation, and peculiar form and dangers, encouraged both personal pride and independence and co-operative and collectivist traditions. Bad geological conditions in South Wales in particular created numerous 'abnormal places' in which profitable working was not immediately possible. Collectivist sentiments were reinforced by the union's role in securing a decent wage and a just and equitable distribution of time spent on the better seams.[49] Local employers adopted an obtuse managerial position to problems of this kind, to safety, and to strike action. Local Liberals did nothing to disassociate themselves from these attitudes. In some areas, and especially in South Wales, union strength was essential in order to extract financial concessions from parsimonious employers (although in the East Midlands, for example, this seemed less necessary). Unions also founded or controlled various social agencies, such as welfare systems and housing clubs, developing, through *collective* action, the basis of *individual* well-being. This was most widespread in South Wales, where around 20 per cent of miners owned their own homes, and where, in large sections of the coalfield, the entire community was included in union-administered medical schemes. In the North-East, where company housing was more common, lodge officials played an important role in ensuring that housing was allocated on the basis of family size and general need.[50] Mutual provision may have generated self-confidence, and an ability to challenge 'Liberal' economic assumptions.[51] The union's role in providing or allocating 'services' also reinforced their function as the protectors of economic interest. A

---

[48] Church, *Coal Industry*, 3, p. 745. The Staffordshire miners sometimes supported 'Tory' solutions.

[49] M. J. Daunton, 'Down the pit: work in the Great Northern and South Wales coalfields, 1870–1914', *Ec.Hist.Rev.* (1981). Despite fragmentation into specialist functions below ground, the system of promotion to hewing in time may have undermined occupational (if not generational) cleavages. See J. E. Benson, *British coalminers in the nineteenth century* (1980), pp. 47–58 for this aspect of work below ground.

[50] M. J. Daunton, 'Miners' housing: South Wales and the Great Northern Coalfield, 1880–1914', *IRSH* (1980), pp. 143–53; R. Earwicker, 'Miners' medical services before the First World War: the South Wales Coalfield', *Llafur* (1981). For lodge involvement in the North-East, esp. Marsden Lodge Mins, 1910–14 *passim*, DMA Mins, Lodge resolutions, 20 July 1912, 16 May 1914.

[51] It also follows that economic dependency would reduce Labour's prospects. See below, p. 220.

party which could build on this experience, and represent it politically, might expect to make some headway.

Nonetheless, potential had to be realised, and experiences were subject to conflicting interpretations. The political consequences of social experience varied according to the purchase of Labour's pronouncements and policies, and to its overall image. Before 1910, the ILP played a central role in Labour's political activity (except in the Lib/Lab seats). Some ILP miners, like J. J. Lawson, W. P. Richardson, or William House in Durham, or Herbert Smith and William Lunn in Yorkshire, were more 'Labour' than 'Socialist', but ethical socialist ideas usually dominated Labour's approach. Ethical socialism drew support from a radicalised Nonconformity, and from the collective individualism particularly apparent in South Wales. Yet property owning religious radicals, or those with a strong sense of moral outrage, were a minority. The social basis for the ILP was thus limited, especially – as in Yorkshire and the North-East – where other factors supported a Liberal allegiance.[52]

Labour was thus hardly a powerful force before 1910. Its organisation in Yorkshire seats like Doncaster and Rotherham, and North-Eastern seats such as Wansbeck and North-West Durham, was extremely weak.[53] On the few occasions that affiliated bodies persuaded the NEC to endorse a campaign at the 1910 elections (Mid and East Glamorgan, Merthyr, the Yorkshire constituency of Morley, and Bishop Auckland in Durham), party 'organisation' could hardly stand the strain. Even Merthyr, Keir Hardie's seat, was not much stronger. The LRC, one local activist noted, 'had no certain income (and) liv(ed) somewhat on its wits and buoyant enthusiasm which, inevitably, sprang into intense activity only during election campaigns'.[54] Hardie relied on 'star' speakers, on the ILP newspaper, the *Merthyr Pioneer*, and the unfailing dedication of a few local activists. The Merthyr position did not subsequently improve. In 1914, NAC organisers had to pull the machine into shape.[55]

This reflected the ethical socialists' limited support. In South Wales, the ILP had failed to deal with the tangible needs and economic interests of 'ordinary' miners. It consisted of clerks, doctors, teachers, ministers, and the autodidact members of the mining elite.[56] Their earnest, improving, moralism set them apart from the rest of the community. In South

[52] See p. 206.
[53] NEC Mins, 20 May 1908, 2 Dec. 1909; F.J. to Baird, 29 Nov. 1909, FJ 09/55.
[54] Edwards, *From the valleys*, p. 112.
[55] K. O. Morgan, *Wales 1880–1980* (Oxford, 1981), p. 145. More generally, J. Parry, 'Trade unions and early Socialism in South Wales', *Llafur* (1985–6), p. 52. For Merthyr, D. Hopkins, 'The Merthyr Pioneer', *Llafur* (1979).
[56] D. Hopkins, 'The membership of the Independent Labour party, 1904–10: a spatial and occupational analysis', *IRSH* (1975), p. 193.

Wales, one activist noted: 'To be an ILP or even an LRC man was to belong to a section, and a rigidly defined section, rather than to belong to a more open group which fed into a wider consensus.' In these circumstances, some activists found 'great compensation' in the ILP's associational life.[57] Entire branches became insular bulwarks against the opinion of the broader community. Some remained determined to preach Socialism; they received limited support from the electorate.

The left's domination of Labour politics was reinforced by the nature of the constituency organisations. The regional mining unions paid little attention to politics even in constituencies targeted for expansion. Although the unions threatened to fight a large number of constituencies following the MFGB's affiliation to the Labour party, this was usually designed to make the Liberals stand down in a smaller number of seats. Ambitious electoral 'plans' were bargaining counters. In the January 1910 election, *all* the mining unions backed down. This reflected both an ideological sympathy with Liberal proposals and (in some cases) a calculated assessment of the electoral position. In the circumstances, a campaign would just be wasted money. Although most lodges in East Glamorgan, for example, had voted in favour of a Labour candidature in 1910, they did not follow this up with their full support. Two lodges failed to affiliate to the Pontypridd TC, which covered parts of both East and Mid Glamorgan, and few affiliated lodges regularly sent delegates to its meetings. The lodges, and other unions, continued to support Lib/Lab municipal candidates. At the Garw colliery in Mid-Glamorgan, a resolution supporting Vernon Hartshorn's parliamentary candidature was passed by a handful of activists. Few South Wales lodges objected when the SWMF insisted Hartshorn stand down 'in order to avoid a three-cornered contest'.[58] There does not appear to have been any substantial lodge dissent in Yorkshire or the North-East, following the executive's similar action. When ILP-dominated, or non-mining, organisations fought the Liberals in East Glamorgan, Bishop Auckland, Morley, and in the semi-mining seats of Gateshead, Holmfirth, and Jarrow in the January 1910 election, Labour came third in every constituency bar Jarrow. The Liberals won every seat. Hardie's personal magnetism made Merthyr – where there was an unofficial second Liberal candidate – the exception. Ethical socialism and nominal union support were not generally enough to dissolve Liberal allegiances.

---

[57] Cited in Stead, 'Labour in Wales', p. 72; Edwards, *From the valleys*, p. 103.
[58] SWMF Mins, 6 Dec. 1909. Only twenty-eight of the 800 miners at the Garw colliery voted at the adoption meeting. For East Glamorgan, Pontypridd TC Mins, *passim* and esp. 11 Sept. 1912, 4 June 1913. In North Monmouthshire, Docker's union delegates were 'dead against running a Labour candidate' even in 1914 (*Free Press of Monmouthshire*, 24 July 1914).

V

The picture in some parts of the 'radical' South Wales, Yorkshire, and North-East coalfields even before 1910 was not universally gloomy. There were localised Labour successes which pointed to a different means of expanding support, even if the lessons were not capable of being directly transferred to other seats. As in the North-West, Labour's success was based not on ethical socialism, but on a Lib/Lab desire for craft representation, coupled to support for aspects of 'Liberal' views and a traditional image. There were three-cornered contests between 1903 and 1906 in Barnard Castle and Chester-le-Street in the North-East, and in the Welsh semi-mining constituency of Gower, because the Liberals refused to accept miners as their candidates. The chosen 'Labour' candidates, Arthur Henderson, J. W. Taylor, and J. Williams, had impeccable Liberal and Nonconformist credentials. They were not Socialists who wished to replace the Liberal party. Taylor stood as 'Independent Labour', Williams as an 'Independent Lib/Lab' candidate. Williams in particular was reluctant to be seen as a 'Labour' man even after the election. In their election campaigns, these candidates emphasised their Liberalism and their moderation, adding an explicit appeal to union solidarity and loyalty. The Lib/Lab tradition had two components – Liberal principles and working-class representation – and they stuck firmly to it. The Liberals had sacrificed union loyalty; inactivity, neglect, complacency, and conservatism had weakened ties of habit, culture, and interest. These 'Labour' candidates were now clearly the better expression of a Lib/Lab culture. All three were returned.[59]

After 1906 Labour tightened its grip on these constituencies, and on some of the Lib/Lab seats which were redesignated 'Labour' following the MFGB's affiliation to the Labour party in 1909. In Barnard Castle, Henderson insisted on the creation of a 'model' organisation, with committees in every ward or polling district, local propaganda campaigns, and organised election and registration work. However, Barnard Castle, lavishly financed by the Ironfounders' union, and only partially a mining seat, was an exception. Neither the mining unions nor local lodges (which could become affiliated to local Labour parties if they so wished) did anything to create a 'Labour' political culture before 1910. There was not even a Labour organisation in West Monmouth or Normanton until

---

[59] Based on the following: Howell, *ILP*, p. 49, A. W. Purdue, 'Arthur Henderson and Liberal, Liberal–Labour and Labour politics in the North-East of England 1892–1903', *Northern Hist.* (1976), pp. 195–217, D. Cleaver, 'Labour and Liberals in the Gower constituency 1885–1910', *Welsh Hist. Rev.* (1985) and Morgan, *Wales in British politics*, p. 244.

1910. Rhondda and Chester-le-Street waited until 1911 and 1914.[60] Before 1910 lodges generally did little other than send delegates to parliamentary selection conferences. Municipal activity consisted of their own sporadic attempts to get miners elected, not of political campaigns. Politics scarcely entered into it.[61]

In 1910 the Liberals (reluctantly) accepted that the miners wished to be part of a Progressive Alliance, and not part of the Liberal party. They allowed Labour a free run in Barnard Castle and Chester-le-Street, and made no effort to oppose former Lib/Lab MPs in Normanton, West Monmouth, South Glamorgan, or the Rhondda.[62] Thereafter the Liberal organisations in these seats went into terminal decline. The Chester-le-Street Liberal association did not meet once between 1909 and 1913. In West Monmouth a Liberal association had to be recreated in 1914. 'Organisations' in other former Lib/Lab seats were equally decrepit.[63]

By 1914, Labour officials thought these seats were invulnerable, and there is no reason to doubt their assessment. Labour had claimed the Lib/Lab mantle, and inherited huge majorities. In the three-cornered contests, the Liberals had polled respectably, despite being defeated, because history and tradition were in their favour, and because they received support from farming and non-mining elements. In Rhondda and West Monmouth, where more than 70 per cent of the electorate were miners, and the farming/non-mining vote was insignificant, Labour's position was probably correspondingly stronger. Local Labour organisations became more active, more 'political', and more successful between 1910 and 1914.[64] Labour's initial growth had rested on its ability to merge linguistic, religious, and cultural factors with support for the unions and for miners' representation. It was now reinforcing this with demands for municipal and state policies which would increase local living standards and improve conditions. Not everyone believed that the solutions could work, but there was no denying whose side Labour supported in these divisions.

[60] See the Barnard Castle Labour Association's annual reports, printed in the *Auckland Chron.*, Mar. of each year. See also, *Rhondda Socialist*, Oct. 1911; Normanton LP *AR* 1911; *N.E.*, 13 June 1914; *Monthly Democrat*, June 1912.

[61] Pontypridd TC Mins, *passim* and esp. 21 June 1911, *Llais Llafur*, 18 May 1914; Eden Lodge Mins, *passim*; Usworth Lodge Mins, *passim* and esp. 22 Feb. 1910; Ironfounders' *MR* Sept. 1911. For municipal activity, *Mid-Rhondda Gazette*, 15 June 1914; Gregory, *Miners*, p. 136.

[62] Gower was the exception. See below pp. 236, 247.

[63] T. Magnay to W.R., 7 Aug. 1913, WR 81; *Llais Llafur*, 28 Mar. 1914.

[64] For increasing electoral strength, compare Normanton LP *AR* 1912 with progressively glowing reports of success, Normanton LP *AR* 1913 and *Wakefield Expr.*, 9 Apr. 1914. For similar improvements in Rhondda, *Rhondda Socialist*, Dec. 1911, 11 Apr. 1912, 12 Apr. 1913. For South Wales generally, Stead, 'Labour in Wales', p. 82 and *Llais Llafur*, 11 Apr. 1914.

The decline of ethical socialism was not confined to the Lib/Lab seats, and there were seats in the North-East, Yorkshire, and South Wales coalfields where Labour consequently made considerable progress after 1910.[65] In South Wales, this could effect major changes in party strength. The pattern of political change in the Mid-Glamorgan constituency illustrates this particularly well. The long-running saga of Vernon Hartshorn's attempt to fight the sitting Liberal MP branded him, and the Labour party, as more extreme than they actually were. Hartshorn's candidature was initially opposed by SWMF moderates. When he was eventually given leave to fight at the March 1910 by-election, the 'Socialist' label stuck. He was defeated by the Liberals in a straight fight by 18 per cent of the vote. Nonetheless, the well-publicised support Hartshorn subsequently received from the former Lib/Lab MPs, Mabon and Brace, and the equally well-publicised support of the Liberal Chief Whip, helped to change popular perceptions. In December the balance between the Liberals' claims and Hartshorn's counter-claim had changed. He appeared more as a 'Labour' and 'union' candidate than a 'Socialist'. The Liberal lead was more than halved and might have been reduced still further if Labour 'removals' could have been traced. The momentum was not allowed to lapse. After the election, lodge officials were first circularised and then organised into groups to discuss organisation and tactics. By 1914, the local miners were more committed than ever to Labour representation.

Mid-Glamorgan was to an extent exceptional. A range of factors were concentrated in such a way that Labour's positive image was substantially reinforced. However, the SWMF was committed to spreading Labour support. The newly appointed 'union' organisers did not concentrate on Mid-Glamorgan and the Labour-held seats. They were encouraged to set up local Labour parties to undertake local political work in *every* coalfield seat, and were moderately successful. By 1914 nearly every union branch in the East Glamorgan constituency, for example, was affiliated to the divisional LRC, which had set up an elaborate network of local committees.[66] Popular support grew. In April 1914 *Llais Llafur* noted that Labour had 'obtained a greatly increased vote in every area' of the coalfield at the UDC elections. Nonetheless, the Liberals retained a good deal of support, as the persistent Lib/Lab tendencies of several mining lodges and some other local unions indicated. Old views, and old percep-

---

[65] For the following: P. Stead, 'Vernon Hartshorn', *Glamorgan Historian* (1969), pp. 88–90, Howard, 'Mid-Glamorgan', pp. 33–40, Gregory, *Miners*, p. 130, *Llais Llafur*, 24 Dec. 1910.

[66] *Mid-Rhondda Gaz.*, 15 June 1914. For the organisers, memo by V. Hartshorn, n.d. 1914, LG C 3/17/4/1, A.H. to J.S.M., 23 Aug. 1912, LP/HEN/08/1/64, SWMF Mins, 16 Feb. 1912.

tions of Labour as a Socialist organisation, also prevented more wide-spread rank and file involvement. In Merthyr, the Liberals still held the Merthyr Vale and Treharris wards (in East Glamorgan for parliamentary purposes). Some parts of Pontypridd – also in East Glamorgan – were Liberal strongholds. In Mid-Glamorgan, Labour actually lost ground to the Young Liberals for a while after 1910; in North Monmouthshire the Liberals were holding their own. The post-war attitude of the SWMF, and of the mining electorate, was far from being evident in 1914.[67]

By 1914, however, Hartshorn calculated that Labour was ahead of the Liberals in Merthyr, on a par with them in East and Mid-Glamorgan, but some way behind in the semi-mining seats, like North Monmouth, where Labour expected only that it would 'give a good account of itself'.[68] The strength of a Liberal tradition, the remnants of an ethical socialist past, and the still limited ability of Labour to deliver an economic alternative, helped limit the degree of change.

To some extent Labour followed a similar path in the North-East. In Bishop Auckland, the Liberal lead fell from 18 per cent to just 4.5 per cent between January and December 1910. House played on his mining credentials, on his opponents conservatism, and on his own proximity to radical Liberal interests. Ethical socialism took a back seat. The Liberals' case weakened; Labours' strengthened; the electoral gap narrowed. The position was subsequently complicated by the revival of Liberal radicalism and House's retirement as candidate. His replacement had to be a miner to satisfy the voters, and an ILP man to satisfy the activists. Smillie was suggested, but declined. The miners withdrew. The ILP – now again institutionally dominant – adopted a local non-miner, Ben Spoor, as candidate. Spoor and other local ILP members were not vague 'hard left' Socialists. Nonetheless, the transformation of Labour's image was inevitably retarded. In 1912, not a good year for Progressives generally it is true, the UDC results were 'a bitter blow to the Labour party'. A subsequent Labour and Tory revival made the position, which had been close in 1910, even closer. Nonetheless, Labour was not pushing at an open door.[69]

The social and political conditions in Bishop Auckland were closer to those in South Wales than was usual in the North-East. The favourable circumstances which enabled Labour to expand in Bishop Auckland were not reflected even in Houghton-le-Spring and North-West Durham, which

[67] *Llais Llafur*, 28 Feb., 11 Apr., 29 May 1914; *Rhondda Socialist*, 12 Apr. 1913.
[68] Hartshorn memo, LG C 3/17/4/1; *Free Press of Monmouthshire*, 15 May 1914. Municipal results in Merthyr confirm that Labour's confidence was not misplaced (*Merthyr Advertiser*, Nov. 1909, Nov. 1913).
[69] *Auckland Chron.*, 4 Apr. 1912 and e.g. 10 Apr. 1913. See also correspondence in the Johnson MS, FJ 1913/234, 288, 291.

Labour fought in 1913–14. The pits were larger, the pit villages more dependent on individual colliery owners or firms. 'Independent' miners were less common; Liberal economic views seemed more valid. Lodge support divided between Liberals and Labour. As a result, the Labour campaign in North-West Durham (as in Houghton-le-Spring) was dominated by an alliance of Socialists and disaffected, formerly Liberal, suffragists whose views were hardly shared by many local miners. The Labour candidate in North-West Durham, G. H. Stuart (Secretary of the Postmen's Federation), was a notorious, anti-Liberal, Socialist.[70] While this did little to strengthen Labour's position, the local Liberals chose radical candidates who in turn reinforced the national reforming image. In these seats, Labour came at the foot of the poll, 12 to 17 per cent behind the victorious Liberals. Houghton-le-Spring, Middleton noted, was 'anything but a rosy prospect'. As Henderson later added, it 'was not theirs for some time to come'.[71] In Northumberland, the position was even worse. The NMA had only agreed to establish constituency Labour organisations in 1914. They started from scratch. In semi-mining seats like Hexham and Tynemouth, other unions had shared the miners' apathy. There were no signs of an imminent breakthrough in the Lib/Lab seats, and a more general breakthrough seemed a long way off.[72]

Yorkshire was historically a more militant coalfield. However, politically the conditions were *less* favourable to Labour than in the North-East and South Wales. The local Liberals were more radical; the economic and social conditions (in most parts of the coalfield) were better. The Tories were also a more serious rival than is sometimes appreciated.[73] Finally, in mining and semi-mining seats like Morley, Barnsley, and Rotherham, railwaymen, gasworkers, and steelworkers were strong enough to prevent the construction of a party image which would satisfy the miners. There were more obstacles to overcome, more interests to balance.

Labour did, nonetheless, make some headway, as municipal results

[70] Gregory, *Miners*, p. 80; *N.E.*, 6 Jan. 1914, Holton, *Feminism and democracy*, pp. 100–12. Henderson had been hoping for a straight fight in Houghton-le Spring (*Auckland Chron.*, 3 Apr. 1913, J.S.M. to his parents, 15 Feb. 1913, MID 11/36). On social matters see also Daunton, 'Miners' housing', p. 154 for the paucity of colliery housing in Bishop Auckland, and Lawson, *A man's life*, pp. 113–14 for the size and nature of pits. Greater 'independence' from the colliery owner may have facilitated an interest in Labour politics.

[71] J.S.M. to W.H., 30 Apr. 1914, LP/ORG/14/2/13; MFGB Mins, 18 Mar. 1915.

[72] NMA, Ec Mins, 16 Dec. 1909, Special Comm. Mins, 20 Nov. 1911, 17 Mar.–13 May 1914.

[73] Cf. their strength in Doncaster and Barnsley, reflected in the high Primrose League membership figures, Pugh, *Tories and the people*, p. 239, and for a similar position in the North-East, e.g. Barnard Castle Cons. ass. ann. meeting, *North Star*, 16 Feb. 1914. For the position in adjacent areas, pp. 230, 235.

indicate. The active Trades Council in Barnsley won three of the six Barnsley wards in the 1913 municipal elections.[74] Rotherham had also showed 'promising' signs of Labour activity before 1910. By 1913, Labour was eroding the Liberals' lead in the mining town of Morley. However, there were no signs of a major Liberal decline in any of these seats (the most attractive from Labour's standpoint) partly because the Liberals controlled the mining areas. When the YMA selected a moderate local miner, T. W. Grundy, as the parliamentary candidate in Rotherham, it was assumed that this position would change. It did not. Five Labour candidates stood at the 1913 municipal elections in Rotherham, but only one was successful. 'The labour movement in Rotherham', one activist explained, 'had been dormant for some time, and it is not to be expected that all the old sting and vigour will come back immediately.'[75] The outlying areas, which made up a substantial proportion of the Rotherham constituency, and half the Barnsley and Morley Divisions, were solidly Liberal. With their strength in the towns far from totally eroded, the Liberals were a formidable force.[76] By 1914 the Rotherham LRC had selected James Walker, a secular Glasgow Socialist, and an organiser from the Steel Smelters' union, as their candidate. His union appointed an agent, and agreed to pay £150 per year towards constituency expenses. This, and institutional changes which gave suffragettes a say in local Labour politics, gave the left and its political interests greater primacy. Grundy's selection had raised hopes; Walker's promised a better organised stagnation.[77] This seemed to be the best that Labour could hope for.

The YMA was only half-committed to political expansion. Its political organisers, who were only appointed in August 1914, were told to concentrate on the Lib/Lab seats, on Doncaster (which new pits and pit settlements were turning into a mining stronghold) and on Holmfirth. This limited commitment reflected the feeling of the rank and file, if not of the activists. In Holmfirth, lodge delegates seldom attended LRC meetings; they also showed little interest in Doncaster, where the position was made worse by the relative indifference of other unions. In both these seats, and in semi-mining constituencies like Osgoldcross, 'Labour'

---

[74] See also comments on the position in 1911 and 1914, *Barnsley Independent*, 2 Sept. 1911; *Barnsley Chron.*, 14 Mar., 11 Apr. 1914.

[75] *Rotherham Express*, 15 Nov. 1913 and also 23 Sept. 1911. AP memo, n.d., NEC Mins (BLPES Coll.).

[76] *Rotherham Express*, 8 and 15 Nov. 1913, 3 Jan. 1914 and reports of some success in Rawmarsh, 11 Apr. 1914. See also reports on the position in Morley, *Morley Obs.*, 22 May, 12 June 1914.

[77] *Rotherham Adv.*, 25 July 1914, BrSS Ec Mins, 12–15 Aug. 1914, MR Aug. 1914. Also Neville (thesis), esp. biographical appendix and Chapter 13.

was weaker than in Barnsley and Rotherham. Infrequent municipal campaigns led to ignoble defeats.[78]

Labour's most pronounced progress in these coalfields came where it took the old Lib/Lab recipe and put together a 'new' version of an old dish. However, there is also some indication that it was beginning to build this into a more positive stance. Some miners at least were also looking at greater state control or involvement in industry as a means to challenge Liberal economic assumptions about the level of economic and social comfort which workers in that industry could reasonably expect. Although Labour or Independent Labour candidates had captured some former Lib/Lab seats with 'old' politics in 1906, the 'new' Labour party made some headway in a few South Wales seats and in Bishop Auckland, and it was this approach which was spreading across the coalfields by 1914. Statist and Labourist politics augmented a changing ethical socialism, and created a sharper, more practical, political image. Nonetheless, neither the party nor the electorate was totally converted. Whatever officials said about the unions' politics, the unions' members (even in South Wales) were not sheep who would follow any lead. Union executives could not, and did not, ignore their members' opinions. Although the NMA and DMA agreed to set up Labour organisations in every constituency, by 1914, as an election approached, they concentrated on securing the Lib/Lab seats of Morpeth, Wansbeck, and Mid-Durham. The YMA and SWMF, despite rhetorical, and in South Wales some practical, attempts to develop organisation, were only a little more expansive once an election seemed imminent.[79] The Liberals were still the more popular party, and Labour could not successfully compete. Until circumstances changed, and Labour could create a more realistic, credible, political image, the radical union leaders had to tread carefully or risk defeat.

VI

In the moderate Midlands coalfields, individual miners *and* many union officials were reluctant to accept *independent* Labour, and particularly Socialist, activity before 1910. Even after (some) members of the unions' executive were converted to Labour representation, they only made half-serious attempts to encourage their members to change. The members did not respond. In the Warwickshire coalfield constituency of Nuneaton,

---

[78] Gregory, *Miners*, p. 119; *Goole Times*, 11 Apr. 1913. For poor UDC results and meetings, *Doncaster Gaz.*, 8 May, 12 June, 7, 17, 31 July 1914. Doncaster contained the newest and the most profitable mines (Neville (thesis), pp. 398–9). For Holmfirth, below, p. 274.
[79] NMA Ec Mins, 20 Mar. 1913, Council meeting, 17 Mar. 1913; DMA Mins, 4 July 1914 and Political Fund Cash Book.

for example, they ignored the union's advice and did not affiliate to the Nuneaton LRC. Local lodges, like other unions in the area, remained apathetic or hostile. 'The progress made is nothing to boast about', one activist reported some time later. Typically, there was virtually no Labour organisation in seats like Hanley (Staffordshire) and North-East Derbyshire before Labour's by-election contests in 1912 and 1914.[80]

The by-election results show that Labour had made virtually no impression. It polled just 12 per cent of the vote in Hanley, formerly a Lib/Lab seat, and 22 per cent in North-East Derbyshire, which contained more miners. However, Labour trailed the Liberals very substantially, and polled far fewer votes than candidates in other coalfields. It had no credible, distinct, policy which could compete against economic prosperity and Liberal reforms. It adopted a radical Liberal approach, and grafted on craft representation and union loyalty. Labour's political claims on these seats were fuelled by well-publicised (Liberal) statements that they should have Labour candidates. Even this was insufficient to undermine Liberal support.[81] There was little that Labour could do. Moderation was so entrenched that Socialist alternatives barely existed. Moreover, when the West Ham Socialist, John Scurr, selected himself as the Socialist parliamentary candidate at the 1913 Chesterfield by-election, the unpopularity of such a position was clearly demonstrated. Union members, voters and officials rallied to the Lib/Lab miners' candidate, who was sent to Westminster with 56 per cent of the vote. Scurr was put on the train back to West Ham having received less than 5 per cent of the vote. The results, and the nature of local Labour opinion, reflected the extent to which the region had been sucked into a Liberal political culture from which it was electorally and individually very difficult to escape.

Despite the conflicts at Hanley and North-East Derbyshire many Liberals had begun to accept the idea of Labour representation by 1914. Local Labour and Trades Council candidates benefited from tacit Liberal support in municipal elections; Liberal/Labour relations were not deteriorating. The Labour campaign in Hanley was forced on a *reluctant* union by the cause of events. The Staffordshire miners were one section of the Liberal and Labour association in Hanley. They had wanted to see their candidate selected as a Lib/Lab and run by the Liberal organisation. The Liberal section of the party were willing to accept this, and their nominee in fact stepped down. In North-East Derbyshire the hurried

---

[80] W. A. Taylor and P. Lake to A.P., 28 Aug. 1912 and n.d., LP/MF/11/11 and 71. The Somerset and Nottinghamshire miners refused to sanction by-election candidatures in the Forest of Dean and West Nottingham. See for this Griffin, *Mining in the East Midlands*, p. 200, Wyncoll, *Nottingham labour movement*, pp. 158–9 and below, pp. 295, 307–8, 312.

[81] e.g. *Daily Chronicle*, 7 May 1914.

lodge votes in favour of a Labour contest were 'even more unrepresentative than usual'. In one colliery, 'only sixteen men were said to have
voted out of several thousand lodge members'.[82] If the Labour candidates
in these contests occasionally made anti-Liberal declarations, this was
not the dominant tone of their campaigns, but a frustrated attempt to
force an electoral opening.[83] The MFGB was pushing its constituent
unions towards the Labour party, but the fiercely independent miners'
unions (to some extent) and their equally independent members (more
generally) were not showing any great inclination to allow institutional
changes at the national level to alter their political views. Labour's future
ascendancy was not inevitable. In 1914, it did not even appear to be
a possibility.

VII

The positive economic and social attractions of Liberalism to some union
members and officials – and Labour's failure to supply an alternative
– helped to limit support for a larger parliamentary campaign in 1914/15,
despite the Liberals' partial deficiencies on mining issues. As in 1910,
the MFGB declined to massively increase its financial commitment, and
allocated only a few additional candidates to each area. In some areas,
– particularly South Wales – the union had been seriously committed
to the idea of a much larger campaign before this decision was made.
Elsewhere, the 'commitment' was largely, or perhaps almost completely,
rhetorical. Many mining unions did not see Progressive conflict as a desirable aim. The DMA's *Monthly Circular* commented favourably on the
MFGB's decision: 'There is no avowed intention of running counter to
(sic) Labour representation, but there is implied caution which is highly
essential in this and many other matters.'[84] Rhetoric aside, Midlands
miners had effectively abandoned the idea of a campaign in Hanley. Union
executives, aware of acute tensions in their unions, were unwilling to
force the issue. Even if the idea of a campaign was not dropped in North-
East Derbyshire, the threatening noises made during the by-election did
not signal the end of a moderate outlook amongst miners in the area.
In the North-West all the Tory mining seats already had Labour candidates, and no Liberal opponents. Most miners in 'Liberal' mining or
semi-mining seats did not wish to see Progressive conflict. Leigh was
the only seat where there was likely to be a three-cornered contest.

[82] Quotations from Gregory, *Miners*, p. 165. See also McKibbin, *Evolution*, p. 61. For
municipal 'concessions', Howe, 'North Gloucestershire', pp. 127–8, Wyncoll, *Nottingham*, pp. 158–9.
[83] Petter, 'Progressive Alliance', p. 56 for the lapse into 'tones worthy of the ILP'.
[84] DMA, *Monthly Circular*, June 1914.

The remaining coalfields were potentially a more significant political problem. However, the strategic position was likely to reflect the fact that Labour's electoral advance was partial and limited. North-Eastern miners decided to concentrate on the Lib/Lab seats and Labour-held Chester-le-Street.[85] In the Yorkshire and South Wales coalfields, despite support for militant industrial action, political aims were more modest and more pragmatic. The YMA concentrated on its Lib/Lab seats, plus Liberal-held Doncaster and Holmfirth. The steelworkers and ASLEF hoped to fight Rotherham and Morley, which the YMA had abandoned all hope of contesting. Mining officials believed they had a 'Progressive' right to contest mining-dominated Doncaster, without Liberal opposition. Since the local Liberal party barely existed, this was not an unrealistic hope. However, the (conservative) sitting Liberal MP foiled Labour's scheme by resisting union and Liberal party pressure to stand down. In Holmfirth, only partially a mining seat, the local prospects seemed poor. Even after Labour's by-election campaign in 1912, the local miners remained unenthusiastic. A proposed campaign may have been a bargaining counter to obtain a free run in Doncaster, a tactic often used in the past.[86] In South Wales, where the activists' enthusiasm had been half-supported by the SWMF, a decision to expand the parliamentary campaign had to be abandoned. Although the final decision on which seats to contest had not been made, the union was almost certainly going to concentrate on Labour-held seats, plus East and Mid-Glamorgan (where a massive percentage of the electorate was engaged in mining). Other unions were not prepared to take on the weaker semi-mining constituencies. Hartshorn had earlier warned Lloyd George that a wider campaign, which would be mutually disastrous, was being considered, presumably as an attempt to reactivate the Liberal offer not to contest one of the two Glamorgan seats. An unofficial 'deal' – or at least (as in 1910) national opposition to a local Liberal campaign – was not an unrealistic hope.[87]

The electoral position in the coalfields, and the fact that the mining unions were not keen to fight every seat at any cost, ensured that the Progressive Alliance was unlikely to fall apart in 1914. There were inevitably some tensions as Labour began to expand, particularly because central Liberal efforts to recognise this with strategic concessions were

---

[85] Alderman House admitted that he had 'had enough' of three-cornered contests (*Daily Cit.*, 21 Jan. 1914).
[86] Rumours in *Rotherham Adv.*, 12 Nov. 1913, and MP's refusal to stand down, *Doncaster Gaz.*, 24 Nov. 1913. For Morley, *Locomotive Journal*, Dec. 1914. The NEC did not think that Morley should be fought (NEC Mins, 16 Sept. 1915, 21 Aug. 1916).
[87] Hartshorn memo, n.d. 1914, LG C 3/17/4/1, and above, p. 218.

not well-received in the constituencies. However, there were few convinced Labour advocates of larger anti-Liberal campaigns, whatever the electoral circumstances or political consequences. The anti-Liberal minority was weakened by defections to Syndicalism and the far left. Labour politics, and gradual expansion of the party's base, were the coming tactics. Until some event, experience, or idea altered expectations and attitudes, Labour had to be satisfied with a gradual and partial erosion of the Liberals' position.

Labour had made some headway in all but the Midlands coalfields by 1914. Outside the North-West, where religious fragmentation was still significant, and the Tories were strong opponents, Labour-held mining seats were secure, even if the Liberals fielded candidates. However, in most mining seats, the Liberals were a more substantial force. Outside South Wales, a Liberal political culture was frequently reinforced by adaptive Liberal organisations, and even in South Wales older Liberal allegiances still had some strength. Labour's appeal to union loyalty, and its ethical socialism, had not been enough to nullify the salience of the Liberals' appeal. Although a more 'practical' Labour stance, and Liberal failure to cope with industrial/wages issues, brought Labour some benefits (because it became more closely identified with the life and prosperity of mining communities) it was still insufficiently distinctive or insufficiently convincing to displace the Liberals in most areas. It was also still too associated with unpopular Socialist ideas. It had not created the grounds for a major realignment, and as a result, there was no serious threat to the strategy of Progressive Alliance. It needed the changed political and ideological climate of the First World War to substantially alter the balance of political loyalties, and to create the symbiotic link between the miners and the Labour party which was so apparent in subsequent years.

Chapter 8

The heavy industrial heartlands

The areas adjacent to the coalfields were as much a part of the Liberals' working-class political base in the 1890s as the coalfield seats themselves. There was a large number of seats on the edge of the North-East and South Wales coalfields which were dominated by iron and steel, docking, shipbuilding, and heavy engineering. Mining was an important supplementary occupation. In many of these seats, trade unions were extremely strong, and workplace relations and conditions were harsh. 'Culturalist' interpretations of Labour's success – and historical hindsight – would suggest that the Liberals would inevitably decline and be replaced by Labour in seats with these social/economic characteristics.

The reality was different. Labour did not dominate the area's politics. Although the Conservatives were not the dominant force in the area, they were far stronger than Labour, particularly in the dockland areas and in some of the steel and shipbuilding towns. While the Tories' support was in part related to a Protestant hostility to the Irish, there was more to it than this. Employment and prosperity in some areas depended on the production of equipment/arms for the military services. Tory employers controlled the prosperity of whole sections of urban constituencies. Economic interest and economic dependency combined with a hostility to outsiders (especially if it was felt they might take employment from the local workforce). Social conservatism and an affinity with the Tories' very masculine views on several other issues (particularly drink) made North-East working-class Conservatism a resilient force.

The Liberals were even stronger. They had deep roots in a broad middle-class/working-class political and social alliance. This was based on shared Nonconformist values and shared economic interests and perceptions. Free trade obviously played a part in this, since much of the shipping, docking, and mining industries owed their prosperity to exports and international trade. Moreover, some very large local firms were so dominant that the attitude of individual (often Liberal) employers could have a pronounced impact on local living standards, particularly during the (frequent) cyclical depressions. This form of economic dependency reinforced Liberal political allegiances. It would be wrong, however, to regard popular Liberalism (or popular Conservatism) as purely functional. The Liberals, like the Tories, built shared interests and values into a political culture which gave voters a means of looking at questions and issues, and a habit of voting in a particular way.

Nonetheless, these allegiances, and this outlook, had to be maintained. Between 1906 and 1914 an 'Old Liberal' ideology, with its history of strong working-class support and institutionalised Lib/Lab contacts, was to differing extents updated by Centrist and New Liberal elements (Section I). However, if a Liberal political culture was being maintained, it was also under attack. Labour's initial response had its roots in the Liberals' own language and values. As in the coalfields, 'ethical socialism' drew on Nonconformist moral values to sanction a critique of social attitudes and conditions. It proved even less successful. Although some ILP branches had begun adopting more materially minded political approaches before 1906, this process – which some wished to take further – was either blocked or hampered by Labour's Socialist wing (Section II).

This changed to some extent after the 1910 election, although the Liberals' own adaptation made it difficult for Labour to break through. Labour developed a sharper and more positive image and a larger electoral base, but only through the support of specific occupational groups, and particularly the miners and railwaymen. These groups were not numerous enough, or so uniformly inclined to vote Labour, that it was possible to forge a general realignment on the left. Other occupational groups were more likely to support the Liberals. The strongly Statist side of Labour's image – which attracted the miners and railwaymen – was not something which most workers found attractive. Liberal reforms created a degree of social security, the market satisfied many of their economic aspirations, and Liberal attacks on the rich satisfied their 'class' perspectives. Labour could not persuade the electorate to demand more than the Liberals could offer (Section III). The result was a limited degree of Labour progress, and a putative electoral campaign which reflected this fact (Section IV). The Liberals remained the stronger of the two parties.

I

In many areas of heavy industry, institutional power in Liberal politics was more concentrated in the hands of a wealthy elite than in areas where radical Liberal ideas made easy progress. Some major Liberal

employers owned plants, shipyards, or mills which dominated entire constituencies. They were often the Presidents of Liberal associations, owners
of Liberal newspapers and MPs. The links between the politics of the
employers and the Liberalism of the workforce were particularly pronounced in towns like Newport in South Wales, and in those parts of
the North-East where these employers adopted a paternalistic approach.
The provision of housing, work-related social and educational facilities,
and other institutional expressions of this bond created an economic
dependency more pronounced than in areas where a diverse local economy
created opportunities and reduced the employers' economic power. However, workers often shared their employers' robust individualism, rooted
as it was in a shared (Nonconformist) belief in personal independence,
self-help, and 'getting on'; they also shared economic ideas, particularly
the value of Free Trade. These ideas outlasted the days when chapel
attendance was common, and when 'Old Liberalism' was an unquestion-
able faith. Liberalism reflected the interests and aims of the often self-
educated, respectable, and skilled workers who were common in these
areas and who had established a degree of social security, social status,
and economic prosperity. Liberal allegiances were not based on a crude
form of social control.[1]

The domination of a single employer was less pronounced in the South
Wales ports. The prevalence of smaller units of production, and the growing political detachment of the few major local magnates 'diluted' the
Liberal elite. Some Liberal associations still preferred wealthy industrialists as candidates (Haslam in Newport, Mond in Swansea) but these
men were not major local employers. They owed their selection to other
factors. In South-West Wales, the leading Liberals were usually Welsh
speaking Nonconformists; they were small employers, lawyers, ministers,
and teachers. They commanded respect in communities which valued
improvement, education, and religious piety. However, this respect was
again based on shared principles; it was not an uncritical deference.[2]

Many of the old Liberal industrialists were Radicals who opposed the
political shift from issues such as educational reform, temperance, and
Disestablishment to the politics of social reform. They were implacably,
and almost uniformly, hostile to the strategy of Progressive Alliance.
Their views, and their attitude to change, would inevitably have a con-

[1] Purdue, 'North-East politics' for details. The results of Liberal/Labour (and Socialist)
clashes in parliamentary elections are given in Appendix 3, p. 455.
[2] Daunton, *Cardiff*, pp. 151–77; T. Brennan, E. W. Cooney, and H. Pollins, *Social change
in South-West Wales* (1954), p. 20, *Llais Llafur*, 6 June 1914. There were large steel
works, generally family firms, in all of the coastal constituencies. The employers had
often moved to the area from the Midlands and Scotland, bringing a section of their
workforce with them.

siderable impact.[3] Nonetheless, local Liberalism had to change. Labour was pushing hard on the Liberals' heels; the Conservatives (more popular than one might think) were moving towards a collectivist stance.[4] The 1906 election exposed Liberal political and organisational weaknesses in seats like Middlesbrough (where Labour thought they were 'practically dead'). In Jarrow, the Liberal organisation was 'in pawn, and Mr Corrie, Secretary of the Northern Liberal Federation, has the Ticket'.[5] The electorate's enthusiasm for Free Trade only half-masked the Liberals' electoral and organisational problems.

Liberal associations became more formalised as they attempted to broaden and expand their membership. They also became more open to pressure from below. This was even the case in Jarrow, a single industry town dominated by Palmer's shipyard and (in the past) by Palmer's (Liberal) politics. The Jarrow Liberal association, reformed in 1908, had an extensive network of local committees by 1914. When war broke out, the party was about to sub-divide these groups in order to work more closely at divining, forming, and organising opinion. Other local parties – less dominated by a single employer – had made the switch much earlier. Liberal political organisation, at least in Stockton, Darlington, and Newcastle, was based on networks of local committees and Liberal working-men's clubs. In Newcastle there had been a Birmingham-style caucus, the 900, for many years.[6] These committees and clubs served Liberals well as an access route to local opinion, and as a means of maintaining activists' support, but they were demanding something in return. Local Liberal groups, often based on a mining lodge, became dominated by working men. They selected municipal candidates who were frequently working-class Liberals. When they were successful, these men dictated local policy. The larger, more working-class, membership also attempted to influence the policy of Divisional executives, through Trades Council pressure, through the Trades Council's representatives on the Divisional executive, or through organisations set up specifically to exert pressure on the Liberal elite. Cardiff's Workingmen's Radical Association and the South Shields Radical Association and Trade Union

---

[3] See above, p. 23.

[4] See e.g. the high Primrose League membership figures in South Shields, Jarrow, and Stockton, cited in Pugh, *Tories and the people,* pp. 127–8, 244–5. Stockton, Darlington, and Sunderland had regularly returned Tory MPs or Liberal Unionists in the 1880s and 1890s. All three seats also returned Unionists at times between 1906 and 1910.

[5] *Jarrow Labour Herald,* 29 June 1906. For Middlesbrough, M. Coates Hanson to J.R.M, 4 June 1905, LRC 24/185.

[6] I owe this information to Bill Purdue. See also *N.E.,* 11 Feb. 1914. For Jarrow, *Jarrow Express,* 14 Feb. 1913, 6 Mar., 3, 4 Apr. 1914.

Representation Committee (two separate organisations) are examples of
the groups which were formed (here and elsewhere) during the late 1890s.[7]

Pressure from working-class Liberal organisations was supplemented
by pressure from 'middle-class' radical groups (like the Young Liberals).
A more formal organisational structure also channelled the radical activists' activities into ward or other local Liberal groups. By 1914 the Swansea Liberal association was reputed to have as efficient an organisation
as the Liverpool Tories, and to be as successful in its integration of the
rank and file. Members' subscriptions, and the bazaars they organised,
also provided a substantial proportion of the average constituency's
annual expenses. Constituency Liberalism was no longer generally the
preserve of a business elite. If some organisations remained oligarchically
controlled, they still had to take local Liberal radicals more seriously.
As Councillors or local representatives they had institutional power. They
also had electoral purchase, and the national party, on their side.[8]

Municipal policy often changed as constituency radicals, and a section
of the Liberal elite, combined to alter the party's political orientation.
A Radical belief in 'thrift' did not govern Liberal policy (although 'waste'
and 'extravagance' were still to be avoided). Although expenditure on
poor relief, for example, was not generous, neither was it parsimonious
by contemporary standards. Liberals were often sympathetic to labour
interests. In Middlesbrough, for example, the Trades Council noted that
its views on municipal matters were 'courteously received and sympathetically considered' by the Liberal Town Council. Liberal Town Councils
on Tyneside commonly introduced fair wages clauses for Council work.[9]
After 1910 in particular, municipal housing schemes became
a focus of Liberal attention, despite bad experiences with previous
attempts at municipal provision. Some Liberals went further. Labour
was more obviously the party of municipal expenditure, and of the
municipal unions, but it was not easy for it to make *minor* Liberal/Labour
differences the grounds for a *major* electoral realignment.[10]

The direction of national and local politics could alienate some Old
Liberals. Walter Runciman senior, father of the Cabinet Minister, a shipping magnate and a leading figure in North-East Liberal circles, was

[7] Daunton, *Cardiff*, pp. 204–8; D. Clark, 'Introduction to South Shields Labour party
   minutes (Wakefield, 1979) [microfilmed records]; Hunter (thesis), pp. 194–9.
[8] *N.E.*, 12, 13 Feb., 17 Apr. 1914 (Sunderland bazaar, Middlesbrough LYL report); *Llais
   Llafur*, 31 Jan. 1914.
[9] Hunter (thesis), pp. 96–100, 224–44; Middlesbrough TC *AR* 1912, Middlesbrough ILP
   Mins, 19 Jan. 1910.
[10] *North-Eastern Daily Gazette*, 30 Oct. 1909, noting some Liberal support for direct
   labour projects and a minimum wage for council workmen in Newcastle. For expenditure
   on housing projects in South Wales, e.g. *Llanelli Mercury*, 12 Mar. 1914.

not unusual in regarding the 1909 Budget as 'a concoction of loot'. Runciman contemplated resigning, but hung on; the wind of change nonetheless blew the industrial magnates and newspapermen, Joicey and Storey, out of the party and towards the Tories. Furness and Charles Palmer, leading Liberal figures and MPs of similar local standing, were equally unhappy with the party's social policy, and worked against it. This, no doubt, was just the tip of an iceberg.[11]

The 'local' and 'national' radicalisation of constituency Liberalism met up when parliamentary candidates were selected. Local manufacturers were still frequently chosen as candidates, but they were increasingly Centrists, New Liberals or political pragmatists who were willing to accept or embrace change. In South Wales, the millionaire former MP for Monmouth Boroughs, Alfred Spicer, was perfectly willing to stand down for a Labour candidate in 1906; his family went on to contribute generously to Labour party funds. Mond (despite his subsequent political course) and Haslam were aggressive Lloyd Georgeites and Centrists.[12] Neither was the North-East unaffected. Russell Rea, the shipping magnate and MP for South Shields, was a member of the Rainbow Circle, as was J. M. Robertson, the Tyneside MP, who was also a prominent secular radical. The ironmaster MPs for Middlesbrough and Stockton, Penry Williams and Jonathon Samuel, based their appeal on more than their local industrial role. The question of the moment, Samuel bravely noted at a Home Rule meeting in 1914, was not Ireland but the redistribution of wealth. A. H. Scott, Darlington's candidate in 1914, was a former Lancastrian MP and a New Liberal. If 'businessmen' were still important, the politics of some of these businessmen at least were changing.[13]

MPs who were pragmatically or ideologically committed to the 'new' politics played an important part in spreading the gospel. Joseph Pease, Arnold Rowntree, and other important local figures had been trying to counter the Radical anti-Progressives since before 1906. Defections, retirements, and new additions to the Progressive ranks reinforced their hand. By 1914, the radical MPs were combining to spread their shared views, aided by the Darlington based, Rowntree-owned, *Northern Echo,* and in South Wales by the Swansea-based *Daily News.* As the largest Liberal newspapers in the North-East and South Wales, they had a powerful

[11] Runciman, *Before the mast,* p. 282; Emy, *Liberals and social politics,* p. 91.
[12] F. H. Heath to J.R.M., 23 Apr. 1901, LRC 2/226. Haslam emphasised his sympathies with labour *(Western Mail,* 9 Jan. 1906, *South Wales Argus,* 18, 23 Dec. 1909). For Mond at this time, Emy, *Liberals and social politics,* pp. 241, 260, and Schneer, *Tillett,* pp. 140–5.
[13] See e.g. Darlington meeting with Scott and Samuel, *Darlington Times,* 27 June 1914 and Scott's Progressive credentials, noted in the *North Star,* 14 Feb. 1914. See also Bernstein, *Liberal politics,* p. 72.

voice. When local parties had to step outside the locality in search of candidates, the radicals again stepped in. It was presumably the Rowntrees who introduced the (extremely) pragmatic radical, and former Rowntree worker, I. T. T. Lincoln, to the Darlington Liberal association. The reforming section of the Liberal elite thus reinforced the efforts of those 'constituency' radicals who wished to push the party further to the left.

Not all MPs, local parties, or newspapers, were as committed to the politics of change. Some Progressive initiatives were defeated.[14] The Lib/Lab MPs, like Wilson in Middlesbrough, were less radical than their Liberal colleagues and successors. However, Stuart, Craig, and Cairns (MPs for Sunderland, Tynemouth, and Newcastle) were solid Centrist reformers; Elverston, the Gateshead MP, was a Manchester radical, if not a Progressive. Moreover, although the Newcastle, Middlesbrough, and South Shields newspapers were hardly carbon copies of the *Northern Echo,* they stood for a Centrist Liberal stance, support for labour interests, and (reluctantly) for some Progressive concessions to Labour.[15] Even in conservative South Wales, promising MPs, such as Llewelyn Williams, the MP for Carmarthen Boroughs, and the Rev J. Towyn Jones, the MP for East Carmarthenshire, were embracing aspects of the radical programme. Towyn Jones was selected as parliamentary candidate *despite* opposition from local Liberal landowners, and against competition from their more conservative, and more affluent, nominee. They represented an evolving 'Welsh' form of Liberal reformism just as the 'reforming' Liberalism practised in the North-East grew from an older, localised, Liberal tradition. Moreover, by 1914 national political campaigns – such as those on land and housing – were introducing evidence of the central party's commitment to intervention and 'practical' politics.[16]

The Liberal image was a composite of varying traditions and influences. An *evolving* party creed could create a *more* popular image than one which simply embraced the most radical proposals currently fashionable with Liberal intellectuals, particularly if 'old' ideas were still the perceived foundations of economic prosperity (although in the North-East, being 'fashionable' and 'intellectual' was probably enough of a handicap without this). The old and the new could mix in differing quantities and with differing degrees of principle and pragmatism. Liberal support for 'old'

---

[14] For one such defeat, Daunton, *Cardiff,* pp. 171–7. There were similar constituency conflicts in North Wales, for which see below, pp. 307.

[15] See Purdue, 'North-East politics', p. 11. For Elverston, and for the Liberal press on Progressivism, *Northern Democrat,* Jan. 1910, *Daily Gazette,* 25 Oct. 1909.

[16] Morgan, *Wales,* p. 139 and *Wales in British politics,* pp. 245, 252.

economic ideas could reflect their continuing salience, or it could involve a blinkered hostility to intervention and attempts to 'moderate' the adverse impact of the market on individual living standards. 'Paternalism' could be a useful adjunct or a stifling reflection of the past's hold. Support from the middle and manufacturing classes could be a useful addition to the Liberals' working-class vote, and was not necessarily incompatible with a crusade against the unproductive and exploiting classes. Gradual change could be as much as the electorate wished to see, a popular merger of the old and the new; it could also be a failure to keep pace with new political demands and interests. The precise impact of the Liberals' position was determined by the nature of local interests and values, and the balance of its approach. Liberalism would also only seriously be threatened if Labour's response revealed chinks in the Liberals' armour which they had the weapons to exploit.

II

The conditions were not favourable from Labour's viewpoint. In the shipbuilding areas, and in the ports, it was difficult for Labour to use union contacts and aims to become rooted in working-class opinion, because working-class fragmentation, between jobs and unions, was so pronounced.[17] Moreover, skilled unionists, used to providing for themselves, and to industrial success, found Centrist Liberal remedies for their (sporadic) problems very attractive. Even craft representation seemed unnecessary to some; state intervention of a broader, 'economic', nature seemed totally irrelevant. It may also have seemed to the unskilled that a Labour party dominated by ILP Socialists who were skilled workers and lower middle-class professionals was hardly any better than the Liberals.

There *were* sections of the workforce, however, which were less likely to find Liberal policies acceptable. Railwaymen, tinplate workers, members of other general unions, and the inhabitants of the mining enclaves which were evident in many of these seats, suffered from less favourable, more permanent, economic problems. Government intervention in their industry was already apparent, but it was (from their point of view) only half-satisfactory. There were also opportunities for Labour to exploit where the internal balance of power in Liberal politics tilted the party further towards the right than was acceptable to the local electorate.

[17] For shipbuilding, Reid (thesis), *passim* and P. L. Robertson, 'Demarcation disputes in British shipbuilding before 1914', *IRSH* (1975), p. 223. For divisions on the South Wales waterfront, Daunton, *Cardiff,* pp. 181–96 and his article, 'The Cardiff Coaltrimmers Union, 1888–1914', *Llafur* (1978). More generally, J. Lovell, *Stevedores and dockers* (1969) and G. Phillips and N. Whiteside, *Casual labour* (Oxford, 1985).

Finally, there were Tory enclaves, especially around the docks, where there were armaments works (as in West Newcastle), in certain shipyards (where Protestantism was still significant) or more generally in seats like Middlesbrough and Darlington where Liberalism was inherently weak. If Labour could adapt, it could expand.[18] Nonetheless, this *potential* Labour support had to be moulded into a single electoral bloc. Labour's political image had to suit groups with different interests, and different political traditions. It could not always do this by emphasising the most locally relevant aspect of a composite image. Constituencies like Jarrow and South Shields contained miners, shipbuilding and other engineering workers, Tory dockland wards and rural and middle-class areas. Finding a language acceptable to all these distinct groups would not be easy. Moreover, the Labour alliance contained elements, particularly the Socialists, whose convictions might prevent them pragmatically adopting a stance which was consistent with local material aims or (conservative) attitudes. The religious commitment and moral force behind ILP activism in Welsh towns like Llanelli and Swansea is well-documented. It is equally evident (if less well-documented) in the North-East, where ILP organisers like the Rev T. E. Moll, and Matt Simm, and the ILP newspaper, the *Northern Democrat,* often harked back to the alleged moral dynamism of the party's ethical socialist past.[19] 'Moral revolutionists' and ethical socialists still had considerable influence in local Labour politics. When Trades Councils and unions were particularly and resolutely attached to the Liberal party, there was less pressure to change. Neither, even if the left accepted change, would the result necessarily convince an electorate which was receiving conflicting messages from the older parties.

The left exercised considerable influence in Labour politics before 1910. In Middlesbrough, the ILP was in effect the only Labour organisation. It supported Lansbury's Independent Labour parliamentary campaign in 1906, despite NEC and NAC advice. The branch continued to sympathise with various 'left' issues, and to support calls for united action with the SDF. The left was also important in Monmouth Boroughs, where James Winstone, who sympathised with many critics of the Labour leadership, was the parliamentary candidate in 1906, and in Stockton, where in the same year Frank Rose, formerly of the Socialist League, stood as Labour's candidate. The small Darlington ILP branch was dominated by critics

[18] For some indication of continuing Tory strength, Blewett, *Peers,* p. 198, noting the excellence of Tory organisation in Sunderland, and Jarrow Cons. Assoc. ann. meeting report, *Jarrow Expr.,* 20 Feb. 1914. The Cardiff District, Monmouth Boroughs, and Swansea seats were marginals.

[19] For South Wales, Griffiths, *Pages from memory,* pp. 13–16, Brennan *et al., South-West Wales,* pp. 49–52, S. Awberry, *Labour's early struggles in Swansea* (Swansea, 1949), esp. pp. 54–5.

of the ILP's national policy.[20] The left was also a force in the unions. Both Rose and Winstone were trade union candidates. The Gasworkers in Jarrow, and the Steel Smelters and several unskilled workers' unions in Swansea, lent support to left-dominated Labour constituency organisations. It is noticeable, however, that they withdrew their support when 'propagandist' and 'Socialist' parliamentary campaigns were suggested. Even when they sympathised with some aspects of the critique, unofficial, often very radical, campaigns were seen as both ideologically unacceptable and a waste of union funds. Moreover, even the dissatisfied did not wish to cut themselves off from Labour moderates by acting against the party leaders; neither were they blind to the benefits of Liberal policy. At the same time, skilled unions like the Boilermakers and the Shipwrights were even more reluctant to embrace these ideas and local miners' lodges generally concurred.[21] In Jarrow, the miners and shipbuilding workers refused to join the Jarrow LRC until it had demonstrated its moderation. The Middlesbrough and South Shields Trades Councils were staunchly Lib/Lab until at least 1910, and harboured Liberal sympathies thereafter. Similar circumstances were not unusual in South Wales.[22]

Socialist organisations were extremely unsuccessful. In Sunderland, a double member borough with an ILP sponsored (but very moderate) Labour MP, there was virtually no Labour organisation before 1910. Despite an enthusiastic local membership, ILP branches in Middlesbrough, Cardiff, and Darlington could scarcely raise the money for a single municipal campaign. In Middlesbrough Lansbury's middle-class allies, led by the formidable Mrs Coates Hanson, supplied the leadership and (occasionally) the funds for branch activity.[23] Lansbury polled 10 per cent of the vote in 1906, 46 per cent less than Wilson, the Lib/Lab candidate. This was the measure of the left's support. Labour organisation

[20] G.L. to J.R.M., 24 Aug. 1905, JRM PRO 30/69/1149, Middlesbrough ILP Mins, 12 Feb. 1906. For Rose, see, p. 57.

[21] Awberry, *Swansea,* pp. 38–42, 48, 53–6, Schneer, *Tillett,* pp. 139, 143–4; A. W. Purdue, 'Jarrow politics, 1885–1914: the challenge to Liberal hegemony', *Northern Hist.* (1982), p. 191. For the ASE's crucial role in the development of Newcastle's excellent Labour organisation, Newcastle LRC *AR* 1905–6, and *AR* 1918–19, 1919–20. For the ASE's refusal to endorse a parliamentary candidate in 1908 without NEC approval, NEC Mins, 10 Sept. 1908.

[22] Purdue, 'Jarrow', p. 187, DMA Marsden Lodge Mins, e.g. 2 Nov., 10 Dec. 1911 (votes of 11–8, 23–19 against affiliation to the Jarrow LRC); Clark, 'South Shields', *passim*; M. Coates Hanson to J.R.M, above, fn. 5, J.R.M. to ? Smith, 29 Dec. 1905, LP GC 17/203, Middlesbrough ILP Mins, 25 Oct. 1908. See also *Stockton Herald,* 16 Nov. 1912, for the Trades Council's eventual, if still rather half-hearted, commitment to Labour representation. For South Wales, e.g. Pontypridd TC Mins, 12 Mar.–22 May 1913.

[23] J. Derbyshire to A.P., 21 Nov. 1908, LP/EL/08/1/159, T. D. Benson to Ensor, 7 Oct. 1909, Ensor MS; Middlesbrough ILP Mins, e.g. 15 Oct. 1906, and A. W. Purdue, 'George Lansbury and the Middlesbrough election of 1906', *IRSH* (1973), pp. 341, 345–6.

in Monmouth Boroughs, where Winstone stood in 1906, was almost non-existent; even the ILP failed to take the campaign seriously. In Swansea and Llanelli, organisation was partial and over-dependent on a handful of middle-class intellectuals who were fiercely committed not to Labour expansion, but to 'making Socialists'.[24] Socialism could not break the Liberals' hold; it also stood in the way of Labour's attempts to find an alternative.

Labour's best electoral performances before 1910 followed campaigns which exploited the deficiencies of the Liberals as representatives of a moderately reforming party which had roots in community sentiments. At the 1906 election, John Williams, an ex-Liberal and Nonconformist lay preacher, stood in Gower as an independent Lib/Lab and miners' candidate. His electoral support came from miners and from the numerous workers in the (depressed) steel and tinplate industries. Williams emphasised his Welshness, his religion, and his Liberalism. He made some references to his class, and more to his occupation. He supported reforms of the kind which national, but not local, Liberals found perfectly acceptable. He narrowly won the contest. It was a victory for tradition. Williams 'reflected a network of community values in which Welshness, nonconformism and, above all, community values played a part'.[25] The Liberals had stepped outside this social nexus. Labour succeeded so completely by occupying the 'Liberal' ground.

Nonetheless, even before 1910 many Labour organisations were beginning to adopt approaches which involved a compromise between 'Socialist' and 'trade union' aspirations. In seats like Gateshead, Newcastle, and Jarrow, ILP branches had always contained elements willing to adopt reforming policies. They had made this evident at the municipal level. The moderate message was also transferred into the parliamentary arena. Hudson, the Newcastle Labour MP, was an ethical reformer and a moderate. Johnson, the former Lib/Lab miners' MP for Gateshead, argued during his 1910 campaign that Labour 'was not a Socialist movement', but a party committed to going 'a bit further' than the Liberals.[26] Even Pete Curran (the Jarrow MP who was a member of the 'radical' Gasworkers' union, and a founder of the ILP) made it clear in the 1907 Jarrow by-election that he stood as a trade unionist. 'He only mentioned Socialism', Bill Purdue writes, 'to deny that he was a Socialist candidate.' The compromise policy bore results. All but one of the trade union

---

[24] *South Wales Argus*, 15, 20 Jan. 1906; D. Cleaver, 'Swansea and District Labour press 1888–1914', *Llafur* (1984), pp. 37–8.

[25] Cleaver, 'Gower', esp. p. 409. The miners made up 20 per cent of the electorate. See also above, p. 216, for comparisons with other mining seats.

[26] *Daily Gazette*, 23 Oct. 1909; Hunter (thesis), pp. 280–4.

branches in Newcastle had affiliated to the LRC by 1908. The Jarrow LRC had likewise attracted a large list of official supporters by the end of the 1907 campaign, in which Curran was also, rather luckily, elected.[27]

Even the more radical ILP branches recognised a need to move closer to the unions, signalling a need to attack material grievances. However, they shrank back from the political consequences. In 1903 the Stockton branch gave up the idea of adopting an ILP parliamentary candidate in favour of a trade unionist – 'a sacrifice for the National Movement'. However, Frank Rose, the candidate they eventually selected, was a radical Socialist. This was a partial shift, not a sweeping change of ideological emphasis. Similarly, although there was a 'reforming' element in the Middlesbrough ILP, the branch as a whole concentrated on the 'radical' issue of women's suffrage, which in seats such as this was hardly a vote-winner.[28] In South Wales, 'moderation' was a little more effective. The formation of the Cardiff LRC in 1908 followed the ILP's decision to give up Socialist unity, and the Trades Council's decision to abandon its support for Lib/Lab municipal candidates. In Swansea, the ILP also shifted a little to the right, a trend reflected in the markedly different attitude of the Socialist newspaper, *Llais Llafur*, to the trade unions.

Nonetheless, there were powerful elements in all these areas that rejected even a limited 'accommodation' with Labour's moderate wing.[29] Some dissident left-wingers in fact stepped up their demands for a more Socialist stance. In Middlesbrough they made several attempts to field municipal 'Labour and Socialist' candidates. The enthusiasm generated by the Right to Work campaign, and by Grayson's success at Colne Valley, suggested to many radical Socialists that a pragmatic acceptance of moderation was no longer necessary. Graysonite Socialist revivalism destroyed what union/ILP 'unity' existed in Stockton, and what organisation and unity there was in Sunderland. In South Shields, ILP/SDF Right to Work candidates opposed trade unionists in the 1908 and 1909 municipal elections.[30] When official support for parliamentary campaigns at Newcastle (1908) and Swansea (1910) was not forthcoming (which reflected the importance of national/local moderate Socialist and trade union opinion), unofficial candidates proceeded and took a more Socialist line.

[27] Purdue, 'Jarrow', pp. 193–4 and *Jarrow Labour Herald*, 4 May 1906; Newcastle LRC *AR* 1907–8, *Northern Democrat*, Sept. 1910. The Liberal vote was divided by an Irish Nationalist candidate.

[28] J. Baker to J.R.M., 30 Apr. 1903, LRC 8/61 and Stockton TC *AR* 1905; Middlesbrough ILP Mins, e.g. 8 Oct. 1906.

[29] Daunton, *Cardiff*, pp. 211–14; Cleaver, 'Swansea Labour press', pp. 38–40. The Swansea left continued to support dissidents as the city's prospective parliamentary candidates.

[30] J. W. Robertson to A.P., J. Baker to A.P., 18, 7 Nov. 1908, LP/EL/08/1/153 and 157. The Sunderland ILP was denounced as a 'bunch of amateur Victor G's' (Derbyshire to A.P., above, fn. 23).

There was some local backing, despite the absence of official endorsement. Tillett's experience in Swansea, however, shows that there were strict limits to the left's support. Although his campaign built on common local working-class views, his rabid anti-semitism (he denounced Mond as 'a German Jew'), and his attacks on the Budget, were too much for many 'respectable' local radicals. His positive proposals, which included extensive nationalisation, equality for women, and the creation of a new Socialist party in Parliament, were neither prominent enough, nor credible enough, to destroy Liberal sympathies. Most unions shied away. Some asked him to stand down, and called on MacDonald to assist. Even 'left-wing' unions, like the Dockers, could not stomach the full Socialist programme.[31]

The Labour party was not very successful before 1910. It had a narrow, and shallow, base. The organisational and electoral position was such that when an election was called in 1910, many constituency parties were unable to begin, or continue, with parliamentary campaigns. If they went ahead, they generally faced a crushing rejection from the electorate. In South Wales, Monmouth Boroughs, fought in 1906, was uncontested in 1910. Despite the election of candidates at Swansea and Cardiff, trade union/NEC consultation resulted in these candidates being withdrawn. The only Welsh coastal, or even semi-mining, seats contested by Labour were South Glamorgan and Gower. They were fought by former Lib/Lab miners' candidates, on Lib/Lab miners' issues. In South Glamorgan, a mixed seat with a large agricultural and middle-class electorate (as well as miners, railwaymen, and dockers), Labour had virtually no organisation and could not have commanded an electoral majority. It relied heavily on the Liberals.[32]

The position in the North-East was no better. Darlington, which also had virtually no Labour organisation, had been fought in 1906 by a former Lib/Lab trade unionist officially reconstituted as a 'Labour' representative. He was defeated, and the campaign was not repeated before 1914. Stockton was more promising. Labour had come just 8 per cent behind the second-placed Liberal in 1906. Nonetheless, local Socialists insisted on supporting an extreme Socialist candidate, whose selection was unconstitutional (his union was not affiliated to the Labour party). The NEC could not grant him official sanction, and the seat went uncontested. South Shields was the only other constituency which warranted serious consideration on the basis of its municipal record and organisational

---

[31] Schneer, *Tillett*, pp. 139–46 and *Llais Llafur*, 15 Jan. 1910.
[32] For Cardiff and Swansea's failed campaigns, NEC Mins, 20 May, 15 Dec. 1908, 2, 17 Dec. 1909, LP *AR* 1910, pp. 59–63, BrSS Ec Mins, 11–13 Nov. 1909, *MR* Nov. 1909. For South Glamorgan, below, p. 245–6.

position, but on neither account was the position sufficiently encouraging for the NEC to sanction a contest.[33]

There were only five Labour campaigns in the North-East in 1910, and only one of these reflected the existence of a strong local Labour base. Sunderland was fought because it was a Labour-held double member borough. The ILP sponsored the campaign, but the only organisation was the Trades Council ('a one man band') and a handful of Graysonites who had little sympathy for the moderate candidate. The Liberals lent a helping hand.[34] Labour also fought the double member borough of Newcastle, again without Liberal opposition, and again this did not reflect a dominant local position. The SDF candidate at the three-cornered by-election contest in 1908 had polled only 10 per cent of the vote. Although the result in nearby Gateshead, where Labour polled a fifth of the vote, was a better indication of the level of Labour support in Newcastle, the Liberals (in both seats) were still considerably more popular. The fourth campaign, in the steel town of Middlesbrough, saw Labour increase its poll from 8 to 14 per cent following the adoption of a moderate from the locally powerful Blastfurnacemen's union. Nonetheless, the very convincing nature of the Liberal victory (by a margin of 36 per cent) suggests that Labour had secured a footing but no more. Labour's only real opportunity arose in Jarrow. The Liberals, facing a potentially hostile electorate, compounded the problem by failing to display the commitment and enthusiasm necessary to convince voters that they were sincere social reformers. Nonetheless, the Liberal/Irish split which had given Labour its chance in 1907 had been papered over and the Liberals consequently regained the seat from Labour in January 1910. By December, although this remained a three-way marginal, Labour had slipped behind the Tories and into third place.[35]

Even by 1910, Labour's 'reformist' stance in Newcastle/Gateshead had failed to create a major electoral realignment. Labour's parliamentary candidate in Newcastle at the 1910 parliamentary elections was elected only because he received Liberal support. The Liberals already occupied too much of the 'Labour' ground. Moreover, both seats contained a number of miners, and Labour's Statist support for the MFGB line was out of line with local interests and views. The local Liberals, who took a very different line, reaped the benefit of supporting the locally dominant

[33] W. W. Robertson to A.P., 18 Nov. 1908, LP/EL/08/1/153; NEC Mins, 12 Oct. 1908. Lib/Lab and Tory politics provided popular alternatives. For this before 1906, P. Harrison to J.R.M., 11 Oct. 1903, LRC 11/158.
[34] T. D. Benson to Ensor, 21 Oct. 1909, Ensor MS, Derbyshire to A.P., above, fn. 23, Blewett, *Peers*, p. 242.
[35] Boilermakers' *AR* 1910 and NEC Mins, 24 Feb. 1910.

view.[36] However, a radical Socialist stance had been even less successful, whilst the partially watered down version evident in Middlesbrough, Stockton, and Swansea had failed to dent the Liberals' lead. A rooted Liberal party with a growing interest in Centrist policies, and some support for New Liberal ideas, grafted greater organisational activity, and a higher profile campaign, on to a strong existing political stock. It was not displaced, or (outside Jarrow) seriously threatened. Labour could not dent the Liberals' appeal, shift the grounds of debate, nor establish the credibility of an alternative emphasis.

III

On the surface, Labour made considerable progress after 1910. Trade Councils in Newport, Middlesbrough, and South Shields ostensibly abandoned their old Lib/Lab ideas. The number of organisations affiliated to constituency Labour parties grew considerably. Yet the institutional changes did not always convince local union branches, or union members, to support Labour with their time, money, and votes. Beneath the surface Labour's rivals were still more popular, and its own internal strains and tensions still hampered change. Electoral progress was limited, being very largely confined to areas and groups where the Statist side of Labour's image was positively attractive.

The growing local and national movement towards a moderate, reforming, stance was vehemently criticised by elements in the ILP after 1910. The Middlesbrough and Darlington branches, for example, backed the more active approach suggested by George Lansbury and Russell Williams (Darlington's prospective Labour candidate).[37] The response of the Middlesbrough ILP to a national ILP circular requesting information on local activity was representative of a broader feeling in local ILP branches. Political work was difficult, the branch resolution recorded, when Labour MPs were 'supporting the Liberals in Parliament continually, even to the detriment of Labour's interests'. These sentiments were not confined to the North-East. When the SWMF refused to conduct a by-election campaign in East Carmarthen during 1912, the local ILP chose Dr J. H. Williams as their candidate. They went ahead with only NAC sanction. Williams' campaign concentrated on the state's misuse of military power

---

[36] The details of Liberal and Labour policy on mining, and the support given by Gateshead miners to the Liberal party, are discussed above, pp. 209–11.

[37] Middlesbrough ILP Mins, voting on NAC elections, 16 Jan. 1911 and motion on LP affiliation, 18 Nov. 1912, M. Coates Hanson to G.L., 26 June 1912, and Coates Hanson to G.L., 31 Oct. 1912, Lansbury MS LL 6 fo. 105, 28 fo. 77.

during the 1911 Llanelli strikes, an issue which, he argued, illustrated the class nature of the whole state apparatus.[38]

One reason for the left's frustration was that union affiliations did not create massive enthusiasm for Labour amongst union branches. In Newport, a town with numerous steelworks and a large docks, only the NUR consistently supported the local Labour party. Meetings were often cancelled because of poor attendances; affiliated union branches refused to allow collections for the Labour party at their meetings. Lib/Lab feeling remained strong. Despite their affiliation to the Labour party, it was not unusual for union branches in many parts of the North-East and South Wales to put forward their own, non-Labour, municipal candidates.[39] When the South Shields LRC adopted a parliamentary candidate in 1914 to oppose the sitting radical Liberal, Russell Rea, at least one affiliated union branch resigned in protest.[40] A handful of individuals generally dominated local parties. Many union delegates nominally on the LRC executive failed to attend a single meeting between 1910 and 1914.

Nonetheless, there was growing party support for careful consideration of 'union' issues. Local ILP radicals, like the national leaders, were determined not to leave the Labour party but to convert it to Socialism from within.[41] Many ILP branches became more active, but concentrated on material issues and the most socially favourable wards in the constituency. In South Shields, Labour focused on four to five mining and dockland wards, whilst dockland wards received the most attention in Newport, Sunderland, and Swansea. The Newcastle LRC concentrated on the mining wards although these were largely in the Gateshead and Tynemouth constituencies for parliamentary purposes. The Middlesbrough ILP accepted the Blastfurnacemen's concentration on the wards dominated by their members (the Blastfurnacemen responded by ignoring them). The Liberals generally did not interfere. Results in the selected wards

[38] Middlesbrough ILP Mins, 8 Jan. 1913; SWMF Mins, 8 Aug. 1912 recording the lodges' decision that they 'did not think that the prospects for the success of a Labour candidate were favourable'. For the position in the constituency, Morgan, *Wales in British politics,* p. 252, F.J. memo, 15 Aug. 1912, ILP MS H.O. Circ./3 and J.S.M. to ?, 16 Aug. 1912 (BLPES Coll., fo. 312).

[39] Newport LP Mins, esp. 11 June 1914 and evidence of continued Lib/Lab problems, 21 Aug. 1913, 30 Jan. 1914. For Darlington, victory of the Lib/Lab ASLEF candidate, *Daily Gazette,* 3 Nov. 1913.

[40] South Shields LP Mins, 1912–14 and *N.E.,* 25 Apr. 1914. As in Yorkshire, some 'respectable' elements, like the co-operators, were firmly Liberal (Morgan, *Wales in British politics,* p. 255 and below pp. 261–2).

[41] See below, p. 338.

improved. Labour elected more Councillors. It had real, but confined, roots.[42]

Specific local circumstances occasionally enabled the Labour party to broaden its appeal by underlining the validity of its political message. In the Carmarthen Boroughs constituency, which was dominated by the steel/tinplate town of Llanelli, local economic depression augmented the substantial existing hostility to the Liberals. It helped provide support for a Trades Council/ILP alliance. However, Labour still needed to establish itself as a serious, credible, working-class, party. Circumstances proved fortuitous. The Llanelli railway strike, and the ensuing rioting and violence, were brutally suppressed by the police. This could not be used successfully to attack state 'militarism', as Williams found in East Carmarthen (where he was heavily defeated in the 1912 by-election) and Tillett himself experienced at public meetings in Llanelli. However, the strikes and rioting *could* be portrayed as a form of communal protest. Labour shunned violence, rioting, *and* the more 'intellectual' arguments of the ILP. Its attitude to the situation reflected communitarian sentiments and a sense of moral outrage at the economic injustice which began the strike and the 'unjust' outside influence which helped end it. As Labour's support for Statist policies also supplied tangible and potentially economically beneficial solutions to the problems, Labour had developed a powerful combination of appeals. The Liberals' half-hearted resistance allowed Labour's case to appear stronger by default. The Llanelli Labour association, backed strongly by the Dockers, the Tin and Sheet Millmen, and the Railwaymen, elected two of their three candidates in the 1913 Llanelli municipal elections despite Liberal and Tory opposition. They were less successful in Carmarthen (a more middle-class town, with little previous Labour history), but with 28 per cent of the vote in three-cornered contests, Labour was not that far behind the Liberals even here. Labour was becoming a solidly protective, loyal, and reforming party. In nearby Gower – where Labour had established a moderate stance in 1906 – local commentators estimated that Labour could poll more than half the total vote in a three-cornered contest by 1914. To a lesser extent, this combination of a sound moral/economic approach, and a particular mix of occupational groups, had helped Labour expand its support in Jarrow. The Liberals – in these circumstances – were being undermined and outflanked.[43]

---

[42] See reports, e.g. *Daily Gazette,* 3 Nov. 1913 (Middlesbrough Ormsby and Newport wards); Hunter (thesis), pp. 92–3. The Middlesbrough ILP minutes suggest that the Blastfurnacemen's union was now directing the show.

[43] D. Hopkin, 'The Llanelli riots 1911', *Welsh Hist. Rev.* (1983), pp. 509, 511, G. H. Stacey to J.S.M., 1 Jan. 1913, LP/AFF 7/318. For election results, *Llanelly Mercury,* 6 Nov. 1913, *Carmarthen Weekly Reporter,* 7 Nov. 1913, 24 Dec. 1910, 23 May 1914.

However, as the Jarrow position also illustrates, it was difficult to turn even this degree of support into a parliamentary majority. In Jarrow, Labour had lost its primacy in 1910. Municipal results suggest that by 1914 it had expanded a little in the mining areas, while the Tories had made up some ground (to an extent at Labour expense) in the rest of the constituency. The skilled unions were still not closely involved with the Labour party. The Labour newspaper had collapsed; Lawson, the Labour agent, wrote later that he knew little of the techniques of party organisation. He also claimed that this made little difference, because there was no organisation to mobilise. There was considerable NEC concern over the local position, which became worse once the prospective parliamentary candidate withdrew in 1914.[44] Labour still had problems in uniting its electoral support, silencing the left, and keeping itself in touch with the race. In most areas, however, Labour's improvement was so limited before 1914 that the question of how to maintain a challenge which just failed never really arose. The mixed nature of the constituencies, class fragmentation, pre-conceived perceptions of what was possible, and the attractions of a moral/material Liberalism, all stood in its way. With social bases which were less favourable, opponents who were more subtle, and Socialists who were less pliable, Labour struggled to make an impression. It struggled in vain.

IV

As an election approached in 1914–15 the Labour/Socialist organisers focused their attention on the local organisational and electoral position. The North-East Divisional ILP took a long look at the position in the constituencies. The verdict was (justifiably) unfavourable. Darlington's attempt to obtain official sanction for their prospective parliamentary candidate was rejected on the grounds of 'evident lack of organisation, funds, and limited trade union support'. Stockton was regarded as the best prospect. It had 150 members, organised into ward committees, and £39 in the bank. It fought around six of the nine municipal wards each year, and was often successful (mainly in the Tory parts of the constituency). This was a far better record than most ILP branches in the area, and it was enough for the NAC to give their support.[45] However, local trade unionists painted a very different picture in their report to the NEC. The LRC Secretary noted that his organisation was 'about (sic) dead as since the Osborne decision the Trade Unions here (are) taking no

---

[44] Lawson, *A man's life,* pp. 175–8, J.S.M. to J. Pointer, 11 Oct. 1913, LP/CAM/13/ 1/114.

[45] J.B.G. Diary, 23 May 1914, NAC Mins, 28 Jan., 28 July 1913.

part in the cause. The only party that is live is the ILP of Stockton and Thornby ... it will take a good many years to get the trade unionists to vote Labour.' This, and the selection of an ILP candidate in the nearby mining seat of Bishop Auckland, killed the hopes of the Stockton candidate, E. P. Wake, who consequently withdrew. He, and the NAC, accepted that the electoral, organisational, and now the financial position made a candidature impossible.[46]

There were few other seats in the North-East, or in South Wales, which were even as attractive a prospect as Stockton. In Middlesbrough and South Shields, two of the most unionised constituencies, the basic structural problem of a limited electoral base had not been remedied. The selection, and enthusiasm, of a local miners' candidate was sufficient to convince some miners' lodges that Labour representation was a good idea. However, miners made up only 15 per cent of the electorate, and this vote was unlikely to be solidly Labour. South Shields, Henderson told the Durham miners, 'was not ready to be contested'.[47] The shipbuilding workers were unenthusiastic. Despite the Trades Council's affiliation to the local Labour party, most individual union members retained their existing political allegiances. The position in Middlesbrough was very similar. The Trades Council's Secretary argued that it was unlikely to change:

The discussion on the question of Labour representation a month ago was not very sanguine, as far as I could gather. In order to have a chance of success, a prospective Labour candidate would have to arouse and educate the constituency for at least a couple of years, & that means a lot of money.

Labour's national headquarters agreed that the 'organisational and general prospects in the constituency are such that the promotion of a candidature is unadvisable'.[48]

The South Wales coastal constituencies were possibly in an even worse position. Class fragmentation was so pronounced that progress was extremely difficult. The Cardiff LRC had to merge with the Trades Council in 1914 to prevent its extinction; the nearby Barry LRC covered just

---

[46] C. F. Barclay to A.H., 12 Jan. 1914, LP/AFF 8/422. See also C. H. Oxberry to F.J., 26 Aug. 1913, J. A. Close to F.J., 9 Oct. 1913, J. Kelsall to F.J., 12 Dec. 1914, FJ 1913/180 and 209, 1914/14.

[47] W. H. to J.S.M., 27 July 1914, LP/ORG/14/2/76; A.H. to W.H., 30 Apr. 1914, LP/ORG/14/2/13, MFGB Mins, 18 Mar. 1915, DMA Council Mins, 18 Dec. 1915. See the equally unfavourable verdict on the semi-mining Gateshead constituency: 'the organisation and general prospects in the constituency are such that the promotion of a candidature is at present inadvisable' (NEC Org, Sub-Comm. Mins, 6 May 1914).

[48] H. Macgregor to A.H., 14 Apr. 1913, LP/AFF 8/286; J.S.M. to W.H., 24 Apr. 1914, LP/ORG/14/2/12. See also Middlesbrough T&LC AR 1914, and Middlesbrough ILP Mins, 31 Jan., 4 Mar., 1 Apr. 1912.

a corner of the sprawling South Glamorgan constituency.[49] Although Monmouth Boroughs had been fought in 1906, the first meeting of the reformed Newport LRC in 1913 had to be adjourned because so few delegates turned up. The attempt to find a substantial number of municipal candidates failed dismally. Ward committees were set up, fell apart, and were reformed with considerable regularity. Registration work was tackled in 1914 but with little success: 'blunders were to be expected as we did not know what to do'. Even in Swansea, from Labour's standpoint the best of the coastal towns, electoral support was limited. Despite the ILP's sterling work, and the support of activists in the dockers', railwaymen's, and tinplate workers' unions, Labour was not the party of the average Swansea working-class voter. As in Cardiff and Newport, support was again confined largely to the dockland wards. However, these wards were just parts of larger constituencies which contained several working-class wards where Labour had failed, and a substantial middle-class vote.[50] Even where the Liberals were extremely conservative – as they were in Cardiff – Labour's position was difficult. To many, prosperity seemed to be dependent on the docks in general, and on an individual's personal abilities and strength in particular. The benefits of Labour representation to voters with these views was unclear. The Labour party floundered.

Labour was not in a position to replace the Liberals or to break out of the Progressive Alliance in 1914. The double member boroughs of Newcastle and Sunderland, along with Gower in South Wales, would certainly have been fought, although only Gower (now an overwhelmingly secure Labour seat) would have been fought on the basis of the party's independent electoral strength. It also seemed likely that candidates would have been sanctioned in (Liberal-held) Jarrow and Carmarthen Boroughs; the remaining constituencies which were seeking candidates were likely to be disappointed.[51] The miners were being persuaded (eventually they were persuaded) not to fight South Shields. The ILP had used up its allocation of candidates on Sunderland and Bishop Auckland. Stockton, Darlington, Swansea Town, and East Carmarthen (all seeking ILP money), were left high and dry. Unions were reluctant to step in. The NUR declined to fill the breach in South Glamorgan, when the sitting Labour MP was transferred to West Monmouth, despite

[49] Daunton, *Cardiff*, p. 214; (Merthyr) *Pioneer*, 28 July 1913, *R.R.*, 22 Jan. 1915.
[50] Newport LP Mins, esp. 19 June 1913, 17 Sept., 1 Oct. 1914; NEC Mins, 11 June 1912. See Pelling, *Social geography*, pp. 352–5, for the social composition.
[51] B. Tillett to J.R.M., 24 Oct. 1912, 26 Feb. 1913, concerning the selection of W. Pugh as Carmarthen Boroughs candidate, LP/CAN/06/1/131 and 137; NAC Mins, 12 Dec. 1913, 27 Jan. 1914. For Labour municipal defeats in three-cornered contests, even in strongholds, see e.g. *N.E.*, 8 Jan. 1914 (Sunderland).

the fact that the local position was improving.[52] If only Jarrow and Carmarthen Boroughs were to be contested by all three parties, the degree of conflict would have been less pronounced in 1914 than in 1910 or in 1906.

The moderation of strategy – like the moderation of policy – was not without its opponents. Often they were one and the same. The dissident radicals, David Williams and T. Russell Williams, were put forward as parliamentary candidates in Swansea and Darlington, but denied sanction. Neither were very pleased. 'If the NAC thinks I am going under without a murmur', Russell Williams wrote to Francis Johnson, 'it makes a mistake.'[53] Yet failure and Syndicalism had sapped the political strength of the left. David Williams had been refused the financial support of his union, the Boilermakers; Russell Williams had lost his place on the NAC two years earlier, as his views became less popular. A 'soft left'/trade union alliance, sympathetic to NEC views, had become more powerful.

Some Liberals also opposed Progressive policies and the Alliance strategy. The most vehement critics were the coalfield anti-Socialists, whose supporters spilled over into the semi-mining seats. Phillips and Edwards, the Welsh anti-Socialist crusaders, had allies in Gower, who were again planning to oppose the sitting Labour MP. This was unlikely to worry Labour, given its impregnable hold over the seat. Other Labour seats were not under threat. The local parties were unlikely to find the money for anti-Labour campaigns, and the Chief Whip was uninterested. Labour was neither a political nor an ideological danger. Liberal attack, and possible Labour retaliation, would only endanger a compromise which was in both parties' interests.

The Liberals' success was based on a still valid Liberal political culture. Economic prosperity seemed to depend on Liberal economic ideas and, in some circumstances, the opinions and actions of individual (Liberal) employers. The Liberals were an evolving party, able to maintain some middle-class support while still being a primarily working-class organisation. The adoption of Centrist and New Liberal reforms kept the party in touch with popular opinion. A new *Labour* form of moral reformism, which was not radically different from a reforming Liberalism, brought it only limited electoral success. Yet Socialist politics had brought even less. Moderation at least enabled the party to secure a parliamentary base and gain some municipal representation. It also held out the carrot

[52] For the Swansea interest, F.J. to J.K.H., 9 Sept. 1913, FJ 1913/189; (Merthyr) *Pioneer*, 14 June 1913; *R.R.*, 16 Apr. 1915 for South Glamorgan.
[53] T. Russell Williams to F.J., 15 June 1914, FJ 1914/170. For Williams' determination to fight, *South Wales Weekly Post*, 18 July 1914.

of some further, gradual, progress if the Liberals slipped. Moreover, there were groups who found the Statist side of Labour's image particu larly attractive, and opportunities to expand where the Liberals failed to accept reform. New experiences – in conjunction with the right political approach – might also cause a Liberal political culture to crack. Nonetheless, in 1914 Labour was expanding only on a limited front. Given the absence of substantial electoral or institutional support for a more extreme alternative – and the positive attraction of Liberal policy – there was no reason to break out of the electoral alliance. Labour had not given up its long-term plan of replacing the Liberals, but it had learned to play for more limited stakes, and to accept the long, hard, slog which seemed to be necessary if it was ever to expand beyond its current limitations.

Chapter 9

Yorkshire

Yorkshire was of paramount importance to both Progressive parties. It was a Liberal stronghold, which had to be retained. It was also the birthplace of the ILP, and the single most important area of its activity and development. If Labour was to expand then Yorkshire was an obvious target. Moreover, extensive Liberal/Labour conflict, not Progressive agreement, always seemed a possible development. A great many Liberal leaders were ideologically and politically opposed to a Progressive Alliance. Moreover, ILP dominated organisations were equally reluctant to accept co-operation with the Liberal party. Yorkshire was a crucial test of the Liberals' viability as a party of the left, and a potentially disruptive element in the Progressive Alliance.

At the same time, however, there were forces which encouraged Progressive unity. The ILP's electoral strength ensured that in some areas at least the Liberals could protect their flanks against attacks from the left by trading seats as part of a reciprocal Progressive arrangement. Similarly, there were areas, particularly in South Yorkshire, where working-class Conservatism was strong and an alliance with Labour might facilitate victories which had previously been impossible or difficult. For Labour, a Progressive Alliance meant a parliamentary foothold, and an alliance with the unions which might help it to gradually erode Liberal support. Nonetheless, given the size of the old 'Socialist' vote, the importance of Yorkshire seats to the vitality of the Liberal party, and the Labour/Socialist desire to expand party support, the Liberals needed to reaffirm their position as the major radical party more urgently here than almost anywhere else.

The institutional pressures which favoured the radicalisation of Liberal politics were as evident in Yorkshire as in other Liberal areas. However, the radical elements were frequently weaker and their efforts more fiercely resisted. Nonetheless, even before 1910 there were signs that the advocates of change were gaining influence. This was most pronounced in a 'block' of radical seats in the southern Pennine textile belt and in a range of more economically diverse seats, with a more Conservative political culture, which were to be found in the area stretching from South Yorkshire through to the East Riding (Section I).

Labour's response to the Liberal revival in the period after 1906 varied considerably. It too faced institutional obstacles which preserved the power of ethical socialists and prevented the party adopting more reformist policies. The party developed its most successful approach in Bradford, where the Socialist moral reformers dominated local Labour politics. By 1906 they had built a substantial organisational and electoral platform. However, this strategy was not easily replicated in the smaller towns, or in the less urbanised seats in the textile belt (Section II). In part this reflected the different social structures and economic conditions in these constituencies. In the Pennines, workers were more isolated, more economically dependent on the success of a single mill, and less able to benefit economically from the municipal interventionism which dominated the Socialist moral reformers programme. Trade unions were often weaker, and this reflected and reinforced a concentration on the 'moral' side of Labour's approach. Institutionally dominant ILP ethical socialists resisted the adoption of 'materialist' policies. Some of the Bradford/Leeds policies were nonetheless pirated, although local parties generally set them in a less radical moral reformist framework. On the other hand, 'Graysonite' Socialism was a disruptive force in the West Riding *and* in the more 'Tory' seats where Labour had considerable electoral potential. In these areas (Section III) institutional disruption from the left was so pronounced that Labour lost ground, despite the occasional and fortuitous parliamentary victory between 1906 and 1910.

After 1910, Liberal radicalisation continued and expanded (Section IV). While this was a general process, the major institutional and political changes were in the southern 'Pennine block' and in the more Tory seats, rather than in the northern textile belt and the nearby cities. A radicalisation from below ensured that Liberal reformers were gaining power and beginning to influence municipal policy. Their efforts were reinforced by New Liberal sympathisers within the Liberal social/political elite, who were also instrumental in promoting more radical policies at the parliamentary level. They helped create a reforming alliance which was broad enough, and flexible enough, to embrace a range of Liberal views without this considerably diluting their radical thrust. Moreover, the conservative Liberal ideas which were dominant elsewhere in the region, and a part of the Liberals' general image in every seat, were not entirely unpopular. Some voters continued to support the fundamental tenets of a Liberal political culture, since this appeared to be the basis of their continued economic prosperity. If the hostility to social reform amongst a local elite consisting largely of Liberal employers was a weakness, their ability to support some Centrist policies, taken with the effects of national radical campaigns, could mean that Liberalism remained a reasonably attractive creed even here.

Nonetheless, Labour also put up a stronger challenge after 1910. In the textile belt, institutional change allowed Labour to take a more positive stance; new issues gave it the opportunity to improve its image. In the cities, the politics of housing reform brought a practical, widely relevant, welfare issue to the fore. Labour inched forward in Leeds and expanded more rapidly in Bradford. By responding to the strikes by miners, railwaymen, and municipal workers with practical Statist solutions, Labour was also able to make considerable progress where these groups, and people with related interests, were concentrated. However, Statist policies seemed inappropriate in areas dependent on private enterprise, while even the workers in these public sector industries were only half-converted. Labour did not substantially improve its position in the bulk of the textile belt (Section V). On the other hand, practical Statist/ welfare politics allowed Labour to improve its position considerably in the Tory areas (Section VI). This was not enough to undermine the Progressive Alliance. On the contrary, it seemed to reinforce its validity. In 1914–15, increased electoral conflict seemed unlikely (Section VII). The Progressive Alliance, and the Liberal party, survived.

I

Yorkshire Liberal politics were being restructured even before 1906. An expanded electorate, and growing electoral competition, meant more work for local Liberal associations. Party membership grew. By the Edwardian period, there were 4–500 Liberal party members in East Bradford and Holmfirth, although 300 was a more common figure and the oligarchical Keighley Liberal association, in the northern textile belt, had only 100 individual subscribers. Minimum subscription rates were reduced. By 1914 it was common for up to 80 per cent of subscribing members to pay less than 2s 6d per annum.[1] Party activists became more important. The Huddersfield Liberals established a propaganda network which involved intense activity along lines pioneered by the ILP. By 1914 a number of southern Pennine Liberal associations had copied their

[1] Cutting on East Bradford, dated 8 Apr. 1905, E. R. Hartley scrapbook, Hartley MS 11DB5/1/13; presentation album from Holmfirth LA members, H. J. Wilson MS 2497, Holmfirth LA AR 1910–11, 1911–12 and report of 1914 ann. meeting, *Barnsley Chron.*, 23 May 1914; Sheffield membership details, circular dated 16 May 1909, Wilson MS 5909; Keighley LA Mins, subscription list, 19 May 1900. The results of Liberal/Labour (and Socialist) clashes in parliamentary contests are given in Appendix 3, pp. 455–6; for the major municipal results, Appendix 4, pp. 461–3.

approach. These 'radicalised' Liberal associations held up to 100 public meetings a year, reinvolved the Liberal Clubs and ward groups in party activity, and developed their municipal programmes. In larger urban centres, at least three-quarters of the municipal wards were usually fought in the annual November elections, almost always more than Labour.[2] This expanded political activity could no longer be organised and controlled by a central clique. Within constituencies, district groups – based on towns, polling districts, or wards – increasingly selected their own municipal candidates and organised their own local affairs. Party activity was co-ordinated through a more formal constituency structure, with local representatives sitting on Divisional executives. In divided parliamentary boroughs, a City Liberal Federation, with representatives from the Divisional executives, might add an extra tier of authority. This created opportunities for less affluent 'new men' to exercise some political power. Even in undemocratic and conservative Leeds, only half of the City Liberal Federation's executive members between 1899 and 1908 were businessmen. Professionals, shopkeepers, artisans, and trade union officials were beginning to assume positions of responsibility.[3]

Those groups who had to secure and mobilise working-class electoral support began to represent their supporters' interests within Liberal politics. Despite the (justified) conservative reputation of the Keighley Liberal association, party members from the division's poorer areas still suggested that the Divisional executive should adopt more radical policies, and form a municipal pact with Labour.[4] Local Liberal groups also increasingly selected radical professionals and working men as municipal candidates. The Divisional Liberal association in Keighley, for example, was regularly paying their municipal candidates' election expenses by 1900, because the candidates were no longer able to pay themselves. By 1906, around 60 per cent of Liberal Councillors in Leeds were from non-business backgrounds, with professionals the single largest group.[5] Liberal Councillors usually determined municipal policy. They also played a significant

---

[2] Holmfirth LA 1914, fn. 1 above. For the strategy and its dissemination, *Lib. Agent,* Oct. 1906, Oct. 1907, Oct. 1908 (all articles by Yorkshire agents); Huddersfield Lib. Councillors' Mins, 16 June 1914, *Lib. Magazine,* Sept. 1908 (Sowerby). See also J. G. Skinner to H.J.W., 13 Feb. and 14 Mar. 1908, H. J. Wilson MS 5905 (Sheffield), noting Wilson's planned, and largely unimplemented, propaganda scheme for Sheffield.

[3] Bernstein, *Liberal politics,* p. 24, Table 1.8. W. P. Byles of the *Yorkshire Observer* encouraged radical 'uprisings'. Charles Ogden, another *Yorks. Obs.* journalist, was active in Elland. Mr James' work on Keighley suggests that, despite the local party's very conservative stance, there were many professionals and skilled workmen active in at least parts of the constituency. I am grateful to Mr James for an advance copy of papers on Keighley, and for permission to use his index of Keighley Liberal activists.

[4] Keighley LA Mins, 14 June 1907 and D. James, 'Philip Snowden and Keighley ILP', in D. James and K. Laybourn (eds.), *Philip Snowden* (1987).

[5] Bernstein, *Liberal politics,* p. 24; Keighley LA Mins, 22 Feb. 1904, 21 Jan. 1913.

role in the Divisional association's general political stance. The radical approach adopted in Huddersfield, for example, was drawn up by the local committee of Liberal Councillors, rather than the Divisional Liberal executive.

It would be a mistake, however, to see these organisational changes as part of a New Liberal initiative, or as evidence of a consistent, organised, replacement of old Liberal politics by new principles. Although there *were* ideological/political conflicts in Osgoldcross, Shipley, Wakefield, and York before 1906, it was not a case of 'New Liberals' fighting against 'reactionaries'. The common thread connecting the more well-known members of the Yorkshire radical camp (men like H. J. Wilson, Arnold Rowntree, and, for a while, Charles Roberts) with radicals in the constituencies was less likely to be a shared New Liberal motivation than a shared 'religious radicalism'. This is important because 'religious radicals' were even more capable than New Liberals of combining with the more conservative Nonconformist Liberals and of creating a political composite which would build on aspects of traditional Liberal beliefs. They were particularly successful in this respect in some areas where the conservative Liberal elite contained a number of Liberal Imperialists.[6] Nonetheless, New Liberal influences and policies made their presence felt through the work of three parliamentary candidates: Herbert Samuel (Cleveland), C. P. Trevelyan (Elland), and F. D. Acland (Richmond). With the reformers, J. H. Whitley (Halifax), A. J. Sherwell (Huddersfield), J. S. Higham (Sowerby), and H. J. Wilson in Holmfirth, they formed a powerful southern Pennine radical force. Their motivations were different, but they increasingly supported the same set of radical policies, and the same set of institutional objectives.

Other, less ideologically committed, but politically ambitious, MPs such as Walter Runciman (Dewsbury), Herbert Gladstone (West Leeds), and Percy Illingworth (Shipley) became Ministers and Whips. They were pragmatic or ideological Centrists, who pushed the party line on the few occasions they actually visited their constituencies. Their views, and positions, stifled local opposition. Other local MPs, such as Tudor Walters (Sheffield Brightside), W. E. B. Priestley (East Bradford), and T. H. Greenwood (York), shifted their ground to suit the new climate.

[6] For radical/Old Liberal tensions and conflict before 1906, Hills, 'The City Council and electoral politics'; Laybourn and Reynolds, *Yorkshire,* pp. 83–5 (Shipley); J.B.G to E. Bruce Glasier, 26 Mar. 1902, JBG 1902/2 (Wakefield); *Y.P.,* 13, 16 Jan. 1900 (Osgoldcross). I owe this last reference to Andrew Thompson of St John's College, Cambridge. There were also many local attempts at forging Liberal/Labour pacts. See E. P. Hennock, *Fit and proper persons* (1973), pp. 254–6, Leeds L.F. Cabinet Comm. Mins, 22 Aug., 9 Nov. 1900, discussion of electoral pact, and Bernstein, fn. 3 above; Howell, *ILP,* pp. 197–9 and Halifax West Ward Lib. Comm. Mins, 2 Dec. 1901.

Greenwood saw radicalism and public popularity as 'the road to power'.[7] Tudor Walters and Priestley, Centrist reformers committed to action on housing and unemployment, further emphasised their radical credentials in order to prevent Labour opposition. Walters also had to contend with members of the Wilson clan, some of whom were active in his constituency. Tudor Walters and Priestley worked hard to prevent Old Liberal anti-Socialists disrupting the Progressive Alliance (and their individual prospects of success) in Sheffield and Bradford. In the rather different climate of the East Riding, C. H. Wilson and T. R. Ferens, the MPs for West and East Hull, merged Nonconformity, paternalism, and collectivism in roughly equal proportions. The radical *Yorkshire Observer* (Bradford) and *Yorkshire Herald* (York), which were owned, edited, and written by Progressives, played an important part in augmenting and expanding party support for the 'new' politics. So too did the backstage activities of New Liberals like C. P. Trevelyan.[8]

Nonetheless, Old Liberals maintained their institutional power, particularly in the northern Pennine seats and in the Leeds/Bradford area. Men like Sir James Kitson, the Leeds manufacturer and Colne Valley MP, and Alfred Illingworth, *bête noire* of Progressive politics in Bradford, were commonly found occupying prominent positions on the executive committees of Liberal constituency associations. In Keighley, the same families of Nonconformist millowners held the principal executive positions on the Divisional association without challenge or change from 1885 to 1918.[9] Constituency Liberal associations in South and West Leeds, and West and South Bradford, were ruled by powerful conservative oligarchies. The City Liberal Federations were not used to counteract this problem (as they were in Manchester). In Leeds, conservative Liberals formed an inner Cabinet which dominated the City Liberal Federation. A committee of Liberal Councillors also determined municipal policy. The retrenching 'business budget' formulated by this group in 1907 had the full co-operation of the Tories, but met with vehement opposition from many Liberal activists. The budget still passed. Despite even Radical hostility to negotiation and agreement with the Tories, municipal conservatism and anti-Socialist pacts were common in Bradford and the sur-

---

[7] E. Vipont, *Arnold Rowntree* (1955), p. 54 and A.R. to M. K. Rowntree, 3 Mar. 1910, AR MS.

[8] *Daily News*, 1, 5 May 1914; Emy, *Liberals and social politics*, p. 153; Howell, *ILP*, pp. 117–20. See also below, pp. 255–6. When Walters was active in Leicester Liberal politics, he had advocated a Labour/Liberal electoral arrangement. MacDonald replied in kind when Walters was threatened with Labour intervention in Brightside (Marquand, *MacDonald*, pp. 82–3). The *Yorkshire Herald* was owned by the Rowntrees. For Trevelyan, below, p. 270.

[9] Data from YLA and Keighley LA minutes. See also James, 'Paternalism in Keighley'. For this more generally, Laybourn and Reynolds, *Yorkshire*, pp. 6–7, 122–4, 132.

rounding seats. Liberal conservatism was reinforced by the archaic politics of influential Liberal papers like the *Leeds Mercury,* and by many of the weekly Liberal papers which were so important in the isolated Pennine seats. Old Liberals also dominated the YLF.[10]

The Old Liberal ascendancy had declined a little by 1910. In Bradford, the death of Alfred Illingworth, and increased Labour pressure, encouraged the half-radical Liberal municipal leader, Alderman Priestman, to adopt a less conservative approach.[11] In Leeds, Radicals and social reformers attacked municipal anti-Socialist alliances. However, if clashes of personality emphasised the divisions between Liberal Imperialists and Radicals, a Radical/reformist alliance similar to those in the south Pennine radical bloc did not take shape as a result of this division in the conservative Liberal camp. In Leeds, as in many north Yorkshire textile seats, the differences between Radicals and Progressives on policy and on Labour representation were too substantial for there to be a *rapprochement.* There were no major shifts in the balance of institutional power in Bradford, Leeds, or in seats like Keighley. The radicals alone were too weak to disrupt the ruling groups' control.[12] A Radical/Centrist alliance still dominated Liberal politics.

Liberal radicalism was a little more developed in York, Wakefield, and Sheffield by 1910, although there had been problems in the shape of a conservative Liberal elite which needed tackling. In contrast to the West Riding, a 'Tory perspective' (a perspective associated with the Tory party) was more prevalent. It drew strength from an Anglican tradition, and from the Tories' historic support for collectivist and materialistic policies. On the Liberal side, the largely Anglican Liberal Imperialists, who controlled Liberal politics before 1910 shared many of these views. The Liberal League, led by Alderman Clegg, supplied the party machinery and directed the work of the city's election agent (an important figure given the weakness of Liberal organisation).

Nonetheless, Liberal Imperialism had little electoral purchase. A radical coup in York had overturned their ascendancy by 1906, leaving the way open for a Liberal municipal assault on poor housing conditions and

---

[10] J. H. Linforth, Leeds agent, report on South Leeds constituency, *Lib. Agent*, Oct. 1908, J. Henry to H.G., 4 Nov. 1907, 23 Jan., 10 Nov. 1908, HG Add MS 46037 fos. 47–55, 97–101, Leeds LF Ec Mins. esp 26 Apr. 1906; Laybourn, 'The ILP in local politics', p. 239. See also YLF Mins, *passim.*

[11] Mounting radical pressure can be adduced, despite the argument of the book, from Laybourn and Reynolds, *Yorkshire*, pp. 6, 68, 80. See also *Bradford Forward*, 19 Dec. 1904, 11, 18 Dec. 1905, *Y.P.*, 2 Nov. 1909.

[12] e.g. J.H. to H.G., 9 Apr. 1907, HG Add MS 46037 fo. 34. The changes made in national policy were still too much for many conservative Liberals. See e.g. Sir James Kitson's refusal to speak for Liberal candidates in 1910, J. Kitson to H.G, 10 May 1909, 8 Jan. 1911, HG Add MS 46028 fos. 157–8.

unemployment which was practical, radical (in contemporary terms) and electorally successful. In Sheffield, the Wilsons were stirred into action in 1909. Clegg wished to form a Sheffield Liberal Federation, and institutionalise the Imperialists' already powerful position. He was pushed more rapidly in this direction by Labour's victory in the Sheffield Attercliffe parliamentary by-election of 1909, a symbol, for him, of the lassitude and misdirection of Sheffield Liberalism.[13] The ensuing battle between Clegg and Wilson, apparently over 'organisation', became a battle for control between groups representing different ideological/strategic ideas about Liberalism's future. At the meeting called to discuss the party's future (including its future organisation) Clegg proposed an anti-Socialist crusade, coupled with opposition to local Labour municipal and parliamentary candidates. Wilson argued that the Liberals should accept Labour victories and work with Labour representatives. However, he also argued for an approach similar to that of the Huddersfield Liberals, and for policies which would contain Labour by keeping the Liberals' radical credentials intact. He predicted that the national party's future agenda would embrace 'New Liberal' collectivisation of land, mines, and railways, and 'Radical' municipalisation of the drink trade. Despite this combination of appeals, the Wilsons were backed by just a quarter of the Liberals attending the meeting, but the purchase of their ideas – and their position in Liberal politics – made them too powerful for Clegg, who immediately backed down. 'The air is cleared', Wilson reported, 'Rebellion is suppressed for the moment.' Although outnumbered, the Progressives were now the dominant group.[14]

A number of Sheffield Liberals had wished to avoid a showdown. Party unity and middle-class support had to be maintained. There was another reason – money. The Sheffield Liberals had severe financial problems; Clegg, one Liberal activist noted, 'has the key to the money boxes'. It would be 'difficult to know how the (Liberal association's) £500 debt (will otherwise) be dealt with'.[15] This financial strength was a significant weapon. Many Yorkshire Liberal associations had an annual income of £3–400 from individual subscriptions and from the Liberal Clubs' contributions. MPs were also expected to contribute at least £100 per year

---

[13] Hills, 'York', pp. 257–61. Mathers (thesis) covers the 1909 Attercliffe election in some detail.

[14] Meeting reports, H.J.W. to Counc. Derry, 24 Mar. 1910, Counc. Gill to C. H. Wilson, 4 Apr. 1910, Wilson MS 5907, 5919. For the conflicting ideological/strategic views, memo by Clegg, 15 Nov. 1909 and Wilson's reply, H.J.W. to Clegg, 2 Dec. 1909, Wilson MS 5906.

[15] O. C. Wilson to H.J.W., 15 Mar. 1910, W. Wilson and J. H. Wilson to H.J.W., 27 July, 3 Aug. 1909, Wilson MS 5906; report of Wilson's attempt to sound opinion, 19 Feb. 1910, Wilson MS 5906.

to constituency funds.[16] Although some seats, like Holmfirth and Huddersfield, became financially solvent, and were thus less open to pressure, most built up debts. Bazaars were one way of solving the problem (and of attaining self-sufficiency).[17] However, in the cities, and in the weaker seats, where rank and file fund-raising was unlikely to succeed, wealthy supporters and MPs had to make larger subscriptions and 'grants' towards municipal expenses to keep the party going. In these circumstances constituency radicals needed support from local radical magnates (like the Rowntrees and Wilsons) or from moderately wealthy MPs, if they were to challenge the conservative Liberal elite. Without this, deference and fear of financial insolvency would underpin the conservatives' position.

The politics of parliamentary candidates changed only slowly. In 1910, the radicalisation of Colne Valley Liberalism resulted in the selection of the Rev William Leach, formerly of the ILP and a confessed 'evolutionary Socialist', as the party's candidate. Arnold Rowntree stood in York. In the East Riding, Dr R. W. Aske and Tom Wing, Nonconformist radicals and land reformers, stood in Hull and Grimsby.[18] The radicals also had to phrase their 'new' policies in a manner which built on older Liberal traditions. Yet they could often do this without compromising their radicalism. Thus C. P. Trevelyan in Elland portrayed the 1910 conflict as a battle 'between the people and the oligarchy, between the poor man and irresponsible wealth'.[19] Given the presence in the area of other committed New Liberals (Herbert Samuel was particularly active) and of many Liberal ministers and whips, party policy in 1910 got a good hearing. Party pragmatists, New Liberals and religious radicals built bridges between the 'new' economic issues behind conflict with the Lords and an 'old' Liberal support for the democratic sovereignty of the people.

The selection of Rowntree's brother-in-law and political ally, T. E. Harvey, in West Leeds did not indicate that politics in the cities and in the adjacent textile seats had been radicalised from below. The Harveys were an important, well-liked, local family. Joseph Henry – the West

[16] Holmfirth LA AR 1910–11, 1911–12; Sowerby Bridge LA and Middleton LA ann. meetings, *Todmorden Adv.*, 24 May 1913; *Cleckheaton Guardian* (Pudsey), 8 May 1914; *Worker* (Huddersfield), 21 July 1914.

[17] e.g., report of Silsden Lib. Club (Shipley), *Keighley News*, 17 Jan. 1914; *Barnsley Chron.*, 23 May 1914; Hudd. Lib. Councillors' Mins, *passim* and H. Snell, *Men, movements and myself* (1938), p. 187. For donations in Leeds and Sheffield as an alternative to a Bazaar, J.H. to H.G., 13 Sept. 1907, 13 Oct., 10 Nov. 1908, HG Add MS 46037 fos. 39, 95, 101; H.J.W. to J. H. Wilson, 22 Feb. 1910, Wilson MS 5906.

[18] Clark, *Colne Valley*, p. 178. Grimsby, although not in the East Riding of Yorkshire, is geographically and politically so close to Hull that it is best examined here.

[19] A. J. A. Morris, 'Charles Trevelyan and two views of "revolution"', in Morris (ed), *Edwardian Radicalism*, p. 141.

Leeds political baron – was a loyal family friend.[20] Harvey was approached by local MPs seeking a local candidate. They did not want – and did not like having – a 'social radical' as their MP. When national trends and policies penetrated Leeds and Bradford, some conservative Liberals did their best to nullify their impact. A portion of the Liberal press, and particularly papers like the *Leeds Mercury,* focused attention on the desirability of less radical views. The *Mercury* bitterly opposed the Budget and the policies and politics associated with it. Most Liberal MPs in Leeds and Bradford, and MPs like Ogden (Pudsey) and Whittaker (Spen Valley), remained solidly Gladstonian. Nonetheless, they held their seats at the 1910 elections. A Radical/Centrist alliance appeared to have some purchase.[21] These elements *could* be an albatross around the Liberal party's neck if they created the image of an out-dated party of the 'right'. However, if Old Liberal politics did *not* undermine Liberal strength, or if Old Liberalism was absorbed by the radicals in such a way that the party maintained some elements of its older electoral constituency, then Liberalism was the stronger for that.

II

Labour's internal politics were no less complex. There were a variety of ideological strands and political responses to the party's problems. The ILP's ethical socialism, and its strategic accompaniment of 'educationalist' propaganda campaigns, still retained enough support to be more than simply a disruptive influence. Some ILP/SDF activists wished to turn support for anti-Liberal assaults into support for a more stridently anti-capitalist approach. By contrast, Labour and Socialist moral reformers wanted to construct 'practical' electoral programmes. They aimed to create broader political bases by building on existing perceptions and interests, and showing that Labour was materially different from the Liberals. 'Labour' moral reformers hoped to do this through an accommodation with the unions which accepted their fundamental aim of raising living standards. The more Socialist moral reformers pushed similar issues much further, attempting to increase working-class living standards and working-class expectations and self-confidence as a prelude to escalating demands. They were particularly keen to use the municipalities' power to feed school children, to provide better pay and conditions for municipal workers, and to provide more generous poor relief to those who had

---

[20] J.H. to H.G., 5 Nov. 1909, 26 Aug. 1911, HG Add MS 46037 fo. 161, 46038 fo. 52.
[21] For the *Leeds Mercury,* J.H. to H.G., 5 Apr. 1908, HG Add MS 46037 fo. 67: 'as a Liberal paper the Mercury is dead'. For Whittaker's opposition to everything the New Liberalism stood for, see his declaration to this effect, A.R. to M. K. Rowntree, 7 Sept. 1910, AR MS.

become destitute. Unlike 'Labour' reformers, they accepted class conflict and a hostility to middle-class behavioural norms. In Leeds, Labour also dealt with the religious/educational grievances of the (largely working-class) Catholic community far more sympathetically than the Liberals. This, like the anti-semitism of James O'Grady, the East Leeds Labour MP, was presumably part of their affinity with the real nature of local working-class culture.[22]

The Bradford/Leeds parties' 'Socialist' moral reformism was the most successful approach, but it did not produce a model policy which could obviously be used to defeat the Liberals. In Bradford and Leeds, Labour made most of its progress *before* 1906, when the Liberals were extremely conservative. At this time there was a clear opportunity for a centre-left party to pick up support, and Labour grasped the nettle. In East Leeds it polled just 5 per cent less than the second-placed Liberal at the 1900 parliamentary election. In the 1905 municipal elections, there was little to choose between the two parties in either East or West Leeds, both having taken votes from the Tories. Moreover, in the 1906 parliamentary contests, Labour came second to the Liberals in South Leeds and won West Bradford despite Liberal opposition. Although the SDF polled well in East Bradford in 1906, municipal results suggest that the level of *Labour* support was even higher. However, this support was not necessarily the result of Labour's radical approach. Labour had paid considerable attention to conventional Liberal issues; it had also operated in a Progressive framework. Jowett had successfully opposed proposals to field an official Labour candidate in East Bradford; Priestley, the East Bradford Liberal MP, had declined to speak for Jowett's Liberal opponent in West Bradford. The Labour victories were not simply the result of the positive attractions of the Labour left.[23]

Labour's inability to create a truly dynamic and positive 'left-wing' appeal became evident after 1906. In South Leeds, fought by Labour in 1906, 1908, and December 1910, the Liberals' *parliamentary* lead was increasing despite a strong Labour municipal performance in the constituency. Moreover, as the Liberals' national image improved, Labour's formerly strong municipal performance in other Leeds seats was undermined,

---

[22] *Leeds Merc.*, 3 Nov. 1909, 26 Oct. 1910, *Lib. Agent*, Apr. 1908. For O'Grady, see J. Buckman, *Immigration in the class struggle* (Manchester, 1983), p. 167. See for Bradford, J. Reynolds and K. Laybourn, 'The emergence of the ILP in Bradford', *IRSH* (1975).

[23] Howell, *ILP*, pp. 193–7. For the 1905–6 electoral position in Leeds, A. Fox to J.R.M., 26 Nov. 1905, J. D. Macrae to J.R.M., 5 Dec. 1905, LRC 5/128, 213, 215. For Socialist reformers' motivations, entries in W. T. Stead, 'The Labour party and the books that helped to make it', *Review of Reviews* (1906), J. Clayton (ed.), *Why I joined the Independent Labour Party* (Leeds, n.d.) and Jowett's biography, A. F. Brockway, *Socialism over sixty years* (1946).

except where its position as the acknowledged anti-Tory party enabled it to mop up anti-Tory support. Thus in (Labour) West Bradford Labour extended its lead, while in (Liberal) East Bradford the Liberals retained their primacy. Similarly, at the 1909 Leeds municipal 'general election', Labour was easily ahead of the Liberals in the (Labour-held) East Leeds division, but 4–5 per cent behind in Liberal-held West and South Leeds. In 1910 politics polarised and made these discrepancies even more pronounced. In the largest of the East Leeds wards, Labour's lead over the Liberals increased from about 8 per cent in 1909 to 22 per cent in the November 1910 municipal elections. By contrast, in a typical ward in (Liberal) West Leeds, Labour slipped from first to third place.[24] Organisationally Labour also stagnated. The Bradford ILP branch had more than 1,000 members, whose constant 'educationalist' propaganda and municipal work gave it a high profile in most parts of the city. However, the East Leeds organisation was 'run on the cheap' throughout this period according to the MP, James O'Grady. Although the Leeds LRC tried to replicate the Bradford approach, it had neither the money nor the support to sustain such extensive campaigns.[25]

The NEC and NAC recognised that Labour had made scarcely any progress since 1906. They declined to sanction additional parliamentary contests in East Bradford and West and South Leeds. Local Liberal retaliation against Labour MPs, they argued, would mean the loss of the East Leeds seat. Peters thought that the proposal to fight the three Leeds seats was 'suicidal': 'If they [the Leeds parties] had their backsides slapped as political babes it would do them good.'[26] While the Bradford/Leeds strategy in municipal politics *was* radical, and *did* have some positive appeal, it was much less successful once the Liberals put up a fight by modifying their image. Labour therefore still needed the protection afforded by the Progressive Alliance if it was to retain its existing parliamentary representation.

[24] In 1909 the election returns in the West Leeds ward of New Whortley closely reflected the municipal results for the constituency as a whole. New Whortley results (constituency results in brackets): Lab 36.16 [32.18]; L 33.58 [36.14]; C 30.26 [31.68]. For further details, Tanner (thesis), pp. 335–6.

[25] For O'Grady's view, *Nafto Record,* July 1917. See also for Leeds, *Nafto Record,* Feb., Mar. 1910, July 1917, Leeds LP Mins, 12 Jan., 17 Dec. 1913, 18 June 1914, *Leeds Weekly Citizen,* e.g. 2, 30 Dec. 1911, and more generally, Woodhouse, 'The working class'. For Bradford, F. Jowett to A.P., n.d., LP/EL/08/1/29, and the constituency report, May 1909, ILP MS H.O. Circ./6. More generally, Reynolds and Layhourn, 'ILP in Bradford', and F. Jowett's article, Bradford T&LC *Year Book* 1905.

[26] A.P. to B. Turner, 1 Mar. 1909, LP/CAN/06/2/240. For the role of the ASRS and of local Labour moderates in rejecting these overtures, *L.L.,* 3 Jan., 7 Feb. 1908, *Locomotive Journal,* Mar. 1910, NEC Mins, 7 July, 2 Dec. 1909, and NAC Mins, 17 Dec. 1909. For similar opposition to campaigns in 1905–6, Layhourn and Reynolds, *Yorkshire,* p. 129.

Labour's response in the Pennine textile belt was conditioned by a different set of economic circumstances. Although mining and textile engineering were important employers, small, paternalistic, family owned textile mills were the most significant local economic institutions. Competition between mills was fierce; conditions and wages were often poor. The work force was highly fragmented even within individual mills. Trade union membership was thin and widely dispersed. Strikes were rare; expectations low.[27] In many of the small, isolated, Pennine villages and small towns, the mill was the only form of local employment, and was central to the life and prosperity of the area. Factory life and discipline reached into the whole community. Millowners might provide schools, chapels, social facilities, even housing. An 'employer's ideology' of 'legitimate' control over the conditions and nature of employment was reinforced by an extremely strong, popular, Liberal/Nonconformist tradition of self-reliance and self-help. Even larger towns, like Keighley, were incestuous hothouses of a pessimistic, insular, culture dominated by 'Chapel and Co-op, Thrift and Low Wages, Higher Education and wretched industrial organisation'.[28] Dissatisfaction with local conditions was tempered by the feeling that nothing could be done to alter the situation. Prosperity was determined by the success of local industry, not by political intervention. Labour campaigns on Statist issues such as the need for fair wages contracts, or higher municipal wages, were hardly of direct interest to workers in these circumstances.

A Liberal political culture so penetrated people's outlooks that challenges to the status quo inevitably came from within that tradition. Unions and workers aimed at securing a 'just' and 'moral' respect from their employers. The ILP's ethical socialism drew its approach from a Nonconformist revivalism, its content from a radical Liberal/working-class sense of a moral entitlement to a degree of security. The Keighley ILP's list of preferred speakers for a proposed lecture tour in 1907 shows clearly that 'moral' politics was still very much alive. They listed the Revs W. B. Graham, W. E. Moll, R. J. Campbell, and Conrad Noel. The only speaker who was not a minister was the personification of ethical socialism, Philip Snowden (who was also born in nearby Cowling). Keighley, like other adjacent seats, was 'a chapel-ridden division'. The ethical/religious emphasis was a general feature of ILP politics in Pennine seats. This attached the ILP to a local language and to a local form of expression. It made it easier to build a political base. However, the similarity between

---

[27] For this and much of the following, J. Bornat, 'An examination of the General Union of Textile Workers, 1883–1922', Essex Ph.D. thesis (1980), pp. 21–32, 86–115.
[28] NAC deputation report, 13 Nov. 1909, Ensor MS. See also James, 'Paternalism in Keighley', T. Mackley to ?, 13 May 1908, Keighley ILP L.B.

ethical socialism and radical Liberalism helped place a ceiling on the level of support which the ILP could attract. Self-development and self-improvement had little attraction to most unskilled workers, many of whom were Tories. Moreover, the Liberals could allege that Socialist support for such unEnglish (and distinctly unYorkshire) notions as free love, for example, made the *differences* between the Socialists and the Liberals rather important. Once the national Liberal party reaffirmed its belief in social reform, the one electoral space which Socialists might exploit narrowed very considerably.[29]

Labour's moral reformism was one valid means of attempting to create a more distinct image. However, the weakness of trade unions in the Pennine seats meant that there was little institutional pressure on ILP branches to become more materially minded. On the contrary, many ILP members regarded union sectionalism with suspicion, and did not wish to abandon the moral emphasis which characterised their ethical socialism. This could even make political sense. As one party official commented on the position in Huddersfield, it was all very well to argue that 'if Williams (the Labour candidate) had not been quite so insistent and had played up the "Labour" aspect more he would have got home ... but it is a difficult line to take with a man like Sherwell (the Liberal), who advocated Socialist measures and renounced the name'.[30]

Nonetheless, a number of longstanding, respected, local ILP leaders – including Herbert Horner, James Parker, and Ben Turner – supported a practical moral reformist stance. They used diplomacy and argument to convince local organisations of the need to accept MacDonald's ideological/strategic trajectory, and to reform ethical socialism on more tangible lines. Neither did they shrink from using their institutional power to reinforce this emphasis. Horner, for example, attempted to stop Grayson speaking at Keighley by passing a resolution banning him from meetings in the division at a thinly attended Executive Committee meeting.[31] However, manipulation was often unnecessary. Many rank and file members were sympathetic to the politics of change. A majority of Huddersfield *Labour* activists thought that their (successive) dissident parliamentary candidates, Russell Williams and Russell Smart, were too radical and too vague. They persuaded them to resign, and chose Harry Snell, a moderate Fabian school-teacher, as their replacement.[32] In Keighley,

[29] Keighley ILP Mins, esp. 31 Mar., 4, 28 July, 8 Aug. 1910; Clark, *Colne Valley*, esp. pp. 124–5, 149, 195.
[30] J.S.M. to his parents, 30 Nov. 1906, MID 7/31. See also *Worker*, 10 Jan. 1914, citing Sherwell's support for New Liberal proposals.
[31] For the moderate left, Keighley ILP Mins, 4 July–8 Aug. 1910.
[32] J. W. Prierley to J. Dawson, n.d. (1911), Huddersfield T&LC Letter Book, Snell, *Men, movements and myself*, pp. 187–90.

although the ILP and the LRC were already very similar in composition
and policy, ILP members attempted to attract support from trade unionists and members of Co-operative Societies, even though this attempt
involved moderating party policy. The branch nominated moderate moral
reformers, not Yorkshire dissident radicals, for NAC positions.[33] Labour
organisations in Sowerby and Holmfirth spent most of their time attempting to secure further trade union affiliations. The Halifax ILP did this
very successfully. By 1910 it had created a powerful constituency machine
which was closely allied to the trade unions.[34]

These political organisations were not always very strong and they
were seldom monolithic. Most Labour/ILP organisations in the Pennines
had about 150 to 250 members, almost all of them in the larger settlements.
However, in the Keighley Division, for example, half the electorate was
scattered over the 'outlying areas'. The Holmfirth LRC was not unusual
in having local committees in just sixteen of the Division's thirty-five
Polling Districts. The small, insular, settlements were inaccessible and
inhospitable, even to people from nearby Pennine towns. They were frequently the chinks in Labour's armour. Even when they could be organised, there could be a cost. Local groups had to be given considerable
autonomy. This could make it difficult for Labour to construct a consistent, moderate, image. In Sowerby, local political work was done by
two Trades Councils, one local LRC, two Socialist branches, and ILP
committees from two Halifax wards which were in the Sowerby division
for parliamentary purposes. Only Halifax had a permanent organiser;
only Keighley, Pudsey, and Huddersfield had newspapers, and only Huddersfield's managed to survive for a substantial portion of the period.
Labour often relied on evangelical lecturers and propagandists to mobilise
and unify its disparate forces.[35]

Local groups, isolated from trade union influences, often doubted
whether a 'practical' strategy should be adopted. Unsurprisingly, Grayson's national campaign for a return to ILP fundamentals began from
a Pennine seat, Colne Valley. His 'educationalist', fire-and-brimstone,
Socialism had some resonance in the area. It was supported by several
senior Yorkshire ILP activists. Russell Williams, Russell Smart, and
Joseph Burgess had helped form the ILP. Smart and Williams still sat

[33]   T. Mackley to J. Dale, 12 Aug. 1905, Keighley ILP L.B., Keighley ILP Mins, 3 Feb.
       1908, 6 Mar. 1909.
[34]   Holmfirth LRC Mins, 1 May, 4, 18 Dec. 1909; Sowerby LRC Mins, 1907–10, *passim*;
       Halifax T&LC Election Comm. Mins, 1906–10, *passim*.
[35]   Sowerby LRC Mins, 25 Feb., 6 May 1911; Holmfirth LRC Mins, 18 July 1908, 1 May
       1909; J. Walker to F.J., 27 Apr. 1908, FJ 08/156; T. Mackley to F.J., H. Walbank,
       A. Garnett, 20 Feb., 3 Mar., 17 June 1906, Keighley ILP Letter Book, fos. 265, 321,
       357, Keighley ILP Mins, 6 Dec. 1909.

on the ILP's Yorkshire Divisional Council. Williams and Burgess were the prospective Labour parliamentary candidates of ILP branches in Spen Valley and Pudsey. Russell Smart moved from Huddersfield to be the candidate of the politically more congenial Elland LRC.

There was a potential audience within the rank and file. 'Educationalism' and 'Socialist unity' were still attractive. In 1906, SDF candidates in East Bradford and Dewsbury were supported by a substantial number of local ILP members, *despite* NEC/NAC policy. Grayson reactivated these feelings. His evangelism, his activism, his idealistic contempt for trade union 'materialism', were parts of the ILP's operational ideology which official ILP policy ignored. Grayson's claim that MacDonald was leading the party into a fossilised and stagnant pact was privately endorsed by many moderate Socialists on the 'soft left'. The NAC's refusal to sanction Grayson's campaign at Colne Valley in 1907 was used in evidence, and it counted against them. There was even support in isolated and 'loyalist' Keighley.[36] More importantly, the *Huddersfield Worker,* which was read throughout the Pennines, lent its considerable weight to the Graysonite cause. The refusal to sanction Burgess' campaign at Pudsey in 1908 was 'almost a second Colne Valley' in that it too created considerable hostility to national policy.[37] When the NAC withdrew permission to fight Keighley, and refused to consider Pudsey, Elland, and other Yorkshire seats in 1910, the dissidents' voices became louder. In Elland the ILP revived the old Socialist ploy of voting for the Tory candidate as a protest against Liberal (and NAC) policy. T. Russell Williams even warned that the NAC's 'attitude to fighting three-cornered contests (was) dangerously near bringing about the secession of the entire Yorkshire movement'.[38]

This was an exaggeration. Moderate ILP reformers, like Horner, the Keighley candidate who was refused NAC sanction in 1910, accepted the party's ideological/strategic stance and its consequent electoral strategy, as did the embryonic organisations in Shipley and Sowerby. ILP branches in Cleveland (where Samuel was the very Progressive MP) lent the Liberals active support, and it is possible that this was as common as the very different attitude displayed by ILP critics of the Progressive position. Although the NAC *had* infringed on the party's operational ideology through the strategy of Progressive Alliance, there were *fundamental* ideo-

---

[36] See e.g. Keighley ILP Mins, 30 Apr. 1910–8 Aug. 1910.
[37] Cutting, *Bradford Argus,* 19 Apr. 1905, Hartley Scrapbook, MS 11D85/1/13, and for adjacent seats, T. Mackley to P.S., 9 May 1905, Keighley ILP Letter Book. For Pudsey, F. Smith to J.B.G., n.d. 1907, JBG 07/94 (misdated, 1908?).
[38] T. R. Williams to F.J., 23 Nov. 1909, FJ 09/535. For Elland, Morris, 'Charles Trevelyan', p. 137. See also Liberal attempts to remove the friction, W.R. to C.P.T., 26 Dec. 1909, CPT 23.

logical reasons, and good tactical excuses, for not supporting the Gray-sonite stance.[39] Moreover, Grayson had undermined his appeal by moving towards the deterministic Socialism practised by his (growing) band of allies in the SDF. These ideas had little purchase with the electorate. The Independent Labour campaign at Pudsey in 1908 had been a disaster. Even Grayson's victory at Colne Valley, Bruce Glasier argued, had more to do with local and national Liberal conservatism than support for 'Socialism'. He and others did not find moderate strategy congenial, but the 'hard left' Graysonites offered only vacant criticism of the status quo, 'struggle', and certain defeat.[40]

The electorate passed judgement in January 1910. Grayson and William Pickles, who sympathised with many Graysonite ideas, were easily defeated by radical Liberal opponents and revitalised Liberal associations in Colne Valley and Holmfirth. Russell Williams was defeated in Spen Valley by T. P. Whittaker, an anti-Budget, anti-Lloyd George, Liberal of Radical/Centrist views. The NEC blamed the 4 per cent decline in the Labour vote at Huddersfield on the disruptive conduct of the Gray-sonite left.[41] Labour polled between 20 and 29 per cent of the vote in these contests, the Liberals between 40 and 50 per cent. There was no Socialist alternative which seemed electorally popular. The moderate moral reformers were confirmed in their resolve.

III

Labour had more potential as a Progressive party in the historically more Conservative area which stretched from South Yorkshire through to the East Riding. Despite a strong Nonconformist/Liberal tradition in some East Riding seats, the major working-class constituencies were ports which usually returned Tories. The Liberals however were not weak. They received support from many of the devoutly Nonconformist fisher-men, and from some merchants and middle-class groups whose prosper-ity, status, and outlook were rooted in Nonconformity and Free Trade. Liberal candidates included the Centrist radicals C. H. Wilson, a ship-owner and merchant, and A. G. Bannister, a former fisherman who was now a trawler owner. In Hull and Grimsby, municipal election results, and

[39] For NEC/NAC supporters, H. Horner to B. Riley, 25 Nov. 1909, FJ 09/542; H. Holgate to J.R.M., 15 Feb. 1909, JRM PRO 30/69/1153 and Sowerby LRC Mins, 11 Nov. 1909, noting approaches to Turner. Turner had already turned down one seat after NEC advice that it was unsuitable. 'Tell me what it is best to do in the interests of the party as a whole', he wrote to MacDonald (B. Turner to J.R.M., 10 Mar. 1909, LP /CAN/06/2/241).

[40] J.B.G. Diary, 18 July 1907. See also the Liberal assessment, cited in the *Worker*, 8 Apr. 1911.

[41] NEC Mins, 24 Feb. 1910, Blewett, *Peers*, pp. 258, 264.

the support which the Trades Council gave to the Liberal machine, indicate that the Liberals received a good deal of support from working-class 'artisans'. Some of this may have resulted from economic dependency on an individual (Liberal) employer, but, whatever its origins, it had created an almost fossilised working-class Liberalism by 1910. There was almost automatic acceptance of Liberal conceptions of the foundations of prosperity and the desirable ends of political action.[42]

Groups with more to gain from Statist policies – particularly the dockers and the railwaymen – were Labour's best hope. However, Grimsby (fought in 1906) contained few members of either group, and in Hull (where there were more dockers and railwaymen) they were not concentrated in a single seat. Labour did not seem to have much chance of success. West Hull, fought at the 1907 parliamentary by-election, was more middle class and more consistently Liberal than either East or Central Hull (the dockland seats which were frequently Tory). However, the ASRS had a substantial number of members in West Hull and naturally chose to concentrate on this constituency. Labour polled just 18 per cent of the vote at the three-cornered contest in Grimsby, but in West Hull, its 29 per cent poll was enough to reduce the Liberals' lead to only 7 per cent. Nonetheless, Labour was not in a good position. The West Hull Labour result was inflated by post-Colne Valley enthusiasm. The momentum could not be maintained. The campaign had been dogged by Labour's internal divisions. It was followed by disagreements over how to proceed. Labour's organisation fell apart. Some ILP elements were sympathetic to Grayson; this ensured that the Trades Council remained firmly Liberal. In Grimsby, some moderates had only backed Labour intervention in 1906 because they believed the Liberals would withdraw; they too backed away after the election.[43] A strong restatement of the Liberal position, and a weak Labour response, resulted in Labour's decline. In 1909, the ASRS contemplated a second campaign in West Hull but withdrew on NEC advice.[44]

Wakefield, York, and the Sheffield constituencies of Attercliffe and Brightside were the only other remotely working-class constituencies in this area. Even Sheffield, despite its Liberal past, had a strong Conservative tradition. Already, before 1906, the Liberals had recognised their weakness and Labour's potential. Wakefield and York were included in the Gladstone–MacDonald pact. However, at the 1906 election,

[42] Pelling, Social geography, pp. 212, 292–5.
[43] R. C. Hall to J.R.M., 28 Mar. 1905; Leeds Merc., 23 Nov. 1907.
[44] A. Bell to M. Middleton, 8 Dec. 1907, MID 7/38, Monthly Labour Journal, Aug. 1909.

Labour came at the foot of the poll in York, a double member borough, in which the Liberals fielded only one candidate; the Liberal came first. In Wakefield, many radical voters respected Labour's position as the Progressive incumbent, and chose not to support the semi-official, conservative, Liberal candidate, but, although Labour held second place, the Tories were successful.[45] Labour's ethical socialism was unattractive to working-class Tories and to middle-class Liberals. Its presumed ability to improve on the Liberals' position was unrealised. Labour performed less successfully than the official Liberal candidates who went on to fight these seats in 1910 and win Wakefield in the December contest for the first time since 1880.

Labour organisations here were also dealt a blow by the Graysonite uprisings. In York, Graysonite fulminations against an iniquitous capitalism contrasted dramatically with the Liberals' practical proposals. The radical left in all these seats attracted enough party support to undermine the smooth running of the machine and foil attempts to moderate the party image between 1906 and 1910. Nonetheless, Statist elements, particularly the miners and railwaymen and to a lesser extent the steelworkers, were advancing very different views. They began to play a more significant role.[46] Nonetheless, the political position was still difficult. Liberal policy was still attractive, even to workers in the public sector. Moreover, although reform-minded trade unionists were concentrated in particular wards, these wards constituted no more than a fifth of the York and Wakefield constituencies and a third of Attercliffe and Brightside. Many of the remaining wards were either regarded as 'hopeless' (like the Park ward in the Attercliffe division), or were contested with devastatingly poor results. Although Labour did well in the 1908 municipal elections, largely at the Liberals' expense, some of this support was subsequently lost. The Liberals either regained their ascendancy or remained strong rivals even in Labour's strongholds. Labour's victory in the four-cornered Attercliffe parliamentary by-election in 1909 was extremely fortuitous. Circumstances inflated its core vote to around 27

---

[45] *York Daily Labour Notes,* 1–13 Jan. 1906, Howell, *ILP,* p. 275. The lack of official support for the Liberal candidate at Wakefield is discussed in the *Wakefield Expr.,* 31 Jan. 1914. At the 1902 by-election, Labour came second to the Tories in a straight fight because middle-class Liberals abstained.

[46] S. Coit to Ensor, 10 Aug. 1909, Ensor MS; G. Friedrich to J.R.M., 12 May 1908, JRM PRO 30/69/1153, B. Lasker to Ensor, 16 Apr. 1908, Ensor MS and Hills, 'York', p. 262; ILP/LRC division in Sheffield, discussed in J. Pointer to J.R.M., 23 Sept. 1905, LRC 25/304, Ward to J.R.M., n.d., LRC 26/357 and ibid., 16 Feb. 1908, 21 Jan. 1909, LP/SHE/08/14 and 69. The Sheffield Trades Council split in 1908, the lighter trades staying in the Lib/Lab Federated Trades Council. (S. Pollard, *A history of labour in Sheffield* (Liverpool, 1959), pp. 198–200).

per cent, and divided its rivals' electoral base.[47] It had not solved the electoral problem.

Labour's weak position was reflected in its attitude to the 1910 election. In Sheffield, Progressive Liberals persuaded the Liberal anti-Socialists that a pact was necessary. Labour moderates – including Pointer, the Attercliffe MP – attached themselves to the Progressive cause. An ILP/SDF/ Gasworkers alliance requested sanction to fight Sheffield Central and Brightside. They were rejected. 'Some of your people', MacDonald told a Sheffield ally, 'think that Sheffield is an oyster lying at their feet.'[48] It clearly was not. As Penny, the ILP agent, informed MacDonald: 'Pointer got through all right, but no thanks are due to the so-called Movement in Sheffield. Attercliffe is a sound Progressive seat, and luckily we have got it. But the "Movement" itself is rotten.' In Wakefield and York, Labour was less fortunate. The Liberals recognised Labour's weakness. They attempted to regain the position of sole anti-Tory party. Labour accepted the inevitable. It did not field a candidate in either seat.[49]

There was little ground for an expansion of the parliamentary campaign in Yorkshire by 1910. Few Labour seats were totally secure: local organisations had not established the electoral base which would make an assault on the Liberals a feasible proposition. York, Wakefield, Grimsby, Keighley, South Leeds, Dewsbury, Pudsey, and West Hull, all contested by Labour or Socialist candidates between 1906 and 1909, were not contested in January 1910. Huddersfield, which was fought twice in 1906, was contested again in January and December 1910. The Labour poll declined. The number of three-cornered contests fell slightly in January 1910, and plummeted in the December. This reflected the electoral position of the party, the changing balance of power and argument within its local leadership, and the ideological and political purchase of Liberal radicalism. The more radical, but 'practical', politics which dominated Labour's attitude to campaigning in Bradford and Leeds had few reflections in the Pennine, South Yorkshire, or East Riding seats. Neither it, nor the Graysonite challenge, developed policies with an obviously broad appeal. There was little to be gained by adopting their preferred strategy of conflict with the Liberal party.

---

[47] Ward to J.S.M., 4 Oct. 1908, LP/SHE/08/54. There were particular local circumstances in 1908 which also favoured Labour.

[48] J.R.M. to Ward, 9 Jan. 1908, LP/SHE/08/9; Sheffield T&LC Mins, 21 Jan. 1908, 22 Feb., 25 May 1910.

[49] J. Penny to J.R.M., 10 Dec. 1910, JRM PRO 30/69/1154, and Penny's fuller report, T&LC Mins, 20 Dec. 1910. For Pointer, Petter (thesis), pp. 171, 186.

IV

Liberal municipal politics continued to change after 1910. Even the more conservative Liberal associations in the northern textile seats and in Bradford and Leeds became more concerned with economic issues. In Bradford, Councillors Smith and Pullin pushed through some social reforms. Conflict between the conservative oligarchies which ruled Leeds politics and an opposition of reformers and Young Liberals came to a head in 1913–14. Liberal Councillors had colluded with the Tories in opposing calls for a higher municipal minimum wage. There was a bitter strike. A section of the Liberal elite opposed minimum wages and also actively supported strike-breaking. The party image suffered, and Labour picked up support in the municipal elections which followed, very largely at the Liberals' expense. The Liberal post-mortem was acrimonious. Liberal radicals attacked 'the dilatory way in which the demands of labour had been dealt with by Liberal Councillors'; for the first time, they obtained a serious hearing.[50] Neither was this conflict confined to Leeds and Bradford. In some of the conservative textile seats local Liberal associations were challenging Divisional executives by adopting a more Progressive approach. They co-operated with Labour in local elections, showed more interest in obtaining a broader membership and adopted more radical proposals. At the same time, many conservative Liberals joined the Tories or left politics altogether. Even here Liberalism was beginning to shift to the left.[51]

Nonetheless, parliamentary Liberalism stagnated. Candidates such as Barrand in Pudsey and Brigg in Keighley were hardly radicals. Barrand was a conventional financier and the director of an Insurance Company; Brigg was a Keighley textile employer and a member of the local Liberal Executive. The candidates in rural seats like Richmond were equally conservative. The conservative Liberal MPs for Spen Valley and Skipton, Whittaker and Clough, were old time Radicals who opposed the Budget in 1914 as they had opposed the Budget in 1909. Candidate selection

---

[50] See esp. Leeds LF EC Mins, 8 Dec. 1913. Previous disputes are mentioned in Leeds LF EC Mins, 26 Apr. 1906, 5 Dec. 1911, with a further report in the *Leeds Cit.,* 25 Nov. 1911. See also J. Henry to H.G., 4 Nov. 1907, 10 Nov. 1908, HG Add MS 46037, fos. 47, 97. The Bradford position is alluded to in the *Bradford Pioneer,* 31 July 1914.

[51] *Cleckheaton Guard.,* 13, 20 Mar. 1914; *Pudsey Advertiser,* 10 Apr. 1914. Oligarchical Keighley was to some extent an exception, but there were protests even here. See e.g. calls for co-operation with Labour, and support for social reform, Keighley LA Mins, 14 Jan. 1907, *Keighley News,* 7 Mar. 1914.

was still largely dominated by the conservative MPs, and by the equally conservative members of the YLF.[52]

In the Pennine radical bloc, the radicals were more successful. Although the Huddersfield Liberal Councillors dragged their heels on housing policy, once they embraced change they moved dramatically. By 1912, the Liberal Council had decided to build 500 houses and immediately rehouse those living in cellar dwellings. The proposals were highly regarded by the ILP elsewhere; the Huddersfield ILP was reduced to saying that the Emperor had stolen their clothes. They accurately and grudgingly recognised that housing reform, the extension of tramways, and improvements in other municipal facilities, pushed the Liberals closer to a 'collectivist' stance than ever before.[53]

Change was not confined to the Pennine seats. When H. J. Wilson retired as the Liberal MP for Holmfirth in 1912, he chose to continue his attempt to radicalise Sheffield Liberalism. He purchased the *Sheffield Daily Independent* as a voice for the Liberal left (and considered helping to set up a radical Liberal paper for Bradford and Leeds).[54] The Sheffield Liberals fought to preserve the principle of model employment, the continuation of the Council's house-building plans, and the commitment to direct labour, against the attacks of the new Tory Council. 'Socialism', the Liberal Alderman Stephenson declared, in his defence of these proposals, 'was just Liberalism one stage further on.' In Wakefield, where five Young Liberal Councillors were part of a growing radical contingent, Liberal municipal policy was equally advanced.[55]

Parliamentary politics were also not allowed to fossilise. Trevelyan played an active part in getting radical issues on the YLF agenda. In 1911, a conference of Yorkshire Liberals argued *against* promoting Home Rule as an election issue. The YLF followed this by noting local apathy over Welsh Disestablishment. It called for particular attention to be focused on land, wages, and the cost of living. In the Pennine belt, new parliamentary candidates, chosen by the local associations, not by

[52] Murray, *People's Budget*, p. 174, *Cleckheaton Guard.*, 9, 16, 30 Jan. 1914, YLF Mins, 10 June 1913, *Darlington Times*, 7 Feb. 1914.

[53] Hudd. Lib. Counc. Mins, 17 Dec. 1912, 23 July 1913, 28 July 1914; *Worker*, 25 Oct. 1913, 10 Jan. 1914. The Wolverhampton LP's favourable comments on the scheme are in the *Wolv. Worker*, Sept. 1913.

[54] Counc. Derry to H.J.W., 28 Feb. 1910. A section of the Wilson clan had discussed mass resignation as one way of fighting Liberal conservatism: H.J.W. to O. Wilson, 23 Feb. 1910, and 23, 24, 26 Feb. 1910. See also H.J.W. to C. H. and W. Wilson, 24, 28 Feb. 1910 (all in Wilson MS 5906). For the Leeds/Bradford press scheme, J.H. to H.G., 13 Sept. 1907, 25 Mar. 1908, HG Add MS 46037 fos. 43, 62, and A. R. to M. K. Rowntree, 24 June 1909, AR MS.

[55] *Sheffield Ind.*, 2 Nov. 1910, 3 Nov. 1913; *S.G.*, 12 Sept. 1913; Lib. ann. meeting in Wakefield, *Wakefield Expr.*, 9 May 1914.

the Whips, reflected the local parties' radical interests. Wilson secured a successor in Holmfirth, Sydney Arnold, who was a land reformer, 'advanced radical', and future Labour finance expert. Other constituencies maintained their position. The Colne Valley Liberals deliberately and carefully selected a radical and local replacement (F. W. Mallalieu) for their radical (but now insane) MP.[56] Pennine radicalism was retaining its capacity to promote reform. Arnold, Sherwell, Trevelyan, Higham, and Mallalieu stood by Lloyd George's proposals, although they were not satisfied to stop there.[57] Higham's only fear on minimum wages was that they would become the employers' *maximum* wage rate; Sherwell, acting with his friends and allies Arnold Rowntree, T. E. Harvey, and a few others, frequently pressurised the Government by moving amendments and voting against its proposals where they stopped short of New Liberal aims. Trevelyan exerted pressure by relaying information on the nature of local popular opinion to contacts in Westminster, particularly Runciman and Percy Illingworth. He also attempted to secure the selection of radical colleagues as parliamentary candidates. H. J. Wilson and Rowntree, who were heavily involved with the Liberal Land campaign, were committed to it becoming a major plank in the Liberals' programme for the next election. Their Yorkshire newspapers pushed questions of land reform and minimum wages to the fore during 1914. These informal links between the radicals and the centre helped create a more uniformly 'radical' image for Yorkshire Liberalism and for the Liberal party in general.[58]

Support for reform was not confined to the Pennine seats. Centrist MPs, like Tudor Walters in Sheffield, enthusiastically embraced the land and housing campaign, and called for action on unemployment. The East Riding MPs and candidates were attentive to material issues, and matters of financial and social insecurity. 'The problem before them', Ferens wrote in 1914, 'was the betterment of the poorer classes – to do away with poverty and suffering.' In Hull in particular, however, Ferens and his allies merged support for new policies with an older Liberal tradition which emphasised toughness, progress through ability, and 'respectable' self-improvement. This put new ideas and policies into a

---

[56] Holmfirth LA *AR* 1911–12, and for Wilson's role in his selection, J. Herbert to W.R., 16 Nov. 1911, WR 44. For Arnold's politics, *The Times,* esp. 20 June 1912. For Mallalieu and declining patience over Home Rule, *Colne Valley Guardian,* 23 May 1914, YLF Mins, 24 May 1911, 21 Feb. 1912, 18 June 1913; C. H. Smithson to C.P.T, 24 July 1910, CPT 26.

[57] *Todmorden Adv.,* 31 Jan. 1913; *Yorks. Herald,* 29 May 1914.

[58] Briggs, *Rowntree,* pp. 67–78 and below pp. 341–3. See also J. Henry to H.G., 26 Aug. 1911, HG Add MS 46038 fo. 152, A.R. to M. K. Rowntree, 23 Nov. 1911, 9 Dec. 1912, 23 June 1914 (action on railway strike, armaments expenditure, taxation), AR MS. For Trevelyan e.g. F. W. Hirst to C.P.T, 14 Oct. 1913, CPT 32, C.P.T. to Grey, 9 Feb. 1910, CPT 27, C.P.T. to W.R., 25 July 1914, WR 135.

familiar language and context. The Hull Liberals still attracted support from traditionally Liberal members of the more affluent classes, as well as from the working classes.[59]

This synthesis was frequently Liberalism's strength. In some of the East Riding seats (and some parts of the northern textile belt) a dour, stolid, paternalistic – although not always *laissez faire* – Old Liberalism remained popular. Old allegiances and patterns of thought in notoriously insular communities were not easily shaken, particularly where no new economic philosophy or circumstances questioned the basis of these views.[60] Labour's considerable local strength, especially in areas of conservative Liberalism, indicates that there was some opposition to Liberalism's more conservative aspects; it does not suggest that the Liberal party itself was redundant.

New Liberals were able to appropriate some old Liberal issues and merge them with their own more radical views on social and economic matters. Religious radicals like H. J. Wilson, Harvey, Sherwell, and Rowntree sympathised with Radical demands on temperance reform and disarmament. Wilson saw nationalisation of railways and land and municipalisation of drink as 'collectivist' proposals, which rested on the same broad principles. Rowntree and his radical allies, and New Liberals like Trevelyan, were part of a foreign affairs group which opposed secret diplomacy and expenditure on armaments. The group also included the conservative Radicals Clough and Whittaker. Trevelyan, formerly a Liberal Imperialist, now agreed with the Radicals in seeking action on Home Rule. The Government had to show that it could stick to its policies and not give in to the establishment. It was now a 'Who Rules' question, like reform of the Lords in 1910. It was invested with a new, radical, meaning.[61] An evolving, composite, Liberal approach ensured that some Radicals at least could remain in a party which was adopting 'unacceptable' ideas on the distribution of wealth and the scale of state intervention. The composite nature of the Liberal party could be a strength.

It depended on the balance. Trevelyan was aware of this. Although he thought the Government could use the Ulster revolt to its own advantage, he did not see it as a desirable issue on which to base a fight. He wanted the Irish problem out of the way, to free the party to concen-

[59] LA meeting, the (Hull) *Daily News*, 27 July 1914, reports, *Hull Times*, 21 Feb., 14 Mar. 1914.

[60] For the strength of Old Liberalism in Keighley, *The Times*, 25, 28 Oct. 1913, *S.G.*, 7 Nov. 1913. See also Clegg's favourable comments on fair wages contracts, *Municipal Journal*, 11 Feb. 1911, p. 126.

[61] C.P.T. to his mother, 16 Oct. 1912, and to Runciman, above, fn. 58. For temperance, e.g. A. E. Dingle, *The campaign for prohibition in Victorian England* (1980), p. 224, and above, p. 257.

UWE Library Services
St Matthias Campus
Tel: 0117 32 84472

XXXX3301

Item Title	Due Date

Sylvia Pankhurst sexual politics and political activism Bar
5005726431   03/05/2011

Rent strikes : people's struggle for housing in West Scotl
7000160560   03/05/2011

* Political change and the Labour Party, 1900-1918 by D
7000130634   23/03/2011

---

* Indicates items borrowed today
www.uwe.ac.uk/library
Overnight loan items are
due back at 12 noon on due date

trate on domestic reform. However, in the northern textile belt, as in Bradford and Leeds, although many conservative Liberals were leaving the party, many stayed *purely* to fight these battles. They were institutionally powerful men, who had bent so far and who were unwilling to bend much further. Despite the apparent, continuing, attraction of a Centrist philosophy, and some support for Radical ideas, the *primacy* of an unchanging Radicalism meant that there was a clear space for Labour to exploit. It could make some headway by restating the paramount importance of social and economic reform. This was a problem which a composite Liberal party always had to face. The price of retaining some Old Liberal support could be a milder stance on social and economic intervention, or a less radical party image. In the face of this, Labour had two choices. It could become a more reformist organisation, exploiting Liberal deficiencies on social reform, and its inattentiveness to certain specific grievances. Alternatively, it could play for higher stakes, provide a more dynamic Socialist alternative, and aim at a fundamental restructuring of the political and social system. Its local actions could influence the extent of electoral change.

V

After 1910, Labour stepped up the pace of party activity. The Leeds/Bradford parties attempted to publicise their particular brand of Labour politics more effectively through newly formed Labour/Socialist newspapers. Housing conditions were elevated to the level of a primary propaganda issue, with Labour rejecting struggle by rent strike in favour of extensive municipal interventionism.[62] The depth *and* breadth of support increased. In East Bradford, the SDP had polled badly in January 1910. However, by November 1913 Labour was out-polling the Liberals in four of the five wards in the constituency.[63] Several wards in West and South Leeds began to elect Labour Councillors in three-cornered contests. Yet the signs were not all favourable. In South and West Leeds, Labour victories were won with a minute turnover of support. As in 1909–10, political polarisation threatened to reduce Labour's lead still further, and once more put the Liberals and Tories in first and second place. In the Labour-held seats of East Leeds and West Bradford, by contrast, a Tory–Labour division had become an institutionalised fact. Labour had continued to

[62] *Bradford Pioneer,* 14 Mar., 4 Apr., 9 May 1913, and *Leeds Cit.,* e.g. 13 Mar., 8 May 1914. See also Englander, *Landlord and tenant,* pp. 153–60 for the support, and defeat, of rent strikes as a Labour policy proposal. There were still organisational problems in Leeds: Leeds LP Mins, 25 July, 6 Sept., 18 June 1914.

[63] Nonetheless, in wards of other Bradford seats, Labour came third in 1913, the Liberals first.

expand. However, even in East Leeds, the constituency's commercial areas (roughly 20 per cent of the seat), and parts of the poorer wards, were sufficiently Conservative to make Labour success dependent on the declining Liberal party.[64] Only East Bradford was in a considerably better position than in 1909–10.

The Bradford/Leeds approach involved issues, particularly housing reform, which could be 'claimed' by the reformers. It combined these with active support for the municipal workers' aims during the 1913 strikes, and a more Socialist rhetoric. It did not remove the Liberals as a rival where they resisted, where they emphasised a continuing commitment to gradual change, and where a skilled workforce did not need Statist policies (as in West Leeds).

Most Labour organisations in the Pennine textile belt adopted similar policies, but without the rhetoric or energy associated with the Bradford ILP. A moderate moral reformism, with Statist overtones where the municipal workers, miners, or railwaymen were significant, became the most common stance. In Dewsbury, Batley, and Sowerby, the trade unions were progressively moving closer to LRCs. In Sowerby, the textile unions took over the party; they put in money and an agent and moderated party policy.[65] Even in 'Graysonite' Spen Valley and Holmfirth there was some change. Holmfirth had been fought when Wilson retired in 1912. However, despite the YMA's decision to fight again at the next election, only three (of at least sixteen) lodges sent delegates to the LRC's meetings. Organisation was primitive, municipal results unencouraging. The radical Liberals were still the principal working-class organisation.[66]

Trade union/Socialist hostility died a long death. The ILP/Trades Council merger at Huddersfield in 1914 prompted a number of moderate union branches to disaffiliate. Moreover, although some Socialists in Huddersfield and Spen Valley regarded close union/ILP links as an opportunity to promote a Socialist form of reformist politics, more were suspicious of 'compromises' with trade union materialism. They had seen 'MacDonaldism' at work in Parliament. They did not like what they saw. They did not believe that MacDonald was moving the country closer to Socialism. The 'materialism' of the Bradford/Leeds parties was too

---

[64] Labour's vote increased by 12 per cent in the Leeds East ward 1909–13, but by 2 per cent in the Armley and Warley ward (Leeds West) and the North-East ward (largely in the Leeds North constituency). The Labour poll in West Leeds had fallen by about 7 per cent in 1909–10 under the polarising impact of a parliamentary campaign (judging from the Armley and Warley result), while the Liberals' increased by 11 per cent. A swing even half this size in 1914–15 would have put Labour in third place.

[65] Sowerby LRC Mins, 29 May 1913, 26 Apr., 28 May 1914 and agent's report, Sowerby LRC MS 51/7; *C.F. T,* 14 Nov. 1913.

[66] *Dewsbury News,* 16 May 1914; Holmfirth LRC Mins, esp. 9 July 1910, 21 Feb. 1913.

easily tarred with the same brush. Moreover, industrial unrest had fired Socialist enthusiasm in the same way that Grayson had done in 1907. Some ILP branches opposed even the formation of Labour organisations. There was considerable unrest in Huddersfield and Colne Valley, where, after lengthy debate and acrimonious conflict, a majority of CVLL delegates voted against joining a putative Colne Valley LRC.[67] Some old Graysonites, like Russell Williams, left the Labour party rather than accept the continuing dilution of its idealism. Others, like Ben Riley, tried to find other ways of preserving the party's soul.[68]

Internal problems were a symptom of a general failure, which they in turn intensified. In Colne Valley, Huddersfield, and Keighley, Labour went into decline. Full-time organisers were regarded as essential to stem the flood; only temporary appointments could be made. Labour's parliamentary support in Keighley remained static between 1906 and 1913, and fell by 4 per cent in Huddersfield between 1906 and December 1910.[69] Although the Liberals subsequently lost support in Huddersfield (for local reasons) in the 1911 municipal contests, Labour did not benefit. It came third in most three-cornered contests, and lost as much ground as it gained (Appendix 4, pp. 461–2). Snell, the Labour candidate, reported that he was unlikely to win in 1914. Prospects were equally poor in Keighley and Colne Valley, where a disintegrating organisation gave up several UDC seats without even a fight and reported that income covered 'only the minimum of expenditure' in 1914. Further activity, the report continued, was pointless until circumstances changed.[70]

The development of a more moderate stance, and of a closer interest in the textile unions' material interests, helped Labour expand a little in the unionised areas which were becoming its strongholds. Nonetheless, it was not overwhelmingly dominant even here. The Liberals were either close behind or a fraction ahead. In the Sowerby Division, the poorest areas, particularly Hebden Bridge, the rural areas, and the middle-class enclaves (such as the Halifax ward of Warley), were all unresponsive. In the Pennine seats generally there were fewer local authority workers, railwaymen, miners, or members of other groups whose interests were

---

[67] *Dewsbury Reporter,* 23 Sept. 1911; *Worker,* 28 Mar. 1914; CVLL Mins, 5 Apr.–27 Sept. 1914. This decision was made after considerable debate, and despite strong arguments from 'moderate' elements. See also the *Worker,* 3, 24 Feb., 30 Mar. 1912, 17 Jan., 26 Sept. 1914.

[68] *Bradford Pioneer,* 10 Apr. 1913.

[69] CVLL Mins, 1910–14 *passim.* For Huddersfield, *Worker,* 6 Apr. 1912; Fabian Soc. Finance Comm. Mins, 17 Oct. 1913.

[70] Hudd. Lab. and Soc. Election Comm. Mins, 21 Feb. 1909, 1 Feb. 1910, 2 Sept. 1913; CVLL, *Half-yearly Report,* Oct. 1913, Apr. 1914, and CVLL Mins, 26 Mar. 1911, 5 Apr. 1914. Reports on Keighley by A.P. and A.H., NEC Mins, n.d. Oct. 1911 (BLPES Coll, fos. 230–1), A.H. to J.S.M., 29, 31 Oct. 1913, LP/HEN/08/1/93–4.

best served by the Labour party. In the small towns, with their more mixed populations, the Labour party fared badly. It could not break the hold of a Liberal political culture with a combination of craft representation and Liberal reforms. Moreover, 'interests' were open to interpretation. The 'solidarities' of mining communities did not translate into solid electoral support for Labour.[71] Two-thirds of Holmfirth's miners reportedly voted Liberal at the 1912 by-election, and Labour's subsequent organisational and electoral deficiencies in the mining sections of this constituency suggest that the problem had not been remedied by changes in union politics. 'Moderation' and trade union support put Labour on a better footing; they were not the answer to its problems.[72]

Labour had no magic cure. The expansion of trade unionism after 1910 did not solve Labour's electoral dilemma. Liberal radicals offered support for general social progress and opportunities for individual improvement. They reached over the heads of an occupational appeal to particular groups, which was Labour's major, distinct, electoral prop. Labour's internal conflicts damaged its image and created organisational problems. Cumulatively, this minimised its ability to exploit (limited) opportunities. However, neither the Graysonite approach nor a material Socialist reformism, gained majority support within the party; they were ideologically and politically inappropriate in the Pennine seats. Even a union-aided, material, stance – which retained an improving, moralistic, rhetoric – did not sweep all obstacles away. Nonetheless, it appeared to be the only way of even denting the Liberals' lead.

VI

In many of the East Riding's rural and coastal seats, Labour barely existed as a political force even in 1914. The Liberals enjoyed an unassailed position on the centre-left. Despite mounting industrial unrest amongst the large numbers of dockers and railwaymen in the semi-industrial ports of Grimsby and Hull, there was little improvement in Labour's position after 1910. The electoral purchase of Centrist Liberalism was too strong. In most local government wards, Labour could not even mount a challenge. Three-cornered contests, even in solidly working-class wards, pro-

---

[71] *Sowerby Chronicle*, 10 Apr. 1914, *Halifax Courier*, 4 Nov. 1911, Sowerby agent's report, Sowerby LRC MS 51/7. The strongest section of the seat was unionised Sowerby Bridge. See e.g. 1913 County Council results: C 35.51, L 33.46, Lab 31.03. For Todmorden (Sowerby Division), *Todmorden Adv.*, 11 Apr. 1913; for Penistone (Holmfirth), *Worker*, 12 Apr. 1913, 11 Apr. 1914; for Goole (Osgoldcross) and Castleford (Spen Valley), *Goole Times*, 11 Apr. 1913; for Pudsey, *Pudsey Adv.*, 9 Apr. 1914. In the Bradford Tong ward, also in the Pudsey division, Labour came third when all three parties clashed in 1911 and 1912.

[72] *The Times*, 22 June 1912. For organisation, see below, p. 279.

duced nothing better than 20 per cent polls and a poor third place. The strikes, Labour's growing contacts with the ASRS and the Trades Council, and the moderation of its policies did not fundamentally alter the position. Members of the ILP turned on the unions and on each other. The Hull organisation, carefully reconstructed after its earlier problems, fell apart.[73]

By contrast, Labour made more headway in York, Wakefield, and Sheffield. Its approach was largely an extension of its previous position. In Sheffield, for example, the steel-dominated Trades Council decided on 'the inauguration of a vigorous policy' in 1912. Attempts were made to appoint an agent and to expand municipal activity. Acrimony and division worked against this, as it did in York and Wakefield. However, the steel unions were now more involved and more committed. The left came under attack. The official Labour newspaper, the *Sheffield Guardian,* attacked the BSP as 'a sort of Italian mafia upon a political scale'. The disaffiliation of hard left elements, the development of a 'realistic' left, and the growing institutional strength of the unions had turned the party around. The NUR in York and Wakefield (aided by some miners in the latter instance) became more involved with Labour organisations following the unrest of 1911–12 and performed a similar function.[74] Labour's expansion in wards dominated by these groups was only slightly delayed even by radical Liberal policies. The members' experience in recent strikes had taught some of them at least the value of state support for their material interest. In November 1913, Labour had a 4 point lead over the Liberals in the steel-dominated Attercliffe and Brightside wards, and a 20 per cent lead over the Liberals in the railway ward of Micklegate in York. Even if this in part reflected a temporary dissatisfaction with the Liberals' national performance (aided by local factors) Labour's lead was substantially higher than in 1909–10, and represented a real expansion of its support amongst a particular section of the electorate.

Nonetheless, Labour's support improved much more gradually and far less completely, in the occupationally very different wards which made up the bulk of these constituencies. Workers in the lighter trades dominated in wards which contained roughly half to two-thirds of the constituency electorate in Attercliffe and Brightside. Here Labour polled 20–5 per cent of the vote on the few occasions when it intervened, the Liberals

---

[73] *Labour Journal,* Nov. 1914 and e.g., Mar., Apr., Nov. 1911, Feb. 1912, June 1913. For the industrial unrest, K. Brooker, *The Hull strikes of* 1911 (East Yorkshire local history society, pamphlet 35 [1979]).

[74] Sheffield T&LC *AR* 1911/12, 1912/13, T&LC Mins, 20 Aug. 1912, 21 July 1915, *S.G.,* 10 Nov. 1911, 3 Apr. 1914, A. Thatcher to F.J., 14 May 1913, 11 July 1914; *Wakefield Expr.,* 8 Nov. 1913. For the NUR in York, H. H. Slessor, *Judgement reserved* (1941), p. 49.

over 30 per cent more. The position was marginally worse in York. Although Labour had a narrow lead in three of the five wards for the first time in 1913, it barely existed in the rest of the constituency. The position was *much* worse in Wakefield, where, even in its mining stronghold, Labour came third (albeit narrowly) in 1913.[75] The rest of the seat was a Labour desert; the party's appeal was too narrow, and insufficiently credible, even amongst its most likely supporters. As York Liberals had demonstrated before 1910, and Wakefield Liberals continued to show, Liberal radicalism could dampen enthusiasm for the Labour party, even in Labour's strongholds. It could eclipse it altogether where Labour could make no specific appeal to Statist occupational groups (Appendix 4, pp. 462–3 for municipal election results).

VII

The NEC and NAC knew the local position. They saw no justification for a major anti-Liberal parliamentary campaign in 1914–15. Only West Bradford, Halifax, and East Leeds could be contested with confidence (and Halifax was a double member borough). Shipley, Dewsbury, and Elland, where ILP activists wished to field candidates, were not even considered by the Yorkshire Divisional Council of the ILP, who regarded Huddersfield, East Bradford, West Leeds, Keighley, and Pudsey as the 'best' ILP seats in the area. Many ILP and Labour officials were far from sanguine about the local prospects even in these constituencies.[76]

The 'justification' for additional candidatures was limited. Despite some progress in Leeds and Bradford, Middleton's feeling was that 'the Leeds people will have all their work cut out to hold the Eastern Division'. They could not risk retaliation by attacking the Liberal-held West and South Leeds constituencies. The poor organisational and financial position provided the excuse. The local party was unhappy, but unable to refute the NEC's arguments. They withdrew their interest. East Bradford, however, was regarded as an attractive proposition by both local and national leaders. The municipal record was better, and West Bradford was securely and convincingly Labour. However, East Bradford had a

[75] *S.G.*, 25 Apr., 2 May, 7 Nov. 1913, *Sheffield Ind.*, 8 Apr. 1913 (Guardians' results), 3 Nov. 1913. The middle-class wards in Wakefield and York were Labour deserts, while the poor Liberal performance was in part the result of (possibly temporary) local factors. See e.g. *S.G.*, 7 Nov. 1913, *Yorks. Herald*, 24 Mar. 1914. For the continued industrial orientation and limited ideological development of the Sheffield LP, T. Adams, 'Working class unrest and the Sheffield labour movement, 1918–21', in C. Wrigley (ed.), *Local studies and local history* (Loughborough, 1982), pp. 16–17.

[76] NAC Mins, 25 Apr. 1913, 24 July 1914 (rejecting Shipley); F.J. to J. Walker, 26 May 1908, FJ 08/212 and *Pudsey Adv.*, 10 July 1913. Pudsey contained roughly 6,000 Leeds freeholders, for which see above, p. 123.

joint SDF/ILP organisation, with limited trade union support. This foiled the prospect of a campaign.[77]

Labour was even weaker in most remaining textile seats. Pudsey, the ILP ruled, could only be considered if plural voting was abolished; without this a campaign would be hopeless. Keighley and Huddersfield (where Snell had been stripped of the Fabians' financial support) thus competed to carry the ILP banner. A further by-election in Keighley was a possibility. The ILP therefore concentrated its attention here, despite three previous electoral defeats, internal problems in the constituency organisation, and the preference of the NAC's own Parliamentary Sub-Committee for a campaign in Colne Valley.[78]

The trade unions were reluctant to fight seats left by the ILP or other adjacent constituencies. Ben Turner's union, the General Union of Textile Workers, declined to support his proposed candidatures in either Colne Valley or Spen Valley, perhaps on NEC advice. Turner accepted the decision: he was increasingly MacDonald's man. Although the YMA arranged for lodge representatives to sit on the Holmfirth LRC Executive for the duration of the forthcoming parliamentary election, there was little local enthusiasm for the Labour party in the mining lodges. A Holmfirth Labour 'campaign' – given local apathy – was unlikely. The Sowerby textile workers, strongly supported by their national executive, took active steps to persuade the NEC that a parliamentary campaign in the Sowerby division was feasible. Their commitment, organisation, and energy were unusual.[79] No other major trade union showed any real interest in fighting a Yorkshire seat.

Few constituencies could contemplate a campaign without ILP or trade union financial support. Nonetheless, it seems probable that Colne Valley and Huddersfield would have raised the money to support parliamentary campaigns, and that the NEC/NAC would not have objected. By August

---

[77] J.S.M. to S.H., 10 May 1914, LP/ORG/14/1/24, T.E.H. to W. Harvey, 19 Jan. 1913, TEH MS, NAC Mins, 28 Jan., 25 Mar., 25 Apr., 28 July 1913; Laybourn and Reynolds, *Yorkshire*, pp. 161–2. For union non-participation, Bradford Workers' Municipal Fed. Mins, e.g. 3 Mar. 1910, 2 Feb. 1911, 4 June 1914.

[78] NAC Parl. Sub-Comm. Mins, 10 Oct. 1913, 21 Apr. 1914, NAC Mins, 12 Dec. 1913, 14 July 1914. For further adverse comments on the position in Keighley, see the views of suffragette organisers active in the 1913 campaign, Holton, *Feminism and democracy*, p. 110. The NAC, and some activists, hoped to remove Grayson as the Colne Valley candidate. This proposal passed at a meeting of the CVLL Executive, but was subsequently rejected by a full meeting of the party (CVLL Mins, 5 Apr., 16 May, 18 July, 27 Sept. 1914). The idea was revived during the war, when there was a move to transfer Wallhead from Coventry.

[79] *Dewsbury News*, 16 May 1914, NAC Mins, 14 July 1914. For Turner, above, p. 265. For Holmfirth and Sowerby, *S.G.*, 21 Feb. 1913, Holmfirth LRC Mins, 13 June–13 July 1914, Sowerby LRC Mins, 29 May 1913–28 May 1914, agent's report, Sowerby LRC MS 51/7, Sowerby LRC *AR* 1913.

1914, the Huddersfield organisations had found enough money, with sufficient ease, to suggest that they would become eligible for an additional ILP election grant. The CVLL, divided over tactics, inactive, and depressed, was reluctant to even try and raise money locally by increasing affiliation fees. Nonetheless, its place in left mythology, and its electoral record, was probably sufficient for it to attract another candidate, or at least another source of money.[80] With the exception of Sowerby, all these seats had already been contested. A major expansion of the parliamentary campaign was not imminent.

In the more Tory areas Labour had more potential and had made more progress. Nonetheless, the Liberals were too strong to be pushed aside in many of the working-class seats. Labour needed Liberal support even if it was to hold Attercliffe (the only Labour seat). It needed Liberal support to gain York (a double member borough with one Liberal and one Tory MP). Labour acted accordingly. The York LRC adopted a candidate, but not an anti-Liberal radical like G. H. Stuart, the candidate who in 1906 had caused so many Liberals to vote Tory. The Fabian, H. H. Schloesser (later Slesser), was a personal friend of Frank Rowntree, and a respected barrister. No Liberal opposition to his campaign was anticipated. Despite a temporary decline in Liberal/Labour relations in Sheffield, Pointer was also unlikely to be opposed in Attercliffe.[81]

Labour was in no position to expand in other Sheffield seats, in Wakefield, or anywhere in the East Riding. There is every indication that the parliamentary campaign in 1914/15 would have reflected these realities. In West Hull, Labour's moderate candidate withdrew in 1914, complaining that he had experienced nothing but 'suspicion and mistrust' at the hands of the local party. A campaign, and any ideas of political success, were a 'forlorn hope'. William Lunn, the miners' prospective parliamentary candidate at Wakefield, in fact withdrew to stand in Holmfirth, and there are no indications that the LRC was able or willing to find a replacement. The NEC rejected proposals to fight Sheffield Brightside, although it hoped to expand here at some time in the future. The Liberals' position was not so strong that they could contemplate attacking Labour, or consider resisting its attempts to contest York, but any further Labour expansion had been temporarily blocked. Nonetheless, the pat-

[80] *Worker*, election fund report, 1 Aug. 1914; CVLL Mins, 18 July, 27 Sept., 12 Dec. 1914, 10 May 1915.
[81] Slesser, *Judgement reserved*, pp. 48–9; Ward to J.R.M., 24 Oct. 1911, LP/MF/11/587, Sheffield T&LC Mins, 6 Feb. 1912.

tern of change was such that Labour activists appeared justified in thinking that their time would soon come.[82]

In 1906, the idea that the Progressive Alliance could survive in Yorkshire seemed improbable. Yorkshire's Liberal leaders were very conservative; the ILP, born in Bradford and historically opposed to any alliance with the Liberal party, was a major local force. Liberal conservatism had provided Labour with a platform; the party seemed set to expand still further. However, in many areas Liberal conceptions of the policies necessary to sustain material prosperity were not easily undermined. Moreover, the adoption of radical policies which were designed to expand opportunities and to provide a degree of security reinforced the salience of an already strong Liberal political culture. The process of radicalisation from above and from below was most complete in a block of southern Pennine seats, but it had an impact in most areas. Labour was left to exploit specific Liberal deficiencies and grievances. It expressed support for groups with interests in specific forms of state intervention, such as the railwaymen, municipal workers, and miners, at a time when they were becoming dissatisfied with the Liberals' attitude to their industry. Labour offered loyal support, and materially relevant 'answers' to the economic problems which underpinned much of the industrial unrest. Institutional structures also changed. Union links often gave Labour moderates the institutional power to adopt or amend 'Socialist' policies, or to couch them in a language which was more acceptable to a local electorate. In the 'Tory' areas where Labour took this line, Liberal radicalism could delay Labour's expansion, especially where Labour's Socialist wing was dominant, or where Labour's support for union solutions, like nationalisation, did not seem credible, materially relevant, or realistic. Nonetheless, Liberal support was being undermined by a cultural/political approach which was protective, defensive, and concerned with material issues which were in the interests of a substantial number of local voters. The prospect of further improvement was indicated by the acceleration of Labour support after 1910. The Liberals had always recognised Labour's potential in these seats. The slight expansion of Labour's parliamentary campaign in 1914, and of Labour representation if the campaigns were successful, was entirely compatible with the idea of a Progressive Alliance. Provided Labour's further expansion was only gradual, and

[82] *Monthly Labour Journal,* Nov. 1914 and *Eastern Morning News,* 6 Nov. 1914; NEC Mins, 24 Jan. 1912. For Wakefield, Holmfirth LRC Mins, 4 July 1914. The LRC had already been co-operating with the Liberals in municipal contests. Lunn's constant movement between Holmfirth and Wakefield may have been influenced by attempts to procure a free run for a YMF candidate either in Wakefield or in Doncaster, for which see above, p. 225.

confined to a few areas, the pact would remain a logical expression of the broad ideological similarities between the two parties and the slight spatial variations in their support.

In Liberal areas, by contrast, Labour's commitment to a practical reformism which would increase working-class security took on a rather different form. Economic conditions and political traditions were very different from seats like York or Wakefield. Support for municipal housing schemes was by far the most important of Labour's practical proposals. In the Bradford/Leeds area, this policy was surrounded with a rhetoric and a philosophy which pointed the party towards a decentralised Socialism. Material questions, in keeping with the party's past, and with the dominant Liberal political culture, were fused with a sense of moral indignation. 'Solutions' depended on municipal intervention and expenditure on practical assistance to the poor. Given poor conditions and low wages in those parts of the city where Labour was popular, this was a realistic approach. In the Pennines, however, there was not a large enough rateable base to support large-scale municipal interventionism. There were fewer municipal workers, and possibly more social stigma attached to the receipt of state benefits. Significantly, economic dependency was also more common. This ensured that Liberal attacks on Socialist 'solutions' to economic problems received sympathetic consideration from an electorate which understood almost by osmosis the alleged importance of Free Trade to local prosperity. Attempts to cater for specific Statist groups could undermine Labour's appeal to other groups of workers. Unable to escape from the hold of a Liberal political culture, Labour policy was closely related to radical Liberal ideas. It lacked a distinct image or a distinct electoral base. Public sector workers were fewer and less committed to Labour than in the cities. Labour's links with the textile and engineering unions were weaker and less effective. Although Labour could exploit the Liberals' deficiencies on social and welfare issues in the northern textile belt, it repeatedly came up against Liberal calls for evidence of its practical alternatives and its own activists' calls for a more 'idealistic' political stance. Outside Bradford and Leeds, where Labour was edging forward, the best that it could hope for was a long hard struggle.

Politics were settling down into a clearer pattern. The anti-Progressive elements in both parties were losing support and (less rapidly) losing institutional strength. The 'left' in the Labour party and the 'right' of the Liberal party could delay the extent of internal change, and hence reduce their party's ability to compete. The Liberal right could also *augment* the party's electoral base; the Labour left could be a valuable fount of ideas. In some circumstances the fact that the Liberal and Labour parties were coalitions was an impediment; in others, the net result was favourable. There was no single, uniform, onward march of a union-based Labour party, no systematic decline of an unadaptive, bourgeois, Liberalism.

Chapter 10

Liberalism's reserve army

Edwardian New Liberals frequently pointed to the existence of a North/ South divide in British politics. They tried to convince their party leaders that they had to cater primarily for the northern and radical side of the party's constituency if the Liberal party was to survive. They may have convinced Lloyd George to tilt the balance of party policy in that direction.[1] Historians have certainly focused on the shift of Liberal support towards the North.[2] Yet the idea of a North/South divide does not do justice to the complexities of the Liberals' political image, and to the nature of their electoral constituency. Shifting the balance towards the North did not involve ignoring the South; being attentive to 'northern' working-class interests did not mean that the party abandoned the idea of organic progress and a broad appeal. On the contrary, the Liberal party was such a strong force because, in addition to its ability to gain support in the industrial areas which we now associate with the Labour party, it had reserves of strength in the South. It returned MPs in a whole range of scattered, varied, 'southern' industrial seats, stretching from East Anglia to Staffordshire and from Exeter to Reading. Labour had to win seats of this kind, or stop the Liberals from doing so, if it was to become the largest party in a three party system; the Liberals had to hold them if they were to remain the party of government.[3]

The Liberals also remained a force in certain rural areas and less industrial parts of England and Wales. Although the 1910 elections saw

[1] J. A. Hobson, 'Sociological interpretation of a general election', in P. Abrams (ed.), *The origins of British sociology* (1968); R. L. Outhwaite to C.P.T., 1 Feb. 1910 and C.P.T to Grey, 9 Feb. 1910, CPT 27. For Lloyd George's analysis, Murray, *People's Budget*, pp. 206–7. For election results in Liberal/Labour (and Socialist) clashes, see Appendix 3, pp. 456–7; for the major municipal results, Appendix 4, pp. 463–4.

[2] Clarke, *Lancashire Liberalism*, pp. 7–9, 397–407, Blewett, *Peers*, Chapter 18 and esp. p. 401.

[3] Labour was so comparatively successful in 1923 and 1929 because of its ability to win seats like Northampton, and prevent the Liberals winning seats like Lincoln and Cambridge.

a pronounced anti-Liberal swing in residential, rural, and mixed seats, in 1914 there were still more Liberal MPs for the many rural/mixed seats than there were Liberal MPs in the North-West. Labour had to capture these areas if it was to fully replace the Liberal coalition.[4]

The seats discussed in this chapter are not part of a single geographical region. Economic structures and social conditions in southern urban and rural areas varied enormously and created a plethora of differing circumstances. Individual local centres contained a range of occupational groups and unique local industries. There was ample opportunity for conflicts of interests within constituencies, and between constituencies. Nonetheless, similar political orientations, principles, or priorities can be detected in a variety of spatially segregated areas where the Liberals were successful. These areas sometimes had similar economic interests and religious orientations; they shared a Liberal political culture and perceived issues in a particular way. They were thus likely to continue with their propensity to support Liberal politicians even after Labour arrived on the scene, *provided* this political culture was updated and shown to be still relevant to their needs and ideas. There were institutional factors which pushed Liberal parties towards a sympathetic consideration of newer, radical, proposals, although equally there were institutional obstacles which could limit their impact (Section I).

It is possible to identify two forms of Liberal politics, which were in turn based on differing economic structures and political traditions. Small-scale, craft-based, and generally light industry was accompanied in some areas during the 1890s (especially parts of the East Midlands and East Anglia) by an 'advanced' Nonconformist Radicalism which was rooted in the independent views and attitudes of the skilled workmen and tradesmen who dominated Liberal politics in that area. It was here that New Liberal ideas and policies took root after 1900. By contrast, Liberals in those areas (particularly the Potteries and the Notts/Derby area) where economic prosperity was dependent on a single, generally factory-based, industry, were traditionally more conservative. After 1906, these Liberals appeared to be more susceptible to a Centrist Liberalism (Section II).

There was a parallel variation in Labour's actions and political image (Section III), and for broadly similar reasons. The popularity of 'Liberal' issues, and the failure of the left to provide an attractive alternative to these ideas, made it difficult for Labour to construct an image which

---

[4] For the anti-Liberal swing in 1910, Blewett, *Peers*, p. 400. The figures cited are based on my analysis of the 1910 election, using Blewett's constituency classification. If Scotland were included, the Liberal 'rural' bloc would be larger still. For Labour's concentration on rural seats in the inter-war years, McKibbin, *Evolution*, p. 151.

was markedly dissimilar from that of the Liberal party. Labour generally replicated the bulk of the Liberals' proposals, while adding support and sympathy for groups seeking to increase their living standards through state or municipal action. However, many of Labour's Statist proposals were either also supported by radical Liberals, or were opposed on the grounds that local economic prosperity would be undermined if they were implemented. This Centrist argument carried great weight, particularly where the electorate was entirely or largely dependent on a single local employer. Where skills were not easily transferable, or when horizons were limited by some other factor, change was not easily contemplated. Whichever way Labour turned, it was half-checked. The Liberals even seemed able to retain substantial support amongst those groups – like the railwaymen and miners – who were Labour's major supporters elsewhere. Labour developed a core of support in a number of seats, but not enough to solve its broader electoral problem. It only made considerable progress where Liberal conservatism created an electoral opening.

The less industrial seats were not untouched by the radicalising tendencies in Edwardian Liberal politics, or by changes in the major urban centres (Section IV). The thrust of Liberal policy was toward the reintegration of rural and urban politics through land reform. In those areas where the Liberal party remained popular in 1910, the land campaign of 1912–14 served to reinforce Liberal allegiances and give the party legitimate hope of regaining some lost ground. Labour did not threaten this position. In rural areas it was not a threat; its role, from the Liberals' viewpoint, was minor but positive. It generally co-operated with the Liberals, made what gains in representation and support it could, and worked for the time when circumstances were more favourable. In 1914–15, despite the enthusiasm of some Socialists, Labour accepted the reality of its position (Section V). Extensive Liberal/Labour conflict seemed unlikely because Labour was still ideologically and politically contained. Far from disappearing beneath the weight of 'Northern' policies, the Liberal party in England and Wales was still a powerful electoral force in many industrial *and* rural constituencies.

I

The scattered and variable nature of urban settlements in the Midlands and southern England ensured that Edwardian Liberals inevitably built on a variety of political traditions. It is nonetheless possible to determine two kinds of Liberal politics in the South, each reflecting different economic and political starting points. The craft economy and Radical tradition was particularly strong in the East Midlands and East Anglia. In Northamptonshire, for example, the Liberal party of the 1880s had its roots in the independent attitudes and views of the largely Nonconformist agricultural and industrial workers and the professional and lower middle classes. Lincoln, Leicester, many other East Anglian towns, and several urban seats in the South (most notably Bristol and Bath) had similar popular Radical traditions. Industrial production was frequently based around a range of light industries, with consumer goods of different kinds being the major element. With a few exceptions, such as Northampton, large factories and a single dominant industry were abnormal.[5]

Liberal political attitudes, and the economic structure which helped sustain them, were rather different in the more heavily unionised towns on the fringes of the East Midlands coalfields (such as Nottingham and Derby) and in the Staffordshire industrial constituencies by 1906. Large-scale manufacture was more common, and major paternalistic employers, like Brunner, Brocklehurst, and Pearce in Cheshire, became MPs for the seats which their employees dominated. They drew in part on the New Liberal ideas and influences which (from their association with Manchester Liberalism) they knew very well. At the same time, however, these and other major local Liberal employers were in essence Centrist paternalists. The concern which they showed for their own workforces and their support for material and social legislation enhanced the economic bond which, they insisted, linked management and workforce. In these areas, relations between Liberals and trade unionists were good – in Nottingham the Liberals' association with the Trades Council was so close that it became notorious.[6] Derby, Stoke, and Hanley, like the nearby coalfields, all had Lib/Lab MPs. A Centrist Liberalism was strongly established.

Given competition from the left, Liberals had to restake their claim to be the major working-class party. However, if the Liberals competed with Labour too forcibly, and opposed all labour representation, they might undermine the claim that they were also labour's friend and ally. If the need to constantly reaffirm the validity of Liberal policies and principles degenerated into an anti-Socialist crusade, the whole strategy of containment would fall apart. The Liberals needed to hold their ground,

[5] J. Howarth, 'The Liberal revival in Northamptonshire', HJ (1969), p. 107; J. W. F. Hill, Victorian Lincoln (Cambridge, 1974), pp. 236–40; M. Elliott, Victorian Leicester (Chichester, 1979), pp. 161–7; H. Spender, The fire of life (1924), p. 210; S. Koss, Nonconformity in modern British politics (1975), pp. 17–18. Northampton had a long tradition of working-class activism. See R. Harrison, Before the Socialists (1965), pp. 179–81, 204.
[6] It was ranked alongside Sheffield and Birmingham as a stronghold of Lib/Lab politics. See comments in J.R.M. to J. Adderley, 25 June 1906, LP GC 5/2 and also W. A. Appleton to J.R.M., 3 Dec. 1902, LRC 6/3.

and concede from strength, if they were to maintain their dominant position in the Progressive Alliance.

The press played an important part in updating the Liberals' image. By the Edwardian period most major southern towns and cities had a Liberal newspaper with a radical tradition. However, some had abandoned their radical past (like the *Leicester Daily Post*) and some more recent additions, like the *Lincolnshire Chronicle*, became a thorn in the flesh of radical Liberal parties. Nonetheless, papers like the *Northamptonshire Daily Echo* and *Northampton Mercury*, the *Leicester Daily Mercury* and the *Staffordshire Sentinel*, remained (to differing extents) true to their roots and evolved into solidly Progressive forces. Moreover, even newspapers which were sceptical about radical policies had to cover the national party's major policy statements; editorial opinion was not in its own right that significant.[7]

Liberals did not rely on local newspapers to project their views. Public meetings, municipal campaigns, and the distribution of pertinent literature, were not the preserve of northern Liberals. Centrally produced leaflets were widely distributed, but Liberal parties in Derby, West Bristol, and probably other urban centres produced localised supplements to the populistic *Liberal Monthly* which reflected local versions of a 'national' platform.[8] Because municipal, parliamentary, and registration campaigns also required the attention of party workers, only a strong, well-supported, organisation could fulfil its task of maintaining Liberal support.

The Liberals were not always equal to the organisational task in the 1890s, and in some areas the Edwardian period did not witness a full recovery. In East Nottingham, for example, the Liberals found it difficult to obtain workers, or to put municipal candidates into the field, after 1910. They won a fortunate 'Free Trade' victory in 1906, but, on the Liberals' own admission, tariff reform was becoming progressively stronger as local industries faced tougher international competition. The Liberals lost in 1910, and had problems finding a new candidate.[9] The eventual replacement, and his successor for the 1912 by-election, were ineffective party hacks. Liberal support disintegrated. The specific problem in 1912 was made worse by the party's national slump, by an ill-prepared register, the failure to trace removals, and Labour abstentions.

[7] A. J. Lee, *The origins of the popular press 1885–1914* (1976), Chapter 5 for the general position.

[8] Derby LA ann. meeting report, *Derby Reporter*, 27 Feb. 1914. This tactic was more widely adopted in rural areas, for which see below, p. 309.

[9] *Nottingham Daily Express*, 2 Nov. 1907, 3 Nov. 1908, 2 Nov. 1909, Wyncoll, *Nottingham*, pp. 155, 158–9. The threatened industries were lacemaking and hosiery, particularly the former.

However, at the root of the problem was the failure to counter a Tory challenge which undermined the economic basis of a Liberal political culture. However, if there was a vacuum on the left in East Nottingham because the Liberals had failed, there were organisational problems in Hanley and Stoke (and to an extent in Leek) because the Liberals had succeeded to such an extent that there seemed little need for formal organisation. The Lib/Lab trade unions did what political work seemed necessary.[10]

II

Despite the openness of the local Liberal elite in areas where there were few major Liberal employers or magnates, there were still some potential institutional obstacles to the spread of radical Liberal ideas. In seats like Leicester and Ipswich, a conservative party oligarchy dominated executive decisions. Years of neglect also meant that some Liberal parties had become financially dependent on a few wealthy subscribers. This could reinforce the influence of the wealthy in constituency affairs. (We should not assume that this was *necessarily* an obstacle to the passage of radical ideas; wealth and radicalism could co-exist.) In Leicester the position became 'serious', on the Liberals' own admission, in 1910. Half of the party's income from subscriptions (c £300) came from the sitting MP. Lincoln's Charles Roberts supplied an even larger percentage of his party's annual income. There were also large donations from members of the Liberal executive in Leicester, and medium-sized donations from the chairman and secretary in Lincoln.[11] Nonetheless, most parties were expanding their membership, both to tackle financial problems and to improve fighting efficiency. In the East Northamptonshire constituency, ward and village organisations were formed specifically to facilitate democratic involvement. Leicester, a large double member borough, had fewer than 200 paying members in 1909, but more than 420 by 1912. Lincoln's membership increased from a higher base of 290 in 1911 to a fairly stable 360–70 by 1914. Northampton had developed ward groups with more than 200 members, and a total membership of several thousand.[12] Derby's ward associations commonly had more than seventy-five

[10] R. H. Davies to C.P.S., 4 May 1912, CPS 332/107; *Lib. Agent*, Oct. 1912. For the Lib/Lab Leek textile unions, J. Sweeney and F. Burchill, *A history of trade unionism in the North Staffordshire textile industry* (Keele, 1971).

[11] C. Beck to C. F. G. Masterman, 20 May 1914, LG C/5/15/5, *Lib. Agent*, July 1914; Leicester LA ARs 1908–12; Lincoln LA Mins, 6 Jan., 21 Oct. 1911, 25 Mar., 3 Apr. 1913. In 1914 Roberts contributed £180 of £280 income (Lincoln LA Subscription Book).

[12] *Kettering Leader*, 17, 26 June 1914; *Northampton Echo*, 20 Jan. 1912. Lincoln and Leicester LA figures derived from the subscription books and annual reports.

active supporters; the Crewe Liberals boasted 700 paying members. Significantly, these seats had far more members than conservative Leicester, which was twice their size.[13]

The Liberals also took to heart the organisation of women and the young. Again Northampton led the way with a 100 strong (and particularly active) Women's Liberal Association, and a 600 strong Young Progressives' League. There were active and growing branches of these organisations in most constituencies by 1914. They did not generally appear to have provided a substantial proportion of constituency income through subscriptions, but their fund-raising activities were a significant factor in making Liberal associations more financially self-sufficient and less dependent on possibly conservative 'benefactors'.[14]

As in other areas, changes in party membership contributed to the institutional recognition of the rank and file's importance. In Lincoln, where the Liberal party was particularly radical, the Divisional executive (roughly twenty strong) was extended to include representatives from the Young Liberals, the WLA, and the Liberal Club. Town Councillors were co-opted. Less is known about equally radical Northampton, but it is clear that the WLA was not just a fund-raising body, and that it took an active part in local political decisions.[15] Even in Leicester, where the local Liberal party was only reluctantly converted to seeking a broader membership, half the Liberal Councillors were already from the professional, artisan, and labouring classes in 1906. Many of the party's new subscribers paid the minimum subscription of 1s od per annum. Even here, membership, and power, was being diluted. In Lincoln, where the decision to seek more small subscribers was made on ideological as well as financial grounds, small subscribers (1s–5s) made up 80 per cent of the party membership. Most members of the Liberal executive did not contribute large amounts to party funds. They were largely tradesmen, retailers, artisans, and professionals.[16]

There is some indication that municipal programmes in the East Midlands and East Anglia began to change as a result, in part, of the upward

[13] *Crewe Chronicle*, 14 Feb., 21 Mar., 23 May 1914; *Derby Rep.*, 13, 20 Feb. 1914.
[14] *Northampton Echo*, 23, 31 Jan., 11–13 Feb. 1912; *Crewe Chron.*, 25 Jan., 31 Mar. 1913. The Leicester Liberal bazaar raised £700 in 1910, a small total in a seat of this size (Leicester LA *AR* 1911). However, the Bedford LA was self-sufficient by 1912, following major efforts to revive party organisation in the area. See esp. H. S. Stanhope to W. Crook, 22 Dec. 1912, F. Kellaway and R. C. Lehmann to Crook, 19 Nov., 3 Dec. 1911, Crook MS Eng. Hist. d. 389 fos. 146–7, 89–91.
[15] Lincoln LA Mins, esp. 19 Oct. 1910, 15 June 1914; *Northampt. Echo*, 12–13 Mar. 1912.
[16] Bernstein, *Liberal politics*, p. 24. The analysis in Elliott, *Leicester*, pp. 162–3 suggests further change by 1914. For Lincoln, Lincoln LA Mins, 3 Apr. 1913, 27 Jan. 1914, 8 Apr. 1915.

filtration of opinion. Liberal municipal programmes were not very innovative, but neither, except in Leicester and Bristol, were they particularly
backward. The Norwich programme was fairly typical. It included municipalisation of the gas and water supply, improved municipal housing,
trade union conditions and fair wages contracts in areas within the Council's jurisdiction, free undenominational education, and a reduction of
municipal borrowing. 'Extreme radicals', usually professionals and
tradesmen, had changed Lincoln's municipal policies, along similar lines,
during the 1890s, although the limited size of the rateable base, and
the extent of support for mutual self-provision, minimised demands for
greater municipal intervention. Nonetheless, by 1914 many Liberal radicals wished to go further than programmes of this kind allowed. The
Norwich Liberal Councillor, Herbert Day, was a good example. Day,
formerly of Toynbee Hall, was a supporter of the Agricultural Labourers'
Union and an advocate of many 'Labour' reforms. He supported municipal provision of meals for school children and shorter hours of work
for Council employees with no loss of pay. However small the threat,
there were good political reasons why policies like this should be accepted
by his less committed but pragmatic colleagues if power and success were
to be retained.[17]

If shifts in the nature of politics were evident, they were not uncontested. The Bristol Liberals were extreme conservatives. Sir Charles Hobhouse, the East Bristol MP, was one of the most vehement Cabinet critics
of Lloyd George's policy and strategy. Coups by local radicals in seats
like Lincoln were easy because moderately wealthy radical Liberals had
few rivals of equal social and financial standing, and because moderate
Liberals had nothing to lose, given past failures. The MP, Charles
Roberts, had already led one constituency revolt in Yorkshire; his financial contribution, and ability to merge 'old' and 'new' issues, were to
be important in convincing some of the more doubtful Liberal voters
that the party was still an acceptable political medium. However, the
Old Liberals could put up a better institutional resistance in seats where
they were wealthier and more established in positions of power.

Leicester supplies the best example of Old Liberal resistance, and of
its electorally damaging repercussions. Whatever the position on the
Liberal Town Council, the constituency Liberal executive was dominated
by Wesleyan businessmen whose radicalism had waned with time. In
1903, the Progressives, led by Edward Wood, a businessman and the
major contributor to party funds, suggested that the party should put

---

[17] Bernstein, 'Liberalism and the Progressive Alliance', pp. 619–20, Howkins, *Norfolk*,
p. 88; Hill, *Lincoln*, pp. 238–40.

forward only one parliamentary candidate at the next election and allow Labour to find the other. Sir Israel Hart, a prominent Liberal conservative, led a rebellion. The anti-Progressives were outvoted, presumably because the pragmatists and party loyalists saw the electoral need, and the Whips' desire, for a pact. However, they bounced back after the 1906 election. Labour's refusal to refrain from anti-Liberal municipal campaigns caused considerable discontent. Even the Progressive *Leicester Daily Mercury* reluctantly agreed that Liberals could not continually back down from the ILP's assaults and concede seat after seat. The party had to preserve its position, even if this meant fighting Labour municipal candidates.[18]

The Leicester Liberals' desire to maintain their ascendancy gained support from across the Liberal spectrum. Progressives knew that they had to dominate the policy debate and make concessions to Labour from a position of strength. The party as a whole agreed to respond by more actively propagating an assertive Liberal gospel. This failed to materialise, in part because the Old Liberals were too conservative, and too powerful, to allow the radicals a say on policy. By 1909, after a brief flurry of activity, the Liberal association resorted to a sterile anti-Socialism and a municipal alliance with the Tories. Some conservative Liberals even wished to adopt a second Liberal parliamentary candidate.[19] There were parallel debates and divisions in other former Radical strongholds, although only Bristol of the major cities had a sufficiently conservative Liberal party, and a sufficiently radical and threatening Labour/Socialist opposition, to create the grounds for conflict.[20]

Liberal anti-Socialists were not allowed to dominate constituency politics. They were attacked even in Leicester and Bristol. In the latter, local radicals received little help from the press, or from the Frys (who unlike their Quaker cousins, the Rowntrees and Cadburys, were not radical patrons) or from their MPs. In Leicester, by contrast, several Liberal ward committees, the *Daily Mercury*, and prominent individual Progressives argued that a municipal alliance with the Tories would polarise politics and allow Labour to absorb yet more of the radical ground. Their analysis was underlined when Liberal defeats at the 1909 municipal elections showed that, for the Liberal party, 'anti-Socialism' lacked electoral

---

[18] *Leicester Daily Mercury*, 3 Nov. 1908, Leics LA Mins, e.g. 9 Apr. 1907. For the selection question, Marquand, *MacDonald*, pp. 81–2.

[19] Leics. LA Mins, 5 Mar. 1907, 8 Feb. 1909 and *AR* 1909.

[20] For problems in Norwich, Bernstein, 'Liberalism and the Progressive Alliance', pp. 620–1, and for Bristol, F. Freeman to J.R.M., 27 Dec. 1910, LP/AFF 5/29: 'In Bristol we are meeting with the determined opposition of the Liberal party. They fight us upon every occasion. In fact, they have expressed themselves as going to wipe us out.' For other areas, see below, pp. 303–4, 312.

purchase.[21] However, if the party was divided, the Old Liberals still dominated the major positions of influence in the constituency. They made it difficult for young aspiring radicals to become the constituency's parliamentary candidate, for example by asking them to contribute at least £200 per year to constituency funds. They eventually adopted the wealthy and pragmatic Young Liberal, Eliott Crawshay-Williams, who angrily and wisely crusaded in favour of Old Liberal licensing reform and New Liberal nationalisation of the railways at the 1910 election.[22] The local MPs, E. Hilton Young and C. M. McCurdy, effected a similar compromise. It was only in Bristol that Hobhouse and his colleagues were able to push Old Liberal issues to the fore.[23]

Most Liberal candidates in the East Midlands and East Anglia backed the radical interpretation of the 1909–10 Liberal programme. The future Labour MPs, H. B. Lees-Smith and L. C. Money (Northampton and East Northants), like Silvester Horne (Ipswich), Herbert Paul (Northampton), and Charles Roberts (Lincoln) were amongst the more prominent Lloyd Georgites. After 1910, they backed policies such as limited nationalisation, land reform, and in some cases a national minimum wage. Some local parties were clearly sympathetic. The Lincoln Liberal executive, for example, declined the offer of speakers for a Welsh Disestablishment campaign in 1912.[24] They supported an ethical (Nonconformist) radicalism which attacked social and economic 'immoralities'; sectarian issues seemed less significant than they had in the past. Moreover, the dominant industries – boot and shoe production, light engineering, clothing, and food processing – were linked to consumer demand, and not to state regulation; and in some areas demand was buoyant.[25] Liberal policies were individually meaningful. They expressed a long-standing hostility to the local establishment. It was supported (in some areas)

---

[21] *Leics. Merc.*, 3 Nov. 1908, 2 Nov. 1909, Elliott, *Leicester*, p. 163; H. E. Meller, *Leisure and the changing city, 1870–1914* (1976), pp. 123, 192–203.

[22] M. Levy (Loughborough MP) to C.P.T., 15 Jan. 1909, CPT 23 (the proposed radical candidate was a friend of Trevelyan's); *Leics. Merc.*, 9 Dec. 1909 and *Lib. Agent*, Oct. 1913. Crawshay-Williams later resigned his seat, marking his departure with a swipe against the Nonconformist conscience, which he had claimed to represent in 1910 (Crawshay-Williams, *Simple Story*, pp. 135–6).

[23] Bristol also claimed Augustine Birrell and Sir W. H. Davies as MPs. For their views during the campaign, and the emphasis (understandable in Birrell's case) on Ireland and education, *Western Daily Press*, 15, 18 Dec. 1909.

[24] Lincoln LA Mins, 12 Apr. 1912.

[25] Pelling, *Social geography*, pp. 88, 204–5. The boot and shoe workers in booming Northampton were doing particularly well. Bristol had a craft tradition through its boot and shoe workers, but its occupational structure was now more varied because of its position as a port, and the presence of a few large firms. It also suffered from fairly high unemployment and low wages. For low wages and extensive poverty in the southern towns of Reading and Oxford, A. L. Bowley and A. R. Burnett-Hurst, *Livelihood and poverty* (1915), Whiting, *Cowley*, Chapter 1.

by the satisfaction born of economic success. This was a good position to be in.

In the Notts/Derby area, and in the Staffordshire/Cheshire industrial belt, and in some other towns, the economic structure, and the political traditions, were rather different. A few factories or plants dominated whole constituencies. Railway works dominated Crewe, for example, while large silk, pottery, and chemical works dominated other Cheshire constituencies. The biscuit and brewing works of Palmer and Simmons were very important in Reading; the railway sheds were the economic mainstay of Peterborough; railway works dominated Swindon and Derby; the Colleges dominated Oxford and Cambridge. Despite the fact that in some seats (particularly the Potteries) the electorate was occupationally homogeneous, physically concentrated in a small area, and held together by family relationships (factors which traditionally are seen as conducive to class solidarity), there was little social cohesion or united class action. Precariously insecure 'craft' elements worked alongside their semi-skilled potential replacements in the factories. Few 'skilled' workers had the ability to move to other (often non-existent) forms of employment. This encouraged a dependence on individual employers, and on economic and individual improvement through the actions of trade unions and friendly societies as means of achieving prosperity and security. This hardly encouraged a sense of unity with the (numerous) less skilled workers, even where the latter were not an economic 'threat'.[26] Liberal support had often evolved from an economic attachment to paternalistic employers and their views, from a general level of prosperity, and from a belief in progress through non-political action. On the other hand, Liberal associations sometimes had to cope with the hold which Tory employers had over their workforce (the position in towns like Crewe, Swindon, and Derby), and here Liberalism became part of a fight for sane progress and 'independence'. The result was a Centrist Liberalism, more attuned to the interests of labour as an industrial force, and to the general need for industrial prosperity, than to notions of moral reform and social unity.

Liberal municipal policy in these areas often involved the provision of services by the municipality (better this than the employers), and demands which reflected the ('sane') interests of local unions. In

[26] See Sweeney and Burchill, *Staffs. textile industry*, p. 79; W. H. Chaloner, *The social and economic development of Crewe* (Manchester, 1950), esp. pp. 153–66; R. Whipp, 'Women and the social origins of work in the Staffordshire pottery industry', *Midland Hist.* (1987), pp. 105–9, W. H. Warburton, *The history of trade union organisation in the North Staffordshire potteries* (1939), pp. 213–16; Whiting, *Cowley*, pp. 11–13. For Cheshire, B. Didsbury, 'Cheshire saltworkers', in R. Samuel (ed.), *Miners, quarrymen and saltworkers* (1977), pp. 83–4.

Nottingham, for example, all Liberal municipal candidates in 1910 supported the introduction of a minimum wage for Council workmen (the
same proposal was put forward by Labour). In Crewe, the radical Councillors Williams, Manning, and Hodgkinson, worked hard to undermine
the idea that the prosperity and social needs of Crewe railwaymen were
best represented and ensured by local railway directors.[27]
  Parliamentary Liberalism was also overwhelmingly Centrist. The
Liberal MPs for many Staffordshire/Cheshire seats – including Brunner
(Northwich), Brocklehurst (Macclesfield), and Pearce (Leek) – were major
local employers. They were able to accept limited nationalisation, the
redistribution of wealth, and minimum wages. In the East Midlands,
men like J. H. Yoxall, the West Nottingham MP and a member of the
NUT, were equally strong on 'labour' issues. Professional politicians,
like the Prime Minister's son, Raymond Asquith (Derby's candidate by
1914), adapted to their surroundings. Asquith's measured radicalism, his
careful cultivation of the railwaymen's leader, J. H. Thomas, and his
support for railwaymen's interests, made him an ideal candidate for the
seat. The NUR here, and in other local seats, was more firmly Progressive
than it was elsewhere. Local Liberals had a more protective image than
the Liberal parties in seats like Lincoln and Northampton and one more
founded on 'economic' than on 'social' politics. They were none the
weaker for that.[28]
  Nonetheless, New Liberals were beginning to appear as parliamentary
candidates, and to lend their weight to the creation of an attractive political image. J. Wedgwood (Newcastle-under-Lyne) and R. L. Outhwaite
(Hanley), often supported by Frances Neilson (a political ally, whose
Hyde constituency was economically more a part of the North-West)
were genuine land reformers. Wedgwood frequently chafed at Labour's
moderation. Although he was regarded as a crank in his own party,
the local ILP respected his radicalism, and the *Daily Herald*'s fearsomely
critical correspondents clasped him to their collective bosom as a fellow

[27] Chaloner, *Crewe*, pp. 218–19, J. M. Lee, *Social leaders and public persons* (Oxford,
  1963), p. 64; Wyncoll, *Nottingham*, p. 154. In Reading, a more mixed seat without
  a threatening Labour movement, Liberal municipal policy was less advanced. Nonetheless, it was changing (A. Alexander, *Borough government and politics: Reading
  1835–1985* (1985), pp. 193, 195–6).
[28] J. Jolliffe, *Raymond Asquith* (1980), p. 178; White (thesis), p. 33; S. Koss, *Sir John
  Brunner: radical plutocrat* (Cambridge, 1970), pp. 206, 256. See also W. H. Hackett
  (Peterborough T&LC) to J.R.M., 17 Dec. 1902, LRC 6/315, supporting G. G. Greenwood, the Progressive MP who was 'entirely with us'. For Yoxall's politics, Emy, *Liberals
  and social politics*, p. 279 fn. 156 and Wyncoll, *Nottingham*, p. 120. In 1914, H. W.
  Moxan, a radical Liberal supporter of nationalising the mines and the railways, was
  selected in West Derbyshire with the full support of the railwaymen (*Daily News*, 25
  May 1914).

rebel. Candidates in the university cities were also seldom Centrists. They had to cater for a mixed audience of academics, university staff, and the (small) organised working-class groups. H. H. Spender (the Cambridge candidate by 1914) found this difficult, but his attempt revolved around New Liberal ideas and a (politically) healthy respect for a (Non-conformist) moral rhetoric.[29]

Although there was some Liberal/Labour conflict in parliamentary by-elections, Progressive co-operation was still a very real feature of local politics. In some areas there were still Lib/Lab municipal candidates even in 1914. More frequently this had given way to union-supported Labour candidates acting in tacit alliance with the Liberals. Concessions of seats to municipal Labour (although not generally Socialist) candidates were common in towns such as Nottingham and Reading.[30] Through judicious combinations of union support, 'Labour' concessions, 'sane' reform, and a new radicalism, the Liberal party was able to present a powerful front to a sympathetic electorate.

III

There was little electoral space for Labour to exploit in the former Radical strongholds. The Liberals had so modernised their image that in general a moderate 'Labour' moral reformism was insufficiently distinctive. An appeal to union solidarity, and the exploitation of a shared occupational language and interest sometimes worked in South Wales mining constituencies (although even here only partially). It was less feasible in the Midlands coalfields and could hardly work in the surrounding non-mining seats, where a diverse economy and fragmented electorate created a plethora of interests and outlooks. Socialist proposals were no solution. It was not easy to establish the credibility and feasibility of proposals which involved fundamental changes in the social and economic structure, especially where capitalism was successfully producing a degree of affluence or security, and Liberals were supporting reforms which would reinforce its beneficial effects. Socialism involved changes which went further than local experience deemed practical; it also (critics argued)

---

[29] H. H Spender to J.R.M., 3 Mar. 1913, JRM PRO 30/69/1157 and his *Fire of life*, Chapter 14. For the traditional Liberal view of Wedgwood and his allies, *Staffordshire Sentinel*, 12 Mar. 1914 and Lord Liverpool to Crewe, 10 July 1912, Crewe MS C1/31. For Wedgwood's radicalism, Wedgwood to E. Pease, 30 June 1908, Fabian Soc. MS A9/2 fos. 86–7. Wedgwood supported Lansbury at the 1912 by-election in Bow and Bromley, and wrote regularly in the *Herald*. He sustained (for two months) a curious alliance with H. G. Wells, Chesterton and Belloc, which was called the 'freedom league' (C. C. Wedgwood, *The last of the Radicals* (1951), p. 93).

[30] Wyncoll, *Nottingham*, pp. 151–9, Alexander, *Reading*, p. 175. For Liberal wooing of the trade unions, e.g. *Crewe Chron.*, 6 June 1914.

infringed on liberties which were personally, as well as economically, essential. Labour could not beat the Liberals on their own terms, and it could not outflank them either. It was in danger of becoming a party which was snapping at the heels of the Liberal party, and becoming, in addition, the voice of those 'sectional' elements who had an interest in forms of state intervention which were only half-accommodated by the Liberal concern with national 'progress'. However, even this approach was undermined by those ethical and radical socialists who opposed such 'practical' considerations. Labour was only really successful where the Liberals failed to live up to their radical capabilities.

In the East Midlands and East Anglia, as in other parts of the country, the formation of the Labour party in 1900 implied a Socialist accommodation with the trade unions and a willingness to moderate programmes and strategies. This was followed by the classic Progressive concession of seats, notably in the double member boroughs of Norwich and Leicester. It even appeared, in both 1906 and 1910, that one of the Socialist organisations in Northampton would field a parliamentary candidate at the Liberals' request. James Gribble, of the SDF and the Boot and Shoe union, was one possibility in 1910; Bruce Glasier was another.[31]

The basis of Labour politics slowly began to change, as local parties abandoned ethical socialism, and its more radical cousins, in favour of a 'Labour' approach. Some unions sometimes still had Lib/Lab local branches, most significantly the ASRS. These increasingly became more involved with Labour politics. By 1914, the Dockers' union (in the ports of Norwich and Ipswich) and the Co-operative Societies (across much of the East Midlands and East Anglia) were also assuming a larger role.[32] Moreover, the Boot and Shoe union's branch activists in Leicester and Northampton toned down their support for Socialism and became more concerned with material issues (the branches in Norwich and East Northamptonshire and a substantial portion of the national leadership were either already moderate, or were increasingly moving in that direction). In Ipswich by 1913, municipal candidates typically argued for greater Labour representation 'because there are hungry children to be fed, honest men requiring work and respectable families unable to obtain a suitable home in which to live'. The formation of Labour organisations in Ipswich

---

[31] The national SDF foiled this plan by insisting that their leader, Harry Quelch, should be the candidate. For these convoluted events, *Northampt. Daily Echo*, 5–7 Dec. 1909, J.B.G. Diary, 6 Dec. 1909, W. Rogers to J.R.M., 9 Dec. 1908, JRM PRO 30/69/1150, F.J. to P.S., 6 Oct. 1908, J. F. Harris to F.J., 4 Dec. 1909, FJ 08/392, 09/585.

[32] Ipswich LRC *AR* 1916 and *New Times*, Nov. 1913; meeting of Wellingborough LP, and selection of R. J. Davies of the Co-operative Society as parliamentary candidate, *Northampt. Daily Echo*, 16 Jan. 1912 and *Kettering Leader*, 8 May 1914; *New Times*, Nov. 1913.

(1908) and Northampton (1914) reflected this perceived need for Socialists and trade unions to co-operate and establish 'practical' programmes. Moderates in East Northampton, led by the railwaymen and Co-operative workers, were moving in the same direction.[33]

At the municipal level this merger of interests could be reflected in the adoption of a very circumscribed electoral strategy. After a series of defeats at the 1907 municipal elections in Norwich, the ILP dropped its wide-ranging assault on the Liberal party, and temporarily shelved its hopes of an ILP/SDF/Trades Council compact. Three wards – all dominated by skilled artisans – were chosen and worked with care. Nonetheless, many Norwich Socialists were unhappy with this approach. Similarly, in Ipswich, the ILP's involvement in the construction of a practical moral reformist approach was grudging and resentful. The branch leaders had little respect for the 'interests' of trade unions and Co-operative societies, and still less for the strategy of municipal concentration.[34] Municipal campaigns were thus only occasionally limited; more often, in Ipswich, as in Northampton, East Northamptonshire, Lincoln, and Bristol, they were as extensive as finances permitted. There was even a strong educationalist under-current in Norwich, which always threatened to provide the basis for an alternative ideological/strategic approach.[35] Even weak or newly formed Labour and Socialist organisations in Bedford, Grantham, and Colchester were unwilling to compromise with radical local Liberals, despite their poor independent position and offers of co-operation.[36]

The most successful Labour organisations, in Leicester and Bristol, were based on large ILP branches. The LRC in each case was simply a channel for union funds. The Bristol ILP had 600 members, the bulk of them in the East Bristol seat; the Leicester ILP had over 1,000, twice as many as the Liberals. The Leicester ILP engaged in a broader municipal campaign and had its own newspaper, the *Leicester Pioneer*. The Bristol

[33] Norwich TC Mins, esp. 31 Jan.–2 Sept. 1907. For the Boot and Shoe workers' apathy in Norwich, F. Whitemore, 'The Labour party, municipal politics and municipal elections in Norwich, 1903–33', Conference paper, University of East Anglia 1986. For Cambridge, Camb. LP Mins, 2 July 1913, Camb. ILP Mins, 13 Feb. 1912. The complexities of NUBSO executive politics are discussed admirably in Howell, *ILP*, pp. 94–108.

[34] Ipswich ILP *AR*, 1906, 1909, F. J. Ellis to A.P., 14 Nov. 1908, LP/EL/08/1/85; R. Jackson to F.J., 3 Nov. 1909, FJ 09/483.

[35] *New Times*, Nov., Dec. 1913, Jan. 1914. See also Whitemore, 'Norwich' and *New Times*, Jan. 1914 for continuing Socialist sympathies.

[36] D. A. Jones to A.P., 8 Nov. 1908, LP/EL/08/1/9; J. Bennett to F.J., 19 Oct. 1914, FJ 1914/352.

LRC also produced an election news sheet, although it tried, and failed, to make it into a permanent weekly.[37]

In both these cities, Labour's electoral strength was concentrated in a handful of wards, which were also spread over several constituencies. The parliamentary results were not poor, but they were not very encouraging. In Leicester, MacDonald polled 20 per cent of the vote in the three-cornered parliamentary contest in 1900.[38] In 1913, with E. R. Hartley as the BSP candidate, the 'Labour' vote was halved, although the lack of official sanction was important here. Similarly, in January 1910, the East Bristol Labour candidate had managed just 17 per cent of the vote. This was substantially behind the victorious, and very conservative, Liberal, Charles Hobhouse.[39] Nonetheless, both parties were stronger than this would suggest, and stronger than Labour organisations elsewhere. In Leicester, Labour elected Councillors in a number of wards following the Liberal/Tory municipal pact in 1909, whilst in East Bristol it gained seats steadily after 1910.[40] What made Labour's 'success' in these seats so different from Labour success elsewhere was that a core of electoral support in a few wards was supplemented by a *broader* sympathy in at least some other parts of the constituency. The Liberals' parliamentary position was far less secure.

Labour organisations in Leicester and Bristol did not have unique approaches. The Bristol ILP leader, W. H. Ayles, echoed Jowett's support for a decentralised municipal Socialism, but this did not dominate campaigns.[41] The crucial factor in party success was the Liberals' conservatism, and in Bristol a level of unemployment which cast doubt on the viability of Liberal economics as a solution for people's material needs. National politics had saved the Liberals in Bristol from greater embarrassment in 1910. Labour's advance at the municipal level, if measured in terms of seats, was still restricted to a few strongholds and to times of Liberal weakness, but in both towns (and especially in Bristol) Labour

---

[37] For Leicester, D. Cox, 'The Labour party in Leicester', *IRSH* (1961), pp. 200–1 and the NAC constituency report included with E. P. Wake to J.R.M., 25 July 1914, JRM PRO 30/69/1158. The Bristol figures are from D. Parker, 'A proper joiner. Marge Evans – memories of the Bristol Labour movement', in Bristol Broadsides, *Placards and pin-money* (Bristol, 1986), p. 5, although I have relied more fully on S. Bryther, *An account of the Socialist movement in Bristol* (Bristol, 1929) for the local position.

[38] Howell, *ILP*, pp. 236–7.

[39] For the by-election, above, p. 74. Labour only regularly fought six of the Leicester constituency's eleven wards. Only four were strongly Labour.

[40] See comments on the 1909 results, *Leics. Daily Merc.*, 2 Nov. 1909. Some Leicester Labour Councillors were returned for wards such as Aylestone and Belgrave, which they could not capture even in the 1920s, because of local Progressive co-operation.

[41] Coverage of the 1910 election, esp. East Bristol Election, *Labour Herald*, Nov. and Dec. 1909, *Western Daily Press*, e.g. 15 Dec. 1909. See also W. H. Ayles, *What a Socialist Town Council should be* (1921).

was a powerful force. They were stronger than the parliamentary results suggested, and could no longer be dismissed as an insignificant force.

The fact that these local Labour parties had achieved some municipal success encouraged them to consider parliamentary expansion. In Leicester, LRC delegates voted 67–8 in favour of an official Labour campaign when the Liberal MP retired in 1913, even though this was very likely to disrupt the Progressive compact which 'gave' Labour and the Liberals one seat each. The NEC declined to sanction the contest, but five ILP Councillors and several other activists supported Hartley, the BSP's candidate. This reflected a combination of genuine anger at NEC mismanagement of the whole affair, and genuine 'educationalist' sympathies. A section of the Bristol and Leicester parties had supported Grayson's activities in 1908, and in 1913 the Bristol ILP seriously debated disaffiliating from the Bristol LRC.[42] Older 'Socialist' tendencies were still a part of the party and of its public image.

The Leicester/Bristol parties had not discovered a 'Socialist' solution which other parties could duplicate. Neither had other southern Socialist parties. In Northampton, Gribble and Quelch, the SDP candidates in the 1910 parliamentary election polled just 10 per cent of the vote. In municipal elections, support for 'Socialism' was an acknowledged handicap. SDP municipal candidates in Northampton succeeded in a few wards, but largely by dropping 'Socialist' proposals. In the constituency as a whole, the SDP/ILP forces found it difficult to poll more than 10 per cent of the vote, and were in decline by 1913 (Appendix 4, Table 1.7). The 100 strong Ipswich ILP branch fought elections on a shoe string. In smaller towns, with newer organisations, enthusiasm was high, but organisation and support almost non-existent.[43]

Despite their electoral failure, Socialist-dominated organisations still only reluctantly accepted their inability to convince national leaders that they should fight parliamentary campaigns. In Ipswich, local ILP leaders only accepted the NAC's decision not to field a candidate against Charles Masterman at the 1914 by-election because they hoped to gain support for a contest at the next parliamentary election. Fred Henderson was contemplating standing as a second Labour/Socialist candidate at the 1914/15 election in Norwich, while at the same time ILP branches in Ipswich and Grantham were renewing their attempts to gain NAC sanction for 'educationalist' campaigns in their (Liberal-held) seats.[44] The

[42] Marquand, *MacDonald*, pp. 152–6; C. Thomas in *Placards and pinmoney*, p. 131 and Bristol ILP Mins, 4, 18 Dec. 1912.

[43] W. R. Smith to A.P., 12 Nov. 1908, LP/EL/08/1/124. For the financial position, Ipswich ILP *Balance Sheet* 1913, 1914.

[44] NAC Mins, 14 Apr. 1914 and Parl. Sub-Comm. Mins, 21 Apr. 1914; Bennett to F.J. above, fn. 36, supplying details of poor organisation, finance etc.

only real electoral progress outside Bristol and Leicester stemmed from moderate campaigning on 'practical' lines, especially in areas where Statist elements were concentrated. Even then the Liberals remained in front.[45]

In those southern seats where a more factory-based economy and Centrist Liberalism combined to minimise working-class hostility to the Liberal party, the ILP was in a weak position. Socialist organisations appeared to be reasonably strong in Nottingham and Derby, and in some of the southern seats, but this does not indicate deep commitment to Socialist principles. The ILP contained many who were very moderate; there was often a huge gap between the handful of radical Socialists and the trade unions. The recently identified moderate nature of post-war Labour organisations in these areas was already apparent before 1914. The 'far off theories' of Socialist branches in Reading, or the activities of the Guild Socialists in Oxford and the Fabians in Cambridge, were far less significant in local politics than the support which local Labour officials gave to 'practical' union interests, to attacks on unemployment, and to other solidly materialist issues. It was these practical issues which dominated Labour's appeal. Similarly, in Cheshire, the ILP was a noisy, dissident, but essentially peripheral organisation. It barely existed in Staffordshire; there was no branch at all in Hanley until after the 1912 by-election.[46]

Before 1910, Liberal hegemony in the Potteries was so complete that Labour organisations struggled to overcome the Lib–Lab tradition and to exist as an independent force. The fact that Labour fought Crewe in 1910 does not nullify this conclusion. When the general election was called, many LRC members encouraged their candidate to withdraw and leave the Liberals to fight the seat. However, Rose, the candidate, insisted on standing. The electorate delivered its own verdict. The Liberals were victorious. Rose polled just 10 per cent of the vote, and was defeated by a margin of 43 per cent. The Crewe LRC fell apart.[47] Although Hanley and Crewe were fought by Labour at the 1912 by-elections, the conflicts

---

[45] Labour's merging of co-operative sentiments with support for the specific grievances of railwaymen led to a degree of success in Kettering, part of the East Northants seat (ward by-election reports, *Kettering Leader*, 26 June 1914). However, UDC results, showing a stronger Liberal position in the smaller towns (ibid., 10 Apr. 1914), provided a counter-incentive to adopting a moderate approach.

[46] Morris (thesis), pp. 201, 225–7, *Lib. Agent*, Oct. 1912; Wyncoll, *Nottingham*, Chapter 11 for the nature of Nottingham Labour politics. For Reading, complaints of the Trades Council Secretary, H. Sanderson to A.P., n.d., LP/EL/08/1/133, details of the 'revolutionary Socialist' candidature at the 1913 by-election, *Government Workers' Advocate*, Dec. 1913, Alexander, *Reading*, p. 175. For Oxford and Cambridge, Whiting, *Cowley*, pp. 20–1 and below, p. 303.

[47] See above, Chapter 2. For the 1910 campaign and the LRC's collapse, *Liverpool Forward*, 15 Nov. 1912.

resulted from national strategic interventions, not from local interests or views.

When the formerly Lib–Lab, now Labour, MP for Hanley died in 1912, members of the the Staffordshire Miners' union put forward their General Secretary, S. Finney, as a Lib/Lab parliamentary candidate. A Liberal candidate consequently withdrew. However, certain land reformers, led by Wedgwood, secured the selection of a colleague, R. L. Outhwaite, as Liberal candidate by whisking the constituency's Liberal leaders away to London, where the Whips and Lloyd George convinced them of the need for a campaign. The local former Lib/Lab compact fell apart. Finney stood as an official Labour candidate. Some local Liberal officials who were not privy to the 'negotiations' between the Whips and party leaders, including the Secretary of the North Stafford-shire Liberal association, resigned in protest at Outhwaite's adoption. The Lib/Lab MP for North-West Staffordshire, one of the Liberals' 'great friends' in the local miners' union, spoke on Finney's platform. Pearce, the Liberal MP for Leek, sent him a letter of support. In the aftermath of the election, the Rugby Liberals moved a resolution which attacked national intervention. Nonetheless, Outhwaite romped home, with Finney polling a little less than 12 per cent of the vote. Labour's aggressive anti-Liberal campaign, featuring Hardie and Lansbury, submerged Finney's moderation. The result, Middleton reported, was 'a bit too strong for the dear old solid, sturdy, Nonconformist Radicals of the Potteries'. The old bonds held good. Liberal radicalism was still attrac-tive.[48] Labour's Socialism, an imported feature of the campaign, was both unrepresentative of local Labour opinion and an electoral failure.

Labour fought Crewe in retaliation. It polled just 19 per cent of the vote – 'an awfully bad result', as Henderson put it. The substantial Labour vote at the 1911 municipal elections evaporated, just as support built up between 1906 and 1910 had disappeared in the 1910 parliamentary contest[49] (Appendix 4, p. 463). Nonetheless, a 19 per cent poll was just enough for the Tories to win the seat on a minority vote. The Crewe LRC again fell apart. There were no Labour municipal contests in 1913. The Crewe ILP merged with the BSP. The best that the Hanley and Crewe Labour organisations could do in 1914 was to move resolutions

---

[48] J.S.M. to his parents, 13 July 1912, MID 10/54. The preceding section based on Petter, 'Progressive Alliance', pp. 52–4, *Lib. Agent*, Oct. 1912, Wedgwood, *Last of the Radicals*, p. 93 and above, pp. 66–7.

[49] A.H. to J.S.M., 21, 28 July 1912, LP/HEN/08/1/51 and 57.

urging the need for better organisation. The position was no better in other railway towns.[50]

Labour had hit an obstacle. The Liberals were not so conservative that Labour had an opportunity to expand. In Crewe, careful campaigning by Labour railwaymen on railwaymen's interests came up against the fact that workers in the repair yards did not have the same interests as those who worked the 'roads'. The former were both internally fragmented and dependent on a single railway company's prosperity. These skilled workers were not essentially concerned with the same issues as the unskilled and the unemployed. The Liberal record on industrial questions, their broader appeal, their ability to determine the nature of workers' expectations and aims (itself in part related to their position in the labour market), and their ability to smear Labour with Socialist paint, gave them a substantial competitive edge. Where these conditions prevailed, Labour made little headway. In Reading, Labour elected a few Councillors in straight fights; in Oxford it could not even manage that.[51]

Labour's only hope was to concentrate on groups whose interests were not being represented by the Liberals' policies. In East Nottingham, Labour made a small breakthrough. Its success was orchestrated by the ILP organiser, Sam Higenbottom. Under his direction, ILP membership expanded rapidly. The break-through came in a three-cornered contest in 1908 after Higenbottom had concentrated all party attention on this single ward (Manvers). In Cambridge, Labour similarly concentrated on the traditionally Liberal, strongly Nonconformist, but railway-dominated, Romsey Town ward. LRC municipal candidates in Romsey were members of the ILP, but they were also railwaymen and Nonconformists. If they shared elements of a 'practical' moral reformist approach with other nearby towns, they also emphasised railwaymen's specific needs and aims. They too achieved a degree of success, but in both seats 'success' in one ward was matched by failure in the rest of the constituency. In Cambridge, although Labour drew a little money and support from university Fabians, middle-class support was unusual before 1918, while the tradesmen and university workers who were a major part of the electorate were actively hostile.[52] In Nottingham, Labour similarly had only a limited base. It had little constructive to offer beyond support for local municipal intervention to remedy the hardship of unemployment.

---

[50] *Staffs. Sentinel*, 15 Jan., 24 Apr., 9 July 1914; letter, *Crewe Chron.*, 18 Jan. 1913, and subsequent press coverage. For other railway towns, Derby LA ann. meeting report, *Derby Rep.*, 20 Feb. 1914. The ILP had scarcely any members in Swindon (C. R. Palmer to A.P., 9 Nov. 1908, LP/EL/08/1/142, F.J. to J.R.M., 16 Jan. 1918, FJ 1918/17).

[51] Whiting, *Cowley*, pp. 16, 22.

[52] Camb. LP Mins, 5 Aug, 5 Sept. 1913, 1, 14 July 1914.

Labour expanded its municipal campaign, in both seats, but with little success. In Nottingham, the position was made worse by Higenbottom's departure in 1912, and by the Osborne Judgement. A new ILP organiser was appointed, but the branch could not afford to pay his wages, and he moved on. By 1914 the ILP was losing the initiative. The newly formed Labour party came together in the most inauspicious circumstances.[53] A core of support in East Nottingham gave Labour an advantage over the Liberals, because in this Tory stronghold any signs of success were unusual. However, this should not indicate that Labour could rival the Tories in East Nottingham, while in Cambridge Labour's support was so confined that it was not even a strong third force. Its limited, localised, success was not an illustration of how it might smash the Liberals' general ascendancy (For municipal results Appendix 4, pp. 463–4).

IV

Liberal support was not confined to industrial seats in the Midlands and Home Counties. Even in the 1880s and 1890s the potential strength of the Liberal party in the less industrial seats worried a great many Tories.[54] To some extent the Liberals' potential reflected the importance of Nonconformity in county life. Religious sentiments remained stronger than in many urban areas. However, Nonconformity was also often an expression of communal identity, and frequently of a clash of interest between farmers and labourers on the one hand and an Anglican gentry on the other. In Scotland, Wales, and even in the South-West peninsula, Liberals also expressed the 'periphery's' feelings of separation from Westminster.[55] In a few areas, Liberals utilised traditional, although not necessarily deferential, allegiances to locally important rural families such as the Aclands and Luttrells in the South-West, or to industrialists like F. E. Guest in Dorset or Charles Henry in Shropshire.[56] The Liberals also drew support from artisans and tradesmen in the market towns, from voters in isolated industrial communities (like the North Wales Quarrymen), as well as the more conventionally 'industrial' elements.

From the 1890s, however, the growing separation of 'urban' from

[53] G. O. Roberts to J.S.M., 19 Jan. 1914, LP/AFF 7/360, Nottingham TC AR 1914; T. Mackley (new organiser) to his parents, 30 Jan. 1914, Keighley ILP MS. For a slightly more favourable account, Wyncoll, Nottingham, pp. 148–61.

[54] E. H. H. Green, 'Radical Conservatism: the electoral genesis of tariff reform', HJ (1985), pp. 675–6.

[55] Morgan, Wales in British politics, p. 212; H. J. Hanham, Scottish Nationalism (1969), Chapter 4 and pp. 94–6. See esp. M. Jones, 'Y Chwarelwyr: the slate quarrymen of North Wales', in Samuel (ed.), Miners, quarrymen and saltworkers, pp. 129–30, for a skilful reconstruction of the views of one tightly-knit community.

[56] Blewett, Peers, pp. 374–6; G. Howard to W.R., 30 Dec. 1919, WR 177.

'rural' interests made it more difficult to sustain this alliance, and Liberal support in rural areas and market towns slumped.[57] Fair Trade and then Tariff Reform offered economic security to areas hit by foreign competition. The defection of Liberal agriculturalists and major local community leaders meant that the employers' power was cast on the Tories' side. Liberal 'pandering' to Catholic demands for Home Rule and educational independence weakened the party in Devon and Cornwall, where Wesleyan community leaders had become Liberal Unionists as a result.[58] When there was no Liberal press, it was frequently very difficult for the Liberals to communicate with potential supporters. Urban influences might attempt to redress the balance with propaganda campaigns and public meetings, but they were not immune to elite pressure or to the economic attractions of Tariff Reform. Their interests and those of the agricultural community were closely related. Liberal organisation also gradually crumbled.

The 1906 election halted this trend; it did not reverse it. The anti-Liberal swing in the 1910 elections was higher in rural seats than in almost any other type of constituency.[59] The mixed rural/urban seats were not far behind. However, in Scotland, Wales, East Anglia, the East Midlands, and in a band of seats from Gloucestershire through to Cornwall, the Liberals either held seats in 1910 or were in a position to regain them with only a minute turnover of support.

Nonconformity was the social foundation-stone of the Liberals' strength, but Liberals still needed to be materially relevant to the electorate's economic needs. Here Free Trade was not entirely disastrous. Dairying and animal fattening, forms of farming common in areas where the Liberals were strong, were profitable because imported feed was cheap. However, the Liberals' new radical thrust added an extra dimension. Proposals for improving the railway network via nationalisation would benefit farmers whose markets, and options, were reduced by geographical isolation, but land reform was the Liberals' major asset. Once agricultural minimum wages and the building of labourers' cottages became party policy, the Liberals had tangible evidence of their commitment to the economic prosperity of agricultural labourers. However, land reform had a broader appeal. Minimum wages would allow labourers to pay farmers a more economical rent for their cottages. Security of tenure was designed to benefit farmers and labourers at the expense of

[57] Howarth, 'Northamptonshire', p. 112; Howkins, *Norfolk*, Chapters 3–4; Pelling, *Social geography, passim*.

[58] D. W. Bebbington, 'Nonconformity and electoral sociology, 1867–1918', *HJ* (1984); Blewett, *Peers*, pp. 374–5.

[59] Ibid. pp. 400–1.

the territorial landed magnates. Neither was land reform solely a 'rural' policy. It would help those small traders in the market towns who occupied leasehold premises at the expense of the lessee. Land reform expressed the traditional hostility of rural Liberals to the old propertied elite, and to everything for which they stood. Moreover, Liberal policy on old Liberal issues, such as Irish Home Rule and Welsh Disestablishment, were being implemented or altered, or (in their original form) were of declining importance by 1914.[60] The Liberal image was set to improve.

Institutional obstacles, particularly a conservative over-concentration on Old Liberal issues, might still prevent the reconstruction of Liberal politics. Some local Liberal officials, and some Liberal Cabinet Ministers (including the President of the Board of Agriculture), were unenthusiastic about the official emphasis on rural minimum wages. Conservative oligarchies were as potentially powerful here as elsewhere. Moreover, regional Liberal Federations were unlikely to override local conservative oligarchies. They were ineffective or redundant (the case in the Welsh, South-West and Eastern Counties), or convinced that abolishing plural voting was the answer to all their problems (the case in the Midlands). National political opinion was often excluded because there was no Liberal press, or because Liberal rural areas were geographically, socially, and in Wales linguistically, isolated.[61]

However, a local radical renaissance had helped to undermine some of the Liberal conservatives' power. The extension of the franchise in 1884–5 was the catalyst. Larger electorates meant that existing associations had to reform and sub-divide if contact with the electorate was to be maintained. In Lincolnshire, these local Liberal associations became more representative of the newly enfranchised labourer's interests. 'If the divisional associations ... looked to the past', Olney writes, 'the local Liberal movements had their eye on the future.' Isolated evidence suggests a movement towards expanding the party membership, and a movement away from a financial dependence on a few wealthy individuals. By the late Edwardian period, many Liberal associations in the Gloucestershire area, for example, had 250–350 members. The lowering

---

[60] Offer, *Property and politics*, pp. 375–6, 390; Morgan, *Wales in British politics*, pp. 273–4; Hutchison, *Scotland*, pp. 234–7. Voters at the South Bucks by-election in 1914 were 'tired' of Irish Home Rule, and 'desired a settlement of the Irish Question' (*Staffs. Sentinel*, 20 Feb. 1914). The St Ives constituency was in the process of 'deselecting' its MP in 1914 because of his opposition to Home Rule (*Daily News*, 29 May 1914).

[61] For the Liberal Federations, G. K. Nelmes, 'Stuart Rendel and Welsh Liberal political organisation in the late nineteenth century', *Welsh Hist. Rev.* (1979), pp. 484–5, Mid.LF Mins, 12 Jan. 1911, Blewett, *Peers*, p. 279. For middle-class oligarchies, Parry, *Gwynedd*, p. 18; K. O. Morgan, 'Cardiganshire politics: the Liberal ascendancy, 1885–1923', *Ceredigion* (1967), e.g. pp. 328–9. The broader importance of these factors is stressed in Howkins, *Norfolk*, pp. 89–109.

of subscription rates to 1s0d suggests a desire to attract a broader party membership. Liberal organisations became more independent. Municipal candidates (and local Councillors) were increasingly less affluent 'new men', with new ideas. More radical policies were adopted as a result. Moreover, radicals from the towns encouraged the dissemination of new ideas throughout the surrounding areas through journals such as the *Cambrian News*, *Y Genedl Gymreig*, the *Stroud Journal*, and the *Gloucester Journal*. These papers attacked both the conservative policies and the system of oligarchical control adopted by Divisional associations. They supported the formation of agricultural trade unions in the rural areas and local branches of other trade unions in the market towns. In Norfolk, home of the agricultural labourers' union, radical Liberals effectively controlled union policy.[62]

Even in the rural areas of North and West Wales, or in isolated market towns like Exeter, where the Old Liberal ascendancy remained intact, it was not unchallenged. In Wales there was considerable internal conflict over the choice of parliamentary candidates. The conservative Liberal parliamentary candidate for Merioneth in 1900 was selected only after nineteen constituency Vice-Presidents were brought in to support his nomination at the final selection conference. Conflict ensued. The Liberal association had to be dissolved and reformed. Although the radicals lost the selection battle again in 1909–10 (as they did in Cardiganshire and Caernarvonshire) the Old Liberal elite no longer had local parties in their pockets.[63] By 1910, the radicals Ellis W. Davies and E. T. John (aided by Lloyd George to an extent) had been selected as parliamentary candidates in Caernarvonshire and East Denbigh. 'The socialist principle', Davis wrote, 'is now an essential part of our national life and the question that remains is not of principle but of degree.' With Ellis Jones Griffith, the Anglesey MP (and from 1912 the Under Secretary of State, Home Office), they formed a small local radical bloc. In the South-West, Exeter's candidate in 1906, George Kekewich, was more representative of the professionals and traders, who were beginning to influence Exeter Liberalism, than of the older elements. However, the 'old politics' still triumphed ideologically and practically. Kekewich was unable to meet the association's demands for a greater financial contribution to local affairs (he could not engage in 'treating'). He was replaced by a wealthy, conservative, local Whig landowner, who had more respect for Exeter's traditional

[62] R. J. Olney, *Lincolnshire politics* (Oxford, 1973), p. 202; Parry, *Gwynedd*, p. 18 and Morgan, 'Cardiganshire', p. 318; Howe, 'North Gloucestershire', pp. 128, 129, 131 and 'Liberal party organisation in Gloucestershire', for full details of party membership and organisation. See also Howkins, *Norfolk*, e.g. p. 109 and, for a similar position in North Wales, D. A. Pretty, *The rural revolt that failed* (Cardiff, 1989), pp. 49–50.

[63] Morgan, 'Cardiganshire', pp. 326–9; Parry, *Gwynedd*, pp. 18–19.

electoral practices. Nonetheless, the radicals were not permanently defeated even in this very conservative city. By 1914, local working-class Liberals were pushing for the kind of municipal interventionism which was common elsewhere.[64]

Nonetheless, local radicalisation *could* spill over into parliamentary politics. When the radical MP for Stroud in Gloucestershire, for example, retired in 1913, the local party turned not to its most affluent and influential supporter, the local industrialist, R. A. Lister (who was a potential candidate), but to the London radical G. A. Hardy. The candidates in nearby Cheltenham and Gloucester, L. J. Mathias and Morgan Phillips Price (the latter a future Communist journalist and Labour candidate), were local men, but also adamant supporters of the full radical programme of land reform, nationalisation, and minimum wages. They were both known for their practical interest in labour and trade union affairs. Their financial contributions to the local Liberal associations were also a useful means of supplementing constituency fund-raising activity (Phillips Price had an identical role when he was the Gloucester Labour party's parliamentary candidate in the 1920s). In Norfolk, E. G. Hemmerde (the land reformer), Noel Buxton, and E. N. Bennett ('a radical of impeccable qualifications') combined to create a local radical parliamentary alliance.[65]

In many rural areas important elements within the existing Liberal elite supported the radical revival. This included the traditionally Lib/Lab labourers' unions where they were strong, and some radical landowners. George Nicholls, the North Northamptonshire MP between 1906 and 1910, was a former labourer who was still active in the agricultural labourers' union. In Devon and Somerset the Aclands and Luttrells led radical local land campaigns in 1913–14. The 'national' land campaign meetings were also reportedly well-received in rural seats like Tavistock and in towns such as Penryn, Falmouth, and Exeter (where the Tories had a one vote majority).[66] The land campaign of 1913–14 also reached over the heads of unsympathetic local leaders through a massive national publicity drive. Eighty lecturers were employed; they held 90 to 120

---

[64] Morgan, *Wales in British politics*, p. 256, and Parry, *Gwynedd*, p. 39 fn. 2, noting Liberal support for a minimum wage in the slate quarrying industry. See also J. Graham Jones, 'E. T. John and Welsh Home Rule', *Welsh Hist. Rev.* (1987), pp. 455–9. Davies' views cited in Parry, *Gwynedd*, p. 28. For Exeter, R. Newton, *Victorian Exeter* (Leicester, 1968) pp. 287, 290–2, 313.

[65] Howkins' comments on Bennett in *Norfolk*, p. 112; Howe, 'North Gloucestershire', p. 134 and 'Liberal party organisation in Gloucestershire', esp. pp. 117–18, and 133 for details of the MPs financial contributions.

[66] G. Wallace Carter to L.G., 28 May 1914, LG C/2/4/22. O. Brett, Lord Esher's son, and a friend of Trevelyan's, became the Liberal candidate at Tavistock (C.P.T. to his father, 11 July 1914, CPT 220 and O. Brett to L.G. LG C/10/1/71).

meetings each day. Ten million leaflets were distributed. The official land campaign was preceded by a WLF land 'crusade', which involved the distribution of localised supplements to the populistic *Liberal Monthly*. The Young Liberals also held their own campaign, with official approval. The land campaign penetrated the leafiest backwaters.[67]

The Tories were worried. 'Unless our party leaders come out with some bold policy of Land Reform as well as Housing Reform', Jesse Collings noted, 'we shall lose very heavily indeed at the next election.' Once food taxes had been dropped, the party had no policy which offered prosperity to both farmers and labourers. In mid 1913, Lansdowne reported that, in the absence of a Tory policy, labourers were 'unsettled', and attracted to the Liberal proposals; farmers were 'discontented'. He talked of the 'serious risk' of losing several rural seats. Liberal candidates and land campaign workers also reported that both farmers *and* labourers were enthusiastic about the Liberals' proposals. The campaign had taken off 'like wildfire'; it would 'sweep the rural constituencies'.[68]

The extent of Liberal electoral support even in traditionally Liberal rural areas is difficult to ascertain. The by-election evidence is patchy, the local government evidence for most rural and semi-rural areas almost non-existent. Hemmerde's victory at North-West Norfolk in 1912 – against the trend – was a proclaimed victory for land reform. Although George Nicholls stood unsuccessfully as a Lib/Lab candidate at Newmarket in 1913, the Liberal vote at the Wycombe by-election in 1914 was higher than in 1910. The reports from party workers, the by-election results, and municipal results for market towns like Gloucester and Exeter, all suggest that the Liberals were at least holding their own.[69] Given that plural voting was soon to be abolished, and the Tories were in disarray, Liberals were justifiably confident. They had a strong southern base, which they showed no signs of losing.

Labour was no rival. Its campaigns, even in 1918, were inspired by Liberal decline, NEC enthusiasm, and the political and economic circumstances arising out of the First World War. Its organisation, even in the 1920s, was weak and dependent on the devoted work of a few activists (particu-

---

[67] J. Aubry Rees to W.R., 8 Jan. 1914, WR 116; WLF *AR* 1914. There are copies of several local Liberal papers in national and local archives e.g. *Suffolk Beacon, East Hants Liberal Monthly*. Land campaign figures from R. Douglas, *Land, people and politics* (1976), p. 160.

[68] Collings cited in Douglas, *Land and politics*, p. 165, Lansdowne, and Liberal reports in Offer, *Property and politics*, pp. 377–8, 380, 382–3.

[69] In Gloucester, the Liberals gained seats in 1912, held them in 1913, and looked forward to regaining control of the Council in 1914. The Conservatives *lost* seats to the Liberals in Exeter old town, but gained seats on the Council because of the incorporation of the (Tory) suburbs.

larly railwaymen, professionals, Nonconformist Ministers, and members of the agricultural labourers' union).[70] In most rural southern seats, Labour only dented the Liberal vote, even after the First World War.

Before 1914 Labour barely existed in most seats. Railwaymen were its most likely supporters, but even the presence of a substantial number of railwaymen did not guarantee success. The Taunton Trades Council, for example, was dominated by the ASRS and campaigned actively on railwaymen's issues, with some impact on Labour's municipal position. It was the exception, not the rule. In other areas where railwaymen were concentrated (such as Bridgwater and Exeter) Labour fared much worse. Elsewhere, without even this group to lend support, it adopted a low profile (so low, in many areas, that it scarcely appeared above the parapet). Clarion vans or ILP cyclists from urban centres paid flying visits to the villages, but most branches in the market towns were too weak to campaign even on their door steps. The Cheltenham LRC disintegrated in 1914 when its Secretary (a wealthy land reformer) moved to another area. The Gloucester ILP, kept solvent by Charles Fox, a local dentist, was inactive: 'it spends its time in internal quarrels or somewhat futile meetings'. There were few permanent Labour branches in North Wales. The 160 ILP members, not enough to organise a single seat, were spread over several urban centres. When Labour and Socialist organisations were established, they enjoyed an embattled, and often brief, existence.[71]

Neither did Labour have a particularly distinctive policy. Its land nationalisation schemes were either regarded as too vague, or as a tame reflection of the Liberals' proposals. The Liberal land campaign had stolen their thunder. In the only Liberal/Labour parliamentary conflict, at Tewkesbury in 1910, Labour polled 2 per cent of the vote, the Liberals more than 40. Occasional, three-cornered, municipal conflicts in Cheltenham and Gloucester saw Labour poll more respectably, but still manage no more than a poor third place. Only in Taunton was Labour able to

---

[70] Howard, 'Expectations born to death', in Winter (ed.), *The working class*, pp. 70–2.

[71] Parry, *Gwynedd*, p. 32. Howkins, *Norfolk*, pp. 105–8, 112 is characteristically optimistic about the strength of these new organisations. Contrast *New Times*, Dec. 1913, Feb. 1914, noting the collapse of Chelmsford ILP and the merger of the LRC and TC in Colchester. See also H. E. Durham to A.H., 24 Jan. 1914, LP/AFF 8/50 (Cheltenham); C. Fox to Ensor, 26 July 1909, Ensor MS, Howe, 'North Gloucestershire', p. 132; reports in *Bristol Times*, 2 Nov. 1911 and *Taunton Echo*, 28 Oct., 4 Nov. 1913 re Taunton. Labour's position in Bridgwater was someway between that in Exeter and Taunton (*Taunton Echo*, municipal and meeting reports, 4 Nov. 1913, 17 Mar., 23 June 1914).

seriously rival the Liberals after 1909, and even this was only in a portion of the constituency. There was no real Labour threat to the Liberal party.[72]

V

By 1914 politics were moving in a broadly Progressive direction. In the formerly 'Socialist' seats, and particularly in the East Midlands and East Anglia, Socialist unrest bubbled beneath the surface, but did not erupt. In Labour-held double member boroughs, the adoption of a second Labour candidate, and Liberal retaliation, would only result in the loss of a seat. The Leicester and Norwich LRCs made no move in this direction; Fred Henderson withdrew from his unofficial campaign in Norwich (allegedly in return for assistance with his municipal career).[73] Moreover, continued Progressive co-operation might yield benefits. In Northampton, another double member borough, the Liberals pointedly selected only one candidate in 1914. Like some Ipswich Liberals, they recognised that Labour held the balance of power in the constituency, and that a 'joint' campaign might be mutually advantageous. The Northampton Labour party was likely to accept the olive branch.[74] There were few other seats where Labour could justify a campaign. Only the East Bristol party made a convincing case, and received official sanction. Despite some local interest in fighting the East Northamptonshire seat, other local Labour groups found it logistically and ideologically impossible to oppose L. C. Money, the sitting Liberal MP. The NEC refused sanction to the prospective Labour candidate.[75]

Neither did the by-election conflicts in Hanley and Crewe indicate that the Progressive Alliance was disintegrating in the remaining industrial centres. It is true that the local understanding which 'gave' Labour Hanley and the Liberals Crewe *had* been disrupted. Although Holmes, Crewe's Labour candidate, tried to negotiate a free run for the 1914–15 election, his public and private overtures to the Liberals were inevitably rejected.[76] The Progressive Alliance simply did not operate in this way. The Crewe

---

[72] i.e., Gloucester Southend ward, 1913: L 47.1, C 42.5, Lab 10.4; Cheltenham East ward 1911: L 52.3, C 40.7, Lab 7. Labour occasionally out-polled the Liberals in the Taunton North ward after 1910.

[73] P. F. Pollard to F. Henderson, 13 Feb. 1914, Henderson MS 15/5.

[74] *M.G.* 9 May 1914 for Liberal comments on the strategic position. For Northampton, memo in the Steel-Maitland papers, MS G.D. 195/202 fo. 234, and Schneer, *Tillett*, p. 165.

[75] NEC Mins, 13 Feb. 1912, 29 June 1914. The rumour that the Liberals would accept a Labour candidature when Money stepped down may have encouraged thoughts of a Labour campaign (Boot and Shoe union *MR* Dec. 1910).

[76] *Staffs Sentinel*, 15 Jan. 1914. Correspondence detailing the negotiations published in the *Crewe Chron.*, 1 Nov. 1913. See also Illingworth's discussion of the overtures, P. Illingworth to A. G. Gardiner, 8 Aug. 1913, Gardiner MS 1/8.

by-election, and the subsequent events, had revealed Labour's true weakness. It now had no means of persuading the Liberals to stand down. Local and national officials withdrew their interest in a campaign. Holmes' attempt to negotiate an alliance, and the support which Wedgwood received from the ILP in Newcastle-upon-Lyme, was the true face of local Progressive politics.[77] Liberal/Labour relations were also cordial in formerly Lib/Lab strongholds like Derby. When local ASRS members proposed fighting Ilkeston at the 1912 by-election, and subsequently in 1914–15, their overtures were dismissed as hopeless. The only (partially) bright spot for Labour was in East Nottingham, where the Liberals' doubts about giving a Socialist Labour candidate (W. C. Anderson, Chairman of the ILP) a free run evaporated in 1914 as the election approached.[78]

In the rural areas, and their adjacent market towns, there was no prospect whatsoever of Liberal/Labour conflict. Even in Norfolk and North Wales, where there was considerable industrial unrest after 1900 in rural and other industries, there was no anti-Liberal backlash.[79] In Cheltenham, Gloucester, and probably other seats, a history of local co-operation and tacit Progressive arrangements in municipal politics was generally translated into Labour support for Liberal parliamentary candidates. There were few signs that this was changing by 1914. The two official pre-war Labour parliamentary campaigns, at Taunton in 1909, and Tewkesbury in January 1910, were not part of a nascent anti-Liberal assault. In the former, Labour did not have a Liberal opponent (although many Liberal voters abstained in protest). In the latter, Fox, the Labour candidate, had anticipated a free run. The Liberals brought out a candidate after a tangled and confused series of events which pleased no one. 'The general opinion', the Liberal *Cheltenham Chronicle* commented, 'is that a hash has been made of things.'[80] Although some middle-class Labour intellectuals occasionally contemplated financing their own Labour candidatures in rural/mixed seats they showed no interest in lost causes or in fighting the Liberals.[81] Tewkesbury and Taunton were not to be con-

[77] For Crewe, NEC Mins, 8 Apr. 1914: 'no candidate (should) be sanctioned for this constituency', and *M.G.*, 18 May 1914. For Newcastle, *Staffs Sentinel*, 2 July 1914.

[78] *R.R.*, 16 Feb. 1912, 17 July 1914; *The Times*, 19, 25 June 1912; Mid.LF Mins, 28 Oct. 1913, 9 July 1914.

[79] Liberal by-election candidates received the agricultural union's endorsement in 1912, despite the opposition of some Labour elements (Howkins, *Norfolk*, p. 118).

[80] Newspaper comment cited in Howe, 'North Gloucestershire', pp. 131, 134–5. See also Fox to Ensor, 1 July 1909, Ensor MS, Gloucester ILP Mins, 15 June 1909.

[81] G. B. Shaw to E. Pease, 28 Oct. 1911, J.K.H. to Pease, 6 Nov. 1911, C. Whitley to Pease, 15 Oct. 1910, Fabian MS A1/1 fo. 48, A7/2 fos. 95–6, B3/3 fo. 4. The Fabians had considered financing the Taunton contest in 1909, but eventually rejected the idea (NEC Mins, 7 July 1909).

tested in 1914–15 (rumours to the contrary were swiftly and convincingly denied).[82] There is no evidence of a concrete intention to run a Labour parliamentary campaign in rural areas. Labour might eventually have been able to fight seats which contained industrial enclaves or groups of unionised agricultural labourers, and the Liberals were unlikely to oppose such limited intervention. There was ample scope for Labour campaigns, given the vast number of 'Tory' seats in the south. However, in 1914 there was little sign that Labour was waiting to take up the challenge.

Labour was not a major threat to the Liberals' position in southern England and rural Wales. The Liberal's new programme attracted support, particularly in the East Midlands and East Anglia, and *reinforced* Liberal allegiances. The idea of a state safety net which would safeguard individual effort successfully updated a Liberal political culture in a manner which suited local interests and outlooks. In those southern industrial seats with a very different economic structure, New Liberal policies supplemented a Centrist approach which had always paid close attention to local labour interests. Liberal economics were seen as the basis of working-class prosperity; the party was now attempting to spread that prosperity still further. Labour had no economic or social policy which could challenge the basis of this support. 'Socialist' campaigns did not convince the electorate that Labour could ensure progress or prosperity. Labour moderates accepted the Liberal hegemony, and adopted a material moral reformism which was (at best) a more 'labour' minded reflection of the Liberals' approach. It sometimes augmented this with an appeal to the Statist interests of particular occupational groups. It made some independent electoral progress on a limited front. However, it did particularly well only when Liberal failure allowed it to appear as the 'better' reforming organisation. Labour had failed to tap the Liberals' reservoir of support.

[82] *The Times*, 28 Oct. 1912, and denial, *Taunton Mail*, 30 Oct. 1912.

Part III   An integrated picture

Chapter 11

The Progressive Alliance in 1914

Many historians argue that the Labour party was a dynamic, because class based, organisation before 1914. They frequently suggest that the party was making substantial organisational and electoral progress, particularly after 1910 when the level of industrial conflict and trade union membership increased. As a result of this progress, they contend, Labour was about to break out of its shackles in 1914, and attack the Liberal party at the forthcoming parliamentary election. Yet, as the foregoing survey has revealed, Labour was not a universally, or even a generally, dynamic organisation. Electoral politics were not so simple; 'progress', was much less pronounced. Labour's preparations for the next election were incomplete when war was declared. Nonetheless, the evidence suggests that the size and geographical distribution of its parliamentary campaign would be compatible with the idea of a Progressive Alliance. Labour had not developed the ideological/political strength to support an expansionist strategy. It had not created a solid 'class' vote, based on cultural unities which were common to working-class voters in all areas. It had not even the uniform support of trade unionists. The assumption that it did is based on inadequate theory and shaky and partial empirical analysis. In reality, electoral politics followed a pattern in which past political practices and current economic interests combined to create an extremely uneven electoral map. The distribution of support was such that it was comparatively strong where the Liberal party was weak, and unable to seriously rival it in most Liberal areas. Co-operation was therefore possible. It was also often seen as desirable, since the Liberals had maintained a political image which made their success advantageous to Labour's supporters. Trade union leaders and members were unwilling to support an assault on the Liberals' position which, in the current electoral climate, would only lead to Progressive defeats. As in 1910, Labour was the Liberals' ally. The electoral, organisational, and strategic position had not so changed that the logic of Alliance had been destroyed (Section I).

The *nature* of Progressive politics in 1914 also requires some comment. Although the Progressive parties had evolved and changed since 1906, neither had changed totally and become a fully acceptable, transformed, social democratic organisation. Labour (Section II) was increasingly dominated by a reforming alliance of moderate moral reformers and various trade union groups; it nonetheless contained other elements, and was institutionally constructed in such a way that they had the potential to influence party decisions. It was a coalition of half-conflicting groups. While the Liberal party (Section III) was also dominated by a reforming alliance, it too was a coalition. Its reforming alliance was subject to immediate attack, as was Labour's, but opposition came quietly and largely from within the party elite. If the institutional structure of the Liberal party was such that Cabinet dissidents could not easily link up with other conservative elements in the constituencies by utilising party machinery, neither could the reforming elite. Neither party was nationally successful enough to command a parliamentary majority, and neither was an institutionally perfect social democratic organisation. The Progressive Alliance allowed the two parties to combine their electoral and ideological assets.

The future of the Progressive Alliance in 1914 was uncertain (Section IV). It seemed unlikely that either the Liberal or Labour parties would split, at this time, along any of their various fissures. The most likely prospect seemed a continuation of the existing pattern of spatially distinct 'spheres of influence', until either proportional representation, or new circumstances or ideas, altered the structure of British politics.

I

The Labour party was not on the verge of replacing the Liberals in 1914. The purchase of Liberal economic policies was reinforced and rendered salient in some areas by the nature of local economic conditions. The Liberal party stood for prosperity, improvement, and security. The Labour left had no *generally* successful response. It had not created a 'class-based' political allegiance which would undermine the Liberal party on a broad front. In whole areas of the country – including heavily industrialised, unionised, iron and steel, engineering, and textile manufacturing areas, and even to some extent in several coalfields – Labour was unsuccessful. Moreover, the Liberal party's approach enabled it to combine a 'northern' working-class constituency with a 'southern' electoral base.

Labour leaders valued Liberal policy. MacDonald remained committed to the ideas of a Progressive Alliance, not withstanding his rejection of a more formal arrangement with the Liberals on several occasions. Labour officials committed the party to fighting more than one hundred seats in 1914–15 to appease the Socialists and frighten the Liberals. The 'commitment' was not indicative of an imminent large-scale conflict. Labour had to show its teeth to gain concessions; signs of weakness would be seized on by the Liberals.[1] To this end, between 1910 and 1914, MacDonald had continued the process of bargaining by public statement and by local demonstrations, or declarations, of strength. Several by-elections were fought as warnings to the Liberals. MacDonald, Henderson, and Vernon Hartshorn sent further private and public messages to the Liberals concerning potential problems in Oldham, West Wolverhampton, and South Wales. Other, scarcely veiled, hints appeared in the press. MacDonald's message to Leicester Liberals in the local Labour newspaper, for example, was carefully reported in the *Daily News*:

Even from your own point of view, and in the interests of your own principles, it is absolutely essential that there should be in the House of Commons a body of men who, knowing what they are driving at, will make it difficult . . . for the leaders of your party to yield to (sic) pressure.

Similarly, the *Daily Citizen*, while rejecting the idea of a formal pact, added that Labour was 'certainly not satisfied with 37 out of 670 seats'; a larger proportion might be different. An increase of Labour's share of an (informal) alliance was (informally) on the negotiating table.[2]

MacDonald had already demonstrated that his interest in expansion was not a commitment to unrestrained Liberal/Labour conflict. He supported by-election campaigns after 1910 under three conditions: when they were inevitable, where Labour had a chance of victory, or when they were pawns in a larger game. The incidence of three-cornered by-elections between 1910 and 1914 did not suggest he was losing control. There was scarcely more conflict than between 1906 and 1910 (fourteen official, nine unofficial campaigns out of around 100, compared to ten official and seven unofficial campaigns from a similar number in the earlier period). Party officials willingly used their emergency powers to prevent candidatures in several working-class seats (e.g. Ilkeston and Ipswich

---

[1] NEC Emergency Committee Mins, n.d. (but *c* May 1914), meeting with NAC delegation. [Filed at the back of the NAC Mins, Vol. 7, ILP MS.] The notion of an expanded campaign has become a text book 'fact'. See the origins of the idea in McKibbin, *Evolution*, pp. 72–7 and reflections of this idea, albeit interpreted differently, in e.g. Hinton, *Labour and Socialism*, p. 5, Burgess, *The challenge of labour*, p. 141. In Scotland, Labour could not implement its bold plans, and a smaller campaign was likely (Hutchison, *Scotland*, p. 265). Hutchison's assessment of the position in Edwardian Scotland parallels my own assessment of Edwardian politics in England and Wales in many respects (see esp. pp. 230–40). For other complementary research on Edwardian Scotland, Hamish Fraser, 'Labour in Scotland', Smith, 'Glasgow and Liverpool'.

[2] *Daily Cit.*, 21 May 1914, *Daily News*, 4 May 1914; *Leicester Pioneer*, 18 Nov. 1911, *The Times*, 2 May 1912.

in England, Glasgow St Rollox and Tradeston in Scotland), despite local opposition.[3]

Conflict was also improbable because Labour's bargaining position within the Progressive Alliance was improving. In three of the fourteen three-cornered by-election contests, the Liberals lost seats to the Tories because of Labour intervention. In July 1914, MacDonald thought that the Liberals might be defeated if there was an immediate election. However, he also knew that the Liberals would not voluntarily hold an election before May 1915, when the abolition of plural voting (or the Tory House of Lords' rejection of this democratic reform) would make the contest more even.[4] After the election, Labour might hold the balance of power. This was an attractive prospect; a Tory victory (the likely outcome of unbridled Progressive conflict) was not.[5]

Labour's strategic actions in 1913–15 reflected this ideological/political judgement. In the Autumn of 1913, the ILP and Fabian Society formed a joint propaganda committee. It aimed to stimulate support for state intervention of a kind which only Labour could satisfy. The committee's War on Poverty campaign was regarded as an 'irresponsible agitation' by Arthur Henderson and the trade union MPs. It was starved of resources by the Labour party and virtually boycotted by the unions. Labour bureaucrats, with the co-operation of some Socialists, organised a separate, concentrated, campaign which focused on improving the electoral/organisational situation in the small number of seats which the NEC had already agreed to contest. The full weight of the party machine was to be thrown behind this campaign. The 'raising of expectations', which might lead to pressure for a wider campaign, was fiercely resisted. Alliance with groups like the women's suffrage societies, which might have served to expand the campaign (*might* because Liberal suffragettes were increasingly dissatisfied with such schemes), were rejected.[6]

Labour also rejected other proposals which could have expanded its potential to conduct anti-Liberal campaigns. Legislation granting MPs a salary freed trade union political funds of a considerable financial burden. These funds could have been used for extra campaigns. The pooling

[3] See e.g. J. S. Taylor to F.J., 2 Dec. 1911, FJ 1911/331.
[4] For the timing of the election, R. Adkins *et al.*, to Harcourt, 5 Aug. 1914, Harcourt MS 444 fos. 124–5, L.G. memo, n.d., Asquith MS 25 fo. 148, *Nation*, 7 Mar. 1914. For Labour perceptions, A.H. to J.R.M., 29 May 1914, LP/MAC/09/1/79 and W. S. Blunt Diary, 22 July 1914, in *My diaries*, ii (1920), pp. 445–6.
[5] P. Illingworth to L.G., 11 June 1914, LG C/5/4/15, for Liberal analysis. Memo by Steel-Maitland, 13 Mar. 1917, Steel-Maitland MS G.D. 193/202 fo. 55 citing a more elaborate contemporary Tory analysis.
[6] Minutes, Standing Joint Committee of the ILP and Fabian Society, ILP MS, and Labour party file, LP/CAM/14/1/; Holton, *Feminism and democracy*, pp. 84, 86–7, 100–1, 111–15.

of union political levies would also have allowed the political funds of smaller unions to be utilised for electoral purposes. It would also have given the NEC the power to spread resources over a larger number of constituencies, rather than concentrate a vast amount of money on a few seats. All these possibilities were rejected (affiliation fees were in fact reduced).[7] Perhaps most strikingly, MacDonald crushed the opposition to his electoral strategy which culminated in a debate at the party conference in 1914. Proportional Representation (as opposed to the Alternative Vote), Labour 'radicals' argued, would enable the party to oppose Liberals on a broad front, and so campaign on distinct (i.e. Socialist) principles. However, with the aid of union leaders, MacDonald 'steamrollered' the opposition. As Beatrice Webb noted, 'the solid phalanx of miners and textiles don't want the Labour members to cut loose from the Liberal party, and MacDonald knows it'.[8]

These sentiments were shared by many other unions (particularly the general unions and those with white-collar memberships). Union executives were divided between those who saw little point in political activity, and those who regarded the Liberals as the best representation of their members' interests.[9] These unions, and even some allegedly committed to the Labour party, demonstrated this by refusing to finance enough Labour parliamentary candidatures to sustain a broad anti-Liberal campaign. There were to be no new candidates in 1914–15 from skilled unions such as the Ironfounders, Shipwrights, and Compositors (who sponsored very few candidates for unions of their size) or from 'radical' unions like the Boot and Shoe operatives or the Steel Smelters. Other unions, including the Bleachers and Dyers, Stonemasons, Coopers, Painters, and Patternmakers were withdrawing from the limited commitment to Labour representation which they had demonstrated in 1910.[10] Limited craft representation, and pressure group action to promote radical Liberal intervention, satisfied most unions' needs. Even some unions who were 'converted' to Labour representation after 1910 backed the idea because they, too, wanted a 'parliamentary representative'. It was demeaning (or

---

[7] In some unions reduction followed a ballot (e.g. Ironfounders' MR Jan. 1911). For the unions' role in the lowering of affiliation fees, and Labour opposition, J.S.M. to F. Chandler [ASC&J], 14 Dec. 1911, J.R.M. to W. Pickles (Painters), 14 July 1910, LP/CAN/06/1/76 and 276, GGL EC Mins, 11, 12 Nov. 1911.

[8] B. Webb Diary, 6 Feb. 1914 (Mackenzie, p. 195).

[9] e.g. Workers' Union, National Union of Clerks, Postal Clerks' Association.

[10] The general source for this, and much of the following, is Labour's own enquiry, the replies to which are recorded in LP/TUA/11. See also *Journal of the Operative Stonemasons Society*, 9 Dec. 1914, Painters' and Decorators' AR 1909.

Table 11.1 *Ballots under the Trade Union Act, 1913, selected trade unions*

Union	For	Against	Turn-out (%)
ASE	20,586	12,740	Less than 25
ASLEF	7,839	3,841	45
Boilermakers	4,752	4,404	14[a]
Boot and Shoe	6,085	1,935	17
Clerks	1,844	540	23
Gasworkers	27,802	4,339	22
MFGB	261,643	194,800	81
Weavers	98,158	75,893	89

Note:
[a] Previous ballots on the principle of Labour party affiliation had even lower turnouts.

Source: P.P. (Cd. 121), Lxxvi, 719 and trade union records.

inefficient) to allow other trade union Labour MPs to put their case on matters related to members' interests.[11]

It would also seem that trade union activists were not forcing their executives to adopt a more expansive approach. Although this pressure did exist, the executives of the Boot and Shoe operatives, Postmen's Federation, Gasworkers, Dockers, and other unions also came under pressure at Conferences from a combination of Syndicalist and Lib/Lab delegates opposed to accepting additional political responsibilities. Indeed, in several unions there were moderately close votes on *disaffiliation* from the Labour party.[12] Ordinary members, as opposed to Conference delegates, were even less enthusiastic. Support for independent working-class representation was not incompatible with a Progressive Alliance, but the ballots held under the Trade Union Act of 1913 still revealed considerable opposition even to this. Forty per cent of those who voted opposed their union having a political fund. Moreover, turnout was usually less than 50 per cent, often less than 25 per cent (Table 11.1). This favoured the radical activists who were organising inside the unions. The 'yes' vote may also have been inflated. Outright pressure, the limited circulation

[11] e.g. Natsopa *Half-yearly statement* June 1914.
[12] A. Fox, *A history of the Boot and Shoe operatives* (Oxford, 1958), pp. 339–40, *Postman's Gazette*, 27 June 1914, GGL, *Report of Biennial Conference* 26–29 May 1914, DWR, Minutes of the Triennial Delegates' Meeting, 1914. See also *Postal Clerks' Herald*, 25 Apr. 1914, H. J. Fyrth and H. Collins, *The Foundry Workers* (Manchester, 1959), p. 127 and Ironfounders' *MR* Mar. 1911.

Table 11.2 *Ballots on funding the Daily Citizen, selected trade unions,*
1913–1914

Union	For	Against	Amount
ASE	13,874	15,288	£5,000
Boilermakers	3,679	2,408	1s per member for three years
Boot and Shoe	2,835	2,147	1s per member for three years
ASC&J	6,553	10,774	?
Gasworkers	27,802	4,339	?
Patternmakers	rejected by maj. of 300		1s per member for three years
Typographical Association	5,672	3,290 (1913)	£500
	5,092	4,149 (1914)	£500

Source: Trade union reports/journals.

of ballot papers, and 'branch voting' – a system by which all votes were
given in favour or against the motion, according to the majority of the
meeting – can all be identified, even if their impact is difficult to ascertain.[13]

The trade union ballots were also votes on a principle. When the members of some unions were asked to put their hands in their pockets (instead
of on their hearts), they were even less enthusiastic about the Labour
party. Some further ballots resulted in union members refusing to sanction
the deductions from their wages which were necessary to create a political
fund. In other unions, as much as *half* the membership contracted out
of their political fund. Moreover, when the Labour party attempted to
raise loans from the unions to finance a national newspaper, the *Daily
Citizen*, a further ballot was necessary before the unions could comply.
Some unions refused to hold a ballot because they anticipated opposition.[14] The ASE, Patternmakers, and the ASC&J unsuccessfully balloted their members. In many other unions, the majority in favour was
extremely small, despite very low turnouts (Table 11.2).

Most union executives respected rank and file opinion. The Patternmakers and the Co-operative Employees, whose members voted against
a political fund, refused to finance Labour parliamentary candidates.
Even when the ballot was narrowly favourable, some union executives

[13] See e.g. Socialist group of the L.S.C., *Socialism and trade unionism*; *Locomotive Journal*,
Dec. 1911, June 1913. For ballot irregularities in an earlier MFGB ballot, *L.L.*., 3 July
1908.
[14] e.g. NAUL Mins, 26 July 1913.

(such as the Compositors) chose not to alienate their members by sponsoring further candidates.[15] The Secretary of NAFTO stated the motive categorically: 'There are [sic] a considerable number of our members who appear to be strongly opposed for the moment at least to the Labour Party, and my E.C. do not feel justified in using our own funds (for this purpose).'[16] The ASC&J reduced its list of candidates from three to one, because contracting out was so extensive. Within the Fabian Society, internal conflict over political activity resulted in the Society withdrawing its financial commitment to fund three candidates.[17]

This is not to argue that no rank and file members and delegates wished to see a larger Labour party or even a larger electoral campaign. 'Socialist' elements, or those more evidently committed to Labour expansion, were becoming a more significant factor in union politics. Several union executives were 'captured' by the left. In some instances they tried to increase their political commitments. The ASE attempted to increase the number of sponsored candidates from five to eleven; the mining unions and the Boilermakers' union took similar action. Nonetheless, their members had other ideas. SWMF and ASE members refused to support the necessary increase in political contributions. The Boilermakers' union – which had voted against a political fund in 1912 – was only able to secure a tiny majority in favour of having a fund in 1914, despite an extremely low turn-out.[18] While the Boilermakers went ahead regardless, both the SWMF *and* the ASE had to restrict their parliamentary action.

There were some more favourable signs. The textile unions, the NUR and the ILP were intending to increase their financial involvement in 1914–15, although in the ILP's case falling membership figures suggested to many (including the national treasurer, T. D. Benson) that this would be impossible.[19] Some smaller unions with interests in state intervention – and particularly in minimum wages – were considering the question

[15] E. Howe and H. E. Waite, *The London Society of Compositors* (1948), p. 324.
[16] A. Gossip to A.H., 5 Dec. 1913, LP/AFF 8/165.
[17] Fabian Soc., Finance Comm. Mins, 20 Nov. 1913, and more generally, N. and J. MacKenzie, *The First Fabians* (1979), Chapter 24; ASC&J, Minutes of the Proceedings of the General Council, 28 Feb., 1 and 11 July 1913, and A. G. Cameron to J.S.M., 13 July 1915, LP/CAN/06/1/92
[18] J. Mortimer, *History of the Boilermakers' Society* (1982), 2, pp. 55–6; B. C. M. Weekes, 'The Amalgamated Society of Engineers 1880–1914. A study of trade union government, politics and industrial policy', Warwick Ph.D. thesis 1970, Chapter 7 and pp. 353–8; *South Wales Weekly Post*, 28 Mar. 1914, and for the lodge resolutions (e.g. Pontypridd and Rhondda no. 2 lodge), *Mid-Rhondda Gaz.*, 19 May 1914. In South Wales the question of finance dragged on. Conference delegates initially demanded a coalfield ballot. This demand was (narrowly) reversed in Feb. 1915, and the levy increased (SWMF Mins, esp. 13 July, 24 Aug. 1914, 13 Jan., 6 Feb. 1915).
[19] NAC Mins, 26 Jan. 1914, ILP CR 1914, pp. 66–8, CR 1915, p. 18. There was press speculation of an impending *reduction* to just eight candidates (e.g. *M.G.*, 2 June 1914).

of funding candidates very carefully, although many still thought that
the Liberals were more likely than Labour to promote their interests.[20]
To some extent there was a hardening of attitudes towards the Liberals.
In the ILP, the development of a 'soft' left, committed to a 'practical'
political stance, was accompanied by concessions to the ethical socialists
and the left on strategy. Labourist unions, the Dockers, whose members
had fewer historical allegiances to the Liberal party, were also financially
encouraging a broader Labour campaign. Nonetheless, and on balance,
there was not enough support for anti-Liberal action to suggest that a
major shift in strategy was possible.

The proof of the pudding should lie in the eating, but since war intervened
and the election was postponed, there is no 'pudding' to eat. Nonetheless,
the structure of Progressive electoral policy for the election in 1914–15
can be partially reconstructed from party and other records. In June 1914,
the NEC was presented with a list of 117 'Present and Prospective' constituencies (Table 11.3). The BSP wished to contest some additional seats
(although its record on carrying out its 'intentions' and its financial position were hardly encouraging) and there were several other constituencies
where candidatures were being contemplated. Most labour historians
have misinterpreted this document. Spurred on by a belief in the growing
strength of the Labour party, they have seen it as evidence of (if not
always commitment to) a putative election campaign involving 150–70
Labour candidates. Moreover, if the underlying assumptions are suspect,
the material 'evidence' of an expanded campaign also requires re-examin-
ation. Lists of this kind should not be taken too seriously. Similar docu-
ments had been produced before the 1910 elections. They were possible
election ingredients, not approved menus. In the January election, only
a portion of the constituencies which Labour hoped to fight were in
fact contested.[21] More detailed examination of the position in 1914–15
confirms that the document, and 'commitments' to an expanded campaign, cannot be taken at face value.

A circumscribed campaign was virtually inevitable. In the first instance,
there were not even 117 Labour candidates. The NEC list had been drawn
up *before* the ILP and MFGB decided which seats to contest. It included
around thirty-five 'new' seats (i.e. in addition to those with sitting Labour

[20] *Journeyman Bakers' Magazine*, Sept. 1913 and Sept. 1914, *Blind Advocate*, Sept. 1914,
U.K. Society of Coachmakers, *Quarterly Report and Journal*, Oct. 1914, *Government
Workers' Advocate*, Dec. 1914. The London tramway workers were considering political
action, despite the Syndicalist views of their executive (*Licensed Vehicle Trades' Record*,
1 Apr. 1914).
[21] e.g. 'Memo on election policy', NEC Mins, 6 Oct. 1909 (BLPES Coll. fos. 118–38)
and NEC Mins, 24 Feb. 1910.

Table 11.3 *Table of 'present and prospective Labour constituencies', 1914*[a]

Labour seat	Sanctioned	Selected	Uncertain
Stockport*			Crewe
Whitehaven			Cockermouth
Derby			Chesterfield
Mid Derby			
Sunderland*	Bishop Auckland	Darlington	Gateshead
Barnard Castle	Jarrow	South Shields	Chester-le-Street
Chester-le-Street		Houghton-le-Spring	
		N.W. Durham	
S. West Ham			Southampton*
			Widnes
E. Manchester	Portsmouth*	Eccles	Accrington
N.E. Manchester	Oldham*	Newton	Rossendale
Blackburn*	Preston*		Kirkdale
Clitheroe	St Helens		West Derby
Barrow	Leigh		
Westhoughton	Wigan		
Gorton			
Ince			
(Bolton*)			
Leicester*		E. Nottingham	Northampton*
Norwich*		E. Bristol	E. Northants
Newcastle*			Morpeth
			Wansbeck
	W. Wolverhampton		Hanley
N.W. Staffs	E. Birmingham	W. Birmingham	Wednesbury
	Coventry		Walsall
			Nuneaton

E. Leeds	W. Hull	York*	Middlesbrough
Normanton	Sowerby	Keighley	Wakefield
Hallamshire		Barnsley	Colne Valley
W. Bradford		Rotherham	Holmfirth
Halifax*		Doncaster	Hallamshire
Attercliffe		Osgoldcross	Pudsey
			Spen Valley
			Huddersfield
			W. Leeds
			Limehouse
			Poplar
Deptford	Bermondsey	Mid-Glamorgan	S. Glamorgan
Woolwich		E. Glamorgan	S. Monmouth
Rhondda		N. Monmouth	Monmouth City
W. Monmouth			
Gower			
S. Glamorgan			
Merthyr*	Camlachie	W. Monmouth	Carmarthen Boroughs
Blackfriars	S. Ayr	Leith	St Rollox
Dundee*	Midlothian	Montrose	N. Aberdeen
W. Fife	S.E. Lanark	W. Lothian	W. Lanark
			S. Edinburgh
			Falkirk
			Greenock

Notes:

* Denotes double member borough.

a Based on the NEC document of the same title, NEC Mins, 23 June 1914. Three constituencies are classified as both 'Labour Seats' and 'Uncertain' contests, because of problems stemming from the Lib.–Lab./Labour split, and one constituency, W. Monmouth, is included under headings 1 and 3. (For an explanation, McKibbin, Evolution, pp. 24–8.) Bolton, wrongly excluded in the original, has been included here.

Table 11.4 *Sanctioned Labour candidates, 1910 and 1914*

Organisation	1910	1914	Not allocated 1914–15
LRC	1	3	
Fabians	2	0	
ILP	14	16[a]	
ASE	5	2[ac]	
ASLEF	1	1	
Blastfurnacemen	1	0[b]	
Bleachers and Dyers	1	0[b]	
Boilermakers	2	4 (1915)	4 (1915)
Boot and Shoe	4	3	3
BrSS	4	3	1
ASC&J	3	1[a]	
Gen. Union of C&J	1	0[b]	
Co-op Employees	0	0[c]	
Coopers	1	0	
DWR	1[d]	2	2
Nat. Union Dock Labs.	1	1	
Gasworkers	2	undecided (2 + ?)	undecided
Ironfounders	1	1	
LSC	1	1	
Stonemasons	1	0	
MFGB[e]	27	23	2[f]
Municipal Employees	1	0	
NAFTO	1	1	
NAUL	0[d]	1	
ASRS/NUR	3	5 (1915)	2 (1915)
Painters	1	0	
Patternmakers	1	0[c]	
Postmen's Fed.	1	1	
Railway Clerks	0	1	
Scottish Ironfounders	1	unknown	unknown
Shipwrights	3	3 (1915)	2 (1915)
Shop Assistants	1	1	
Tin & Sheet Millmen	1	unknown	unknown
Typographical Ass.	1	1	
UTFWA	3	6	
Watermen and Lightermen	0	1 (1915)	1 (1915)
	91	84	17

Source: The political plans of all unions which sponsored candidates in 1910 and 1918 have where possible been determined. The results are based on LP ARs, trade union journals, reports, minutes, and histories, and especially the replies to the LP circular, LP/TUA/11/37–92. Most unions had declared their intentions in 1914 on the basis of what funds would be available by 1915. Those unions whose political funds would not match their political ambitions until 1915 at the earliest are marked '(1915)'.

Notes:
* Excludes Northern Ireland.
a Financial problems permitting.
b Probable situation.
c Situation created by ballot of the membership.
d A candidature, or an additional candidature, was contemplated, but not agreed when the election was called.
e Includes LCMF/local parties in mining constituencies. Excludes Lib./Lab. MPs, 1914.
f South Wales only.

MPs) which had candidates or organisations seeking ILP or MFGB financial sanction.[22] Yet these organisations were only financing perhaps a dozen additional candidatures. Other organisations – like the ASE and Fabians – had *reduced* their commitment, leaving a substantial number of seats which were on the NEC list without a financially sanctioned candidate. As Table 11.4 demonstrates, the best estimate suggests that there were fewer Labour candidates seeking seats in 1914–15 than in 1910. It would thus be almost impossible to undertake a wider campaign, given the limited ability of constituency organisations to fill the gap.

A circumscribed Labour campaign took concrete shape between April 1914 and January 1915. During this time, 80 per cent of the available candidates found seats and received NEC sanction for their involvement. Many of the unions involved sought NEC advice on the particular seats in question before accepting financial responsibility for prospective campaigns. The NEC and NAC encouraged them to concentrate on seats with a Tory tradition, on mining constituencies (which MacDonald accepted as a legitimate area of Labour expansion), on double member boroughs, and on 'Liberal' seats where Labour was a generally powerful Progressive rival. The overwhelming majority of candidates were in 'approved' areas. Of the fifty-nine sanctioned candidates, all but sixteen were unlikely to face Liberal opposition (Table 11.5). The incidence of Liberal–Labour conflict would have been higher if the Liberals had carried

---

[22] Roughly calculated from Gregory, *Miners*, NEC and NAC minutes, and other sources. Some seats had no particular or known candidate in mind.

Table 11.5 Constituencies with sanctioned Labour candidates, c. January 1915

Constituency	Sponsor	Lib. Opp. Likely	Constituency	Sponsor	Lip. Opp. Likely
Deptford	LSC	No	Monmouth W.	MFGB	No
West Ham, South	Gasworkers	No	Rhondda	MFGB	No
			Gower	MFGB	Yes
Woolwich	None[a]	No	Merthyr*	ILP	No
Bermondsey	ILP	Yes			
			Attercliffe	ILP	No
Birmingham E.	LRC[b]	No	Bradford W.	ILP	No
Birmingham W.	ILP	No	Halifax*	ILP	No
Wolverhampton W.	Railway Clerks	No	Leeds E.	NAFTO	No
			York*	LRC[c]	No
Coventry	ILP	Yes	Doncaster	MFGB	Yes
			Keighley	ILP	Yes
Barrow	ASE	No	Morley	ASLEF	Yes
Blackburn*	ILP	No	Rotherham	BrSS	Yes
Bolton*	UTFWA	No	Sowerby	UTFWA	Yes
Clitheroe	UTFWA	No			
Gorton	BrSS	No	Chester-le-Street	MFGB	No
Ince	MFGB	No	Newcastle*	NUR	No
Manchester E.	MFGB	No	Sunderland*	ILP	No
Manchester N.E.	ILP	No	Barnard Castle	Ironfounders	No
Newton	Shop Assistants	No			
Oldham*	UTFWA	No	Bishop Auckland	ILP	Yes
Preston*	UTFWA	No	Durham N.W.	Postmen	Yes

Constituency		
St Helens	Dock Labourers	No
Stockport*	NUR	No
Westhoughton	ASC&J	No
Whitehaven	MFGB	No
Wigan	MFGB	No
Accrington	UTFWA	Yes
Eccles	ILP	Yes
Leigh	MFGB	Yes
Hallamshire[d]	MFGB	?
N.W. Staffordshire	MFGB	No
Normanton	MFGB	No
Holmfirth	MFGB	Yes
N.E. Derby	MFGB	Yes
Houghton-le-Spring	MFGB	Yes
Morpeth[d]	MFGB	?
Derby*	NUR	No
Leicester*	ILP	No
Norwich*	Typographical Association	No
Bristol E.	ILP	Yes
Portsmouth*	LRC	No
Scotland		
Blackfriars	ASE	No
Dundee*	Shipwrights	No
Fife W.	MFGB	No
Aberdeen N.	ILP	Yes
Lanark N.E.	MFGB	Yes
Midlothian	MFGB	Yes

Notes:

* Denotes double member borough.

[a] No Fabian Society funds available, but deliberately not announced by Crooks. (Fab. Soc. Parl. Sub-Comm. Mins, 16 Jan. 1914).

[b] Nominally LRC, actually by the candidate. (Birm. LRC Mins, 14 Feb. 1914).

[c] Nominally Fabian Society, actually by the candidate. (Fab. Soc. Parl. Sub-Comm. Mins, 16 Jan. 1914).

[d] The MFGB had decided to sponsor a candidate when the sitting Lib/Lab MP retired; the question of when these MPs would retire was undecided. So too was the likely reaction of local Liberal associations.

Source: NEC/NAC Mins and local press and party records.

out the threats of retaliation which were made between 1913 and 1914; but these ideas were disparaged and rejected by Liberals at the centre throughout the latter half of 1914. Threatened campaigns were part of the process of public negotiation which characterised the Progressive Alliance. There is little evidence of alleged anti-Labour campaigns becoming realities.[23]

This is not to suggest that the centre had perfect control over the size of the electoral campaign. Elements within the party leadership disapproved of prospective Labour campaigns in (for example) Liberal-held Keighley, Eccles, Sowerby, East Bristol, and Houghton-le-Spring. They had previously expressed doubts over the position in several other seats the DMA to fight Chester-le-Street (where the locally financed Labour MP was retiring) instead of Liberal-held South Shields, and persuaded other unions not to proceed with 'improbable' campaigns. Moreover, as in 1910, some candidates in 'hopeless' seats might well have withdrawn before the contest.[24]

There were several months to go before a possible election. It seems unlikely that the availability of seventeen unallocated candidates would have substantially increased the degree of Liberal/Labour conflict. The organisational and electoral position in the 'Liberal' areas was unencouraging (as the chapters on constituency politics demonstrate). In some historically Liberal areas (examined in Chapters 7 to 10 and in some sections of Chapters 5 and 6) the reaffirmation of Liberal ideas was sufficient to perpetuate Liberal support. However, the progressive appearance of a Centrist Liberalism demonstrated that Liberal ideas on the production of wealth were not incompatible with support for legislation which would create a greater degree of social security. New Liberals went further. They added support for the redistribution of, and not just the production of, wealth to the Liberal package. Moreover, members of both these reforming strands accepted the presentation of policy as an attack on the rich (although Centrists might object to some more radical pronounce ments). Reformers – of both types – were evident in almost all constitu-

---

[23] See above, pp. 92–3, 319. I have also discounted rumours of conflict in Merthyr, Barnard Castle, and Gower, as there is evidence of central opposition, and no evidence of actual campaigns in the local press.
[24] See above, pp. 57–9. MFGB Mins, esp. 18 Mar., 10 Aug. 1915. For union/NEC co-operation, R. Spencer to J.R.M., 14 Mar. 1912, LP/CAN/06/1/230 and NAUL Ec Mins, 27 Sept. 1912, 20 May 1913. The NAUL expressed an interest in fighting only 'if the chances of success are reasonable'. After delegates raised the matter at the union conference, the Bakers' executive agreed to hold a Conference vote before a parliamentary seat could be contested by the union's candidate (*Journeyman Bakers' Magazine*, Sept. 1914).

ency organisations, although the internal political balance depended on local economic and institutional factors. An organic, reforming, ideology also helped create a broad alliance of 'older' and 'newer' Liberal traditions and supporters. Labour, unable to challenge this synthesis of ideas with a national and class-based appeal, tended to reflect the broad drift of Liberal policy at the national level. Despite some general differences in tone, Labour developed an independent, successful, and distinct image, based on rather different ideas, only in certain areas. Its progress was limited.[25]

The NEC and NAC recognised that the Liberals' ability to update their appeal made them almost invulnerable in many parts of the country. They flatly refused to sanction contests in at least five of the remaining seats from 'Liberal' working-class areas which appeared on the election 'blueprint' in 1914.[26] In several other Liberal-held seats on the list, local organisations withdrew 'voluntarily',[27] or were engaged in 'candidatures' which were entirely fatuous.[28] There are strong indications in some additional seats that candidates were unlikely to obtain financial and political backing. The various textile workers' unions declined to contest Spen Valley and Rossendale, a Liberal seat also rejected by the LCMF; the NUR refused to fight 'Liberal' Ilkeston or South Glamorgan.[29] Organisations turning to the ILP (as very many did) found that they had allocated all their candidates to seats by January 1915.

At the same time, the Liberal party was a less complete obstacle in the traditionally Tory parts of the country and in the coalfields. In the former, even fairly materially minded New Liberal ideas were only half-relevant to areas where local economies were in crisis, where Free Trade had not brought prosperity, or where local perceptions of policy were governed by a very different political language. Labour had the capacity to expand in the coalfields, in the Tory areas, and in some other seats where its advocacy of state intervention and 'ordinary' outlooks represented a distinct and relevant image, rooted in the dominant local political culture. Nonetheless, it did not have the political and economic credibility or the economic teeth to make rapid progress in the face of concerted Liberal opposition. Its potential was not yet realised.

The bulk of the seventeen unallocated candidates were likely to find their way to seats in the coalfields and in the more Tory areas where

---

[25] See below, Chapters 5–10.
[26] i.e. Crewe and East Northants in southern Britain, Gateshead, Darlington, and West Leeds in the north (NEC Mins, 8 Apr., 29 June 1914, NAC Parl. Sub-Comm. Mins, 21 Apr. 1914). See also below, pp. 278–80.
[27] i.e. Hanley, Crewe, Cockermouth (see above, pp. 301–3, 204).
[28] i.e. Walsall, Monmouth Boroughs, Middlesbrough (see above, pp. 187–8, 238, 241–2).
[29] *Dewsbury News*, 16 May 1914; *Daily Despatch*, 10 June 1914; *R.R.*, 22 Jan. 1915.

the NEC was happy to sanction campaigns. In some mining areas, which the NEC identified as 'Labour' territory, the NEC supported campaigns even if this was likely to involve a degree of Liberal/Labour conflict. Some mining seats which the MFGB was unable to contest already had non-mining candidates.[30] In other semi-mining seats, such as the Carmarthen Boroughs and Jarrow, Labour had a strong base amongst mining *and* non-mining elements. The NEC responded favourably to unions which expressed an interest in fighting these seats.[31] Nonetheless, limited Labour progress in the Midlands, North-East, and Yorkshire coalfields in particular made considerable expansion difficult even here. In fact, the potential for compromise with the Liberals became evident when the DMA withdrew its candidate from South Shields. The NMA similarly indicated its strategic moderation by concentrating on obtaining control of the Lib/Lab seats of Morpeth and Wansbeck without conflict. The suppression of Liberal 'campaigns' in Merthyr, Gower, Chester-le-Street, and Barnard Castle, and of *Labour* interest in fighting North-East Derbyshire, Chesterfield, and Nuneaton, revealed that rhetoric, and the enthusiasm of the parties' dissident elements, was unlikely to dominate the logic of a Progressive strategy. Even South Wales and Yorkshire miners were seeking some form of informal compact which would enable a degree of Labour expansion, rather than Progressive conflict.[32] An increase of Liberal/Labour conflict in South Wales and Yorkshire was likely, but it would have been limited and perhaps balanced by compromise in other coalfields. It was also unlikely to disrupt the Progressive Alliance.

This strategic stance reflected Labour's electoral and organisational position in the mining constituencies. It had begun to merge practical reform, a Statist appeal, and craft representation with respect for locally dominant political cultures. By 1914 it was very slowly and partially beginning to create a *Labour* political culture from new and old ingredients. This made the party sufficiently similar, and sufficiently different, to justify a change of political allegiance. Nonetheless, Labour's positive policies were not such that a Liberal party committed to social reform and anti-Tory policies could be swept aside, especially if (as in the Midlands) its appeal was reinforced by the apparent and continuing salience of Liberal economic ideas. In short, Labour had made some progress in

---

[30] i.e. North-West Durham, Morley, Rotherham.

[31] E. A. Spicer to J.S.M., 14 Feb. 1914, and B. Tillett to J.R.M., 24 Oct. 1912, LP/CAN/06/ 1/385 and 129B, G. H. Stacey to J.S.M., 1 Jan. 1913, LP/AFF 7/318. Jarrow was to have been contested by the ASC&J. Although they withdrew in 1914, and there were some local problems, this was a former Labour seat, and a three-way marginal. It was therefore likely to attract a candidate.

[32] See above, pp. 221–6.

South Wales in particular, without making the coalfields their own. The prospective electoral campaign reflected this fact.[33]

The positive attractions of a Labourist or Statist political image created political opportunities in some 'Tory' areas which were also reflected in Labour's prospective electoral campaign. Labour had demonstrated by January 1915 that it could secure Liberal withdrawals in seats like West Wolverhampton, West Birmingham, and York which it had not fought in December 1910. Several other 'Tory' seats on the NEC list were likely to attract some of the remaining candidates. East Nottingham had a candidate waiting in the wings. The two Liverpool seats on the list, Kirkdale and West Derby, were approaching unions whose candidates had not yet found seats. None of these seats would have been fought by the Liberals.[34] Moreover, some Tory seats which were not on the NEC list (e.g. Handsworth) could have been fought, and almost certainly without Liberal opposition. In East Nottingham, Liverpool West Derby, and Liverpool Kirkdale, like York, West Birmingham, West Wolverhampton, and the double member boroughs of Oldham and Portsmouth, which also had sanctioned Labour candidates, Labour would very probably have had no Liberal opposition if it fielded a candidate. None of these seats had been fought by Labour in 1910. These new 'concessions' demonstrated that Labour could advance *within* the Progressive Alliance where it demonstrated it was a strong force or a useful ally.[35]

There was little prospect of a broader Labour campaign in these areas at a 1914–15 election. In potentially Labour seats (those with a substantial Tory working-class vote, e.g. Sheffield Brightside, Wakefield, Widnes, or Wednesbury) a campaign in 1914–15 was impossible, as trade unions and other organisations asked to contest these seats noted.[36] There was some short-term prospect of further expansion in London, the West Midlands, West Lancashire, and in the southern ports (where one prospective Labour campaign at least was blighted by the local party's internal problems), and even in some Tory rural seats/market towns. In the longer term, however, Labour clearly had the potential to go beyond this and rival the Liberals more generally in the Tory working-class areas. This potential was not ready to be realised in 1914.[37]

---

[33] See above, Chapter 7.
[34] See Liverpool LRC Mins, 1 May 1914, discussing an approach to Bellamy of the NUR, and *R.R.*, 16 Apr. 1915 for his selection as an NUR candidate. There is no indication, however, that he had accepted (or rejected) the Liverpool offer. See also above, pp. 307, 158–9.
[35] See above, pp. 158–9, 187–9, 192, 280, 303.
[36] See above, pp. 159, 280.
[37] See above, pp. 193–5, 312–3.

The Liberals' radical stance in many Tory areas stood in the way of Labour's expansion. Local circumstances were hostile to *all* Progressive organisations, so it took time for Labour to emerge as a political rival. It only became successful as an anti-Tory organisation (i.e., a serious threat to Tory domination of the seat) in certain social/political circumstances. It could at times construct an image which embraced economic relevance, social policies, and an awareness of the need for a 'working-class' political identity. This was true even for 'Liberal' areas, particularly seats in the Bradford/Leeds area, parts of the East End of London, in Salford, and to some extent in Glasgow. Here, unusually, Labour was willing, and occasionally able, to become the party of action on general local problems such as abject poverty or squalid housing conditions, and to be the party which expressed this through a language of plebeian opposition to uncaring (middle-class) outsiders. It could nullify the view that the Liberals had cornered the market in materially significant forms of intervention. Nonetheless, the circumstances, and the dynamic Labour organisations which produced these results, were unusual. The Liberals were unlikely to oppose Labour candidates in Bow and Bromley and West Salford, and the Progressive parties were considering an arrangement in Glasgow. However, adaptive, radical, Liberal parties *usually* seemed to offer as credible an approach and to present a serious obstacle even in the inner-cities.[38]

Some additional seats in 'Liberal' areas would probably have been added to the list of sanctioned seats by January 1915. Northampton (a double member borough) was to be fought by a Liberal *and* a Labour candidate.[39] There were also some constituencies (such as Burnley, Huddersfield, and Colne Valley), where Labour had developed a substantial organisational and electoral base by emphasising local Liberal deficiencies, by building on the work of ethical socialists and Socialist moral reformers, by adopting Statist ideas, or through combinations of these factors. In the instances identified above the response of local Labour groups to appeals for funds suggested that money may not have been a problem. All three seats had been fought in 1910 (Burnley by a member of the SDF), and were likely to be fought again.

A substantially wider and more anti-Liberal campaign than in 1910 was unlikely. There was little prospect of a major expansion beyond the sixty-five seats which had sanctioned candidates by January 1915. Available evidence suggests some increase in Tory areas, in certain coal-fields and in a few additional seats where Labour was a powerful force.

[38] See above, pp. 156–7, 193. For Glasgow, D. Howell, *Leaders lost* (Manchester, 1986), pp. 235–7. For a possible Progressive arrangement, Hutchison, *Scotland*, p. 265.
[39] See above, p. 311.

Some candidates may not have found seats which would merit the expenditure of union funds and attract NEC approval, and (as in 1910) some may have chosen to keep their powder dry.[40] The BSP and ILP were in no position to support further action. Few local organisations could finance a parliamentary contest from their own financial resources (those that claimed this usually had other sources of funds).[41] The Labour party was not riding the crest of a constituency wave which was inexorably forcing it into conflict with the Liberals. In January 1910, Labour fielded sixty-seven candidates in England and Wales, nineteen of whom faced two opponents. In 1914–15, the campaign would probably have been a little larger, the degree of Liberal/Labour conflict a fraction more pronounced. Labour was as committed to 'Liberal' policies in 1914 as it had been in 1910. It had no new ideological perspective. It had made only limited organisational and electoral progress even in some seats which would be fought. As the municipal evidence indicates, it had often expanded on a limited front by consolidating a hold over a small proportion of a constituency (and amongst particular occupational groups within the working class). Major progress was confined to Labour-held seats, some constituencies with a large Tory working-class vote, and a few mining seats. The overall position in 1914 was not much different than in 1910.

History was about to repeat itself.

II

The Liberal blockage in MacDonald's scheme for a gradual realignment on the left, and the ideological/political failure of Edwardian Socialists, ensured that expansion would be limited. This failure fuelled internal conflicts which MacDonald's strategy had initially masked. Discontent, anguish, and acrimony are increasingly apparent. For many in the Labour party, change in the nature of Labour/Socialist aims, in pursuit of (elusive) electoral success, meant that the soul of the party was sacrificed for little return.

The left attempted to crystallise this opposition. Yet despite the fact that Jowett's 'vote-on-principle' policy was accepted at the ILP Conference in 1914, the left appeared leaderless and without concrete ideas. It was already a declining force. As one left activist wrote to Lansbury (who had virtually dropped out of politics by 1914), 'the one outstanding fact

[40] In 1910, fourteen officially sanctioned candidates did not find a seat. Unions often opposed fighting 'frivolous' campaigns. See above, fn. 24 and pp. 56–60, 149, 239.
[41] For financial problems, J. MacTavish to J.R.M., 15 July 1914, JRM PRO 30/69/1158 (Portsmouth); Edinburgh TC AR 1913/14; Newport LP Mins, 18 June 1914; J. C. Hendry to J.K.H., 14 Apr. 1908, FJ 08/147 (Montrose).

is the absolute chaos of the Labour and Socialist parties – all of them ... Everything is mixed and chaotic in the extreme.'[42] An independent Socialist alternative, the BSP, had been formed and had failed. Even 'hard left' elements were trickling back to the Labour camp; the BSP itself was attempting to affiliate. This was in part a victory for those Socialist moral reformers – like Irving – who had always wanted to fight for Socialism within the Labour party. However, these elements were trying to re-enter Labour politics at a time when they had evidently failed as an independent organisation. If their attempt to affiliate succeeded (which was by no means certain) their moral (and numerical) strength would have been less evident than in 1906.

Paradoxically, by 1914 a section of the Socialist left had developed a comparatively sophisticated critique of state centralism. The New Liberal emphasis on reconciling intervention with freedom via democracy, they argued, had not penetrated the crucial areas of industry or Parliament. A collectivism propelled forward by material aspiration and electoral competition ensured that reforms were handed down by paternalistic technocrats. Moreover, the limited nature of Liberal sympathy for democracy was evident from Liberal ambivalence towards women's suffrage. Liberal reforms were based on the dictatorship of the intellectuals and the Civil Service bureaucrats. They were not designed to create working-class self-confidence and individual self-sufficiency.[43]

Labour's Socialist moral reformers wished to bring about Socialism and improve material conditions while increasing individual liberty. Municipal action – their chosen stance – could only take them so far. *National* political action, they argued, was imperative. However, while the left's critique of national bureaucracy was well-received amongst intellectuals, they had no means of making ideological criticism electorally attractive. Some hoped that industrial unrest would inspire a 'spirit of alienation'. They were disappointed. They increasingly fell back on the need to capture the party machine, not to win the intellectual and political argument. The rank and file had to be given more freedom from the centre; they had to influence the 'national' politicians. There had to be 'some modification of the existing Labour party organisation which will give real Socialists . . . a greater chance of getting to the top'.[44]

The institutional structure of the Labour party was such that the politics of the machine *could* influence party policy. Despite the fact that the ILP's 'Big Four' used the party bureaucracy, its control of the press and

---

[42] H. Burrows to G.L., 27 Nov. 1912, and for Lansbury's detachment, A. Salter to G.L., 27 Sept. 1914, Lansbury MS 6 fo. 229, 7 fo. 172.
[43] See above, pp. 71–2.
[44] H. D. Harben to B. Webb, 8 Dec. 1913, Webb MS II 4F fo. 166.

the party Conference, and appeals to party 'loyalty' to stifle opposition, the machinery for influencing national policy existed and could not be removed. The NAC and its executive positions were open to election. The NAC controlled the number and distribution of ILP parliamentary candidates, and had a say in the editorial policy of the party press (unlike the NLF). The ILP Conference (again unlike the NLF Conference) made party policy. It was not *easy* for dissident leaders to organise against the leadership. There was no forum for constituency organisations; attempts to organise branch opinion were seen as 'disloyal'; the party leaders used their influence with Labour/Socialist newspapers to stifle opposition; they could manipulate the national conference agenda. However, it was not impossible for dissidents to have their say. They could canvass ILP branches, gaining support for individual conference resolutions (as they did in 1908 over Grayson, and again in 1910 over the Green Manifesto) prior to the party conference. Despite Brunner's attempt to use NLF circulars to effect a similar result, the Liberals were less subject to institutionalised dissent.[45]

Permeation of the party machinery could also influence decisions taken at the Labour party conference, which made policy for the party as a whole. Although ILP delegates could be outvoted by the trade unions, Socialist permeation of trade union delegations might engineer support for dissident politics.[46] Socialist permeation of the unions, and influence in the ILP, could in turn help to determine the composition of the parliamentary party. MPs such as Keir Hardie, Fred Jowett and Lansbury had senior positions on the NAC and NEC. Other ILP MPs, like Snowden, occasionally showed signs of also opposing official Labour policy. Socialist dissidents or sympathisers, like McLachlan, Smart, and Wallhead were parliamentary candidates in 1910. Trade union candidates and MPs, such as F. H. Rose, Thomas Gribble, Ben Tillett, G. H. Stuart, James Winstone, and James O'Grady, were ideologically and politically closer to the critics of party policy than they were to MacDonald (although they were by no means a homogeneous bloc). There was also a wider and sympathetic body of opinion within the party which, despite fundamental ideological differences, the left could attempt to exploit. Some shared with the more radical left a belief in elements of the party's 'historic' operative principles.[47] Others objected to the centralisation of power, and the separation of the PLP from the party as a whole. This applied

[45] Koss, *Brunner*, pp. 248–9; Morris (thesis), Chapter 8 and p. 182.
[46] See above, p. 323.
[47] Labour's political idiom is expertly discussed in Drucker, *Doctrine and ethos*, and L. Minkin, *The Labour party Conference* (1978). See also Morris (thesis), pp. 231–2 for this in 1909–10.

most obviously to moderate members of the ILP but even Statist
reformers, like the Webbs, were dissatisfied with the Labour party as
a medium for radical change, and could act in concert with more vehement
critics of party policy on some issues. There was a general sense of stagnation. As Beatrice Webb wrote in 1914:

> What annoys me is the absence of any relation, good or bad, between the Labour
> M.P.s and the Labour Movement in the country. The Labour M.P.s seem to
> be drifting into futility – a futility that will be presently recognised by all whom
> it may concern. J. R. MacDonald has ceased to be a Socialist; the Trade Union
> M.P.s never were Socialists. Snowden is embittered and Lansbury is wild.[48]

The Webbs' complaint concerned the intellectual capacity of the union
leaders, and MacDonald's lack of commitment to extensive state intervention. However, although they also wished to change people (witness hopes
for the industrial unrest, and co-operation with the ILP over 'raising
expectations'), Sidney Webb increasingly emphasised the need for a better
organised state, and a better organised Labour party.[49] Paradoxically,
many union leaders with Statist aims found the Webbs' ideas acceptable.
The Statist elements were a powerful and growing voice in the country
and in Labour politics.

The various ideological components of the Labour party were all represented institutionally at the political centre and in the country. Labour's
institutional machinery was such that they could hope one day to alter
the balance of power, and capture the party machine. In 1914, the Mac-
Donaldite, moral reformist, wing had formed an alliance with moderate
trade unionists, including many Statist elements. This should not imply
uniformity. MacDonald, like the Webbs, had doubts about the union
leaders' abilities and interests.[50] He was also far from being a Statist
reformer. His support for 'improving' Liberal welfare policies, his desire
to work at the pace of opinion, to respect middle-class talents and interests, and to create the grounds for ethical change, rather than pursue
material benefits as an end in their own right, was shared by many ILP
moderates and the leaders of many (largely skilled) trade unions. However, Labour was a shifting coalition. Party leaders would always have
to consider this fact when discussing policy. They would also have to
guard against the intellectual and institutional assaults of those groups
who were waiting to rescue the party from 'unprincipled compromise'
or 'political betrayal'. Beneath a surface agreement over collectivism

[48] B. Webb Diary, 11 Oct. 1912 (Mackenzie, p. 180).
[49] Winter, *Socialism and war*, pp. 31, 33–9. See also above, pp. 72, 320.
[50] Cf. J.R.M. Diary, 1 Oct. 1914.

Labour was divided over what kind of state the party was trying to create. The divisions were not disappearing.

III

The Liberal party was also a coalition. Many influential Radicals and Liberal Imperialists clung to older views. Their wealth and position gave them considerable power over the formulation and expression of policy, and hence over the party image. They also still enjoyed a degree of electoral support, and this reinforced their significance in the party machine.

New Liberals were very much in the minority; they did not dominate politics at the centre or in most constituency organisations. The New Liberal thrust in Cabinet emanated from a few individuals, with support from Centrists and party pragmatists.[51] The power of a Centrist/New Liberal alliance in Cabinet, in Parliament, and in the constituencies, was growing, but they were not omnipotent. Their ideas were often watered down. The Alliance was not incapable of being undermined more substantially by alternative arguments. Liberal 'national' policy was a synthesis of competing, and partially distinct, aims. In this sense, Labour, Liberals (and the Tories) were in the same position.

New Liberals recognised that the composition of their party was a problem. They were dissatisfied at the pace of change in party policy; some were also unhappy at the nature of Liberal collectivism. There was some support for democratic control of foreign policy, and for Jowett's proposed reforms of Parliament. Individual radicals supported full suffrage, proportional representation, the referendum, and greater individual participation; the Government was less enthusiastic.[52] Significantly Churchill, in direct opposition to many democratic New Liberal principles, argued that bureaucratic state intervention commanded more confidence than devolved, more accountable, municipal interventionism. Popular participation and hostility to bureaucracy were not uppermost in all areas of Liberal policy.[53] A party which contained an institutionally and electorally successful Centrist strand, committed to the production, not redistribution, of wealth, tied the New Liberals' hands. The fact that New Liberal theorists, and even candidates and MPs like Harben and Wedgwood, thought that the division of parties did not reflect the

---

[51] See above, pp. 60–70.
[52] J. A. Hobson to C.P.S., n.d., June 1914, CPS 333/92, Acland, *Adult suffrage*, Pugh, *Electoral reform*, p. 12. For Jowett and Liberal radicals, see the *Nation*'s views, cited in *Bradford Pioneer*, 10 July 1914.
[53] e.g. W.C. to W.R., 2 June 1909, WR 301. The position was better in education, where New Liberals like Acland were more involved in policy discussions. See Thompson (thesis).

division of ideas in politics, that the victory of the ideas was paramount, might indicate a further weakness. Nonetheless, the New Liberals wished if possible to change Liberal policy and convert the Liberal party, not to join Labour or start a new organisation. There were four major reasons for this. The first was sheer pragmatism. The Liberal party was in power; it was a major force with a strong electoral base. It was thus the most effective medium for those who wished to alter aspects of the current system.[54] The second was related to the nature of Liberal moral reformism. Although moral reformers were ideologically capable of moving as far to the left as public opinion dictated, its exponents knew that rational conviction and conversion was a slow process. They were occasionally tempted to push reforms through irrespective of public opinion, or to embrace a moral populism which allowed them to dabble with 'irrationalism' and 'sentiment', as means of securing support for Liberal policies. Ultimately, however, they believed in rational choices, conviction, and intellect, and therefore wished to convert their party and its 'rational' members.[55] Ideologically, and politically, they regarded compromise with party conservatives as essential.

The third reason for accepting the Liberal party – with all its faults – was the nature of the Labour party, its principal rival on the left. The point of contention was the trade union movement – 'a heavy log difficult to move ... chiefly occupied, with questions of organisation and internal squabbles' as Ponsonby put it. Trade unions, they argued, were embedded in the competitive nature of capitalism, and concerned with little more than wages and hours. The Statist elements in particular were concerned with Government intervention, but not with how that was compatible with the interests of the economy or of the community as a whole.[56] There was a fourth reason. To an extent, New Liberal ideas were a rationalisation of interests and self-perceptions. The trade unions' independent (or in Liberal terms 'sectional') activity represented a culture, and aspirations, which the New Liberals could not accept. Despite their emphasis on 'democracy', many New Liberals did not want policy to reflect existing popular attitudes or material interests, which (when not making allowances) they generally disparaged. The reviled Fabians were hardly more elitist. Their corporate stance recognised acquisitiveness, and sought to control it through the machinery of the state. Many Fabians (including the Webbs) were at least as pleased as

[54] See above, p. 67, fn. 1, for the limited commitment of radicals such as Harben and Wedgwood to the Liberal party *per se*.
[55] See above, pp. 25–7, 70, 284, and below pp. 375–80.
[56] A. Ponsonby to J.R.M., 19 Aug. 1914, JRM PRO 30/69/1158, and L.G.'s views, C.P.S. Diary, 3 Feb. 1913.

New Liberals to see popular demonstrations of hostility to the 'dehumanising' industrial system, despite their association with 'bureaucracy'. A large part of the New Liberals' objection to 'Fabianism' was the Fabians' advocacy of an *administrative* (Fabian) not an intellectual (New Liberal) elite, and the Fabians' partial support for working-class affluence as an end in its own right. New Liberals felt uneasy with labour elements who thought, spoke, and behaved very differently from the intellectual elite, and whose conception of change placed an emotional hostility to capitalism's impact on human dignity above intellectual assessments of how the position could be changed. This was a cultural hostility to the ethos of the Labour party as much as an ideological hostility to corporatism. Labour was not powerful enough, nor ideologically attractive enough at this stage, to persuade New Liberals to swallow their objections to a party based on the organised working class.

Nonetheless, Liberal radicals wanted to move their party to the left; they wanted the power necessary to implement their beliefs. Some (although not usually the theorists) recognised that the purchase of ideas alone was not enough. The formation of Dilke's Radical Committee – which included radical back-benchers such as Alden, Money, Ponsonby, Higham, and Trevelyan – in the 1890s, was a recognition of the need for an internal, organised radical bloc. Their attempts to 'capture' the NLF and other party institutions were equally part of the process of institutionalising radical policy.[57] It was necessary to bring pressure on the Cabinet because of the institutionalised power of the party conservatives.

The Liberal party had to be 'radicalised' from above *and* from below if it was to become the efficient social democratic mechanism which the New Liberals wished to create. To this end, it was necessary to bring pressure to bear on parties in the constituencies because they too had a strong conservative component. To an extent, 'radicalisation from below' *was* altering the composition and power structure of local parties, the local presentation of policy, and the nature of the parliamentary party. In some areas there had been substantial progress by 1914. London, Manchester, Huddersfield, and Northampton were centres of radical thought. They acted as political fulcrums and (potentially) as sources of radical political initiatives. Nonetheless, these areas were not typical, and they could not dictate policy to the national party. There was no automatic line to the party as a whole, or even to the leadership. The New Liberals at the centre and in the constituencies had no fully adequate institutional means of bringing pressure on a reluctant, conservative, party elite. Policy

[57] See esp. C.P.T. to H. Samuel, 12, 18 May 1895, *CPT* 4.

emanated from the top. By 1910, the New Liberals were beginning to become more involved in the process of policy formation. They moved closer to the centre of power, becoming private secretaries, Whips, junior ministers, and Cabinet ministers. This (like 'Fabianism') may have been more 'efficient' than converting party opinion; it avoided giving power to a party conference which, while it might have institutionalised radicalism, could also have become a thorn in the leadership's flesh. Nonetheless, reforming strands were not uniting together or looking to the future. Even in 1910 many radical back-benchers felt distant and uninvolved in Liberal policy discussions. Power was insecurely held by slender threats. The Liberal party's composition and structure made it an imperfect social democratic mechanism. The self-proclaimed aristocracy of intellect no doubt felt flattered by its greater power after 1910; in failing to recognise the importance of institutionalising that power, they sacrificed the future to the present.

IV

In 1914, British social democracy had an uncertain future. Four possibilities stand out. One widely discussed at the time was the disintegration of the Labour party, the collapse of an organisation no longer able to maintain the alliance between moderate collectivists, trade unions, and Socialists. MacDonald, Snowden and others shared many of the ideas, aims, and dislikes of the Liberal moral reformers. MacDonald noted later that he might have joined a Liberal Government in certain circumstances at this time. A New Liberal/Revisionist alliance was mooted before, during, and after the First World War.[58] There was also speculation that the trade unions' support for Liberal reforms, and the virulent opposition of some Labour Socialists to these policies, would remove the grounds for a Labour/Socialist alliance.[59] 'Labour' might have split along either of these fissures. Despite internal tensions, it did not appear to be doing so in 1914.

The second possibility was that the Liberal party would become dominated by a Centrist/Old Liberal alliance, with the New Liberal wing deserting to Labour. This too seemed unlikely on the eve of war, even though the balance of power in Liberal politics had shifted a little towards the right. The third possibility – the most likely – was the continuation of the 'MacDonaldite' strategy of Progressive Alliance. The rationale of

[58] J.R.M., *Socialism after the war*, p. 39 and Conrad Noel's illuminating pamphlet, *How to win* (1914). For the revival of this during the war, below, pp. 365, 370, 378.
[59] *Postman's Gazette*, 1 Nov. 1913, Burrows to Lansbury, above, fn. 42, B. Webb Diary, 5 July 1913 (Mackenzie, p. 188).

Alliance was undisturbed. The cross-party ideological coalition was still a strong force. It was even reinforced by changing attitudes within each organisation, and by the prospects of expanded Labour representation held out in 1914. From Labour's standpoint, the Liberal party still had certain defects. However, Labour representation was a useful stick with which to promote Liberal action, an interim benefit on the way to a more pronounced realignment. The left might not like the nature of the party's aims or the rate of its advance, but they had no alternative. Moreover, it was possible for them to hope that in future, they could either convince the party of the need for a more radical stance, or capture its principal executive positions and dictate policy. Gradual expansion, until the conditions for realignment were apposite, was still an attractive proposition to many sections of the party.

As things stood, Labour's progress would be slow. The Progressive Alliance was not about to disintegrate through rank and file pressure, sweeping ideological solutions to Labour's problems, or minor shifts leading to the expansion of Labour's electoral base. The leaders were not being forced into a larger parliamentary campaign by the unions. Limited commitment to Labour politics and aims amongst many unskilled unions, some skilled unions, and most white-collar unions, coupled with widespread contracting-out, and the use of political funds for non-political activity, ensured that there was no simple correlation between the expansion of trade unions and the expansion of Labour's electoral campaign. It would need *increases* in political levies, a politicisation of many unions, and a massive upsurge in branch solvency before a very widespread campaign was possible.[60] There was no suggestion that anything on this scale was imminent in 1914.

A *gradual* expansion of the Labour campaign, and of the Labour vote, was a more serious proposition. Labour stalwarts like the MFGB and UTFWA were hoping to finance more candidates. Executive politics, the desire for craft representation, activists' pressure, and the sheer existence of a political fund meant that *some* additional candidates would be available in the future. Moreover, the Liberals' inability to forge real roots in some Tory areas, the increasingly 'Labour' inclinations of some miners, and the development of Labour support amongst public sector workers, suggested a growing capacity to 'justify' electoral campaigns in certain parts of the country and particular types of seats. The country might indeed have become divided into two nations. It would nonetheless

---

[60] DWR, Minutes of delegates' meeting 1917 (suspension of the political levy); Watermen and Lightermen, *AR* 1915 (transfer to general funds); NAUL EC Mins, 5 Mar./6 Aug. 1909 (use of political funds for strike support). For contracting out, below, pp. 393–4, 401–3.

doubtless be difficult to ensure – after a time – that the expansion of Labour's campaign was confined to these areas. Pressure from constituency organisations was mounting. Organisational efficiency would become more general; encouraged by Labour officials, some unions already made financial provision for local Labour action by their members, and rather more were contemplating similar action.[61] This would not create organisational uniformity, but it would make it more difficult to channel activity into 'acceptable' areas. The party leaders recognised this, but saw it as an inevitable by-product of the desire to expand. However, there is no evidence that local organisations had succeeded in creating a powerful and popular constituency base by 1914, or that they were moving rapidly in that direction.

The fourth possibility was electoral reform. The NEC, bitterly divided over the issue, had avoided discussing it since 1910, but had to do so at the party conference in 1914.[62] Some Socialists supported Proportional Representation because they thought it would encourage Labour to field more candidates and adopt a distinct, non-Liberal (i.e. Socialist) approach. There would be no virtue in (pre-election) compromises with the Liberals. Others indicated that Proportional Representation would permit the formation of a single Socialist party which could act in partial alliance with Labour representatives, enabling Socialists to put forward their case without permanently undermining the prospects of their more moderate, but broadly acceptable, colleagues. Some more conservative Labour politicians supported the Alternative Vote, which (opponents argued) would still enable it to co-operate with the Liberal party. Despite a Conference vote which rejected both changes (by narrow majorities), it was an issue marked for further consideration, with the Alternative Vote the more likely option.[63]

Although individuals in the Liberal party supported such a change in the electoral system, it was not party policy in 1914. Nonetheless, growing Liberal/Labour conflict, the threat of Tory victories because of a split Progressive vote, and the desire of Liberal associations to field candidates even where Labour was the Progressive representative, ensured that it would remain on the Liberal agenda. Important provincial organ-

---

[61] *Locomotive Journal*, July 1914, *Bakers' Magazine*, July 1915, *R.R.*, 3 Apr. 1914, *Typographical Circular*, July 1915, Railway Clerks *AR* 1916, SWMF Mins, 1 Mar. 1915. See also discussion of local political finance, LP *AR* 1917, pp. 12–14. The Prudential Agents' Assoc., the Gasworkers, and other unions were committed to new or additional candidates when their political funds were larger (*Daily Cit.*, 30 May, 3 June 1914).

[62] See J.R.M. *et al.*, *The Labour party and electoral reform* (1914).

[63] This was MacDonald and the PLP's preference and it was backed by important unions like the Steel Smelters (Pugh, *Electoral reform*, pp. 8–11, BrSS *MR* Feb. 1914). The PLP also supported an A.V. Bill later in 1914. The 'radical' ASE, like many Socialists, backed P.R. (Burgess, *Bradford Pioneer*, 15 Aug. 1913, ASE *MR* Feb. 1914).

isations were urging its consideration. In 1912, several members of the Cabinet were reportedly sympathetic.[64] Despite this, neither Labour nor the Liberals adopted the idea. They did not need to. Labour was still a limited organisational and electoral threat. The Progressive Alliance served both parties' purpose. As that changed, party policy could well change with it.

The Progressive Alliance was still intact in 1914. Despite potential fissures in the Liberal and Labour coalitions, it appeared that an immediate and fundamental realignment of forces was unlikely. The formation of the Alliance in 1906 reflected the growing ascendancy of social democratic ideas in both parties. It was also an acknowledgement of the fact that, despite this common social democratic core, there were also important differences between these two composite organisations. These differences meant that each party could add something to a Progressive electoral coalition and increase its electoral strength. United the two parties might stand as a powerful anti-Tory force; divided they would almost certainly fall. The Liberals, on their own, were economically and culturally unsuited to breaking the Tories' hold over working-class opinion in several parts of the country. Yet the Liberal party had an electoral base which included several working-class areas and substantial middle-class and rural support. Labour's as yet half-formed, but still positive, appeal to certain groups and areas was insufficient to make it a major anti-Tory party in the country as a whole; yet its limited, distinct, strengths complemented those of its Progressive ally. A pact united forces in areas where neither party could win unaided, and prevented potentially damaging conflicts in seats where only the Tories would benefit from Progressive disarray.

Nonetheless, Labour was not happy to remain as a junior partner in a Progressive Alliance indefinitely. Beneath the surface of Progressive co-operation, it attempted to gradually expand its base and to replace its Progressive ally. The electoral future of the Liberal and Labour parties as competing organisations would be determined by their ability to serve the material interests and social outlooks of voters. Even in 1914, Labour's ability to replace the Liberals was geographically and occupationally confined. If it had a sizeable base in many areas of Liberal strength, it could seldom gain seats in 'Liberal' working-class areas. Co-operation seemed half-justified by the ideological similarities between the parties; it was also politically essential. There seemed little prospect that this division of labour would disintegrate in the near future. In time, however, the

[64] Pugh, *Electoral reform*, pp. 11–16, Mid.LF Mins, 5 Mar. 1914, LCLF Mins, 10 Sept. 1912, Scottish LF motion, cited in Petter (thesis), p. 50.

expansion of the Labour machine may had led to further conflict. Both parties, at some point, would have to consider the growing demand for electoral reform as a means of securing Progressive co-operation and political independence. In 1914, neither party wished to sacrifice the possibility of securing a more complete ascendancy. The Labour left placed its hope in ideological 'progress', in gaining institutional control of the Labour machine, or in a form of proportional representation which would guarantee its ideological purity. The Labour centre/right hoped that in the near future the Liberals would lose their grip. Meantime they would keep plugging away.

The *nature* of the parties was also not written in tablets of stone. They were coalitions of potentially shifting groups. Neither group was an ideologically or institutionally perfect vehicle for social democratic aspirations. Labour was open to influence from the unions and the left. This, social democrats argued, might undermine its credibility and create divergent aims and interests. It was constructed in such a way that these groups had a ready access route to institutional power. The Liberals, by contrast, were creating a reforming alliance at the centre and in the constituencies. However, this alliance was divided and vulnerable. Some elements at least might easily link up with other sections of the party in a changed political climate. The institutional strength of the most radical elements, the social democratic New Liberals, was insufficient to guarantee that the party maintained its current direction. They were over-dependent on the purchase of their ideas and the power of Lloyd George for their new political prominence. The New Liberals had been influential in creating an electoral coalition which took the party from almost permanent opposition in the 1890s to a position of primacy in the Edwardian period. They had helped reinforce the party's position in 'Liberal' areas. They had helped it win hitherto Tory seats. They had encouraged the adoption of an approach which kept the Liberal reforming alliance, and the Progressive Alliance, together. The New Liberalism would be less functional if, through its own ideological failings or Labour's positive attractions, the 'Tory' areas were lost. The First World War thus provided a stimulus and a test to both the New Liberalism and the 'new' Liberal party.

Part IV The politics of change

Chapter 12

Industry, politics and the Progressive
Alliance, 1914–18

It is commonly assumed that the First World War caused considerable
social and political upheaval. Changes in the industrial sphere and a
compression of the class structure are generally identified as the major
causes of a change in Labour's strength and position. In reality, while
there were some changes, there was not a complete rupture with the
past. Social and economic conditions did not create a homogeneous working class, or a uniform class experience (Section I). Workers were not
discontented with an oppressive state (as some Marxist historians would
have us believe). They did not display a sense of oppositional class unity.
Neither did participation in the war effort transform the British working
class (Section II).

Nonetheless, there was the potential for social/political discontent during the war, and parties could not afford to let their political position
slip. Labour attempted to maximise its prospects by supporting the military and industrial changes which Governments argued were necessary
to win the war, while insisting at the same time that these changes should
not adversely affect domestic living standards and liberties. Many Labour
proposals for the home front reflected traditional Liberal concerns. However, while Labour's support for the provision of public housing, and
its concern that the burden of war should fall on the rich were 'moral'
issues which built on pre-war (Liberal) campaigns for economic justice,
it had developed concrete proposals (nationalisation, the capital levy)
which improved its credibility as a reforming party. It now had relevant,
and emotive, rallying cries because the wartime experience of profiteering
and personal loss made proposals for redemptive intervention seem 'just',
and it appeared to have the means to turn emotion into action. Nonetheless, Labour was still so close to a Liberal tradition, and offered so little
that was really economically distinctive, that older allegiances and rival
(Tory) rallying cries were more potent means of attracting working-class
support in many parts of the country. At the same time, however, Labour
support for the war effort, and for retaining economic gains made during

the war, especially through greater state involvement in industry (an idea also made credible to certain occupational groups by the experience of war), made it seem more positively attractive to the unskilled and to workers in areas dominated by voters with Statist interests. Its comparative electoral potential improved dramatically, particularly in the Tory working-class areas and the coalfields, although even here it had not found all the political answers (Section III). This was a rapid escalation of pre-war trends. The war did not create a uniform class experience which might make 'class politics', and the ideas of the left, a realistic possibility. Unless the left developed new ideas, Labour would still need a political image which satisfied and represented spatially and occupationally distinct experiences and interests. It had not supplied this by 1918. Social experiences and improvements in Labour's approach at least ensured that it was in a better position to build on its strengths as a partial, localised, expression of particular sets of ideas and interests.

The Liberals' position was just as complicated. They tried to manage and to win the war while maintaining support for a degree of liberty, equality, and tolerable living conditions on the home front (Section IV). This was always a difficult path to tread. In 1916 the party split when Lloyd George took over and attempted to prosecute the conduct of the war more vigorously. Although the split was not at this stage as serious as some historians have suggested, the balancing process subsequently became more difficult and a bad political situation for the Liberals became worse. The nature of Government action made Lloyd George's Coalition Liberals appear as a party of the right, focusing primarily on military 'necessity' at the expense of the home front.

The Asquithian Liberals suffered ideologically and politically from their perceived inability to overcome obstacles to the achievement of full military efficiency. They also failed to maintain the radical domestic political focus which before 1914 ensured that they were perceived as the major party of the left in most parts of the country. After the split, they were wary of becoming a party of opposition. The composition of the party and its institutional structure made it difficult for party radicals to act as a torch which would keep the flame of radical Liberalism alight. The Liberals' hold slipped just as Labour restaked its claim to parts of the pre-war Liberal electoral constituency. It was this which made Labour's limited progress so politically significant.

I

For many years social and labour historians saw the First World War as a cause of huge social and political changes, as the cause of greater working-class unity and of a more popular working-class party. Recent accounts have identified a more complex relationship between war and social change, and have stressed the continued fragmentation of the working class. Yet many aspects of the war remain to be examined. Historians are not always clear as to how the war affected those not employed in the munitions industries. Neither do they always recognise that, as the war was experienced in different ways, there could be variations in how particular groups of workers responded to differing political initiatives.

On the home front, the workers most likely to be affected by the war were those engaged in essential war work, particularly manufacturing and metals. Some labour historians argue that these workers were subject to considerable state control, and to a major restructuring of work practices. This created a degree of class unity and a consequent political radicalism which existed despite official labour attempts to blunt its impact. Moreover, Government action drew the whole nation into war, raising expectations and encouraging class sentiments. The state acquired powers to intervene in every aspect of life. The Defence of the Realm Act granted the Government power to intervene in order to maximise war production. The Treasury agreement of March 1915, which made strikes and restrictive practices on Government contracts illegal, was enforced with the official co-operation of the TUC and the unions. Wage rates were centrally arranged and 'war bonuses' centrally negotiated; dilution of labour and alterations in working conditions were agreed in principle. Job mobility and enlistment were controlled, particularly after the introduction of conscription, by the use of leaving certificates and exemption badges. The state took the power to influence prices and to improve general welfare through restrictions, controls, and reforms. Through the control of the press, it could influence the individual's capacity to construct informed criticism. Eventually, once conscription was introduced, Government had to some extent power over life and death itself.[1]

In practice, the impact of the war even on war workers was less pronounced, and less uniform, than this might suggest. The Government *claimed* it intervened in order to maximise military production. In reality intervention was piecemeal and cautious.[2] The dilution of labour,

---

[1] For the conventional analysis, J. Hinton, *The first shop stewards movement* (1973), Burgess, *Challenge of labour*, Chapter 5, Cronin, *Labour and society in Britain*, Chapter 2.

[2] For an overview, Clegg, *Trade unions*, 2, pp. 118–212 and C. J. Wrigley, 'The trade unions during the first world war', in Wrigley (ed.), *History of industrial relation*', ii. More specifically, H. Jones, 'The Home Office and working conditions, 1914–40', London Ph.D. thesis 1983, pp. 40–61. The social impact of war has also received considerable recent attention. See especially J. Winter, *The Great War and the British people* (Cambridge, 1986) and Waites, *Society at war*.

through the introduction of new technology and the erosion of skill and union control, was not so pronounced that there was a second industrial revolution or a remaking of the working class. There were many jobs which most women were physically incapable of assuming. In the iron-founding industry, for example, the number of women employed rose from 2 to just 8 per cent during the war. Definitions of 'acceptable' female work, and union opposition to the introduction of female labour, further limited the tasks which women were asked to perform. Dangerous work – such as mining – was ruled out.[3] Unions, anxious to protect their (male) members' jobs, kept female labour out through agreements with local employers. In the Boot and Shoe industry, for example, where industrial change had already eroded craft control, dilution was 'practically a dead letter' before 1917. Although restrictions were eased later, female labour was introduced only on the most menial work.[4] The absorption of around 5 million men into the armed forces meant that the unskilled worker, previously at the mercy of an over-staffed and under-unionised labour market, was now in a strong bargaining position. This, and the high profits which employers could make on war work, gave the unskilled workers' unions a previously unknown strength.

The craft unions were in an even better position to resist Government intervention. With skilled labour in such short supply, management could not afford to introduce changes which would encourage union members to seek employment elsewhere. The 'State' and 'Capital' did not collude to remove workers' skill as a joint response to the problem. They were not so sophisticated or so unified. Individual sectors of the capitalist economy had different interests. Far from there being a uniform 'deskilling' of labour, management, and unions in varying industries (and even firms) conducted a series of quite separate negotiations, and produced a widely varying pattern of agreed industrial practices.[5]

War did not transform the position of skilled workers. First, they frequently, and successfully, rejected dilution of labour. In some instances this involved finding alternative means of tackling increased work. It could involve the introduction of new technology (as in shipbuilding) or (as in the printing industry) more rapid promotion and the relaxation

---

[3] Neville (thesis), p. 493, Williams, *Derbyshire miners*, pp. 539–40; Fyrth and Collins, *Ironfounders*, p. 145; BrSS, *MR* Jan. 1917.

[4] Fox, *Boot and Shoe Union*, pp. 369–70.

[5] J. Zeitlin, 'Industrial structure, employer strategy and the diffusion of job control in Britain, 1880–1920', in Mommsen and Husung (eds.), *Trade unionism in Great Britain and Germany*, pp. 325–37; J. Turner, 'The politics of "Organised Business" during the First World War', in J. Turner (ed.), *Businessmen in politics* (1984), pp. 37–49. This was the case even in the South Wales coal industry, G. Holmes, 'The First World War and Government Coal Control', in C. Baber and L. J. Williams (eds.), *Modern South Wales* (Cardiff, 1986), pp. 215–16.

of some apprenticeship regulations for male workers.[6] Secondly, women were largely employed on repetitive munitions work, which disappeared at the end of the war and did not fit them to compete with skilled craftsmen. Roughly 60 per cent of men and 54 per cent of women on munitions work were dilutees, compared to just one third of men and one fifth of women in other divisions of the metals and chemical industries. Thirdly on Clydeside at least (and probably elsewhere), few employers were interested in putting untrained women into skilled jobs, particularly if this meant losing production or workers because of union hostility to the proposals.[7]

This was also the position in the mining and transport industries, which were even more heavily controlled by the state. Following a series of strikes or threatened strikes in South Wales, the Government was forced to take control of production, initially in the South Wales coalfields, and subsequently over the major remaining coalfields. This appeared the only way to resolve obdurate industrial relations problems. Management of the docks and the railways was also 'unified' by the state. This did not facilitate greater repression and create class antagonism. Working conditions were not substantially altered. There were some changes in shift systems and promotion structures; on the railways, for example, shunters became drivers more rapidly than in the past. There was more flexibility between jobs. On the docks, casual labour and job specialisation declined; in the mines, hewers might be expected to do the work of 'putters' and 'fillers' (where labour had been so divided) and the subcontracting 'butty system' was abolished in the East Midlands and South Yorkshire.[8] There was little 'dilution', and even after conscription was introduced, workers in these areas were initially able to gain exemption. Later, when more cannon fodder was needed, the 'combing out' process was restricted to 'new' labour. Even the exhortations to work, the attacks on absenteeism and heavy drinking, were largely kept within the unions;

---

[6] S. Higenbottom, *Our Society's history* (Manchester, 1939), pp. 196–7; Musson, *Typographical Association*, pp. 366–8; Mortimer, *Boilermakers' Society*, ii, p. 88.

[7] Reid, 'Dilution during the First World War', pp. 50–3. See also Hyman, *Workers' Union*, p. 85. The opposite argument was developed by G. D. H. Cole and later by James Hinton. The figures for October 1917 are from Waites, *Society at war*, p. 196.

[8] Mining: B. E. Supple, *The history of the coalmining industry*, 4 (1987), Chapters 2–3, and esp. pp. 48, 78–86, Neville (thesis) p. 512; Docks: Phillips and Whiteside, *Casual labour*, Chapter 4, E. Taplin, *The Dockers' Union* (Leicester, 1985), Chapter 9, Schneer, 'British dockers during 1914–18', pp. 102–7; Railways: P. S. Bagwell, *The Railwaymen* (1963), pp. 345–56, and *Locomotive Journal*, Aug. 1917.

there was little outside interference or major threats to the unions' 'independence'.[9]

Rather than proposing dilution, or introducing new technology, many employers advocated a shift to piece work as a means of improving production. Some unions, such as the Carpenters, Engineers, and Ironfounders, were very suspicious of this, even though it was a growing trend before 1914, because it gave employers the power to dictate earnings. Others, like the Boilermakers, had already accepted it as inevitable.[10] Even within these unions, however, responses varied with local practices and positions. It was not unusual for unions to 'permit' change in areas of 'new' industry, like Coventry, where it was already general practice, or to 'exchange' a move to piece work in return for some management concession on wage rates. High wages on piece work presented a potential expansion of earning capability for many workers. Although unions were sufficiently suspicious to seek terminal dates for these arrangements, it was often impossible to retain the members' support for (less remunerative) time rates. Nonetheless, 'dilution' and new working conditions passed by many centres of heavy industry.[11] This was not because of union resistance to technological change. There is little evidence of a technological explosion during the war or of employers displaying an interest in 'scientific management' which was thwarted by the unions. Moreover, unions in growing areas (like Coventry) were not always compliant, while unions in the 'older' industrial areas (like the North-East) did not mindlessly resist change.[12] For whatever reason, the work-experience of that section of the skilled working class engaged in war-production

---

[9] Supple, *Coal Industry*, 4, pp. 71–2; Phillips and Whiteside, *Casual labour*, pp. 120–1, Schneer, *Tillett*, Chapter 9, Waller, *Liverpool*, pp. 271–2. For railways, Howard (thesis), Chapter 4.

[10] Higenbottom, *Our Society's history*, p. 208; Zeitlin, 'Engineers and compositors', p. 271; Ironfounders' *MR* Aug. 1917. Union attitudes are discussed further below, pp. 363–5.

[11] For Coventry, J. Haydu, 'Factory politics in Britain and the United States: engineers and machinists, 1914–1919', *Comparative studies in society and history* (1985), pp. 60–3 and Whiting, *Cowley*, pp. 6–7. Cf. the engineering industry in the North-East, Waites, *Society at war*, p. 154 and J. F. Clarke, 'Labour in World War One. Some experiences in engineering and shipbuilding on the North-East coast 1914–18', *Bulletin of the North-East group for the study of labour history* (1980), p. 42.

[12] For the general wartime position and the exceptions (principally ironfounding) to the rule that industry was not substantially altered technically, S. Pollard, *The development of the British economy 1914–67* (1969), pp. 53–62. Although Lewchuk has argued that union strength prevented the introduction of 'Fordism' in car production, the evidence is disputed (W. Lewchuk, 'Fordism and British motor car employers, 1896–1932' in H. Gospel and C. Littler (eds.), *Managerial strategies and industrial relations* (1983) and S. Tolliday, 'The failure of mass production unionism in the motor industry, 1914–39', in Wrigley (ed.), *Industrial relations*, II, pp. 311–12. More generally, Littler, *Labour process*, pp. 97, 187).

was not generally altered in a manner which reduced its autonomy, status, or control.

At the same time, the material well-being and living standards of those engaged in war work, and particularly the unskilled, were far better in 1918 than in 1914. Earnings were more regular, overtime more common, and supplementary work for family members was more freely available. As increases in hourly wage rates often only kept incomes in line with inflation, more regular work was probably the major source of improvements in real incomes. State imposed minimums in agriculture, and in the docks (where a minimum working week was also established) and a more vigorous Trade Boards Act also had a positive impact.[13] Workers in Government arms factories and a wide range of small enterprises experienced marked improvements in wages and conditions. Government social intervention had a positive impact. There were considerable improvements in health and in life expectancy.[14] ʏ

Yet changes in wage rates and apparent changes in living standards are an unsatisfactory means of determining the real impact of war on the working class. Most historians of the First World War, unlike historians of earlier and later periods, have still to deal with factors other than national wage rates in discussing the economic side of the standard of living. They do not take full account, for example, of the regional/sectoral nature of change. Some understanding of the fact that the experience of war was mixed, and that the interpretation of that experience was equally variable, is vital to an appreciation of the varying attitudes which workers displayed to the Government and its policies in 1917–18.

The position for skilled war workers was not as disastrous as older accounts suggest, although the general thrust of recent research confirms that differentials narrowed during this period. Dr Winter's recent calculations suggest that wages for skilled groups kept ahead of the inflation which raged in 1918. Miners and railwaymen were particularly successful in this respect. To some extent this reflected market conditions. However, in their (state-controlled) industries, company wage increases were replaced by national agreements, and forms of intervention by the state which benefited the workers. Industrial action and other union overtures brought concessions. 'The government' a War Cabinet document noted, 'could not embark on a conflict with the miners when they were not certain to bring it to a victorious issue . . . A great strike would be equiva-

[13] R. Penn, 'The course of wage differentials between skilled and non-skilled manual workers in Britain between 1856 and 1964', *British Journal of Industrial Relations* (1983), p.76 (Rochdale); Howkins, *Poor labouring men*, pp. 121–2; Stuart and Hunter, *Taylors' union*, p. 148; Taplin, *Dockers' Union*, pp. 129, 132.

[14] Winter, *The war and the people*, pp. 153, 244–5. See also L. M. Barnett, *British food policy during the First World War* (1985).

lent to a military defeat.'[15] Moreover, increased family income as a result of better employment opportunities for women, increased overtime, and more regular earnings also affected skilled workers. In North-Eastern shipbuilding towns, sporadic or more permanent unemployment (a problem before 1914) became less serious. Some skilled workers moved to piece work, others were promoted. Despite the movement towards national wage bargaining it seems likely that in skilled occupations – as in mining and docking – the level of real local earnings would depend on the nature and extent of local supplements to national wage agreements, or on local means of calculating payments. Local prices and other costs would also influence perceptions of 'affluence'. Differential housing costs in particular could erode living standards when changes in wage rates would suggest improvements. In addition to those areas where housing costs had been increasing before 1914, areas such as Coventry, Luton, Birmingham, and Glasgow expanded because of munitions or war work at a time when the decline of housebuilding, and new family formation, was putting extra pressure on the existing housing stock. Private landlords and coal companies declined to deal with repairs or to consider investment in housing. Equally, however, workers in some towns *benefited* from the restriction of rent increases imposed by national legislation.[16]

The experience of those in 'non-essential' employment was less favourable. They were more likely to be conscripted. As Dr Dewey notes, the 'soldiers of the First World War were as likely to have been clerks or shop assistants in civilian life as to have been miners or engineers'. Those who remained worked longer hours in worse conditions, with few financial incentives. Post Office workers, for example, were moved from one kind of work, or one office, to another, worked unsociable split shifts, and had to make way for casual, 'temporary', and female workers. Like railway clerks, and possibly others, they were poorly paid, or not paid at all for compulsory overtime. Nonetheless, in the major 'non-essential'

---

[15] Cited in K. Middlemass, *Politics in industrial society* (1979), p. 103. Government involvement in the strikes is discussed in Supple, *Coal Industry*, 4, pp. 62–77.

[16] A. L. Bowley, *Prices and wages in the United Kingdom 1914–20* (Oxford, 1921), p. 92, Winter, *The war and the people*, Chapter 7, Boilermakers', *AR* 1915. Instances of a *widening* real earnings gap between skilled and unskilled workers in some sectors are cited in A. Reid, 'The impact of the First World War on British workers', in J. Wall and J. Winter (eds.), *The upheaval of war* (Cambridge, 1988), pp. 225, 232 and note 10. For housing costs, McLean, *Red Clydeside*, Chapter 2, Englander, *Landlord and tenant*, pp. 236–7, Melling, *Rent strikes*, esp. Chapter 7. Compare Waites, *Society at war*, p. 173 for the local impact of rent restriction legislation. For differential earnings, Taplin, *Dockers' Union*, pp. 132–5, Supple, *Coal Industry*, 4, p. 103.

manufacturing industries – cotton and woollen textiles – there were few major changes in working conditions.[17]

There were also seldom compensating financial benefits for sacrifices by workers in this sector. Wage increases for printers, building workers, cotton operatives, railway and postal clerks, and teachers were below the rate of inflation. At the same time, the income tax threshold was lowered to £120. Moreover, although some groups – like the cotton operatives – were excluded from making national insurance payments, the extension of the scheme ensured that new categories of workers, including many in these sectors, faced irksome deductions from their wages for the first time.[18] Equally, future employment may have seemed less secure. In some white-collar industries, and in industries – such as pottery or textiles – where women workers were already important, the proportion of women workers in the industry expanded dramatically. In cotton textiles at least they were even promoted to senior positions.[19] For these women, unlike most women war workers, war work was no doubt a significant positive change; for the male workforce, it was a potential disruption to their status, if not to their families' immediate welfare (many women workers in cotton, and in other 'family' industries like the railways, were related to existing workers, so family income often increased). Union leaders were also concerned that women would not be replaced by men at the end of the war, and would become a source of cheap labour.

Managements' reactions to wartime circumstances also varied, and became a significant contributory factor to the workers' perception of their position. In cotton textiles, for example, little changed. The system for coping with unemployment was not dramatically altered. The state kept out of the industry's affairs. Co-operative industrial relations and a Centrist perspective on the causes and nature of economic success remained intact. By contrast, those who were part of a nationalised industry, such as railway or postal clerks, were plunged into national wage negotiations. They saw manual workers in their industry benefit considerably from arrangements negotiated by the unions. If their 'status' aspi-

---

[17] P. E. Dewey, 'Military recruiting and the British labour force during the First World War', *HJ* (1984), p. 221; Clinton, *Post Office workers*, p. 191; *Railway Clerk*, 15 Jan., 15 Aug. 1915, 15 Oct. 1917. For textiles, Bornat (thesis), pp. 246–70, A. Fowler, 'War and labour unrest', in A. Fowler and T. Wyke (eds.), *The barefoot aristocrats* (Littleborough, 1987), Chapter 8.

[18] Clinton, *Post Office workers*, pp. 193–4, A. Tranter, 'The Railway Clerks Association: its origins and history to 1921', Cambridge Ph.D. thesis 1979, pp. 253, 257–8; BrSS *MR* Feb. 1917; N. Whiteside, 'Welfare legislation and the unions during the First World War', *HJ* (1980), pp. 862–4, noting opposition to the extension of national insurance.

[19] G. D. H. Cole, *The payment of wages* (1918), pp. 9–12, Bornat (thesis) pp. 209, 269–70, 420; Savage, *Preston*, pp. 93–4; Whipp, 'Pottery workers', pp. 110–16.

rations meant they still saw themselves as a distinct, white-collar, group, they learnt the economic value of collective action within a state regulated industry.[20]

The potential benefits of state involvement as a means of securing better wages and conditions were increasingly evident to many occupational groups. Company profits, and local employment on the railways, were maintained by suppressing the market mechanism. Governments also recognised, and institutionalised, the unions' new position (union recognition was a major issue before 1914). State intervention was of tangible benefit. Although it was the market position of labour which was most important in securing financial improvements during the war, few union leaders thought that this position could last. They remained fearful that 'unfavourable' intervention (such as the restriction of the right to strike) might outlast the end of the war, while 'favourable' intervention (such as national wage rates) might not. Moreover, the unions, even in state 'controlled' industries, did not get all their aims. ASLEF, for example, did not get its eight hour day. State control *could* be in the workers' economic interests; their life did not have to be governed by the vagaries of the market. However, if state control was combined with direct access to politically sympathetic decision-makers, then even more improvements in wages and conditions, or at least the stabilisation of wartime improvements, might be achieved.[21]

There is one other aspect of the period which impinged on everyone's life – the war itself. Around 6 million men served in the armed services. They suffered an experience which was unprecedented and of incalculable effect. Moreover, there was scarcely a family which did not indirectly face the repercussions of war through the involvement, death, or wounding of a family member. Three-quarters of a million men died; a larger number suffered (often permanent) injury. Yet many were there voluntarily. Like the majority of workers on the home front, their patriotism was never in question. They were not a disaffected proletariat. On the other hand, soldiers were also concerned with more mundane circumstances. Pay was worse for British than Commonwealth and especially US soldiers; food was sparse, conditions poor, discipline severe and swift. Boredom was a fact of life; it left time to contemplate questions such as the level of state provision for wives and dependents (which was

---

[20] Fowler, 'War and labour unrest', pp. 148–9; Hopwood, *Lancashire weavers*, pp. 81–2; Tranter (thesis), chapter 7.

[21] Supple, *Coal Industry*, 4, pp. 82–6, 108–11; Bagwell, *Railwaymen*, pp. 345–56. See also Holmes, 'Government coal control' for a convincing account of the continuity in management which contributed to the attitude of miners to state intervention.

Table 12.1 *Stoppages and working days lost, GB, 1910–1918*

	No. of stoppages	No. of work days lost (million)
1910	521	9.87
1911	872	10.16
1912	834	40.89
1913	1,459	9.80
1914	972	9.88
1915	672	2.95
1916	532	2.45
1917	730	5.65
1918	1,165	5.88

Source: H. Pelling, *A history of British trade unionism* (2nd edn, 1971), pp. 280–1.

less than generous).[22] Even the soldiers' experience was not without the capacity to sustain discontent with the Government.

II ⌐

The complex nature of working-class reaction to the war and wartime experiences suggests that notions of a uniform oppositional class consciousness are misplaced. Far from creating a climate of dissatisfaction, wartime industrial relations reflected labour's quiescence. The unions leaderships' decision to temporarily renounce the right to strike was generally respected. Fewer working days were lost by strike action during the war than in any year since 1909, as Table 12.1 demonstrates. As the Fabian Socialists Susan Lawrence and Beatrice Webb noted, assertive working-class action was regarded as 'sordid and unpatriotic' by the workers themselves, who displayed a 'curious self-complacency' and trust in the Government. ILP pacifists, who suffered at the hands of patriotic mobs, would have heartily concurred.[23]

Many union leaders and members were emphatically patriotic, to the point, in some instances, of xenophobia. Union leaders were involved in recruiting and in the administration of domestic policy. It was workers who would die from shortages of war material, they argued, not

[22] Winter, *The war and the people*, pp. 285–304 and D. Englander and J. Osborne, 'Jack, Tommy and Henry Dubb: the armed forces and the working class', *HJ* (1978), esp. p. 601; Wilson, *The myriad faces of war*, esp. Chapter 60.

[23] Quotations from J. Horne 'Labour leaders and the post-war world', Sussex D.Phil. thesis 1979, p. 56. See also Marquand, *MacDonald*, p. 197.

employers. When differences arose between workers and management, negotiation seemed morally just. The Boilermakers' union agreed to act 'with loyalty and unselfishness ... We are (sic) going to continue doing our best for comrades in the fight and for our country which we love.' The NUR journal, the *Railway Review*, supported a 'vigorous prosecution of the war'. For the super-patriotic Ben Tillett, war produced an almost redemptive strength and unity, 'a new relationship between the classes ... a new spiritual sense of being ... a closer bond of fairer, sweeter human ties of friendship'.[24] The executive of the Ironfounders' Society reluctantly accepted changes designed to increase productivity because the 'alternative is a cruel and wasteful sacrifice of our best manhood'. On the railways, union leaders accepted that 'a strict code of discipline' was essential and that changes were 'necessary and inevitable'. Observers of conditions at the front spoke with equal enthusiasm of the developing bonds between those who daily faced the same conditions and dangers.[25]

There is no reason to dismiss these statements as the inaccurate views of interested parties. As early enlistment figures indicate, voluntary recruitment campaigns were very successful; controls had to be introduced to prevent further damage to the labour supply in 'essential' industries. When the Germans launched their Spring offensive in 1918, even the most radical union leaders (successfully) discouraged strike action.[26] Pacifists were unpopular. The Nottinghamshire miners, for example, considered censuring Smillie, the MFGB's President (who opposed the 1914–18 war), and disaffiliating from the national union because the 'pacifist' ILP wing allegedly exercised too much influence over its actions. The DMA was equally hostile. ILP pacifists were so unpopular that the *Railway Review* argued for a change in the construction of the Labour party after the war. Local Labour parties and Socialist groups found that pacifism could damage their health. They often ceased to hold public meetings in order to prevent this being taken any further.[27]

Working-class support for the war, and for the benefits of full employment, was so pronounced that industrial changes were often freely accepted by the workforce. Leaders of the Ironfounders' union complained

---

[24] Boilermakers' *AR* 1914, *R.R.*, 7 Aug. 1917. Cf. Shipwrights' *AR* 1917. Tillett's observations cited in Thorne (thesis), p. 56. For further instances, Waites, *Society at war*, p. 189.

[25] Ironfounders' *MR* Oct. 1915; *R.R.*, 12 Feb. 1915, *Railway Clerk*, 15 June 1915; Englander and Osborne, 'Armed Forces', pp. 594–5.

[26] Waites, *Society at war*, pp. 186–7, 232.

[27] A. R. Griffin, *A history of the Nottinghamshire Miners' Unions* (1962), pp. 22–3, DMA *Monthly Circular*, Nov. 1915, Jan. 1916, May 1918; *R.R.*, 9 June 1916. Cf. Wyncoll, *Nottingham*, p. 171, Bristol ILP Mins, 30 Apr. 1916.

that local branches did not relay information concerning dilution agreements to head office. They also noted that many branches objected to local funds being used to oppose dilution even through official channels:

I want to urge upon all our members the absolute necessity of declining to allow the specious promises, made under the pretext of patriotism, to influence them in the slightest degree; there is a loyalty due to each other in the workshop, and an industrial betrayal will react upon our brothers in the trenches. Wherever and whenever a change in working conditions takes place let it be with the full knowledge and sanction of your local officials, and upon a collective basis.[28]

The Ironfounders' members demonstrated a willingness to accept dilution, even on private work, and to accept cash increases as payment for accelerated output. Other unions with suspicious leaderships, like the Postmen, noted their members' willingness 'to accept onerous duties'. Again, higher wages were acceptable compensation. New technology was accepted if it produced more work or (as in the aircraft industry) if it created new skills. Change could be a source of opportunity. Even in the engineering industry, workers on Tyneside, for example, demonstrated a 'tolerance and acceptance of wartime conditions' which blocked the development of rank and file protest movements.[29]

'Patriotism' was not a means of sublimating class consciousness. It was a more permanent feature of working-class attitudes. So too was class fragmentation. 'Craft' unions – even the engineers – frequently resented the improvements secured by unskilled workers. In May 1915, for example, the ASE rejected closer links with the Workers' Union, which was rapidly expanding by enrolling unskilled engineering workers. On the contrary, the ASE secured an agreement with the employers which ensured that skilled workers alone were exempt from military service. Even when this agreement was relaxed, the Workers' Union (along with many others) complained bitterly of the 'secret diplomacy on the Man-Power question' which ensured that many ASE members continued to be exempt from conscription.[30] The ASE also attacked the NUR, another general union, over recruitment in railway workshops, while the ASE's members in the docks complained of 'poaching' by skilled unions like the Shipwrights and Plumbers. ASE exclusivity did not disappear on Clydeside or in Coventry, where rank and file 'general' committees of all workers, organised by the shop stewards, fell apart. Moreover, as Hinton acknowledges, the shop stewards movement (which allegedly undermined this exclusivity) was insignificant in engineering centres like

[28] Ironfounders' MR Nov., Aug. 1917. See also MR Nov. 1916.
[29] Ibid., Apr. 1915, Jan. 1917; Postman's Gazette, 29 May 1915; Musson, Typographical Association, p. 370; Clarke, 'Labour on the North-East coast 1914–18', p. 42.
[30] Workers' Union Record, Sept. 1917, Martin, TUC, pp. 142–5.

Woolwich, because ASE members adopted 'a contemptuous superiority towards the less skilled'.[31] Even in engineering, there is little evidence of united rank and file action against the state and against a (compromised) leadership.

What was true for engineering was even more true for other industries. The railway drivers' union, ASLEF, and the NUR continued their feud. On one occasion ASLEF accused the NUR of 'Prussianism' over its attempts to monopolise the union/management Conciliation scheme. The NUR sued for libel. The printers' union kept its distance from the union of printers' assistants, the ASC&J from the general union which catered for the industry's less skilled members. Friction between skilled unions in shipbuilding was as apparent as ever, whilst increasingly broadly based unskilled unions like the Workers' Union came into conflict with other 'unskilled' unions, like the Agricultural Labourers, which catered for just one group.[32]

In fact strikes aimed at *preserving* differentials were common in the engineering industry, and were behind the strikes of ironfounders and boot and shoe workers in 1917–18. Several unions, including the Railway Clerks, sought war bonuses which reflected existing differentials.[33] The poor nature of women's work, and the nature of the unions' response to women's involvement, was hardly likely to forge a common class bond between male and female workers in the same industry. Few union leaders identified a cohesive class movement. James O'Grady, the Leeds MP and General Secretary of the new National Federation of General Workers, warned of 'the old evil of differentiation between workers ... a division in the ranks of organised labour with internecine warfare and the growth of capitalistic power over a "class" so divided'.[34] Patriotic unity, Government concessions, the continued existence of economic fragmentation, and the greater prosperity of some working-class groups, was hardly conducive to the creation of an oppositional consciousness. Nonetheless, public sentiment was not entirely satisfied. There was a degree of dissatisfaction amongst skilled unions, and a growing confidence amongst general unions experiencing unprecedented growth and affluence. There was a broad, if unspecific, feeling that improvements had to be protected and

[31] ASE, *MR* Mar. and Aug. 1918; Reid, 'Dilution and trade unionism', pp. 53–4, 66–9; Haydu, 'Factory politics', pp. 71–2; Hinton, *Shop stewards*, p. 185.

[32] *Locomotive Journal*, Mar. 1917, *R.R.*, 4 May 1917; Musson, *Typographical Association*, pp. 434–9; Reid, ibid. The tensions between the two labourers' unions became acute (H. D. Harben to C.P.T., 15 Apr. 1920, CPT 120).

[33] Fyrth and Collins, *Foundry workers*, p. 148; Fox, *Boot and Shoe workers*, pp. 390–1; Tranter (thesis), pp. 251–2, 256.

[34] National Federation of General Workers' *AR* 1918. See also Tranter (thesis), pp. 259–60, for the support amongst lower paid clerks for the NUR and its policy of flat rate increases.

in the longer term that the war should not be fought for nothing. There was a potential conflict between sentiments which dictated support for the Government, and sentiments which could be mobilised by an opposition party.

III

The politicians' function is to draw lines of contact between people's experiences and their political views, and, despite the political truce, they did not abandon this task. In 1914, MacDonald had wanted to oppose the war and the foreign policy which he and others believed had created the conflict. In due course, MacDonald had argued, Labour would become the 'rallying centre for those who wish that this war should not have been fought in vain'. In 1914, he advocated dropping his pre-war strategy of supporting the Liberal party on essentials, but disagreeing over details. He wanted to cut loose, ally with those Liberal radicals who opposed the war, and attack the whole tenor of Liberal policy. MacDonald, the whipping boy of the left in 1914, became its hero overnight (despite the fact that MacDonald had different reasons for opposing the war than many Socialists). Henderson, the voice of the unions, opposed what he clearly perceived as a woolly middle-class radicalism, which was insufficiently grounded in working-class opinions and values. Opposing the war would be morally wrong and politically impossible. If Labour continued its pre-war approach, Henderson argued, of staying in contact with public opinion by being as patriotic as the rest, but voicing its disapproval of specific Government failures on the home front, it would inevitably benefit. Most MPs, union leaders, and many moderately left-wing reformers agreed with Henderson. For some in the Labour party, as in the Liberal party, war justified 'illiberal' actions which had to be reluctantly accepted. For others, a belief in 'reason' and the moral reformist philosophy advanced by men like Hobson or MacDonald was matched by a less articulate but powerfully felt need to defend the state, the country, and their families from attack. For some, like Tawney, the two could be reconciled. This was a war, he argued, against the irrationalism and brutality which the Prussians had seen within men and erected into an official Governmental outlook. Yet Tawney did not as a consequence see 'rationalism' as the sole source of good (as some Liberals did). For him 'irrational' forces (religious faith, sin, patriotism) were a fact of life, and could display the better side of men's nature, as well as its darker aspects. Many Labour politicians were less articulate but equally, if not more, confident in working-class 'decency' and 'good sense'. Like Tawney, they did not *reluctantly* abandon a 'rational' moral reformism. They started, like him, from a partial acceptance of the non-rational. MacDonald was defeated, and resigned as Chairman of the PLP.[35]

While Labour party *leaders* entered the Coalition Government from 1915, and allowed their opposition to the Government to lapse, party *organisers*, like Middleton and Higenbottom, wanted Labour to maintain its opposition status by concentrating on the Government's poor domestic administration of the war.[36] 'Domestic' activity should be encouraged:

it will pay us to do less of the actual recruiting. The men will be got anyway. We can score if our people will vigorously deal with problems arising from the War ... It is for us to drive home that we are the only people who can be looked to for protection. That we are doing the work *now* and will do it after ... (I) have watched the change in feeling, and feel confident that if we give a line distinct from either (the) Lib. or Tory Party, we shall score well.[37]

This was also the best way to obscure Labour's differences over the war and over the party's long-term future. Materially minded Socialist moral reformers (like Jowett and Lansbury) could accept a fight for better economic and social conditions which was based on the municipality. Labour's desire to turn local relief committees into 'citizens organisations', rather than arms of Government, was compatible with their pre-war philosophy. 'War problems', the radical Manchester Central ILP branch noted, were 'a worker's question.' Relief should not be administered by those 'dominated by COS ideas' who 'often conduct the work in an intolerant and inquisitorial spirit which is both offensive and degrading to the recipients'. By arguing for higher dependants' allowances, controlled food prices, and rent control, Socialists would 'set up a standard of comfort which will influence our whole social and industrial life and leave permanent results after the present crisis has passed'.[38]

In keeping with this, Labour devised a 'Pound a week' campaign, intended to secure better state provision for the wives and widows of soldiers soon after the outbreak of war. The War Emergency Workers National Committee encouraged, and ran, campaigns against increases

[35] Howard, 'MacDonald and Henderson', pp. 882–4. See also D. Newton, *British labour, European Socialism and the struggle for peace* (Oxford, 1985), Chapter 6, Winter, *Socialism and war*, pp. 154, 156, discussing the non-pacificist views of R. H. Tawney.

[36] A.H. to J.S.M., 20 Aug. 1915, discussing the proposal that Henderson should resign as Secretary of the party, and draft pencil reply, n.d., MID 13/47 and 48; *Locomotive Journal*, Jan. 1917.

[37] S.H. to J.S.M., 22 May 1915, LP/ORG/14/1/144.

[38] Manchester Central ILP Mins, 22 Oct. 1914. For this approach, J. Bush, *Behind the Lines* (1984) [East London], esp. p. 39, R. Harrison, 'The War Emergency Workers National Committee, 1914–20', in Briggs and Saville (eds.), *Labour history*, ii, pp. 211–59.

in food prices. These campaigns did not create class unity. Rent control, the most potent demand, became a major focus of complaint only in some areas of the country, and particularly on Clydeside. Even then, Labour's solutions were not original. They consisted largely of calls for Government loans to encourage municipal schemes. Significantly, however, the methods and ideas employed by O'Grady, Irving, Wheatley, Jowett, and Lansbury before 1914 were now spreading, albeit shorn of the humanistic Marxist rhetoric (and analysis of the Servile State) with which they had previously been associated. Even before 1914, this approach had helped create support for Labour amongst the unskilled and poorly paid.[39] The changed nature of the labour market inspired greater confidence amongst the less skilled and raised their aspirations. There was every incentive for elements on the left to once again become involved in Labour politics and to argue that this approach could work.[40]

The idea of patriotic sacrifice in the interests of victory was a powerful counterpressure acting against the development of a war-time opposition to the Government. Labour had to have a moral justification if its opposition was to be successful, and unlike the Liberal moral reformers, Labour's moral reformers and moral revolutionaries were able to supply it. They had not lost their faith in the morality of the working class, and hence in catering for their interests. By January 1915, George Lansbury was finding evidence of their essential humanity in the self-sacrificing bravery and unselfish care which soldiers bestowed on their comrades at the front. Ordinary workers, like the soldiers, were both patriotic *and* humane. Within industry, they sought 'just' settlements of grievances and the eradication of immoral economic exploitation of their patriotic sacrifice. They sought what was no more than human decency. By 1917, even MacDonald periodically regarded the 'spirit of rebellion' which insisted on these standards as a desirable attitude. It represented a healthy belief in freedom and an independence from the state and its dictates.[41] The 'moral economy' of the civilian population, a 'fluctuating code of

---

[39] D. Kirkwood, *My life of revolt* (1935), p. 120; Melling, *Rent strikes*, Chapter 4 and above, pp. 71–4, 147, 177–9, 258–60, 274–5. Nonetheless, in Burnley and Glasgow in particular the ILP before 1914 was more a skilled man's party. See Trodd (thesis) and McLean, *Red Clydeside*, Chapters 13–14.

[40] Whiteside, 'Welfare and unions', pp. 862–4. Guild Socialists and some Marxists still had their doubts. See e.g. A. W. Wright, *G. D. H. Cole and Socialist democracy* (Oxford, 1979), pp. 44–7 and A. Clinton, *The trade union rank and file* (Manchester, 1977), p. 73.

[41] *D.H.*, 2 Jan., 27 Feb. 1915; Winter, *Socialism and war*, pp. 238–9. Cf. Middleton's opposition to state interference as an infringement of this morality: men would make sacrifices, he argued, 'if they are treated as men and a little less like children or machines' (J.S.M. to his parents, 18 July 1915, MID 13/43).

negative rather than positive injunctions', became the basis of Labour and trade union opposition to certain Government dictates.[42]

The trade unions and the Labour party couched their opposition to Government industrial policy in the language of a just hostility to infringements of a (tacit) reciprocal arrangement. The Railway Clerks' President, for example, declared that union members objected 'to their patriotism being exploited'. Dilution of labour had been accepted by union members, but the union suspected a Government desire to take this further. This was unacceptable:

So long as women are not used by railway officials to undermine existing conditions we shall not object to their employment, but we shall certainly resist to the utmost any and every attempt to use them for monetary profit instead of the nation's need.[43]

In 1915, the South Wales miners also used the language of 'just' demands and infringed 'contracts' to explain their willingness to strike. They called for wages which reflected the sacrifices workers were making, individually and through their brothers at the front, to the war effort. They were 'guarding' jobs and living standards which they held in trust for the fighting miners. The mine owners had chosen profiteering above patriotism by attempting 'to beat down the men's wages under cover of the "national crisis"'. 'Profiteering' entered the language and became part of a new radical rhetoric which had nothing to do with a Socialist anti-war movement. Members of the SWMF and the ASE, the unions most involved in state action, distanced themselves from anti-war elements and even from the moderate left.[44]

Campaigns against high rents and profiteering became subsumed into campaigns which focused on 'the essential selfishness and unsatisfactoriness of Capitalism, and the patriotism and unselfishness of labour'. The Herald made the point with graphic cartoons and stinging articles:

The people with the two mites have stood by their country in this war as never men stood; and yet no sooner have their men-folk gone forth, strong in faith and limbs, to give their all for their country, than the men of substance have taken advantage of their sacrifice and absence and swooped down and ruthlessly and shamelessly robbed their wives and children of their bread and their fire. And when they have done their devil's work and filled their coffers, they actually

[42] E. M. H. Lloyd, *Experiments in State control* (Oxford, 1924), p. 5.

[43] *Railway Clerk*, 15 June 1915. See also H. Jones, *Politics, health and industry* (forthcoming, Manchester, 1991), Chapter 3.

[44] *D.H.*, 30 Jan. 1915 and A. Mòr O'Brien, 'Patriotism on trial: the strike of the South Wales miners, July 1915', *Welsh Hist. Rev.* (1984), pp. 92–5; ASE *Journal* Feb. and Mar. 1918; *Commission of enquiry into the industrial unrest*, P.P., 1917–18, xv, Cd 8663; Cd 8664, p. 2; Cd 8665, p. 9; Cd 8666, p. 2. See also Waites, *Society at war*, pp. 68–70.

attempt to justify their conduct by citing the law of Supply and Demand, as if children were articles of merchandise, and as if there were no moral connection between their own full storehouses and fuller pockets and the empty pockets and empty stomachs of their neighbours.[45]

The 'rich' and their air of class superiority became the focus for Labour and trade union propaganda. The *Railway Clerk* noted how wealthy upper-class ladies had the ability 'to dine thoroughly well before they motor down to address meetings of tired munition workers ... about war savings and economy'. The *Herald* called for an end to this hypocrisy, and drew a 'Socialist' message 'that what one person has another person cannot have: that money spent on luxury cannot be spent on the war, neither can it be spent on providing the necessities of life for the poor'.[46]

For the *Herald* and many others on the left, the aim of Labour propaganda was to create a *class* movement, committed to the development of working-class self-confidence and a fundamental redistribution of wealth and opportunity. It might seem to some that the Labour party was recast in this image, and that the left's political propaganda had the desired social effect. The Capital Levy and nationalisation were now firmly on Labour's post-war agenda. The contemporary activist G. D. H. Cole (who significantly became the major historian of labour unrest in the First World War) saw the development of rank and file 'all grades' movements, based on workshop politics, as a sign that the old fragmentation of the working class was being undermined. A unifying political theme, and unifying social and economic changes, were coming together. The Russian Revolution supplied the vital injection of both confidence and Socialist ideology. Labour adopted a 'Socialist' constitution in 1918.[47]

There are two major problems with this analysis. First, the *social* basis is questionable. It may be that these changes helped to produce a greater level of class *awareness*, that people began to think of 'the rich' and 'the Government' as colluding groups who opposed the interests of the workers. However, there is a danger of overstating the erosion of status distinctions during the war. It has already been argued that the industrial 'lessons' of war were not unifying, that the ideas and interests of sections of the working class differed. It is also important not to assume a correlation between social and political changes. Internal class divisions became more acute after 1918 (skilled groups often reestablishing wage differentials, for example), but with no adverse electoral consequences for the

---

[45] *D.H.*, 27 Feb. 1915.
[46] *Railway Clerk*, 15 June 1916; *D.H.*, 27 Feb. 1915.
[47] G. D. H. Cole, *Workshop organisation* (Oxford, 1923), Wright, *G. D. H. Cole*, p. 44.

Labour party. 'Class awareness' and a unifying 'class consciousness' should not be confused.[48]

The second problem with seeing the war as a radicalising factor is the nature of Labour's response. The 'political' lessons of the war were not, even in Labour's eyes, the need to create a 'Socialist' opposition to capitalism, and the *Herald*'s interpretation of events involved pushing a common set of Labour sentiments towards a much less common conclusion. The moderate moral reformers and the Statist elements in the Labour party had a very different interpretation of wartime experience, and they reasserted their primacy in Labour politics as the war went on.

MacDonald was a reluctant participant in the process of reconstruction. In 1914, he had hoped for an amalgam of anti-war organisations which would be 'one of the biggest things we have seen in our time'. However, although he still regarded the 'feeble' unions as a 'terrible incubus', he had no faith in the anti-war Liberals' ability to provide a basis for an alternative party.[49] Despite his new belief in a spirit of opposition, it was the need for a concrete policy which dominated his writing during the latter half of the war, and brought him back into the political mainstream and into Labour activity.[50] By 1916, he had began to embrace the idea that capital should make an equivalent material contribution to the war effort as labour.[51] He regarded this as a practical proposal, a view (significantly) shared by radical Liberals.[52] Other moderates were also concerned with post-war reconstruction. Henderson, Sidney Webb, and the WNC had been considering post-war policy since at least 1916. By 1918 the Labour party had taken over the WNC's plans and its policy-making functions. The *New Statesman* could proudly proclaim that Labour had a programme, published as *Labour and the New Social Order*, and the will to put that programme into effect.[53]

These ideas were little more than radical Liberal policy. Labour's 'Memorandum on War Aims' was almost a UDC document, and was supported by many radical Liberal moral reformers. Its action on Free Trade, Ireland, conscription, the treatment of alien immigrants, and on

[48] A point well-made in Waites, *Society at war*, p. 22.
[49] J.R.M. to G. Murray, 26 Aug. 1914, Murray MS 153 fo. 8, J.R.M., *Socialism after the war*, p. 41; Winter, *Socialism and war*, p. 235, M. Swartz, *The union of democratic control in British politics during the First World War* (Oxford, 1971), p. 154.
[50] See his pamphlets, *War and the workers, The war and the mind of labour, The conscription of wealth* and *Socialism after the war*, all cited in Horne (thesis), pp. 381–3.
[51] The Webbs and MacDonald had both written non-propagandist papers on this by 1917.
[52] J.S.M. to WNC, 17 Sept. 1917, WNC 9/1/225.
[53] A.H., 'Labour after the war', *Labour Year Book 1916*; Winter, *Socialism and war*, pp. 216–19; *New Statesman*, 27 Jan. 1917, 23 Nov. 1918.

issues of liberty and freedom raised by press censorship, attracted many radical Liberals to the Labour party. Labour had maintained the balance between support for military intervention and support for liberty which the Liberal party had been unable to maintain; Socialists had maintained their idealism and principles, and their support for a just peace. Former villains became heroes. Lansbury's ideas were widely praised by Liberal moral reformers, his hostility to capitalism being buried by his hostility to an over-powerful state and the immorality of war. Moral reformist journals, like the *Nation*, saw Labour as the embodiment of its 'Liberal' principles.[54] Liberal moral reformers could co-exist even with Labour's more Socialist elements. On social issues, on the war, and on the attitude and danger of the state, they held similar views. The Labour party itself became more united, some older problems becoming submerged by new concerns. It became more attractive to radical Liberals. It did not have a 'class' experience to draw on, and it did not have a programme which emphasised class conflict. Instead it had a programme which was attentive to a Liberal political language, which was hardened by new policies (principally the capital levy) and which could hope to mobilise some of the partial hostility to Government domestic policy which became more evident in the closing stages of the war.

Labour moral reformers were already supplying a 'practical' interpretation of working-class experience in their work on the domestic front during the war. They tapped some similar sentiments and traditions to the Socialist reformers (or at least enough to create a degree of party unity) and put forward similar solutions. In the longer term, they still had very different ideas of how Labour should proceed. The Labour moderates' call for social reform, land reform, the extension of pension provision, and other reforming initiatives were designed to create a practical programme for the future. Even the capital levy, sold as a proposal which would hit the 'unearned' and 'immoral' profits of the rich, was entirely compatible with pre-war moral reformist rhetoric. It was also compatible with Liberal economics, since the money could be used to pay off the War Debt (not to provide services to the poor) and to soak up inflation.[55] The importance of profit to investment and prosperity was not challenged. The levy was not to be permanent. On the contrary, in the longer term, some union leaders, and some Labour financial

---

[54] J. M. Kenworthy to G.L., 24 June 1917, A. MacLaren to G.L., 20 Dec. 1917, Lansbury MS 28 fos. 358, 378. For the local impact, C. Parry, 'Gwynedd and the Great War', *Welsh Hist. Rev.* (1988), pp. 92–5.

[55] R. C. Whiting, 'The Labour party, capitalism, and the national debt, 1918–24', in P. J. Waller (ed.), *Politics and social change in modern Britain* (Oxford, 1987).

experts, saw the levy as a threat to the prosperity which the market alone could provide.[56]

Labour also became a more positively attractive party to Statist occupational groups, like the miners and railwaymen. Labour's support for greater state control, and the now more evident need for a party which represented the economic interests of workers in these industries, combined to sharpen and improve its political position.[57] Labour support for nationalisation of the railways and mines, and greater state control of docking, were policies which reflected union interests in prescribed national wage scales, consolidated minimum wages, and limited working weeks.[58] Indeed, since only state control of the coal industry created uniform wages and improved conditions, only its maintenance could hold wages above a market value for unprofitable pits and ensure continued support for safer working practices. Yet the MFGB only sought a less bureaucratic form of state intervention than the old Coal Control. Several mining areas were likely to do well from a revived market position. Regional pay settlements and a less pronounced emphasis on uniformity were therefore not unpopular.[59] Similarly, it was not clear that all railwaymen would benefit from nationalisation. State control vied with a belief in the market. At best, there was support for the corporate idea that the workers needed a friend in Government to negotiate and organise on their behalf. The conservative, protective, side of Labour's image in some areas was reinforced by the mining, dockers', and railwaymen's unions, who also pushed the party towards supporting the war. Support for 'Socialist' state control was the preserve of the few.

Just as the capital levy and Labour's other policies gave it a stronger, more credible, 'practical' moral reformist stance, so the experience of war collectivism, and Labour's support for its continuation in some areas, improved the party's ability to develop support amongst 'Statist' elements. Events and politics did not create a uniform working class, or a uniform or overwhelmingly positive Labour appeal. They did, however, allow 'moderates' and 'radicals' to come together behind particular stances which submerged the fact that the old internal divisions had not been solved. They put Labour in a better competitive position.

[56] See below, p. 434, fn. 33.
[57] The part played by Smillie and Thomas is documented in C. J. Howard, 'Henderson, MacDonald and leadership in the Labour party 1914–22', Cambridge Ph.D. thesis 1978, pp. 119–30.
[58] Clegg, *Trade unions*, 2, p. 212, *New Statesman*, 14 Apr. 1917, Winter, *Socialism and war*, p. 238, Phillips and Whiteside, *Casual labour*, p. 144. See also, pp. 393–4, 400.
[59] The MFGB programme of immediate aims fell short of nationalisation, aiming at a less bureaucratic form of joint control. This is discussed in Supple, *Coal Industry*, 4, pp. 109–10. For the continuing support for non-national settlements in affluent regions, Griffin, *Notts Miners*, p. 30.

IV

Labour was not riding the crest of a new 'class' wave, and its political rivals were not swept aside. Indeed, initially it appeared that they would do very well. Asquith's Government portrayed their actions as a war against 'Prussianism', an aristocratic willingness to smash opponents at home and enemies abroad with a force and callousness which allowed it to commit appalling atrocities. The invasion of 'little Belgium', and the horrors committed by the 'evil Hun' against its people, were carefully exposed by the press and by official Government propaganda institutions. 'Opponents' of war dramatically switched and became active supporters of intervention.[60] The Liberal party machine was thrown into a moral crusade against Germany. Liberals recognised that politically they should 'not let patriotism get identified with Toryism or militarism'.[61]

Fighting a major war involved trampling on many elements of the party's operational ideology. Liberty was curtailed through the Defence of the Realm Act, the restriction of press freedom, the muzzling of Parliament, and ultimately by conscription. Free Trade suffered in the Budget of 1915, food supply increasingly came under Government control. Runciman and McKenna, politically pragmatic Liberals before 1914, took the initiative in changing Liberal policy, with support from even the most conventional Liberal forces: 'We place no limits,' the *Westminster Gazette* noted in 1915, 'on the claims of the State to the service of its individual citizens in a struggle in which its honour, and it may be its existence, is at stake.'[62] Initially at least, Government policy provoked surprisingly little reaction.

The Government also sought to promote full working-class involvement and co-operation in the war effort. Labour leaders were given places in the Government. There were concessions to Labour opinion on food policy and rationing. Government leaders intervened over the heads of businessmen to ensure that wage settlements rewarded the workers for their sacrifices. Just as patriotism should not be associated with the Tories,

---

[60] J. M. Read, *Atrocity propaganda* (New York, 1941), Chapter 8; M. Saunders and P. M. Taylor, *British propaganda during the First World War, 1914–18* (1982), pp. 139–47. For this in Cabinet, K. Wilson, *The policy of the entente* (Cambridge, 1985), Chapter 8; for a regional example, Parry, 'Gwynedd and the Great War', pp. 83–4.

[61] M. Bentley, *The Liberal mind* (Cambridge, 1977), p. 18. For further examples of the Liberal/Nonconformist reaction, Koss, *Nonconformity*, pp. 129–30.

[62] Cited in Freeden, *Liberalism divided*, p. 20.

Masterman noted, so defence of the working man should not be uniquely associated with Labour.[63]

It was not easy to maintain this position. When the war was not 'over by Christmas', when shortages of shells and other materials blocked effective prosecution of the war, the Liberals took the blame. As C. P. Scott noted, 'the truce of parties certainly doesn't apply to the party press'. The Tory newspapers laid the blame squarely on the Liberals' alleged refusal to prepare the country for war. Haldane, doubly condemned as the War Minister up to 1912 and an enthusiastic Germanist, was pilloried by the Northcliffe press.[64] The *National Review* and *John Bull*, in particular, gloried in attacks on aliens resident in Britain, and the 'selfish shirkers' who pursued 'leisure, treasure and pleasure' by striking while their braver comrades died at the front. The Tory party leadership did little to hold them back even if they did not actively encourage the assaults. The Liberals were under political attack.

The Tories were assisted by the Liberals' public division over the war. For those reluctantly converted in 1914, war – even against 'Prussianism' – involved a cruel conundrum. To support a war for liberty when this involved stepping on every domestic freedom was agonisingly difficult. War also increasingly involved crushing precious freedoms, and whipping up 'irrational' sentiments which were inimicable to the Liberal emphasis on ethical motivation and reason.[65]

The real test, however, came when conscription was introduced in 1916. This turned many Liberal *supporters* of the war (like J. A. Simon or R. D. Holt) into ardent opponents of Government policy. There were heated debates in the Liberal press. The *Daily News* opposed the idea; the *Manchester Guardian* was unenthusiastic. Those who accepted it did so reluctantly. It was a necessary, but undesirable, answer to the failure of voluntarism. Many Liberals portrayed their hesitation as a 'reasonable' reluctance to prescribe mass slaughter. Such subtleties were nothing to the Tories. 'Rational' regard for liberty, coupled with support for living standards on the home front, was portrayed as weakness, as

---

[63] Masterman to L.G., 5 Nov. 1914, LG C/5/15/8.

[64] C.P.S. to L. T. Hobhouse, 2 Nov. 1914 (Wilson edn., p. 109), H.H.A. to V. Stanley, 29 Nov. 1914 (Brock edn., p. 324): 'Poor old boy', Asquith had observed, with typical disregard for the potential political outcomes. For the Conservative press attack on Haldane, S. Koss, *Haldane* (1969), esp. pp. 131–2.

[65] Clarke, *Liberals and Social Democrats*, pp. 181–2; Freeden, *Liberalism divided*, pp. 21–6.

an unpatriotic disregard for the defence of the country and the lives of British troops.[66]

The Liberals also needed to counter Labour's propaganda. Their major problem was balancing the needs of the home front with the necessities of war. Liberal policy needed a dynamic presentation. Asquith's defence of working-class living standards was dry and legalistic. 'It never seems to dawn upon their kind', Middleton wrote, 'that it is a positive scandal and a disgrace to the civilisation that we are defending that families of five should have to struggle on these wages.' Asquith, Spender later wrote,

> was wholly sceptical as to the value of either agitation or imprecation in winning the war, and he thought it of high importance that both the Government and the public should keep an equal mind in face of adversity. Mr Lloyd George ... believed in constantly whipping up both the Government and the public to effort and more effort.

Lloyd George and the party radicals, in war as in peace, had to assume the propagandist's role. As Denman wrote, they had to prepare for the future, to hold out the candle of Liberalism for the public to see. In war, Governments had 'to abrogate their normal function of moulding public opinion ... to the Private member'.[67] Party radicals would have to do the job.

This was not easy. Many Liberal radicals – including the religious radicals Rowntree, Harvey, and Baker, and the moral reformers, Morel, Trevelyan, Ponsonby, Outhwaite, and Morrell – opposed the war and so took no part in party politics. Some, including Outhwaite, Trevelyan, and Harvey, had effectively been 'deselected' by their constituency Liberal associations.[68] In the Liberal party, unlike the Labour party, 'pacifists' were a very substantial proportion of the group concerned with an effective domestic policy. This severely weakened the Liberals' attention to the home front.

Nonetheless, there were radical elements (including Hobhouse, Scott, and the M.G.) who still supported the Government, and who wished to promote an active domestic policy. However, there was no formal mechanism through which they could influence party policy or public opinion. What agencies there were had disappeared. The maintenance of party principles and support was hampered. The Liberal Publication

---

[66] For Holt, M. W. Hart 'The decline of the Liberal party in Parliament and in the constituencies, 1914–31', Oxford D.Phil. thesis 1982, p. 27; J.S.M. to his parents, 18 July 1915, MID 13/48, Daily News, 15 July 1915.

[67] J.S.M. to his parents, 5 Mar. 1916, MID 13/78; Spender cited in Hazlehurst, Politicians at war, p. 214; R. D. Denman to ?, 11 May 1915, Denman MS 1/C.

[68] Morris, Trevelyan, pp. 129–30, J. Henry to H.G., 26 Nov. 1916, 30 Dec. 1917, HG Add MS 46038 fos. 118, 121, Hart, 'Liberals, war and the franchise', p. 826.

Department had closed down. The Young Liberals and associated Liberal groups had virtually disappeared. The party in the country stagnated.[69] Resolutions were passed, but Liberals found it impossible to influence or pressurise their Government. Discussion of the future was largely left to the 'pacifist' radicals, often in conjunction with Labour MPs (New Liberal theorists had never respected the institutional division of opinion). The Liberal party trod a thin line. It was in danger of losing its balance. As the Chief Whip warned, it was both bitterly divided and in danger of losing popular support.[70]

One final point needs to be made. Liberal radicalism lacked its old conviction. Some radical Liberals had developed an even greater respect for Labour following the ILP 'pacifists'' opposition to war, the opposition of some trade unions to conscription, and the party's general policy towards Free Trade, Ireland, and individual liberty. On the whole, Labour seemed more attentive to elements of the Liberals' operative ideology than their own leaders.[71] At the same time, the New Liberal theorists who had inspired pre-war radicalism grew more sceptical about human rationality, the law of progress, and their ability to change Liberalism, people, and the Liberal party because of the jingoistic wave sweeping the country. Here they differed significantly from moral reformers such as Tawney. Like Labour's more Socialist elements New Liberals, saw an over-powerful state as an obstacle to individual development. Collectivism – before 1914 the policy of progress – became the enemy of freedom. Unlike the Socialist reformers, however, they did not see class control of the state as the answer. At a time when most groups within the Labour party were still convinced of the innate superiority of working-class values, or of the primacy of satisfying working-class economic needs, and were *attacking*, some Liberal moral reformers drew back from the view that the working class was capable of the role which they had hitherto been ascribed. Ideas were vital to create true progress. Their enthusiasm for the organised working class, evident before 1914 as 'moral populism', sometimes became stronger (encouraging them to move further towards Labour) and sometimes (under the impact of jingoism) gave way to despair. Whichever way, the Liberal left was ideologically and politically

---

[69] J. Gulland and J. M. Hogge to W.R., 4, 26 Jan. 1919, W.R. to McKenna, 27 Jan. 1919, WR 171; H.G. memo, n.d. July 1925, WR 197.

[70] For Liberals urging Fabians and ILP/UDC groups to plan post-war reconstruction, B. Webb Diary, 22 July 1915 (MacKenzie edn., p. 236); memo by Gulland, n.d. 1915, Asquith MS 82 fos. 130–4. For Liberal organisation in 1918, below, pp. 404–6.

[71] See below, pp. 407–14.

weaker than ever before. Labour's competitive position improved. The Liberal party was squeezed from the left and the right.[72]

Lloyd George's ousting of Asquith in December 1916 was a politically logical and justified step given the need to stem attacks from the right and left, and the difficulty of effecting either without control of the leadership, although doubtless it also reflected his personal interest in power. It was not well-received by many Liberals. Pease noted in his diary that his thoughts on Lloyd George's action, written down, would 'burn a hole in this paper'. Yet before the end of the war he was seeking a place in the Coalition Government. Many others only retrospectively traced their disagreement with Lloyd George back to the split in 1916.[73] Even Asquith kept his options open by pledging 'organised support' if Lloyd George stuck to Liberal principles. In the period after 1916, Lloyd Georgeites and Asquithian Liberals adopted a similar line on many issues because there was still a shared core of aims and objectives. Moreover, many Asquithian Liberals thought it would be unpatriotic, and therefore electorally damaging, to oppose the new Coalition. It would also make permanent a division which many hoped would be temporary. Lloyd George promised a more active prosecution of the war; with his reconstruction proposals he promised active, and radical, preparation for the peace. Many (even Asquithian) Liberals had been hoping for this since 1914.[74]

Lloyd George was now the head of a primarily Conservative Coalition. As war progressed, its centre of gravity moved to the right. Effective prosecution of the war dominated effective prosecution of the peace. This seemed, in propaganda terms, to be a 'Conservative', not a 'Liberal' Government, and some Asquithian Liberals shared this view.[75] Lloyd George was too willing to infringe liberty, too ready to sacrifice the Liberals' operational ideology, too willing to sacrifice domestic living standards, too unwilling to negotiate a peace treaty or to consider President Wilson's peace proposals. Yet, while these Liberals could and did act as a ginger group, the 'Asquithians' as a party were poorly placed to attack. It was difficult enough to attack a Government which had some Liberals in it, but even more difficult to do this without drawing attention

---

[72] For the New Liberals' views, J. A. Hobson, *Democracy after the war* (1917), pp. 5–7; Collini, *Liberalism and sociology*, p. 250. Wartime by-elections, fought by Independents of various hues, have to be treated very carefully, but they do not suggest a widespread patriotic revolt against the Liberals. However, candidates opposed to conscription did fairly well in 1916.

[73] Pease Diary, 25 Jan. 1917, Gainford MS 41 and Pease to W.C., 20 Dec. 1918, Gainford MS 91.

[74] Wilson, *The downfall of the Liberal party*, p. 106.

[75] A point well made in Hart, 'Liberals, war and the franchise', p. 821.

to the Asquithians' own 'failure' to prosecute the war and prevent infringements of liberty and contractions of living standards on the home front. Calls for a negotiated peace were open to devastating counter-attack.[76] The Liberal remnant needed drive, a skilful balancing of tactics, and a subtle appreciation of the popular mood. Asquith was more ill-fitted to this task than ever. War had taken its toll. He spent a good deal of time in Oxfordshire, where he 'sat in the garden and in his room a good deal reading Shakespeare's England'. He was 'no longer keenly interested'.[77] He seldom went near the Commons, and almost never spoke. The remaining party leaders were not much better. McKinnon Wood was silent, Runciman was ill, and although Samuel was a little better (and had more radical and considered views) he was hardly a dynamic and popular figure. Simon, who had resigned over conscription, and Grey, whom many blamed for the war, were asked to give a lead by that section of the party which admired their principled stance. Both declined to give one. The Liberal Front Bench acted, according to the Nation, 'intermittently or not at all'.[78] It was truly a line of extinct volcanoes.

There was a leadership vacuum on the 'Asquithian' side of the party. The radicals' difficulty in influencing policy, evident before 1914, and again between 1914 and 1916, became even worse. They were numerically weaker than before 1914. Progressive 'pacifists' were in no position to take the lead. Many were also unwilling to try. Some even contemplated forming a new 'Democratic' party with MacDonald. However, many Labour 'pacifists' disagreed with some ideologically similar Liberals over tactics, and with others (like the 'Cobdenite' Francis Hirst) on domestic policy.[79] By 1917, MacDonald saw 'no prospect' of an anti-war reaction at the end of the war, and doubted whether alliance with the scattered, divided, Liberal elements was politically sensible. The Liberal Progressives

---

[76] See e.g. C.P.T. to A. Ponsonby, cited in Marquand, *MacDonald*, p. 195.

[77] Pease Diary, 29 May–June 1917, Gainford MS 41 fo. 23, Haldane to his mother, 27 Apr. 1917, Haldane MS 5997; Morrell, *Memoirs*, p. 54.

[78] Leif Jones to J. A. Simon, 2 May 1918, Simon MS 55 fos. 113–4; *Nation* observations, 10 Aug. 1918; for Samuel's views, H. Samuel, *The war and liberty* (1917) and Samuel to W.R., 19 Oct. 1919, WR 191 (pro capital levy).

[79] For the idea of a 'new' organisation, J.R.M., *Socialism after the war*, p. 40 and White (thesis), p. 326, and for hostile trade union reactions to the notion of a UDC/ILP 'peace party', R.R., 11 June 1915, 9 June 1916. For the 'war resisters' and the distinction between various forms of 'pacifism', M. Ceadal, *Pacifism in Britain 1914–45* (Oxford, 1980), p. 48, and for division in the ILP, Morgan, *Keir Hardie*, pp. 267–8. The 'New Liberal' or 'Radical' group of MPs, formed to watch over the nature of Government intervention at home and abroad, could not agree over basic questions. For Radicals, the extent of shared beliefs with Labour was always 'more apparent than real' (Minutes of meetings, Denman MS 4/3; Beauchamp to Simon, 27 Jan. 1918, Simon MS 54 fos. 106–7).

declined as a force. Some (like Morrell and Harvey) became heavily involved in the cases of individual pacifists who sought military exemption. Others formulated peace plans and set up discussion groups. While Labour campaigned, the Liberal radicals formed Clubs; eventually many moved (reluctantly) towards their old Progressive ally.[80] Money, Martin, King, Outhwaite, Hemmerde, and Wedgwood (all in favour of the war) and the 'pacifists' E. T. John, Trevelyan, and Morel, had joined or nearly joined the ILP by 1918. Hobson considered this after he resigned from the Liberal party over Free Trade in 1916, as did Harvey and Denman. Several Progressives saw Labour as an expression of the Liberal beliefs which the Coalition had abandoned. Others, including Trevelyan, Morel, and Ponsonby, argued (like MacDonald in one of his wartime incarnations) that the war had demonstrated a need for more drastic changes than had previously been contemplated, 'that the existing foundations of society are utterly rotten' and that 'only profound and revolutionary changes . . . can alter things and give the bulk of humanity the opportunities to which they are entitled'.[81]

Many Liberals nonetheless hesitated before joining Labour because they thought Statist elements would dominate Labour politics, and that Labour would not serve the ideal of humanity 'as well as it served the immediate interests of a class'. Labour was still 'somewhat class-bound and creed-bound'. While the *Nation* saw its cause as 'the chief moral attraction of our politics', not all New Liberals were convinced that Labour was the right medium for their message.[82] Even those who eventually joined Labour, like Ponsonby, found it 'extremely difficult to know what to do', in 1918. Ponsonby tried to prompt Asquith into action, but failed. He hoped to free Lloyd George 'from the nationalist war point of view', to move him away from 'the working of the machine' towards the 'considerations that really count'; but he failed here too. He and Trevelyan moved closer to Labour, hoping that other radicals would follow them and 'make a great party for the future'. They still realised that Labour did not have all the answers. It was not a 'perfect' organisation. It did not place enough emphasis on ideas and the national

---

[80] Morrell, *Memoirs,* p. 47; White (thesis), pp. 325–6. MacDonald was hardly entirely happy with the Labour party. See diary entries, 12 Feb., 12 June 1918, JRM PRO 30/69/1173.

[81] R. L. Outhwaite to F. W. Jowett, 23 Mar. 1916, FJ 1916/48A. For the Progressives' comments, *Sheffield Ind.,* 12 Dec. 1918, *Liv. Post,* 9 Dec. 1918, White (thesis), pp. 341, 350, 323, 319–20.

[82] *Nation,* 7, 21 Dec. 1918.

interest. The powerful sense of loyalty and decency which they identified was only one attribute of a social democratic party. In the short-term, until they learnt the value of ideas, Labour would make 'a horrid mess of it'.[83]

Some radical Liberals remained in the Liberal party because they were so uneasy about the unions, or because they were socially uneasy about the idea of a proletarian party which did not give pride of place to intellect (and to intellectuals like themselves). F. D. Acland, Pringle, Hogge, Harvey, Wedgwood Benn, and others stuck to Asquith. Some radicals, particularly those with Fabian inclinations, like Alden and Addison, found the Coalition's Liberalism perfectly acceptable. The Coalition also claimed the pre-war radical leaders, Lloyd George and Churchill. The radical Liberal thrust was diminished by apathy, depression, and division.[84]

What was true for politics at the centre was true for politics in the constituencies. Many Liberals supported the Coalition. Liberal moral reformists flocked to Labour in the Nonconformist strongholds. In areas where Liberal organisations had been weak, and consisted of small but active groups of radical Progressives, this defection was so swift and complete that Liberals were left with almost no constituency organisation. In West Lancashire, the West Midlands, London, and the dockland seats on the south coast, the Liberal party had almost ceased to exist by 1918.

In the constituencies, as at the centre, not all Progressives left the sinking ship. They stayed, but saw danger in the party's indecision, in the Coalition's pursuit of Statist reforms and in the 'control' of democracy by the Coalition system. They too attempted to put pressure on the Asquithian leadership to provide an alternative. The Manchester and Huddersfield parties developed their own radical programmes, which they publicised in an attempt to gain wider constituency support. A 'Radical Council' consisting largely of radical Liberal MPs (including some who were contemplating joining Labour) put forward thirty-two proposals aimed at the 'fundamental re-organisation of society'. The radical Liberal press made encouraging noises. If Liberals could not win the next election,

---

[83] Record of interview with L.G., 27 June 1918, C.P.T. to Ponsonby, 30 Dec. 1918, Ponsonby MS Eng Hist c 667 fos. 62–6, 121; C.P.T. to E. Acland, 24 May 1919, cited in R. Douglas, *A history of the Liberal party* (1971), p. 152, and his article 'Can Radicalism and Socialism unite?', *Nation*, 2 Feb. 1918, cited in Morris, *Trevelyan*, p. 140. See also C. Addison, *Four and a half years* (1934), p. 602.
[84] See below, pp. 406–7.

they argued, they would not lose everything if they took the bull by the horns.[85]

Support for action also came from men like Leif Jones, Holt, Buckmaster, Charles Mallett, and Charles Hobhouse who had opposed, and continued to oppose, Progressive policies.[86] They called for a Radical/Centrist alternative to the Coalition and with a degree of success. This wing of the party was institutionally even more preponderant in the constituencies and amongst the party leadership. Moreover, whereas the New Liberalism and Progressivism had been necessary as a means of securing support from working-class radical Liberals and Tory working men before 1914, these groups of voters no longer supported the Liberals to anything like the same extent. New Liberal policies were thus no longer so essential to the party's survival. The purchase of Centrist/Radical ideas, as a means of holding an existing base, correspondingly increased. When the party leaders half-heartedly responded to pressure they advanced Radical/Centrist views. Runciman, now the principal active Liberal leader, and the NLF produced policy statements in January and July 1918. Their statements satisfied Radical/Centrists, but not Progressives. Runciman's points were good, the editor of the Progressive *Northern Echo* noted, 'so far as they went' but they did not go far enough. He suggested 'a more concrete policy ... especially with regard to Trade Union restoration', the extension of national insurance, a policy for state housing, a radical stance on the taxation of the wealthy and recognition of 'the strong demand for the Nationalisation of the Railways'. The NLF statement, the *Nation* noted, was 'vague and colourless'.[87] The Liberal party was ideologically retreating into its (moderate) electoral heartlands.

By the end of the war Labour had to an extent improved its position. The qualification is important. War was not a perfect political opportunity for a party with such a strong 'pacifist' element. 'Patriotism' gave Labour's rivals a pathway into popular opinion which reinforced old electoral loyalties and won new support. Equally, conditions on the home front did not produce a homogeneous, class conscious, working-class,

---

[85]   For policy proposals, MLF Mins, 24 Apr.–6 Nov. 1918, A. A. Haworth to W.R., 19 Jan. 1918, WR 169, *M.G.*, 13 Dec. 1917, 15 Mar. 1918, *Nation*, 27 July 1918. For the Radical Committee, White (thesis), pp. 321–3. Even pro-war Liberals, like C. P. Scott and Josiah Wedgwood, were ready to participate in organisations which looked forward to the peace (Morris, *Trevelyan*, p. 131 and C.P.S. Diary, 3–4 Sept. 1914, Wilson edn., p. 103). Progressives were quite willing to accept a capital levy, and even limited nationalisation.

[86]   Hart (thesis), pp. 52–4, 62, 79.

[87]   W.R., 'The Radical outlook', *Contemporary Review* (1918), pp. 1–7; C. Starmer to W.R., 15 Jan. 1918, WR 169; *Nation*, 7 Sept. 1918. The Radicals in 1918, as in 1914, believed that a Radical/Centrist policy would be popular.

unity. Labour made some headway because its reiteration of radical Liberal views and its support for 'just' changes in national financial and housing policy, allowed it to reaffirm forcefully its position as a practical moral reformist force. It maintained its roots in a radical Liberal political culture, but made itself a more attractive expression of these sentiments and views. At the same time, Labour's commitment to protecting gains made during the war was popular and backed (following the experience of wartime collectivism) with ideas which were now *positively* attractive. Its stance on the war in many areas ensured that the party could not be labelled 'unpatriotic', and this continued to reinforce its image as the party of the ordinary person. It was more attractive than ever in the areas where it was already strong before 1914; it was now socially and in some areas, *economically* rooted. Yet its appeal was still partial; it still lacked a fully credible economic alternative which would rupture habitual political outlooks and allegiances, especially amongst the unskilled workers and those with a Tory past.

At the same time as Labour became a more serious positive political force, the Liberals became a less serious opposition. The 'balanced' Liberal approach of concern for both the war and home front was overtaken by events. The Liberals began, even before 1916, to let the Tories assume the role of the 'patriotic' party. Following the split in 1916, Coalition Liberalism slipped to the right by concentrating (like the Tories) on the need to fight the war. Lloyd George was 'imprisoned'. He, and his allies, became tainted by their association with the 'right'.

The Liberals needed to maintain their reputation as a party committed to individual and economic liberties, and to the improvements in living standards which attracted its social democratic and religious/moral support. They were allowing the Labour party to usurp this role even before 1916; after the split, it became even more difficult to maintain this side of the party image. The Asquithians were seriously hampered by the end of the New Liberal/Centrist alliance. Many New Liberals were either disillusioned or moving towards Labour. Others were part of the Coalition, and silent on *party* (as opposed to Coalition) policy. Although the remaining radicals tried to jog Asquith's hand, they failed. In so far as a 'party' policy emerged, it emanated from a Radical/Centrist grouping.

The Liberal party was always likely to lose some support during the war. Before 1914, it had been a broad and complex coalition. Its middle-class, conservative, support was already being undermined; it was also losing ground to Labour in mining areas, in the Tory regions, and in some poverty-stricken seats where the Liberal style of intervention was only partially relevant. It fought hard to keep Labour in check in these areas, and half-succeeded, but with evident difficulty. The war made the Liberals' difficulties more pronounced, and accelerated their inability to convincingly repel Labour's opposition. The Liberals' wartime problems were also unlikely to go unnoticed in the party's electoral heartlands.

A second Liberal weakness also became more evident during the war. The institutional structure of the Liberal party was a handicap in this difficult task. Its radical left had not captured or radicalised the party. It had dominated the party through its ideas and through Lloyd George's dynamism. During the war, the left's ideas lost their shine. The internal, institutional, position declined. Bringing *public* pressure to bear on the Government to consider domestic policy (the prevalent tactic before the war) became almost impossible. There was no *institutional* structure which the reformers could utilise. After the split in 1916, the Asquithians fell back on the ideas of a Radical/Centrist alliance which was now institutionally unassailable and electorally more feasible. The New Liberal ideas, and the Progressive strategy which had helped make the party so successful even in Tory areas, was redundant now that Labour was a practical alternative force whose leaders refused to act as part of an alliance. The party was thrown back on its heartlands and its traditional supporters. War collectivism had a less pronounced impact on those industries (textiles, shipbuilding, iron and steel, consumer goods, and agriculture) which were more common in the 'Liberal' areas. Radical/ Centrist ideas were still electorally and institutionally significant in these areas and with these groups, but the party still needed a radical leaven if they were to hold these areas, let alone regain support in seats where they had shallower political roots. As the end of the war and the 1918 election approached, the Edwardian Liberal coalition appeared to be falling apart. In so far as the Liberal party had a policy, it reflected the half-changed ideas of its older, more traditional, electoral constituency.

Chapter 13

The end of the Progressive Alliance

The post-war electoral competition took place within a new framework. The franchise had been extended. Constituency boundaries had been redrawn. While franchise extension did not substantially alter the electoral framework in Labour's favour, boundary revision did. It created more seats with a high concentration of working-class voters, and proportionally more mining constituencies. These were the seats which Labour was most likely to win (Section I). Despite this, structural changes alone cannot explain Labour's development. Within the labour elite, support for an increased commitment to Labour politics before 1917 was partial. Statist groups displayed increased interest (Section II), but a more general increase in support was not evident before the last stage of the war. Arthur Henderson sought to break out of the Progressive Alliance (Section III) not because of changes in union opinion or improvements in constituency organisation but because of new political circumstances (Section IV). Even by 1918, Labour organisation was weak in most of the formerly Liberal working-class areas because it had not 'solved' its old problems. Similarly, it had made organisational progress only in *parts* of the mining and Tory areas where before 1914 it seemed to have more potential than the Liberals as an anti-Tory force. Statist policies, and Statist unions, were not strong enough to create substantial organisations even in areas where Labour had a comparative advantage. Henderson had to canvass non-Statist unions and persuade them to finance more parliamentary candidates. He also had to ignore the financial and organisational problems which in the past had justified a limited campaign, and actively encouraged local organisations to fight even when the organisational and financial position was extremely poor.

There were two major factors in changing Henderson's attitude and that of other party members. The first was the positive effect of war collectivism on Labour's competitive standing. The second was the Liberals' difficulties, which ensured that they would be less effective opponents even in their traditional heartlands by the end of the war. This assessment was proved accurate by events. Although Liberals in those radical centres which had developed policy initiatives put up a fight, the Liberal party generally disappeared in the Tory and mining areas, and was seriously weakened elsewhere (Section V). The Asquithians did not field a full quota of candidates, or present a consistent face to the electorate. They often appeared to side with the Coalition, but were usually opposed by Coalition candidates. Their political image was blurred, but failure and an association with the 'right' were reportedly the most popular impressions. This was reflected in the election results (Section VI). A large portion of the Liberal vote went Tory. However, Labour also outpolled the Liberals in 1918, though not because it received the full 'Progressive' vote, or because its pre-war support was augmented by the vast majority of new male voters enfranchised in 1918. It did not mobilise support because a more pronounced sense of class consciousness could find expression following the extension of the franchise. Closer examination of the election results (Section VII) confirms that Labour had become the major anti-Tory party in areas where it had always had some potential (the mining and Tory areas). Its progress in Liberal areas was apparent, but more limited. It made some localised headway with a 'practical', but 'radical' approach. However, in general the Liberal party was not eradicated. Labour was not so positively attractive in most formerly Liberal working-class areas that Liberalism no longer seemed a viable creed. Labour's limited progress here, and more substantial success elsewhere, was still sufficient to firmly establish it as the major Progressive party. The Tories and Labour between them had shattered the Edwardian Liberals' electoral coalition. Labour had made its breakthrough by inheriting a portion of that estate.

I

There was substantial pressure for a new Reform Act before the end of the First World War. The Liberals had only failed to pass a Franchise and Registration Bill in 1912 because the Speaker refused amendments which would include women voters in the measure. The parliamentary timetable allowed no scope for a redrafted Bill.[1] Nonetheless, franchise extension was gaining support in the Liberal party. Liberal party members and parliamentary candidates increasingly favoured reform.[2] The problem, however, was that the bulk of the Tory party would oppose universal

---

[1] D. Morgan, *Suffragists and Liberals* (Oxford, 1975) for the background to this measure. For the 'unforeseen' action of the Speaker, Haldane to his mother, 24 Jan. 1913, Haldane MS 5989 fo. 26, H. Samuel to his mother, 26 Jan. 1913, Samuel MS A/156/427.
[2] WLF memo, n.d. Jan. 1914, L.G. C/17/3/27, Pugh, *Electoral reform*, pp. 22, 32.

suffrage for men and women. However, once war was declared and conscription introduced, it was politically impossible to allow men to die for their country, but not to have a say in its political future. The Speaker's Conference called in 1916 was designed to smooth the passage of a new Reform Bill through the Commons. It was a means of circumventing opposition from Tories and from Liberal anti-suffragists.[3] The result was an enquiry into the whole electoral system which investigated everyone's pet schemes and proposals. The ensuing report was a compromise, which had a considerable impact. Although it was not binding on Parliament, its moral force was supplemented by the guiding hand of the party whips.[4]

The report suggested a complete redistribution of parliamentary seats, the adoption of the Alternative Vote, full extension of the franchise to men, and a limited extension of the franchise to women. Support for the first two proposals came from both convinced supporters and from those who saw these changes as safeguards against the likely effects of franchise extension. The franchise stipulations themselves were a compromise. Women over thirty or thirty-five who qualified as local government electors, either in their own right or through their husband's entitlement, would now be registered for the municipal *and* parliamentary vote. This, many considered, would minimise the extent and consequences of female enfranchisement, and of the political disruption: the women's electorate would consist of former municipal voters and the wives of pre-war parliamentary voters, who would vote for the same parties as their husbands. However, the municipal franchise for men had also been altered. The residence period was to be cut from twelve to six months. A large number of previously disfranchised male householders (and their wives) would be added to the register. The women's vote was thus larger than calculations based on the exact pre-war position had suggested. Although Parliament accepted the bulk of the report, there were amendments and amplifications which materially altered the electoral arrangements.

The Conference's neat women's franchise scheme was thus not so easily implemented. The women's franchise depended on the nature of the municipal franchise. The Conference suggested that the pre-war English household franchise should be adopted for all *municipal* contests in the United Kingdom. By advocating one uniform municipal franchise – household suffrage – it had suggested a tidier system, but one which

[3] Dr Pugh's *Electoral reform in war and peace* contains a complete discussion of the Conference, its aftermath and context, on which much of the following is based.

[4] Ramsden, *Balfour and Baldwin*, pp. 120–1, Pugh, *Electoral reform*, Chapter 6. See also G. Locker Lampson to Lady Cave, W. Long to Sir G. Cave, both 7 Dec. 1917, Cave MS 62503, emphasising the importance of Cave's management of the Bill in the Commons as a means of defusing Tory opposition.

involved taking voting rights away from those people in Scotland, Ireland, and London who had previously qualified as lodger and service voters. This was unpopular with several powerful organisations. Amendments preserved a good deal of the lodger vote (an estimated 65 per cent in London) by allowing the enfranchisement (throughout the country) of lodgers who were tenants of unfurnished rooms. Service voters and those who had received poor relief were also included. Only inhabitants of furnished rooms were excluded.[5]

Despite these amendments, the new municipal franchise (the basis for the women's franchise) and the former parliamentary franchise were very similar. The vast proportion of the 8 million new female voters (roughly 78 per cent of women over 30) were the wives of men who would have qualified before 1914. The male increase – largely previously unenfranchised householders and tenants of unfurnished rooms – was concentrated in cities like London, where mobility and multi-occupancy were common. Of the 4 million men who obtained the parliamentary vote, the majority were young men living in furnished rooms. They were not therefore eligible for the municipal franchise.[6] At the parliamentary level, change was more dramatic, in terms of numbers, but the political impact needs to be examined carefully. The increased number of male and female parliamentary voters was spread fairly evenly across the country, with concentrations in areas of pre-war low enfranchisement. Most 'new' voters were thus the sons or wives of previously enfranchised male voters. The political disruption, given household voting patterns in which fathers, wives, and sons voted for the same party, was not likely to be substantial. It was only in areas of pre-war low enfranchisement, largely the inner-cities, that the increase was likely to include a larger number of older men who had not been enfranchised in 1914 (the alleged 'sub-class' which featured in so much contemporary propaganda).

In calculating the 'class impact' of franchise changes, several aspects of the post-war electoral system need to be borne in mind. Even by 1921 (when full figures became available) male suffrage was not universal. Only 93 per cent of the adult male population in 1921 had the vote. A little over 500,000 men remained unregistered. They were concentrated in areas where multi-occupation was the norm, particularly inner-city seats (both working class *and* middle class) and the coastal resorts. If this, and the continued exclusion of 20–5 per cent of women over thirty who inhabited furnished rooms, had no 'class' impact (a point which will be established later) and allowing for a plural vote of around 250,000, then 78 per cent of the post-war parliamentary electorate was working

[5] *Hansard*, 18 June 1917, c. 1531, 15 Nov. 1917, c. 680.
[6] See references in fn. 16 below.

class.[7] The *national* change was from around 70 to 78 per cent. If the (largely concentrated) plural vote is discounted before and after the war, the change was from 76 per cent to 80 per cent. In the *average* constituency, which before and after 1918 had only a small plural vote, the 'class' impact of franchise change was negligible.[8]

The male voters enfranchised in 1918 were only significantly different from the existing electorate (in class terms) in the inner cities, where a variety of factors had altered the nature of disfranchisement before 1914. The social balance of inner-city electorates was now tilted a little more towards the unskilled and the poor, although in some seats this was countered by an expanded inner-city business vote (the result of Tory back-bench amendments passed in November 1917). Nonetheless, most inner-city working-class seats were overwhelmingly working class even before 1914, and the franchise changes did not consequently have a pronounced political impact. The constituencies most affected by franchise reform were those, like Pudsey, where working-class electorates were no longer swamped by the (now abolished) urban freehold vote.[9]

The nature of the municipal franchise merits closer attention. The municipal and parliamentary franchise for women was almost identical, but the municipal and parliamentary franchises for men were very different.[10] In 1921 there were around 7.25 million men on the municipal register (an increase of around 1.25 million compared to 1915). Much of this increase was concentrated in the former areas of low enfranchisement, but most especially in London, where not only formerly excluded householders, but also formerly excluded tenants of unfurnished lodgings and those in receipt of poor relief, were now able to qualify. On the other hand, in many provincial towns the increase was comparatively small. This reflected the fact that there were few householders who had been excluded by the residence requirement or the receipt of poor relief, and few lodgers who lived in unfurnished rooms.[11] The increase in the level of enfranchisement was so pronounced in London that after 1918

[7] For the low level of male parliamentary enfranchisement, *Statistical Review* 1929, text, p. 136. Electoral figures from the Autumn Register, Registrar-General's *Statistical Review* 1921.

[8] See above, pp. 119–23.

[9] Ramsden, *Balfour and Baldwin*, p. 121. See also above, pp. 100, 279.

[10] The parliamentary register contained about 120,000 women registered through their husband's business vote (although they were only entitled to one vote, they could choose to exercise it in one of two locations). They were not registered twice for the municipal vote. However, the municipal register did contain around 100,000 women aged twenty-one to thirty who qualified as local government voters in their own right (S. Vivien to A. S. Hinsleywood, 19 Mar. 1928, PRO HO 45/13153).

[11] Electoral registers for 1910–15 show that frequently more than 85 per cent of lodgers in provincial seats occupied *furnished* rooms, compared to perhaps 35 per cent in London.

proportionally more voters had the vote here than in any other part of the country.[12] However, as Table 13.1 demonstrates, there was a strong correlation between the pre-war parliamentary and post-war municipal levels of enfranchisement outside London. Three-quarters of the 4 million men who received the parliamentary vote were still ineligible to vote in local elections. A number of previously disfranchised mobile householders were now included. The bulk of the voteless before 1914 had been young lodgers; young lodgers still, by and large, did not get the vote. Despite the 1918 Reform Act, many of the features of the Edwardian parliamentary franchise continued at the municipal level. It was still usually necessary to be a householder in order to qualify. Being a householder still correlated with being older, and with being married.[13] Age, marriage, and enfranchisement still went hand in hand. This is most clearly seen in the women's franchise. In the sixty constituencies for which full and accurate *Census* data on gender, age and marital status is available, there was a very strong correlation between marriage and enfranchisement.[14] Moreover, the level of municipal enfranchisement rose from 76 per cent in 1918 to 80 per cent in 1921, during the post-war marriage boom, and fell to around 73 per cent in 1929, when the age qualification was lowered to twenty-one. A smaller proportion of the twenty-one to thirty age group was married, and lived as householders or in unfurnished rooms and fewer consequently got the vote.[15] As contemporaries agreed, it was single people, of all classes, who failed to qualify for the municipal franchise.[16]

The inclusion of the Alternative Vote in the Speaker's Conference report threatened to effect a more fundamental change in the electoral structure. However, it was unpopular with large sections of all parties, particularly the Tories. There was a long and complex battle between the Commons

---

[12] Tanner (thesis), p. 336 for tabulated levels of enfranchisement.
[13] One additional factor in determining the level of enfranchisement may have been a reduced but continuing party involvement (e.g. South-East Surrey Cons. Ass. Mins., Organisation Comm., e.g. 12 Sept. 1922, *Cons. Agents' Journal*, July and Oct. 1918, Oct. 1919, Manchester LP *AR* 1925).
[14] A rank correlation test produces a coefficient of 0.71, with 1 being a 100 per cent correlation and 0 indicating a nil correlation.
[15] Intercensal population figures are estimates derived from the Registrar-General's *Decennial Supplement*. All electoral figures are taken from the Autumn Register, as printed in the *Statistical Review*, except those for 1918, which are from *P.P.* 1918 (Cd. 138), xix, 925. See also Tanner, 'Parliamentary electoral system', pp. 214–15.
[16] 'No democrat', it was declared in the *Athenaeum* (Mar. 1917) 'can object to this form of franchise on the grounds that it is undemocratic or favours one class more than another, since marriage and widowhood are facts common to all ranks.' For the excluded women, *Labour Woman*, Apr. 1928, *Woman's Leader*, 20 Aug. 1926, *Liberal Monthly*, Aug. 1920. For the excluded men, *The Times*, 23 Sept. 1918 and 7 Nov. 1922, *Liv. Post*, 25 Oct. 1924, *Daily Telegraph*, 9 Nov. 1922, *Forward*, 2 Dec. 1922, *Yorks. Obs.*, 17 Nov. 1922.

Table 13.1 *Continuity between the pre-war parliamentary electorate and post-war male municipal electorate, 1911 and 1921*[a]

Constituency	1911 Pre-war parl. enfranchisement (minus furnished lodgers)	1921 Post-war male municipal enfranchisement	Degree of discontinuity
Deptford	50.94	75.73	+ 24.79
Bethnal Green (two seats)	45.73	68.64	+ 22.91
Barrow	52.83	65.78	+ 12.95
Gateshead	61.21	71.89	+ 10.68
Walsall	59.88	70.52	+ 10.64
Blackburn	62.77	70.01	+ 7.24
Ipswich	63.86	68.93	+ 5.07
Warrington	56.31	58.24	+ 1.93

Note:

[a] The level of enfranchisement has been calculated for both dates with plural voters included, because accurate constituency figures for all these constituencies in 1911 do not exist. For the purposes of this table, lodger voters who were tenants of furnished rooms in 1911 have not been taken into consideration when calculating the 1911 figue, thus enabling more accurate comparison with the position in 1921. (Franchise changes ensured that the post-war 'household' franchise excluded lodgers in furnished rooms). By calculating the pre-war position minus lodgers living in these circumstances, the figure in column 4 can be seen as indicative of the real increase in the number of new male voters between 1911 and 1921 (whereas making no adjustment would *increase* the figure in column 1, and thus understate the *increase* in new voters).

Source: Population figures are from the 1911 and 1921 *Census*. 1911 electoral figures are from *P.P.* (1911), with furnished lodgers counted from the electoral register. Figures for the local government electorate in 1921 are from the Autumn register, Registrar-General's *Statistical Review* (1921), pp. 96–114.

and the Lords over the proposal. The Bill itself was jeopardized by its inclusion. The offending clause was therefore dropped. As we shall see, however, the assumption that it would be implemented had a considerable impact on the Labour party.[17]

The third element in the Conference report, and perhaps the most significant, was boundary revision. In discussions of the Commissioners' rubric for redistribution, the Tories secured changes which ensured that consideration of an area's 'economic interest' was a factor in creating new boundaries. This had two effects, one desired and one not even contemplated. The first was to protect agricultural constituencies with declining populations. This benefited the Tories, who had estimated the original proposals would halve the number of rural seats. The second effect was the creation of more economically homogeneous industrial constituencies, a fact which helped Labour.[18] Whether local parties *also* succeeded in altering the precise nature of boundaries in a politically advantageous way is an interesting question. They *did* submit counter-proposals to the Boundary Commission's local reports, and they were aware that 'small' changes in boundaries could influence political outcomes. Whether they drew up their recommendations accordingly, and whether they were accepted, is something which contemporaries disagreed over, and local historians might well ponder.[19]

The Boundary Commission restructured the electoral map. It (rightly) created more suburban seats particularly around London, where some of the older constituencies had enormous electorates by 1914. Wandsworth, a single seat, became *five* new constituencies; several other seats were divided in two. The number of seats in Kent, Surrey, Essex, and Middlesex increased from fifteen to forty. There were smaller increases in other cities, particularly Liverpool, Newcastle and Birmingham.[20]

[17]   Pugh, *Electoral reform*, pp. 83–4, 180, Ramsden, *Balfour and Baldwin*, pp. 120–2.

[18]   *The Times*, 6 June 1917, *M.G.*, 19 June 1917. More generally, Ramsden, *Balfour and Baldwin*, p. 121. The politics of redistribution are discussed in J. Turner, *British politics and the crisis of war 1916–18* (forthcoming, Yale). See also below, p. 413.

[19]   For accusations of political manoeuvring, and claims of partiality, *The Times*, 7 June 1917, *M.G.*, 11 July 1917. See also K. W. D. Rolf, 'Tories, tariffs and elections: the West Midlands in English politics 1918–35', Cambridge Ph.D. thesis 1974, pp. 46, 234. For consideration of the details from a party standpoint, e.g. memo by the Sec. of Liverpool Constitutional Ass. (n.d. 1916), Salvidge to Bonar Law, 1 Nov. 1917, Bonar Law MS 82/5/7 and 21/4/9. See also, for the impact of changes on one (rather important) seat, S. Ball, 'Asquith's decline and the general election of 1918', *Scottish Historical Review* (1982), pp. 48–9, 60–2.

[20]   Birmingham, 7 to 12; Liverpool, 9 to 11; Newcastle, one seat (two members) to four seats. For the London suburbs, Ramsden, *Balfour and Baldwin*, p. 123. The precise increase in middle-class seats (and in working-class seats) is difficult to calculate. Existing estimates of the pre- and post-war position use different criteria. Moreover, Census statistical data covers whole cities, not its parliamentary divisions. All current estimates of the position in these seats are therefore based on impressionistic data.

The 'economic' argument preserved some Liberal seats in the Celtic fringe, but the preservation of Tory rural seats and the creation of new (potentially 'Labour') mining seats was the major effect. The number of seats with more than 30 per cent of the male workforce in mining increased from around thirty-five to fifty-five. A number of South Wales seats were sub-divided. There were nearly twice as many mining seats in South Wales in 1918 as there were in 1914.[21] Some of this was justified because the seats were so large before the war. The Boundary Commissioners and coalfield Labour organisations between them ensured that mining communities were not divided by constituency boundaries. In Derbyshire at least this enabled a more favourable political distribution of the Labour vote.[22]

Redistribution also created more – and more predominantly working-class – constituencies. Warrington, Nelson and Colne, and Smethwick, for example, lost, or were lifted out of, rural/middle-class surrounds. In Wales, aggregations of boroughs (e.g. Monmouth Boroughs, Carmarthen Boroughs) lost their middle-class areas to produce several more clearly working-class divisions. In the cities, few real working-class 'ghettos' were produced, because in general the housing developments which facilitated this came later. Even so, redistribution probably produced more thoroughly working-class seats in cities like Newcastle and Leicester.[23] Many new working-class suburban constituencies were also created around London because the borough freehold vote was abolished. Perhaps a third of all constituencies in post-war Britain were dominated by working-class and mining groups, compared to a little over a quarter before 1914.[24] Labour was in a structurally better position.

II

Even before the details of redistribution became available, Labour was preparing to exploit advantages over the Liberal party which, for the first time, put it in a better competitive position. At the Labour party

[21] I have based my calculations on the (admittedly imperfect) figures in Gregory, *Miners*, Appendix B and M. Kinnear, *The British voter* (2nd edn., 1981), p. 116.

[22] Williams, *Derbyshire miners*, p. 543.

[23] See discussions, *Leics. Merc.*, e.g. 12, 13, 18, 21, 28 July 1917. For Lancashire seats, *M.G.*, 6, 12, 18 July 1917.

[24] D. H. Close, 'The realignment of the British electorate in 1931', *History* (1982), p. 393 fn. 2. The pre-war Blewett/Pelling social class index is based on the number of domestic servants per 1,000 households. Professor Close's use of occupational data from the 1931 *Census* is more elaborate and sophisticated, but using this information might overstate the number of working-class seats in the years 1918–22, for the growth of council estates by 1931 transformed several constituencies. I am very grateful to Dr Close for allowing me to consult his full constituency index.

conference in June 1918, Henderson argued that it was time to seize the political opportunity, break out of the Progressive Alliance, and reconstruct the party and its electoral strategy. He 'made no apology for this attack upon electoral positions not previously contemplated by the party', and fixed no limit on the number of constituencies to be contested: 'They would not be doing their duty to the Movement if they allowed these new electors to be denied the choice of a Labour candidate and then imposed upon local Labour people the responsibility to wean them from any allegiance they may have formed.'[25] This strategic change was not inevitable. It did not result from uniform changes in class consciousness, rank and file pressure, or growing militancy. At the outbreak of war in 1914, there were many unions which sponsored only a few candidates each; others none at all. Although there was some pressure to expand political activity, it was by no means universal. Initially the experience of war only extended the commitment of those groups who were moderately enthusiastic before 1914.[26] In 1915, the SWMF finally (and narrowly) agreed to increase its political levy in accordance with MFGB dictates. Local activists, encouraged by local events, immediately pressed for increased financial assistance from the MFGB and the Labour party so that more candidates could be adopted.[27] In 1916, a ballot of Nottinghamshire miners confirmed even their support for Labour representation. Nonetheless, the MFGB pledged itself to just six extra candidates at the Annual Conference in July 1916. Conference rejected this by sixty-three votes to sixty-two; the North-East and South Wales miners wanted more candidates in their areas than this small increase would allow. The question of further candidatures was deferred pending publication of the Speaker's Conference Report, with its provision for the Alternative Vote, the redistribution of boundaries, and the payment of returning officers' expenses.[28]

By 1917, activists and leaders in transport and supply industries were also more committed to Labour representation. The Railway Clerks' Association, hitherto lukewarm on parliamentary representation, balloted its membership on the need for more candidates; Tillett's dock workers also conducted a ballot under the Trade Union Act of 1913.[29] All ballots were successful. A few skilled unions also managed to increase their commitment. The 'radical' ASE reballoted its members on parliamentary representation and, like the LSC, now achieved a majority in

[25] LP AR 1918, p. 27.
[26] NEC Mins, 28 Apr. 1915 for affiliation fees. See also above, pp. 324, 345.
[27] SWMF Mins, 6 Feb. 1915, NEC Mins, 30 June 1915, 22 Feb. 1916.
[28] Wyncoll, Nottingham, p. 171; MFGB Mins, 23 Nov. 1916, 18 Apr. 1917.
[29] R.R., 23 July 1915, Tranter (thesis), pp. 184–91, Railway Clerks' AR 1915, 1916; Dockers' Record, Apr. and July 1915.

favour of having a political fund. The ASE immediately selected fourteen additional candidates.[30]

Nevertheless, it would be misleading to see this as evidence of a major and widespread conversion of the trade unionists to the Labour party. The vote and turn-out in the ASE and LSC ballots was lower than on previous occasions.[31] Moreover, it was one thing to obtain votes in favour of parliamentary representation, another to raise the money. The Railway Clerks' annual conference initially declined to accept the increase in subscriptions which was essential if the planned expansion of political activity was to be realised. The SWMF's call for increased political contributions was only (narrowly) carried on a card vote. If few miners subsequently declined to pay their levy, even this was better than in transport/supply industries.[32] No levies were collected from a third of all NUR branches in 1915. By mid 1917, less than 15 per cent of NUR members and a third of ASLEF members were paying their political levy, and again many branches, some 'in our great Trade Union centres', were making no contribution.[33] Other unions, as we shall see, were even less enthusiastic.

Nor was there an enormous blossoming of constituency organisation in the initial phases of the war. Political activity on 'domestic' issues was 'not the success we (the Labour party proponents of such work) were entitled to expect'.[34] Labour organisers concentrated on seats which had candidates or MPs before 1914, but even then Higenbottom could only report (slow) progress in a few seats (e.g. Oldham, Newton, North-East Manchester, and West Wolverhampton).[35] In the latter, there was a slow, steady increase in the number of affiliated societies, a process repeated in Sheffield and other 'Tory' areas where Labour had been improving its position before the war, and in some Labour-held seats. Candidates were being selected, and the post-war situation was being considered.[36]

These improvements were both limited and geographically restricted.

[30] ASE *Monthly Journal*, Feb., May 1916; NEC Mins, 11 Oct. 1916; LSC Polit. Comm. Mins, 22 June 1915, LSC *AR* 1916.

[31] ASE: 13,299 to 11,474; LSC: 2,558 to 2, 120.

[32] *Railway Clerk*, 15 June 1916. For (e.g.) the Northumberland miners (341 non-payers/ 30,000 1914, 266/25,130 1916), *R.R.*, 23 Jan. 1915, 19 Jan. 1917.

[33] *Locomotive Journal*, Feb. 1917 (referring to 1915), Dec. 1917 (referring to that year); *R.R.*, 22 June 1917. See also below, p. 401.

[34] J.S.M. to J. T. Abbott, 28 Feb. 1917, WNC 9/1/210. More generally, R. Harrison, 'The War Emergency Workers National Committee, 1914–20', in Briggs and Saville (eds.), *Essays in Labour History*, ii, p. 236.

[35] S.H. to J.S.M., 20 and 24 Apr. 1915, LP/ORG/14/1/130 and 133; Northampton TC *AR* 1915, Nottingham TC *AR* 1915.

[36] S.H. to J.S.M., 19, 21, 22 Apr., 17 and 18 May 1915, LP/ORG/14/1/127–8, 131–2, 142, Railway Clerks' *AR* 1916; Sheffield T&LC *AR* 1917/8, NEC Mins, 14 Nov. 1917.

The first meeting of the Labour agents' society set up in 1915 attracted just thirty people. By 1917 the society had only fifty members. There were organisational problems even in many Labour seats. Only a little over eighty constituencies had a branch of the Women's Labour League; over thirty seats with Labour MPs or candidates – around half the total – had no organisation of Labour women.[37]

In many of the seats which Labour was actively cultivating before 1914, there were few signs of major improvements. In the North-East, for example, some miners and coal mechanics withdrew from the South Shields Labour party, because of the 'lack of interest of their members (and the) inability to secure Delegates'. The position was worse in the South. In Portsmouth, a dozen affiliated organisations had left by 1917. The Coventry LRC suffered from its delegates' sporadic attendance. Although the Northampton Trades Council reported (slow) progress in breaking 'the ties which bind men to (other) political parties', it nearly fell apart on several occasions. The East Bristol ILP, like other ILP branches, suffered for its 'pacifist' stance.[38]

Labour's leaders responded with caution before 1917. In Scotland, sympathetic activists and organisers restrained those, particularly in Glasgow, who wished to select more parliamentary candidates. The NEC advised against selecting candidates in Doncaster and Tyneside. In short, in the early part of the war, Labour's organisational expansion was prompted largely by groups with Statist interests, and *occasionally* by changes in the politics of union activists. Reports suggested only localised progress in established areas; the NEC's attitude to parliamentary candidatures reflected that fact.[39]

III

Three factors helped change opinion within the Labour party: the split in the Liberal party, and its apparent move to the right; the proposed boundary revision and introduction of the Alternative Vote, and the Russian revolution in 1917. It is difficult to disentangle these factors, and ascribe a dominant influence to any particular one. Snowden focused on 'the merging of Liberal and Tory with' (he added in a typically condescending way) 'that portion of the Labour Party which never had any

---

[37] For the appointment of Labour agents, E. P. Wake to J.S.M., 19 Dec. 1915, JSM 13/67 and *Wolv. Worker*, 1 Feb. 1917.

[38] South Shields LP Mins, 1 Dec. 1915, 8 Feb. 1916, 13 Feb. 1917; Howard (thesis), pp. 142–3; Northampton TC *AR* 1916; Bristol ILP Mins, e.g. ann. meetings 18 Apr. 1915, 30 Apr. 1916.

[39] J.S.M. to B. Shaw, 20 Oct. 1916, LP/SAC/14/218 & 239; NEC Mins, 30 July 1915, 10 Oct., 21 Aug. 1916. See also Parry, 'Gwynedd and the Great War', p. 110.

sound grasp of political and economic principles'. Henderson warmed to the Alternative Vote, which he thought might avoid the problem of restricting local Labour enthusiasm for fielding parliamentary candidates. He was distressed when it was dropped.[40] Few Labour officials anticipated Liberal annihilation, although they expected to do better than in the past. Labour's strategic planning, even in 1918, consequently proceeded with cautious regard for Liberal feelings.[41]

Prior to the Stockholm Conference, however, the party leaders were still only willing to consider candidatures in mining seats and in seats where there was some evidence of fairly successful Labour activity before 1914.[42] Lloyd George's attempt to prevent Henderson attending the Stockholm Conference showed him that Labour's independence was not safe while it remained in the Coalition. It further suggested to him that Lloyd George was unlikely to become the standard bearer of a rival, democratic, reforming political organisation.[43] The Russian Revolution may also have convinced other party and union leaders that change was possible. Middleton for one argued that the Leeds Conference in 1917 demonstrated that 'the feeling of the general public is not the same since the Russian Revolution. There is a great chance for a new world after this.'[44]

Henderson set about reconstructing the party. Two days after the NEC endorsed his proposals, a Labour deputation asked the MFGB's executive to rescind the resolution which limited the number of its parliamentary candidates. Henderson also received permission to address constituent mining unions on the need for them to finance additional campaigns. Henderson's organisers began nationwide tours, meeting union committees and constituency executives. Henderson himself spent a week in the North-West and South Wales, in which he 'urged the need for

[40] P.S., in Blackburn T&LC *YB* 1916–17; C.P.S. Diary, 11–12 Dec. 1917 (Wilson, p. 317); NEC Mins, 13, 22 Feb. 1918. Henderson had been one of the sponsors of an A.V. Bill introduced in February 1914.

[41] Memo by J. Gulland, Liberal Whip, 9 Oct. 1918, Samuel MS A/63 fos. 15–17.

[42] NEC Mins, esp. 28 June 1915 (Hanley, Staffs), 2 Nov. 1916 (Mansfield, Notts), 19 Dec. 1916 (Yorkshire, Cleveland), 12 Nov. 1916, 5 Mar. 1917 (North Monmouth), 14 Aug. 1917 (East Northants). Cf. NAC Mins, 21 Apr. 1916, suggested move of Wallhead from Coventry to (marginal) Jarrow. Even by 24 April 1918 there were only 115 fixed candidates according to the NEC minutes.

[43] C.P.S. Diary, 11–12 Dec. 1917 (Wilson, p. 317): 'Speaking of the future of the Liberal party he asked how was it possible that Lloyd George could now ever hope to lead it. Up to a year ago he might have done, but he had taken a thoroughly undemocratic attitude towards the Russian Revolution . . .'.

[44] J.S.M. to his parents, 10 June 1917, MID 14/9. Snowden and Bruce Glasier shared Middleton's views (J.B.G. to E. Bruce Glasier, 30 Apr. 1915, JBG 1915/17). For the Stockholm Conference and the Labour leadership, Winter, *Socialism and war*, pp. 240–63.

an increased number of candidates' from the LCMF, and made a similar
appeal to the UTFWA, the Ironfounders, and the SWMF. He also spoke
to delegates in a number of constituencies and cities. The smaller, or
less obviously 'industrial', unions were not neglected.[45]

Henderson also attempted to co-ordinate activity with the ILP. He
was concerned that they would adopt large numbers of alleged pacifists
(whom he wanted to keep out of the picture). The NAC agreed to support
no more than one sixth of all candidates, although Henderson did his
best to restrict this even further.[46] Labour's Head Office also informed
the branches that it would help them bear the financial weight of a parliamentary campaign. Henderson attacked with gusto.

IV

Henderson's stance was not based on a revolution in popular attitudes
towards the Labour party. In many former Liberal strongholds, despite
Labour's new, more credible, practical, moral reformism, it went into
the 1918 election as a weak 'replacement' for the Liberal party. The position was particularly poor in the rural areas and southern towns (discussed in Chapter 10). F. E. Green, historian of the agricultural labourers'
union, noted that in rural areas, 'very few candidates possessed any shred
of political organisation, or even an agent, before the campaign started'.
Candidates were appointed with breakneck speed. In some seats, like
Cambridgeshire, they failed to meet the deadline for official sanction;
in Holland-with-Boston, the local party adopted the dissident sitting Tory
MP. In Market Harborough, Labour had forty-four workers in nineteen
villages; there were sixty-five villages in the constituency.[47] Middle-class
seats were no better. There was 'little or no organisation' in Blackpool.
In Maidstone 'organisation and finance had to be created as we proceeded'.[48] In more industrial seats, the NUR played a vital role in sustain-
ing flimsy local organisations. It raised the money (with difficulty) to
fight Reading and Luton. In Northampton, the NUR tried to convert
other unions, but a month before the campaign there was 'no organisation
worth a mention'. Where the railwaymen were more numerous, as in
Derby or Crewe, or where the miners or sympathetic middle-class Progressives could help out, as in Leek, Hanley, or Nottingham, the position

[45] MFGB Mins, 28 Sept. 1917; NEC Mins, reports of 14 Nov. and 12 Dec. 1917.
[46] NEC Mins, 28 Nov. 1917, 8 Oct. 1918; memo, 18 June 1918 (misdated 1919), Ensor
     MS. (I owe this reference to Michael Hart).
[47] Cited in Howard (thesis) p. 209, and Dr Howard's 'Introduction to Cambridgeshire
     LP Minutes' (E.P.Microform, Wakefield, 1979); *Postal Record*, 2 Jan. 1919.
[48] Gen. Union of Textile Workers, AR 1918; *R.R.*, 17 Jan. 1919. See also Champness,
     Frank Smith, p. 42, for a similar position in Balham.

was much better. Despite localised improvements, however, in huge areas of southern and rural Britain Labour was not riding a popular wave.[49]

Labour also, and more seriously, showed an inability to establish strong organisations in many centres of heavy industry and in large areas of industrial Yorkshire, where before 1914 the Liberals had been a powerful, rooted, force (Chapters 8 and 9). Thus in the steel/dock towns of Cardiff and Newport in South Wales, Lib/Lab strength and general Liberal sympathies made Labour organisation embarrassingly inefficient. The Penistone LRC in Yorkshire was the old Holmfirth ILP branches under another name (although they now had financial support from the miners). The South Shields Labour party in the North-East had no individual members, and was reluctant to consider any change along these lines. It was still extremely divided between trade unionists and Socialists.[50]

Nonetheless, the position was better than in southern and rural seats. Pro-Labour unions (like the textile workers, the ASE, NUR, and the miners) were much stronger. The ILP was more active than ever. Its anti-war stance, and support for domestic liberties, had enabled it to absorb some middle-class Liberal support. It had become a half-way house for those radical Liberals whose ethical moralism had been 'betrayed' by their party during the war.[51] The result of these various changes was strong, union-based, organisations in seats where Labour had already been doing well (such as Colne Valley, Sowerby, or Newcastle) and a series of well-supported, if still 'Socialist-dominated', organisations in seats like Middlesbrough, Swansea, and Bradford.[52] When the election came in 1918, these organisations were able to obtain funds from local sources with considerable ease. The Bradford Labour appeal attracted donations of £5–£30 from ILP Clubs, local union branches, and middle-class sympathisers. The Colne Valley election appeal actually made a profit.[53]

In most parts of the North-West, the West Midlands, and London where the Liberals were strongly established before 1914 (discussed in

[49] R.R., 3, 10 Jan. 1919; Leek Post, 4 Jan. 1919, Leek Times, 4 Jan. 1919, Staffs. Sentinel, 28 Dec. 1918; Wyncoll, Nottingham, p. 182. For the pre-war position, see above, Chapter 10.

[50] R.R., 27 June 1918, Newport LP Mins, 24 May, 8 Aug. 1917; Holmfirth LRC Mins, esp. 17 Aug., 2, 16 Nov. 1918; South Shields LP Mins, e.g. 22 July 1918.

[51] e.g. statement of Rev. R. Quick, a 'Gladstonian Liberal', supporting Labour and 'taking the most religious action he had ever taken. The Labour party programme was a religious document' (Leek Times, 14 Dec. 1918). For clerical involvement more generally, Howard (thesis), pp. 258–62.

[52] R.R., 10 Jan. 1919 (Middlesbrough). For strong union involvement and financial/organisational strength, Worker, 9 Nov., 7 Dec. 1918 and Colne Valley LP AR 1919; Newcastle LP AR 1919; C.F.T., 8 Feb. 1918 (Sowerby).

[53] Bradford Pioneer, 6 Dec. 1918, 15 Jan. 1919.

parts of Chapters 5 and 6) the old pattern of politics did not disappear. In the cotton spinning districts, union officials still appeared on Liberal platforms. In the Black country seat of Walsall, even NUR members spoke for the Liberals, and the Trades Council opposed the idea of a Labour parliamentary campaign.[54] Labour was not automatically successful in London. A Centrist/New Liberal perspective in these 'radicalised' Liberal areas still had considerable validity and support. Labour organisation was often correspondingly weak.[55]

In a climate of general Liberal weakness, it was important for Labour to consolidate its pre-war base, and to realise its pre-war potential in the Tory areas where the Liberals had hitherto held sway as the second party despite their intrinsic weakness. Labour had not overcome its problems *or* realised this potential in many Tory areas by 1918. Old obstacles to its expansion remained significant. Some in fact became *more* pronounced. The 'pacifist' views of some local Labour parties, for example, seemed to reflect the continuing influence of Socialists who found some working-class attitudes (such as patriotism) 'distinctly nauseating'. This helped perpetuate an image of the party as an 'ethical', 'moral', 'unrealistic', and 'alien' organisation (a problem evident in some areas before the war). Significantly, much of the support for the 'Trade Union Labour party' which some contemplated forming in 1918 came from Labourist areas like the North-West. So too did the opposition to individual membership, with the attendant threat to Labour's protective, conservative, working-class role. As George Milligan, of the Liverpool Dockers' union put it: 'They did not want middle-class or higher-class leaders to come and tell them what to do, or theorists like Mr H. G. Wells and Bernard Shaw.'[56]

Many Labour organisations in Tory areas were still dominated by Socialists, relied on middle-class Socialists for funds, and suffered from shortages of party workers. Organisational deficiencies in many 'Tory' areas went unchecked. The Birmingham party could not even find a list of members. Nearby seats, such as West Wolverhampton, West Bromwich, and Smethwick, were in a slightly better organisational position (politically they were more moderate, and the unions were stronger).[57] In Liverpool, however, Labour scarcely even considered the election before October 1918. Labour organisations in some East London seats

[54] UTFWA *AR* 1919; *R.R.*, 24 Jan. 1919; Walsall T&LC Mins, 20 Mar. 1918.
[55] *L.L.*, 19 Dec. 1918; H. Morrison, *An autobiography* (1960), pp. 72, 77–8.
[56] *C.F.T.*, 9 Aug. 1918. Crinion (UTFWA) and Sexton were both prominent in this movement.
[57] Champness, *Frank Smith*, p. 42, Birm. LP Mins, e.g. 11 Nov. 1919; *Typographical Circular*, Feb. 1919, *Smethwick Telephone*, 4 Jan. 1919; *Wolv. Worker*, e.g. 30 Aug., 26 Sept. 1918.

like Limehouse had to cope with ethnic divisions, both within the electorate and within the party. The London Labour 'machine' was painfully inadequate; in the blossoming outer-London working-class seats, such as East Leyton, the election found Labour 'without organisation and quite unprepared'.[58]

Nevertheless, it was not unknown for local Labour organisations in the North-West, London, and the West Midlands (the major 'Tory' areas) to blossom during the war. The excellent pre-war organisations in Manchester and Clitheroe retained their strength. Some radical, campaigning, organisations established or extended their organisational base; Lansbury in Poplar and Dan Irving in Burnley were backed by organisations which had been active throughout the war.[59] Their practical Socialist moral reformism began to produce results.

Labour's greatest potential source of immediate strength was the (now more numerous) mining constituencies, particularly as the mining unions had become more committed than ever to Labour representation. Early in 1918, the mining unions in South Wales and the North-East developed a remarkably positive political approach to the next election. In South Wales, each ward in seats with a SWMF candidate was to have six conveners. Municipal organisation was to be tackled immediately, and miners with local knowledge and support were to be established as agents and secretaries. There was little chance of miners' views not being represented. Miners' lodges and associated groups (Colliery Mechanics, Deputies' Association, Colliery Co-operative Employees and Societies) totally dominated the local Labour parties.[60] In Durham, the union provided funds, and appointed paid election agents, sub-agents, polling agents, and clerks. Few Durham mining seats (except Barnard Castle, which had a 'model organisation') had less than twenty-five paid miners involved in the 1918 campaign. Some, like Sedgefield, had over fifty (Appendix 5). There was no doubt that Labour was an extension of the union, and that its purpose was to protect miners' interests, economic needs, and broad aspirations by political means. This involvement surpassed anything which had been evident before the war. It was associated with a further shift to the centre-right in the local Labour parties' political stance. Even in mining areas, however, the pre-war pattern was not subsumed by wartime developments. The Derbyshire miners were slow to set up new organisations; the Yorkshire miners were slow to provide substantial funds and assist-

[58] C. R. Attlee, autobiographical notes, Attlee MS 1/8 (Churchill College, Cambridge); R.R. (East Leyton), 27 Dec. 1918.
[59] Bush, East London, pp. 86–8; Burnley Expr., 11, 14 Dec. 1918.
[60] Pontypridd T&LC Mins, esp. 5 June, 9 Oct. 1918; Houghton-le-Spring LP AR 1918, 1919, 1920, Blaydon LP AR 1919, 1920, Durham LP Mins, 9 Feb. 1918 and LP AR 1920.

ance. In the Forest of Dean and in Warwickshire, there was little organisation in the mining areas.[61]

In the country as a whole, poor constituency organisation in part reflected the limited commitment of trade unions to Labour representation,
even after the events of 1916–17 had made Labour the only real alternative
to the Coalition. In 1917, the NUR had to formally cease discussing
the possibility of financing more Labour candidatures at the next election
because, with only one eighth of members paying the political levy, funds
were too low. Even by 1918, less than half the union's membership were
paying the political levy. ASLEF managed to finance some extra candidates, but only a quarter of its members paid the political levy. The
members of some moderate mining unions contributed reluctantly. Older
political ties, patriotism, and doubts about the credibility of Labour policies such as nationalisation, encouraged some, even in the leadership,
to draw back.[62]

Members of other unions were often even more circumspect. Leaders
of unskilled unions tried to convince their members of the need to support
the Labour party (despite personal reservations in some cases). However,
affluence (by comparison with pre-war circumstances), patriotism, and
Labour's association with moral improvement and the skilled unions were
not necessarily likely to radicalise union members. Despite positive
responses to ballots, many unions declined to take a major part in Labour
politics. Some did not use all their political funds in 1918.[63] Blue-collar
and white-collar unions were often hostile to the Labour party. When
NAFTO sought information on the non-payment of political contributions by union members, many branches failed to make the returns.
Several branches questioned the value of Labour affiliation; only a quarter
of the membership paid the levy even in 1918.[64] Similarly, although members of the postal workers' unions, and the Co-operative Employees,
voted in favour of a political fund, the unions proceeded cautiously,
fearful that a combination of militants and moderates would object if
political action was pushed too hard. This was a common view amongst
unions of this kind. 'We shall have to face the fact', the Bakers' Magazine
noted in June 1917:

[61] Williams, *Derbyshire miners*, p. 546; Neville (thesis), pp. 782–3; R.R., 3 Jan. 1919;
    Champness, *Frank Smith*, p. 45 and e.g. *Nuneaton Observer*, 20 Dec. 1918.
[62] *Locomotive Journal*, Feb., Dec. 1917, June, July 1918, Mar., Apr. 1919; R.R., 29 June,
    31 Aug. and (letter) 28 Dec. 1917, 28 June 1918. The scattered nature of railway union
    membership seems to have contributed to problems in creating Labour sentiments, and
    to problems in collecting political contributions.
[63] Henderson's observations on the limited contribution made by General Unions, LP
    AR 1919, p. 133. See also *Dockers' Record*, Dec. 1918, Oct. 1919; Workers' Union
    AR 1918. The dockers financed only four candidates, the Workers' Union two.
[64] NAFTO *MR* Mar. and Apr. 1915, Mar. and July 1917; NAFTO *AR* 1918.

that the majority of our members remain unconvinced as to the necessity of political action ... They are loth to cut themselves adrift from the old parties, and such a word as 'Socialism' is imagined to be something not quite respectable.[65]

Unionisation did not imply 'proletarianisation'. Moreover, some white-collar and blue-collar unions, which at executive level were dominated by the far left, took a distinctly anti-Labour stance, with the result that political activity under the Labour banner was not encouraged.[66]

Several skilled unions raised large political funds simply because of the size and affluence of their membership. The size of a union's political fund was not an indication of rank and file commitment to the Labour party. The ASE's narrow majority in favour of political action has already been noted. The Boilermakers' members were also uninterested in political activity: 'Our political effort, like our political fund', the Secretary reported in 1919, 'has never been more than a half-hearted thing.' The union's members objected to the political radicalism of their General Secretary, and, although few contracted out of the political levy, there was the usual problem of non-payment.[67] Members of the ASC&J called for the termination of their political fund, and a large proportion of members claimed exemption. The GUCJ had a voluntary parliamentary fund which produced scarcely any income. Although the Ironfounders' membership voted five to one in favour of financing more parliamentary candidates, no more than 15 per cent of adult members voted in the ballot, and more than a third of all branches made no return.[68] In printing, a substantial proportion of the Typographical Association's members, and at least one eighth of the Compositors, contracted out of their political levy.[69] Even skilled unionists were not necessarily enthusiastic.

Many unions only considered financing parliamentary candidates after

---

[65] *Postal Record*, 28 Nov. 1918; *Postman's Gazette*, 24 June 1916, 12 Oct. 1917; W Richardson, *A union of many trades* [USDAW] (Manchester, 1979), p. 74; *Journeyman Bakers' Magazine*, June 1917.

[66] See also comments on Labour candidates, *Licensed Vehicle Trades Record*, 14 Nov. 1917, 20 Mar. 1918. White-collar unions often had radical leaderships and a membership with a functional attitude to unionisation. For the clerks' union, Waites, *Society at war*, pp. 260–1.

[67] See above, pp. 322 and 324, for the earlier position. For the political funds, Boilermakers' *AR* 1919 and *MR*, Mar. and Nov. 1918 (*c* 1/3 contracted out). Results were also influenced by the method of collection. Frequently all members who did not fill in exemption forms were said to 'pay' the political levy, in that a set amount per head was then set aside from general funds. They did not 'see' the money being allocated. However, where a 'political' component of a union subscription was collected *separately*, there was more scope for non-payment by members who had not taken the effort to contract out (see e.g. *R.R.*, 27 June 1919).

[68] Ironfounders' *MR* Nov. 1917; ASC&J Gen. Council Mins, 24 July, 7 Aug. 1916, GUCJ, *AR* 1917.

[69] Typographical Ass., Delegates' Meeting, 17 June 1918; LSC, Polit. Comm. Mins, 26 May 1916, and membership figures, *AR* 1916.

Henderson's impassioned request. The Bakers' executive considered it 'in answer to a request from Mr A. Henderson' at their meeting on 14 October 1917; the Vehicle Workers 'at the instigation of the Labour party'.[70] Henderson had to make further requests before the UTFWA (despite some reservations) and the Railway Clerks increased the number of their candidates. It was only after a second request that the Postal Clerks, Natsopa, and moderate and small unions such as the Midland Textile Association and the Instrument Makers actively responded.[71]

Several unions felt it necessary to offer incentives to members asked to pay additional political dues. 'In order to stimulate interest', NAFTO announced, branches could keep a quarter of their political contributions. The Ironfounders and the Typographical Association followed suit (the latter considered refunding half the levy); the Boilermakers and the Railway Clerks used local payments to sugar the pill of increases in their political contributions, although in the latter instance the membership repudiated the executive's decision, and opted for a lower levy.[72]

In the 1918 election, trade unions directly financed half of Labour's candidates, roughly 160 individuals, and more than twice the pre-war union commitment. Half the candidates were sponsored by the miners (fifty-one), and ASE (sixteen) and the railway unions (fifteen).[73] It is likely that without the experience of war (for the Statist unions) and the attendant collapse of the old political system (for many others), the unions' commitment would have been even more limited. Union opinion, popular support, and organisational expansion did not 'force' Labour to attack the Liberals. Labour had *some* support amongst Statist unions and voters, but there were still limits to its appeal. Liberal failure gave it the chance to move beyond this and grasp the nettle.

The remaining candidates in 1918 were financed by affiliated groups and constituency organisations, with a degree of help from the party at the centre. The ILP sponsored fifty candidates, four times as many as in 1910. It had acquired many new members during the war, often from the Liberals. Although previously it had few wealthy backers, it

---

[70] *Journeyman Bakers' Magazine*, Nov. 1917; *Licensed Vehicle Trades' Record*, 14 Nov. 1917. See also *Dockers' Record*, Dec. 1917.

[71] *C.F.T.*, 5 Apr., 21 June 1918; *Railway Clerk*, 15 Mar. 1918; *Postal Record*, 23 May 1918; Amalgamated Instrument Makers' *AR* 1919; Burchill and Sweeney, *North Staffordshire textile industry*, esp. pp. 79–80; R. B. Suthers, *The story of NATSOPA* (1929), p. 59.

[72] NAFTO *MR* Oct. 1916 and Apr. 1918, vote of 830–657 in favour of more than one candidate, on a turn-out of less than 20 per cent; Ironfounders *MR* Oct. 1917; Typographical Ass. Delegates' Meeting 17 June 1918; Boilermakers' *MR* Feb. 1917, and May 1917 vote of 2,663–1,059 in favour, turnout less than 10 per cent; *Railway Clerk*, 15 June 1916.

[73] All figures based on LP *AR* 1919, pp. 187–93.

was now able to attract donations from reasonably affluent recruits.[74] Again, this reflected wartime developments, and had few pre-war precedents. Local Labour organisations supported 140 candidates, financed by increased local affiliation fees, donations from local union branches (especially the candidate's union), and from middle-class sympathisers. Contributions from wealthy local activists and the parliamentary candidate or his associates were particularly important in the weaker seats. Frequently campaigns strained constituency resources. In Sheffield and Penistone for example, local organisations bit off more than they could chew, and ran up debts which they could not logically hope to pay.[75] Birmingham raised a political fund three times larger than in 1915, but largely from the NUR and wealthy individuals. Organisations in middle-class areas were even more dependent on a few sympathisers.[76] There were again no pre-war precedents of even this limited degree of 'improvement'.

No doubt some change in Labour's position and strength was inevitable. The war may only have *accelerated* changes in several unions and in several regions (particularly the coalfields). War allowed Labour to develop policies which, although not carefully formulated, were sufficiently attractive, and yet sufficiently vague, to provide a unifying focus for party activists, some union members, and a section of the anti-Tory electorate. Yet Labour's appeal was not totally attractive to groups in areas even where it had considerable pre-war potential, let alone the 'Liberal' areas, where to some extent the nature of the local economic, and occasionally political, situation still suggested that the Liberals were a viable force. There was also the powerful counter-attraction of the Coalition. Ultimately, however, as Henderson recognised, there was a vacuum which the Liberals were unlikely to fill, and an opportunity finally to break out of the Progressive Alliance and become the principal anti-Tory party. Labour seized that opportunity.

V

The 1918 election came as a shock to the Asquithian Liberals. They had been hoping for and discussing Liberal reunion, and unlike Labour were

---

[74] For the changing role of middle-class wealth compare T. D. Benson to Ensor, 15 May 1909, Ensor MS with R. E. Dowse, *Left in the Centre* (1966), pp. 333–4, and e.g. H. H. Markwald to J.R.M., 6 Feb. 1920, JRM PRO 30/69/1164.

[75] Sheffield T&LC Mins, e.g. 22 Sept. 1918 (candidate's offer to part-fund an agent), 12 Nov. 1918, 21 Jan. 1919; Penistone LP Mins, 16 Nov. 1918, 23 Oct. 1920. There were also candidates from the BSP and some self-financed campaigns in University seats.

[76] Birm. T&LC *AR* 1918 and Birm. LP Mins, 11 Nov. 1919; Koss, *Brunner*, p. 256; Howard, 'Cambridge LP'; Gloucester LP Mins, e.g. 18 July 1922.

not anticipating an immediate appeal to the electorate. Once the election was called, they were placed in a dilemma. There were Liberals in the Coalition, who were supporting a Government which had won the war and was now offering to construct a 'Liberal' post-war world. To oppose this would be akin to punching oneself on the nose; it might also crystallise a separation which many hoped would only be temporary. Yet Lloyd George allocated so few 'coupons' to the Liberals that most Liberal candidates faced Coalition opposition. There was little time to reform organisations to suit the new boundaries, or to mobilise old members and supporters.[77] The party floundered in complete disarray. The leaders fumed. Strategic decisions needed to be made, but Asquith passed the buck. Constituency organisations, he argued, should act as they saw fit. If they chose Coalition Liberal candidates, Liberal voters should support them; if they chose 'Free' Liberals, this candidate should get the Liberal vote. Where there was no Liberal candidate, Liberals were free to act as they pleased.

The official Asquithian Liberal attitude to the Coalition was neither clear nor inspiring. Asquith argued that he would support the Coalition in so far as it pursued Liberal policies, although 'Free Liberals' would not be 'fettered' to the Coalition and its views and forced to give it uncritical support. The provincial Liberal press generally reflected these views, as did Asquithian Liberal candidates.[78]

This approach had serious consequences for the Liberals' role as an anti-Tory force. There were only 276 non-Coalition Liberal candidates in 1918. In whole areas of the country, support for the Coalition, general organisational weakness, or a reluctance to split the Progressive vote restricted the size of the Liberal campaign. In several cities (such as Leeds and Bristol) the Liberals and Tories formed an electoral pact.[79] Where before 1914 the Liberals were weak, already flimsy organisations crumbled. A substantial number of constituencies in West Lancashire, and especially in Liverpool, went uncontested.[80] In the West Midlands, 'local

---

[77]   W. Royle to E. D. Simon, copy, 29 Oct. 1918, MLF MS M/283/1/3/3, and MLF Mins, 11 July 1918; Lancs. and Cheshire Soc. of Liberal Agents Mins, 5 Sept 1918; Rolf (thesis), pp. 162–4. In Yorkshire, there were few problems by 1916, but redistribution and Coalition had a disruptive impact (YLF Mins, 14 July 1916, reply to NLF circular on constituency organisation; Dugdale (thesis) pp. 56–7; Leeds LF Mins, 15 Nov., and e.g. 8 Dec. 1920). For Labour's anticipation of an election, e.g. J.R.M. to F.J., 1 July 1918, FJ 1918/85, S. Webb to Ensor, 16 July 1918, Ensor MS.

[78]   Wilson, Downfall of the Liberal party, pp. 164–70. For e.g. Maclean and Simon, Daily News, 23 Nov. 1918, M.G., 30 Dec. 1918. For provincial press opinion, e.g. Sheffield Ind., 19, 25 Nov. 1918, North Mail, 19, 22 Nov. 1918.

[79]   Reports in the Star, 19 Nov. 1918 and the Daily News, 23 Nov. 1918, on official policy.

[80]   Liv. Post, speeches by Bowring, Muspratt, and Russell, 30 Dec. 1918. See also e.g. 26 Nov. 1918 (Waterloo).

pressure and the fear of (a) Coalition wave' persuaded some Liberal candidates to stand down in favour of the Tories. Other Liberal organisations, divided and disillusioned, resolved to wait for a better occasion.[81] Still others supported Labour. Dr Hazel, the West Bromwich Liberal candidate in 1914, and several other Liberal figures, publicly supported their old Progressive rivals (Hazel withdrew his nomination). A Progressive Alliance also still operated in parts of the West Midlands and Lancashire.[82] Moreover, there were few Liberals who were willing to fight in the Home Counties or Greater London. Nearly half the campaigns fought in 1918 were financed partly by the Whips, the bulk of these being in the former Tory areas of Lancashire, the West Midlands, the Home Counties and (surprisingly) in Scotland. The central organisation had to prop up a collapsing constituency machine.[83]

The position was made worse by local division and disunity. Many pacifist Liberals were repudiated by their Liberal associations. Some of these stood as Independents, with the support of a portion of the local Liberal machine. Disagreements within local organisations could also result in rival factions bringing forward Coalition and 'Free' Liberal candidates. Thus, while many seats had no Liberal candidates, a number had two.[84] This was hardly good propaganda. Events on the national stage, the widespread reporting of the Liberal party as a spent force (even in Liberal papers) and its failure to present a policy, all reinforced Labour's contention that politics were now a question of capital versus labour, of the 'Coalition of Interests' against the representatives of morality and honest toil.[85]

Asquithian Liberals did not always make a positive attempt to capture

[81] Mid.L.F. Mins, 31 Jan., 17 Oct. 1919; *Liv. Post*, 10 Dec. 1918 (Shrewsbury); *Birm. Gazette*, 23 Nov. 1918 (Kidderminster).
[82] *Birm. Gazette*, 28 Nov. 1918, and vote of thanks to Hazel and the *Gazette*, *Typographical Circular*, Feb. 1919. *Birm. Gazette*, 29 Nov. 1918 on Labour support for a Progressive Liberal in Duddeston, and Labour withdrawal in Lancaster. See also reports of Labour's limited campaigns in Manchester, *C.F.T.*, 29 Mar. 1918, and decisions to field only one candidate in a double member borough, Oldham LP Mins, e.g. 7 May, 13 Aug. 1918.
[83] In much of Surrey and Middlesex, Labour was the only opposition because of the local Liberals' pro-Coalition sympathies (e.g. reports in *Surrey Times*, 22 Nov. 1918, Hart (thesis), p. 95). For pro-Labour withdrawals in London, *Star* 30 Oct., 22 Nov. 1918. Details of Liberal payments from Asquith MS 141.
[84] On some occasions Coalition Liberals stood against Asquithians either as a result of internal division or because Coalition Liberals were adopted by Tories. For the former, e.g. *Newcastle Daily Chronicle*, 11 Dec. 1918 (Bishop Auckland) and *Liv. Post*, 30 Dec. 1918 (Yorks., Buckrose); for the latter, e.g. *Bristol Times*, 28 Nov. 1918 (East Bristol), *M.G.*, 11 Dec. 1918 (Huddersfield). Other Coalition Liberals spoke against Liberal candidates (memo, Asquith MS 148 fos. 82–4).
[85] *D.H.*, 16 Nov. 1918, and for local reflections, e.g. W.C.A. in Sheffield, *Sheff. Daily Tel.*, 7 Dec. 1918. Turner at Dewsbury, *Dewsbury Reporter*, 4 Jan. 1919.

some of the 'radical' vote by creating a distinct image. Almost all 'Free' Liberals in the North-West, for example, described themselves as 'Liberal Coalitionists'. Others complained bitterly that they had not been given the Coalition 'coupon', and continued to support the Coalition and its programme without qualification. Liberals across the country fought hard to show that they were on the side of the angels, rather than attempting to be a rallying point for those only half-satisfied with the Coalition.[86]

Some radical Liberals recognised that this was not enough. Asquith was 'motivated by the highest patriotism', the *M.G.* noted:

> But it was perhaps not fully appreciated or even understood . . . that the prolonga- tion of his forbearance after the gage had definitely been thrown down by the Prime Minister had a depressing and even paralysing effect not only on the elector but on the candidate.[87]

The *Nation* replied to the Asquithian failure by supporting Labour as the only alternative to the Coalition, and the heir of true Liberalism. The *Daily News* advocated voting against the Coalition, as did Progressive papers in Birmingham and the North-East. In some cases this involved supporting Labour in preference to Coalition Liberals.[88] Other Liberals, especially those in the Pennine radical bloc, in London, and in the Man- chester area adopted radical programmes. As they acknowledged, this aligned them with the Labour party in broad outlook, although some at least still recognised major differences.[89] Labour's past links with Liberalism, its attitude during the war and its programme for the peace, could be taken by some Liberal voters as evidence of its soundness as a radical party. When several Liberal newspapers and former Liberal politicians endorsed Labour, its credibility increased still further. Where Liberals failed to select an alternative candidate, the choices became even simpler. Labour's propaganda was reinforced by the actions and

---

[86] *The Times*, 10 Dec. 1918 (Yorkshire); *Liv. Post*, 25 Nov., 13 Dec. 1918; *M.G.*, 22 Nov 1918; examples from Essex, London and Wolverhampton, Hart (thesis), pp. 96–7, and for other parts of the West Midlands and the North, *Mid. Daily Tel.*, 27 Nov. 1918, *North Mail*, 20 Nov. 1918.

[87] *M.G.*, 30 Dec. 1918.

[88] *Nation*, e.g. 23 Nov. 1918; *Daily News*, 14 Dec. 1918, and for the suggestion that Labour was the heir of Liberalism, 25 Nov. 1918; *N.E.*, 14 Dec. 1918.

[89] For Yorkshire, e.g. Arnold and Less-Smith, *Sheffield Ind.*, 20, 29, 30 Nov. 1918. Even the Keighley Liberal association was reformed in a manner which would suggest a recognition of the need to break down the hold of party conservatives (Keighley LA Mins, 28 June, 2 Sept. 1918). For Manchester, MLF Mins, 24 Apr.–6 Nov. 1918 and A. A. Haworth to W.R., 16 Jan. 1918, WR 169, noting contacts between Huddersfield and Manchester Liberals. Cf. Mid.LF Mins, 31 Oct. 1919, noting that in 1918 the Man- chester programme 'had not had time to take root' in the Midlands area before the election was called. For the positive results of attempts to oppose the Coalition (e.g. by putting up a Liberal candidate), A. H. Taylor, 'The effect of electoral pacts on the decline of the Liberal party', *British Journal of Political Science* (1973).

pronouncements of their former radical allies in the Progressive Alliance. When this was taken in conjunction with its *positive* attractions as a 'patriotic', Statist, party, or as a *more* moral and now more economically sustainable practical moral reformist organisation, Labour was clearly in a better competitive position than ever before.

V

The election results confirmed that a process of realignment was under way. After the election, Labour became the official opposition, with just 21 per cent of the vote and only fifty-seven MPs. The party of government in 1914, elected in 1910 with well over 40 per cent of the vote, managed to poll just 13 per cent of the vote and to elect just thirty-three MPs in 1918 (Table 13.2).

It is extremely difficult to determine precisely where Labour support came from. The election was fought in great confusion and on an inaccurate register. There were a great many minor parties, some of whom, in particular circumstances, polled very well. Turn-out was low (57 per cent). It seems unlikely that the newly enfranchised voters (the wives and sons of existing voters) formed a distinct pro-Labour bloc. On the contrary, in many areas the enfranchisement of women may have harmed Labour's prospects. Yet it also seems unlikely that the entire Liberal vote simply transferred to Labour, because mass defections are so unusual and because the pre-war Liberal coalition included many who were unlikely Labour voters.[90]

Most newly enfranchised male voters did not vote for anyone in 1918. Being young and single they were very likely to be conscripted soldiers. Only a quarter of military personnel still at the front (the overwhelming majority) actually voted. In some constituencies the figure was even lower.[91] Neither were the areas where there was a major increase in the level of enfranchisement areas where Labour did well.[92] It is thus difficult to see new male voters as the source of Labour's expansion.

[90] Francis and Peele, 'Reflections on generational analysis', noting estimates of anti-Labour bias amongst women in the inter-war years. See also Rasmussen, 'The flapper vote', pp. 57–8, Savage, *Preston*, pp. 172–3. These accounts are littered with technical problems, and the pattern of voting by gender remains an open question.

[91] 'Absent' (i.e. military) voters were registered for the constituency where they were normally resident. Their votes were counted separately, and the turn-out figures for each constituency regularly figured in the local press. See e.g. *M.G.*, 30 Dec. 1918 (Lancs.); *Star*, 30 Dec. 1918 (London); P. R. Shorter, 'Electoral politics and political change in the East Midlands 1918–35', Cambridge Ph.D. thesis 1975, pp. 214–15 (East Midlands).

[92] Hart, 'Liberals, war and the franchise', pp. 823–4. See also J. Turner, 'The Labour vote and the franchise after 1918', in P. R. Denley and D. I. Hopkin (eds.), *History and computing* (Manchester, 1987).

Table 13.2 *Liberal and Labour electoral performance, 1918 parliamentary election (GB)*

	Candidates	Votes cast[a]	% vote	Votes per candidate	MPs
Liberal[b]	276	1,388,784	13.00	5,031	36[c]
Labour	361	2,245,777	20.80	6,221	57

Notes:

[a] Excludes four unopposed Liberals, eleven unopposed Labour.

[b] Asquithian Liberals only.

[c] Nine of these took the Coalition whip upon election, even though they were not Coalition Liberal candidates. Only fourteen consistently opposed the Government.

The most telling evidence in support of this argument, however, is derived from post-war municipal elections, in which three-quarters of the new male voters could not vote. If the 4 million newly enfranchised men were the principal source of Labour's post-war support, then Labour should have fared very much worse in municipal than in parliamentary elections. It should have floundered; instead it flourished. In 1919, Labour won a landslide victory in the municipal elections, gaining over 400 seats. Before 1914 there were only forty-eight Labour councillors in London: after the municipal 'general election' of 1919 there were over 550. Over half of all Labour candidates in London were returned, and the party controlled twelve of the twenty-eight Borough Councils. This success cannot be attributed solely to the new voters. In Camberwell, Greenwich, and Southwark (where there were a substantial number of new male voters), the number of Labour councillors increased from none to thirty-two, twenty, and thirty respectively. In Battersea, high pre-war levels of enfranchisement meant that there were few new male voters: Labour increased its representation nonetheless from none to forty-one. Similar successes were also recorded in the provincial boroughs, where the increase in the number of new voters was comparatively small. Labour gained seventeen seats in Manchester, eleven in Birmingham, and ten in Bradford, Liverpool, and Swindon.[93] These were no freak results. Although Labour lost some support in 1922, in all other years before 1930 it increased its number of elected councillors.

It is clear that Labour was not at a critical disadvantage in municipal politics. True, Labour's municipal improvement did not always match its parliamentary advance. There were towns and cities which it captured at the parliamentary level, but which were Tory in local government. Some of this may have resulted from elections being fought on differing boundaries, and with different candidature patterns. Local factors, and the timing of elections, could also be significant. However, contemporaries suggested a more serious bias, arguing that the young were more inclined to vote Labour, and consequently that municipal elections understated Labour support.[94]

It is possible to determine the extent of this bias because in 1922 municipal and parliamentary elections were held within weeks of each other, and because in a number of seats boundaries and candidature patterns permit exact comparisons between Labour's parliamentary and municipal

[93] *The Times*, 3 Nov. 1919; C. Cook, 'Liberals, Labour and local elections', in G. Peele and C. Cook (eds.), *The politics of reappraisal 1918–1939* (1975).

[94] J. S. Rowett, 'The Labour party in local government: theory and practice in the inter-war years', Oxford D.Phil. thesis 1979, pp. 11–12; *The Times*, 7 Nov. 1922, *Daily Telegraph*, 9 Nov. 1922, *Yorks. Obs.*, 17 Nov. 1922, *Forward*, 2 Dec. 1922.

Table 13.3 *Municipal and parliamentary election results in comparable units, 1922*

	Municipal	Parliamentary
England and Wales		
Labour	46.15[a]	47.66
Conservative	53.85[a]	52.34
Glasgow		
Labour	60.67[b]	61.87[b]
Conservative	39.33	38.13

Notes:

[a] The polls of Independents who achieved 1 per cent of the vote or less have been equally redistributed between the parties. The figures are an average of the share of the vote achieved in the wards of fourteen parliamentary constituencies, mainly the divisions of provincial cities and London boroughs.

[b] Small Communist vote included with Labour's. The analysis is based on data from the four constituencies for which results are broadly comparable.

vote. The results, summarised in Table 13.3, suggest an anti-Labour bias of around 1.5 per cent of the vote in municipal elections. Labour was thus only marginally less successful in municipal than in parliamentary politics. It was 'converting' older voters (who had the municipal vote) in roughly the same proportions as their sons who held the parliamentary franchise.

This should hardly be surprising. Political organisers noted the existence of a household vote, and political sociologists have supported this notion. It seems entirely plausible that, when some older voters defected to Labour (a fact reflected in the party's municipal support), their sons did so too. The slight disparity in Labour's municipal and parliamentary support is entirely consistent with the greater volatility of younger voters.[95]

This does not mean that Labour support came from a simple Progressive switch. As Table 13.4 suggests, only a portion of the former Liberal vote, swollen by the votes of these voters' wives and sons, switched to Labour. Many new Labour supporters (a fifth in Table 13.4) were former Tories. Moreover, perhaps half the Liberal vote did not switch to its old Progressive ally. Of course, too much weight should not be attached to evidence of this kind. The constituencies covered by the table are

[95] *Liberal Monthly*, Aug. 1920, Butler and Stokes, *Political change in Britain*, *passim*. For the importance of political fluidity in 1918, Miller, *Electoral dynamics*, pp. 103–7, 224–5, Crewe, 'Political change', pp. 65–6.

Table 13.4 *Effect of Labour intervention 1922 on January 1910 parliamentary poll, comparable constituencies, 1910 and 1922 (%)*

January 1910		1922 result		Change
Liberal	52.71		31.32	−21.39
Conservative	47.29		41.83	−5.46
		Labour	26.85	+26.85

not a weighted sample, for example, and the figures disguise shifts between parties and between voting and non-voting. However, the table reinforces the notion that Labour was only moderately attractive, is consistent with the idea that Labour was a *positive* force in 'Tory' areas, and supports the idea that the circumstances which prompted change require more careful explanation.

VII

There was no single 'rise of Labour', no single transfer of support made possible by franchise extension or by a 'rational' electoral switch from a Progressive Liberal party to a Progressive Labour party. The pattern, on the contrary, was more fragmented, reflecting the pre-war determinants of political behaviour, as modified by the new ideas, policies, and circumstances which arose during the First World War. The major increase in Labour strength was in the mining areas where it had polled fairly well before 1914. Nearly two-thirds of the Labour MPs elected in 1918 sat for mining constituencies, mainly in South Wales, the North-East, Lancashire, and Scotland. However, there were some successes in mining areas which hitherto had been solidly Liberal. Broxtowe, Mansfield, and West Nottingham in the Notts/Derby coalfield, Kingswinford and Leek in Staffordshire and the Forest of Dean in the Somerset coalfields, all returned Labour MPs (Table 13.5). Although some of these seats contained a number of non-mining elements, all local analysis suggests that the mining vote was decisive.[96] Even where Labour was not successful in mining areas it nonetheless performed well. In a few former Lib/Lab seats, particularly Morpeth and Chesterfield, and some Durham mining seats, the Liberal vote held up, but generally the Liberal party failed to put up candidates or fared substantially worse than Labour. The increase in Labour majorities in areas (such as the North-West) where the Liberal vote had already disappeared could only have been achieved

[96] e.g. *Leek Times*, 4 Jan. 1919; Hutchison, *Scotland*, p. 283; Mid.LF Mins, 31 Jan., 17 Oct. 1919.

Table 13.5 *Seats captured by Labour, 1918 election*

Mining seats		Non-mining seats	
North-West	4	North-West	10
South Wales	9	West Midlands	3
North-East	5	South-East	3
Yorkshire	5	Others (held pre-1914)	2[a]
Scotland	3	Others (gained 1918)	6[b]
Other mining	7		
Total	33		24

Notes:
[a] Leeds South-East, Derby.
[b] Glasgow, Govan; Edinburgh, Central; Ayr, North; Northants, Kettering; Northants, Wellingborough; Lincs, Holland with Boston.

by Conservative defections. However, in the main the mining areas had been very solidly Liberal and the scale of Liberal defections was generally very considerable.

Labour also consolidated its hold over the formerly Tory industrial areas. Events augmented its pre-war appeal and vastly speeded up the process of removing Liberal opposition. In many Tory parts of London, West Lancashire, and the West Midlands, radical Liberal activists switched to Labour. In Black Country industrial towns (as in the Midlands mining areas) Liberal voters followed suit. The 'great bulk' of the Liberal vote in West Bromwich, one Liberal argued, went Labour (as the former radical Liberal candidate and the Liberal press recommended).[97] Moreover, Labour now had a more sharply defined, more independent, image. It had policies which (in some areas) reinforced its stance. When it could suppress its radical/pacifist/moralistic wing, it was strong enough to win such seats as Preston, Bolton, Salford North, Wednesbury, West Bromwich, and Smethwick. Its assimilation to local views had been reinforced by the institutional primacy of groups, like the ironfounders and textile workers, who were committed to strong support for the war, and a protective stance on the home front (part and parcel of their conception of patriotism). Raised living standards and expectations in poor areas like Salford were not nullified by the party's *national* image as a skilled workers' party (as they were elsewhere) because the local party's stance so completely contradicted it. Labour was seen as the party committed to protecting the gains made by the dockers, to protecting the threatened position of male workers in the textile and pottery industries,

[97]   e.g. *Birm. Gazette*, 28 Nov. 1918, Mid.L.F. Mins, 31 Jan. 1919.

and which was a genuinely sympathetic, practical, and ordinary organisation. The Liberals either vanished or (where they did fight) were easily defeated.[98] However, party organisers rightly argued that Labour had also drawn support from the Tories, in addition to mopping up the Liberal vote. London Tories in particular noticed the 'huge turn-over' in their support by 1919, and there was a general, almost hysterical, Conservative reaction to the Labour 'threat'.[99] Labour did not create as substantial an electoral base in the Tory areas as it had in the mining areas. However, it had finally established its position as the major anti-Tory party in a large proportion of the Tory areas which before 1914 it was only slowly capturing. It had a solid presence in a large proportion of the electoral map.

The Liberal–Labour electoral conflict in the remaining industrial areas was very different. The Liberals had a stronger, more secure, position which in some areas (even in 1918) they attempted to maintain. The areas of heavy industry, the Yorkshire and Lancashire textile belts, many urban and some rural parts of the South, and some parts of London, had a more Liberal political culture. Labour's problems in these areas had not gone away. The party's moderate moral reformism was not far removed from radical Liberalism; it shared Nonconformist roots and economic views. A Centrist Liberalism, with its emphasis on industrial prosperity through union/management co-operation and Free Trade, had been topped up in some areas by New Liberal politics; in others, the New Liberalism was the dominant force. The salience of Liberal ideas had not been undermined by the experience of war. Labour's Statism seemed inappropriate. Old allegiances were not easily ruptured, particularly where the Liberals put up a fight. To the unskilled, particularly in London, a radical Liberal moral populism seemed more acceptable than Labour's mixed recipes for prosperity. A *radical* Labour attempt to by-pass these problems by emphasising what the municipality could do to affect living standards had brought some success before 1914. It had also utilised pride, and a hostility to middle-class interference, to portray working-class material improvement as moral justice. There were echoes of this in the war-time fight for improvements on the home front,

---

[98] In Birmingham the Liberals came third in six three-cornered contests. In Liverpool they fought only one of the eleven seats. For Labour's approach in Lancashire, Savage, *Preston*, p. 164, M.G., 12, 14 Dec. 1918.

[99] *London Municipal Notes*, Dec. 1919 and *Conservative Agents' Journal*, Nov. 1919 for a similar verdict; for this position in the West Midlands, and for Labour's progress, S. Drinkwater to J.R.M., 13 June 1919, JRM PRO 30/69/1163. For 1918, cf. Amery Diary, 29 Dec. 1918 in J. Barnes and D. Nicholson (eds), *The Leo Amery Diaries*, i (1980), p. 248.

combined (in some instances) with a deep pride in the working-class contribution to winning the war.

These tactics did bear some fruit in 1918 and in the immediate post-war years. Poplar and West Ham became more securely Labour. The four West Ham seats provided two Socialist/Labour MPs in 1918, and Poplar, Stepney, and West Ham itself were to be a solid Labour power bloc in the following years. Neither Bradford nor Leeds – where Labour employed a similar approach – could match this performance either in 1918 or subsequently, perhaps because local social/economic conditions were much better than in London. However, O'Grady was elected in Leeds for his old (slightly changed) constituency, and the more Labour parts of both Bradford and Leeds continued to produce a higher Labour vote. Moreover, other exponents of these policies were also successful. Dan Irving, the BSP candidate, captured Burnley. On Clydeside, where rent strikes and housing politics had been expertly forged into a Labour political allegiance, Neil Maclean was elected in Govan and Labour polled well in (some) other Scottish seats. However, Labour had not found an ideologically radical answer. Several more Socialist parties subsequently slipped to the right, as the West Ham LRC had done before 1914. A strident materialistic Socialism and a protective Labourism were sometimes only separated by rhetoric.[100]

The approach adopted by Lansbury and others helped to create a popular and successful alternative to the Liberal party in some Liberal areas, but the conditions were not always so apposite, nor the political application so skilful. Many moderate Labour parties took the campaigning opportunities offered by the idea of a capital levy, and the circumstances of war, to attract substantial Liberal support on moral reformist lines. Labour obtained a good deal of support in Liberal areas like Yorkshire. In Rotherham, for example, the Liberals polled only 4,000 votes in 1918, compared to 12,000 in 1910, despite the doubling of the electorate. It 'would be folly', one local newspaper noted, 'to shut our eyes to the fact that Labour has taken a large number of Liberal votes'. The illustration, and the conclusion, could be repeated. Defections even affected those Liberals who tried to present some kind of radical Liberal alternative. Sowerby, 'where Mr Higham, a sound Radical of long standing, is displaced, is a good example', the *M.G.* noted. He came at the foot of the poll, despite his radicalism, because 'a large part of the normal

---

[100] Bush, *East London*, pp. 89–98, and Chapter 7, Gillespie (thesis), Chapter 8; McLean, *Red Clydeside*, pp. 154–77 and Hutchison, *Scotland*, esp. p. 279; *Burnley Expr.*, 11, 14 Dec. 1918, *Burnley News*, 1 Jan. 1919.

Liberal vote has clearly been transferred to Labour'. [101] Labour defeated
Liberals in seats where it had shown no previous ability to erode the
Liberal ascendancy (Appendix 6). Where the Liberals failed even to field
a candidate, as they often did even in former strongholds, Labour staked
its claim to be the major Progressive force without even token opposition.

The extent of Labour's progress in 1918 can be exaggerated. Its proximity to a radical Liberal political culture enabled it to make up some
ground, but its 'deficiencies' were such that the transfer of support was
less than complete. Labour captured few seats in the formerly 'Liberal'
areas. The Liberals returned as many MPs in these areas as Labour (and
more in Scotland). They threatened or out-polled the Labour party in
a substantial number of constituencies in all the old Liberal working-class
areas, and not just in the rural/southern seats (Appendix 6). [102] Moreover,
some at least of the Coalition Liberal vote in 1918 came from Liberal
partisans. The 'Asquithians' performance thus understates the level of
Liberal party support. Labour went on to improve its position in 1922
and 1923, but the Liberal decline, and Labour's ability to find an attractive
alternative, developed slowly. Labour had captured the mining and Tory
areas; it had put a foot in the door in the old Liberal working-class
heartlands, but it was not always unchallenged or unchallengeable. If
it now had the substantial advantage of being the official opposition to
the Coalition, with a launching pad from which to expand, it was not
capable of absorbing all the old Liberal coalition. The other half of the
Progressive constituency was still uncertain as to which way it should
tilt.

The Progressive Alliance ended in 1918, but not because Labour was
riding a wave of popular indignation and protest. Neither did it end
because Labour had found an ideological solution to its pre-war impasse.
Rather the Alliance disintegrated because Labour finally came into its
(Liberal) political inheritance. It captured that half of the pre-war Progressive electoral constituency where it had been slowly gaining ground
before 1914. In these areas it had proved itself to be not only a 'better'
Progressive party, but also a positively attractive and distinctive force.
However, although a practical Socialist reformism helped it generate
some positive popular support in 'Liberal' cities dominated by particular
economic circumstances, elsewhere conditions were less favourable to

[101]   *Rotherham Adv.*, 4 Jan. 1919; *M.G.*, 30 Dec. 1918. For a similar analysis of the position
in the East and West Midlands, Shorter (thesis), pp. 219–26.
[102]   See Taylor's points concerning 'major party status', in 'Electoral pacts', p. 245 and
R. Lupton's original local study, 'The decline of the Liberal party 1918–24, with special
reference to South-East Lancashire', Cambridge B.A. dissertation 1986 for the continuing potential strength of the Liberal party.

this approach. Labour gained a foothold in the Liberal half of the old Progressive coalition through the more coherent and credible combination of material and moral issues which characterised its moderate moral reformism. It was unable to break the hold of a Liberal political culture or totally overturn the Liberal party, despite its rival's national weakness, because even this approach was not so distinctive, economically meaningful, and politically credible that an often radical Liberal party was an unacceptable alternative. It had made a major breakthrough; it could not go back. But could it, ideologically and electorally, go forward?

Conclusion

In 1906 the Liberal party won a landslide electoral victory. Labour, usually acting in alliance with the Liberals at the parliamentary level, but always attempting to erode its ally's position in the constituencies, was at best a small third force. In 1918, however, Labour broke out of this alliance and became the major opposition to the Government. In discussing how and why the pattern of politics changed, scholars have always recognised that two wider questions underpin their analysis. They have identified changes in the determinants of political behaviour and in the nature of the parties. A switch from 'religious' to 'class' based allegiances was encouraged, or reflected, by the rise of mature, 'national', parties. For some, the Liberals were a class-based, and hence 'viable' party by 1910. New Liberal ideas created a materially attractive party image through the politics of social reform. For others, a working-class cultural unity – and/or experience of trade union action – created a 'collectivist' outlook and a form of class consciousness which found its 'natural' expression in the Labour party. For both schools, dynamic forces (ideas or class consciousness) swept away the old politics. In the process, they also altered the *nature* of that political party. The Liberals became a social democratic force (for Dr Clarke); Labour became the voice of the trade unions and a non-revolutionary sense of class solidarity (for Dr McKibbin). The specific historical debate thus masks a broader concern with the determinants of political behaviour and with the forces which governed the general political orientation of the parties in question.[1]

The analysis in this book suggests a different interpretation of the causes, extent, and nature of realignment. It thus has (different) implications for the same narrow and broader concerns. The evidence presented here suggests that the process of change was more fragmented.

[1] McKibbin, *Evolution*, esp. pp. xiv, 236 and his 'Marxism in Britain'; Clarke, *Lancashire Liberalism*, esp. p. 406, and his articles, 'Electoral sociology of modern Britain' and 'Social democratic theory of the class struggle'.

The Liberals were not an entirely 'viable' force, but Labour's capacity to replace them was not so evident that major electoral changes were inevitable. There were areas of Labour growth before 1914, and areas of Liberal success. The political system was an elaborate jigsaw. The pieces fit together but not in a manner that can adequately be explained by existing accounts. Neither a single set of ideas (the New Liberalism) nor a collective consciousness born of social change and trade union membership, can be judged the primary motive force in the process of realignment. The *dynamics* of change were different, and so, as a result, was the character of the parties which change produced.

I

Politics were not nationalised, and elections did not become class based (as conventionally understood) between 1900 and 1918. Class fragmentation was as significant as cultural unity. There was a multiplicity of working-class circumstances which might point individual workers in different political directions. Even the organised working class did not share a single outlook or interest. The context of social experience, and of economic expectations, was local, not national.[2] However, politics was also important in determining electoral patterns. The agents of socialisation taught not one but a series of contradictory lessons, and politics gave form to particular aspects of that experience.[3] However, political approaches, like social experiences, were not uniform. Strands within each party attempted to form, or represent, differing local interests, beliefs, and outlooks. Each political strand emphasised different interpretations of a common core of principles. Local parties, matching local experiences, emphasised different aspects of that party's aims. The political standing of local organisations was influenced by perceptions associated with the voter's past political views. Current economic and social conditions could interact with new ideas to create the capacity for change, but newer, more radical approaches (Liberal or Labour) were not necessarily more attractive, or more successful.[4] People were not blank slates. Existing allegiances were not easily ruptured. Social and economic con-

---

[2] This reflects points made in several chapters above, and particular conceptions of how social forces influence political actions. See Reid, 'Politics, economics and the British working class', the debate between Price and Joyce (*Social History* 1983–4) and Giddins, *Constitution of society*. For the ambiguities of individual experience, e.g. Moore, *Pitmen, preachers and politics*, pp. 169–90.

[3] Stedman Jones, *Languages of Class*, pp. 21–2 and Heath *et al.*, *How Britain votes*, p. 171. I would argue, however, that particular combinations of past traditions and current experiences make some outcomes far more likely than others.

[4] These conditions would include the level of prosperity and a worker's perception (related to his skill and occupation) of the determinants of that prosperity.

ditions did not always alter in such a way that new outlooks were easily sustained. The more radical policies were not suited to all conditions.[5] Provided entrenched parties adopted some measures of reform, moving with and updating existing outlooks, they would be seriously threatened only where the economic foundations, or social purchase, of their ideas were evidently and clearly challenged. Even then, as Edwardian reformers such as Hobson, Hobhouse, MacDonald, and Bernstein recognised, a new political culture could not be created overnight. The new and the old had to merge to gain popular acceptance. It took time for parties advocating economically more advantageous stances to also become a fair representation of local social views. Only when a new economic validity was supported by social continuity were parties securely based.[6]

As the electorate's interests and attitudes were not transformed, and as 'bourgeois' parties were not reactionary, class conflict did not dominate politics. The past continued to influence the present. In simplified terms, there were two political nations. In traditionally Tory areas, and in areas where voters had a particular economic interest in state intervention (largely coalfields and railway centres), the Labourist and Statist side of Labour's image became gradually more pronounced, and more popular. The institutional involvement of these groups in Labour politics helped create the *social* roots which the Liberals lacked. A tough, unsentimental, Labourism was more closely related than a moralistic Liberalism to the dominant Tory political culture. In many mining areas, with their more Liberal past, Labour's social roots were forged through support for social attitudes associated with the Liberal party (particularly Nonconformity), but also through an image which embraced the toughness, independence, loyalty, and mutual support associated with the miners' own associational life. However, Labour's social roots were not so strong that its growing support could be turned into electoral victories before the war. It was increasingly the party of local views and local working-class interests, but it was also still too negative an organisation to become the major anti-Tory organisation if the Liberals resisted with a radical approach. Its vision of the future lacked the economic credibility which might make more moderate views unattractive.[7]

In most traditionally Liberal areas, by contrast, the dominant Labour

---

[5] See above, pp. 139, 153, 211–13, 261, 286–7, 304–5, 412–16.
[6] While voting patterns relate to occupations, and to economic factors, I am thus not arguing that the *broad* pattern of change was determined by a calculated, 'rational', economic choice, whatever effect this may have had at the margins. For social continuity as an important factor in electoral politics, above, pp. 10–12, 82–4. For the significance of social continuity in the 1920s, e.g. Moore, *Pitmen, preachers and politics*, pp. 189–90, Macintyre, *Little Moscows*, pp. 157–63, 192.
[7] See Chapters 5–7; and pp. 265–8, 276–8.

approach – a moderate moral reformism – was much closer to a radical Liberal tradition. The two parties had similar social roots. However, the Liberals had a more attractive and distinctive economic appeal. This was not because New Liberal ideas had transformed Liberal politics. In many traditionally Liberal areas Old Liberal/Centrist alliances almost matched the perceived interests and the views of local non-Tory voters. The *generation* of wealth – the concern of these particular groups – could prove as popular as the New Liberals' greater concern with its redistribution. When local parties in these areas also displayed a concern for social reforms which would reinforce and make more secure the benefits of Liberal economic success, either under New Liberal influence or not, there was little scope for even limited Labour expansion.[8] In discussing the efficacy of Edwardian Liberalism, Dr Clarke's error was not so much in spotting that the Liberal party was stronger before 1914 than previous historians had allowed – although he went too far in this respect – or even in spotting that the New Liberalism was a significant force, but in seeing the first simply as a function of the second. The extent to which the New Liberalism influenced an area's politics was not the touchstone of the Liberal party's viability. The existence of a *balanced* local appeal – one which matched local experiences and views – was a more significant indication that the Liberals held a strong position. The New Liberalism could be an important component of that image; it could reinforce the party's interest in reform and encourage a more populistic approach, but it was not the only attractive feature of Liberal politics.[9] In these circumstances, Labour chipped away at the Liberals' lead, exploiting its local deficiencies as a representative of local interests and views, and mobilising support from small enclaves of Statist/Labourist voters.

This attention to spatial variations in conditions and in political stances should not suggest that all areas were 'unique'. There were core similarities between areas with politically similar pasts, and a certain kind of economic and social structure. Neither should it suggest that 'national' and 'local' politics were unconnected. On the contrary, they influenced each other. A 'national' party image and national institutional forces (e.g. the party head offices) influenced the party's local image. Moreover, the local electoral purchase of competing internal strands gave representatives of that particular approach a more powerful position in *national* politics. New Liberals and Centrists thus had a powerful voice in Cabinet politics

[8] See esp. Chapters 8–10, but also pp. 144, 157–8, 173–4, 186, 213, 222.
[9] The conclusions of many local studies which have used the presence or absence of New Liberal ideas as an index of viability are thus themselves in need of revision.

before 1914, while the Statist and Labourist elements in the Labour party were becoming politically, as well as electorally, more significant.[10]

Institutional factors also influenced the distribution of power and hence the direction, and presentation, of local and national party policy. Parties responded to their members, as well as their voters. Old Liberal (Liberal Imperialist and Radical) elements in the Liberal party – and Socialists in the Labour party – thus exercised influence out of all proportion to their more limited electoral appeal.[11] In the constituencies, Old Liberal influence was particularly evident where the leading Liberal figures were also part of the area's industrial elite. However, the presence of so many 'moralistic' radical Socialists and moral reformers even in Labourist/Statist areas was a damaging feature of Labour politics in these areas. The composite nature, and institutional structure, of the Labour party hardly helped its attempts to match and form local views in an acceptable manner. The problem was even more pronounced in areas where Socialist traditions were more strongly felt, and where moderate elements were institutionally weak. Changes in the attitudes of national leaders, and the democratisation of constituency parties, were radicalising the Liberal party, but the process was incomplete by 1914.

Labour constituency organisations were also changing and becoming more 'moderate', in some areas at least. However, Labour's traditions and structure also ensured that the left received a (public) hearing for its views, and that these views would not be regarded unsympathetically in some quarters. Moreover, Socialist moral reformers seemed to be successful in a number of areas, and to offer the prospect of a fight with capitalism, rather than acceptance of its impact. The left could not easily be controlled by institutional means (although this did not prevent party leaders trying). There was a developing tension between the party leaders/bureaucracy on the one hand and radical, and even moderate, constituency activists on the other, because of these infringements of the party's *operative* ideology. If the Liberals did not have this problem, their institutional structure made it difficult for national leaders to remove Old Liberal obstacles to newer ideas, or to call on rank and file support for their views. Changes in policy often had to be forced through by covert means and the pressure of public opinion.[12]

Despite these problems, reforming alliances dominated both parties on the eve of war in 1914. The Cabinet's reforming coalition of New

[10] In Labour politics, the physical representation of particular, localised, approaches was further facilitated by the importance of large, and frequently *localised,* unions (e.g. mining, UTFWA, dockers).

[11] See Chapter 2 and Chapter 11.

[12] For Labour, pp. 54, 73–4, 85–6, 144, 174–5, 202–3, 264–5. For the Liberals, pp. 48–50, 64–8, 86–90, 302.

Liberals and Centrists was still intact. The New Liberals were preparing to push the party still further to the left. They had defeated a Radical/Centrist attempt to put party policy on a more moderate course in part through the electoral purchase of their ideas, but also because their approach linked 'Old' and 'New' Liberal concerns, and was thus institutionally more powerful. New Liberals were democrats and libertarians, as well as interventionists. They took several Radical interests and invested them with a populistic meaning. This gave potential Radical opponents an excuse to accept the drift of electorally more attractive policies. It also ensured that the party retained a broader electoral appeal; a purely New Liberal, class-based, party would have had a *smaller* electoral base. The ability to evolve towards new goals, and embrace a variety of appeals, helped the Liberal party hold traditionally Liberal, but socially mixed, rural/middle-class seats, at the same time that its major support came from industrial areas. The Liberal reformers combined a variety of economic/social appeals with traditional Liberal concerns to create an attractive composite image. They were able to retain the support of a Labour party which contained groups with additional, and distinct, contextual appeals. The Progressive Alliance was an almost uniquely attractive anti-Tory force.[13]

There was an important potential problem: Labour expansion. The Liberals' difficulty in countering the Statist and Labourist side of Labour's appeal, and their occasional lapses or local weaknesses on social reform, gave Labour some opportunity to expand. It consequently made some headway between 1906 and 1914. This had little to do with class consciousness, the expansion of trade unionism, or the influence of the left. The map of Labour's support did not reflect areas with the highest trade union density. Neither had Labour become a party whose appeal was based on class awareness, despite the aims of the left. Occupational homogeneity and high union density *could* help Labour where Labour was a credible expression of the values and interests of workers in a particular industry. However, some prosperous and occupationally unified areas were securely Liberal, while some relatively ununionised areas could sustain high levels of Labour/Socialist activity. With a few local exceptions, where the left donned a 'practical' mantle and adopted material campaigning issues with a broad appeal, and a moral rhetoric, the left's ideas were unconvincing and unpopular. They failed to gain majority support amongst skilled or unskilled workers, let alone to unify the two groups.

Neither had the left's strategy of conflict with the Liberals convinced most party leaders that the Alliance should be terminated. In most areas,

[13] See above, pp. 68–9 and e.g. 272, 304–10. The Liberals won three successive elections between 1906 and 1910, and they had a chance of success in 1914–15.

unions did not accept the left's analysis of their problems, or their proposed remedies for the situation. The national party's moderating influence was also spreading through the country, and national moderates were gaining powerful allies in the constituency organisations. The reforming groups in both parties had enough in common, and enough institutional power, to make Progressive co-operation *ideologically* desirable and politically possible, even if their control was incomplete.[14] Moreover, Labour's positive appeal was so localised (and so complementary to that of the Liberal party) that co-operation between parties sharing similar goals was *pragmatically* sensible. There was not the ideological/ strategic basis (given the failure of dissidents in both parties to provide an alternative) nor the organisational and electoral justification, for a policy of conflict. Neither were the dissidents so institutionally powerful, or the points of friction between the parties so significant, that co-operation could be made unworkable. The Progressive Alliance remained intact in 1914.[15]

The Progressive Alliance was not, however, without weaknesses. The existence of two political nations made the Liberal coalition potentially weak. Liberal policy was only partially attractive to Labourist and Statist voters, and to those influential individuals in the Labour party who voiced Labourist and Statist views. Even the New Liberalism could not give them all they required. The Liberal party also contained too many conservative elements to satisfy even those Labour activists who had a great deal in common with Liberal reformers. The radicalisation of the Liberal party was going ahead, but pressure from the centre and pressure from within constituency parties did not always result in political/institutional changes. A composite Liberal party, which had to cater for a variety of groups, could not always respond swiftly enough for radical voters. It was thus potentially weak in Liberal areas. It was not a perfect social democratic machine, and it did not have an electorally flawless ideology. Labour groups closer to the radical Liberal tradition were waiting in the wings, anxious to exploit any decline in the Liberals' local standing, and emphasise the moral reformist side of Labour's platform.

The Liberals' position contained a potentially more serious weakness. The party contained Old Liberal elements who were very dissatisfied with the current approach, and others, including many Centrists, who were at least partially dissatisfied. A substantial portion of the party, attached firmly to no one particular strand, might equally waver towards

---

[14] There were some differences. For tensions over industrial questions, and for Liberal/ Labour conflicts, pp. 23, 26–7, 62–5, 149–51, 185–7, 209–11, 269, 319, 337. But see also e.g. pp. 154, 158, 261.
[15] See Chapter 11.

the centre-right. If the nature of the NLF as a party institution did not give them the opportunity to attack *publicly*, they had the power to attack from within. The composite nature of the Liberal party and its institutional structure was a *strength* while the radicals managed to hold these elements in check, but it was likely to be a problem if (as eventually happened) the position was reversed, and it was the radicals who had to influence a more conservative leadership.[16] However, Labour also had its problems. There were few signs that the Progressive Alliance was collapsing in 1914, rather more that Labour was under considerable stress.[17] As party leaders recognised, the Liberals were in a powerful position.

II

During the war the Progressive Alliance fell apart. Labour's position in the formerly Tory and mining areas became much stronger. Local Labour parties increasingly came under the influence of expanding trade unions with an enhanced interest in the Labour party. They encouraged whole-hearted support for the war (pushing Socialists out in the process if necessary), and reinforced Labour's *social* roots. The *economic* impact of war also helped Labour's competitive position. War collectivism made state involvement in (particularly) the coal and railway industries seem a viable means of altering wages and conditions. The affected workers became more confident in the method (the impact of which was more individually demonstrable), less confident in the parties currently governing its practical application. Labour – more committed than ever to local interests – became an attractive force.[18] Its commitment to protecting the gains made by the unskilled workers who often dominated Tory areas also gained some credibility from the experience of war collectivism. To many, Labour seemed the party most likely to protect these gains.

Labour was building an electoral core of support through its Labourist and Statist appeals, particularly in Tory and mining areas. It was evidently a closer expression of local views, and since its ideas had more credibility following the experience of war, it was in a much stronger position. It was also the most viable Progressive party. It had not, however, entered the promised land. It still had to cope with class fragmentation. Even within individual industries or unions, differing areas and groups had differing interests. The scepticism of some trade unionists, particularly those who fared well under market conditions, about the economic rationality of Statist solutions was one facet of this. At the same time, others,

---

[16] See pp. 68–9, 88, 151–2, 207, 233, 254, 307.
[17] See pp. 325–41.
[18] See pp. 361–5, 368, 372, 392–4, 400, 403, 412–13.

including many leaders of the least skilled, thought their views might be submerged within the Labour party by the weight of 'skilled' unions. The Socialists, and their likely impact on policy, were a further handicap to Labour's electoral success.[19]

Other political factors also significantly influenced the pattern of change. Between 1914 and 1918 the Liberal party came under considerable stress. On the one hand, a patriotic Tory party advocated fighting the war with gusto and at all costs. On the other hand, Labour concentrated on domestic conditions (while additionally, in most areas, declaring its support for 'the boys at the front'). This dual threat from the right and the left was always likely to erode *some* of the Edwardian Liberals' electoral base.[20] However, the structure of the Liberal party made it difficult to counter these political challenges. The needs of workers on the home front were likely to suffer, even if the military situation did not seem to require the largest allocation of resources. The Radical/Centrist party leadership was not temperamentally inclined to address these problems; nor was it likely to adopt a populistic presentation of its achievements.[21] The internal pressure to act on these lines was not as pronounced as it had been before 1914. The New Liberals were numerically and politically weaker (many, as 'pacifists', were discredited). They were also less ideologically committed and personally less enthusiastic about material reforms if this meant increasing state power. It seemed to many New Liberals, for a while at least, that rationalism had indeed been beaten to its corner, and that the state was buying popular acquiescence. Whatever their views (and some *were* pushing for action) they had little power.

The party also lost support to the right because of its 'weak' commitment to military victory. The New Liberals were not alone in their doubts about the war. Radicals were concerned that individual liberties should be respected. Members of both groups (and some Centrists) publicly opposed several measures, including conscription. At the same time, even discussion of the need to adopt such measures seemed absurd to those for whom victory was the sole aim. The Tories – as the champions of this course – became more politically attractive, especially when military shortages or defeats encouraged popular criticism of the Government. Labour's growing potential in half the political map, the decline of the

---

[19]   This contributed to Labour's limited organisational expansion: pp. 363–5, 395–404.
[20]   For the indications that this drift was localised and limited before 1914, above, pp. 344–8.
[21]   See pp. 373–5.

New Liberals, and the Tory appeal to patriotism, put the old Liberal electoral coalition under considerable pressure.[22]

The pressure became even more significant because the Liberal party divided over these issues. Asquith's perceived failure to tackle the management of the war effectively, Lloyd George's desire to get on with this task (an aim shared by other Liberals) and the temperamental and institutional obstacles to an agreed means of overcoming this problem, cumulatively led to a split in the party. There was a Radical/New Liberal core to the 'Asquithian' group, while Liberal Imperialists and Centrists were more likely to support the Coalition. The division reflected disagreements over foreign policy (evident since before 1900) and doubts about the 'Prussianisation' of the state, not an ideological reluctance to accept state intervention.[23] New Liberals had been quite happy to accept intervention before 1914. Although the division was precipitated by the split in the leadership, it revealed that there were deep fissures within the party. Nonetheless, there was a continuing core of agreement between many 'Asquithian' and Coalition Liberals. The boundaries between the two were fluid. Some New Liberals (for example) supported the Coalition, whatever their doubts about aspects of its policy. The Asquithian/Coalition 'blocs' were hardly ideologically coherent or rigid. It did not seem inevitable that the split would continue.[24] The split did not show that a fracture of this kind had always been a probability, or that a partial revival was an impossibility.

The Liberals' position worsened between December 1916 and November 1918. The Coalition Liberals' membership of a Tory coalition made them appear as a party of the right. The divided, disillusioned and uncommitted nature of the 'Asquithians' ensured that (despite attempts by New Liberals) their 'party' could not stand as an independent organisation of the 'left'. The *nature* of the Liberal party – an advantage before 1914 – became a handicap. A more radical stance was necessary if only to show that the party still had a *positive*, popular, aim. However, a composite Liberal party with few radicals at the top and no institutionalised radical bloc was incapable of such actions. Liberal leaders fell back on the more traditional voters and activists whose views they could

[22] See pp. 374–80.
[23] i.e. it was in part about democracy, liberty, and the form, legitimacy, and limits of state intervention. See above, pp. 365–70, 373–7. For details of the broad pre-war Radical/New Liberal agreement over foreign policy, Clarke, *Liberals and Social Democrats*, Chapter 3. Bernstein, *Liberal politics*, Chapter 8.
[24] M. Fry has recently discussed the policy disputes underpinning the split ('Political change in Britain, August 1914 to December 1916: Lloyd George replaces Asquith: the issues underlying the drama', *H.J.* (1988)). Forthcoming books by Turner and Hart will no doubt clarify the process and discuss more fully the relationship between ideology, policy and personal factors in Liberal politics during this period.

more easily represent. They did little at national *or* local level to maintain party allegiances. The decision to hold an election in December 1918 – and the results of Lloyd George's allocation of the 'coupon' – made the rupture seem irremediable.

The Liberals' deficiencies would have been less significant if Labour's political response had been ineffective except in Tory and mining areas. However, in addition to the Statist and Labourist components of its image, Labour improved its standing as a moderate moral reformist organisation. The hard core of Liberal working-class voters was at risk. Labour often embraced policies on housing, the capital levy and state intervention which created a degree of internal unity and an impression of greater political dynamism. Party leaders used their institutional power to give the national party a broad appeal. In Liberal areas, these and other issues were used to make Labour appear as an attractive, contemporary, version of the Liberal party, at the same time that Liberals were divided, indecisive, tainted with failure and locally often non-existent as a political force. However, Labour had been, and still was, too close to the Liberal tradition, too tainted with Socialism, too tied to the unions, and too incapable of providing an economic justification for defection, to obliterate the Liberals in areas where Liberalism had strong roots. The Liberal party was sufficiently cohesive and attractive to survive the 1916 split. Even Lloyd George's allocation of the coupon, which institutionalised the divisions and badly damaged the party, did not destroy its capacity to survive, or obliterate its popular appeal.

This was reflected in the 1918 election. The Liberal party collapsed in those areas where its local appeal had always been limited, and where the Statist/Labourist side of the Labour party was an attractive alternative. Although the situation in 1918 was such that Labour won comparatively few seats, even in the coalfields, it had assumed its role as the major anti-Tory force in a substantial section of the electoral map.[25] Labour fared much worse in the traditionally Liberal areas, except in some instances where it was already the main, or at least a very significant, anti-Tory force, or where its Socialist moral reformism succeeded in creating a distinct 'Labour' image. Labour out-polled the Liberals in some areas where they had hitherto been very strong, and where Labour scarcely even existed before 1914. Its *moderate* moral reformism was not, in 1918, as unattractive, or as lacking in economic teeth, as in 1914. In many respects, Labour was tapping a Liberal tradition of hostility to the unproductive rich.

At the same time, however, the *extent* of Labour's improvement could

[25] Labour was helped in some mining areas by the favourable attitude of Coalition leaders to its former Labour supporters.

reflect a negative protest against the Liberals' deficiencies.[26] It did not reflect a *positive* attraction to a distinct party, except where other aspects of the party image may have attracted enough Statist or Labourist support to create (given the relatively high rate of Liberal abstention) a sound competitive position. Labour did not have a positive economic attraction to many of the skilled workers in these areas. Labour assumed the position of the major anti-Tory organisation in British politics, but not because it was a nationally powerful, and dynamic, organisation. It had not found the answer to its pre-war problems. It was a party with a strong moral base, a localised, but positive appeal, and a powerful commitment to improving the material condition of the people. Unified in 1918, especially through the capital levy and nationalisation, the party had a sense of direction and a purpose which it had hitherto lacked. However, Labour was presented with a half open door and it took the opportunity to obtain a hearing in areas where hitherto it had had the door slammed in its face. It became a larger, more significant, force than it need have done because of the Liberals' failure and its own ability to duplicate aspects of the Liberal appeal. It had not removed old causes of tensions. On the contrary, even before 1918 many party leaders recognised that balancing Statist/Labourist aims against those of the still numerous social democrats and ethical socialists, whilst also minimising the influence of the various Socialist elements, would not be easy.

It is significant that even the chaos of the 1918 election did not wipe out the Liberal party. Neither of its rivals could make such a case that longstanding Liberal allegiances, and Liberal ideas, seemed totally obsolete. Some Asquithian Liberals resisted the attempt to turn the election into a Labour/Coalition conflict. A few topped up old allegiances with radical plans for social reconstruction. Almost despite the party leaders, radical Liberals attempted to keep the party alive. However, the institutional structure of the Liberal party was such that these local initiatives did not influence national policy.[27] The Asquithians thus lacked a sense of movement and contemporary credibility. They did not fare well. However, there were more localised successes and competent performances than some suggest. In some 'radicalised' areas, such as the Yorkshire Pennine seats, the East Midlands and London, Liberals polled respectably, as they did in parts of the Lancashire textile belt where Centrist ideas had continuing purchase. There was still an electoral space which in theory the Liberal party could occupy, and which all three parties would have to try and capture if they were to be the major element

---

[26] Limited Labour organisational progress indicates, in part, its real position.
[27] See pp. 379–81, 404–8.

in a three-party system. However, the Asquithians' ability to compete
even here was now severely impaired. In defeat, the weaknesses of the
Edwardian Liberal party became progressively more serious.

I have argued in this book first for a more fragmented view of *electoral*
change. This reassessment has stemmed largely from my conception of
how the political system functioned between 1900 and 1918. The motive
force of electoral and political change was not war and a class consciousness stemming from cultural unities. Social change was not given political
expression simply by Labour's links with the trade unions. Local social
structures and interests, in conjunction with local political actions, created
powerful political languages and cultures. When 'modernised' these continued to influence perceptions of what was attainable or desirable. New
ideas, particularly where they satisfied economic interests or a desire for
social security or improvement, could break the hold of the past, and
this gave Labour a hold over a section of the electoral map. However,
Labour did not succeed in creating a nationally applicable appeal which
could rupture old ties through the creation of a new agenda. The working
class did not cling to Labour automatically and as if by instinct, and
even the organised working class did not flock to Labour as the party
which would express their views and protect their interests. The 1918
election marked the end of a formative stage in some areas. It marked
a sharp, unheralded, electoral breakthrough in others. It was not the
final victory in either section of the electoral map.

I have also argued for a more fragmented picture of *political* change.
The Liberal party was a broad reforming coalition. There were few signs
that this coalition was about to collapse in 1914. Nonetheless, the party
was *potentially* weak. Its appeal was not universal; its composite nature
ensured that it could not easily adopt radical measures. Events during
the First World War caused its localised electoral weaknesses to become
more significant, and allowed the radicalising trend to be abandoned.
Divisions over the war showed that it was not easy to maintain a coalition
of groups with such diverse, half-contradictory, views. Unlike the elements of the Labour party, the Liberals did not share a fundamental
commitment to improving working-class living standards which could
hold the party together whatever the divisions over the war. There was
a form of social democracy more usually associated with Liberal thinkers
and reformers which, in war time conditions, was less resilient than the
social democracy practised by Labour. The party split made attempts
to find a unifying theme more difficult; new issues and conditions ensured
that some on the left and on the right did not wish to try. Old problems
became more serious. Before 1914 the New Liberal/Centrist coalition

had merged the religious and economic case for Liberalism with a populistic concern for labour interests and views. Once a Radical/Centrist group was in control, and the dog wagged the New Liberal tail, the party was less well equipped to stand and fight as a working-class party.[28] Labour, united over its domestic approach during the war, gained from wartime experiences which made the Statist/Labourist side of its policies more attractive. These groups became stronger as a result. At the same time, it had not ceased to be a coalition. Moderate moral reformers had also been electorally successful, and were likely to be important in attempts to convert more Liberal voters. The left had a degree of success, and were rallied to the party by (amongst other things) the possibility that nationalisation and the capital levy were genuine radical policies. Labour seemed more united in 1918 than ever before, but war had not in reality made the party a more cohesive organisation; it had not removed the party's capacity for internal ideological conflict.

III

The story does not end in 1918. Although the dynamics of change in the subsequent period require detailed analysis in their own right, there is enough evidence to suggest that the political system continued to be influenced by the interactive processes outlined here.[29] 'Religious' allegiances had not simply given way to 'class' politics (as conventionally understood) rather later than historians have hitherto assumed. The interactive nature of politics continued to produce a political system which needs more complex analysis. Varying socio-economic circumstances, economic needs, and matching political appeals continued to affect the electoral competition. Moreover, the parties continued to contain varying ideological tendencies. It is true that in the Labour party a sense of partial ideological unity had developed between some soft left activists and trade unionists at the centre and in the constituencies before 1914. It is even fair to say that the points of contact between this group and the more Socialist elements had become more pronounced by 1918. Some historians argue that this 'unity' continued into the 1920s, either because of shared aims or because of organisational pressures from the centre. Yet the internal clash between ideological strands continued to dominate political decisions, and was reflected in the detail and direction of policy, especially when issues of substance had to be faced. The conflict between capital

---

[28] See pp. 433–4.

[29] I am aware that there were quite probably changes in the relationship between local and national politics between 1918 and 1931, and in the nature of society. My brief attempt to show the continuing importance of the broad themes of this book is not meant to preclude further analysis.

and labour (even organised labour) is a poor guide to the subsequent pattern of electoral changes and political actions. The bare bones of a more viable analysis (which other historians are creating and fleshing out) are offered below.

Labour expanded almost immediately after the 1918 election. The 1919 municipal elections saw landslide Labour victories in many parts of the country as voters turned against the Coalition. Labour subsequently lost a good deal of this support. However, continued economic problems, even for some skilled workers (the result of declining trading opportunities and over-capacity induced by war), coupled with Labour's growing local and national ability to create a more protective political image, allowed it to secure a hold over certain areas. Unemployment and wage cuts in particular worked in its favour. In the coalfields (where Labour's 'Mines for the Nation' campaign and the Sankey Commission's deliberations together produced a politically attractive situation for Labour), in some Tory areas, and in parts of some major cities (such as Sheffield, London, and Glasgow), Labour was an entrenched force by 1922.[30] It had a large electoral 'cushion' of seats, which made it a permanent feature of the electoral competition. Institutional changes – principally the absorption of unskilled workers' representatives (including Irish community leaders) and leaders of other groups attracted primarily by a tough Labourism – had allowed it to seize the opportunity.

By contrast, in most 'Liberal' areas, Labour did not immediately become so attractive that supporters of the older parties, or new additions to the electorate, could easily break family voting patterns. The capital levy was a useful propaganda instrument, because it combined 'moral' attack on the rich with an apparent means of financing reform (as the Liberals had done in 1909–10). It was not a revolutionary idea, especially in Mac-Donald's hands. It could be – and was – justified by MacDonald, and by many radical Liberals, as a means of soaking up inflation in the period immediately after 1918.[31] It did not become part of a wider strategy for creating class unity through a substantial redistribution of wealth. Despite the Liberals' growing conservatism, and Labour's ability to claim

---

[30] Supple, *Coal Industry*, 4, Chapter 3 and Howard (thesis), pp. 225–7; Adams, 'Sheffield', pp. 16–26; Gillespie (thesis), Chapter 8; McLean, *Red Clydeside*, Chapter 14.

[31] Whiting, 'Labour and the National Debt' for the general position. See also J.B.G. to F.J., 9 Apr. 1916, JBG 1916/43, noting MacDonald's conception of the capital levy: 'It is not what I, and I fancy the NAC and the movement had in view when we talk of the "Conscription of Wealth" ... doubtless MacDonald is looking at the thing as a practical proposal, whereas we are urging our (version) as propaganda.' For Liberal radicals and the capital levy, H.S. to W.R., 13 Oct. 1919, WR 177, E. Dodds, *Is Liberalism Dead?* (1920), p. 101, C. F. G. Masterman, *The New Liberalism* (1920), p. 79, *Nation*, 1 May 1920, voting on Commons' motions, noted in M. Kinnear, *The fall of Lloyd George* (1973), pp. 169–71, comments by Ramsay Muir, *M.G.*, 3 Nov. 1922.

that it was now the major anti-Tory force, the Liberal party declined
only slowly. In Liberal strongholds, such as East and West Yorkshire,
North and South-West London, and the East and South-West Midlands,
in heavily industrialised areas such as the southern Lancashire spinning
belt and the North-East, Liberals often performed well. In middle-class
areas and in most rural seats they scarcely declined at all (vis-à-vis
Labour).[32]

There was close competition between the Progressive forces in many
of the formerly Liberal industrial areas. In 1923 the Liberals polled just
1 per cent of the vote less than Labour in the country as a whole, and
managed a number of victories in working-class seats. However, Labour's
cushion of seats in the other half of the electoral map, and its ability
to undermine the effectiveness of the Liberal performance in its old strongholds, ensured that it was the larger and more secure party. It had a
core of safe seats, and a broad popular base. Labour formed a minority
Government with Liberal support. It was only after this, in the 1924
election, that many 'Liberal' seats became more securely 'Labour'.

The breakthrough in 1924 had nothing to do with a new approach,
little to do with declining class fragmentation, or growing class consciousness, and much more to do with the Liberals' official support for the
Tories at the national level. The Liberal party effectively admitted that
it had little distinctive to say. It 'betrayed' its working-class support by
siding with the Tory 'enemy'. This was a serious mistake. It seemed
to demonstrate what Labour was saying at every opportunity – that the
fight was now between the Tories and Labour. A choice had to be made
between the two. Labour's advance in some Liberal areas was checked
by a different approach, and it seems likely that some at least of the
Liberal decline could have been prevented, even after 1918, by a more
adaptive Liberal party. The economic, and religious, case for a Liberal
political approach was still recognised in many rural, but also in some
working-class areas, and by some working-class leaders.[33] However,
the majority of major Liberal figures paid little attention to potentially
popular, even left-Centrist proposals (of the kind associated with Ramsay
Muir, for instance), while New Liberals like Masterman and Hobson,
or innovative thinkers like Keynes, were given even less opportunity to
influence policy in the immediate post-war period. The Liberals' claim
to be the voice of 'sane labour' was less credible than ever. The party

---

[32] Hart, 'Liberals, war and the franchise', pp. 827–8 notes some of these regionalised
trends as a positive feature, but this is unusual. Labour's limited organisational development is discussed in Howard, 'Expectations born to death'.

[33] Miller, Electoral dynamics, Chapter 6. For economic outlooks, e.g., comments by
Mosses of the Patternmakers' union, W. Mosses, History of the Patternmakers,
pp. 360–1 and The Times, 3, 6 Nov. 1922 (J. R. Clynes and W. Graham).

leaders had not exploited the capital levy as an electioneering tool even while there was an economic case for its implementation, in part because party moderates found it unacceptable.[34] The continuing absence of an institutionalised radical forum meant that those who disagreed over policy could not bring pressure to bear on the leadership. Yet vague statements on the need to revive trade and free the market were not enough to inspire broader support or to maintain the party's position in working-class areas. The fact that the Liberal party was a broad coalition was of value when the party had a dynamic thrust, but it made it vulnerable to polarisation and subject to considerable internal resistance from entrenched conservative sections of the party. The Liberals needed ideas which could help them at least retain a hold over traditionally Liberal areas; given an internal structure which had been frozen since 1914, and the strength of convention and moderation in the party, it was necessary for these ideas to be imposed by the party leadership. It did not have this dynamic thrust until the later 1920s, when it was too late.[35]

By 1924, Labour was firmly established in radical Liberal eyes as the inheritor of the Liberal tradition.[36] However, it had not swept old views – and old allegiances – out of the way with a dynamic, class-based, appeal. The left had not found a means of unifying the working class and making them into a Labour/Socialist electoral bloc. Crucially, the left lacked either a distinctive, but credible, means of suggesting that greater economic prosperity was around the corner, or of 'justifying' higher taxation of the rich to pay for benefits for the poor. In the absence of this, Labour's economic policy was dominated by men with no wish to depart from the classical Liberal text. When falling inflation removed the 'Liberal' economic case for a capital levy, Labour dropped this potential obstacle to its absorption of (lower middle-class) Liberal support. Higher taxation was rejected for similar reasons.[37] Labour moderates, who aimed at creating a national (not class-based) party, were effectively attaching themselves to economic policies which even Liberal Centrists would find acceptable. They were attempting to recreate the old Progressive electoral coalition, without the need for a tactical alliance with the

[34] Elibank to D. Maclean, 10 June 1919, Maclean MS c 465 fos. 184–6, and his continuing opposition, *Lib. Magazine*, June 1919, p. 293, *Daily News*, 3 Nov. 1922, MLF Mins, 8 Apr. 1919, YLF Mins, 16 Feb. 1921. For the following, Tanner (thesis), pp. 353–8.

[35] Freeden, *Liberalism divided*, and Bentley, *Liberal mind*, pp. 94–9, 110–11 throw differing light on elements of this situation, but see Hart (thesis) for a fuller account.

[36] e.g. *Nation*, 14 Oct. 1922, Wedgwood Benn Diary, 29 May 1924, Stansgate MS ST 66/2, comments cited in Clarke, *Liberals and Social Democrats*, p. 237.

[37] R. Lyman, *The first Labour Government* (1957), pp. 50–9; M. E. Short, 'The politics of personal taxation: budget-making in Britain, 1917–31', Cambridge Ph.D. thesis 1985, Chapter 6.

Liberals and without having to accommodate the Liberal right. This tactic operated on two levels: at the level of party ideology (which has already been discussed) and at the organisational level. In this latter respect, the introduction of individual membership, and the formation of advisory committees, were an attempt to include middle-class Progressives in the party structure. Attempts to force Communists out of the party were the reverse side of the same coin.

Labour was not, however, ideally equipped to rebuild the old Progressive electoral coalition. Its internal composition and institutional structure differed from the Liberals (which was not necessarily a bad thing) but in such a way that it had equally serious, if rather different, problems. Unions with Statist interests were a major element in the party, and voters with these interests were a major part of the party's electoral base. The Webbs – with their corporatist views on the merits of state involvement – were significantly more influential in Labour policy discussions than they had been before 1914.[38] After an initial reluctance to get involved, the gradually larger role played by the general unions of unskilled Labourist workers also enhanced Labour's role as a conservative, protective, force. Although supporters of moderate moral reformist ideas appeared to be an important part of the current electoral base, and Centrist economic ideas might appeal to Liberal voters, attempts to impose these views were not always popular; neither were attempts to convert the party easy, given its disparate structure and aims. Statist elements insisted on national support for their industry. The Labourist elements supported a protective conservatism.

Policy discussions and ministerial appointments were inevitably influenced by their strength in the party.[39] Policy options in education, agriculture, and defence at least were strictly limited as a result. A general climate of anti-intellectualism hardly helped the party develop a means of countering the limitations imposed by the conventional Civil Service view of what constituted desirable policy.[40] Neither did a tendency to concentrate economic decision-making in Snowden's hands, or in large committees of interested parties, provide a good alternative.[41] The left

[38] Winter, *Socialism and war*, Chapters 7–8.
[39] In forming the 1924 Labour Government, Henderson had 'pointed out the inadvisability of omitting the textile industry' and added that 'South Wales had to be represented by Hartshorn' (S. Webb, 'The First Labour Government', *Political Quarterly* (1961), p. 15).
[40] Barker, *Education and politics*, p. 60; Howard (thesis), p. 264; D. Carlton, *MacDonald versus Henderson* (1970), pp. 17–18, Lyman, *Labour Government*, p. 271, G. Blaxland, *J. H. Thomas* (1964), p. 170 and the relayed comments on Thomas' subservience to Civil Servants, cited in L. Radice, *Beatrice and Sidney Webb* (1984), p. 282.
[41] See F. W. Pethwick-Lawrence to Dalton, 4 Mar. 1924, Pethwick-Lawrence MS 1 fo. 192, discussing Labour's finance committee.

also still clashed with Labour's reforming alliance at the municipal *and* national level. Some argued that it was imperative to attack Capitalism with a vibrant policy of wealth redistribution which had material teeth, to create a 'class', rather than a 'national' party. This was unattractive to most party moderates. Violent public discussion of such ideas did not help the party's prospects, even though they seldom became official policy. Liberals in middle-class and rural areas in particular held aloof, while more than 60 per cent of working-class voters failed to vote Labour.[42]

Labour's progress after 1924 had little to do with trade union expansion (union membership fell between 1924 and 1929, whereas Labour's vote increased substantially). Politics were more significant. The moderate moral reformers, like other sections of the party, were at last developing a more assertive and practical *social* policy. The legislative acknowledgement of state responsibility for *social* matters during the war (including education, housing, and even health, to a limited extent) may have made better state provision of these facilities (via local authorities) seem a realistic aim, in the same way that increased state *economic* intervention during the war increased support for Statist *economic* ideas. The collective provision of facilities (either for individual improvement or as preparation for the next step towards Socialism) became politically feasible, and a potentially unifying theme. Labour's powerful moral critique of limited educational opportunities and poor housing provision, coupled with practical ideas for their improvement, helped it expand its electoral base to areas, and amongst voters, whose ties to more economistic Labour policies were limited. Its support – and membership – became less predominantly working class. Party organisation improved and spread. The party's electoral base was less entirely based on areas of heavy industry. The strategy of catering for a broader set of *social* interests seemed to be working. It was this success, the existence of a shared core of beliefs, and the absence of a credible left alternative, which made MacDonald seem so secure, rather than an imposed uniformity or a total ideological transformation of the party.[43] Nonetheless, there were still variations in the stances adopted by local Labour parties. The old distinctions

---

[42] For the left's parliamentary opposition, Marquand, *MacDonald*, pp. 326, 420, 452–5. For the most well-known municipal examples of 'Socialist' municipal campaigns, Ryan, 'Poplarism' and Gillespie (thesis), Chapter 8, S. R. Williams, 'The Bedwellty Board of Guardians and the Default Act of 1927', *Llafur* (1979). For the level of working-class support, Pugh, *Making of modern British politics*, pp. 255–6.

[43] Savage, *Preston*, pp. 195–8 and Chapter 7. For these developing social policies, Whiting, *Cowley*, pp. 137, 147, 149, M. Daunton (ed.), *Councillors and tenants*, Adams, 'Sheffield', pp. 16–17 for Sheffield 1918–22, and summary of J. Rowett's paper on later Sheffield politics, *BSSLH* (Autumn 1979).

between Labourist, Statist, moderate reformist, and Socialist reformist approaches did not disappear.[44]

The left had failed to counter the dominant reforming drift of policy. This was not, as some argued, because the party had lost its soul to the pursuit of Mammon. It was not 'a machine without a spirit' as Mac-Donald claimed, or an unidealistic organisation interested only in 'beer, bread, and 'baccy'. Party activists retained their religious/ethical motivations, and the party retained its moral rhetoric. While there was some constituency opposition to the exclusion of Communists from the party, and, despite an untheoretical rejection of orthodox economics which the ILP expressed and built on with its 'Living Wage' campaign, revolts against party policy were limited. The left could not turn general unease into a party revolt.[45]

In 1929 Labour entered an election in which the Tories' limited economic success (and programme for success) was easily contrasted with major progress by Labour in municipal politics. It developed a sharper national image. Following the election, Labour again formed a minority Government, but with an increased share of the vote and a larger cushion of seats than before. The Labour Government did not mark time. It immediately set out to improve educational and social provision, particularly pensions.[46] Yet whatever the progress on social policy, Labour had no means of countering the approaching *economic* crisis. Its failure to cope with the crisis reopened old internal divisions. The twists and turns of party politics show the problems of unifying a party – and an electoral constituency – which did not in reality have identical aims and interests. Labour's economic policy in office, while essentially 'Liberal', was still influenced by Statist and Labourist considerations. Labour made unorthodox attempts to maintain wages above market rates (in the mining industry). Although the conclusions of its inquiry into the cotton industry argued for prosperity via productivity increases and rationalisation (a very 'Liberal' argument) the report also managed to convey the impression that Government would intervene to prevent the attendant pay cuts (a very Labourist solution). Labour also attempted to keep unemployment benefits above the rates common in other countries, and to considerably extend the number of people eligible for relief (although it faced internal

---

[44] A point made, despite the emphasis on the growing uniformity of municipal policy, in the excellent thesis by J. Boughton ('Working class politics in Birmingham and Sheffield', Warwick Ph.D. thesis 1987, pp. 121–3). See also Gillespie (thesis), Chapter 8.

[45] J.R.M. Diary, 12 Oct. 1921, PRO 30/69/1753; S. Desmond, *Labour: the giant with the feet of clay* (1921), pp. 2, 42–7. For the social base, Miller, *Electoral dynamics*, p. 173.

[46] B. B. Gilbert, *British social policy* (1970), pp. 251–2 (pensions), 96–7 (unemployment benefit).

opposition for not going further).[47] It followed neither a deflationary nor an economically expansionist policy.

The fact that there was no obvious basis in economic theory for a counter-cyclical programme is beside the point. Neither is it particularly significant that Labour's political make up prevented it from concerted efforts at deflation (which was neither economically nor politically the answer). Labour's problem was its attitude to the unorthodox and the innovative. All parties contained people who were questioning old ideas, or who were at least willing to ignore theoretical doubts in the search for a *politically* acceptable stance to economic problems. Labour's composition, and its divisions, were significant because they stifled attempts to consider the alternatives. They prevented the party taking steps which might have maximised its prospects and minimised the political damage.

By 1931, Labour was in poor condition. Internal tensions had ensured that leading figures in local and national politics had used all the institutional power at their disposal to combat the left and ensure the primacy of their own views. The party's fund of good will and tolerance was low.[48] Half-formed ideas associated with the left – particularly increased decentralisation of financial and social policy to the municipalities, the development of a more active, campaigning stance to the impending crisis, and the discussion of those (limited) economic programmes which were being put forward as a means of fighting the slump – had been rejected.[49] More significantly, sound or potentially attractive elements of these programmes were not absorbed into the moderate leadership's thinking. The aggressive tactics of some Socialists contributed to this polarisation of opinion. They divided the party into those who were *for* MacDonald (and a cramping infatuation with unadapted conventional economic views) or *for* the left (and rabid attacks on Capitalism in general and

---

[47] Supple, *Coal Industry*, 4, pp. 333–7 (mining); A. Fowler, 'Spinners in the inter-war years', in Fowler and Whyte (eds.), *Barefoot aristocrats*, pp. 172–3. See also R. I. McKibbin, 'The economic policy of the Second Labour Government, 1929–31', *Past and Present* (1975), pp. 112–14.

[48] For tensions within the party, E. Shaw, *Discipline and discord in the Labour party* (Manchester, 1988), Chapter 1. For the left and Cabinet posts, Webb, 'First Labour Government' and Marquand, *MacDonald*, pp. 492–3. For the constituencies, e.g. Hutchison, *Scotland*, pp. 296–303, Kinnear, *British voter*, p. 110 fn. 14 (London), Wyncoll, *Nottingham*, pp. 187, 192, W. David, 'The Labour party and the "exclusion" of the Communists: the case of the Ogmore Divisional Labour party in the 1920s', *Llafur* (1983), Macintyre, *Little Moscows*, pp. 32–5.

[49] Rowett (thesis), pp. 57–8; B. Webb diary, 17 Aug. 1925 (MacKenzie, p. 54); R. Skidelsky, *Politicians and the Slump* (1969), pp. 50, 180–2.

party leaders, as its instrument, in particular).[50] There was more sub-merged support (in all parties) for politically and economically fighting the crisis than has often been suggested.[51] MacDonald, and party finan-cial experts like L. C. Money and Willie Graham, may have been willing to consider policy changes, and especially the introduction of tariffs. However, other expert advice seemed more attractive. Sympathy for con-ventional economic views was reinforced by the exasperation of men subjected to constant criticism from within their own party. The structure of policy making was such that they did not have to consider constructive ideas from party intellectuals.[52] When the crisis came, Labour's options were consequently limited. The Labour Cabinet could not cut expenditure on unemployment relief (the policy which economic orthodoxy dictated and which even many Statist/Labourist elements and their Fabian allies deemed to be economically 'correct'). These latter groups could not sacri-fice their supporters. Their function was to protect, not to destroy, and loyalty was more central to their ideology than respect for economic ideas. For them, and for many party activists, middle-class ideas, and these ideas in particular, could not be seen as a blueprint for Labour policy. However, the party leaders were no longer able to consider other options. Their existing views, their willingness to accept what was deemed intellectually rational and correct, and the isolation from alternatives which was in part a consequence of Labour's complex internal politics, ensured that they lacked the will and the ability to manage the crisis in the party, or the ideas and approaches which might have papered over the cracks or given it a positive line. Most other Labour moral reformers, with their stronger commitment to the working class than MacDonald, were unable to join the National Government which was

[50] See e.g. Pethwick-Lawrence's observation that the left's attacks on MacDonald, culmi-nating in violent and extreme censure motions, caused him to withdraw his own partial criticisms of MacDonald's approach (*Fate has been kind* (1942), p. 149). Some on the left later accepted the tactical mistake (e.g. Kirkwood, *Life of revolt*, pp. 249–50).
[51] The Webbs canvassed Keynes' opinions but treated them with little respect (B. Webb diary, 9 Aug. 1926 [MacKenzie, pp. 93–4], B. Webb to W. Robson, 11 Sept. 1931 [Mac-Kenzie, p. 365]). For sympathy for Keynes ideas at this time, Clegg, *Trade unions*, 2, pp. 500–2, E. Durbin, *New Jerusalems* (1985), pp. 66–8. Some Cabinet figures from the centre-left were willing to consider unconventional views (K. O. and J. Morgan, *Portrait of a Progressive*, pp. 202–3, Pethwick-Lawrence, *Fate has been kind*, pp. 163–6), or to support Mosley's scheme (Skidelsky, *Politicians and the Slump*, p. 170).
[52] W. Janeway, 'The economic policy of the second Labour Government 1929–31', Cam-bridge Ph.D. thesis 1971, pp. 223, 281–2, Short (thesis), pp. 277–9; V. Brittain, *Pethwick-Lawrence* (1963), p. 103 and P-L to P.S., n.d. 1931, Pethwick-Lawrence MS 5 fo. 41. Thomas was also known to favour protection. MacDonald, according to Snowden, considered fighting a precipitative election campaign on a 'fight the slump' platform in 1930 (P. Snowden, *An autobiography*, 2 (1934), p. 923).

formed to implement the cuts.[53] Labour split, and the scars went deep. It appeared that both Progressive parties had been destroyed.

The rise of Labour between 1885 and 1931 cannot be explained by an expanding class consciousness. Labour was not a dynamic organisation, riding the crest of a unifying social wave. The interactive nature of politics, and the inability of the left to produce a strategy which made popular sense of a 'class' experience, led to the creation of two anti-Tory parties. Both parties were coalitions. There was a broad area of agreement between reforming groups in each organisation. Yet as composite units, both parties were different. In alliance, they had been a powerful force, but the existence of the alliance was always under threat. The Liberals found it difficult to satisfy all the Progressive Alliance's constituent elements. However, the Progressive Alliance did not crumble until war put it under considerable stress. Labour emerged as the major anti-Tory organisation with a larger share of the Progressive vote than seemed likely before the war. It was not, however, able to absorb all the Progressive vote and rival the Tories. Separated, neither Progressive Party was a satisfactory, potentially successful, opposition, because neither party was a perfect reforming mechanism for the varying needs of a varying electorate. Neither party had the ideological and economic means, or the political commitment, to square the circle and recreate the old Progressive coalition. In 1918, Labour had a localised base, which was augmented because good fortune, and a slightly different, newly credible, conception of social democracy, attracted some Liberal votes in circumstances when obstacles or alternatives to supporting Labour were easily overlooked. Labour was more clearly committed to improving living standards and social opportunities, and more in tune with the climate of opinion.

The party expanded between 1918 and 1929 because it continued to develop (partially differing) stances which catered for a variety of practical needs and ambitions. It combined a moral outrage at inequality with (partially differing) practical ideas for improving living standards. These ideas were often half-contradictory, but they were sincerely meant, locally relevant, and individually appreciated. Labour support was based largely on the economic protection of the less affluent, and the extension of social opportunities to those who could not obtain them without state provision. Labour still lacked a broad, positive, and *economic* appeal, and a means of mobilising support from more affluent voters. Under

[53] e.g. Snell, *Men, movements and myself*, pp. 251–3. Loyalty to the party – part of Labour's operational ideology – was also evidently a factor in the opposition to MacDonald. For rank and file views, Boughton (thesis) Chapter 7 and M. Dickie, 'The ideology of Northampton Labour party in the inter-war years', Warwick M.A. thesis 1982.

pressure it became more difficult for varying aims and ideas to be reconciled within this particular institutional framework, or for alternative ideas to be deployed. This is not to denigrate Labour's strengths and achievements. It is not to suggest that other parties would have done better. It is to argue that Labour's expansion was based on morally and practically relevant ideas, not simply on class consciousness. It is to argue that elements within the Labour party have always been concerned with practical issues and practical remedies, with the immorality of capitalism, and not just with the Socialist millennium. It is to suggest that – in particular circumstances – this allowed it to expand and grow to the position of major anti-Tory party. It is also to suggest that Labour did not have the economic edge necessary for it to become the largest party in the state. It was not the emergence of a class-conscious electorate in 1918, or the inevitable attractions of Labour as the working-class party and the party of the trade unions, which caused Labour's expansion before 1931. It was defeat in 1931, war in 1939, and the development of a new economic confidence which created a truly attractive, 'national', electoral platform for the Labour party, and which, for a time at least, masked many of its internal divisions.

The Scottish parliamentary electoral system

The Scottish electoral system differed from that in England and Wales in a number of respects. There were differences in electoral law, some of which were comparatively minor. For Scottish leaseholders, for instance, conditions as to the length of the lease and value of the property, which were essential to the granting of the vote, were stricter than in England and Wales. On the other hand, all aspirants to the property franchise could vote in respect of their wives' property. More significantly property owners voted for the constituency in which they qualified; there was no Scottish equivalent of the English freeholder who voted for the county division adjacent to the borough in which his property was situated.[1] There were consequently fewer plural voters.

There were far fewer differences in the electoral law regarding tenants and lodgers. There were some differences in the qualifying dates and in the residence laws.[2] Lodgers, for instance, were allowed to move within the same borough without disqualification according to statute law. However, Scottish law was not always more generous. The Scottish system of rate collection involved a division of responsibility between the owner and tenant of houses rated over £4 per year, both being responsible for a portion of the amount due. The rates had to be paid before a vote could be granted. This resulted in a considerable number of potential voters (about 1,000 per constituency, or a total of 50–65,000) being unable to qualify in the 1890s.[3]

It was the registration system, however, which differed the most. The electoral register was compiled not by Poor Law overseers, but by an assessor or electoral registration officer, whose main duty was to value property for revenue purposes.[4] Ratepayers were identified, and since the payment of rates was the necessary prerequisite of enfranchisement, the system tracked down the vast number of eligible occupiers. Moreover, parties and assessors co-operated to remove errors before the lists were published and without recourse to claims.

[1] *Lib. Agent*, July 1898. Details of the number of non-resident voters in each constituency are given in *P.P.* 1895 (Cd 388), Lxxix, 319. However, like the 1888 return in England and Wales, different definitions between areas make the return unreliable. For the problem, Clarke, *Lancashire Liberalism*, p. 114, fn. 1.
[2] The Scottish register came into effect in November rather than January.
[3] Lowell, *Government of England*, i, pp. 212–13. For the figures, see the parliamentary return of men disfranchised by non-payment of rates, *P.P.* 1898 (Cd 376), Lxxix, 755.
[4] The appointments were made by the Inland Revenue from the 1890s, but incumbents were allowed to continue.

Thus in Glasgow, with an electoral roll of 87,000, the average number of occupier claims received by the local Sheriff (the Scottish equivalent of the revising barrister) between 1894 and 1898 was 128. In 1897 there were seventeen claims in Dundee, forty-four in Edinburgh and twenty-seven in Aberdeen. In most instances, the occupiers' claims were sustained. There were more claims in county divisions because ownership voters were not automatically included as voters in the electoral register. By the Edwardian period, although there were more 'ordinary' claims, detailed annual listings of local court proceedings show that this was the exception, not the norm.[5]

As in England and Wales, the lodger vote dominated party involvement in the registration process. The well-known prevalence of tenements in Glasgow and Edinburgh ensured that there were a large number of potential lodger voters in these cities, but tenements were a more widespread feature of the Scottish housing scene, and there were consequently a large number of lodgers in seats such as Dundee and Kilmarnock, and in the Lanarkshire coalfield.[6] Other obstacles still had to be circumvented. Traditionally lodger claims were settled by agreement between the parties and the Sheriff on the basis of a pre-arranged formula. As in England and Wales, however, there were as many interpretations of the £10 basis to the franchise as there were Sheriffs. Usually a value for the house was set below which no lodger claims would be entertained. This could be as low as £7 10s, but when the amount set reached £12 (which was not uncommon) 'hundreds' of working-class men were unable to qualify, even where housing conditions ensured that lodgers proliferated.[7] However, party differences in 1910, and Labour intervention, led to the breakdown of old arrangements. Often these were settled by negotiation between the parties, although Labour intransigence (and legal decisions) made these arrangements more difficult.[8] Nonetheless, because property was regularly assessed, the value of lodgings was seldom in dispute, and objections to claims were again less frequent than in England and Wales.[9]

It is difficult to assess the precise impact of these differences on the level of enfranchisement. The overall figures for England and Wales and Scotland were not greatly dissimilar, allowance having been made for the greater proportion of plural voters in England. There are three major reasons why the difference between law and procedure did not produce a greater discrepancy. First, if the lodger franchises' more generous successive occupation clause added some voters from the poorer classes, the requirement for rates to be personally paid creamed

[5] *Lib. Agent*, Apr. 1898; *Falkirk Mail*, 10 Oct. 1914; annual lists in the *Scotsman*, Sept.–Oct. 1910–14.
[6] See e.g. J. Butt, 'Housing in Scottish cities', in Gordon and Dicks, *Scottish urban history*.
[7] *Hansard*, 25 Oct. 1917, c. 1201, 26 Nov. 1917, c. 1796; Leith Burghs Branch LP, *Third Annual Report*, 1909.
[8] See e.g. Glasgow LP Mins, 28 Nov. 1912, 8 May 1913, 2 July 1914, *Scotsman*, 5 Oct. 1910, 5 Oct. 1911, 8 Oct. 1912.
[9] *Lib. Agent*, Apr. 1898 for 500 claims and no objections in Glasgow.

off a number of poorer voters.[10] Secondly, as far as occupiers were concerned, the overseers in England and Wales were becoming more efficient, and the disparity between the efficiency of Scottish and non-Scottish officials, which had previously caused so much comment, was diminishing by 1914. Thirdly, because lodgings were prevalent, enfranchisement was generally lower. Attempts to lower the predetermined amount at which lodgers qualified allowed more miners, for example, to gain the vote in Fife, Lanarkshire, Ayr and Midlothian, but, except where the Sheriff was willing to accept claims at rateable values of below £5, there was a low ceiling on how much could be done.[11] In Scottish and Welsh (but not other) mining areas, the housing structure and the interpretation of local officials allowed a fairly large number of lodgers onto the electoral roll in a few areas. Nonetheless, this was not the norm, and the structural problem of young men sharing accommodation with older miners was not overcome.[12] There were stronger similarities than differences between the two systems.

In general it would appear that the level and nature of enfranchisement was a reflection of local housing conditions, with better Scottish procedure and differences in electoral law raising the level of enfranchisement in some areas above what one might expect. Thus, enfranchisement in Glasgow stood a little above that for many London boroughs, the nearest comparable example, mainly because the officials who drew up the occupiers' lists were more efficient. Similarly, the wider successive occupation clause for lodgers may have caused the enfranchisement of perhaps 5–15 per cent of the lodger electorate, depending on the fluidity of the local population.[13]

[10] These were not necessarily Irish voters, many of whom already had the vote (J. McCaffrey, 'The Irish vote in Glasgow in the later Nineteenth Century; a preliminary survey', Innes Review (1970), pp. 33–5, and his essay 'Politics and the Catholic community since 1878', in D. Roberts (ed.), Modern Scottish Catholicism (Glasgow, 1979)). Neither was the exclusion of some Irish voters an obvious handicap to Labour, because Irish voters did not automatically support the Labour party (above, p. 433).

[11] W. Hamish Fraser, 'Labour in Scotland' in Brown (ed.), First Labour Party, p. 58. Not all attempts to lower the predetermined amount were made by Labour, and not all successful attempts benefited the Labour party. See returns of claims by party, Scotsman, 4, 6 Oct. 1910, 3 Oct. 1911, 4 Oct. 1912.

[12] Ten per cent of houses in the North-East and South Wales coalfields were sub-let (Benson, British coalminers, p. 106). See also People's Suffrage Federation, Leaflet No. 22, 'Adult suffrage and the possibilities of franchise reform', pp. 3–4.

[13] Scottish electoral registers do not identify successive occupiers, as some English registers do. Consequently, it has been suggested that the extent of successive occupation amongst lodgers may be within the same parameters as that for English occupiers, given on p. 103. In Haddingtonshire, the constituency examined in Chapter 4, it seems unlikely that the population would have been particularly mobile. The level of successive occupation was likely to have been nearer the lower end of the scale, as it was in the Gower constituency in Glamorgan, which had a similar social composition.

The politics of the plural vote, 1910

Selected constituencies, December 1910

Constituency	C.	Rad.	Constituency	C.	Rad.
Bucks, North	432	152	Leics, Melton	900	290
Cambs, West	743	466	Lincs, Gainsboro'	1,221	546
Cambs, East	375	136	Lincs, Horncastle	882	235
Cheshire, Altrincham	733	453	Lincs, Louth	490	161
Cheshire, Eddisbury	740	346	Lincs, Spalding	874	320
Cheshire, Hyde	324	205	Lincs, Stamford	738	177
Cheshire, Macclesfield	202	65	M'sex, Tottenham	1,471	281
Cornwall, Bodmin	385	138	Norfolk, Mid	450	110
Cumberland, Egremont	380	121	Northants, Mid	257	121
Cumberland, Eskdale	675	270	Northumb., Hexham	549	204
Derby, High Peak	337	146	Notts, Bassetlaw	448	105
Devon, Mid	437	78	Oxford, Mid	809	360
Devon, Tavistock	1,642	792	Oxford, North	283	85
Devon, Torquay	232	61	Somerset, Frome	827	428
Dorset, North	254	112	Suffolk, Lowestoft	559	217

Constituency			Constituency		
Durham, Jarrow	964	653	Suffolk, Stowmarket	574	208
Essex, Saf. Walden	305	88	Suffolk, Woodbridge	1,086	506
Gloucs, Stroud	334	162	Warwicks, Nuneaton	918	280
Gloucs, Tewkesbury	1,495	917	West'land, Kendal	413	90
Hereford, South	500	189	Wight, Isle of	291	61
Hunts, North	374	123	Wilts, Chippenham	223	74
Hunts, South	261	63	Wilts, Cricklade	318	74
Kent, Dartford	1,045	207	Worcs, Droitwich	706	394
Lancs, Accrington	256	214	Worcs, North	870	583
Lancs, Darwen	1,563	867	Yorks, Buckrose	378	118
Lancs, Lancaster	376	153	Yorks, Holderness	1,482	614
Lancs, Newton	520	293	Yorks, Pudsey	2,663	1,593
Lancs, N. Lonsdale	802	342	Yorks, Skipton	409	156
Lancs, Stretford	3,438	959			
Leics, Loughboro'	445	104	Total	41,658 (70.70%)	17,266 (29.30%)

Source: Memos by W. A. Gales of Conservative Central Office (n.d., probably late 1917), Steel–Maitland MS G.D. 193/202, fos. 238–41.

449

Conservative seats held by the plural vote, December 1910

Constituency	C maj. Dec. 1910	C. maj. on plural voters	Rad. maj. without plural voters
Cheshire, Altrincham	119	280	161
Cheshire, Eddisbury	289	394	105
Cornwall, Bodmin	41	247	206
Cumberland, Egremont	250	259	9
Cumberland, Eskdale	370	405	35
Derby High Peak	184	191	7
Devon, Mid	354	369	15
Devon, Tavistock	390	850	460
Devon, Torquay	130	171	41
Dorset, North	32	142	110
Gloucs, Tewkesbury	432	578	146
Hereford, South	121	311	190
Hunts, South	148	198	50
Lancs, Darwen	215	696	481
Lancs, Newton	144	227	83
Lancs, N. Lonsdale	74	460	386
Leics, Melton	372	610	238
Lincs, Horncastle	107	647	540
Lincs, Stamford	339	561	222
Norfolk, Mid	37	340	303
Notts, Bassetlaw	215	343	128
Oxford, Mid	392	449	57
Suffolk, Stowmarket	191	366	175
Suffolk, Woodbridge	560	580	20
West'land, Kendal	308	323	15
Wight, Isle of	223	231	8
Wilts, Chippenham	26	149	123
Worcs, Droitwich	72	312	240
Yorks, Holderness	381	868	487

Source: Memo by W. A. Gales (n.d., 1917), Steel–Maitland MS G.D. 193/202, fo. 62. The Liberals produced a very slightly different list, but with no information about the size of the majority (e.g. *Liberal Monthly*, Feb. 1911).

Liberal/Labour (and Socialist) conflict in parliamentary elections, 1906–1914

	Labour	Liberal	Tory/LU
The North-West			
Ashton (J1910)	5.0 (I.Lab.)	49.3	45.7
Burnley (1906)	32.5 (SDF)	34.8	32.7
(J1910)	30.2 (SDP)	34.6	35.2
(D1910)	23.8 (SDP)	38.7	37.5
Carlisle (J1910)	11.3 (SDP)	47.7	41.0
Manchester, North-West (4/1908)	2.6 (SDF)	46.7	50.7
Manchester, South-West (J1910)	16.6	41.0	42.4
Rochdale (1906)	19.5 (I.Lab.)	45.9	34.6
(J1910)	12.6 (SDP)	48.8	38.6
(D1910)	14.5 (SDP)	44.6	40.9
Salford, West (J1910)	17.3 (I.Lab.)	44.9	37.8
Cheshire, Hyde (J1910)	21.2	39.5	39.3
Cumberland, Cockermouth* (8/1906)	14.5	39.3	46.2
Cumberland, Cockermouth* (J1910)	14.5	39.3	46.2
Lancs, Accrington	38.3 (SDF)	56.8	4.9 (I.Lab.)
Lancs, Eccles (1906)	26.4	38.8	34.8
(J1910)	20.3	41.0	38.7
Lancs, Rossendale (J1910)	5.1 (I.Lab.)	57.4	37.5
The Tory regions			
LONDON			
Bethnal Green, South-West (7/1911)	2.5 (I.Lab.)	50.4	47.1
Bethnal Green (2/1914)	5.3 (I.Lab.)	47.1	47.6
Deptford (1906)	52.2	6.1^a	41.7
Hammersmith (1906)	8.4 (I.Lab.)	43.2	48.4

Lambeth, Kennington (J1910)	5.5 (I.Lab.)	47.6	46.9
Shoreditch, Haggerston (8/1908)	17.7 (SDF)	30.9	51.4
Shoreditch, Haggerston (J1910)	11.1 (SDP)	48.0	40.9
Southwark, Bermondsey (10/1909)	15.9	36.6	47.5
Tower Hamlets, Bow and Bromley (J1910)	33.5	24.6[a]	41.9
Tower Hamlets, Poplar (2/1914)	11.6 (BSP)	46.0	42.4
Croydon (1906)	20.2	38.3	41.5
Croydon (3/1909)	4.2	38.4	57.4
SOUTH COAST			
Chatham (D1910)	8.9	34.7	56.4
Gravesend (1906)	16.2	26.2	57.6
Portsmouth† (1906)	17.6	22.6	17.1
		22.0	16.1
Portsmouth† (J1910)	6.1	21.3	28.7
		17.1 (4.0 Ind.)	26.8
Southampton† (1906)	8.0 (SDF)	26.4	21.5
		23.4	20.7

The Coalfields

THE NORTH-WEST

Whitehaven (J1910)	28.8	29.7	41.5
Wigan (1906)	28.7 (I.Lab.)	24.7	46.6
Cumberland, Cockermouth* (8/1906)	14.5	39.3	46.2
Cumberland, Cockermouth* (J1910)	18.9	35.9	45.2
Lancashire, Eccles* (1906)	26.4	38.8	34.8
Lancashire, Eccles* (J1910)	20.3	41.0	38.7
Lancashire, Leigh (J1910)	24.7	40.2	35.1

	Labour	Liberal	Tory/LU
NORTH-EAST/YORKSHIRE/SOUTH WALES			
Gateshead* (J1910)	21.4	40.7	37.9
Durham, Bishop Auckland (J1910)	27.9	42.1	30.0
Durham, Bishop Auckland (D1910)	33.2	37.6	29.2
Durham, Chester-le-Street (1906)	45.6 (I.Lab.)	26.3	28.1
Durham, Houghton-le-Spring (3/1913)	26.2	43.6	30.2
Durham, Jarrow* (1906)	38.8	61.2	
Durham, Jarrow* (7/1907)	33.1	24.4 (14.9 Nat.)	27.6
Durham, Jarrow* (J1910)	33.5	34.0	32.5
Durham, Jarrow* (D1910)	32.7	34.0	33.3
Durham, North-West (1/1914)	28.2	40.6	31.2
Yorks, Morley (J1910)	16.1	59.0	24.9
Merthyr† (1906)	31.9	43.7	
		24.4	
Merthyr† (J1910)	36.7	41.0 (9.7 I.Lib.)	12.6
Carm., Eastern* (D1910)	12.6 (I.Lab.)	62.6	24.8
Carm., Eastern* (8/1912)	10.3 (ILP)	57.8	31.9
Glam., East (D1910)	24.1	47.0	28.9
Glam., Gower* (1906)	42.8 (I.L./Lab.)	40.0	17.2
Glam., Gower* (D1910)	54.8	45.2	
Glam., Mid (3/1910)	41.0	59.0	
Glam., Mid (D1910)	44.5	55.5	
MIDLANDS			
Hanley* (7/1912)	11.8	46.4	41.8
Derby, Chesterfield (8/1913)	4.2 (I.Lab.)	55.8	40.0
Derby, North-East (5/1914)	22.5	37.8	39.7

The industrial heartlands

Gateshead* (J1910)	21.4	40.7	37.9
Middlesbrough (1906)	8.4 (I.Lab.)	52.6	39.0
Middlesbrough (J1910)	14.2	50.5	35.3
Newcastle (9/1908)	10.4 (SDF)	41.1	48.5
Stockton (1906)	23.1	31.4	45.5
Durham, Jarrow* (1906)	38.8	61.2	
Durham, Jarrow* (7/1907)	33.1	24.4 (14.9 Nat.)	27.6
Durham, Jarrow* (J1910)	33.5	34.0	32.5
Durham, Jarrow* (D1910)	32.7	34.0	33.3
Carmarthen District Borough (1/1912)	2.3 (I.Lab.)	58.6	39.1
Monmouth Boroughs (1906)	16.5	44.7	38.8
Swansea, Town (J1910)	12.2 (I.Lab.)	50.8	37.0
Carm., Eastern* (D1910)	12.6 (I.Lab.)	62.6	24.8
Carm., Eastern* (8/1912)	10.3 (ILP)	57.8	31.9
Glam., Gower* (1906)	42.8 (I.L./Lab.)	40.0	17.2
Glam., Gower* (D1910)	54.8	45.2	

Yorkshire

Bradford, East (1906)	22.8 (SDF)	45.6	31.6
Bradford, East (J1910)	12.0 (SDP)	53.3	34.7
Bradford, West (1906)	39.1	28.2	32.7
Dewsbury (1906)	21.3	54.7	24.0
Dewsbury (4/1908)	20.2	46.1	33.7
Great Grimsby (1906)	17.8	32.0	50.2
Huddersfield (1906)	35.2	38.2	26.6
Huddersfield (11/1906)	33.8	36.0	30.2
Huddersfield (J1910)	31.6	39.8	28.6
Huddersfield (D1910)	29.0	37.5	33.5

	Labour	Liberal	Tory/LU
Hull, West (11/1907)	29.1	36.2	34.7
Leeds, South (1906)	32.6	50.2	17.2
Leeds, South (2/1908)	19.4	41.7	38.9
Leeds, South (D1910)	21.5	48.2	30.3
Sheffield, Attercliffe (5/1909)	27.5	24.6 (21.7 I.C.)	26.2
Sheffield, Brightside (J1910)	4.7 (SDP)	56.6	38.7
York† (1906)	19.7	22.7	26.3
Yorks, Colne Valley (7/1907)	35.2 (I.Lab.)	33.7	31.1
Yorks, Colne Valley (J1910)	27.1 (I.Lab.)	40.7	32.2
Yorks, Holmfirth* (J1910)	14.9	57.5	27.6
Yorks, Holmfirth* (6/1912)	28.2	42.0	29.8
Yorks, Keighley (1906)	26.6 (I.Lab.)	45.7	27.7
Yorks, Keighley (10/1911)	28.9	39.0	32.1
Yorks, Keighley (11/1913)	29.8	38.7	31.5
Yorks, Pudsey (6/1908)	10.7 (I.Lab.)	44.2	45.1
Yorks, Spen Valley (J1910)	23.3	44.8	31.9
Liberalism's reserve army			
Bristol, East (J1910)	17.2	52.0	30.8
Ipswich (5/1914)	3.1 (I.Lab.)	46.3	50.6
Leicester (6/1913)	11.4 (BSP)	47.8	40.8
Northampton† (1906)	11.7 (SDF)	20.7	18.8
	10.9 (SDF)	19.5	18.4
Northampton† (J1910)	7.7 (SDP)	23.3	19.8
	7.0 (SDP)	22.9	19.3

Cheshire, Crewe (J1910)	9.5	53.3	37.2
Cheshire, Crewe (7/1912)	17.7	37.7	44.6
Cornwall, Camborne (1906)	1.5 (SDF)	65.0	33.5
Gloucs, Tewkesbury (J1910)	2.1	44.7	53.2
Northants, East (D1910)	9.2 (I.Lab.)	47.8	43.0

Notes:

* Semi-mining constituency.

† Double member borough with two seats being contested.

a Liberal candidate without central party support.

Source: Craig, *Parliamentary election results, 1885–1918.*

Appendix 4 Municipal election results in selected three-cornered contests, 1907–1913

Because of the uneven nature of local political intervention, and other technical problems, the simple aggregation of municipal results – the method of analysis adopted in many local studies – is generally unhelpful. In examining municipal results, the pattern of change has to be carefully assessed from a series of contests (or non-contests) with differing candidature patterns and different contexts. The results are illustrations of points made in the text, rather than the full (and necessarily lengthy) compilation of returns which would constitute a complete picture of each unit's electoral history (for examples of this, see Tanner, (thesis), Chapters 3–4). For a discussion of the problems and techniques of analysing municipal results, see D. M. Tanner, 'Elections, statistics, and the rise of the Labour party, 1906–1931', *Historical Journal* (forthcoming 1991)'.

In the following tables, party polls in double member wards are an average of both 'scores' where there were two candidates. 'Socialist' votes are included with 'Labour' polls where appropriate. Footnotes are provided which note the rare occasions when these practices may not be justified. Figures for cross-voting between parties in double member wards suggest that Labour was likely to benefit from Liberal support where it fielded only one candidate. In some instances its vote may therefore overstate the true level of its support.

THE NORTH-WEST

HYDE

	Year	Lab.	L.	C.		Year	Lab.	L.	C.
Godley	1907	32.16	26.57	41.28*	Werneth	1907	23.80*	37.88*	38.32
	1909	46.23	23.22	30.55		1909	30.07	34.83*	35.16*
	1910	23.90	35.35	40.67*		1910	14.08	40.44*	45.48^a
	1911	27.21	37.11*	35.68†		1912	32.59	37.06	30.35*
	1913	20.55†	39.72†	40.03					
Newton	1907	34.78	25.80	39.42	All wards	1907	30.46	29.84	39.70
	1909	25.97	35.38	38.66		1909	33.80	31.28	34.92
	1910	23.97	35.34*	40.69*		1910	20.33	36.73	42.94
					Parl. El.	J.1910	21.20	39.50	39.30

BURNLEY

	Year	Lab.	L.	C.		Year	Lab.	L.	C.
St Andrews	1907	44.48	42.13	13.39	Gannow	1909	42.60^d	30.66	26.74
	1909	29.43	48.92	21.65		1910	35.74	28.52	35.74
						1911	34.57	24.57	40.86
Burnley Wood	1910	26.80	33.47	39.73	Danehouse	1909	26.19	41.42	32.39
	1911	23.87	36.09	40.04					
	1912	18.10	43.65	38.25	Lowerhouse	1908	29.36	47.45	23.19
	1913	32.20	28.81	38.99					
Stoneyholme	1910	20.10	38.76	41.14	Fulledge	1913	18.66	36.78	44.56

OLDHAM

	Year	Lab.	L.	C.		Year	Lab.	L.	C.
St Pauls	1910	19.91	45.75	34.34	Coldhurst	1912	20.63	36.32	43.05
	1911	23.80	33.16	43.04					
Hartford	1913	17.51	51.42	31.07	Hollingwood	1912	13.26	37.41	49.33

		Lab.	L.	C.			Lab.	L.	C.
Mumps	1913	13.70	44.82	41.48	Clarkesfield	1909	15.24	38.12	46.64
ACCRINGTON									
South	1909	16.46	41.07	42.47	Peel Park	1912	31.50	48.35	20.15
West	1907	20.62	39.13	40.25					
	1908	19.25	42.96	37.79					
BURY									
East	1907	35.76	34.69	29.55	Moorside	1910	37.81	24.78	37.41
	1908	30.15	32.05	37.80*		1911	23.58	28.57	47.85
	1909	19.49	41.77	38.74		1912	30.52	32.56	36.92
	1913	22.47*	42.33	35.20					
Elton	1907	26.96	37.56	35.48*					
	1908	15.35†	36.91	47.74					
CARLISLE									
Newtown	1908	27.86	33.89	38.25	Caldewgate	1908	21.55	37.36	41.09
	1912	32.24	34.87*	32.89					
Denton Holme	1912	35.14	33.82	31.04*					
ROCHDALE									
Wardleworth W.	1907	26.88	28.67	44.45	Wardleworth E.	1907	21.39	40.00	38.61
	1910	28.41	39.47	32.12					
	1911	39.02^c	31.98	29.02					
BLACKBURN									
St Matthew	1907	48.21	10.82	40.97	Trinity	1907	35.59	9.51	54.90
	1909	33.30^b	26.38	40.32		1908	42.33	8.20	49.47

Place	Year			
St Lukes	1911	21.37	29.80	48.83
St Pauls	1911	7.11	44.75	48.14
TORY REGIONS				
COVENTRY				
All Saints	1913	48.30	32.27	19.43
Swanswell	1908	23.76	32.88	43.36
	1909	9.05	59.16	31.79
YORKSHIRE				
HALIFAX				
North	1907	46.72	28.34	24.94
Southowram	1907	38.06	41.38	20.56
	1911	27.27	38.60	34.13
	1913	47.76	32.49	19.75
Pellon	1907	28.17	36.19	35.64
Illingworth	1911	15.19	28.46	56.35
HUDDERSFIELD				
Lindley	1907	42.45	40.05	17.50
	1912	37.25	41.15	21.60
Moldgreen	1907	31.97	30.24	37.79
	1908	26.34	37.55	36.11
	1910	29.49	28.70	41.80

Place	Year			
St Johns	1907	9.64	40.14	50.22
St Marks	1910	18.38	30.98	50.64
	1911	10.94	37.01	52.05
Harnall	1908	38.54	24.22	37.24
Stoke	1907	22.21	22.84	54.95
	1909	11.24	36.67	52.09
	1911	9.43	41.35	49.22
Copley	1907	40.26	25.73	34.01
	1912	41.83	38.38	19.79
Kingston	1907	31.75	35.51	32.74
	1908	30.25	31.38	38.37
	1909	30.78	37.95	31.27
	1911	21.34	36.44	42.22
Ovendon	1907	28.51	34.14	37.35
Newsome	1912	39.85	29.15	31.00
Lockwood	1908	34.63	39.35	26.02
	1911	23.08	33.63	43.29

		Lab.	L.	C.
North Central	1908	27.16	28.22	44.62
	1909	31.82	25.89	42.29
Marsh	1907	23.60	41.54	34.86
Crosland Moor	1912	22.05	39.26	38.69
YORK				
Micklegate	1907	27.23*	37.63	35.14
	1908	26.58	32.23	41.19
	1909	35.36	27.64	37.00
	1910	28.43*	41.32	30.25
	1911	39.48	32.79	27.73
	1913	38.18*	19.88*	41.94
WAKEFIELD				
BelleVue	1909	27.78ᶠ	37.96†	34.26
	1913	31.41	36.15	32.44
Primrose Hill	1911	32.40	23.47	44.13
Kirkgate	1908	19.48	38.74	41.78
SHEFFIELD				
Attercliffe	1907	39.03	40.67	20.30
	1908	30.02	23.96	46.02

		Lab.	L.	C.
Longwood	1911	30.53	38.63	30.84
	1912	27.86	45.13	27.01
Paddock	1913	30.25	29.87	39.88
Almondley	1908	22.66	36.31	41.03
West	1907	20.30	41.79*	37.91*
Walmgate	1911	30.44	42.08	27.48
	1913	35.95	32.65	31.39
Bootham	1913	27.61	25.72	46.68*
Eastmoor	1910	31.23	25.28	43.49
Calder	1909	29.51	31.31	39.18
S. Westgate	1913	11.14	32.07	56.79
Brightside	1908	40.79	25.66	33.55
	1911	34.58	38.75	26.67

Ward	Year			
	1911	42.62	1.39[i]	55.99
	1913	37.37	33.09	29.54
Burngreave	1907	21.42	44.36	34.22
	1911	16.83	53.40	29.77
Darnall	1912	22.24	50.35	27.41
Broomhall	1913	17.06	28.38	54.56
Neepsend	1912	9.83	45.25	44.92

Ward	Year			
	1912	29.47	35.25	35.28
	1913	36.94	33.22	29.84
Healey	1907	20.24	34.15	45.61
	1908	24.54	24.73	50.73
	1909	20.62	34.15	45.23
	1911	14.34	37.71	47.95
Walkley	1908	16.32	40.46	43.22

LIBERALISM'S RESERVE ARMY

NORTHAMPTON

Ward	Year			
North	1907	45.42	6.50	48.08
Castle	1908	36.95	33.69	29.36
	1909	34.99	21.20	43.81
Kingsthorpe	1907	27.72	29.36	42.92
	1908	27.96	36.22	35.82
	1909	15.44	49.25	35.31
St James	1907	21.15	42.95	35.90
	1908	20.00	37.61	42.39
	1913	12.61	56.84	30.55
Far Cotton	1909	6.50	51.78	41.72
	1911	3.57	50.95	45.58
Abington	1912[g]	21.72	40.11	38.17
	1913	12.61	56.84	30.55

Ward	Year			
St Crispins	1907	28.03	31.83	40.14
	1908	33.51	29.50	36.99
	1909	33.98	25.61	40.41
	1913	28.79	34.03	37.18[e]
St Michael	1908	27.47[c]	24.71	47.82
	1909	17.26	26.78	55.96
	1911	9.25	46.87	43.88
St Edmunds	1908	14.21	46.85	38.94
	1909	13.38	36.41	50.21
	1913	8.54	45.58	45.88[e]
St Lawrence	1912[g]	21.08	35.90	43.02
	1913	18.75	35.78	45.47
Kingsley	1913	11.05	51.84	37.11

		Lab.	L.	C.
CREWE				
North	1907	39.73	34.69	25.58
	1909	25.38	37.84	36.78*
Central	1909	24.81	41.76	33.43*
	1911	31.30	35.61	33.09†
NOTTINGHAM				
Manvers	1908	37.45	25.49	37.06
	1910	38.13	16.77	45.10
	1912	34.66	15.75	49.59
Byron	1907	11.96	35.95	52.09

		Lab.	L.	C.
West	1907	32.24	25.09*	42.67
	1911	39.44	37.62†	22.94
St Ann's	1907	16.83	29.48	53.69
Woolaton	1912	13.47	48.25	38.28

Notes:

* Average vote.

† Average vote of two candidates with markedly different polls.

[a] Independent, supported by Tories.

[b] Ind. Lab., supported by Labour.

[c] Combined Labour and (larger) Socialist vote.

[d] Combined Labour and (small) Socialist vote.

[e] Boundary revision, and therefore all three seats contested. No comparison with previous contests possible.

[f] Boundary revision . . . 2 L, 3 C, 3 Lab. candidates.

[g] Boundary revision . . . 3 L, 2 C, 1 Lab. candidates.

[h] Boundary revision . . . 3 L, 3 C, 1 Lab. candidates.

[i] Candidate withdrew after nomination.

[j] Opposed by ward Liberals.

Source: local press and party records.

Appendix 5 Organisational assistance funded by the Durham Miners' Association, 1918 election

	Election agent	Sub- agent	Polling agent	Clerks
Spennymoor	/	6	25	8
Blaydon	/	10	0	14
Sedgefield	/	22	23	11
Houghton-le-Spring	/	12	0	15
Seaham	/	9	12	11
Barnard Castle	/	7	8	6
Durham	/	10	39	97

Source: Durham Miners' Association Cash Books, DMA 79.

Favourable Labour electoral performances, 1918 election

Three-cornered contests: Labour seats won

In fifteen constituencies Labour won in three-cornered contests and in five our candidate polled more than the combined vote of his opponents. The following is the list:

		Votes polled	Opposition	Results
Deptford	C. W. Bowerman	14,073	Ind. U.	9,711
			Ind.	2,106
Stoke-on-Trent (Burslem)	S. Finney	7,474	Co. U.	6,301
			L.	3,108
Wigan	J. A. Parkinson	12,914	Co. U.	11,584
			L.	2,434
Wednesbury	A. Short	11,341	Co. U.	10,464
			L.	988
Bishop Auckland	B. C. Spoor	10,060	Co. L.	7,417
			L.	2,411
Houghton-le-Spring	R. Richardson	7,315	L.	6,626
			Coa.	6,185
Clitheroe	Alfred Davis	9,578	U.	8,419
			Co. L.	3,443
Ormskirk	James Bell	6,545	C. U.	6,080
			Agr.	4,989
Broxstowe	G. A. Spencer	11,150	L.	4,681
			Coa.	4,374
Kingswinford	C. H. Sitch	10,397	U.	7,509
			L.	3,943
Rother Valley	T. W. Grundy	9,917	Coa.	4,894
			L.	3,177
Rothwell	W. Lunn	9,998	Co. U.	6,621
			L.	4,909
Wentworth	G. H. Hirst	13,029	Co. U.	5,315
			L.	3,453

466

		Votes polled	Opposition	Results
Holland with Boston	W. S. Royce	8,788	Co. U.	7,718
			L.	5,557
Govan	N. Maclean	9,577	Co. U.	8,762
			L.	1,678

Four-cornered contests in which Labour beat Liberal candidate

There were nineteen contests with four candidates, seven of which were won by Labour. In eleven instances we secured second place and in only one case third place.

Constituency	Name	Position	Lab. vote	Lib. vote
Battersea (South)	Col. A. Lynch	2	3,383	2,273
Fulham (West)	R. M. Gentry	2	4,435	1,139
Derby	J. H. Thomas	1	25,145	13,408
Edmonton	F. A. Broad	2	3,575	2,245
Oldham	W. C. Robinson	3	15,178	9,323
Preston	Tom Shaw	1	19,213	18,485
Reading	T. C. Morris	2	8,410	3,143
Rotherham	J. Walker	2	9,757	3,805
Hanley	H. Parker	2	7,697	1,459
Wallasey	W. M. Citrine	2	4,384	4,055
Cardiff (Central)	J. E. Edmunds	2	4,663	4,172
Workington	Tom Cape	1	10,441	2,968
Barnard Castle	J. Swan	1	5,468	2,180
Mansfield	W. Carter	1	8,957	4,000
Frome	Capt. Gill	2	10,454	2,004
Nuneaton	I. Gregory	2	6,269	5,707
South Ayrshire	J. Brown	1	6,358	4,555
Hamilton	D. M. Graham	1	6,988	(I) 504
Lanark (North)	J. Sullivan	2	5,673	3,068

*Three-cornered contests: Labour seats not won but higher polls than
Liberal candidate:*

There were 68 three-cornered contests in which the Labour candidate polled
a heavier vote than the Liberal. The following is the list:

		Votes polled	Liberal
Bow and Bromley	G. Lansbury	7,248	988
Mile End	W. Devenay	2,392	1,119
Wandsworth (Central)	G. P. Blizard	3,382	(Co.l)2,988
Birkenhead (East)	J. Finigan	5,399	1,787
Birkenhead (West)	W. H. Egan	5,673	1,755
Ladywood	J. W. Kneeshaw	2,572	1,552
Moseley	Dr R. Dunstan	3,789	3,422
Bournemouth	Rev. F. J. Hopkins	5,302	1,854
Bradford (Central)	W. Leach	7,636	4,304
Bradford (East)	F. W. Jowett	8,637	4,782
Bradford (North)	J. H. Palin	6,499	4,688
Bristol (East)	L. Bateman	8,135	1,447
Dewsbury	B. Riley	5,596	5,130
Gateshead	J. Brotherton	7,212	5,833
Huddersfield	H. Snell	12,737	11,256
Ilford	Rev. H. Dunnico	4,621	3,261
Ipswich	R. Jackson	8,143	3,663
Kingston-on-Thames	T. H. Dumper	2,502	2,325
Lincoln	A. Taylor	6,658	5,550
Wavertree	C. Wilson	5,103	2,484
Ardwick	T. Lowth	5,670	3,510
Blackley	A. Townend	3,569	2,986
Devonport	F. Bramley	4,115	3,930
Sutton	W. T. Gay	5,334	3,488
Chatham	D. Hubbard	4,134	2,778
Rossendale	G. W. Jones	7,984	5,837
Salford (South)	J. Gorman	3,807	1,994
Wakefield	A. Bellamy	5,882	2,448
Wallsend	J. Chapman	6,835	3,047
Walsall	J. Thickett	8,336	4,914
Walthamstow (West)	V. McEntee	4,167	2,707
Upton	B. W. Gardner	3,186	2,380
Willesden (East)	H. J. Lincoln	4,941	2,757
Willesden (West)	S. Viant	7,217	1,697
Cardiff (South)	J. T. Catworthy	4,303	4,126
Camlachie	H. B. Guthrie	7,192	860
Maryhill	J. W. Muir	5,531	2,363
St Rollox	J. Stewart	6,147	1,521

		Votes polled	Liberal
Springburn	G. D. Hardie	7,996	1,669
Buckingham	John Scurr	7,481	3,250
Stalybridge and Hyde	W. Fowden	6,508	6,241
Torquay	Maj. A. E. Trestrail	4,029	3,173
Blaydon	W. Whiteley	7,844	1,064
Sedgefield	J. Herriotts	5,801	3,333
Maldon	G. Dallas	6,315	1,490
South-East Essex	J. Cotter	5,343	1,372
Watford	G. Latham	4,952	3,395
Tonbridge	J. Palmer	5,006	1,851
Farnworth	T. Greenall	9,710	3,893
Lonsdale	D. Hunter	4,472	4,276
Royton	J. Crinion	4,875	4,451
Brigg	D. J. Quibell	4,789	4,475
Enfield	W. E. Hill	6,176	1,987
Finchley	J. R. Leslie	3,140	2,221
Uxbridge	H. Gosling	6,251	545
Wood Green	Tudor Rhys	4,539	2,957
Peterborough	J. Mansfield	8,832	3,214
Hexham	W. Weir	4,168	3,948
Rushcliffe	C. Harris	6,180	3,673
Yeovil	W. T. Kelly	7,589	2,743
Eastbourne	T. B. Hasdell	4,641	1,852
Swindon	J. Compton	8,393	2,460
York, North Riding (Cleveland)	H. Dack	8,610	7,089
Sowerby	J. W. Ogden	7,306	6,778
Bute and Northern Ayr	R. Smith	5,848	2,059
Berwick and Haddington	R. W. Foulis	4,783	2,557
Dumbarton	W. H. Martin	7,072	3,048
Stirling and Clackmannan (Western)	T. Johnston	3,809	2,582

Source: Labour Party *AR 1919*, pp. 192–3, with corrections made.

Bibliography

This book is based on two types of source material. First, and principally, on national and local Liberal, Labour and trade union records, and the papers, biographies, contemporary writing and memoirs of national and local political figures. I have used newspaper reports where these records were sparse, some standard reference works, national newspapers, and various government reports and publications throughout the book. A second category of source material was equally important, but generally only for specific sections of the book. I have gained valuable information from a survey and compilation of parliamentary and municipal election results and campaign details from the period 1906–22, supplemented by consideration in some instances of UDC and other election results. I have also made considerable use of the now very large published and unpublished material on aspects of Liberal and Labour politics in this period. This bibliography reflects only the first type of source material consulted. (For a partial list of newspaper and secondary material, see my Ph.D. thesis, pp. 386–8, 393–9). There are two exceptions to this general principle. I have included a list of those electoral registers which I have consulted, since these are an under-utilised source, and details of their location may be useful to other researchers. I have also listed unpublished theses and papers, since these too may not be well-known. I hope my very considerable debts to certain general texts are suffi-ciently recognised in the Acknowledgements and the Introduction, and that my specific debts to key secondary works on certain areas are recognised in the foot-notes. All collections of microfilm material have been consulted at the BLPES. The place of publication of printed material is London unless otherwise stated. Pamphlet material is listed under the author's name.

PRIVATE PAPERS

At Blackburn Central Reference Library:
  S. Higenbottom.
At the Bodleian Library:
  Dr C. Addison; H. H. Asquith; W. Crook; R. D. Denman; R. C. K. Ensor;
    L. Harcourt; D. Maclean; A. Ponsonby; J. A. Simon.
At Bradford District Archives:
  E. G. Hartley.

At the British Library:
  J. Burns; G. Cave; C. Dilke; H. Gladstone; H. D. Harben; C. P. Scott;
  J. A. Spender.
At the BLPES:
  E. H. J. N. Dalton; A. G. Gardiner; G. Lansbury; S. and B. Webb.
At Cambridge University Library:
  Lord Crewe.
At Friends House:
  T. E. Harvey; A. Rowntree.
At the Greater London Record Office:
  W. H. Dickinson.
At the House of Lords Record Office:
  A. Bonar Law; D. Lloyd George; H. Samuel; Viscount Stansgate (W. Wedg-
  wood Benn).
At Liverpool University:
  J. Bruce Glasier.
At Manchester University:
  C. P. Scott correspondence.
At the National Library of Scotland:
  Murray of Elibank; R. B. Haldane.
At Newcastle University:
  W. Runciman; C. P. Trevelyan.
At Norfolk CRO, Norwich:
  F. Henderson.
At Nuffield College, Oxford:
  Lord Gainford (J. A. Pease).
At the PRO:
  J. R. MacDonald.
At Ruskin College, Oxford:
  J. S. Middleton.
At the Scottish Record Office:
  Sir A. Steel-Maitland.
At Sheffield Central Library:
  H. J. Wilson.
At Southwark Record Office:
  C. Hesse.
At Trinity College, Cambridge:
  F. W. Pethwick-Lawrence.
Microfilm:
  F. Johnson (*The Archives of the Independent Labour Party* series, Harvester
  Microfilm).

OFFICIAL PAPERS

Cabinet Papers: PRO CAB 23, 24
Home Office Papers: HO 45.

Parliamentary Debates, Fifth Series.

Parliamentary Papers:

Report of the Boundary Commission (England and Wales), P.P. 1884–5 (Cd 4287), xix, 297.

Return of resident and non-resident voters, England and Wales, P.P. 1888 (Cd 394–5), xxix, 907–19.

Return of resident and non-resident Burgh voters, Scotland, P.P. 1895 (Cd 389), Lxxix, 315.

Return of resident and non-resident County voters, Scotland, P.P. 1895 (Cd 388), Lxxix, 319.

Return of those disfranchised in respect of non-payment of rates, Scotland, P.P. 1898 (Cd 376), Lxxix, 755.

Report of a Board of Trade enquiry into working-class rents, housing and retail prices, P.P. 1908 (Cd 3864), cvii, 319.

Return of women municipal voters (England and Wales), P.P. 1908 (Cd 364), xci, 533.

Return of parliamentary voters, P.P. 1911 (Cd 4975), Lxii, 679; 1914–16 (Cd 120), Lii, 585.

Reports of the Chief Registrar of Friendly Societies for the year 1912 (and 1913), P.P. 1913 (Cd 89), Lvii, 759; 1914 (Cd 121), Lxxvi, 719 (results of ballots under the Trade Union Act of 1913).

Reports of the Commission of Enquiry into Industrial Unrest, P.P. 1917–18 (Cd 8662–8696), xv.

Reports of the Boundary Commissioners for England and Wales, P.P. 1917–18 (Cd 8759), xiv, 47.

Return of Parliamentary voters, P.P. 1918 (Cd 138), xix, 925.

Census 1911, 1921.

Annual Reports of the Registrar General/Registrar General's *Statistical Review*/ Registrar General's *Deccenial Supplement*, 1911–21.

PARTY RECORDS

CENTRAL

British Socialist Party:
Report of the Annual Conference (1912 etc.) [AR].

Conservative party:
Minutes of the National Society of Conservative Agents (Westminster City Archives).

Fabian Society:
Report of the Executive [AR].
M.B. of Committees and Sub-Committees and correspondence (Fabian Society Archives, Nuffield College, Oxford).

Independent Labour Party:
Report of the Annual Conference [CR].
NAC M.B., Head Office Circulars (BLPES).

Miscellaneous archival material (ILP Archives, Harvester Microfilm).

Report and M.B. of the Joint Committee of the ILP and Fabian Society (Harvester Microfilm).

Labour party

Report of the Annual Conference [*AR*].

NEC M.B., correspondence and other material (Labour party archives, Walworth Road).

'Infancy of the Labour party collection' (Bryan MS, BLPES).

Liberal party:

AR and *Transactions of the National Liberal Federation*

M.B. of the Society of Certified and Associated Liberal Agents (Leeds Archives, Sheepscar Branch).

LOCAL AND REGIONAL

All printed reports consulted at the BL, BLPES, Labour party Archives and TUC unless otherwise stated. Dates are given where there are incomplete runs of printed material for this period. Several sets of minutes have been microfilmed (E.P. Microform series, *Origins and development of the Labour Party in Britain at local level* [E.P. Microform, Wakefield, 1979]). This now includes several sets of minutes which I originally examined at local repositories.

Conservative party:

Reigate/Surrey South East Division M.B. (Surrey CRO).

Labour party:

Accrington and District T&LC *AR & BS* 1905.

Barnsley and District TC/T&LC *AR* 1907, 1915.

Barrow LRC *AR & BS* 1905—6.

Birmingham ILP Federation M.B.; Hay Mills ILP Branch, Kings Heath ILP Branch M.B.; Birmingham LRC/LP M.B.; Birmingham TC M.B. (Birmingham Central Reference Library).

Blaydon LP *AR* 1919, 1920 (Durham CRO, Shotton Coll.).

Bolton TC *AR* 1914.

Bradford and District T&LC *Year Book* 1908, 1914.

Bradford TC M.B.; Workers' Municipal Federation M.B. (Bradford District Archives).

Bristol ILP Federation M.B. (Microfilm, BLPES).

Cambridge ILP M.B. 1906–12; Cambridge LP M.B. 1913– (Cambridge CRO).

Clitheroe Division LP *Agent's Annual Report* 1915.

Colne Valley Socialist League (later Labour League), M.B. and *AR*s (E.P. Microform).

Coventry LP *AR* 1910, 1911, 1913, 1914; T&LC *AR* 1913.

Durham LP M.B. and *AR* 1918– (Durham CRO, Shotton Coll.).

Edinburgh LP *AR & BS* 1914.

Glasgow LP M.B. (E.P. Microform), *AR* 1914–15, *Year Book* 1915–16.

Gloucester ILP M.B. 1906–16 (E.P. Microform).

Halifax T&LC Election Committee M.B. 1906–10 (Calderdale Borough Library).

Houghton-le-Spring LP *AR* 1918–20 (Durham CRO, Shotton Coll.).

Huddersfield Labour and Socialist Election Committee M.B., Letter Books; T&LC M.B., Letter Books (Huddersfield Library).

Ince Division LP *Rules* 1911.

Ipswich ILP *AR* 1906, 1909, 1913, 1914 and miscellaneous material (Ratcliffe Collection, Suffolk CRO, Ipswich).

Keighley ILP M.B., Letter Books (Keighley Library).

Leeds LP M.B. (Leeds Archives, Sheepscar); T&LC *AR* 1904–9.

Leigh Division LP *AR* 1915 (Durham CRO, Shotton Coll.).

Liverpool LRC M.B. (Liverpool Record Office).

London District Council ILP M.B. and correspondence (BLPES).

Manchester Central ILP M.B.; Manchester & Salford LRC *AR* 1904–15, 1925 (Manchester Central Reference Library).

Middlesbrough ILP M.B. 1906–14 (Cleveland CRO); Middlesbrough TC *AR* 1911–14 (Middlesbrough Reference Library).

Newcastle & District LRC *AR & B* 1903–8, LP *AR* 1918–19, 1919–20 (Durham CRO, Shotton Coll.).

Newport LP M.B. (Swansea University Library).

Normanton Division LP *AR* 1911–13.

Northampton TC *AR* 1911–20; LP *AR* 1915, 1920.

Norwich TC M.B. 1906–9 (Norwich Record Office).

Nottingham LP *Year Book* 1912; TC *Annual Report and Year Book* 1914, 1915.

Oldham LP M.B. and miscellaneous material; T&LC M.B., Fair Contracts Sub-Committee M.B., *AR* (Oldham Local Studies Centre).

Pontypridd TC M.B. (E.P. Microform).

Sheffield LP M.B.; Sheffield ILP M.B., and ILP ward committee M.B. (E.P. Microform).

South Shields LP M.B. (E.P. Microform).

Sowerby Division Labour Representation Association *AR & BS* 1913; M.B. and miscellaneous records (Calderdale Borough Library).

Stockport ILP M.B. and miscellaneous records (E.P. Microform).

Stockton TC *AR* 1905.

Walsall TC M.B. (Walsall Borough Library).

Wolverhampton TC M.B. (Wolverhampton Borough Record Office).

Woolwich Labour Representation Association *Year Book* 1908, *AR* 1912–14.

Liberal party:

Coventry LA M.B., *AR* and miscellaneous material (Coventry Borough Record Office).

Halifax West Ward Liberal Committee M.B. (Calderdale Borough Library).

Holmfirth LA *AR* 1911–13 (H. J. Wilson MS, Sheffield Central Library).

Home Counties Liberal Federation *AR* 1898–1903, 1905, 1908, 1910, 1925 (BLPES and Bristol University Library).

Huddersfield Liberal Councillors M.B. (Huddersfield Library).

Keighley LA M.B. (Keighley Public Library).

Lancashire and Cheshire LF M.B.; Lancashire and Cheshire Liberal Agents M.B. (Manchester Central Reference Library).
Leeds LF (EC and other committees) M.B. (Leeds Archives, Sheepscar).
Leicester LA M.B. and *AR* (Leicester CRO).
Lincoln LA M.B. and Subscription Book 1909– (Lincoln Archives Office).
Manchester Liberal Union/Federation M.B.; Manchester Progressive Association M.B. (Manchester Central Reference Library).
Midlands LF M.B. (Birmingham University Library).
Stockport LA M.B. (Stockport Library).
Walsall LA M.B. (Walsall Borough Library).
Yorkshire LF M.B.; Yorkshire Liberal Agents M.B. (Leeds Archives, Sheepscar).

TRADE UNION RECORDS

All printed reports, Bishopsgate Institute, BL, BLPES, TUC and Modern Records Centre, Warwick University unless otherwise stated. Dates are given where isolated items only have been used. Some minutes are in printed form, others are manuscript.
National Agricultural Labourers' and Rural Workers' Union *AR*.
Amalgamated Society of Engineers *AR*, *Quarterly Report*, *MR*.
Amalgamated Society of Locomotive Enginemen and Firemen *AR*.
National Federation of Blastfurnacemen, Ore Miners, and Kindred Trades, Cumberland and Lancashire District *AR* 1913.
Amalgamated Society of Bleachers, Dyers and Finishers *AR* 1914, 1918.
United Society of Boilermakers and Iron and Steel Shipbuilders *AR*, *MR*.
National Union of Boot and Shoe Operatives *CR*, 1906, 1910, *MR*.
British Steel Smelters *AR*, M.B. of Quarterly Meetings, *MR* with EC minutes.
Amalgamated Society of Carpenters and Joiners *AR*, *MR*, Minutes of the Proceedings of the General Council 1912–14, circulars and other miscellaneous material (MRC, Warwick).
General Union of Carpenters and Joiners General Council and EC M.B. (MRC, Warwick).
Chainmakers and Strikers' Association *Rules* 1889, *AR* 1922.
National Union of Clerks *AR & BS*.
United Kingdom Society of Coachmakers *Quarterly Report and Journal* 1910, 1914, 1919, EC M.B. (MRC, Warwick).
Cardiff, Penarth and Barry Society of Coal Trimmers *AR*.
Cumberland Iron Ore Miners and Kindred Trades Association, Lodge *Balance Sheet* 31/3/1916.
National Union of Dock Labourers *AR* 1914, 1918, EC *Report* (MRC, Warwick and Nuffield College, Oxford).
Dock, Wharf, Riverside and General Workers' Union of Great Britain and Ireland *AR*, M.B. of the Triennial Delegates' Meetings (MRC, Warwick).
Durham Miners' Association M.B., Circulars, *MR*, Political fund cash books (Durham CRO and Durham Miners' Offices).

Durham Miners' Association Lodge M.B.: Dean and Chapter, Eden, Marsden (Durham CRO).

National Union of Gasworkers and General Labourers *Quarterly Report and Balance Sheet*, Biennial Conference M.B., EC M.B. (GMBATU, Woodstock College).

Amalgamated Society of Instrument Makers *AR* 1918, *Half-Yearly Report*, March 1919.

Friendly Society of Ironfounders *AR* 1912–15, *MR*.

London and Provincial Licensed Vehicle Workers *AR* 1916–19.

London Society of Compositors *AR*, Political Committee M.B. (MRC, Warwick).

Miners' Federation of Great Britain *AR*, EC M.B. (Swansea University Library).

National Amalgamated Union of Labour M.B. (GMBATU, Woodstock College).

National Union of Railwaymen *AR*.

National Amalgamated Society of Ship Painters and Decorators *AR*.

Northumberland Miners' Association M.B., Circulars, Letter Books (Northumberland CRO).

United Patternmakers' Association *AR*.

National Society of Printers' Assistants *Half-Yearly Statement*.

Railway Clerks' Association *AR & BS*.

Shipconstructors' and Shipwrights' Association *AR*, *Quarterly Report*.

South Wales Miners' Federation EC M.B. (Swansea University Library).

General Union of Textile Workers *AR*.

Trades Union Congress *AR*.

Typographical Association *Half-Yearly Report*.

United Garment Workers *Rules* 1914, *AR* 1919, 1920.

United Textile Factory Workers' Association *AR* 1910, 1919.

Amalgamated Society of Watermen, Lightermen and Bargemen *AR*.

Workers' Union *AR*.

NEWSPAPERS AND JOURNALS

NATIONAL PARTY PUBLICATIONS

Conservative party:
Conservative Agents' Journal (Conservative Central Office).
Fabian Society:
Fabian News.
Labour party:
Labour Organiser.
Labour Woman.
Liberal party:
Liberal Agent (Bristol University Library).
Liberal Magazine.
Liberal Monthly.
Young Liberal.

LOCAL PARTY PUBLICATIONS

Conservative party:
London Municipal Notes.
Labour party/ILP:
Monthly Messenger (Bermondsey) at Southwark Record Office.
Blackburn Labour Journal.
Workers' Tribune (Blackburn).
Labour Advocate (Blackpool).
Bradford Forward at Bradford Reference Library.
Bradford Pioneer.
Labour Herald (East Bristol).
Forward (Glasgow).
The Worker (Huddersfield).
Monthly Labour Journal (Hull).
Jarrow Labour Herald.
Keighley Labour Journal.
Leeds and District Weekly Citizen.
Leicester Pioneer.
Liverpool Forward.
Liverpool Labour Chronicle.
Llais Llafur (Swansea).
Manchester Weekly Citizen.
New Times (Colchester).
Northern Democrat (Newcastle).
Pioneer (Merthyr).
The Pioneer and Labour Journal (Woolwich).
Rhondda Socialist.
Sheffield Guardian.
Wolverhampton Worker.
York Daily Labour Notes (1906 election).
Yorkshire Factory Times.
Liberal party:
East Hants Liberal Monthly.
The Suffolk Beacon.
Y Gwerinwr: Monthly Democrat.

TRADE UNION PUBLICATIONS

(Agricultural Labourers) *The Labourer.*
(ASE) *Monthly Journal.*
(ASLEF) *Locomotive Journal.*
Journeyman Bakers' Magazine and Chronicle.
(Birmingham and District Municipal Employees' Association) *The Municipal Employees' Monthly.*
(National League of the Blind) *The Blind Advocate.*

(National Union of Dock Labourers) *The Docker's Record.*
(London and Provincial Licensed Vehicle Workers) *Licensed Vehicle Trades' Record.*
Journal of the Operative Stonemasons Society.
(National Association of Furnishing Trade Operatives) *Nafto Record.*
Postman's Gazette.
Postal Clerk's Herald.
Railway Clerk.
Railway Review.
(Royal Army Clothing Employees) *The Government Workers' Advocate.*
(Ship Stewards, Cooks, Butchers and Bakers) *The Marine Caterer.*
The Shop Assistant.
Typographical Circular.
The Workers' Union Record.

NATIONAL PAPERS AND JOURNALS

Christian Commonwealth.
Clarion.
Daily Citizen.
Daily Herald.
Daily News.
Labour Leader.
Manchester Guardian.
Municipal Journal.
Nation.
New Statesman.
Reynolds Newspaper.
Socialist Review.
Westminster Gazette.

ELECTORAL REGISTERS

Electoral registers were not compiled in a uniform way, so some are more useful than others. Although I have used a substantial number to obtain information about the composition of constituencies, the following list refers only to those which contained information of use in Chapter 4. All registers consulted are from the British Library collection of current and 'dead' registers unless stated otherwise.

LONDON CONSTITUENCIES

Bethnal Green, North East.
Bethnal Green, South West.
Hampstead.
Islington, South.

Paddington, North.
St Pancras, East.

PROVINCIAL CONSTITUENCIES

Barrow.
Bolton.
Bradford, East.
Bradford, West.
Brighton.
Buckinghamshire, Aylesbury.
Cheltenham.
Colchester.
Gateshead.
Glamorgan, Gower.
Haddingtonshire.
Leeds, East.
Leeds, West.
Linlithgowshire.
Liverpool Record Office.
   Liverpool, Scotland
   Liverpool, West Derby
Manchester Reference Library.
   Manchester, East
   Manchester, North-East
   Manchester, South-West
Walsall.
Wednesbury.
West Fife.
Worcester.

REFERENCE WORKS

Craig, F. W. S., *British parliamentary election results 1885–1918* (1974).
   British general election manifestos 1900–1974 (1975).
   British electoral facts 1885–1975 (1976).
   British parliamentary election results 1918–1945 (1983).
Dictionary of Labour Biography.
The Labour Party, *The Labour Who's Who 1924* (1924).
Law reporter.
Maps from the British Library collection.
Mitchell's Newspaper press directory.
Municipal Year Book 1911–.
Rogers on Elections (Vol. I, 17th edn, 1909 and Vol. II, 18th edn, 1906).
Saint's registration cases.
Warwick guide to British labour periodicals (Brighton, 1977).

Year Book of social progress 1913–14.

CONTEMPORARY WORKS

Acland, F. D., *Adult suffrage. An address to democrats* (1910).
Ayles, W. H., *What a Socialist Town Council should be* (1921).
Benson, T. D., *Socialism and service* (1906).
Bowley, A. L. and Burnett-Hurst, A. R., *Livelihood and poverty* (1915).
Bradford Liberal Association, *A programme of municipal reform* (Bradford, 1894).
Buxton, S. C., *Political questions of the day* (11th edn, 1903).
Clayton, I. (ed.), *Why I joined the Independent Labour Party* (Leeds, n.d.).
Dalton, E. H. J. N., *The Capital Levy explained* (1923).
Desmond, S., *Labour: the giant with the feet of clay* (1921).
Dilke, C., *Electoral reform. Address to the National Liberal Club, 1909* (1909).
Dilke, C., *Woman suffrage and electoral reform* (1910).
Dodds, E., *Is Liberalism dead?* (1920).
Fyfe, H. H., *The British Liberal party* (1928).
Hall, L., *et al. Let us reform the Labour Party* (Manchester, 1910).
Hardie, J. Keir, *The citizenship of women* (2nd edn, 1906).
Hobson, J. A., 'The general election: a sociological interpretation', *Sociological Review*, iii (1910).
Jowett, F. W., *The Socialist and the city* (1907).
  What is the use of Parliament? (1909).
  What made me a Socialist (1925).
King, J., *Electoral reform* (1908).
King, J. and Rafferty, F. W., *Our electoral system: the demand for reform* (1912).
Liberal Party, *Memorandum on Liberal re-organisation* (1900).
  Liberal policy (1918).
London Labour Council for Adult Suffrage, *Adult suffrage* (1917).
Lowell, A. L., *The Government of England* (2 vols, 1908 and 1912).
MacDonald, J. R., *The Socialist movement* (1911).
  The conscription of wealth (Manchester, 1917).
  Socialism after the war (Manchester and London, 1917).
  Socialism: critical and constructive (1921).
MacDonald, J. R., Roberts, G. H. and Anderson, W. C., *The Labour party, and electoral reform: Proportional Representation and the Alternative Vote* (1914).
Marr, T. R., *Housing conditions in Manchester and Salford* (Manchester, 1904).
Masterman, C. F. G., *Youth and Liberalism* (LYL Pamphlet, No. 9).
  The condition of England (1909).
  The New Liberalism (1920).
Money, L. C., *Things that matter* (1912).
Muir, J. R. B., *The New Liberalism* (1923).
Noel, C., *How to win* (1914).

Ostrogorski, M., *Democracy and the organisation of political parties* (translated F. Clarke, 2 vols., 1902).

Parker, F. Rowley, *The powers, duties and liabilities of an election agent* (2nd edn, 1891).

People's Suffrage Federation, *Facts about franchise: working women and the limited suffrage bill* (1910).

Prescott, C. W. D., *Young Liberalism* (LYL Pamphlet, No. 10).

Rea, R., *Social reform versus Socialism* (1912).

Rees, J. Aubrey, *Our aims and objectives* (LYL Pamphlet, No. 1).

Rosenbaum, S., 'The general election of January 1910 and the bearing of the results upon some problems of representation', *Journal of the Royal Statistical Society*, Lxxiii (1910).

Schloesser, H. H., *The twentieth century Reform Bill* (1911).

Seager, J. R., *The Franchise Act 1884* (1885).

Notes on registration (1903).

Shaw, F. J., *Facts about Newcastle* (Newcastle, 1907).

Smart, T. R., *Revolution or reform* (1917).

Snowden, P., *Socialism and Syndicalism* (1913).

Labour in chains: the pest of industrial conscription (Manchester and London, 1917).

Socialist group of the L.S.C., *Socialism and trade unions* (n.d.).

Stead, W. T., 'The Labour party and the books that helped to make it', *Review of Reviews* (1906).

Terry, G. P. W., *The Representation of the People Acts, 1918–28* (1928).

Walters, C. Ensor, *The social mission of the church* (1906).

Williams, R., *London rookeries and collier's slums* (1893).

PUBLISHED DIARIES AND LETTERS

Addison, Dr C.

Addison, Dr C., *Politics from within 1911–18* (2 vols, 1924).

Addison, Dr C., *Four and a half years* (2 vols, 1934).

Amery, L. A.

Barnes, J. and Nicholson, D. (eds), *The Leo Amery diaries* (1980).

Asquith, H. H.

Brock, M. and Brock, E. (eds), *H. H. Asquith, Letters to Venetia Stanley* (Oxford, 1982).

Asquith, R.

Joliffe, J., *Raymond Asquith* (1980).

Blunt, W. S.

Blunt, W. S., *My diaries*, vols i and ii (1919, 1920).

Ede, C.

Jefferys, K. (ed.), *Labour and the wartime coalition* (1987).

Hobhouse, Sir C. E. H.

David, E. (ed.), *Inside Asquith's Cabinet* (1977).

Riddell, Lord
  Riddell, Lord, *More pages from my diary, 1908–14* (1934).
  Riddell, Lord, *Lord Riddell's intimate diary of the Peace Conference and after, 1918–1923* (1933).
Sanders, Sir R.
  Ramsden, J. (ed.), *Real Old Tory Politics. The political diaries of Sir Robert Sanders, Lord Bayford, 1910–35* (1984).
Scott, C. P.
  Wilson, T. (ed.), *The political diaries of C. P. Scott, 1911–28* (1970).
Webb, B. and S.
  MacKenzie, N. (ed.), *The letters of Sidney and Beatrice Webb*, iii (1978).
  MacKenzie, N. and MacKenzie, J. (eds), *The diary of Beatrice Webb*, iii (1984).

BIOGRAPHY AND MEMOIRS

Acland, A. H. A. and Acland, F. D.
  Acland, A., *A Devon family* (1981).
Addison, Dr C.
  Morgan, J. and Morgan, K. O., *Portrait of a Progressive* (Oxford, 1980).
Aldred, G. A.
  Aldred, G. A., *No traitor's gait* (1955).
Asquith, H. H.
  Jenkins, R., *Asquith* (1964).
  Koss, S. E., *Asquith* (1975).
Attlee, C. R.
  Attlee, C. R., *As it happened* (1953).
  Harris, K., *Attlee* (1982).
Barclay, T.
  Barclay, T., *Thirty years* (1914).
Bateson, W.
  Bateson, W., *The way we came* (1924).
Benn, J.
  Gardiner, A. G., *John Benn and the Progressive movement* (1925).
Bernstein, E.
  Bernstein, E., *My years of exile* (1921).
Bigham, C. C.
  Bigham, C. C., *A picture of life* (1941).
Brunner, Sir J.
  Koss, S. E., *Sir John Brunner: radical plutocrat, 1842–1919* (Cambridge, 1970).
Burgess, J.
  Burgess, J., *A potential poet (Joseph Burgess) his autobiography and verse* (Ilford, 1927).
Burns, J.
  Brown, K. D., *John Burns* (1971).
Buxton, C.
  de Bunsen, V., *C. R. Buxton* (1948).

Churchill, W.
  Churchill, R. S., *Winston S. Churchill* (1967).
  Pelling, H., *Winston Churchill* (1974).
Clynes, J. R.
  Clynes, J. R., *Memoirs, 1869–1937* (2 vols, 1937).
Cole, G. D. H.
  Wright, A. W., *G. D. H. Cole and Socialist democracy* (Oxford, 1979).
Crawshay-Williams, E.
  Crawshay-Williams, E., *Simple story* (1935).
Dalton, E. H. J. N.
  Dalton, E. H. J. N., *Memoirs: call back yesterday, 1887–1931* (1953).
Desmond, T. Shaw
  Desmond, T. S., *Pilgrim to Paradise* (1951).
Dickinson, W. H.
  White, Hope C., *W. H. Dickinson: a memoir* (1956).
Edwards, W. J.
  Edwards, W. J., *From the valleys I came* (1958).
Elibank, Murray of
  Murray, A. C., *Master and brother* (1945).
Fox, R. M.
  Fox, R. M., *Smokey crusade* (1937).
Glasier, J. Bruce and Glasier, K. Bruce
  L. Thomson, *The enthusiasts* (1971).
Gosling, H.
  Goslind, H., *Up and down stream* (1927).
Griffiths, J.
  Pages from memory (1969).
Hardie, J. K. H.
  MacLean, I., *Keir Hardie* (1974).
  Morgan, K. O., *Keir Hardie: Radical and Socialist* (1975).
  Reid, F., *Keir Hardie: the making of a Socialist* (1978).
Harris, Sir P.
  Harris, P., *Forty years in and out of Parliament* (1947).
Henderson, A.
  Hamilton, M., *Arthur Henderson* (1938)
  McKibbin, R. I., 'Arthur Henderson as Labour leader', *IRSH* (1978).
Hobson, S. G.
  Hobson, S. G., *Pilgrim to the left* (1938).
Hodge, J.
  Hodge, J., *Workman's cottage to Westminster* (1931).
Hudson, Sir R.
  Spender, J. A., *Sir Robert Hudson. A memoir* (1930).
Jones, J.
  Jones, J., *My lively life* (1927).

Jowett, F. W.
  Brockway, A. F., *Socialism over sixty years: the life of Jowett of Bradford* (1946).
Kirkwood, D.
  Kirkwood, D., *My life of revolt* (1935).
Lansbury, G.
  Lansbury, G., *Looking backwards - and forwards* (1935).
  Postgate, R. W., *The life of George Lansbury* (1951).
Lawson, J. J.
  Lawson, J. J., *A man's life* (1932).
Lidgett, J. Scott
  Davies, R. E. (ed.), *John Scott Lidgett* (1957).
Linforth, J. H.
  Linforth, J. H., *Leaves from an agent's diary* (Leeds, 1911).
Lloyd George, D.
  Grigg, J., *Lloyd George: the people's champion* (1978)
  Grigg, J., *Lloyd George: from peace to war* (1985)
MacDonald, J. R.
  Marquand, D., *Ramsay MacDonald* (1977).
Massingham, H. W.
  Havighurst, A. F., *Radical journalist. H. W. Massingham* (Cambridge, 1974).
Masterman, C. F. G.
  Masterman, L., *C. F. G. Masterman* (1939).
Mond, A.
  Mond, A., *Industry and politics* (1927).
Morel, E. D.
  Cline, C. A., *E. D. Morel* (Belfast, 1980).
Morrell, Lady O.
  Morrell, O., *Ottoline at Garsington: memoirs of Lady Ottoline Morrell 1915–1918* (1974).
Murray, G.
  Wilson, D., *Gilbert Murray* (Oxford, 1987).
Paton, J.
  Paton, J., *Proletarian pilgrimage* (1935).
Pethwick-Lawrence, F. W.
  Pethwick-Lawrence, F. W., *Fate has been kind* (1942).
Rowntree, A.
  Vipont, E., *Arnold Rowntree* (1955).
Rowntree, S.
  Briggs, A., *Social thought and social action* (1961).
Salter, A.
  Brockway, A. Fenner, *Bermondsey story* (1949).
Sanders, W. S.
  Sanders, W. S., *Early Socialist days* (1927).
Slessor, H. H.
  Slessor, H. H., *Judgement reserved* (1941).

Smillie, R.
  Smillie, R., *My life for labour* (1924).
Smith, F.
  Champness, E. I., *Frank Smith M.P. Pioneer and modern mystic* (1943).
Smith, H.
  Lawson, J. J., *The man in the cap: Herbert Smith* (1941).
Snell, H.
  Snell, H., *Men, movements and myself* (1936).
Snowden, P.
  Snowden, P., *An autobiography* (2 vols, 1934).
Soutter, F. W.
  Soutter, F. W., *Fights for freedom* (1925).
Spender, H. H.
  Spender H. H., *The fire of life* (1924)
Spender, J. A.
  Spender, J. A., *Life, journalism and politics* (2 vols, 1927).
Thomas, J. H.
  Blaxland, G., *J. H. Thomas* (1964).
Thorne, W.
  Radice, G. and Radice, L., *Constructive militant* (1974).
Tillett, B.
  Schneer, J., *Ben Tillett* (1982).
Tomlinson, G.
  Blackburn, F., *George Tomlinson* (1954).
Trevelyan, C. P.
  Morris, A. J. A., *C. P. Trevelyan, 1870–1958* (Belfast, 1977).
Turner, B.
  Turner, B., *About myself, 1863–1930* (1930).
Webb, B.
  Webb, B., *My apprenticeship* (1938).
  Webb, B., *Our partnership* (1948).
  Radice, L., *Beatrice and Sidney Webb* (1984).
Wedgwood, J. C.
  Wedgwood, C. V., *The last of the Radicals* (1951).
Wilson, H. J.
  Fowler, W. S., *A study in Radicalism and Dissent* (1961).

THESES

Bornat, J., 'An examination of the General Union of Textile Workers, 1883–1922', Essex Ph.D. thesis, 1980.
Boughton, J., 'Working class politics in Birmingham and Sheffield', Warwick Ph.D. thesis, 1987.
Dickie, M., 'The ideology of Northampton Labour party in the inter-war years', Warwick MA thesis, 1982.

Dugdale, K., 'Conservatives, Liberals and Labour in Yorkshire, 1918–29', Sheffield MA thesis, 1976.

Ellins, R. E., 'Aspects of the New Liberalism', Sheffield Ph.D. thesis, 1980.

Feldman, D. M., 'Immigrants and workers, Englishmen and Jews: Jewish immigration to the East End of London 1880–1906', Cambridge Ph.D. thesis, 1986.

Hart, M. W., 'The decline of the Liberal Party in Parliament and in the constituencies, 1914–31', Oxford D.Phil. thesis, 1982.

Hill, J., 'Working-class politics in Lancashire: a regional study in the origins of the Labour party', Keele Ph.D. thesis, 1969.

Horne, J., 'Labour leaders and the post-war world', Sussex D.Phil. thesis, 1979.

Howard, C. J., 'Henderson, MacDonald and leadership in the Labour party 1914–22', Cambridge Ph.D. thesis, 1978.

Hunter, I. G., 'Workers' participation in local government on Tyneside to 1919', Newcastle M.Litt. thesis, 1979.

Janeway, W. H., 'The economic policy of the Second Labour Government 1929–31', Cambridge Ph.D. thesis, 1971.

Jones, G. A., 'National and local issues in politics: a study of East Sussex and the Lancashire spinning towns, 1906–10', Sussex D.Phil. thesis, 1964–5.

Langford, K., 'Success, failure and division – the Liberal electoral performance in East Anglia (with specific reference to the Suffolk county division) 1885–95', Cambridge BA dissertation, 1985.

Lupton, R., 'The decline of the Liberal party 1918–24, with special reference to South-East Lancashire', Cambridge BA dissertation, 1986.

Marriott, J. W., 'London over the border: a study of West Ham during rapid growth', Cambridge Ph.D. thesis, 1984.

Mathers, H. E., 'Sheffield municipal politics, 1893–1926: parties, personalities and the rise of Labour', Sheffield Ph.D. thesis 1980.

Meadowcroft, M. J., 'Transition in Leeds City Government, 1903–26', Bradford M.Litt. thesis, 1978.

Morris, D., 'Labour or Socialism? Opposition and dissent within the ILP, with special reference to Lancashire', Manchester Ph.D. thesis, 1982.

Neville, R. G., 'The Yorkshire miners 1881 to 1926: a study in labour and social history', Leeds Ph.D. thesis, 1974.

Rolf, K. W. D., 'Tories, tariffs and elections: West Midlands in English politics, 1918–35', Cambridge Ph.D. thesis, 1974.

Rowett, J. S., 'The Labour party in local government: theory and practice in the inter-war years', Oxford D.Phil. thesis, 1979.

Scott, I., 'The Lancashire and Cheshire Miners' Federation 1900–14', York Ph.D. thesis, 1977.

Short, M. E., 'The politics of personal taxation: budget making in Britain, 1917–31', Cambridge Ph.D. thesis, 1985.

Shorter, P. R., 'Electoral politics and political change in the East Midlands 1918–35', Cambridge Ph.D. thesis, 1975.

Stevens, C. P., 'Urban Conservatism in Yorkshire', 1885–1906', Oxford D.Phil. thesis in progress.

Tanner, D. M., 'Political realignment in England and Wales, *c.* 1906–22', London
    Ph.D. thesis, 1985.
Thompson, A., 'The Liberal party and English Nonconformity, *c.* 1895–1914,
    with particular reference to education and licensing reform', Cambridge
    Ph.D. thesis in progress.
Tranter, A., 'The Railway Clerks Association: its origins and history to 1921',
    Cambridge Ph.D. thesis, 1979.
Trodd, G. N., 'Political change and the working class in Blackburn and Burnley
    1880–1914', Lancaster Ph.D. thesis, 1978.
Weekes, B. C. M., 'The Amalgamated Society of Engineers, 1880–1914', Warwick
    Ph.D. thesis, 1970.
White, A. D., 'Radical Liberals and Liberal politics 1906 – *c.* 1924', Kent Ph.D.
    thesis, 1980.
Wright, R. A., 'Liberal party organisation and politics in Birmingham, Coventry
    and Wolverhampton, 1886–1914, with particular reference to the develop-
    ment of independent Labour representation', Birmingham Ph.D. thesis, 1978.

Index